LIVING  LITURGY™

Spirituality, Celebration, and Catechesis for Sundays and Solemnities

Year C • 2019

Brian Schmisek
Katy Beedle Rice
Diana Macalintal

LITURGICAL PRESS
Collegeville, Minnesota

www.litpress.org

✠ CONTENTS

Brian Schmisek is professor and dean of the Institute of Pastoral Studies at Loyola University Chicago. Prior to coming to Chicago in 2012, he was the founding dean of the School of Ministry at the University of Dallas. His published works include *The Rome of Peter and Paul: A Pilgrim's Handbook to New Testament Sites in the Eternal City* (Pickwick), *Ancient Faith for the Modern World: A Brief Guide to the Apostles' Creed* (ACTA), *Resurrection of the Flesh or Resurrection from the Dead: Implications for Theology* (Liturgical Press), many other books coauthored for biblical study, and articles.

Katy Beedle Rice is a catechist and writer who lives with her husband and three children in Boise, Idaho. She is a formation leader for the National Association of the Catechesis of the Good Shepherd, training catechists who work with children ages three through six. Rice is also a contributing preacher for the Dominican Podcast *theWord* (https://word.op.org), writes for Celebration Publications, a division of the National Catholic Reporter Publishing Company, and blogs about motherhood, ministry, and the Eucharist at blessedbrokenshared.blogspot.com.

Diana Macalintal has served as a liturgist, musician, author, speaker, and composer for the last twenty-five years, and her work can be found in *Give Us This Day* and many other publications. She is the author of *The Work of Your Hands: Prayers for Ordinary and Extraordinary Moments of Grace*, *Joined by the Church, Sealed by a Blessing: Couples and Communities Called to Conversion Together*, and *Your Parish Is the Curriculum: RCIA in the Midst of the Community* (Liturgical Press). Macalintal is a cofounder of TeamRCIA.com with her husband, Nick Wagner.

 **PREFACE**

Renewal

Last year Liturgical Press gave a new look and feel to this popular resource. We spoke of it with the metaphor of a new house, or even a renovation. So we have been in this renovated house for a year now, and so begins year two. With the renewed look and feel of *Living Liturgy*™ last year, we heard many good things including some constructive feedback. We remain indebted to the work that Sr. Joyce Ann Zimmerman, CPPS, director of the Institute for Liturgical Ministry (now closed, unfortunately), and Sr. Kathleen Harmon, SNDdeN, did by launching this resource nearly twenty years ago. Much of the structure they gave the work has remained the same. In fact, in this 2019 edition we largely return to the format they were using, especially concerning "Focusing the Gospel, Connecting the Gospel, and Connecting the Responsorial Psalm." We tried a slightly different model in 2018 but now return to the tried-and-true earlier format for those sections. It's worth another look at this new home as it were.

Artwork

We like the artwork in this new edition and received positive reviews. So it stays! Liturgical Press brought back the three artists from the 2018 edition: Deborah Luke, Tanja Butler, and Ned Bustard. The artwork, like that for 2018, is new and original, commissioned especially for this 2019 edition. We hope you enjoy this as much as you did the artwork in last year's edition.

Reflecting on the Gospel and Living the Paschal Mystery

Based on surveys and feedback, we know that the most frequented part of the book is "Reflecting on the Gospel," followed by "Living the Paschal Mystery," true to Sr. Joyce Ann's insight. Brian Schmisek wrote these pieces again, as he did last year, with that in mind. Especially because we are in the year of Luke, many of the themes tend to reflect the social tradition of the church, as well as Pope Francis's focus on mercy.

Focusing the Gospel, Connecting the Gospel, Connecting the Responsorial Psalm, Prompts for Faith Sharing, and Homily Points

Pages 2–3 of the material each week remain widely used. Katy Beedle Rice, an author new to this project, wrote these sections, drawing on the former structure including "Key words and phrases" and "To the point," as well as model prayers. Her insights as a mother, wife, and catechist shine through these sections.

Liturgy

Liturgy remains a primary focus of the book, and it is our good fortune to have Diana Macalintal's experience and knowledge forming the gist of this section. She continues to share her insight and practical advice honed by years of parish and diocesan ministry. From musical selections to commentary on the General Instruction of the Roman Missal, her words are filled with wisdom.

Purpose

The three authors for this book, Brian, Katy, and Diana, continue to retain its original and primary purpose: "to help people prepare for liturgy and live a liturgical spirituality (that is, a way of living that is rooted in liturgy), opening their vision to their baptismal identity as the Body of Christ and shaping their living according to the rhythm of paschal mystery dying and rising. The paschal mystery is the central focus of liturgy, of the gospels, and of this volume." We are humbled and privileged to be carrying on this task. We hope this work with its artful imagery assists many in living a liturgical spirituality. We are open to feedback and look forward to hearing from you about this renovated home for *Living Liturgy*™.

SEASON OF ADVENT

SPIRITUALITY

GOSPEL ACCLAMATION
Ps 85:8

℟. Alleluia, alleluia.
Show us, Lord, your love;
and grant us your salvation.
℟. Alleluia, alleluia.

Gospel

Luke 21:25-28, 34-36; L3C

Jesus said to his disciples:
"There will be signs in the sun, the
moon, and the stars,
and on earth nations will be in
dismay,
perplexed by the roaring of the
sea and the waves.
People will die of fright
in anticipation of what is com-
ing upon the world,
for the powers of the heav-
ens will be shaken.
And then they will see the Son
of Man
coming in a cloud with power and
great glory.
But when these signs begin to happen,
stand erect and raise your heads
because your redemption is at hand.

"Beware that your hearts do not be-
come drowsy
from carousing and drunkenness
and the anxieties of daily life,
and that day catch you by surprise
like a trap.
For that day will assault everyone
who lives on the face of the earth.
Be vigilant at all times
and pray that you have the strength
to escape the tribulations that are
imminent
and to stand before the Son of Man."

Reflecting on the Gospel

Most of us look for meaning in the signs and events of daily life. We wonder how God might be acting in our lives. Was this a chance meeting with an old friend, or part of something greater? Was it a coincidence that I was thinking of this person when I received a call from him or her? Did the inclement weather keep me at home so I was able to spend time with my family? Not only we, but generations of those who have gone before us, discerned meaning in the events of daily life. The ancient pagan Romans looked at the sky for omens, and read the entrails of slaughtered chickens to discern how the gods were acting in their world.

The gospel reading for today gives the reader signs that will accompany the end times, the coming of the Son of Man. But we would be mistaken if we took these passages literally. And it's certainly true that hundreds if not thousands of people have done just that—looked for these signs to be fulfilled literally.

The message of this passage sought to give hope to a beleaguered people, the Christians, who anticipated their redemption. Many of them desperately wanted to see the coming of the Son of Man who would establish justice and peace. Many of the early Christians were on the bottom of the social ladder, experiencing tribulations and trials. Jesus himself had faced a violent end at the hands of the state. The Christians needed to be reminded that their salvation would come, and that they also needed to be vigilant, watching for that same salvation. And at the time this gospel was written there were many other Christians who may have lost hope or grown weary of waiting. This message was for them; and the message is also for us.

For us, the watching for the coming of the Son of Man has been not merely decades, as it was for the early Christians, but two millennia! Do we really believe that the end is near? that Jesus might return any day? It might be more worthwhile for me to imagine my own personal end (death) rather than the end of the world. In that way, it might be easier to see that my own personal end could catch me "by surprise like a trap." And when I live with the expectation that my end is near, or at least unknown, it can be easier for daily anxieties to dissipate. This is not to say we have no cares for the world, but rather, we have our eyes set on something greater as we live by a different set of values. Ideally, we serve more than we are served; we give more than we receive. And in that way we imitate Christ, whose disciples we are.

Living the Paschal Mystery

How would I live today if I knew it was my last day on the earth? What priorities would guide my choices and decisions? The church gives us the reading from Luke to start this Advent season in part so that we might call to mind the "end times" and the concurrent coming of the Son of Man. When our minds are drowning in lists, shopping, groceries, and gifts, we might pause, raise our head above these pressing concerns, and reflect from another point of view. In the end, what does it all mean? What is driving my actions and behaviors? Am I watchful, vigilant for the Lord's coming? And what would such watchfulness look like? The dying and rising of Christ gives meaning to my own personal death and resurrection each season, when I set aside my own desires and aims and focus on something eternal, something lasting. It is then that we recall the relationships forged and celebrated on this earth endure forever. The coming of the Son of Man means death to an old way of life, and resurrection of hope and life everlasting.

Focusing the Gospel

Key words and phrases: But when these signs begin to happen, / stand erect and raise your heads / because your redemption is at hand.

To the point: We begin a new church year with a gospel that seems intent upon shocking and startling us out of complacency. Jesus speaks of signs that will accompany the coming of the Son of Man. These signs are so terrifying that "[p]eople will die of fright," and yet, in the midst of it, we hear a word of hope: though these calamities may occur, "stand erect and raise your heads / because your redemption is at hand." To prepare for this redemption, Jesus counsels us to be vigilant in waiting and in prayer.

Connecting the Gospel

to the first reading: The prophet Jeremiah also preaches a word of hope, this time to the people of Israel in exile in Babylon. Even though they have seen their homeland taken over by foreign armies and their temple destroyed, Jeremiah reminds the people that their God has not forgotten them. Indeed, "[t]he days are coming . . . when I will fulfill the promise / I made to the house of Israel and Judah."

to experience: Jeremiah proclaims that God has a plan for Judah to be saved and for Jerusalem to dwell in safety. When we hear these words of comfort, taken together with today's gospel that speaks of calamities and dismay, we can know that the God of Jeremiah and Jesus, our God, is one who desires peace and for all people to dwell in safety. How might we preach peace, safety, and hope when we encounter panic, chaos, and despair?

Connecting the Responsorial Psalm

to the readings: The theme of hope and trust is evident in today's psalm. The psalmist prays, "[G]uide me in your truth and teach me, / for you are God my savior, / and for you I wait all the day." Like the prophet Jeremiah, the psalmist proclaims the constancy of God who is eager to guide the humble along the path of life. And how might we characterize this path of life in its essence? In the second reading, Paul, writing to the community in Thessalonica, gives us a clue. He concludes a prayer for their community by stating, "May the Lord make you increase and abound in love / for one another and for all." This abounding love will strengthen the hearts of the community and shape them in holiness. It is abounding love that will allow them (and us) to stand erect to greet the Son of Man when he comes.

to psalmist preparation: This psalm is one of deep longing to know the ways of the Lord and to live in God's covenant. We are called to a practice of waiting within Advent—to live in the here and now, and also to yearn and work for the coming of the kingdom of God in its fullness. How do you practice a spirituality of waiting? How do you come to know the Lord?

PROMPTS FOR FAITH-SHARING

What is an action or practice of preparation you can embrace this Advent? It could be an action of preparing for Christmas, preparing for Jesus' second coming, or preparing our world to become more like the kingdom of God.

_____

_____

_____

_____

As Christians living in the year 2018 we realize that our own personal end will likely come before the second coming of Jesus. Thinking about your own mortality, how would you live this coming year if you knew it was your last on earth?

_____

_____

_____

_____

Advent is a time of preparation and a time of waiting. What spiritual practices make waiting fruitful for you?

_____

_____

_____

_____

Though today's gospel can seem disturbing, we are called to be people of hope and joy. As a Christian, how do you preach safety, peace, and hope when you encounter panic, chaos, and despair?

_____

_____

_____

_____

Model Penitential Act

Presider: In today's gospel Jesus speaks of the coming of the Son of Man. As we begin a new church year, let us ask for God's mercy and forgiveness, so as to be ready to greet Jesus when he comes again . . . [*pause*]

> Lord Jesus, you are Son of God and Son of Man: Lord, have mercy.
> Christ Jesus, you are the fulfillment of God's promise: Christ, have mercy.
> Lord Jesus, you show us the path of holiness: Lord, have mercy.

Homily Points

• Advent is a season of preparation. We prepare our hearts and homes to celebrate the feast of Christmas. We prepare spiritually to greet Christ when he comes again. And we also look to how we can prepare our world to become more and more like the kingdom of God where love and justice rule. Advent is a time when we live this preparation in an intentional manner, but waiting and preparing are constant hallmarks of the Christian life.

• In the second reading, the apostle Paul reminds us that we have never arrived in this life. Our preparation is never complete. He exhorts the community in Thessalonica that even as they are conducting themselves in a way pleasing to God, that they "do so even more" (4:1). The conduct that Paul calls the community to is one that has "abound[ing] . . . love" as its foundation and guide. As Christians, we never have a reason to be bored or complacent. Our work is never finished as we collaborate with Jesus in building a kingdom of love and peace.

• Despite the foreboding nature of our gospel reading today, as Christians we believe in a radical promise—that light is stronger than darkness, love is stronger than hate, and life is stronger than death. We are called to be signs of hope in a world at times overcome with fear. As we begin the physical preparations for Christmas by lighting our Advent wreaths, buying gifts, planning our feasts and parties for the Christmas season, let us also consider, how might we prepare ourselves to be light, love, and life to those around us?

Model Universal Prayer (Prayer of the Faithful)

Presider: Let us present our needs to the Lord, confident in his love and mercy.

Response: Lord, hear our prayer.

That the church be a beacon of hope in troubled times . . .

That all people throughout the world dwell in safety and work for justice . . .

That those who suffer from depression, anxiety, and mental illness might know the love and tender care of the God of hope . . .

That each of us here might give up our daily anxieties so as to live more fully into God's promise of peace . . .

Presider: God of abounding love, you call us to live with you in holiness and peace. Grant our prayers that we might grow closer to you each day. We ask this through Christ our Lord. Amen.

COLLECT

Let us pray.

Pause for silent prayer

Grant your faithful, we pray, almighty God,
the resolve to run forth to meet your Christ
with righteous deeds at his coming,
so that, gathered at his right hand,
they may be worthy to possess the heavenly Kingdom.
Through our Lord Jesus Christ, your Son,
who lives and reigns with you in the unity of the Holy Spirit,
one God, for ever and ever. **Amen.**

FIRST READING

Jer 33:14-16

The days are coming, says the LORD,
    when I will fulfill the promise
    I made to the house of Israel and Judah.
In those days, in that time,
    I will raise up for David a just shoot;
    he shall do what is right and just in the land.
In those days Judah shall be safe
    and Jerusalem shall dwell secure;
    this is what they shall call her:
    "The LORD our justice."

RESPONSORIAL PSALM
Ps 25:4-5, 8-9, 10, 14

℞. (1b) To you, O Lord, I lift my soul.

Your ways, O LORD, make known to me;
    teach me your paths,
guide me in your truth and teach me,
    for you are God my savior,
    and for you I wait all the day.

℞. To you, O Lord, I lift my soul.

Good and upright is the LORD;
    thus he shows sinners the way.
He guides the humble to justice,
    and teaches the humble his way.

℞. To you, O Lord, I lift my soul.

All the paths of the LORD are kindness and
        constancy
    toward those who keep his covenant
        and his decrees.
The friendship of the LORD is with those
        who fear him,
    and his covenant, for their instruction.

℞. To you, O Lord, I lift my soul.

SECOND READING
1 Thess 3:12–4:2

Brothers and sisters:
May the Lord make you increase and
        abound in love
    for one another and for all,
    just as we have for you,
    so as to strengthen your hearts,
    to be blameless in holiness before our
        God and Father
    at the coming of our Lord Jesus with all
        his holy ones. Amen.

Finally, brothers and sisters,
    we earnestly ask and exhort you in the
        Lord Jesus that,
    as you received from us
    how you should conduct yourselves to
        please God
    —and as you are conducting
        yourselves—
    you do so even more.
For you know what instructions we gave
        you through the Lord Jesus.

About Liturgy
Be vigilant: We may be able to control our own personal practices and even our parish culture, but we will never be able to control how other people observe the weeks leading up to Christmas. We can ensure that we omit the Gloria at Mass during Advent (except for solemnities, weddings, and confirmation), but people will still sing and play Christmas songs in their homes and social gatherings. No matter how long you refrain from putting up your own Christmas tree, many others will have theirs fully decorated by Thanksgiving! And no amount of preaching will convince the majority of your parishioners that they should be spending more time in quiet prayer than in shopping for gifts and going to Christmas parties.

As much as we want all Christians to keep prayerful, sober watch in anticipation of the coming of the Lord, we cannot become "Advent police," because the exhortation to vigilance goes both ways. We, too, must be vigilant that our behavior and attitudes help us "increase and abound in love / for one another and for all" (1 Thess 3:12). One way you can do this is to learn and participate in some of the Advent practices of cultures that are different from yours. For many Hispanic and Asian communities, Advent is a time of prayer and parties, of joyful music and quiet contemplation. There is a beautiful grace, too, in this kind of waiting for the day of the Lord.

As those who help shape the unique spirit of Advent in our communities, let us help one another be attentive to God's presence all around us so that our hearts may not become drowsy from our anxieties.

About Initiation
Today is not a beginning: Although today is the beginning of the new liturgical year, it is not the beginning of RCIA. There is no formal "beginning" to the first period of the Rite of Christian Initiation of Adults, which is the period of evangelization and precatechumenate. We should be evangelizing all year long and be ready to meet seekers every day of the year! To help your community understand that evangelization is year-round and to avoid any misconception that catechumens are formed on a school-year calendar, do not schedule a Rite of Acceptance for this Sunday. Instead, plan to celebrate it a few times during Ordinary Time throughout the year.

About Liturgical Music
Meter and melody: Because the Advent season is so short, it is a good time to incorporate seasonal songs that are used every Sunday of Advent. This helps your assembly become more familiar with the music over the weeks, especially if you may have more visitors and newcomers this time of year. It also sets a musical "environment" that is both constant and developing. One way to strike this balance is to use a seasonal hymn tune for the entrance song, such as CONDITOR ALME SIDERUM, and each week pair it with different texts. To do this, find texts that match the tune's meter, which is 88 88, meaning there are four phrases of eight syllables each. Some text examples from *Sacred Song* might be "Creator of the Stars of Night," which is the most common for this tune; "O Lord of Light" by Melvin Farrell; "Lift Up Your Heads, You Mighty Gates," translated by Catherine Winkworth; "On Jordan's Bank," translated by John Chandler. As you explore your own music resources, be sure that the stressed syllables of the text match the natural stresses of the tune.

R̸. Alleluia, alleluia.
Hail, Mary, full of grace, the Lord is with you;
blessed are you among women.
R̸. Alleluia, alleluia.

Gospel   Luke 1:26-38; L689

The angel Gabriel was sent from God
  to a town of Galilee called Nazareth,
  to a virgin betrothed to a man named
      Joseph,
  of the house of David,
  and the virgin's name was Mary.
And coming to her, he said,
  "Hail, full of grace! The Lord is with
      you."
But she was greatly troubled at what was
    said
  and pondered what sort of greeting
      this might be.
Then the angel said to her,
  "Do not be afraid, Mary,
  for you have found favor with God.
Behold, you will conceive in your womb
      and bear a son,
  and you shall name him Jesus.

Continued in Appendix A, p. 263.

See Appendix A, p. 263, for the other readings.

Reflecting on the Gospel

The immaculate conception is a difficult concept for adults to grasp, much less children. Though it is a basic element of faith, it is the source of never-ending confusion and much explanatory catechesis. Frankly, the issue is not made easier when the reading for this solemnity narrates the conception of Jesus (also known as the annunciation) and not the immaculate conception (the conception of Mary). But as we know, there is no scriptural passage that narrates the conception of Mary, so the church gives us the story about the conception of Jesus! No wonder confusion abounds.

We recall that every Marian title ultimately says more about Jesus than it does about Mary. And that is certainly true with the immaculate conception, which claims that the salvific effects of what God has done in Christ preserved Mary from sin from the moment of her conception. Thus, the salvific power of the Christ-event transcends time, reaches back as it were, and has an effect on Mary herself as she is conceived.

For most of the history of the church this doctrine remained in the realm of theological inquiry and/or speculation. Not until the mid-nineteenth century was this formally proclaimed as doctrine by Pope Pius IX.

Upon reading the gospel for the day we may turn our attention to Mary's faith in God and her openness to the Lord's will. Mary is known and celebrated throughout the world for this characteristic, among many others. Her yes (in Latin, *fiat*, or "let it be done [to me]") shows her willingness to cooperate with God for the salvation of humanity. Her attitude and character were called "immaculate" by many early church fathers even if they were not referring to her conception. She was so open, pure, and devoted to God that she was willing to become an unwed mother in an age when that meant punishment and death under the law. Her character was understood to be immaculate from the moment of her conception by a singularly unique gift.

We can understand and appreciate some confusion regarding the meaning of this feast, which celebrates Mary's immaculate character from the moment of conception, by reading from the gospel about the conception of Jesus by Mary's own word of *fiat*.

Living the Paschal Mystery

Ours is an adult faith with fairly sophisticated concepts and theological insights. Not only do we have sacred texts, but we have a tradition of faith with a capital "T" carried through the ages by saints, martyrs, popes, and the people of God. For some it becomes something of a theological parlor game to know and recite Catholic trivia with names, dates, historical underpinnings, and whimsical theories consigned to the dustbin of theological inquiry. But our faith is much more than an intellectual head-trip. Faith in Christ is about doing much more than knowing, though both have their rightful place. Never once in the gospels does Jesus say people will be judged by what they know. Instead, he often admonishes his audiences about what they do, or rather, do not do. On this feast day of the Immaculate Conception we certainly nod to the theological history and development of doctrine that gives us today's celebration. But we might also remind ourselves that we are to be doers of the word, and not mere hearers.

Focusing the Gospel

Key words and phrases: [F]or nothing will be impossible for God.

To the point: In the second reading we hear God's plan of salvation, which is that we were chosen "before the foundation of the world, / to be holy and without blemish before him." In Mary we see this plan perfected. She is sustained by Gabriel's promise that "nothing will be impossible for God." We, too, believe in a God of infinite possibilities and can trust in this plan of salvation.

Model Penitential Act

Presider: In today's second reading we hear that we have been chosen before the foundation of the world to be holy and without blemish before God. Let us pause to ask for God's mercy and pardon for the times we have not lived up to this call . . . [*pause*]

Lord Jesus, you are Son of God and son of Mary: Lord, have mercy.

Christ Jesus, you have blessed us with every spiritual blessing: Christ, have mercy.

Lord Jesus, you call us to holiness: Lord, have mercy.

Model Universal Prayer (Prayer of the Faithful)

Presider: Let us bring our intentions before the Lord, believing as Mary did that nothing is impossible for God.

Response: Lord, hear our prayer.

That the church be a spiritual mother for all who seek comfort and shelter within her arms . . .

That all people might know of the love and mercy of God . . .

That those in need, especially pregnant women, might find support and security. . .

That all those gathered here might renew their commitment to let it "be done to me according to your word". . .

Presider: God of infinite love, for whom all things are possible, you call us to be holy and without blemish in your sight. Hear the prayers we bring to you today for ourselves and for our world, through Christ Jesus our Lord. Amen.

About Liturgy

Holy Days of Obligation: In the United States when January 1, August 15, or November 1 fall on a Saturday or Monday the obligation to attend Mass is removed. But because December 8 is the patronal feast day for the United States it is always observed, except when it falls on a Sunday. When that happens, the observance is transferred to the following Monday, but the obligation is removed. This year December 8 falls on a Saturday and the obligation remains.

This Saturday evening Mass may be celebrated using the readings and prayers for December 8. However, most people attending your parish's Saturday night Mass will expect to hear the readings and prayers for Sunday.

Therefore you will likely be asked: Can a person fulfill both obligations (December 8 and Sunday) by attending a Saturday evening Mass? The short answer is "no" because only one obligation is fulfilled by participating at a Mass, regardless of the readings and prayers used at that Mass. Thus, this weekend we are called to participate in two Masses. This may be a hardship for most people; however, it can also be an opportunity to invite people to make an additional effort for Advent.

COLLECT
Let us pray.

Pause for silent prayer

O God, who by the Immaculate Conception of the Blessed Virgin
prepared a worthy dwelling for your Son,
grant, we pray,
that, as you preserved her from every stain
by virtue of the Death of your Son, which you foresaw,
so, through her intercession,
we, too, may be cleansed and admitted to your presence.
Through our Lord Jesus Christ, your Son,
who lives and reigns with you in the unity of the Holy Spirit,
one God, for ever and ever. **Amen.**

FOR REFLECTION

• In Mary we find a model of discipleship. Just as Mary was invited to bear Christ to the world, we are also called to be Christ-bearers. How do you bear Christ to the world?

• The angel Gabriel proclaims to Mary, "[N]othing will be impossible for God." Where do you need to hear this proclamation in your own life?

• As God protected Mary from sin from the moment of her conception, he also desires to wash all sin from us. What spiritual practices reveal God's forgiveness to you?

Homily Points

• The church fathers have taught us that in her immaculate conception the Blessed Virgin Mary was protected from Original Sin from the very moment of her creation in the womb of her mother Anne. In the first reading today we witness Adam and Eve in the Garden of Eden making choices that separate them from the ideal relationship they enjoyed with God up to that point. Now, instead of walking with God in the garden, Adam hides as God calls, "Where are you?"

• In our lives as Christians we, too, are invited to walk with God. In what areas in our lives does God call to us, "Where are you?"

✚ SPIRITUALITY

GOSPEL ACCLAMATION
Luke 3:4, 6

℟. Alleluia, alleluia.
Prepare the way of the Lord, make straight his
    paths:
all flesh shall see the salvation of God.
℟. Alleluia, alleluia.

Gospel

Luke 3:1-6; L6C

**In the fifteenth year
    of the reign of
    Tiberius Caesar,
when Pontius Pilate was
    governor of Judea,
and Herod was tetrarch of Galilee,
and his brother Philip tetrarch
    of the region of Ituraea and
    Trachonitis,
and Lysanias was tetrarch of Abilene,
during the high priesthood of Annas
    and Caiaphas,
the word of God came to John the
    son of Zechariah in the desert.
John went throughout the whole region
    of the Jordan,
proclaiming a baptism of repentance
    for the forgiveness of sins,
as it is written in the book of the
    words of the prophet Isaiah:
*A voice of one crying out in the
    desert:
"Prepare the way of the Lord,
    make straight his paths.
Every valley shall be filled
    and every mountain and hill
        shall be made low.
The winding roads shall be made
    straight,
    and the rough ways made
        smooth,
and all flesh shall see the salvation
    of God."***

Reflecting on the Gospel

After his introductory material, including the infancy narratives in chapters 1 and 2, Luke picks up the gospel story he inherited from Mark. That is, today's reading from Luke is based on the opening verses of the Gospel of Mark with important additions. Beginning with John the Baptist's preaching, Luke situates the Christ-event in a particular historical time and place, for, as he tells us in Acts 26:26, these things did not happen in a corner. And it is precisely because of Luke's desire to give us the historical details that scholars can be fairly confident of their dating. Luke cites both civil and religious leaders to situate the Christ-event in history. The Emperor Tiberius, who reigned from AD 14 to 36, succeeded Caesar Augustus, which means that the fifteenth year of Tiberius's reign could be anywhere from AD 27 to 29 depending on how one counts the years. This is the most specific date given by Luke in this passage; the other figures named by Luke all fall within a wider range than that. For example, Pontius Pilate served from AD 26 to 36.

The historical details do much for the modern Christian (and ancient Christian for that matter) in demonstrating that Jesus was a historical figure. The Christ-event is not a mere myth like so many other Greek and Roman tales. Jesus was a living, breathing Jewish human being who lived in the Roman Empire in the province of Judea. These things did not happen in a corner (cf. Acts 26:26).

Once the events are situated in their historical setting, Luke continues the narrative with the story about John the Baptist, whose birth is recounted in the first chapter. There we hear the story of Zechariah and Elizabeth having a child even though Elizabeth is barren. It is Luke who essentially makes John a cousin of Jesus, a detail found nowhere else in the New Testament. The appellation of John as "son of Zechariah" (Luke 3:2) is a nod to the story in the first chapter.

These details alone—the historical setting and the familial relationship between John and Jesus—tell us we are dealing with a unique author who has his own theological insights to convey. Luke is a gifted storyteller, theologian, and evangelist. We do well to read his story carefully.

Living the Paschal Mystery

Christians believe in the person Jesus, the Christ, the son of the Living God. Jesus walked this earth, breathed the air, enjoyed the sunshine, had meaningful relationships, and ultimately suffered death at the hands of the state. His story really happened: it is not myth, make believe, or something we simply tell children so they will be nice to one another. Luke is an evangelist who gives us the details, which allow scholars to situate the life of Jesus in a historical context. The names of civil and religious leaders like Tiberius, Pontius Pilate, Herod, Philip, and others throughout the gospel are known by ancient pagan sources as well. They form something of an anchor or peg upon which to hang a timeline for Jesus and his ministry. In the language of another gospel, this is the story of the Word made flesh in a given time and place.

Jesus lived in a province ruled by Rome and was executed by that ruling power. Though put to death by the state he was raised up by God, giving us the paschal mystery. On this Second Sunday of Advent we pause to reflect on Jesus' historical circumstances and our own, knowing that death is not the end.

Focusing the Gospel

Key words and phrases: [T]he word of God came to John the son of Zechariah in the desert. . . . *Prepare the way of the Lord.*

To the point: Earlier in the Gospel of Luke we hear of John the Baptist's childhood in which "[t]he child grew and became strong in spirit, and he was in the desert until the day of his manifestation to Israel" (1:80; NABRE). This desert time is important for John's formation as the preacher we hear in the gospel today. In the desert one must listen. John proclaims the words of the prophet Isaiah to the people, *"Prepare the way of the Lord"!* These words were addressed originally to the Israelites in exile in Babylon. The way being prepared was the way the Lord would lead them out of exile and restore them to their homeland. Now John invites his listeners to undertake an interior way of repentance.

Connecting the Gospel

to the first and second readings: In the gospel we hear of John the Baptist drawing close to God in the desert. In the first two readings both the apostle Paul and the prophet Baruch are undergoing their own "desert" experiences. Paul is writing to the Christian community at Philippi from a prison. Baruch preaches a word of hope to the people of Israel in exile in Babylon.

to experience: While difficult, desert experiences often serve to sharpen our faith and put our lives into focus. Where is the desert in your life right now? How might God be speaking to you in the desert?

Connecting the Responsorial Psalm

to the readings: Psalm 126 is one of pure joy and exultation. A people that were taken captive and exiled to another land are restored to security and prosperity in their homeland. This exultation is echoed by the prophet Baruch in the first reading. Baruch speaks to the city of Jerusalem mourning the loss of her children in the Babylonian exile. Baruch reassures her, saying, "[L]ook to the east and see your children / gathered from the east and the west / at the word of the Holy One, / rejoicing that they are remembered by God." Another prophet raises his voice in the gospel reading: John the Baptist. Unlike the psalm and the first reading, the gospel sounds harsher in some ways. Broaching no nonsense, John calls the people to a baptism of repentance. His call, though, is also reason to rejoice. Our God is one who does not turn his back on sinners. Instead, God wishes to restore all those who have fallen "captive" to sin. And when that happens "[t]hose who sow in tears / shall reap rejoicing."

to psalmist preparation: As you prepare to sing this psalm, reflect on moments of great joy in your own life. When has your mouth been filled with laughter and your tongue sung for joy? How might you express this overflowing joy to those in the assembly?

PROMPTS FOR FAITH-SHARING

As we prepare the way for Jesus to be born anew into our hearts this Christmas, what are the valleys we are called to fill in? Which mountains within our lives (pride, greed, anger) must be made low?

In his letter to the Philippians St. Paul writes, "And this is my prayer: / that your love may increase ever more and more / in knowledge and every kind of perception, / to discern what is of value" (1:9-10). How might we fulfill that prayer within our own lives?

Both John and Jesus experience a period of time in the desert before taking on their public ministry. Where might you cultivate desert places in your life where you go to be with God in solitude and prayer?

As a parish how might you prepare to welcome with love and joy the people who will join your community to celebrate Christmas?

Model Penitential Act

Presider: In today's gospel John the Baptist proclaims a baptism of repentance for the forgiveness of sins. For the areas in our own lives crying for repentance and forgiveness, we ask for God's mercy. . . [*pause*]

Lord Jesus, you are the way, the truth and the life: Lord, have mercy.

Christ Jesus, you show us the way of salvation: Christ, have mercy.

Lord Jesus, you call us to repentance: Lord, have mercy.

Homily Points

• The word of God comes to John the Baptist in the desert. We are not told what this word is but we see the result: John leaves his life of solitude and prayer to proclaim a baptism of repentance for the forgiveness of sins. As the forerunner of Jesus, John's work is to prepare the people to receive the one who is coming, the one who is "the salvation of God." John has been prepared for his mission by his life in the desert. Later Jesus will also follow this path. After being baptized in the Jordan, he will be led into the desert by the Spirit where he will fast and pray for forty days and forty nights.

• A few hundred years later, around the third century AD, a group of monks and nuns return to the desert to live lives of solitude and prayer. These Desert Fathers and Mothers left behind words of wisdom and a model for living the spiritual life. Although we may not be able to follow their austere example, we can cultivate areas of stillness and quiet in our own lives.

• Advent and Lent, our two seasons of preparation in the church year, provide annual opportunities for us to enter into the desert on retreat. We are given time to follow in the footsteps of Jesus, John, and the Desert Fathers and Mothers to listen to God away from all distractions. Where can you find space in your life to cultivate interior silence and contemplation? How might you set aside time for deep listening to the word of God?

Model Universal Prayer (Prayer of the Faithful)

Presider: Heeding the call of John the Baptist, we pray for the strength and wisdom to *"[p]repare the way of the Lord."*

Response: Lord, hear our prayer.

That the Church offer welcome to those seeking the way of repentance . . .

That all peoples of the world realign their lives with mercy and justice . . .

That those who are experiencing imprisonment or exile might know the unchanging love of God. . .

That each of us here may undertake the work of preparing a way for the Lord in our own lives. . .

Presider: God of justice and mercy, you speak a word of hope and promise to us in the desert areas of our lives. Hear our prayers that we might draw ever nearer to you in this season of Advent. Through Christ our Lord. Amen.

COLLECT

Let us pray.

Pause for silent prayer

Almighty and merciful God,
may no earthly undertaking hinder those
who set out in haste to meet your Son,
but may our learning of heavenly wisdom
gain us admittance to his company.
Who lives and reigns with you in the unity
    of the Holy Spirit,
one God, for ever and ever. **Amen.**

FIRST READING
Bar 5:1-9

Jerusalem, take off your robe of mourning
        and misery;
    put on the splendor of glory from God
        forever:
wrapped in the cloak of justice from God,
    bear on your head the mitre
    that displays the glory of the eternal
        name.
For God will show all the earth your
        splendor:
    you will be named by God forever
    the peace of justice, the glory of God's
        worship.

Up, Jerusalem! stand upon the heights;
    look to the east and see your children
gathered from the east and the west
    at the word of the Holy One,
    rejoicing that they are remembered by
        God.
Led away on foot by their enemies they
        left you:
    but God will bring them back to you
    borne aloft in glory as on royal thrones.
For God has commanded
    that every lofty mountain be made low,
and that the age-old depths and gorges
    be filled to level ground,
    that Israel may advance secure in the
        glory of God.
The forests and every fragrant kind of
        tree
    have overshadowed Israel at God's
        command;
for God is leading Israel in joy
    by the light of his glory,
    with his mercy and justice for company.

RESPONSORIAL PSALM

Ps 126:1-2, 2-3, 4-5, 6

R̸. (3) The Lord has done great things for us; we are filled with joy.

When the Lord brought back the captives
of Zion,
we were like men dreaming.
Then our mouth was filled with laughter,
and our tongue with rejoicing.

R̸. The Lord has done great things for us;
we are filled with joy.

Then they said among the nations,
"The Lord has done great things for
them."
The Lord has done great things for us;
we are glad indeed.

R̸. The Lord has done great things for us;
we are filled with joy.

Restore our fortunes, O Lord,
like the torrents in the southern desert.
Those who sow in tears
shall reap rejoicing.

R̸. The Lord has done great things for us;
we are filled with joy.

Although they go forth weeping,
carrying the seed to be sown,
they shall come back rejoicing,
carrying their sheaves.

R̸. The Lord has done great things for us;
we are filled with joy.

SECOND READING

Phil 1:4-6, 8-11

Brothers and sisters:
I pray always with joy in my every prayer
for all of you,
because of your partnership for the
gospel
from the first day until now.
I am confident of this,
that the one who began a good work
in you
will continue to complete it
until the day of Christ Jesus.
God is my witness,
how I long for all of you with the
affection of Christ Jesus.
And this is my prayer:
that your love may increase ever more
and more
in knowledge and every kind of
perception,
to discern what is of value,
so that you may be pure and blameless
for the day of Christ,
filled with the fruit of righteousness
that comes through Jesus Christ
for the glory and praise of God.

About Liturgy

Prepare the way: I do a lot of airline travel so I'm quite familiar with airport security protocols and I know the best ways to get through screening lines quickly and without much hassle. Except during the holidays. That's when all the once- or twice-a-year travelers come out. They always bring way too much luggage, never have their IDs and boarding passes ready, and usually end up right in front of me in the security line. I used to roll my eyes every time I saw them and grumble under my breath. Why couldn't they know more about airport etiquette and be a road warrior like me?

That is until I had a conversation with a harried single mom while waiting in line at security. She was taking three excited kids and a sullen teenager to Disneyland. She had scraped and sacrificed for several years to save up just enough to pay for the entire trip on her own. Yet the airport was the hardest part of the journey for her because she was deathly afraid to fly. None of her kids had been on a plane before, and she hadn't flown since she was a child herself, but she was determined to give her children a bit of joy after so many years of just getting by. Her story, grit, and courage helped me see my inexperienced travel companions with a bit more compassion and even admiration.

How might it change our perception of those Christmas and Easter Catholics who start making their way to our parishes this time of year if we saw them less as a nuisance or burden and more like Christ for whom we wait? What if the road we are called to make straight is meant to be for them? What if we made every effort to ease their path to Christ with sincere and radical hospitality? We will not know how many obstacles they have had to navigate just to get to our doors unless we long for them with the affection of Christ. Then perhaps all those of us who are travelers on the road will see the salvation of God together.

About Liturgical Music

Singing by ear and by heart: Many people today do not read music. It is simply a reality. While we need to do our part to promote more music-reading literacy in our communities, we should also aid those who may feel discouraged or put off by music they perceive to be complicated. This doesn't mean that we need to water down our liturgical music. It simply challenges us to look for melodies that can be learned easily by ear and are grounded in strong texts, and with settings that are flexible enough to be enhanced by a choir or additional instruments. Two such pieces for this Sunday are found in *Sacred Song*. First, "Prepare the Way of the Lord" (Taizé Community) is a four-part round that can be learned quickly by an assembly. Once the assembly is confident with the melody, the choir can complement the assembly line with the canon. You could even invite the entire assembly to join in the canon as well, dividing parts by men and women or by sections of the church. The refrain of "Arise Jerusalem, Stand on the Height" (Collegeville Composers), with its exhortation to "open your hearts," can be a powerful antiphon the assembly sings during the communion procession while cantors or a schola lead the verses.

DECEMBER 9, 2018
SECOND SUNDAY OF ADVENT

✠ SPIRITUALITY

GOSPEL ACCLAMATION
Isa 61:1 (cited in Luke 4:18)

R̸. Alleluia, alleluia.
The Spirit of the Lord is upon me,
because he has anointed me
to bring glad tidings to the poor.
R̸. Alleluia, alleluia.

Gospel   Luke 3:10-18; L9C

The crowds asked John the Baptist,
   "What should we do?"
He said to them in reply,
   "Whoever has two cloaks
   should share with the person
      who has none.
And whoever has food should do
      likewise."
Even tax collectors came to be bap-
      tized and they said to him,
   "Teacher, what should we do?"
He answered them,
   "Stop collecting more than what
      is prescribed."
Soldiers also asked him,
   "And what is it that we should do?"
He told them,
   "Do not practice extortion,
   do not falsely accuse anyone,
   and be satisfied with your wages."

Now the people were filled with
      expectation,
   and all were asking in their hearts
   whether John might be the Christ.
John answered them all, saying,
   "I am baptizing you with water,
   but one mightier than I is coming.
I am not worthy to loosen the thongs of
      his sandals.
He will baptize you with the Holy Spirit
      and fire.
His winnowing fan is in his hand to
      clear his threshing floor
   and to gather the wheat into his barn,
   but the chaff he will burn with un-
      quenchable fire."
Exhorting them in many other ways,
   he preached good news to the people.

Reflecting on the Gospel

We hear the preaching of John the Baptist today, the Third Sunday of Advent. We are moving toward the imminent coming of the Son of Man. John would have been a fine preacher of the fire and brimstone variety, motivating his audience to action. Three times different groups ask him, "What should we do?" And three times John has an answer founded in justice and mercy. Follow the rules; share with those who have not. This is fairly simple and straightforward advice. And because of it he was thought to be the Messiah.

We can almost feel the crowd's anticipation and excitement. Here is someone who is preaching justice and mercy. By the crowd's ready reception of this message we might imagine that justice and mercy were in short supply. Soldiers might have taken more than their due, as did the tax collectors. Mercy, giving another a cloak when you have two, seems to have been wanting. The reception of the message tells us something about the crowds, who likely were on the lower economic rungs of society.

Furthermore, John tells them that this is only the beginning. Another is coming. Rather than a message of peace, John tells them that the one to come bears a winnowing fan. Though today many might not be familiar with the term, a winnowing fan was a fork-like shovel. The winnower used the fan to throw wheat grains into the air. The heavy kernels would fall to the ground and the lighter chaff would be blown away, gathered up, and burned. John the Baptist used this vivid image to speak of what the "one who is to come" would do.

Being burned in an "unquenchable fire" seems a distant image from the "lilies of the field" Jesus that Luke will narrate later in his gospel. This might cause us to wonder, were John's expectations met? Perhaps in his fire-and-brimstone preaching he was hoping for a fiery judgment. And this could be the reason he sent messengers to Jesus later in the gospel asking him, "Are you the one who is to come, or should we look for another?" (Luke 7:19; NABRE). John's own expectation of a Messiah who would bring judgment, wrath, and an "unquenchable fire" might not have been met by Jesus. John would not be the first to have dashed expectations and hopes. Jesus has another way. Still, John's essential message of practicing justice and mercy are good ways to prepare for Christ's coming.

Living the Paschal Mystery

John the Baptist's simple message of justice and mercy has global ramifications in the modern world. Though it's easy to glance backward and recognize the challenges faced by those in the ancient world, John's message is for us too. There are those today who are cheated out of wages and/or benefits by others who game the system. Many of us might even benefit (intentionally or not) from a system that encourages unjust practices when it comes to labor conditions or wages and benefits. Those in the developed world have the equivalent of multiple cloaks while many throughout the world go without. While it might be rare for us to see outright pilfering of wages, more often we can encounter poor working conditions, a minimum wage that requires 120 hours of work each week to support a family, or cheap goods whose real costs are borne an ocean away. What are the values that guide our lives? How are we to live in preparation for the coming of the Son of Man? Justice and mercy are a sure foundation.

Focusing the Gospel

Key words and phrases: The crowds asked John the Baptist, / "What should we do?"

To the point: After hearing John's preaching, the people who have gathered around him are inspired to take action in their own lives. Three times we hear the question repeated in this gospel passage, "What should we do?" The crowds, then the tax collectors, and finally the soldiers ask. And three times John replies to this question. He tells the crowds to share their excess with those that have nothing. He instructs the tax collectors and soldiers to practice fairness and prudence in their professions. John's good news requires action and sows seeds for the kingdom of God of which Jesus will preach.

Connecting the Gospel

to the first and second readings: In today's set of readings we have an unusual situation where the Old Testament and epistle connect seamlessly with each other while the gospel seems to be on its own. In the first two readings we hear the theme of rejoicing loud and clear. The prophet Zephaniah tells us to "[s]hout for joy . . .!" while the apostle Paul exhorts, "Rejoice in the Lord always." Both readings announce the nearness of God and tell us not to be afraid. In the gospel, John the Baptist strikes a sterner tone. He gives clear examples of the actions the people must take in order to demonstrate their repentance. He ends with a powerful image of Jesus with winnowing fan in hand ready to gather the harvest while destroying the chaff. This gospel, however somber, is also a reason to rejoice. John's call from God to preach to the people shows that it is not too late for them to return to God. They, too, can have lives free from fear and full of rejoicing. The One who is the source of complete joy and peace calls to them.

to experience: The season of Advent is halfway over and Christmas is drawing near. How does God call to you to let go of anxieties and make room for the joy of Christmas?

Connecting the Responsorial Psalm

to the readings: The psalm today comes from the book of the prophet Isaiah. These verses cap off a section in Isaiah called the Book of Emmanuel (6:1-12:6). The name Emmanuel, which means "God with us," is not directly heard in the psalm or the readings for today, but we hear echoes of this theme. The prophet Zephaniah proclaims, "The LORD, your God, is in your midst." The apostle Paul writes, "The Lord is near." And in the psalm itself we hear, "Shout with exultation, O city of Zion, / for great in your midst / is the Holy One of Israel!"

to psalmist preparation: We are approaching Christmas, the feast of the Incarnation, when God chose to become a human being to draw near to us. As you prepare to proclaim this psalm of thanksgiving and joy, pause to reflect on how you have experienced Emmanuel, "God with us," in your own life.

PROMPTS FOR FAITH-SHARING

The prophet Zephaniah tells us, "The LORD, your God, is in your midst." How have you experienced God in your midst this past week?

In today's second reading St. Paul exhorts us, "Have no anxiety at all." What anxieties are you dealing with right now in your life? How might you give these anxieties over to God?

In today's gospel the people ask John the Baptist, "What should we do?" As you enter into the final nine days of Advent, what is one action you might take to serve Jesus' mission of mercy and justice?

This is Gaudete Sunday, a Sunday for joy even as we continue the season of Advent preparing our hearts and minds for Christmas. Are there Christmas preparations that are causing you stress and worry? Can you trade them in or let go of them in order to allow room for more joy?

Model Penitential Act

Presider: On this Gaudete Sunday, we are reminded to rejoice always in the Lord. As we prepare to enter into this celebration, we reflect on how we have lived this call to joy. . . [*pause*]

Lord Jesus, you baptize with the holy Spirit and fire: Lord, have mercy.

Christ Jesus, you are the promised Messiah: Christ, have mercy.

Lord Jesus, you show us the way of kindness and joy: Lord, have mercy.

Homily Points

• In her book, *The Religious Potential of the Child*, theologian Sofia Cavalletti says, "It is only in love, and not in fear, that one may have a moral life worthy of the name." In the gospel we hear the people gathered around John the Baptist ask him, "What should we do?" They want to offer a fitting response to the baptism of repentance they have experienced. Today we have the stern exhortations of John paired with the injunction from the apostle Paul, "Rejoice in the Lord always. / I shall say it again: rejoice!" We are called not only to do good but to do good with joy and love.

• In today's readings we hear the source of our joy proclaimed: "The Lord is near" and God is in our midst. Our belief in Emmanuel, "God with us," is central to our lives as Christians. It shapes our relationship with God and others and calls us to be living signs of God's presence in the world. When we live from this central belief we naturally desire to do what is right in honor of our relationship with God.

• John the Baptist lifts up the image of Jesus with winnowing fan in hand, ready to "gather the wheat into his barn" and burn the chaff "with unquenchable fire." Advent can be seen as a time to clear away the chaff in our own lives. Out of love for God and for our neighbor we can ask, what are the things that separate us from experiencing God in our daily lives? Where have we failed to live the moral life with joy and love? We are now over halfway through with Advent. As Christmas draws closer may we intensify our prayer for Jesus to send the fire of his love to purify our hearts and minds anew.

Model Universal Prayer (Prayer of the Faithful)

Presider: Today St. Paul exhorts us, "Have no anxiety at all, but in everything, / by prayer and petition, with thanksgiving, / make your requests known to God." In this spirit let us offer our petitions.

Response: Lord, hear our prayer.

That the church may be a sign of joy in the world . . .

That all people may know "the peace of God that surpasses all understanding" . . .

That those who are experiencing loneliness and despair in this Advent season might be comforted . . .

That each of us here may open ourselves to the question, "what must I do?" and be prepared to take action to spread joy and kindness in our families and communities . . .

Presider: God of joy, you call us to let go of our anxieties and to trust in your bountiful love and peace. Hear our prayers that we may become living signs of your tender care for all. Through Christ our Lord. Amen.

COLLECT

Let us pray.

Pause for silent prayer

O God, who see how your people
faithfully await the feast of the Lord's
    Nativity,
enable us, we pray,
to attain the joys of so great a salvation
and to celebrate them always
with solemn worship and glad rejoicing.
Through our Lord Jesus Christ, your Son,
who lives and reigns with you in the unity
    of the Holy Spirit,
one God, for ever and ever. **Amen.**

FIRST READING
Zeph 3:14-18a

Shout for joy, O daughter Zion!
    Sing joyfully, O Israel!
Be glad and exult with all your heart,
    O daughter Jerusalem!
The LORD has removed the judgment
    against you,
    he has turned away your enemies;
the King of Israel, the LORD, is in your
    midst,
    you have no further misfortune to fear.
On that day, it shall be said to Jerusalem:
    Fear not, O Zion, be not discouraged!
The LORD, your God, is in your midst,
    a mighty savior;
he will rejoice over you with gladness,
    and renew you in his love,
he will sing joyfully because of you,
    as one sings at festivals.

RESPONSORIAL PSALM

Isa 12:2-3, 4, 5-6

R⃒. (6) Cry out with joy and gladness: for
   among you is the great and Holy One
   of Israel.

God indeed is my savior;
   I am confident and unafraid.
My strength and my courage is the LORD,
   and he has been my savior.
With joy you will draw water
   at the fountain of salvation.

R⃒. Cry out with joy and gladness: for
   among you is the great and Holy One
   of Israel.

Give thanks to the LORD, acclaim his name;
   among the nations make known his
      deeds,
   proclaim how exalted is his name.

R⃒. Cry out with joy and gladness: for
   among you is the great and Holy One
   of Israel.

Sing praise to the LORD for his glorious
      achievement;
   let this be known throughout all the
      earth.
Shout with exultation, O city of Zion,
   for great in your midst
   is the Holy One of Israel!

R⃒. Cry out with joy and gladness: for
   among you is the great and Holy One
   of Israel.

SECOND READING

Phil 4:4-7

Brothers and sisters:
Rejoice in the Lord always.
I shall say it again: rejoice!
Your kindness should be known to all.
The Lord is near.
Have no anxiety at all, but in everything,
   by prayer and petition, with
      thanksgiving,
   make your requests known to God.
Then the peace of God that surpasses all
      understanding
   will guard your hearts and minds in
      Christ Jesus.

About Liturgy

No sourpusses allowed: In Joy of the Gospel, Pope Francis quotes Pope John XXIII's speech at the opening of Vatican II and his statement that we must disagree with "those prophets of doom" who see nothing hopeful in the world. Then Francis says, "One of the more serious temptations which stifles boldness and zeal is a defeatism which turns us into querulous and disillusioned pessimists, 'sourpusses'" (85). You have to love a pope that uses the word "sourpusses" in an official papal exhortation! Earlier that year, in one of his intimate daily Mass homilies at the Vatican's Casa Santa Marta, Francis said, "We can't proclaim Jesus with funeral faces" (May 31, 2013). And still again at an earlier homily, "Sometimes these melancholic Christians' faces have more in common with pickled peppers than the joy of having a beautiful life" (May 10, 2013).

I wonder if someone took a picture of your liturgical ministers at Sunday Mass, would the pope's words ring true? Would you see sourpusses and pickled peppers? I know I have at many of the Masses I've been to in my life and I was probably one of those pickled peppers! When we get so focused on the details of doing the liturgy and getting it all just right, sometimes we can look like those melancholy Christians. We don't mean to, but oftentimes our faces don't match what we're trying to communicate, that is, glad tidings and good news.

Pope Francis's entire pontificate has been marked by joy. It is one of the four behaviors, the pope says, by which Christians will be known. (The other three are love, harmony, and suffering.) The pope also says that the Spirit is the "author of joy, the creator of joy" and this joy of the Spirit "gives us true Christian freedom" (May 31, 2013). Today of all days, Gaudete "Rejoice" Sunday, we must keep the sourpusses and prophets of doom in ourselves at bay. As you prepare to minister today pray to the Spirit to free you from any anxiety, worry, or sadness that might dampen the good news you want to communicate through your words and actions. Your prayer might even be a simple refrain from today's second reading: "Rejoice in the Lord always. / I shall say it again: rejoice!" (Phil 4:4).

About Initiation

The parish is *the curriculum:* In their 1999 pastoral plan on adult faith formation the United States bishops said, "[W]hile the parish may *have an* adult faith formation program, it is no less true that the parish *is* an adult faith formation program" (Our Hearts Were Burning Within Us 121, emphasis original). Although they weren't referring specifically to the RCIA, this statement gives catechumenate teams a deeper understanding of what the Rite of Christian Initiation of Adults means when it says that the initiation of catechumens "takes place within the community of the faithful" (4).

Formation of those preparing to live the Christian way of life doesn't happen in a classroom. It happens where other Christians are doing what Christians do: wherever they reflect on the Word together, strive to live and work in harmony and joy with one another, gather to pray, and especially, proclaim the good news to those in need.

About Liturgical Music

Suggestions: These last nine days before Christmas are the traditional times for singing the O Antiphons. Today "O Come, O Come, Emmanuel" with a joyfully sung refrain at a non-funereal tempo, would be an appropriate song to conclude the Mass and begin this final period of Advent. Also, look at *Psallite*'s "Rejoice in the Lord, Again Rejoice!" as a possible communion procession.

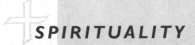

SPIRITUALITY

GOSPEL ACCLAMATION

Luke 1:38

R⁷. Alleluia, alleluia.
Behold, I am the handmaid of the Lord.
May it be done to me according to your word.
R⁷. Alleluia, alleluia.

Gospel

Luke 1:39-45; L12C

Mary set out
and traveled to the hill country in haste
to a town of Judah,
where she entered the house of Zechariah
and greeted Elizabeth.
When Elizabeth heard Mary's greeting,
the infant leaped in her womb,
and Elizabeth, filled with the Holy Spirit,
cried out in a loud voice and said,
"Blessed are you among women,
and blessed is the fruit of your womb.
And how does this happen to me,
that the mother of my Lord should come to me?
For at the moment the sound of your greeting reached my ears,
the infant in my womb leaped for joy.
Blessed are you who believed
that what was spoken to you by the Lord
would be fulfilled."

Reflecting on the Gospel

We are only days away from Christmas when we celebrate the fourth Sunday of Advent this year. This season is especially short and can make for a hectic, frenetic pace as we consider all that needs to happen before the holiday. Some are preparing homes to receive guests, others are preparing meals, and many are doing both! Still others are setting out on their travels to see loved ones during these holy days. We are busy with many tasks.

We might imagine Mary and Elizabeth sharing these feelings in this reading from Luke. Mary visits her cousin and Elizabeth has certainly been preparing for her guest. The greeting is joyful and Luke tells us that Elizabeth was filled with the Holy Spirit. For Luke the evangelist the Holy Spirit is active not only in Jesus' ministry but before Jesus was born, in preparation for it. Recall that Mary conceives by the power of the Holy Spirit, and after Jesus is raised from the dead Luke will recount how the Holy Spirit was poured out on the assembled disciples at Pentecost as tongues of fire. Some have even said Luke's Acts of the Apostles would be better termed the Acts of the Holy Spirit. So it is significant here that Elizabeth, too, is filled with the Holy Spirit. Not only that but essentially she proclaims the baby in Mary's womb to be "Lord." Here again Luke is displaying his theological insight that Jesus was not merely Lord at the moment of his baptism (as Mark might have it), but he could rightfully be called Lord before he was even born. Even the baby John in Elizabeth's womb shares the joy.

This gospel passage calls to mind for us how important human relationships are. Amidst all the travel, preparation, meals, and general business, the bonds of human love bind us together. When we consider the holiday season with its pressing demands let us recall the ultimate reason for our cares and concerns. We have in mind those we love and care for. May the relationships we celebrate this season, especially the relationships we have in Christ, inspire us to live in a meaningful way.

Living the Paschal Mystery

In this the first chapter of Luke's gospel we learn that Elizabeth was filled with the Holy Spirit. Luke has a concern for women as we shall see in reading his gospel. Luke often gives women pride of place, or at least shows them with a status equal to that of men. This story is an example of that. We hear virtually nothing about Zechariah, who has been struck speechless. Instead, this is an encounter between two women, each filled with the Holy Spirit, having a profound meeting and reflecting theologically on that.

Like these women, we are to recognize the work of the Holy Spirit in our lives. Whether it may be the miraculous birth of a child or the bringing forth of other new life, the Holy Spirit is as active today as in days of old.

When the daily activities of life seem to overwhelm us, as they might at this time of year, it is good to pause and to reflect on the lives of these women who were open to God's activity in their lives.

Focusing the Gospel

Key words and phrases: Mary set out / and traveled to the hill country in haste.

To the point: Our gospel today begins with a journey. Mary, having heard from the angel Gabriel of Elizabeth's pregnancy, sets out to visit her kinswoman. This was no small expedition. Tradition holds that Zechariah and Elizabeth lived in Ain Karim, a little town in the hill country of Judea about five miles from Jerusalem. The journey from Nazareth was nearly one hundred miles: traveling on foot or by caravan, it would have taken three to five days. Not only did Mary believe the news Gabriel had brought her, but she puts this faith into action immediately, traveling in haste to be close to Elizabeth and to share the good news that invites us all to "[leap] for joy."

Connecting the Gospel

to the first reading: The prophet Micah speaks to the people of Israel exiled in Babylon and tells them of a leader who will be raised up for them. This ruler will be a "shepherd" whose "greatness / shall reach to the ends of the earth." Finally, Micah tells us, "[H]e shall be peace." In the gospel we see this prophecy coming true. When Mary reaches Elizabeth's house, Elizabeth is alerted to the presence of Jesus by the infant leaping within her own womb. By the Holy Spirit she proclaims that this is, indeed, "the mother of my Lord." John the Baptist, who will later point to Jesus with words and actions, begins his task of pointing to Jesus by leaping for joy.

to experience: As we near the end of Advent our joy grows ever greater. We, too, prepare to herald Jesus, the Prince of Peace, in word and action.

Connecting the Responsorial Psalm

to the readings: The first reading and the gospel speak of God's promise (first reading) and the fulfillment of that promise (gospel) to send a savior to God's people. Micah prophesies a ruler who will shepherd the people out of exile into a place of security and peace. John the Baptist announces the presence of this ruler in the womb of the Virgin Mary when he leaps for joy. Today's psalm has a different tone, however. As a lament, it calls upon God to come to the aid of a nation in shambles. The psalmist demands that God "[r]ouse your power, / and come to save us."

to psalmist preparation: This is a song of faith and of desperation. The psalmist demands that God protect God's people in a time of near annihilation. As you proclaim this psalm to the people of God today, think of a time when you yourself have been desperate for God's protection, love, and care. Use this experience to convey both the urgency in the psalm as well as the faith that God will do what God has promised and restore the people once again.

PROMPTS FOR FAITH-SHARING

In the second reading, the letter to the Hebrews proclaims that "we have been consecrated / through the offering of the body of Jesus Christ once for all." To be consecrated is to be set apart for a holy purpose. How do our lives give testimony to being consecrated?

Just as in the birth of Jesus, the Holy Spirit is active in our own time. How do you experience the Holy Spirit working in your life?

John the Baptist first prophesies to Jesus' presence by leaping for joy in Elizabeth's womb. In this season of Advent and Christmas does your joy point to the risen Lord? How?

Mary and Elizabeth share each other's joy and offer strength to one another in their pregnancies. In our spiritual life we need companions who can point out where God is working in our lives. Other times we are called to be the one who bears witness to Christ's presence in another. How might we cultivate these spiritual friendships?

Model Penitential Act

Presider: In today's gospel Elizabeth tells Mary, "Blessed are you who believed / that what was spoken to you by the Lord / would be fulfilled." Let us prepare to enter into this liturgy by opening ourselves up to the transformative word of God. . .[*pause*]

Lord Jesus, you are Son of God and son of Mary: Lord, have mercy.

Christ Jesus, you shepherd us into life: Christ, have mercy.

Lord Jesus, you are the Prince of Peace: Lord, have mercy.

Homily Points

• There is a theme that runs throughout all salvation history of God choosing the small and humble to do great things. We see this in the gospel where the woman chosen to be Jesus' mother is not the wife of the high priest who lives close to Jerusalem, but is instead a young unmarried woman from Nazareth, a small settlement in the northern part of Israel. And yet it is this woman who says "yes" to the angel's request that she bear a child who will be, "Son of the Most High."

• In the first reading the prophet Micah calls Bethlehem-Ephrathah "too small to be among the clans of Judah," but then goes on to say "from you shall come forth for me / one who is to be ruler in Israel." Jesus will be born not in Jerusalem, the holiest and most important city in Israel, but in little Bethlehem. When we gather together in a few days to celebrate the Nativity of the Lord we will hear that arriving in Bethlehem, with no room available at the inn, his family must seek shelter in the place where animals are kept. The first people to visit his manger-cradle are not the local elite or dignitaries but shepherds fresh from the fields.

• All of these details of Jesus' conception and birth reveal to us the character of God. If it is God's way to choose the small and humble, then it must be ours as well. How might we find a way to embrace this preference in our own lives and in our celebration of Christmas?

Model Universal Prayer (Prayer of the Faithful)

Presider: Let us pray for the faith of Mary, who believed that what was spoken to her by the Lord would be fulfilled.

Response: Lord, hear our prayer.

That all members of the church may faithfully follow Jesus, the Shepherd . . .

That all people of the world might dwell in peace . . .

That those who are shut-in or experience isolation might be embraced in the community of God's love . . .

That each of us here may joyfully recognize Jesus within the small and humble of society . . .

Presider: Faithful God, you gave us Mary as a model of belief and discipleship. Hear our prayers that we might follow her example. Through Christ our Lord. Amen.

COLLECT

Let us pray.

Pause for silent prayer

Pour forth, we beseech you, O Lord,
your grace into our hearts,
that we, to whom the Incarnation of Christ
      your Son
was made known by the message of an
      Angel,
may by his Passion and Cross
be brought to the glory of his
      Resurrection.
Who lives and reigns with you in the unity
      of the Holy Spirit,
one God, for ever and ever. **Amen.**

FIRST READING

Mic 5:1-4a

Thus says the LORD:
You, Bethlehem-Ephrathah
      too small to be among the clans of
            Judah,
from you shall come forth for me
      one who is to be ruler in Israel;
whose origin is from of old,
      from ancient times.
Therefore the Lord will give them up, until
      the time
      when she who is to give birth has
            borne,
and the rest of his kindred shall return
      to the children of Israel.
He shall stand firm and shepherd his flock
      by the strength of the LORD,
      in the majestic name of the LORD, his
            God;
and they shall remain, for now his
      greatness
      shall reach to the ends of the earth;
      he shall be peace.

RESPONSORIAL PSALM
Ps 80:2-3, 15-16, 18-19

R℣. (4) Lord, make us turn to you; let us see
    your face and we shall be saved.

O shepherd of Israel, hearken,
    from your throne upon the cherubim,
        shine forth.
Rouse your power,
    and come to save us.

R℣. Lord, make us turn to you; let us see
    your face and we shall be saved.

Once again, O Lᴏʀᴅ of hosts,
    look down from heaven, and see;
take care of this vine,
    and protect what your right hand has
        planted,
    the son of man whom you yourself
        made strong.

R℣. Lord, make us turn to you; let us see
    your face and we shall be saved.

May your help be with the man of your
    right hand,
    with the son of man whom you yourself
        made strong.
Then we will no more withdraw from you;
    give us new life, and we will call upon
        your name.

R℣. Lord, make us turn to you; let us see
    your face and we shall be saved.

SECOND READING
Heb 10:5-10

Brothers and sisters:
When Christ came into the world, he said:
    "Sacrifice and offering you did not
        desire,
      but a body you prepared for me;
      in holocausts and sin offerings you took
        no delight.
      Then I said, 'As is written of me in the
        scroll,
    behold, I come to do your will, O God.'"

First he says, "Sacrifices and offerings,
    holocausts and sin offerings,
    you neither desired nor delighted in."
These are offered according to the law.
Then he says, "Behold, I come to do your
    will."
He takes away the first to establish the
    second.
By this "will," we have been consecrated
    through the offering of the body of
        Jesus Christ once for all.

About Liturgy

Hail, Mary: The gospel for the Fourth Sunday of Advent in each liturgical year focuses on Mary, the Mother of God. Today's passage from Luke gives us a Marian set of beatitudes: "Blessed are you among women"; "blessed is the fruit of your womb"; and "[b]lessed are you who believed." What an overwhelming and powerful way to be greeted—with blessing after blessing!

    This visitation scene reminds us that greetings are opportunities for blessings and for recognizing the presence of Christ in one another. How appropriate then that in the days when we give our season's greetings that we take time to recognize these as more than just mere formality or holiday tradition.

    First, in the liturgy we have the ritual greeting and response, "The Lord be with you"; "And with your spirit." Here presider and people recognize the presence of Christ in one another and bless each other for the work that they are about to perform. This dialogue occurs at five key moments of the Mass: at the beginning, before the gospel proclamation, at the start of the eucharistic prayer, just before Communion, and at the dismissal. Each of these moments requires focused attention and commitment from all the people of God whatever their role is in the body of Christ. This ritual dialogue does not serve as a nicety like "Good morning." Rather they are words reminding us of the profound responsibility we each have in bearing Christ to the world. As Christians we are called to do this through our witness in communal prayer, proclamation of the good news, priestly offering of ourselves in union with Christ's sacrifice, working for peace, and finally, by bringing that peace to the ends of the earth.

    Second, we can bring this blessing through the greetings we share each day, whether spoken, written, or silent. If we can make these few seconds moments of intentional connection and blessing, we, too, just might leap for joy.

Marian prayers at Mass: In some places it has become a practice to insert the Hail Mary as a prayer of the assembly during Mass. Often this happens as a conclusion to the universal prayer or perhaps after Communion. This practice, however, does not align with any rubrics from the Roman Missal. The Mass is always christological in that our prayer reflects on our salvation in Christ. Even when our readings or the liturgical feast emphasize Mary the Mother of God, our praise is centered on Christ. We might use Mary's own words, as in, for example, the *Magnificat*, but the focus remains on God.

About Liturgical Music

Suggestions: Any setting of the *Magnificat* would be appropriate for today, even though we do not get that specific text in this part of the gospel reading. One image that we do get from today's readings is Mary as the one who does God's will. One lovely piece that communicates the joy of doing God's will is *Psallite*'s "Come, All You Good and Faithful Servants" (*Sacred Song*). The refrain text is "Come, all you good and faithful servants, share in the joy, the joy of the Lord." This is interspersed with verses from Psalm 34, which makes it a perfect communion processional. Another possible *Psallite* antiphon is "Let the Word Make a Home in Your Heart," which serves as a connection to the Word made flesh we will hear in John's gospel on Christmas Day and with Mary who pondered all these things in her heart.

SEASON OF CHRISTMAS

The Lord entered her, and became a servant;
the Word entered her, and became silent within her;
thunder entered her, and his voice was still;
the Shepherd of all entered her;
he became a Lamb in her, and came forth bleating.

—St. Ephrem the Syrian

✟ SPIRITUALITY

The Vigil Mass

GOSPEL ACCLAMATION
R̹. Alleluia, alleluia.
Tomorrow the wickedness of the earth will be
destroyed:
the Savior of the world will reign over us.
R̹. Alleluia, alleluia.

Gospel

Matt 1:1-25; L13ABC

The book of the genealogy of
Jesus Christ,
the son of David, the son
of Abraham.

Abraham became the
father of Isaac,
Isaac the father of Jacob,
Jacob the father of Judah
and his brothers.
Judah became the father of Perez and
Zerah,
whose mother was Tamar.
Perez became the father of Hezron,
Hezron the father of Ram,
Ram the father of Amminadab.
Amminadab became the father of
Nahshon,
Nahshon the father of Salmon,
Salmon the father of Boaz,
whose mother was Rahab.
Boaz became the father of Obed,
whose mother was Ruth.
Obed became the father of Jesse,
Jesse the father of David the king.

David became the father of Solomon,
whose mother had been the wife of
Uriah.
Solomon became the father of Rehoboam,
Rehoboam the father of Abijah,
Abijah the father of Asaph.

Continued in Appendix A, p. 264, or
Matt 1:18-25 *in Appendix A, p. 264.*

See Appendix A, p. 265, for the other readings.

Reflecting on the Gospel and Living the Paschal Mystery
Key words and phrases:
"Jesus Christ, the Son of David, the Son of Abraham." "Emmanuel, God with us."

To the point: This evening's reading gives lectors trouble. It is worth taking time to practice the pronunciation of the names—while also learning rhythm and emphasis—in proclaiming Matthew's three sets of fourteen generations. All too often the names are lost in the struggle to pronounce them properly. It is critical that those who proclaim the Word of God practice their proclamation skills.

All that being noted, it is significant that Matthew traces Jesus' lineage to Abraham, the father in faith. When Luke has the chance to convey Jesus' lineage he traces it back to Adam! Each evangelist is writing for his own audience: Matthew for a Jewish Christian audience (thus Abraham) and Luke for a Gentile Christian audience (thus Adam). Moreover, Matthew values an orderly and numerically significant count of generations that Luke does not address at all. Neither agrees on his genealogy, the number of generations, or even the names in the generations, including the name of Jesus' paternal grandfather (the father of Joseph)! In fact, students of Scripture are often given the task of comparing the genealogies of Matthew and Luke to recognize these significant and irreconcilable differences. But the differences point to something more profound, which is each evangelist's theological perspective on Jesus.

One important matter to learn by a compare-and-contrast exercise is not the names of the generations, but rather that Jesus was born of human stock, in a human lineage. He was a human being (Adam), Jewish (Abraham) of the tribe of Judah, and in the line of David. Though David lived one thousand years before Jesus, the promise of a new David is fulfilled in Jesus.

To ponder and pray: How many of us remember waiting as children for Christmas morning, or waiting for a special birthday, or a visit from family or friends? The wait seemed interminable. And yet the object of our anticipation finally and inevitably arrived. In one sense this evening's gospel tells the story of another wait, but this time for one thousand years! The promised Son of David, the sprout from the stump of Jesse, has appeared. Jesus, the fulfillment of the promises made of old, is Son of David and also Emmanuel, God with us. The divine has become human and humanity is thereby infused with divinity.

This opening chapter of Matthew sets the stage for the theological understanding of Jesus. At the conclusion of the gospel Jesus will tell his disciples that he will be with them always. He who bears the title Emmanuel is "God with us" not only once two thousand years ago but also now and eternally. When we celebrate the birth of the Messiah we recognize the fulfillment of all of our longings, all of our anticipation, all of our expectations. Only Emmanuel, God with us, can satisfy these existential yearnings. For that, we celebrate and are grateful.

SPIRITUALITY

Mass at Midnight

GOSPEL ACCLAMATION
Luke 2:10-11

R̸. Alleluia, alleluia.
I proclaim to you good news of great joy:
today a Savior is born for us,
Christ the Lord.
R̸. Alleluia, alleluia.

Gospel

Luke 2:1-14; L14ABC

In those days a decree went out from
    Caesar Augustus
  that the whole world should be
      enrolled.
This was the first enrollment,
  when Quirinius was governor of Syria.
So all went to be enrolled, each to his
      own town.
And Joseph too went up from Galilee
    from the town of Nazareth
  to Judea, to the city of David that is
      called Bethlehem,
  because he was of the house and fam-
      ily of David,
  to be enrolled with Mary, his betrothed,
      who was with child.
While they were there,
  the time came for her to have her child,
  and she gave birth to her firstborn son.

Continued in Appendix A, p. 265.

See Appendix A, p. 266, for the other readings.

Reflecting on the Gospel and Living the Paschal Mystery

Key words and phrases: She wrapped him in swaddling clothes and laid him in a manger.

To the point: The gospel for midnight Mass contains the scene we connect most readily with Christmas. Jesus, Son of God and son of Mary, is born in Bethlehem, but since there is no room at the inn he has no cradle for a bed. Instead, a feedbox becomes his resting place. We've pictured this scene so many times that maybe it has stopped shocking us. It certainly would have shocked Jesus' first visitors. This baby, whose birth is proclaimed by an angel, is to be found with his mother and father sleeping among the animals. This one, whom the shepherds are told is "Savior," "Messiah," and "Lord," enters the world as a helpless baby who must depend on others for all of his physical needs.

To ponder and pray: That God chose to become a human being is remarkable, but that God chose to become a human being born in a barn to poor parents is even more so. This child of whom angels sing is born into the messiness of human life. Can we also find him there?

✝ SPIRITUALITY

Mass at Dawn

GOSPEL ACCLAMATION
Luke 2:14

R̸. Alleluia, alleluia.
Glory to God in the highest,
and on earth peace to those
on whom his favor rests.
R̸. Alleluia, alleluia.

Gospel

Luke 2:15-20; L15ABC

When the angels went
    away from them to
    heaven,
the shepherds said to
    one another,
"Let us go, then, to
    Bethlehem
to see this thing that has
    taken place,
which the Lord has
    made known to us."
So they went in haste and
    found Mary and Joseph,
and the infant lying in the
    manger.
When they saw this,
    they made known the message
    that had been told them about this
    child.
All who heard it were amazed
    by what had been told them by the
    shepherds.
And Mary kept all these things,
    reflecting on them in her heart.
Then the shepherds returned,
    glorifying and praising God
    for all they had heard and seen,
    just as it had been told to them.

See Appendix A, p. 266, for the other readings.

Reflecting on the Gospel and Living the Paschal Mystery
Key words and phrases: [T]hey went in haste. [T]hey made known the message. [R]eflecting on them in her heart.

To the point: The story of Christmas does not end with the angels' song glorifying God. Here we see the shepherds' response to the revelation given to them by that heavenly host. They "went in haste," which echoes Mary's swift response after her own angelic visit in the previous chapter. Having seen for themselves what had been revealed to them, the shepherds did not stay long at the manger despite what our nativity scenes capture. The shepherds keep moving, making known the message about the child Jesus and glorifying God as they returned to their flocks. Although they remained shepherds, they had been changed. They were now the first evangelists of the in-breaking of God into human history.

In this same passage, we see another kind of response to the message of salvation. Mary's silent contemplation, we know, will not remain silent for long. Though she has few words recorded in the gospels after the birth of her son, she, too, communicated the saving message not only by her words but also by her presence at the cross and among the apostles.

On this Christmas morning the gospel calls us to respond to God's action in our lives. That response requires both quiet contemplation and bold proclamation.

To ponder and pray: Christmas morning finds many of us unwrapping gifts that have been waiting all Advent to be opened. Once the adrenaline of surprise and wonder has passed, we experience a "gift coma" that lulls us into a pleasant and carefree mood.

In this time with family and friends we can bask in their presence and take pleasure in the things we have received from loved ones. However, a true gift given in love is one that obligates the receiver to action, that is, to return the gift—not as a kind of payment or equal exchange but as a loving response of thanksgiving, acknowledging both the gift and the giver.

When our heavenly Father is the one who bestows the gift, and the gift given is Jesus his only Son, what "return gift" could we possibly give?

Today we can look to the humble shepherds who had nothing to give but their presence and their courageous witness to any who would hear their message—that God is with us! We also can follow the example of Mary whose "return gift" was her very heart in which she allowed the message to dwell and shape her life and actions.

In his famous poem Howard Thurman says, "When the song of the angels is stilled . . . the work of Christmas begins" ("The Work of Christmas," *The Mood of Christmas and Other Celebrations*). We still have much work to do this Christmas.

SPIRITUALITY

Mass during the Day

GOSPEL ACCLAMATION

R7. Alleluia, alleluia.
A holy day has dawned upon us.
Come, you nations, and adore the Lord.
For today a great light has come upon the earth.
R7. Alleluia, alleluia.

Gospel

John 1:1-18; L16ABC

In the beginning was the Word,
   and the Word was with God,
   and the Word was God.
He was in the beginning with God.
All things came to be through him,
   and without him nothing came to be.
What came to be through him was life,
   and this life was the light of the human
      race;
the light shines in the darkness,
   and the darkness has not overcome it.

A man named John was sent from God.
He came for testimony, to testify to the
      light,
   so that all might believe through him.
He was not the light,
   but came to testify to the light.
The true light, which enlightens everyone,
   was coming into the world.
   He was in the world,
      and the world came to be through him,
      but the world did not know him.
   He came to what was his own,
      but his own people did not accept him.

But to those who did accept him
   he gave power to become children of
      God,
   to those who believe in his name,
   who were born not by natural
      generation
   nor by human choice nor by a man's
      decision
   but of God.

Continued in Appendix A, p. 267, or
John 1:1-5, 9-14 *in Appendix A, p. 267.*

See Appendix A, p. 267, for the other readings.

Reflecting on the Gospel and Living the Paschal Mystery
Key words and phrases:
In the beginning was the Word. And the Word became flesh.

To the point: Those expecting a gospel reading about the nativity may be surprised to hear high-minded, sophisticated, theological discourse from John's prologue. This is perhaps the most subtle, nuanced, and erudite expression of the dynamic relationship between the Word and God. A pinnacle is reached when we read, "And the Word became flesh," which is true incarnation theology. The eternal unchanging word underwent change and became time-bound flesh. There is nothing here about Mary, Joseph, angels, or shepherds. Instead, we have refined theology, which is not wedded to story.

To ponder and pray: The incarnation is a central mystery of faith and belief in it marks one as Christian. In Jesus the divine becomes human, raising humanity to divinity. Lowly, changing, finite flesh is the place of the exalted, unchanging, eternal God. This central insight from John's prologue means that all humanity, as well as each human person, is worthy of respect, dignity, and care because every human person is the reflection of and dwelling place of the divine. How we treat our fellow human beings is therefore an expression of our worship of God. It is not possible to worship God and mistreat one's fellows. By the incarnation our humanity is exalted to divinity.

Model Penitential Act

Presider: We gather to celebrate the birth of Emmanuel, God with us, now and forever. As we prepare to enter into the mystery of the incarnation let us pause to ask for pardon and healing . . . [*pause*]

    Lord Jesus, you bring light into gloom and darkness: Lord, have mercy.

    Christ Jesus, wrapped in swaddling clothes and laid in a manger, you are the savior of the world: Christ, have mercy.

    Lord Jesus, you fill the earth with glory: Lord, have mercy.

Model Universal Prayer (Prayer of the Faithful)

Presider: With hearts full of gratitude for the gift of Jesus, we lift our prayers to God.

Response: Lord, hear our prayer.

That the church be a sign of peace and hope within a world in need of healing . . .

That the rulers of the world might lead with justice and peace . . .

That those in need may have shelter and food, and find a generous welcome this Christmas . . .

That each of us here might be renewed in our lives as Christians this Christmas by accepting anew God's gift of love . . .

Presider: Glorious God, we praise you for the gift of your Son, the savior who came for all people to bring peace and justice. We ask you to hear our prayers and grant them through Jesus Christ, Lord forever and ever. Amen.

About Liturgy

Facets of the Nativity: There are four different sets of readings and prayers assigned to four different times of day in the Roman Missal and the Lectionary for the celebration of the nativity. The Vigil Mass is used in the evening on December 24, and the gospel comes from Matthew's genealogy. On Christmas Day there are three options: the Mass during the Night, which proclaims the beginning of Luke's nativity narrative; the Mass at Dawn, which continues Luke's account; and the Mass during the Day, which gives us John's prologue.

Although the Roman Missal prayers are set for each time of day, the readings may be chosen from among the various options given. Many will choose to proclaim Luke's gospel at all the Masses on these two days because it gives the Christmas story that most people expect. However, there is great wisdom in using each assigned set of readings at their proper times because these give us a fuller picture of who this newborn king truly is. By bookending the Nativity feast with the complexity of Jesus' family tree and John's poetic description of the Logos, one sees a deeper way of understanding Christmas that goes beyond the familiar manger scene.

COLLECT

(from the Mass during the Day)
Let us pray.

Pause for silent prayer

O God, who wonderfully created the dignity
    of human nature
and still more wonderfully restored it,
grant, we pray,
that we may share in the divinity of Christ,
who humbled himself to share in our
    humanity.
Who lives and reigns with you in the unity of
    the Holy Spirit,
one God, for ever and ever. **Amen.**

FOR REFLECTION

• Sometime during Christmas Eve, Christmas Day, or throughout the Christmas season you will likely sing "Silent Night." Where and when do you find silence to celebrate the birth of Christ?

• On Christmas we celebrate how "the Word became flesh / and made his dwelling among us." How do you experience Jesus as flesh and blood in your own life?

Homily Points

• On this feast of the Nativity of the Lord we are given four different gospels to be read on the vigil, midnight, dawn, and day of Christmas. Each reading invites us into a unique facet of the mystery of the incarnation. The vigil reading from Matthew shows Jesus as the pinnacle of a long line of ancestors from Abraham through forty-two generations to the Messiah, the long-awaited one. The gospels for midnight and dawn contain the birth of Jesus and the adoration of the shepherds found in Luke. Luke's historical details assure us that this event actually took place in Bethlehem over two thousand years ago. He also shows us that the Savior of the world made his dwelling first among the poor and lowly. In John's gospel, Jesus' genesis is told in a different way: the Word that was with God from the very beginning "became flesh / and made his dwelling among us."

✠ SPIRITUALITY

GOSPEL ACCLAMATION
Col 3:15a, 16a

℟. Alleluia, alleluia.
Let the peace of Christ control your hearts;
let the word of Christ dwell in you richly.
℟. Alleluia, alleluia.

Gospel Luke 2:41-52;
L17C

Each year Jesus' par-
ents went to Jeru-
salem for the feast
of Passover,
and when he was
twelve years old,
they went up accord-
ing to festival
custom.
After they had completed
its days, as they were
returning,
the boy Jesus remained behind in Jerusalem,
but his parents did not know it.
Thinking that he was in the caravan,
they journeyed for a day
and looked for him among their relatives and acquaintances,
but not finding him,
they returned to Jerusalem to look for
him.
After three days they found him in the
temple,
sitting in the midst of the teachers,
listening to them and asking them
questions,
and all who heard him were astounded
at his understanding and his answers.

Continued in Appendix A, p. 268.

Reflecting on the Gospel

A missing child is a parent's worst fear. We can imagine being in a grocery store, a department store, or even an amusement park and the panic that would overtake us if a child in our care was nowhere to be found. We might have been relying on someone else to keep an eye on this young one, only to realize that was a misunderstanding. Such things happen occasionally and often the child is found shortly thereafter. Other times it results in tragedy. But in today's gospel story the Holy Family had lost Jesus in the capital city of Jerusalem! This is a reminder that though Jesus' family is holy it was not without challenges, like any family. Joseph and Mary dealt with parenting a preteen who thought he was fine on his own. Obviously miscommunication was a challenge for them as it might be for us as well.

It can be simple for us to imagine that the Holy Family was perfect, something to which we could never measure up. But Luke gives us a story of a family with real-life challenges and problems. In fact, this is a challenge we would not wish upon anyone, losing track of a child for days in a major city.

Even so, such a story might give us hope as we deal with daily activities in family life, striving not for perfection, which is an unattainable ideal. But instead, we recognize that family life can be messy, punctuated with misunderstandings, miscommunication, and mistakes. Such events are not "sinful" and they were obviously part of life for the Holy Family. It is signifi-cant that Luke tells us not only that Jesus was obedient to his parents but that he also grew in wisdom. He was not born fully formed and all knowing. As a human being he naturally learned things. And simply reflecting on this fact can be the source of profound meditation on our part. We who believe that Jesus was divine also believe that he was human. He was not a divine puppet but a flesh-and-blood human being who was raised in a family and grew in wisdom. Our own families are places of sanctity. We will have challenges as the Holy Family did. But we can deal with them forthrightly, knowing that the relation-ships we have in this most basic human unit are a means of sanctification.

Living the Paschal Mystery

The family has been called the "domestic church" as it is the first encounter children have with the Gospel, and it is the dwelling place of faith and lived Christian relationships. But oftentimes we hear such ideas and think that a fam-ily must therefore be a place of perfection, and we all know from our own ex-periences that families (or churches for that matter) are anything but places of perfection. So the idea can be daunting and seem unattainable. But Luke gives us an image of family life that might be more relatable. Even the Holy Family had their share of challenges, and so we have hope for ourselves and our own family situations. We know from experience—confirmed by research—that we learn more by imitation and example than we do by preaching and teaching. In other words, one's actions speak more loudly than words. How we live the gospel message in the midst of family life says much more about our faith com-mitment than what we say about the Gospel. Our homes and families ought to be places of security, welcome, love, care, concern, and forgiveness. Speaking about such things does not mean as much as living them. The same can be said for the Holy Family. Their behaviors spoke more loudly than their words. Today on this feast of the Holy Family, we might pause to consider what message we convey by our actions.

Focusing the Gospel

Key words and phrases: Did you not know that I must be in my Father's house?

To the point: In many ways this seems like an odd gospel to choose for the feast of the Holy Family. Mary and Joseph lose their adolescent son in a big city not just for an hour or an afternoon but for three days. This hardly seems like an example to lift up or emulate for tranquil family life. But perhaps that is part of the point. Jesus is born into a human family. Out of all of the places in the world God chose a faithful Jewish couple living in Israel to raise his son. Jesus' growing up years are often called the "hidden life in Nazareth." Much of family life is hidden and often involves misunderstandings and anxieties. Can we claim all parts of this life as holy?

Connecting the Gospel

to the first reading: In the first reading from First Samuel we see many parallels to the gospel. Another mother and another son approach the "Father's house." Hannah, who was also only able to conceive through the intervention of God, now takes this long-awaited child (for whom she prayed for so fervently that the high priest accused her of being intoxicated) and gives him to the Lord. Whereas Mary and Joseph find their son in the temple, Hannah leaves her child in the house of the Lord. In toddlerhood (Samuel) and early adolescence (Jesus) each son was unique, set apart for a special purpose and consecrated to the Lord.

to experience: In Hannah's devotion and Mary and Joseph's anxiety and misunderstanding we see the struggle of parents who love their child but also know this child is not theirs but God's. Within the Holy Family, Mary and Joseph were blessed with closeness to Jesus but also challenged and at times saddened by his vocation that would take him away from them. In our own lives, how can we follow the examples of Hannah and Mary and Joseph and hold those that we love most dear gently, realizing that they are gifts that do not belong to us but to God?

Connecting the Responsorial Psalm

to the readings: Today's psalm is one of joy and anticipation, fitting for a pilgrim to Jerusalem who longs to dwell in the house of the Lord. Jesus also finds joy and contentment in the temple, not wanting to leave after journeying to Jerusalem for the feast of Passover.

to psalmist preparation: For the pilgrim there is joy in the journey and joy in the ultimate destination. This psalm is a prayer for pilgrims going up to Jerusalem for one of the three pilgrimage feasts of the year. As you proclaim it, infuse your words with longing and with joy so as to remind the assembly of where their true home lies—in the house of the Lord.

PROMPTS FOR FAITH-SHARING

How do you experience your family as a "domestic church"?

Where do you find "holy imperfection" in your own family?

How does your family support each other in times of stress and sadness?

In the gospel Jesus calls the temple, "my Father's house." Do you feel at home in your church community? How do you experience it as a place of shelter and welcome? How might you help it grow to be even more a house of God?

Model Penitential Act

Presider: Today we celebrate the Holy Family of Jesus, Mary, and Joseph. We also remember that we are children of God and therefore members of God's family. For the times that have not lived up to this identity, we ask for pardon and healing . . . [*pause*]

Lord Jesus, you command us to love one another: Lord, have mercy.

Christ Jesus, you are a member of the Holy Family with Mary and Joseph: Christ, have mercy.

Lord Jesus, you call us to remain in you: Lord, have mercy.

Homily Points

• Even in the Holy Family there were misunderstandings and anxieties. We are told in the gospel that after Mary and Joseph found Jesus in the temple and questioned him, they did not understand it when he said, "Did you not know that I must be in my Father's house?" If Mary and Joseph did not always understand Jesus, we can be assured that misunderstandings will occur among our own family members. What is most important is how we respond to these misunderstandings. How might we practice love and respect, especially when confusion and anxiety arise?

• In the 1930s a new religious community grew up in the Roman Catholic Church called the Little Brothers of Jesus and the Little Sisters of Jesus. These communities, inspired by the work and writing of Blessed Charles de Foucald, take as their model the hidden life of Jesus of Nazareth. Brother Charles wrote, "I did not feel that I was called to imitate Jesus in his public life and preaching, but understood that I should imitate the hidden life of the humble and poor workman of Nazareth." How might we also take as our model the hidden life of Nazareth where Jesus lived with Mary and Joseph and "advanced in wisdom and age and favor / before God and man"?

• Mary, Joseph, and Jesus were a family deeply immersed in the rituals and traditions of their people. In today's gospel we hear of how they keep the feast of Passover by traveling to Jerusalem to celebrate this holy day. In our own lives we are given a family and also the family of the church, the people of God. In both our domestic family and our church family relationships are strengthened through the celebration of rituals. How might we invite more ritual into the life of our families?

Model Universal Prayer (Prayer of the Faithful)

Presider: As children of God, we bring our intercessions to the Lord with confidence, knowing we will receive what we need.

Response: Lord, hear our prayer.

That all members of the church seek to live out in peace and tranquility their call to be the family of God . . .

That the countries of the world seek to safeguard and protect the earth, our common home . . .

That families in crisis might find the help and support they need to flourish and thrive . . .

That all gathered here might strive to be faithful and loving members of the families we belong to . . .

Presider: God, Father of all, through your son Jesus, you invite us to claim our rightful places as your beloved sons and daughters. Hear the prayers we bring before you, that through the intercession of the Holy Family we might become a sign of your love in the world, through Jesus Christ our Lord. Amen.

COLLECT

Let us pray.

Pause for silent prayer

O God, who were pleased to give us
the shining example of the Holy Family,
graciously grant that we may imitate them
in practicing the virtues of family life and
    in the bonds of charity,
and so, in the joy of your house,
delight one day in eternal rewards.
Through our Lord Jesus Christ, your Son,
who lives and reigns with you in the unity
    of the Holy Spirit,
one God, for ever and ever. **Amen**.

FIRST READING

1 Sam 1:20-22, 24-28

In those days Hannah conceived, and at
    the end of her term bore a son
  whom she called Samuel, since she had
    asked the LORD for him.
The next time her husband Elkanah was
    going up
  with the rest of his household
  to offer the customary sacrifice to the
    LORD and to fulfill his vows,
  Hannah did not go, explaining to her
    husband,
  "Once the child is weaned,
  I will take him to appear before the LORD
  and to remain there forever;
  I will offer him as a perpetual nazirite."

Once Samuel was weaned, Hannah
    brought him up with her,
  along with a three-year-old bull,
  an ephah of flour, and a skin of wine,
  and presented him at the temple of the
    LORD in Shiloh.
After the boy's father had sacrificed the
    young bull,
  Hannah, his mother, approached Eli and
    said:
  "Pardon, my lord!
As you live, my lord,
  I am the woman who stood near you
    here, praying to the LORD.
I prayed for this child, and the LORD
    granted my request.
Now I, in turn, give him to the LORD;
  as long as he lives, he shall be dedicated
    to the LORD."
Hannah left Samuel there.

RESPONSORIAL PSALM

Ps 84:2-3, 5-6, 9-10

℟. (cf. 5a) Blessed are they who dwell in
  your house, O Lord.

How lovely is your dwelling place, O Lord of hosts!
My soul yearns and pines for the courts of the Lord.
My heart and my flesh cry out for the living God.

R⒎ Blessed are they who dwell in your house, O Lord.

Happy they who dwell in your house!
Continually they praise you.
Happy the men whose strength you are!
Their hearts are set upon the pilgrimage.

R⒎ Blessed are they who dwell in your house, O Lord.

O Lord of hosts, hear our prayer;
hearken, O God of Jacob!
O God, behold our shield,
and look upon the face of your anointed.

R⒎ Blessed are they who dwell in your house, O Lord.

SECOND READING
1 John 3:1-2, 21-24

Beloved:
See what love the Father has bestowed on us
that we may be called the children of God.
And so we are.
The reason the world does not know us is that it did not know him.
Beloved, we are God's children now;
what we shall be has not yet been revealed.
We do know that when it is revealed we shall be like him,
for we shall see him as he is.

Beloved, if our hearts do not condemn us,
we have confidence in God and receive from him whatever we ask,
because we keep his commandments and do what pleases him.
And his commandment is this:
we should believe in the name of his Son, Jesus Christ,
and love one another just as he commanded us.
Those who keep his commandments remain in him, and he in them,
and the way we know that he remains in us
is from the Spirit he gave us.

See Appendix A, p. 268, for optional readings.

CATECHESIS

About Liturgy
The domestic church: This Sunday is a good time to help your households reflect on how they are the church in miniature. The Dogmatic Constitution on the Church says that the family is "regarded as the domestic church" (*Lumen Gentium* 11). In the family Christian spouses signify the unity between Christ and the church, help one another attain holiness through the love they share in their marriage, and build up the church by raising children in the faith.

These kinds of households, made up of married spouses with children, hold a special place among the people of God. This does not mean, however, that other kinds of households cannot be holy as well. Homilists and liturgy planners need to be aware that many in their assemblies today will not reflect this "ideal" image of a holy family. Thankfully, today's gospel reading can give us a glimpse into the "holy imperfection" even the Holy Family experienced! For what makes a family holy is not perfection but love that is shown in compassion, kindness, humility, gentleness, patience, perseverance, and forgiveness. All of us in our own households can surely reflect and inspire that kind of holiness.

A domestic church calendar: As we near the end of the calendar year and the solemnity of the Epiphany when calendars might be blessed, you could invite all your households to prepare their own domestic church calendar. In addition to Sunday, the premier holy day, and the holy days of obligation, this calendar would have all the spiritual days that are important for that specific household to remember and observe with prayer. Here are some days that could be included in a domestic church calendar: birthdays of family members, baptismal anniversaries, wedding anniversaries, death anniversaries of loved ones, first Communion and confirmation anniversaries, one's patron saint days, and one's parish or diocesan patron saint day. Invite households to bring their domestic church calendar to the Epiphany Masses next week to be blessed.

About Initiation
Formation at home: Although you might not be meeting with catechumens and candidates during this Christmas season, you can still help them to be formed in the Christian faith. Give them "mystagogical" questions they can reflect on by themselves or with their family and sponsors during the holidays. These are questions that prompt them to look for Christ in their daily lives and to reflect on what their encounters with Christ mean. When you come together again you can share your responses.

Here are some question ideas: Read through your Christmas cards. How do you hear "good news" in those greetings? How did you see God today, and did it remind you of a story from the Bible? What was the most memorable moment from church in these past few weeks, and what did that say to you about who Jesus is?

About Liturgical Music
Singing at home: Today's second reading option from Colossians invites us to sing psalms, hymns, and spiritual songs with gratitude to God in our hearts. As music ministers we do this mostly at church in the liturgy. Yet we can also be models of sung prayer in our homes as well.

One place where communal singing can easily be incorporated into home life is at mealtime prayer. You can help your parish households sing their table blessings by teaching them simple refrains they could use at home. One such refrain that would be appropriate as a communion song for today is *Psallite*'s "We Receive from Your Fullness."

DECEMBER 30, 2018
THE HOLY FAMILY OF JESUS, MARY, AND JOSEPH

GOSPEL ACCLAMATION
Heb 1:1-2

R꒒. Alleluia, alleluia.

In the past God spoke to our ancestors through
    the prophets;
in these last days, he has spoken to us through
    the Son.

R꒒. Alleluia, alleluia.

Gospel

Luke 2:16-21; L18ABC

**The shepherds went in haste to Bethle-
    hem and found Mary and Joseph,
    and the infant lying in the manger.
When they saw this,
    they made known the message
    that had been told them about this
        child.
All who heard it were amazed
    by what had been told them by the
        shepherds.
And Mary kept all these things,
    reflecting on them in her heart.
Then the shepherds returned,
    glorifying and praising God
    for all they had heard and seen,
    just as it had been told to them.**

**When eight days were completed for
    his circumcision,
    he was named Jesus, the name given
        him by the angel
    before he was conceived in the
        womb.**

See Appendix A, p. 269, for the other readings.

Reflecting on the Gospel

Catholics are known for having a devotion to Mary, the mother of Jesus. In many RCIA classes the topic of Mary consumes a great deal of the room's oxygen. Mary's role is also a flashpoint in discussions between Catholics and other Christians, especially Protestants. There is much room for confusion over Marian titles; in fact, they are often misunderstood. A good rule of thumb is that any title for Mary says much more about Jesus than it does about Mary. And that is certainly the case today when we celebrate the solemnity of Mary, the Mother of God.

On its face such a title, Mother of God, can be perplexing. How can God, who exists from all eternity, have a mother? Where is that in the Scriptures? But of course, the statement says more about Jesus, who is the enfleshment (incarnation) of the Word of God.

These questions also perplexed the church fathers who were debating the terms "Mother of God" or, literally, "God-bearer" (*Theotokos* in Greek), and whether it was appropriate to apply them to Mary. Many theologians objected to "Theotokos" (bearer of God) being applied to Mary and instead preferred "Christotokos" (bearer of Christ). These theologians said it was better to refer to Mary as the one who bore Christ rather than as the one who bore God. On the other side of the argument were theologians who said that Jesus was the incarnation of God to such a degree that Mary could legitimately be called "bearer of God." And to make a long story short, the latter group carried the day as our commemorating this feast today certainly indicates.

But it would be too easy to become caught up in this Marian title as another example of outsized Catholic devotion to Mary. Instead, this title has its roots in the fifth century, one thousand years before Catholics and Protestants. Ultimately, like so many other Marian titles, this says more about Jesus and his identity than it does about Mary. And the claim is simply and profoundly this: that Jesus was the incarnation of God from the moment of his conception so that Mary can rightly be said to have borne the divine. Christianity is an incarnational and sacramental faith. Matter, earth, and world are the place of divine revelation. It is not that humanity must raise itself up to divinity, but rather, divinity humbles itself and enters into humanity to become human. All the created world, most especially each human being, is a locus of the divine.

Living the Paschal Mystery

When we recognize that all of creation is a place for God's indwelling we see that the sacred is infused within the secular. There is not such a sharp distinction any longer between the holy and the profane, for by the incarnation the divine has become human, the eternal time-bound, and the immortal mortal.

We now treat not only humans but all creation with the respect and humility that it deserves as a place for the divine. Despite all the evidence to the contrary—wars, disease, poverty, selfishness, and even death itself—God has the last word, which is eternal life. God who is all powerful is also all vulnerable. God suffers with creation when it is desecrated. God is not far removed and otherworldly. God intimately knows human life and the human struggle for justice, dignity, and equality. Jesus, the incarnation of the Word of God underwent the paschal mystery of dying and rising. By so doing he gave new meaning to these most fundamental aspects of our world. Death now leads to life, as the created world is infused with the divine.

Focusing the Gospel

Key words and phrases: Mary kept all these things, / reflecting on them in her heart.

To the point: On this solemnity of Mary we are given only a small snippet of her life. In the gospel all we hear is that she "kept all these things, / reflecting on them in her heart." Many times there will be things we don't understand in life. Today Mary's response is lifted up for us to contemplate. When faced with the infinite mystery of God become human, Mary holds it close to her very core, safe in the center of her heart.

Model Penitential Act

Presider: As we gather today to consecrate this New Year to God through the intercession of Mary, the Holy Mother of God, let us pause to acknowledge our own sinfulness and need of God's mercy. . . [*pause*]

Lord Jesus, you are Son of God and son of Mary: Lord, have mercy.

Christ Jesus, through you we are able to call God "Abba, Father!": Christ, have mercy.

Lord Jesus, you give us every spiritual blessing: Lord, have mercy.

Model Universal Prayer (Prayer of the Faithful)

Presider: As we enter into this New Year let us offer our intentions to God, assured of his love and faithful blessing.

Response: Lord, hear our prayer.

That the church might be a sign of the merciful, compassionate, parental love of God . . .

That this New Year might bring peace and overflowing blessings to all the nations of the world . . .

That, through the intercession of Mary, those who have lost their way might come home to God. . .

That each of us here might be a tangible blessing to all we meet . . .

Presider: Loving God, we commend this New Year to your merciful care, along with all of our needs, hopes, and dreams. We ask this through Jesus Christ our Lord. Amen.

About Liturgy

Blessings: Today's readings give us an opportunity to reflect on what the church teaches us about blessings. You may already know about the *Book of Blessings*, which is the universal church's official ritual text for blessings used throughout the liturgical year and for specific occasions in a parish's or household's life. To get a substantial understanding of the theology of blessings, read the "General Introduction" to this ritual book. From those introductory notes we learn that God has been blessing us from the very beginning of creation. It is simply what God does. "He who is all good has made all things good, so that he might fill his creatures with blessings" (1). Christ is "the Father's supreme blessing upon us" (3); and those who become God's children through Christ are given the Spirit of Christ "in order to bring God's healing blessings to the world" (3).

On this first day of the year, when we give praise to God for the blessings we have received through Christ by his coming into human history through the life of a woman, Mary, let us recommit to being a blessing for others and to bring God's healing blessings to the world.

COLLECT

Let us pray.

Pause for silent prayer

O God, who through the fruitful virginity of Blessed Mary
bestowed on the human race
the grace of eternal salvation,
grant, we pray,
that we may experience the intercession of her,
through whom we were found worthy
to receive the author of life,
our Lord Jesus Christ, your Son.
Who lives and reigns with you in the unity of the Holy Spirit,
one God, for ever and ever. **Amen.**

FOR REFLECTION

• In the first reading Aaron is instructed by God on how to bless the people. In this New Year, how might we dedicate our lives to be a blessing for all those around us?

• In the second reading from Galatians we hear God referred to as "Abba, Father!" In your prayer life how do you address God?

• We can imagine how the shepherds' lives might have changed that night they drew close to Jesus in the manger. How has your faith grown and deepened this Christmas season?

Homily Points

• In the gospel we are told the shepherds "went in haste" to confirm the angel's message to them. Mary, after hearing her own earth-shattering news from an angel, goes "in haste" to visit her cousin Elizabeth. The good news shared with Mary at Jesus' conception and with the shepherds at Jesus' birth motivates the ones who hear it to immediate action. This overflowing joy and wonder demands to be shared.

• This haste is counterbalanced by Mary's response to the shepherds' news: "Mary kept all these things, / reflecting on them in her heart." How in our lives as Christians can we balance the need for haste and the need for reflection? How might we invite both of these states into our lives this New Year?

33

✠ SPIRITUALITY

GOSPEL ACCLAMATION

Matt 2:2

R̸. Alleluia, alleluia.
We saw his star at its rising
and have come to do him homage.
R̸. Alleluia, alleluia.

Gospel

Matt 2:1-12; L20ABC

When Jesus was born
   in Bethlehem of
   Judea,
  in the days of King
   Herod,
  behold, magi from the
   east arrived in Je-
   rusalem, saying,
  "Where is the newborn
   king of the Jews?
We saw his star at its
   rising
  and have come to do
   him homage."
When King Herod heard
   this,
  he was greatly troubled,
  and all Jerusalem with him.
Assembling all the chief priests and the
   scribes of the people,
  he inquired of them where the Christ
   was to be born.
They said to him, "In Bethlehem of Judea,
  for thus it has been written through the
   prophet:
    And you, Bethlehem, land of Judah,
    are by no means least among the
     rulers of Judah;
    since from you shall come a ruler,
    who is to shepherd my people
     Israel."

Continued in Appendix A, p. 269.

Reflecting on the Gospel

The feast of the Epiphany is celebrated in many cultures and oftentimes more prominently than Christmas! At a time when many homes have taken down decorations and put away special dishes from the season, we are reminded that there are still celebrations to be had. This story of the visit from the magi is unique to Matthew's gospel and when read on its own terms it can be especially revealing. Often, however, we read this gospel with preconceived notions. For example, the text doesn't say how many magi there were but because they gave three gifts (gold, frankincense, and myrrh) artists, preachers, and homilists through the centuries talk about there being three kings. Aside from fulfilling Scripture (e.g., Isa 60:6), the gifts are symbolic, as they were given to kings or divinities in antiquity. Gold is a precious element representing kingship, frankincense a perfume, and myrrh a costly balm or ointment.

And this leads to the term, "king," which is not used in the gospel text. Instead, the term is "magi," which designated the Persian (modern-day Iran) priestly caste. Thus, Matthew foreshadows the postresurrection mission to the Gentiles by showing Gentiles (Persians) coming to worship the child Jesus. Ultimately, this is a story about who Jesus is and what his mission will be.

It is also significant that the magi worship the *child* Jesus. Matthew does not use the term infant here for Jesus is no longer an infant. And it's clear from the story that Mary is at her *house*, not in a manger as Luke would have it. Again, when we read these stories on their own terms without importing "what we know" from other stories, a different picture emerges, and that can be a picture that conforms more closely to the theology that the evangelist wanted to impart.

In the story following today's gospel, Matthew tells us of the Holy Family's flight into Egypt to escape Herod slaughtering all the male children in Bethlehem up to two years old (Matt 2:16; NABRE). This is a clear indication that the magi visited the home about two years after the birth of Jesus. And the point here is theological. Jesus is brought to Egypt so that the Scripture passage might be fulfilled, "Out of Egypt I called my son" (Matt 2:15; Hos 11:1; NABRE). So in today's gospel reading we see the mission to the Gentiles and the universal scope of salvation foreshadowed by the visit of the magi to worship the child Jesus. Salvation knows no bounds. This is a cause for celebration indeed!

Living the Paschal Mystery

Both children and adults enjoy giving and receiving gifts: it seems to be part of the human condition. For the receiver there is an element of surprise. What could it be? Perhaps some anticipation comes with opening the gift and there is a sense of wonder. For the giver there is the joy of generosity, in seeing the look on the face of the one who receives. There is the joy that comes in simply thinking of the other and providing something for the other not because it was earned, but instead because it comes from a place of generosity. Stories of gifts given and received are numerous in the Scriptures, antiquity, and history. They come to be part of family and friend lore as well. It's likely that many of us can quickly call to mind gifts that we've given or received. The gifts given by the magi in some way represent or symbolize the best physical objects that humanity has to offer. And Jesus is the best that God has to offer. By the conclusion of the gospel story humanity will have executed Jesus, the gift of God, only to have God raise him up from the dead. This expression of the paschal mystery guides our thoughts today when the magi present the best of human intentions.

Focusing the Gospel

Key words and phrases: They were overjoyed at seeing the star.

To the point: In today's gospel creation itself proclaims the birth of Jesus to the magi, the kings who are strangers in the land of Israel. They follow the star in their search for this newborn king, and when they find him not in the palace in Jerusalem but in a humble home in Bethlehem, they worship this baby and offer him kingly gifts. The magi respond with joy to the revelation of Jesus, unlike Herod who is "greatly troubled." Unable to receive the gift of Jesus or to offer Jesus the gift of himself he remains hostage to his greed and lust for power.

Connecting the Gospel

to the first and second readings: For the first time in our Advent and Christmas gospel readings the gift of Jesus is extended to the Gentiles. This is foreshadowed in Isaiah's prophecy to the people of Israel, "Nations shall walk by your light." Jesus, the light of the world, born to the Jewish people, invites everyone, Jews and Gentiles, into the light of God's love. The apostle Paul proclaims in his letter to the Ephesians, "[T]he Gentiles are coheirs, members of the same body, / and copartners in the promise in Christ Jesus through the gospel."

to experience: Paul proclaims the radical inclusivity of God's kingdom ushered in by the mystery of the incarnation: God become human, longing to draw all of creation to God-self. How do we practice this radical inclusivity in our own lives? How might we not only welcome the stranger but also reverence the stranger's wisdom, understanding, and right to be among us?

Connecting the Responsorial Psalm

to the readings: Psalm 72 is a prayer for the king of Israel, asking that the entire world might receive blessing through him as a representative of God and God's divine judgment and justice. In the gospel we see this prayer brought to fulfillment. The psalmist prays, "All kings shall pay him homage, / all nations shall serve him." In the gospel the magi (representatives from foreign lands) come and do just this—prostrate themselves before Jesus and do him homage. The psalmist proclaims that this king of great glory who rules all nations is concerned with the poor and the lowly, and then in the gospel we see that the king is in fact one of the poor and the lowly. Jesus is not found in a lavish palace with guards, wealth, and an army at his command. He is a defenseless child born to commoners.

to psalmist preparation: Today's feast marks the opening of the covenant to all the people of the world. Just as the magi welcomed the sight of the star with great joy, we, too, are invited to joyfully accept this humble child as our king and Lord. The psalm you proclaim today lauds the glory of this king and also extolls his compassion to the poor and the oppressed. How might you proclaim God's glory and compassion within the acts of your daily life?

PROMPTS FOR FAITH-SHARING

The prophet Isaiah tells us, "Rise up . . . ! Your light has come." When have you had the opportunity to be a light for others?

The magi follow a star that leads them to Jesus, God with us. In your life, how has creation helped you to know God?

The magi, strangers from a foreign country, travel to the land of Israel and are welcomed into Jesus' home. In your life of faith when have you encountered different cultures and/or religions? How has this experience changed your understanding of God and humanity?

In today's second reading St. Paul proclaims the inclusivity of God's kingdom where both Jews and Gentiles are welcome. How do you welcome those of different backgrounds into your home or parish?

Model Penitential Act

Presider: On this great feast of Epiphany we are invited anew to walk in the light of the Lord. Let us seek God's mercy for the times we have preferred the darkness to this saving light . . . [*pause*]

Lord Jesus, you are the light of the world: Lord, have mercy.

Christ Jesus, creation itself heralds you as the king: Christ, have mercy.

Lord Jesus, you are ruler and shepherd of the world: Lord, have mercy.

Homily Points

• Throughout the Advent and Christmas gospels we have seen God communicate with people in many different ways. Mary, Joseph, and the shepherds in the fields of Bethlehem all receive angelic visitors to tell them of Jesus' birth. Elizabeth and John the Baptist know of Jesus' presence in the womb of Mary by the power of the Holy Spirit. In today's gospel the scribes and priests know the Messiah's birthplace through the prophecies they have studied their entire lives. For the magi, creation itself points the way to God through their study of the stars and the new star they have charted and followed.

• Of the many people who hear of the Messiah's arrival, there is one who does not receive the news with joy and wonder. The magi arrive in Jerusalem looking for the newborn king of the Jews and instead they find Herod, a power-hungry ruler. It has been said that the gospel is meant to "comfort the afflicted and afflict the comfortable." Herod is certainly not comforted by the news of a newborn king but instead is "deeply troubled." In the gospel Herod becomes the first of many who will reject Jesus' light, life, and love.

• The gifts of the magi reveal the nature of Jesus to us. Gold is a gift befitting a king. Frankincense was a precious incense burned at the temple as a sign of the presence of God. Myrrh is mentioned in the gospels surrounding Jesus' death. It is offered to Jesus on the cross mixed with wine, which he refuses to drink, and it is among the perfumes and spices that Nicodemus brings to prepare Jesus' body for burial. The gifts proclaim Jesus king, God, and human. From creation to angelic messages to small details in the gospel, it seems that God desires to communicate God-self to us through whatever means available. The question is, are we listening?

Model Universal Prayer (Prayer of the Faithful)

Presider: On this feast of Epiphany we lift up our prayers and petitions to the God of light.

Response: Lord, hear our prayer.

That the church might shine as a light, inviting all nations into the peace and justice of the Lord . . .

That the nations of the world might attend to the oppressed and needy within their midst . . .

That those who walk in the darkness of greed, jealousy, and lust for power might be touched by the merciful light of God . . .

That all of us gathered here might welcome the light of God into our lives to eradicate the darkness of sin . . .

Presider: God of creation, you call to us through the radiance of the sun and the stars to fashion our lives after that of your son Jesus, the light of the world. Hear and grant our prayers through Christ our Lord. Amen.

COLLECT

Let us pray.

Pause for silent prayer

O God, who on this day
revealed your Only Begotten Son to the
    nations
by the guidance of a star,
grant in your mercy
that we, who know you already by faith,
may be brought to behold the beauty of
    your sublime glory.
Through our Lord Jesus Christ, your Son,
who lives and reigns with you in the unity
    of the Holy Spirit,
one God, for ever and ever. Amen.

FIRST READING

Isa 60:1-6

Rise up in splendor, Jerusalem! Your light
    has come,
    the glory of the Lord shines upon you.
See, darkness covers the earth,
    and thick clouds cover the peoples;
but upon you the Lord shines,
    and over you appears his glory.
Nations shall walk by your light,
    and kings by your shining radiance.
Raise your eyes and look about;
    they all gather and come to you:
your sons come from afar,
    and your daughters in the arms of their
        nurses.

Then you shall be radiant at what you see,
    your heart shall throb and overflow,
for the riches of the sea shall be emptied
        out before you,
    the wealth of nations shall be brought
        to you.
Caravans of camels shall fill you,
    dromedaries from Midian and Ephah;
all from Sheba shall come
    bearing gold and frankincense,
    and proclaiming the praises of the Lord.

RESPONSORIAL PSALM

Ps 72:1-2, 7-8, 10-11, 12-13

℟. (cf. 11) Lord, every nation on earth will adore you.

O God, with your judgment endow the king,
   and with your justice, the king's son;
he shall govern your people with justice
   and your afflicted ones with judgment.

℟. Lord, every nation on earth will adore you.

Justice shall flower in his days,
   and profound peace, till the moon be no more.
May he rule from sea to sea,
   and from the River to the ends of the earth.

℟. Lord, every nation on earth will adore you.

The kings of Tarshish and the Isles shall offer gifts;
   the kings of Arabia and Seba shall bring tribute.
All kings shall pay him homage,
   all nations shall serve him.

℟. Lord, every nation on earth will adore you.

For he shall rescue the poor when he cries out,
   and the afflicted when he has no one to help him.
He shall have pity for the lowly and the poor;
   the lives of the poor he shall save.

℟. Lord, every nation on earth will adore you.

SECOND READING

Eph 3:2-3a, 5-6

Brothers and sisters:
You have heard of the stewardship of God's grace
   that was given to me for your benefit,
   namely, that the mystery was made known to me by revelation.
It was not made known to people in other generations
   as it has now been revealed
to his holy apostles and prophets by the Spirit:
that the Gentiles are coheirs, members of the same body,
and copartners in the promise in Christ Jesus through the gospel.

About Liturgy

Blessing of calendars: Closely connected to this solemnity of the Epiphany is the focus on the blessing of time. We see this in the tradition of the announcement of Easter and the moveable feasts, sung this day after the proclamation of the gospel. We also see it in the traditional inscription used to bless a home at Epiphany, in which the date of the new calendar year is written above a home's door, along with the initials of the wise men's names: "C," "M," and "B" according to tradition. Perhaps it is because of the beginning of the new year, or because the magi used their keen observation of the movement of the stars that we mark the passage of time with blessings on this day.

If you had invited your community to create their own domestic church calendar (see feast of the Holy Family), today might be a good day to bless these calendars or to send home a blessing prayer people can use to bless their daily calendars. There is no official text found in the Book of Blessings for such a blessing, but you can find a "Blessing of Calendars on the Feast of the Epiphany" in *The Work of Your Hands* (Liturgical Press).

About Initiation

Copartners in the promise: Today's second reading from Ephesians gives us the crux of the meaning of Epiphany. The revelation given to St. Paul to steward is this: "that the Gentiles are coheirs, members of the same body, / and copartners in the promise in Christ Jesus through the gospel" (Eph 3:6). No longer is God's chosen limited to only one people: God's promise is given to all who seek God in Christ, and they become members of the same body of Christ. In light of this revelation, today may be an opportune time to celebrate a Rite of Reception of Baptized Christians into the Full Communion of the Catholic Church. The ritual may take place within or outside of Mass; however, it is preferable that the newly received also celebrate the Eucharist. Although the rite is relatively simple and does not take too much time, it is best to schedule this rite for a Mass at which there are no other additional rites, blessings, or lengthy presentations.

About Liturgical Music

Beyond "We Three Kings": No Epiphany celebration can go by without singing "We Three Kings." However there are many other carols that can take us beyond the literal retelling of the magi story. Songs to look for are those that focus on the promise of God given to all people, such as those that complement the message of today's psalm refrain, "Lord, every nation on earth will adore you" (Ps 72). Also look for songs that pick up the images from today's first reading of light rising over all.

Some song suggestions are: "Epiphany Carol" with text by Francis Patrick O'Brien set to the tune of BEACH SPRING (GIA); the traditional carol, "Good Christian Friends, Rejoice"; *Psallite*'s "Our City Has No Need of Sun or Moon."

Announcing Easter: Even though we're not done with Christmas yet, the church reminds us today that the fulcrum of the entire liturgical year is the Easter celebration of the Lord's resurrection. Don't forget to consider preparing to sing the Announcement of Easter and the Moveable Feasts, which are found in appendix I of the Roman Missal. This may be led by the deacon or a cantor.

✝ SPIRITUALITY

GOSPEL ACCLAMATION
cf. Luke 3:16

R︎. Alleluia, alleluia.
John said: One mightier than I
    is coming;
he will baptize you with the
    Holy Spirit and with fire.
R︎. Alleluia, alleluia.

Gospel

Luke 3:15-16, 21-22; L21C

**The people were filled
    with expectation,
and all were asking in
    their hearts
whether John might be
    the Christ.
John answered them all,
    saying,
"I am baptizing you
    with water,
but one mightier than I
    is coming.
I am not worthy to
    loosen the thongs of his sandals.
He will baptize you with the Holy Spirit
    and fire."**

**After all the people had been baptized
    and Jesus also had been baptized and
    was praying,
heaven was opened and the Holy
    Spirit descended upon him
in bodily form like a dove.
And a voice came from heaven,
    "You are my beloved Son;
    with you I am well pleased."**

Reflecting on the Gospel

The baptism of an infant is the cause of much joy, celebration, and love among family and friends. The baby is welcomed into the Christian community, a community of grace, support, and encouragement in the face of all that life can bring. This ritual action has its roots not only in Jesus but in John, "the Baptist" who was so named precisely because of this action he performed at the Jordan River. The early followers of Jesus recognized that Jesus' own ministry began after he was baptized by John, a story first recounted in the Gospel of Mark, which states that John preached a baptism of "forgiveness of sins." This story is echoed in Luke as well (Luke 3:3).

Thus, we (and the early Christians) experience a theological quandary. Why did Jesus, who is said to be without sin, submit to baptism by John? To what purpose or to what end is a baptism of forgiveness of sins to one without sin? Responses to this question were as varied as the gospel writers and church fathers themselves. Matthew says that it is "to fulfill all righteousness" (Matt 3:15; NABRE). The Gospel of John simply neglects to say that Jesus was baptized by John. Instead, John the Baptist merely testifies to Jesus without baptizing him at all. Luke places the baptism of Jesus in the passive voice and almost as an afterthought: "After all the people had been baptized / and Jesus also had been baptized" (Luke 3:21). Other than the Synoptics, neither Paul nor any other New Testament authors mention Jesus being baptized.

As indicated by the gospels, the ministry of Jesus began at or shortly after his baptism. And Luke shows that the Holy Spirit was active at this time, descending upon Jesus "in bodily form like a dove." Though Matthew says the Spirit descended upon him like a dove, only Luke says, "*in bodily form* like a dove." This phrase reflects Luke's tendency to objectivize the supernatural and it is something we will notice throughout this gospel. Further, Luke is also the only evangelist to say that Jesus was at prayer during this event. Prayer is another Lucan theme that we will see throughout his gospel: Luke shows Jesus at prayer more than any other evangelist. Luke will also show the early Christian community at prayer in the Acts of the Apostles.

So in these four short verses we have Lucan theology bursting from the page. Jesus is baptized by John (passive voice) though John preaches a baptism of forgiveness of sins. Luke objectivizes the supernatural by saying the Holy Spirit descended in bodily form like a dove, and Luke shows Jesus at prayer.

Living the Paschal Mystery

When we are about to make an important or life-altering decision we certainly pause to give it some thought. Before accepting a new position, a big move, or making a commitment to someone or something we likely ask God's guidance and wisdom. Some state simply that this is a prayer. And it seems Jesus did the same: he prayed before he embarked on his ministry.

If Luke is certain to show us that Jesus prayed, we are sure to see this as an example for our own lives. We are to pray. Significantly, Luke does not tell us what Jesus prayed only *that* he prayed. And this has ramifications for us too.

We are to be a people of prayer who consult and communicate with the Almighty, seeking direction, guidance, wisdom, and insight before embarking on our way.

When we pray we imitate Jesus and the relationship he lived with the Father. We also imitate the early Christians. We recognize that prayer is not limited to the liturgy or to formal recitation of memorized texts. Instead, it is a reflection of the relationship we have with God.

Focusing the Gospel

Key words and phrases: You are my beloved Son; with you I am well pleased.

To the point: In the beginning of Luke's gospel Jesus is named "Son of God" by the angel Gabriel, "my Lord" by Elizabeth, and "Messiah" by the angel of the Lord. Now, after being baptized in the River Jordan, Jesus is given another name, "beloved Son." Assured of God's love and approval, Jesus is ready to begin his public ministry.

Connecting the Gospel

to the second reading: In the Acts of the Apostles we see the moment of the baptism of Jesus, which was first witnessed by the people of Israel and then opened up to all people. Peter, the quintessential Jewish apostle, is called to visit the Roman centurion Cornelius, a Gentile. Through prayer, mystical vision, and meeting with Cornelius, Peter is finally able to proclaim, "God shows no partiality." Even though the good news of Jesus first came to the people of Israel, it is meant as a gift for all.

to experience: It is easy in life to want to divide the world into "us" and "them." As human beings we are naturally more comfortable when surrounded by people and places that are familiar to us. As Christians, however, we are called to proclaim a God who shows no partiality. How might we live this good news in our lives?

Connecting the Responsorial Psalm

to the readings: This psalm gives praise to God, whose might and glory is shown by his command of the waters of the earth. This water is destructive at times through flooding, but water also brings life into the dry desert. We hear that "[t]he voice of the LORD is over the waters" and remember how in the beginning the Holy Spirit hovered over the waters of the earth. We hear that "[t]he LORD is enthroned above the flood" and remember God promising Noah and his descendants never again to send water to wipe out creation. In the gospel a new moment in salvation history is narrated and it, too, contains water. Jesus steps forward to be baptized in the waters of the Jordan River and when he comes out we again hear the "voice of the LORD . . . over the waters." This heavenly voice proclaims, "You are my beloved Son; with you I am well pleased," and we can picture Jesus at prayer "enthroned" at the Jordan River as he lives more fully into his kingship as God's beloved.

to psalmist preparation: Proclaim this psalm with awe and wonder. The God we serve and worship is the God of all creation. Remember a time when you were awestruck by nature. Perhaps it was during a beautiful sunset, seeing the view from a mountaintop or gazing out at the ocean for the first time. Our God is creator and ruler of all this. As part of his creation let us, too, cry, "Glory!"

PROMPTS FOR FAITH-SHARING

On this feast of the Baptism of the Lord, consider your own baptismal day. What do you remember or what have you been told about the day you were baptized?

_____

_____

_____

_____

This feast day officially marks the last day of the Christmas season. Looking back on the weeks since December 25th, what has been most meaningful for you this Christmas? What traditions would you like to continue? Looking forward to next year, what would you like to do differently?

_____

_____

_____

After being baptized, Jesus prays. In Luke's gospel we often see Jesus in prayer. How would you like to enrich your own prayer life this year?

_____

_____

_____

At his baptism Jesus hears the voice of God saying, "You are my beloved Son; with you I am well pleased." Is it easy or difficult for you to believe that you are God's beloved? Why do you think this is?

_____

_____

_____

Model Rite for the Blessing and Sprinkling of Water

Presider: On this feast of the Baptism of the Lord we recall the grace of our own baptism. As we are sprinkled with holy water let us prepare ourselves to enter into this celebration with joy and a renewed commitment to our own baptismal promises . . . [*pause*]
  [*continue with* The Roman Missal, *Appendix II*]

Homily Points

• The baptism that John preaches in Luke's gospel is "a baptism of repentance for the forgiveness of sins" (3:3; NABRE). Having no need for repentance, conversion, or forgiveness, Jesus nevertheless joins the crowds on the banks of the Jordan River.

• In an action that prefigures the cross and resurrection, Jesus bears the sins of all others as he goes down into the Jordan and then reemerges to be named the "beloved Son" of God. Pope Benedict XVI tells us, "To accept the invitation to be baptized now means to go to the place of Jesus' Baptism. It is to go where he identifies himself with us and to receive there our identification with him. The point where he anticipates death has now become the point where we anticipate rising again with him" (*Jesus of Nazareth*). In Jesus' baptism and our own, we touch the place where humanity and divinity, as well as mortality and immortality, meet.

• Jesus' baptism also marks the beginning of his public ministry. In his book *Life of the Beloved*, Henri Nouwen says, "Self-rejection is the greatest enemy of the spiritual life because it contradicts the sacred voice that calls us the 'Beloved.'" When we embrace and live into the reality that "being the Beloved expresses the core truth of our existence," we are ready to go forth, following in the footsteps of Jesus to love and serve others. In baptism we are configured to Jesus, named children of the light, and commissioned to go forth as beloved sons and daughters of God.

Model Universal Prayer (Prayer of the Faithful)

Presider: As beloved sons and daughters of God we dare to bring our petitions before the Lord.

Response: Lord, hear our prayer.

That the church might be a voice of justice for those neglected and oppressed in the world . . .

That nations might work together to protect clean water sources and provide adequate drinking water for all people . . .

That the forgotten of society, especially prisoners, the mentally ill, and the disabled might be treated as beloved sons and daughters of God . . .

That all of us here might be renewed in the grace of our own Baptism to follow in the footsteps of Jesus . . .

Presider: God of mercy, you never cease to call us to repentance and fullness of life. Hear our prayers as we strive to follow the way of Jesus. We ask this through Christ our Lord. . Amen.

Let us pray

Pause for silent prayer

Almighty ever-living God,
who, when Christ had been baptized in the
    River Jordan
and as the Holy Spirit descended upon
    him,
solemnly declared him your beloved Son,
grant that your children by adoption,
reborn of water and the Holy Spirit,
may always be well pleasing to you.
Through our Lord Jesus Christ, your Son,
who lives and reigns with you in the unity
    of the Holy Spirit,
one God, for ever and ever. **Amen.**

FIRST READING
Isa 42:1-4, 6-7

Thus says the LORD:
Here is my servant whom I uphold,
    my chosen one with whom I am pleased,
upon whom I have put my spirit;
    he shall bring forth justice to the
        nations,
not crying out, not shouting,
    not making his voice heard in the street.
A bruised reed he shall not break,
    and a smoldering wick he shall not
        quench,
until he establishes justice on the earth;
    the coastlands will wait for his teaching.

I, the LORD, have called you for the victory
        of justice,
    I have grasped you by the hand;
I formed you, and set you
    as a covenant of the people,
    a light for the nations,
to open the eyes of the blind,
    to bring out prisoners from confinement,
    and from the dungeon, those who live in
        darkness.

RESPONSORIAL PSALM

Ps 29:1-2, 3-4, 9-10

℟. (11b) The Lord will bless his people
   with peace.

Give to the LORD, you sons of God,
   give to the LORD glory and praise,
give to the LORD the glory due his name;
   adore the LORD in holy attire.

℟. The Lord will bless his people with
   peace.

The voice of the LORD is over the waters,
   the LORD, over vast waters.
The voice of the LORD is mighty;
   the voice of the LORD is majestic.

℟. The Lord will bless his people with
   peace.

The God of glory thunders,
   and in his temple all say, "Glory!"
The LORD is enthroned above the flood;
   the LORD is enthroned as king forever.

℟. The Lord will bless his people with
   peace.

SECOND READING

Acts 10:34-38

Peter proceeded to speak to those gathered
   in the house of Cornelius, saying:
   "In truth, I see that God shows no
      partiality.
Rather, in every nation whoever fears him
      and acts uprightly
   is acceptable to him.
You know the word that he sent to the
      Israelites
   as he proclaimed peace through Jesus
      Christ, who is Lord of all,
   what has happened all over Judea,
   beginning in Galilee after the baptism
   that John preached,
   how God anointed Jesus of Nazareth
   with the Holy Spirit and power.
He went about doing good
   and healing all those oppressed by the
      devil,
   for God was with him."

*See Appendix A, p. 270, for additional
readings.*

About Liturgy

Epiphany, part two: In the Eastern church Epiphany (or Theophany, meaning "manifestation of God") evokes three different scenes in the life of Christ. First is the visitation of the magi and the epiphany that God's promise is given to all people. Second is today's manifestation at the Jordan of God's chosen one in Jesus. Third is next week's revelation of God's glory made visible in the first public miracle of Christ at a wedding at Cana. This triptych is often seen together in religious art and gives us a profound insight into the meaning of Christmas.

For most people Christmas is a children's holiday and a time for adults to return to the innocence and joy of their childhood. The emphasis in both secular and religious imagery on the Christ-child in Bethlehem reinforces this idea. However, the Christmas feast of the Baptism of the Lord counterbalances that notion. It reminds us that the child in the manger becomes an adult on mission, and that mission will eventually lead not only to a feast filled with rich food and choice wine but also to suffering and death. This is one reason why it is important that we mark this Sunday as the final day of Christmas.

This triple-revelation gives us a summary of Christ's mission and, thus, the mission of every disciple who follows him into those same baptismal waters. As we memorialize the baptism of Jesus today let us also remember our own baptism and call to mind our participation in Christ's mission "to open the eyes of the blind, / to bring out prisoners from confinement, / and from the dungeon, those who live in darkness" (Isa 42:7).

About Initiation

Remembering our baptism: The Rite of Christian Initiation of Adults (RCIA) is primarily for the initiation of those who are unbaptized. However, baptized persons who were baptized as infants as Roman Catholics or in another Christian community but did not receive any further formation in the Christian way of life may benefit from a similar process for catechesis as that of the catechumens. Nonetheless, their formation must always be seen as post-baptismal and mystagogical, recalling that they already are members of the church and children of God by their baptism. (See especially RCIA 400 to 403.)

One way to honor the baptism of these candidates preparing for reception or for confirmation and Eucharist is to help them recall their baptism. Although some may have no actual memory of the event, you can still help them through their imagination to picture some of the symbols of their baptism: water, light, oil, name, garment, godparent, minister. Then have a prayerful discussion on what each of these symbols means to them and to the church. This is also a good exercise for all the baptized to do today!

If you have baptized *uncatechized* adults (as described in RCIA 400), today might be a good day to celebrate the optional Rite of Welcoming. If you have baptized *catechized* adults preparing for reception or confirmation, today might be a good time do a simple blessing for them as they continue in their preparation. Although both of these groups are baptized, you should not combine uncatechized and catechized persons together in the rituals because they are at different levels in their journey of conversion.

About Liturgical Music

Christmas isn't over yet: The Christmas season officially ends after the Baptism of the Lord. Although it may seem strange to sing Christmas carols in the middle of January, be sure to include at least a few songs that mark this day as the last day of Christmas.

ORDINARY
TIME I

✚ SPIRITUALITY

GOSPEL ACCLAMATION
See 2 Thess 2:14

℟. Alleluia, alleluia.
God has called us through the Gospel
to possess the glory of our Lord Jesus Christ.
℟. Alleluia, alleluia.

Gospel   John 2:1-11; L66C

There was a wedding at Cana in
Galilee,
and the mother of Jesus was
there.
Jesus and his disciples were also
invited to the wedding.
When the wine ran short,
the mother of Jesus said to him,
"They have no wine."
And Jesus said to her,
"Woman, how does your con-
cern affect me?
My hour has not yet come."
His mother said to the servers,
"Do whatever he tells you."
Now there were six stone water jars there
for Jewish ceremonial washings,
each holding twenty to thirty gallons.
Jesus told them,
"Fill the jars with water."
So they filled them to the brim.
Then he told them,
"Draw some out now and take it to the
headwaiter."
So they took it.
And when the headwaiter tasted the
water that had become wine,
without knowing where it came from
—although the servers who had drawn
the water knew—,
the headwaiter called the bridegroom
and said to him,
"Everyone serves good wine first,
and then when people have drunk
freely, an inferior one;
but you have kept the good wine until
now."
Jesus did this as the beginning of his
signs at Cana in Galilee
and so revealed his glory,
and his disciples began to believe in him.

Reflecting on the Gospel

How many of us have been to a wedding party preceded by the groom's dinner, which is itself preceded by a number of festivities celebrating the bride and groom and their new life together? There are standard elements in most wedding celebrations, including the exchanging of vows (within a Mass or not) and usually a dinner or some food is served to the guests. Quite often there is dancing or some other activity. It's a day to remember for the guests, the hosts, the bride and groom, and their families. Family stories will be told for many years after each wedding, as legends become lore.

In antiquity, marriage celebrations followed a pattern as well, as reflected in today's gospel. One such cultural element that is still followed today(!) is that the best wine is served before a lesser quality wine. Such norms are the background setting for Jesus' first sign, as narrated by the Gospel of John. (In the Gospel of John, Jesus performs seven signs rather than a myriad of miracles, and the signs are indications of his true identity.) Interestingly, this gospel is the only one to tell this story. The Synoptic Gospel writers neglect this story: they may not have been aware of it.

Although liturgically we are in Year (or Cycle) C when we read from the Gospel of Luke, we begin Ordinary Time with this reading from the Gospel of John, which does not refer to Jesus' mother by name, for she is never named in this gospel, but rather, Mary is called "the mother of Jesus." According to this gospel, not only is she present at the beginning of Jesus' ministry, but she will be present at the cross too, accompanied by the Beloved Disciple (who, like the mother of Jesus, remains nameless). For the Gospel of John, the emphasis is on Jesus to such a degree that the other characters do not even have names!

And this is a good point for us. Namely, our emphasis should be on Jesus and his true identity. It is easy to be drawn away from him and look to novelties or curiosities. But in the Fourth Gospel we have stories of seven signs that Jesus performs, each revealing his identity as Son of God, the Word made flesh. We need look no further. For the disciple, and certainly for the evangelist, the focus is on Jesus for he is the incarnation of the Word of God and his words are life eternal.

Living the Paschal Mystery

Jesus was a living, breathing human being with a mother, father (Joseph), brothers, and sisters according to the Synoptics. According to today's gospel reading, he attended a wedding feast, and we can probably assume this was not his first or last wedding feast. In the shortest of all the Bible verses, according to many translations, the Gospel of John later tells us, "And Jesus wept" (11:35; NABRE). In sum, Jesus was a human being rather than a divine puppet. He experienced emotions from celebrating at a wedding to weeping at the death of a friend. Ultimately, he faced death itself, as each of us will. By undergoing his passion and death, which led to resurrection and life, he gives us the promise of life eternal. In Jesus, divinity became humanity thus exalting humanity to the divine. The paschal mystery nourishes our faith with the knowledge that our own personal death will lead to eternal life because of what God has done in Christ.

Focusing the Gospel

Key words and phrases: Jesus did this as the beginning of his signs in Cana in Galilee and so revealed his glory, and his disciples began to believe in him.

To the point: In the Gospel of John we do not hear of Jesus performing "miracles"; instead he offers "signs" that reveal his own identity and the nature of the kingdom of God. From this first sign in Cana we can glean that the kingdom is like a wedding feast where the wine will never run out and the joy grows ever deeper.

Connecting the Gospel

to the first reading: The wedding theme of today's gospel is echoed in the first reading in which the prophet Isaiah assures Israel that "[a]s a young man marries a virgin, / your Builder shall marry you; / and as a bridegroom rejoices in his bride / so shall your God rejoice in you." Just as a wedding feast is an apt image for the kingdom of God, marriage is a metaphor used in both the Old and New Testaments to symbolize the relationship God desires with God's people. This relationship is not without its difficulties. But even after infidelity—when the people of God turned away from the covenant and worshiped idols—God remains faithful.

to experience: All relationships, especially marriage, require work and celebration to keep the relationship vital. How do you set aside time to nurture and celebrate your relationship with God?

Connecting the Responsorial Psalm

to the readings: The psalmist enjoins us, "Sing to the LORD a new song." In the first reading from Isaiah, the prophet announces that Israel will receive a new name. Instead of "[d]esolate" or "[f]orsaken," Israel shall now be called "[e]spoused." Isaiah tells the nation, recently brought out of exile in Babylon, to begin again in their homeland to live out the covenant with their God. At the wedding feast in Cana we encounter Jesus who is also on the edge of something new. At the behest of his mother, he performs his first public sign and begins to reveal his identity to those closest to him. Our God is one of new beginnings and we are called to be a people of hope who believe that newness is possible: new behaviors, new actions, new love, and new life.

to psalmist preparation: In worship, we often return to the songs that we know and love to express our adoration for God. Today the psalmist reminds us to sing something new. The creator God invites us to embrace our own God-given creativity. Where are you being called to newness in your own life?

PROMPTS FOR FAITH-SHARING

In the first reading from Isaiah we see our relationship to God as that of a bride and bridegroom. One metaphor alone cannot contain the mystery of our covenant with God. In what ways is this metaphor helpful and true for you in your spiritual journey?

In the psalm we are encouraged to "sing to the LORD a new song." Where might God be calling you to "newness" in your own life?

Read through the list of spiritual gifts in the second reading (1 Cor 12:8-10). What gifts do you recognize in your own life and community? Which gifts are your community in need of at this moment in time?

Jesus' signs disclose himself and the kingdom of God to us. What does today's gospel about the wedding feast in Cana reveal to you about Jesus' nature and kingdom?

Model Penitential Act

Presider: In today's gospel reading Mary instructs the servers at the wedding feast in Cana, "Do whatever he tells you." These words are addressed to us as well in the life of faith. For the times that we have not listened attentively to the voice of Jesus calling us to righteousness, we ask for God's pardon and healing . . . [*pause*]

Lord Jesus, you invite us to collaborate in your saving work: Lord, have mercy.

Christ Jesus, you call us to newness of life: Christ, have mercy.

Lord Jesus, you provide for all our needs: Lord, have mercy.

Homily Points

• In the first half of the Gospel of John, Jesus performs seven signs that reveal Jesus' identity to us, as well as the nature of the kingdom of God. In these signs Jesus turns an abundance of water into wine, cures the sick and the lame, feeds the hungry, walks on water, and raises Lazarus from the dead. Through these signs we see that the kingdom of God is one where there will be no more illness, hunger, grief, destruction, or death. As children of the kingdom we are called to be signs of this kingdom of peace and abundance.

• We are given direction in becoming "kingdom people" in today's second reading. As human persons we've all experienced moments of feeling self-righteous about our own talents or envious of another's. St. Paul counsels us against this mind-set. When we compare ourselves to others we set up distinctions. We are either better or worse and we are usually not peaceful about either. St. Paul offers us another way: all abilities are given as gifts by the Holy Spirit, and all gifts are meant to be used for the good of the community.

• Mary also shows us the way to the kingdom. Despite Jesus' first dismissive remarks to his mother, Mary tells the waiters at the wedding feast, "Do whatever he tells you." Mary knows Jesus' generous nature. She probably wasn't surprised when her son, instead of supplying a small portion of wine for the wedding feast, converted upward of 120 gallons of water into wine. Later, Jesus will tell his disciples, "I came so that they might have life and have it more abundantly" (10:10; NABRE). When we listen to Mary's command, we, too, encounter life in abundance.

Model Universal Prayer (Prayer of the Faithful)

Presider: With confidence in the God of abundance who provides for our every need we bring our prayers before the Lord.

Response: Lord, hear our prayer.

That the church be a sign of the joy of the Kingdom of God by providing hospitality and welcome to all seekers . . .

That the nations of the world adopt a spirit of cooperation and generosity in dealing with both need and plenty . . .

That married couples renew their commitment to each other and find an abundance of joy in their covenant relationship . . .

That all of us here strive to use the spiritual gifts we have been given for the good of all . . .

Presider: God of the covenant, you invite us to live as people of the Kingdom of God in joy and hope. Increase our confidence in your goodness and help us see the abundance that surrounds us spiritually and materially, and to use it for your glory. We ask these prayers through Christ Jesus our Lord. Amen.

COLLECT

Let us pray.

Pause for silent prayer

Almighty ever-living God,
who govern all things,
both in heaven and on earth,
mercifully hear the pleading of your
    people
and bestow your peace on our times.
Through our Lord Jesus Christ, your Son,
who lives and reigns with you in the unity
    of the Holy Spirit,
one God, for ever and ever. **Amen.**

FIRST READING

Isa 62:1-5

For Zion's sake I will not be silent,
    for Jerusalem's sake I will not be quiet,
until her vindication shines forth like the
        dawn
    and her victory like a burning torch.

Nations shall behold your vindication,
    and all the kings your glory;
you shall be called by a new name
    pronounced by the mouth of the LORD.
You shall be a glorious crown in the hand
        of the LORD,
    a royal diadem held by your God.
No more shall people call you "Forsaken,"
    or your land "Desolate,"
but you shall be called "My Delight,"
    and your land "Espoused."
For the LORD delights in you
    and makes your land his spouse.
As a young man marries a virgin,
    your Builder shall marry you;
and as a bridegroom rejoices in his bride
    so shall your God rejoice in you.

RESPONSORIAL PSALM

Ps 96:1-2, 2-3, 7-8, 9-10

R℣. (3) Proclaim his marvelous deeds to all
the nations.

Sing to the LORD a new song;
sing to the LORD, all you lands.
Sing to the LORD; bless his name.

R℣. Proclaim his marvelous deeds to all the
nations.

Announce his salvation, day after day.
Tell his glory among the nations;
among all peoples, his wondrous deeds.

R℣. Proclaim his marvelous deeds to all the
nations.

Give to the LORD, you families of nations,
give to the LORD glory and praise;
give to the LORD the glory due his name!

R℣. Proclaim his marvelous deeds to all the
nations.

Worship the LORD in holy attire.
Tremble before him, all the earth;
say among the nations: The LORD is king.
He governs the peoples with equity.

R℣. Proclaim his marvelous deeds to all the
nations.

SECOND READING

1 Cor 12:4-11

Brothers and sisters:
There are different kinds of spiritual gifts
but the same Spirit;
there are different forms of service but
the same Lord;
there are different workings but the
same God
who produces all of them in everyone.
To each individual the manifestation of
the Spirit
is given for some benefit.
To one is given through the Spirit the
expression of wisdom;
to another, the expression of knowledge
according to the same Spirit;
to another, faith by the same Spirit;
to another, gifts of healing by the one
Spirit;
to another, mighty deeds;
to another, prophecy;
to another, discernment of spirits;
to another, varieties of tongues;
to another, interpretation of tongues.
But one and the same Spirit produces all
of these,
distributing them individually to each
person as he wishes.

About Liturgy

What happened to the First Sunday in Ordinary Time?: You might have thought that last Sunday, the Baptism of the Lord, was the *First* Sunday in Ordinary Time. But the liturgical books are clear that the Baptism of the Lord is part of the Christmas season and that "Ordinary Time begins on Monday after the Sunday following 6 January" (Lectionary 103).

This rubric isn't just a calendar instruction but also a theological statement. We call Sunday both the first and eighth day of the week. For Christians it is both the chronological and spiritual beginning and end of our week. When we talk about "ordinary time," we aren't referring to a quality of being mundane but to something being ordered—put into right relationship. The weeks between the seasons of Advent/Christmas and Lent/Easter are ordered toward the "ordinary" or normative mystery of Christ, a mystery that pervades every moment. Striving to be aware of Christ's enduring presence reminds us to live in constant right relationship. Thus, the Lord's Day on which we gather orders gives us the lens for how we are to see Christ's presence in the days that follow.

Since these last six days are rightly called the days of the first week of Ordinary Time, today, January 20, is rightly called the Second Sunday in Ordinary Time for it orders and directs us how to live this coming week aware of Christ's presence.

Epiphany, part three: In the ordinary event of a wedding feast, we encounter today the third traditional epiphany of Christ. God, who has sanctified all human life by the incarnation, shows us that holiness is not confined to the sacred space of the church or to the vocation of a few people but is readily poured out wherever people hear Jesus' words, believe, and follow him.

About Initiation

Preparation for Purification and Enlightenment: Not everyone who has become a catechumen this past year will be ready for baptism this coming Easter Vigil. Ideally, catechumens are given an entire liturgical year for encountering the mystery of Christ in the Sunday celebrations and feasts of the Lord and the saints. During these next seven Sundays of Ordinary Time pay special attention to the catechumens and look for markers of conversion as they are listed in RCIA 120. These behavioral and spiritual changes are required before one can celebrate the Rite of Election at the beginning of Lent. Those who need more time to develop these hallmarks of conversion continue through the liturgical year, encountering Christ and allowing him to change their hearts.

About Liturgical Music

Setting a musical environment: As we discussed at the beginning of Advent, music can also set a liturgical environment in the same way that liturgical colors and décor enhance the liturgical season. One way to begin doing this is to start with just three Mass settings a year. The first is a musical setting for Ordinary Time. This would be something that can be flexible enough to accommodate a variety of ensemble arrangements, from a single cantor to an SATB choir, but presents itself as simple yet substantial. One such example is "The *Psallite* Mass: At the Table of the Lord" (*Sacred Song*), which employs both metered and chanted melodies. Because winter Ordinary Time is relatively short, it is best to introduce new Mass settings over the summer and fall weeks to give the assembly time to become familiar with a setting before it is changed with the season.

Then select two other settings: one that complements the sobriety of the preparatory seasons of Advent and Lent, and one that expresses the exuberant festivity of Christmas and Easter.

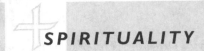

SPIRITUALITY

GOSPEL ACCLAMATION
See Luke 4:18

R̸. Alleluia, alleluia.
The Lord sent me to bring glad tidings to the
    poor,
and to proclaim liberty to captives.
R̸. Alleluia, alleluia.

Gospel   Luke 1:1-4; 4:14-21; L69C

Since many have undertaken to
    compile a narrative of the
    events
  that have been fulfilled among
    us,
  just as those who were eye-
    witnesses from the
    beginning
  and ministers of the word have
    handed them down to us,
I too have decided,
  after investigating everything
    accurately anew,
  to write it down in an orderly
    sequence for you,
  most excellent Theophilus,
  so that you may realize the certainty
    of the teachings
  you have received.

Jesus returned to Galilee in the power
    of the Spirit,
  and news of him spread throughout
    the whole region.
He taught in their synagogues and was
    praised by all.

He came to Nazareth, where he had
    grown up,
  and went according to his custom
  into the synagogue on the sabbath day.
He stood up to read and was handed a
    scroll of the prophet Isaiah.
He unrolled the scroll and found the
    passage where it was written:
  The Spirit of the Lord is upon me,
    because he has anointed me
    to bring glad tidings to the poor.

Continued in Appendix A, p. 271.

Reflecting on the Gospel

When embarking on an important work, task, or life choice, we often indicate so. Presidential candidates declare their candidacy in symbolically significant places. One proposes marriage to another in a meaningful way that is remembered. And special events like birthdays, baptisms, and anniversaries are marked by rituals. Afterward, we settle into routine. Luke does something similar when he begins his gospel. He opens with a four-verse prologue that is one long sentence in Greek! And the Greek he writes is florid, high in style, and reminiscent of classical Greek. After these four verses he descends from that style to the more common (*koinē*) Greek.

There are many things to note in this brief opening to the gospel, but it is significant that Luke says he is relying on the eyewitness of others, and thereby indicates that he was not an eyewitness himself. Otherwise, he might have said something like "and my own eyewitness." But it is clear that he is at least a second-generation Christian, who has looked into this story and told it so the believer Theophilus (the name means "God-lover") might have surety. And in fact, the word "surety" (*asphaleian* in Greek) concludes the first four-verse sentence in Greek, indicating its importance. By this emphasis on surety, even the modern reader recognizes that the story of Jesus is no mere myth. As Luke says later in Acts, "[T]his was not done in a corner" (Acts 26:26; NABRE). The events of Jesus' life, death, and resurrection really and truly happened.

But the church is not content to give us only the first four verses of the gospel on this Sunday. The second significant item to note is that we also read about Jesus' preaching in the synagogue at Nazareth in chapter 4. Luke is intent to show that the Scriptures of old are fulfilled in Jesus. Jesus reads the prophet and proclaims that the message is fulfilled in their midst. The message will be Jesus' guiding light. He will refer to it again when John the Baptist's followers come to Jesus and ask if he is the one they should expect. Jesus causes the blind to see and proclaims glad tidings to the poor. In so doing, he is the fulfillment of the hopes and expectations of the prophets, for the Spirit of the Lord is upon him.

Living the Paschal Mystery

How do we imagine the ministry of Jesus? What was it that he did? We know it ultimately ended in his passion, death, and resurrection, but what about his work among the people? Today's gospel reading, with Jesus quoting the prophet, gives us an indication as to what occupied the mind and thoughts of Jesus as he performed his ministry. He brings glad tidings to the poor, liberty to captives, sight to the blind, and freedom for the oppressed. This was the message of the prophet and to use a modern term, it is the mission statement of Jesus' ministry. If we want to be his followers, it is up to us to take on this mission statement as well. This ministry is in conformity with the prophets. It animated Jesus himself, and it should animate his followers. Jesus does not talk here about prayer, or doing liturgy, or even going to church. The ministry of Jesus is action in the world. And this action, as indicated by the mission statement, upends the powerful and the privileged. It ultimately (and fairly quickly) leads to Jesus' death. Faced with such a leader, will we be followers as well, undergoing our own paschal mystery? Or are we content to read about his ministry rather than do it, hear about it rather than practice it?

Focusing the Gospel

Key words and phrases: Today this Scripture passage is fulfilled in your hearing.

To the point: Following his baptism in the Jordan and time of temptation in the desert, Jesus returns to his hometown of Nazareth to worship in the synagogue. After reading from the scroll of Isaiah the people look at Jesus intently as he tells them, "Today this Scripture passage is fulfilled in your hearing." When we read the Bible we remember the history of this great book. We think about the context in which these words were first written and proclaimed. But then we go further for we believe the *living* word has something to tell us today. How can these words of comfort and justice for the poor and oppressed be fulfilled in our time? What role do we have in making these words come alive here and now?

Connecting the Gospel

to the first reading: The prophet Nehemiah lived in a time of great upheaval for the people of Israel. Following the Babylonian exile the Israelites were gradually allowed to return to their homeland. They returned to find Jerusalem in ruins. The walls that protected the city are no longer standing. Hearing of the distress of his fellow Israelites, Nehemiah also returns to Jerusalem to lead the restoration efforts. Under Nehemiah's leadership the people repair the walls to the city so they might once again dwell in safety and begin the task of restoring their homes and the temple. The first thing Nehemiah does once the walls are repaired is to gather all of the people together and to have Ezra, the scribe, read to them from the Torah. This is the moment we hear about in today's first reading. In Ezra we can see a precursor to Jesus' proclamation of Scripture in Nazareth. Ezra reads the words to the people to remind them of who they are. They are the people of God, God's beloved. Because of this they are called from their desolation and mourning into joy, for through "rejoicing in the LORD" they will regain their strength.

to experience: In today's first reading and gospel we see the people listening to the word of God. We are called to be formed by this word as well, to encounter it deeply and to invite it to change our lives.

Connecting the Responsorial Psalm

to the readings: Today's passage from Psalm 19 is a hymn to the beauty and value of the law. When the psalmist sings in praise of the law, it is not just the Ten Commandments that are being lauded. The "law of the LORD" refers to the Torah, the first five books of the Bible and the most precious books to the Jewish people. These books form the Jewish people in their identity. In today's first reading Ezra reads to the people from "daybreak till midday . . . the book of the law." Though the people have been in a time of desperation and mourning as they work to restore Jerusalem, they are reminded to rejoice, for their most precious possession, one that can never be taken away or destroyed, is the law of the Lord.

to psalmist preparation: Consider what it would be like to sing these words in the midst of difficult times—in grief, sorrow, or uncertainty. What does it mean to place your trust and hope in the law of the Lord and to count it as your greatest treasure?

PROMPTS FOR FAITH-SHARING

As it says in the book of Nehemiah, Ezra reads from the book of the law of Moses to the people from daybreak to midday and "all the people listened attentively." What helps you to listen attentively to the word of God?

St. Paul tells us, "[Y]ou are Christ's body, and individually parts of it." How do you see this metaphor within your life? How does your family and/or community respect and encourage the gifts of all?

In the gospel, Jesus reads from the scroll of the prophet Isaiah what could be considered his mission statement, one that all of us as followers of Christ could also consider *our* mission statement. What is one action you could do this week to help bring about the liberty, justice, freedom, and healing that Isaiah talks about?

Jesus tells the people, "Today this Scripture passage is fulfilled in your hearing." How have you experienced the word of God being fulfilled in your own life?

Model Penitential Act

Presider: In today's second reading the apostle Paul tells us we are all members of Christ's body. For the times we have not acted in a way befitting of the body of Christ, we ask for pardon and forgiveness . . . [*pause*]

Lord Jesus, you are the fulfillment of the law and the prophets: Lord, have mercy.

Christ Jesus, you are the anointed one: Christ, have mercy.

Lord Jesus, you proclaim liberty to captives and free the oppressed: Lord, have mercy.

Homily Points

• Jesus goes to the synagogue in Nazareth "according to his custom." Jesus prepares for his ministry, as all prophets must, by first listening to God and becoming immersed in God's word. Synagogues are places of worship as well as places of study. We, who have been anointed "priest, prophet, and king," must also be immersed in the word of God. This is the only way we will be able to bring "glad tidings to the poor" and "proclaim liberty to captives."

• There is a beautiful prayer attributed to St. Teresa of Avila called "Christ has no body." She tells us, "Christ has no body but yours, no hands, no feet on earth but yours." In today's gospel we hear that Jesus is the fulfillment of the prophet Isaiah's words, "The Spirit of the Lord is upon me, / because he has anointed me / to bring glad tidings to the poor." As the body of Christ we are called to fulfill this prophecy in our time.

• We cannot do this work on our own, however. One of the apostle Paul's themes in his letter to the Corinthians is unity. The Christian community at Corinth struggled with divisions as members clamored to claim superiority over one another. Today we hear Paul's analogy of the Christian community as the Body of Christ. Within a body all parts are necessary and no part is expendable. Only when we work together in concert and under the guidance of the Holy Spirit do we see the kingdom of God, a kingdom of justice and peace, break forth.

Model Universal Prayer (Prayer of the Faithful)

Presider: As members of the Body of Christ we lift up our prayers to God.

Response: Lord, hear our prayer.

That the church recognize and respect its diversity of members and the importance of all their gifts and talents . . .

That rulers of nations embrace a preferential option for the poor and oppressed . . .

That all those experiencing poverty, whether materially or spiritually, know the abundance of the Lord. . .

That all gathered here might, in gratitude and joy, use our gifts to build up the body of Christ . . .

Presider: Gracious God, you have called us, as members of the body of Christ, to bring glad tidings to the poor and to proclaim freedom to the captive and the oppressed. Hear our prayers that we might live into the fullness of this call. We ask this through Christ our Lord. Amen.

COLLECT

Let us pray.

Pause for silent prayer

Almighty ever-living God,
direct our actions according to your good
   pleasure,
that in the name of your beloved Son
we may abound in good works.
Through our Lord Jesus Christ, your Son,
who lives and reigns with you in the unity
   of the Holy Spirit,
one God, for ever and ever. **Amen.**

FIRST READING

Neh 8:2-4a, 5-6, 8-10

Ezra the priest brought the law before the
   assembly,
   which consisted of men, women,
   and those children old enough to
      understand.
Standing at one end of the open place that
   was before the Water Gate,
   he read out of the book from daybreak
      till midday,
   in the presence of the men, the women,
   and those children old enough to
      understand;
   and all the people listened attentively to
      the book of the law.
Ezra the scribe stood on a wooden
   platform
   that had been made for the occasion.
He opened the scroll
   so that all the people might see it
   —for he was standing higher up than
      any of the people—;
   and, as he opened it, all the people rose.
Ezra blessed the LORD, the great God,
   and all the people, their hands raised
      high, answered,
   "Amen, amen!"
Then they bowed down and prostrated
   themselves before the LORD,
   their faces to the ground.
Ezra read plainly from the book of the law
   of God,
   interpreting it so that all could
      understand what was read.
Then Nehemiah, that is, His Excellency,
   and Ezra the priest-scribe
   and the Levites who were instructing
      the people
   said to all the people:
   "Today is holy to the LORD your God.
Do not be sad, and do not weep"—
   for all the people were weeping as they
      heard the words of the law.

He said further: "Go, eat rich foods and
    drink sweet drinks,
    and allot portions to those who had
        nothing prepared;
    for today is holy to our LORD.
Do not be saddened this day,
    for rejoicing in the LORD must be your
        strength!"

RESPONSORIAL PSALM
Ps 19:8, 9, 10, 15

R͡. (cf. John 6:63c) Your words, Lord, are
    Spirit and life.

The law of the LORD is perfect,
    refreshing the soul;
the decree of the LORD is trustworthy,
    giving wisdom to the simple.

R͡. Your words, Lord, are Spirit and life.

The precepts of the LORD are right,
    rejoicing the heart;
the command of the LORD is clear,
    enlightening the eye.

R͡. Your words, Lord, are Spirit and life.

The fear of the LORD is pure,
    enduring forever;
the ordinances of the LORD are true,
    all of them just.

R͡. Your words, Lord, are Spirit and life.

Let the words of my mouth and the
        thought of my heart
    find favor before you,
O LORD, my rock and my redeemer.

R͡. Your words, Lord, are Spirit and life.

SECOND READING
1 Cor 12:12-14, 27

Brothers and sisters:
As a body is one though it has many parts,
    and all the parts of the body, though
        many, are one body,
    so also Christ.
For in one Spirit we were all baptized into
        one body,
    whether Jews or Greeks, slaves or free
        persons,
    and we were all given to drink of one
        Spirit.
Now the body is not a single part, but
    many.
You are Christ's body, and individually
    parts of it.

or 1 Cor 12:12-30

See Appendix A, p. 271.

About Liturgy

Observing the liturgy: If you truly want to assess the quality of your Sunday liturgy, at some point you will need to be an objective observer. This can be difficult if you're also trying to pray and be part of the assembly. So these Sundays before Lent may be a good time to schedule two or three times when you will attend one of your parish Masses as an outside observer and just watch and take notes discreetly, looking for specific areas for improvement. Here are some points that will help you get started.

First, it may be easier to do this with a small group of people doing the observation. This group might be made up of other liturgical ministers, but also be sure to include other parishioners as well whose only Sunday role is in the assembly. Have each person sit in a different place of the church than they are used to sitting in order to get a better sense of the variety of perspectives your assembly has each Sunday. In addition, you might set up a couple of stationary video cameras, one focused toward the sanctuary and one focused toward the assembly. This is to help you observe the body language of the people and the ministers.

Second, use a worksheet to help you look for specific points. Immediately after the Mass is over gather with the team and share your notes while it is fresh. You might watch the video, too, while you do this. As you notice things in the video, write down the time marker and notate what you saw.

Third, be sure to let all the liturgical ministers and pastoral staff know that these observations will be taking place. Also let them know that follow-up gatherings will be scheduled where they will be able to hear about what you observed and view any specific parts of the videos you want to highlight. Assure everyone that these observations are to help everyone see where the parish is strong and where it can improve: it is not to critique any one person.

Finally, when you gather with all the liturgical ministers and staff set some ground rules for the discussion. Comments should begin with what went well, including what each person saw they themselves did well during the liturgy. Any criticisms of how someone did their ministry should be limited to the points on your worksheet and be given kindly. If you feel that the discussion might get too negative, try facilitating these discussions in smaller groups. Always end the gatherings with inviting everyone to share a few simple next steps each person can take to improve and what the entire liturgy team will commit to doing to continue improving.

In these next few Sundays we'll look at specific items to observe in each part of the liturgy.

About Liturgical Music

Helping the Body of Christ: "If one part suffers, all the parts suffer with it; / if one part is honored, all the parts share its joy" (1 Cor 12:26). One way ministers can help one another is to take some time to share in supportive feedback of one another. This can be done with cantors in a master class format in a rehearsal. Each cantor prepares a psalm and leads it while the choir members act as an assembly, facing the cantor. The "assembly" pays attention not only to what they hear but also to gestures, body posture, and facial expression. Then they give the cantor constructive feedback, starting first with what the cantor did well, followed by one or two specific points for improvement.

✝ SPIRITUALITY

GOSPEL ACCLAMATION
Matt 4:18

℟. Alleluia, alleluia.
The Lord sent me to bring glad tidings to the
    poor,
to proclaim liberty to captives.
℟. Alleluia, alleluia.

Gospel

Luke 4:21-30; L72C

**Jesus began speaking in the
    synagogue, saying:
"Today this Scripture pas-
    sage is fulfilled in
    your hearing."
And all spoke highly of him
    and were amazed at the
    gracious words that
    came from his mouth.
They also asked, "Isn't this
    the son of Joseph?"
He said to them, "Surely you will quote me
    this proverb,
    'Physician, cure yourself,' and say,
    'Do here in your native place
    the things that we heard were done in
        Capernaum.'"
And he said, "Amen, I say to you,
    no prophet is accepted in his own native
        place.
Indeed, I tell you,
    there were many widows in Israel in the
        days of Elijah
    when the sky was closed for three and a
        half years
    and a severe famine spread over the en-
        tire land.
It was to none of these that Elijah was sent,
    but only to a widow in Zarephath in the
        land of Sidon.
Again, there were many lepers in Israel
    during the time of Elisha the prophet;
    yet not one of them was cleansed, but
        only Naaman the Syrian."
When the people in the synagogue heard this,
    they were all filled with fury.
They rose up, drove him out of the town,
    and led him to the brow of the hill
    on which their town had been built,
    to hurl him down headlong.
But Jesus passed through the midst of them
    and went away.**

Reflecting on the Gospel

It can be difficult to be surprised by the familiar. We experience it regularly; it is customary. We follow routine and habit. Even people we encounter can become familiar to the point of predictability. We expect certain reactions from those we know. So when someone familiar does something unexpected or different we can be puzzled. The actions did not follow the script; the person did not meet my expectations. What follows can be problematic. In these cases, it's usually best for us to reassess our expectations and reexamine our habits.

Something similar happens in today's gospel when Jesus preaches in his hometown synagogue. The audience thought they knew him: "Isn't this the son of Joseph?" But what he preached, the fulfillment of the Scriptures, was shocking to the point of their attempting to silence him for good. In the face of such objection, Jesus does not change his message. On the contrary, he says that "no prophet is accepted in his own native place." By this, Jesus refers to himself as a prophet in the manner of Elisha and Elijah.

The reference to Elijah going to the widow in Zarephath and Elisha to Naaman the Syrian prefigures Jesus' own ministry to those who are not Jewish. Luke is foreshadowing the eventual Gentile mission and demonstrating that it, too, is rooted in Scripture. Just as Elijah and Elisha went beyond the bounds of the Israelites, Jesus will too. Luke's story of Jesus is rooted in the prophets, especially the ministry of Elijah and Elisha who raised the dead, fed multitudes, and ministered to non-Israelites. For Luke more than any other evangelist, the prophets, John the Baptist, and Jesus himself in his ministry, passion, death, and subsequent entrance into glory follow "God's plan" (Luke is the New Testament author who uses the term "God's plan" more than any other New Testament author). Jesus behaves in a way wholly unexpected by those in his hometown who ostensibly knew him best. Rather than seek to silence him for good, they might have reassessed their own preconceptions. But as we know, such a task is difficult. It's much easier to believe what I already "know" to be true.

On this Fourth Sunday in Ordinary Time may we be open to the unexpected, for it might simply be the plan of God.

Living the Paschal Mystery

Mark Twain once said, "What gets us into trouble is not what we don't know. It's what we know for sure that just ain't so." Our brains are wired to be comfortable with the familiar. We don't need to think about walking; we simply walk. We don't need to invest much mental energy in routine tasks simply because they are so familiar. The human brain spends minimal mental energy on the routine. And this is a good thing as the brain can then spend its mental energy on other more critical tasks.

But this can also be a problem in that the unexpected, by definition, does not conform to routine. So being open to the unexpected is probably a good habit for us to cultivate. Aware that we are hardwired for routine, it takes extra energy to be open to new things and new experiences, even new information that does not conform to what we already know or even "know for sure that just ain't so."

When we take in new information that causes a change in our way of thinking we experience a *metanoia*, to use a favorite term of Luke. We die to our old preconceived notions and allow something new to rise up. But sometimes our first reaction can be like the townspeople of Nazareth, and we can seek to destroy the messenger. Allowing new information to influence us and ultimately to shape or even change our minds is a difficult process. We let go of the past; we let go of our old ways of thinking. We let go of what "just ain't so" and embrace something new. This is a kind of paschal mystery.

Focusing the Gospel

Key words and phrases: They . . . asked, "Isn't this the son of Joseph?"

To the point: It is often difficult to see something (or someone) that we know well with fresh eyes. Jesus returns to his hometown and the people there see him as they always have, as the son of Joseph the carpenter. Jesus tells them, "[N]o prophet is accepted in his own native place." Prophets, by their very nature, are called to shake people out of their complacency and to point out when something new is happening. Like the people of Nazareth, we might feel like we know Jesus. His words may not sound radical to us. As Christians we must continually strive to be open to the words of Jesus, the prophet, who would like to show us something new.

Connecting the Gospel

to the first reading: Jeremiah is also a prophet who finds no welcome in his hometown. He receives the call from God as a young man and is given the difficult task of prophesying the coming Babylonian exile to the king and temple court. It does not go well. At one point Jeremiah, unlike Jesus who is able to pass through the midst of those who wish to hurl him over a cliff, is actually tossed into a pit. Even though Jesus and Jeremiah both face resistance, God continues to be with them. As God tells Jeremiah, "They will fight against you but not prevail over you, / for I am with you to deliver you."

to experience: The prophet's life is not one of popularity and acclaim, but often includes derision and solitude. When it is difficult to follow the path of Jesus and to speak the word of God to others we, too, can hear God's instruction to Jeremiah, "But do you gird your loins; / stand up and tell them / all that I command you. / Be not crushed on their account."

Connecting the Responsorial Psalm

to the readings: Today's psalm reinforces the theme of reliance on God in difficult times. The psalmist proclaims, "In you, O Lord, I take refuge; / let me never be put to shame." This hope in the Lord has been founded on an experience of God's love even from infancy: "On you I depend from birth; / from my mother's womb you are my strength." In the reading from Jeremiah we hear how God has known and dedicated the prophet even before he was "formed . . . in the womb." In the gospel Jesus' neighbors, who have witnessed his own growth from child to manhood, ask each other, "Isn't this the son of Joseph?" The psalm reminds us that no matter how intimately we might know a person or for how long a time, it is God alone who has accompanied this individual from the secret life of the womb.

to psalmist preparation: In the gospel Jesus encounters resistance to his ministry and even the threat of violence. In this passage we see the foreshadowing of the cross when Jesus will not "[pass] through the midst of" the angry crowd but will give himself up to be crucified. Today's psalm speaks of radical trust in God. When have you relied on the Lord to be a refuge in times of struggle?

PROMPTS FOR FAITH-SHARING

In the first reading God tells the prophet Jeremiah, "[B]efore you were born I dedicated you, / a prophet to the nations I appointed you." What work has God dedicated you for?

_____

_____

_____

In the second reading St. Paul expounds on the true nature of love beginning, "Love is patient, love is kind." In your family and/or parish community where is this love present? Where is it lacking?

_____

_____

_____

_____

Jesus' hometown crowd is shocked at the words he speaks to them. They ask, "Isn't this the son of Joseph?" Are there areas in your life where you feel stifled by people's preconceptions of you? How might you embrace the freedom of God to be who he is calling you to be?

_____

_____

_____

At the end of today's gospel Jesus passes through the midst of the angry crowd and goes away. Are there areas of conflict in your life where you are being called to walk away?

_____

_____

_____

_____

Model Penitential Act

Presider: Today we read the beloved words of the apostle Paul, "Love is patient, love is kind." We pause to reflect on the times we have not embodied this love that "endures all things" . . . [*pause*]

Lord Jesus, you are our rock of refuge: Lord, have mercy.

Christ Jesus, you call us to faith and hope: Christ, have mercy.

Lord Jesus, you show us the way of perfect love: Lord, have mercy.

Homily Points

• Today's first reading presents the call of the prophet Jeremiah. God tells Jeremiah, "Before I formed you in the womb I knew you, / before you were born I dedicated you, / a prophet to the nations I appointed you." God has created each one of us with intentionality and gifts to use for the building of the kingdom of God.

• In the gospel we see Jesus at the beginning of the work for which he has been dedicated and already he is facing resistance and violence. In this first altercation he is able to pass through the midst of the angry mob. He has work to do and a mission to accomplish. At the end of his ministry in Jerusalem instead of passing through the crowd he will submit to it and give his life. In all that he does, Jesus is animated and led by love, the love that St. Paul talks about in his letter to the Corinthians.

• Often we hear the second reading from St. Paul at weddings. It might lead us to associate Paul's words with romantic love and, indeed, this is the kind of love necessary to sustain a lifelong covenant between two people. Far from exclusively romantic love, however, Paul is telling us of the love that must surround and infuse our entire lives as Christians. Without this love Paul says, "I am nothing." In our lives as Christians we are called to follow the examples of Jeremiah, Paul, and Jesus. To accept the work God has dedicated us to and to strive to meet all the circumstances of our lives with patient and enduring love.

Model Universal Prayer (Prayer of the Faithful)

Presider: Trusting in the all-encompassing love of God, which sustains and surrounds us, we offer up our prayers.

Response: Lord, hear our prayer.

That the church strive to be a living model of the love of God . . .

That leaders of nations listen to present-day prophets who point the way to hope, faith, and love . . .

That those who grieve the loss of a family member or friend be comforted . . .

That all gathered here might heed our baptismal call to be prophets of God's love . . .

Presider: Gracious God, hear the prayers we bring before you today and in your generous love, grant them. We ask this through Christ our Lord. Amen.

COLLECT

Let us pray.

Pause for silent prayer

Grant us, Lord our God,
that we may honor you with all our mind,
and love everyone in truth of heart.
Through our Lord Jesus Christ, your Son,
who lives and reigns with you in the unity
   of the Holy Spirit,
one God, for ever and ever. **Amen.**

FIRST READING

Jer 1:4-5, 17-19

The word of the LORD came to me, saying:
   Before I formed you in the womb I knew
      you,
      before you were born I dedicated you,
      a prophet to the nations I appointed
         you.

   But do you gird your loins;
      stand up and tell them
      all that I command you.
   Be not crushed on their account,
      as though I would leave you crushed
         before them;
   for it is I this day
      who have made you a fortified city,
   a pillar of iron, a wall of brass,
      against the whole land:
   against Judah's kings and princes,
      against its priests and people.
   They will fight against you but not
        prevail over you,
      for I am with you to deliver you, says
         the LORD.

RESPONSORIAL PSALM

Ps 71:1-2, 3-4, 5-6, 15, 17

℟. (cf. 15ab) I will sing of your salvation.

In you, O LORD, I take refuge;
   let me never be put to shame.
In your justice rescue me, and deliver me;
   incline your ear to me, and save me.

℟. I will sing of your salvation.

Be my rock of refuge,
   a stronghold to give me safety,
   for you are my rock and my fortress.
O my God, rescue me from the hand of the
      wicked.

℟. I will sing of your salvation.

For you are my hope, O Lord;
   my trust, O God, from my youth.
On you I depend from birth;
   from my mother's womb you are my
      strength.

℟. I will sing of your salvation.

My mouth shall declare your justice,
    day by day your salvation.
O God, you have taught me from my
    youth,
    and till the present I proclaim your
      wondrous deeds.

R̷. I will sing of your salvation.

SECOND READING
1 Cor 13:4-13

Brothers and sisters:
Love is patient, love is kind.
It is not jealous, it is not pompous,
    it is not inflated, it is not rude,
    it does not seek its own interests,
    it is not quick-tempered, it does not
      brood over injury,
    it does not rejoice over wrongdoing but
      rejoices with the truth.
It bears all things, believes all things,
    hopes all things, endures all things.

Love never fails.
If there are prophecies, they will be
      brought to nothing;
    if tongues, they will cease;
    if knowledge, it will be brought to
      nothing.
For we know partially and we prophesy
      partially,
    but when the perfect comes, the partial
      will pass away.
When I was a child, I used to talk as a
      child,
    think as a child, reason as a child;
    when I became a man, I put aside
      childish things.
At present we see indistinctly, as in a
      mirror,
    but then face to face.
At present I know partially;
    then I shall know fully, as I am fully
      known.
So faith, hope, love remain, these three;
    but the greatest of these is love.

or 1 Cor 12:31–13:13

See Appendix A, p. 272.

About Liturgy

Observing the Introductory Rites: Here are a few points to notice and include in your observation and evaluation worksheet for your community's introductory rites (see previous Sunday). Although the Mass starts with the entrance chant, there are many things before Mass, which you could also observe.

Hospitality: Were there greeters outside the church, at the church doors, and inside the church welcoming people as they arrived? Did assembly members greet each other in a friendly and genuine way as people gathered in and around their seats? Would a visitor or newcomer feel welcomed? Would a visitor leave the Mass having been personally greeted, welcomed, and invited to return by at least one other person? Are the locations of restrooms clearly marked so that visitors know where to find them? Is there "code language" in your bulletin, such as "RCIA" or "ICF dinner"? Can visitors easily find the parish phone number and a name of someone to talk to if they are new to the parish? Do you have to be an insider to know where meeting rooms are? Are the parking lot, gathering areas, and church space clean and inviting? Do those in wheelchairs have easy access to all parts of the church grounds? Are worship aids or projected materials printed clearly in type that is easily read? Do all who use the microphones use them effectively so that all can hear well?

Silence: If there is a music rehearsal, announcements, or welcome before Mass, is there some period of silence before the entrance chant begins? Was there an ample amount of silence at the beginning of the penitential rite and after the invitation, "Let us pray," in the collect? Describe the quality of the silence, for example, uncomfortable, deep, rushed, peaceful, etc.

Procession: Did the entrance procession look like a procession? Did the ministers walk with dignity? Were the cross, book of the gospels, and other items carried and placed with dignity? Did the ministers walk slowly or hurriedly? Did they all move gracefully? Was the assembly instructed to "greet Father" by singing the opening song, or were there other ways that the procession focused on the celebrant rather than the assembly?

Prayers: Was the sign of the cross done slowly with large dignified and deliberate movements? Did the celebrant add extraneous words, such as a greeting before the sign of the cross, or "thank you" or "good morning" after the assembly's response, "And with your spirit"? Was the opening prayer proclaimed clearly, slowly, and solemnly in a way that felt like prayer?

About Liturgical Music

Liturgical music observation points for the Introductory Rites: If someone rehearsed music with the assembly before Mass, did they do it respectfully, encouraging and not scolding people? Are song numbers clearly marked? Are there enough hymnals in every pew? Can visitors find books and song numbers easily? Was the entrance chant familiar, known and sung by all, even those in the procession? Did the entrance chant accomplish the task of gathering the assembly? Were enough verses sung to do this, or did the opening song end once the ministers arrived at their places? Did the assembly know and sing the Gloria? Did the presider, deacon, and altar servers sing all the music? Did the accompaniment support and enable the full participation of the assembly in sung prayer? Was the music and the way it was played and sung joyful?

SPIRITUALITY

GOSPEL ACCLAMATION
Matt 4:19

℟. Alleluia, alleluia.
Come after me
and I will make you fishers of men.
℟. Alleluia, alleluia.

Gospel   Luke 5:1-11; L75C

While the crowd was pressing
in on Jesus and listening
to the word of God,
he was standing by the
Lake of Gennesaret.
He saw two boats there
alongside the lake;
the fishermen had dis-
embarked and were
washing their nets.
Getting into one of the
boats, the one belonging
to Simon,
he asked him to put out a short distance from the shore.
Then he sat down and taught the
crowds from the boat.
After he had finished speaking, he said
to Simon,
"Put out into deep water and lower
your nets for a catch."
Simon said in reply,
"Master, we have worked hard all
night and have caught nothing,
but at your command I will lower the
nets."
When they had done this, they caught a
great number of fish
and their nets were tearing.
They signaled to their partners in the
other boat
to come to help them.
They came and filled both boats
so that the boats were in danger of
sinking.

Continued in Appendix A, p. 272.

Reflecting on the Gospel

Hometown monuments, markers, and memorials sometimes go by different names. For example, people who grew up in one era might recall an earlier name for a stadium or a building. In Chicago, the Sears Tower became the Willis Tower in 2009. Investors bought it several years later and were considering another name change. But many locals still refer to it as the Sears Tower. Many stadiums undergo name changes as well based on naming rights sold to the highest bidding corporation. These names are a reflection of our culture and can be difficult for foreigners or others to follow. Just imagine some talking about the Willis Tower when others know it only as the Sears Tower. Are we speaking of the same thing? Where is the Willis Tower?

We see something like this happening in the Gospel of Luke today, when we hear about the Lake of Gennesaret, which is also known as the Sea of Tiberias and the Sea of Galilee! The New Testament uses three different names for the same body of water, which makes it challenging for those of us reading about this two thousand years later and more than an ocean away.

Such is the setting for the call of Simon as Luke tells it. This story is different from that told in Mark, Matthew, or John. Here Luke has a focus on Simon, without his brother Andrew. In fact, Luke mentions Andrew only in the list of the twelve (Luke 6:12; Acts 1:13) where he calls him the brother of Simon. Otherwise we hear nothing of Andrew from Luke. Luke also tells us in this story that Simon was "Simon Peter," prior to Jesus naming him "Peter." And we also hear about James and John, the sons of Zebedee, partners of Simon. According to Luke, this was not Simon's first encounter with Jesus. Immediately prior to the story in today's gospel, Jesus healed Simon's mother-in-law (Luke 4:38-39). So this provides more background to Simon's appeal to Jesus, "Depart from me, Lord, for I am a sinful man." Simon has encountered the power of Jesus in the healing of his mother-in-law and now in the miraculous catch of fish. Faced with this Simon is utterly aware of his own humanity and humility. Jesus responds with a line that has reverberated through the centuries, "Do not be afraid; / from now on you will be catching men." What a difference this story is in the hands of the master storyteller Luke. From Mark (1:16-20) he inherited a story about Jesus' call of Simon, Andrew, James, and John, all of whom immediately dropped their nets to follow him. Luke instead places the focus squarely on Simon *Peter* to the point that we lose Andrew and only hear of James and John in the closing verses. Furthermore, by preceding this story with the healing of the mother-in-law, Simon's leaving everything to follow Jesus becomes more plausible. We are in the hands of a remarkable theologian and evangelist. We would do well to read his story carefully and with attention to detail.

Living the Paschal Mystery

So often today's gospel story is read symbolically so that the tearing nets mean one thing and the great number of fish mean something else. The boat's near sinking is sometimes interpreted symbolically too. But it can be more fruitful simply to read Luke's story on its own terms, without fishing for meaning so to speak.

Jesus provides more than enough. There is bounty with Jesus who surpasses every expectation. When experience teaches Simon that there is no hope, or no use in trying, Jesus encourages him nonetheless and provides excess. This dramatic scene captures something of the initial excitement, humility, and genuineness that often accompanies the early stages of true discipleship. It is then that we die to our own preconceived notions and our own experience, and open ourselves up to the munificence of the divine. That is when our cup overflows with the good things God wants to provide. In the face of such generosity, we can only be humble. Simon knows he did not earn this miraculous catch, but it was a free gift. May we, too, die to our own self-importance and grandiosity and recognize that the good things we have are a gift of God.

Focusing the Gospel

Key words and phrases: Depart from me, Lord, for I am a sinful man.

To the point: After witnessing the miraculous catch of fish Peter begs Jesus to leave him. Knowing his own sinfulness, Peter believes he is not worthy to be in the presence of the Lord of life. Jesus has other ideas, however. Throughout salvation history we witness God's pattern of choosing the small and weak, and yes, even sinful, to fulfill God's plan. Jesus responds to Peter's plea by reassuring him, "Do not be afraid." Jesus knows our sinfulness, loves us, and calls us to follow him anyway.

Connecting the Gospel

to the first and second readings: In the first and second readings, both the prophet Isaiah and the apostle Paul echo Peter's words of self-reproach. When Isaiah receives a heavenly vision of seraphim surrounding God's throne he cries out, "Woe is me, I am doomed!" Isaiah cites his "unclean lips" as a reason he cannot possibly be a prophet for the Lord of Hosts. In Paul's litany of the appearances of the risen Lord to the apostles he ends with Jesus' appearance to himself, but adds, "I am the least of the apostles, / not fit to be called an apostle, / because I persecuted the church of God." Just as with Peter, the failings of Isaiah and Paul do not dissuade God from calling them to be of service.

to experience: As human beings we all possess flaws and weaknesses. Rather than being a cause for shame, these flaws might be a way that God is speaking to us. The musician Leonard Cohen says that cracks allow light to get in.

Connecting the Responsorial Psalm

to the readings: In the gospel and the first reading Peter and Isaiah encounter the living God and respond in awe and fear. While Isaiah experiences a mystical vision, Peter comes face to face with the Lord who can cause the very fish in the Sea of Galilee to flock to his net. Today's psalm is a hymn of gratitude and praise for the Lord of all. Oftentimes the most authentic prayer is one of wonder. Words can escape us upon witnessing the grandeur of God through nature or miraculous intervention. Even speechless, we can turn to the Lord in gratitude and simply be in the presence of God.

to psalmist preparation: Today's psalm is one of simple and exultant praise. Pope Francis tells us, "Praise is the 'breath' which gives us life, because it is intimacy with God, an intimacy that grows through daily praise" (address to Catholic Fraternity, Oct. 31, 2014). How do you praise God in your daily life?

PROMPTS FOR FAITH-SHARING

In the first reading we hear of the call of the prophet Isaiah. Isaiah responds, "Here I am . . . send me!" Where in your life do you hear the call of God? What do you need in order to respond to this call as Isaiah did?

In the second reading, St. Paul reminds the Corinthians of the witness he has provided to them of Jesus' life, death, and resurrection. In your own life, who has been a witness of faith for you? How are you a witness for others?

In the life of faith we are called to persistence. Where might Jesus be calling you to try one more time to put out your nets for a catch?

In response to Peter's protestations of his own sinfulness, Jesus tells him, "Do not be afraid." Are there places in your own life where fear of failure keeps you from attempting something new? Can you hear Jesus telling you, "Do not be afraid"?

Model Penitential Act

Presider: In today's gospel Jesus calls Peter, James, and John to be his first disciples. Peter responds by crying out, "Depart from me, Lord, for I am a sinful man." For the times we have let our own sinfulness prohibit us from following Jesus, we ask for mercy and forgiveness . . . [*pause*]

Lord Jesus, you call us to leave everything and follow you: Lord, have mercy.

Christ Jesus, you died for our sins: Christ, have mercy.

Lord Jesus, you invite us to be fishers of men: Lord, have mercy.

Homily Points

• Today Jesus urges Peter not to be afraid of his own sinfulness, his self-perceived unworthiness. We hear this phrase, "Do not be afraid," again and again throughout the Scriptures. In the First Letter of St. John we are given a clue as to why. John tells us that "perfect love drives out fear" (4:18; NABRE). God desires perfect love in his relationship with us, and in perfect love there is no room for fear.

• In the life of faith we are also called to persistence and perseverance. Sometimes things seem hopeless. We have tried again and again to repair a relationship or conquer a bad habit, but to no avail. Jesus tells Peter to put out his nets into the deep for a catch, and even though he has been fishing all night and caught nothing, he acquiesces to Jesus' request. His success is beyond his wildest imagining. He catches such an abundance of fish he must call other fishermen to partake.

• As seen in the gospel encounter between Peter and Jesus, Christianity is a religion passed on through relationships. The last part of St. Paul's first letter to the Corinthians is a discourse on the resurrection of Christ. Today we begin this discourse, which we will read for the next three Sundays. In building his case for the resurrection of Jesus, Paul cites the many people whom Jesus appeared to after his crucifixion. All of these people passed on what they had heard and seen to invite others to faith. Today, we believe because of what we have experienced, read, and most importantly, because of the testimony of others in our lives. Despite our own failings and weaknesses, we are called like Isaiah, Paul, and Simon Peter to witness to Jesus through our persistence, relationships, and a love that casts out fear.

Model Universal Prayer (Prayer of the Faithful)

Presider: In today's gospel Jesus reassures Peter, "Do not be afraid." With faith in the goodness of God, let us lift our prayers to the Lord.

Response: Lord, hear our prayer.

That the pope, the successor of Peter, might point the way to Jesus with fidelity . . .

That all the peoples of the world come to know the glory and majesty of God . . .

That all those who feel overwhelmed by sin receive the grace to live in righteousness . . .

That all gathered here might be renewed in our commitment to leave everything and follow Jesus . . .

Presider: Good and gracious God, throughout history you have called human beings to collaborate with you in your work of salvation. Hear our prayers, that we might be strengthened in your grace to continue to serve you. We ask this through Christ our Lord. Amen.

COLLECT

Let us pray.

Pause for silent prayer

Keep your family safe, O Lord, with
    unfailing care,
that, relying solely on the hope of
    heavenly grace,
they may be defended always by your
    protection.
Through our Lord Jesus Christ, your Son,
who lives and reigns with you in the unity
    of the Holy Spirit,
one God, for ever and ever. **Amen.**

FIRST READING

Isa 6:1-2a, 3-8

In the year King Uzziah died,
    I saw the Lord seated on a high and
        lofty throne,
    with the train of his garment filling the
        temple.
Seraphim were stationed above.

They cried one to the other,
    "Holy, holy, holy is the LORD of hosts!
All the earth is filled with his glory!"
At the sound of that cry, the frame of the
       door shook
    and the house was filled with smoke.

Then I said, "Woe is me, I am doomed!
For I am a man of unclean lips,
    living among a people of unclean lips;
    yet my eyes have seen the King, the
       LORD of hosts!"
Then one of the seraphim flew to me,
    holding an ember that he had taken
       with tongs from the altar.

He touched my mouth with it, and said,
    "See, now that this has touched your
       lips,
    your wickedness is removed, your sin
       purged."

Then I heard the voice of the Lord saying,
    "Whom shall I send? Who will go for
       us?"
"Here I am," I said; "send me!"

RESPONSORIAL PSALM

Ps 138:1-2, 2-3, 4-5, 7-8

℟. (1c) In the sight of the angels I will
    sing your praises, Lord.

I will give thanks to you, O LORD, with all
    my heart,
    for you have heard the words of my
       mouth;
    in the presence of the angels I will sing
       your praise;

I will worship at your holy temple
   and give thanks to your name.

R℣. In the sight of the angels I will sing
   your praises, Lord.

Because of your kindness and your truth;
   for you have made great above all things
   your name and your promise.
When I called, you answered me;
   you built up strength within me.

R℣. In the sight of the angels I will sing
   your praises, Lord.

All the kings of the earth shall give
      thanks to you, O Lord,
   when they hear the words of your mouth;
and they shall sing of the ways of the Lord:
   "Great is the glory of the Lord."

R℣. In the sight of the angels I will sing
   your praises, Lord.

Your right hand saves me.
   The Lord will complete what he has
      done for me;
your kindness, O Lord, endures forever;
   forsake not the work of your hands.

R℣. In the sight of the angels I will sing
   your praises, Lord.

SECOND READING
1 Cor 15:3-8, 11

Brothers and sisters,
   I handed on to you as of first
      importance what I also received:
   that Christ died for our sins
      in accordance with the Scriptures;
   that he was buried;
   that he was raised on the third day
      in accordance with the Scriptures;
   that he appeared to Cephas, then to the
      Twelve.
After that, he appeared to more
      than five hundred brothers at once,
   most of whom are still living,
   though some have fallen asleep.
After that he appeared to James,
   then to all the apostles.
Last of all, as to one born abnormally,
   he appeared to me.
Therefore, whether it be I or they,
   so we preach and so you believed.

or 1 Cor 15:1-11

See Appendix A, p. 272.

About Liturgy

Observing the Liturgy of the Word: Here are items to look for as you continue to observe and evaluate your Sunday Mass.

Silence: Was there an ample amount of silence before the first reading to allow people to be settled and ready to hear the Word? Was there a good amount of silence after the first and second readings? Was there silence after the homily?

Proclamation of the readings: Did the lector, deacon, or priest proclaim the reading clearly and confidently? Did they have good eye contact with the assembly? Did they project well, speaking so all could hear? Did they convey the emotion and meaning of the reading? Describe the pace of their reading. Was it too fast or too slow? Describe their posture at the ambo. Did they look attentive? Did they slouch? Describe their gestures. Did they do anything distracting? Was there a different reader for each reading? Did the readers use the microphone well? Are there areas in the church space where the proclamation sounds unclear?

Procession: Did the procession during the gospel acclamation look like a procession? Did the ministers walk with dignity? Was the book of the gospels carried with dignity in the procession?

Homily: Did the homily connect and interpret the people's lives with the Scriptures proclaimed at that liturgy? Did the homily strengthen people's faith to participate in Communion or whatever blessing or sacrament was being celebrated at that liturgy?

Prayers: Did the profession of faith feel like a "profession" by the whole assembly? Did the universal prayer include prayers for the church, the world, the needs of the community, the needs of those suffering or oppressed? Were the prayers written thoughtfully? Did they include prayers for current important events in the neighborhood, city, or world? Were they announced by the reader prayerfully and clearly? Did the presider seem confident in leading the prayer of the people? Did the presider engage the assembly in prayer?

Assembly: During the readings did the assembly read along in a missalette, or did they actively listen to the proclamations? During the songs did the assembly listen to the choir, or did they actively sing the responses and acclamations? Did the assembly seem engaged during the homily and the universal prayer?

About Liturgical Music

Evaluating the Liturgy of the Word: During the Liturgy of the Word, the music ministers serve in a role similar to that of the lectors in that one of their main liturgical actions is to proclaim the Scripture through music. Here are some points to watch for as you evaluate your music ministry this week:

Did the assembly sing the responsorial psalm well? Did the assembly sound like they knew the music? Did the assembly know when to sing? Did the assembly sing confidently? Did a cantor lead the responsorial psalm from the ambo? Did the cantor communicate the meaning of the text through both their voice and body? Did the assembly sing the gospel acclamation well? Was the verse of the gospel acclamation sung or spoken? If the response of the universal prayer was sung, did the assembly sing it confidently?

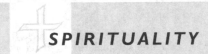

✝ SPIRITUALITY

GOSPEL ACCLAMATION
Luke 6:23ab

℟. Alleluia, alleluia.
Rejoice and be glad,
your reward will be great in heaven.
℟. Alleluia, alleluia.

Gospel

Luke 6:17, 20-26; L78C

Jesus came down with the Twelve
and stood on a stretch of level ground
with a great crowd of his disciples
and a large number of the people
from all Judea and Jerusalem
and the coastal region of Tyre and Sidon.
And raising his eyes toward his disciples he said:
"Blessed are you who are poor, for the kingdom of God is yours.
Blessed are you who are now hungry, for you will be satisfied.
Blessed are you who are now weeping, for you will laugh.
Blessed are you when people hate you, and when they exclude and insult you, and denounce your name as evil on account of the Son of Man.
Rejoice and leap for joy on that day!
Behold, your reward will be great in heaven.
For their ancestors treated the prophets in the same way.
But woe to you who are rich, for you have received your consolation.
Woe to you who are filled now, for you will be hungry.
Woe to you who laugh now, for you will grieve and weep.
Woe to you when all speak well of you, for their ancestors treated the false prophets in this way."

Reflecting on the Gospel

When parents leave children on their own for the first time it can be a big decision. Instructions are clear, often written down on a sheet of paper. Maybe a mobile phone or a home phone is available so the parties can stay in touch. And oftentimes the children remember or misremember instructions, reaching out to parents for additional clarity. Did the parents say no dessert? Or no dessert until after dinner? Did they say no TV/screen time, or limited TV/screen time? Some might remember the instructions differently.

Today in the Gospel of Luke we have Jesus' Sermon on the Plain as opposed to Matthew's Jesus who gives the Sermon on the Mount. Luke's Jesus preaches to a great crowd of disciples (indicating there were more than twelve) whereas Matthew's Jesus preaches to the disciples (and there were only twelve in the Gospel of Matthew).

But perhaps one of the greatest differences in the two versions of this story is not the setting or the audience but the message itself. Both Luke and Matthew begin with four beatitudes, but Matthew concludes with additional beatitudes. Luke, on the other hand, matches the four beatitudes with four woes that are frankly disturbing to the moderate, middle-class listener from the developed world.

We might ask what's wrong with being well off, having our fill of food and laughter, and being spoken well of? This might even be the goal of the so-called prosperity gospel we hear about so often in popular culture. But Luke sees it differently. Blessings are for those who are poor, hungry, weeping, and those hated. For whom is this good news? The rich and content? Hardly. Luke's Sermon on the Plain echoes themes introduced in Mary's *Magnificat* in the opening of the gospel. The hungry are fed while the rich are turned away empty. Jesus' values are not those of the world. To be countercultural means identifying with those who are blessed, not clawing one's way to keep company with those who are destined for woe.

Luke has something to say to us today. This message is not limited to the time of Jesus. It is for us. Where do we find ourselves? In the four beatitudes or the four woes? This message is as much for us as it is for the disciples, if we dare to carry that name.

Living the Paschal Mystery

Sometimes it can be difficult to imagine why Jesus faced suffering and death. Often there is a popular idea that would have Jesus preaching only love, peace, kindness, and lilies of the field. The thinking goes that in the face of such preaching he was put to death by those who were against love, peace, and kindness. Such is too facile an explanation.

Jesus' preaching was certainly about love, but it was about much more. Somebody preaching love is no threat to the establishment, no threat to the powerful. Somebody preaching love can easily be dismissed as a dreamer and best left alone.

Today's gospel gives us some of Jesus' preaching that likely created enemies for himself. His preaching favored the poor, hungry, weeping, and hated. He upended not only ancient cultural norms and values but modern ones too. Rather than simply give a verbal pat on the head to those on the bottom rungs of society, he also pulls down the mighty and issues woes that apply just as much to us as they did to those in power in antiquity. In so doing, Jesus creates enemies, not of the poor but of the powerful. It is they who will ultimately put him to death. But as we know, his suffering and death is not the end. God raises him up to glory, giving us the paschal mystery. His followers find themselves allied with those blessed by Jesus.

Focusing the Gospel

Key words and phrases: Blessed are you who are poor, / for the kingdom of God is yours.

To the point: Jesus begins his famous Sermon on the Plain in Luke (a companion to Matthew's Sermon on the Mount) by turning the world on its head. In the kingdom of God the blessed are those who are marginalized and oppressed in our societies. And those who enjoy favor now will not find it in God's kingdom. Today Jesus gives us a choice. Do we glory in the richness of the kingdom of God or in what our world counts as riches? Do we stand with the hungry and grieving, or are we too busy feasting and laughing to notice their pain?

Connecting the Gospel

to the first reading: The cursed and the blessed are also mentioned in the first reading from the prophet Jeremiah. Here the distinguishing feature centers on trust. While the cursed trust in fallible humanity, the blessed trust in God. Jeremiah prophesied during a time of great peril in Israel's history. Instead of remaining faithful to the covenant, many of the people had begun to worship idols. Through Jeremiah, God invites the people to once more be faithful to the covenant of their ancestors and to trust in him alone.

to experience: At times it is difficult to trust in God, whom we do not see, when there are so many products and people assuring us that by turning ourselves over to their patented formula, three-step method, or unique program, all will be well. Where in your own life might God be calling you to trust in him alone?

Connecting the Responsorial Psalm

to the readings: Today's psalm, the first in the book of Psalms, also contrasts the just with the wicked, the blessed with the cursed. Whereas Luke separates these groups by what they have and experience, and Jeremiah separates them by whom they trust, the psalmist makes a distinction in how they are rooted—in the law of the Lord or in the ways of the wicked. This psalm can be seen as an introduction to the entire book of Psalms and it states its thesis quite clearly: Happy is the one who is rooted in God. This person "meditates on his law day and night." The "law" in this case can be read as "Torah," the first five books of the Old Testament, traditionally attributed to Moses by the people of Israel. In today's gospel we see allusions to Moses, the lawgiver, coming down from Mount Sinai. Jesus returns from the mountain where he has chosen twelve of his disciples to be apostles and preaches God's law to the great multitude of people who are gathered. As the psalmist proclaims, Happy is the one who "delights in the law of the LORD / and meditates on his law day and night."

to psalmist preparation: Like the gospel, this psalm clearly lays out two ways for us to choose from—the way of the just or the way of the wicked. This choice is before us always, in every decision and action that make up our daily lives. Let your love for God's law and desire to remain rooted in God shine through as you proclaim this psalm.

PROMPTS FOR FAITH-SHARING

In the reading from the prophet Jeremiah and in the psalm, there is a common image: the one who trusts in God and meditates on God's law is like a tree planted beside flowing water. Nourished deeply by the living water of God's love, the just one flourishes and bears fruit. Where do you find living water in your own life? How might God be inviting you to drink even more deeply?

In the Nicene Creed we state: "I look forward to the resurrection of the dead." How does belief in the resurrection of the dead affect your faith life?

In your daily life what are some actions you can take to align yourself with those Jesus proclaims as blessed: the poor, the hungry, the grieving, and the outcast?

In Luke's Sermon on the Plain Jesus includes statements of woe after the more familiar statements of blessing that are also included in Matthew's Sermon on the Mount. Why do you think these statements are included? How do they challenge you in your life of faith?

Model Penitential Act

Presider: Today, Jesus lays out for us the path to blessedness. For the times we have not followed this path by aligning ourselves with the poor and the hungry, we ask for pardon and forgiveness . . . [*pause*]

Lord Jesus, you show us the way to blessedness: Lord, have mercy.

Christ Jesus, you call us to identify with the poor and hungry: Christ, have mercy.

Lord Jesus, you are the risen one: Lord, have mercy.

Homily Points

• In today's readings we are offered a choice: trust in God or trust in humans (the first reading), the way of the just or the way of the wicked (the psalm), belief in or denial of Christ's resurrection, and blessing or woe (the gospel). There is no middle ground. Instead, our decisions will define the course of our lives.

• In the reading from the First Letter to the Corinthians, the apostle Paul continues to set down his arguments for the improbable occurrence of Jesus' resurrection from the dead. We, who have come to this mystery so long after the historical event, might find it difficult to conceptualize Jesus' resurrection. And yet, we choose to trust in God and believe that life is stronger than death in both Jesus of Nazareth and also in those who share his light land life.

• In three weeks we will be celebrating the First Sunday of Lent. Today's gospel and those for the next two weeks are taken from Jesus' Sermon on the Plain. Jesus' words emphasize the closeness of God to those who are poor, oppressed, and grieving. As we approach the season of Lent, a time of prayer, fasting, and almsgiving, we might begin to consider how we could use that holy time to align ourselves with those whom Jesus proclaims as blessed. In every decision and action that make up our daily lives we have an opportunity to encounter blessing or woe, justice or wickedness, trust in God or trust in the things of the world that are passing away. The choice is ours.

Model Universal Prayer (Prayer of the Faithful)

Presider: Today Jesus shows us the way of blessing and the way of woe. Let us pray for the strength to choose the way of blessing.

Response: Lord, hear our prayer.

That the church might be aligned with the poor and oppressed of society, and as such, show the way of blessing to all . . .

That leaders of nations not seek their own success but work tirelessly for the needs of all . . .

That those who hunger and grieve be fed and comforted by their neighbors . . .

That all of us here might align ourselves with the poor, hungry, grieving, and excluded within our families, our community, our nation, and our world . . .

Presider: Loving God, you sent your son to show us the way of holy living. Hear our prayers that we might become ever more people of your way. We ask this through Christ our Lord. Amen.

COLLECT

Let us pray.

Pause for silent prayer

O God, who teach us that you abide
in hearts that are just and true,
grant that we may be so fashioned by
     your grace
as to become a dwelling pleasing to you.
Through our Lord Jesus Christ, your Son,
who lives and reigns with you in the unity
     of the Holy Spirit,
one God, for ever and ever. **Amen.**

FIRST READING
Jer 17:5-8

Thus says the Lord:
    Cursed is the one who trusts in human
        beings,
        who seeks his strength in flesh,
        whose heart turns away from the
            Lord.
    He is like a barren bush in the desert
        that enjoys no change of season,
    but stands in a lava waste,
        a salt and empty earth.
    Blessed is the one who trusts in the
        Lord,
        whose hope is the Lord.
    He is like a tree planted beside the
        waters
        that stretches out its roots to the
            stream:
    it fears not the heat when it comes;
        its leaves stay green;
    in the year of drought it shows no
        distress,
        but still bears fruit.

RESPONSORIAL PSALM
Ps 1:1-2, 3, 4, 6

R℣. (40:5a) Blessed are they who hope in
   the Lord.

Blessed the man who follows not
   the counsel of the wicked,
nor walks in the way of sinners,
   nor sits in the company of the insolent,
but delights in the law of the LORD
   and meditates on his law day and night.

R℣. Blessed are they who hope in the Lord.

He is like a tree
   planted near running water,
that yields its fruit in due season,
   and whose leaves never fade.
Whatever he does, prospers.

R℣. Blessed are they who hope in the Lord.

Not so the wicked, not so;
   they are like chaff which the wind
      drives away.
For the LORD watches over the way of the
      just,
   but the way of the wicked vanishes.

R℣. Blessed are they who hope in the Lord.

SECOND READING
1 Cor 15:12, 16-20

Brothers and sisters:
If Christ is preached as raised from the
      dead,
   how can some among you say there is no
      resurrection of the dead?
If the dead are not raised, neither has
      Christ been raised,
   and if Christ has not been raised, your
      faith is vain;
   you are still in your sins.
Then those who have fallen asleep in
      Christ have perished.
If for this life only we have hoped in
      Christ,
   we are the most pitiable people of all.

But now Christ has been raised from the
      dead,
   the firstfruits of those who have fallen
      asleep.

About Liturgy

Rare readings: Today and the next two Sundays give us the opportunity to hear a set of readings we don't often hear because of the logistics of the liturgical year. The last time we celebrated the Sixth Sunday of Ordinary Time, Year C, was in 2010; the Seventh Sunday, Year C, in 2007; and the Eighth Sunday, Year C, in 2001! These are a lovely set of readings from Luke, so be sure to alert your homilists and lectors to how special these coming Sundays are.

Observing the Preparation of Gifts and the Eucharistic Prayer: We continue our observation of the liturgy with these points to pay attention to in the preparation of gifts and the Eucharistic Prayer.

Gifts: Were the gifts of bread and wine brought to the altar by assembly members from the midst of the assembly, or were they simply retrieved from a side table by the priest or assistant? Were the vessels used for the bread and wine of genuine, beautiful, and dignified quality? Was enough bread and wine for the whole assembly brought to the altar?

Procession: Did the procession of gifts look like a procession? Were the gifts of bread, wine, and money processed to the altar with care and dignity? Was money collected in a graceful, unhurried, efficient manner? Were additional gifts other than bread, wine, and money brought forward? Why?

Eucharistic Prayer: Did the priest lead the Eucharistic Prayer clearly and confidently? Did the priest engage the assembly in the Eucharistic Prayer through graceful gestures and appropriate tone of voice and eye contact? Describe the pace of the Eucharistic Prayer. Was it spoken too quickly or too slowly? Did the priest convey a sense of praise and thanksgiving through his voice, posture, and gestures during the Eucharistic Prayer? Did the priest chant or sing any parts of the Eucharistic Prayer? In your opinion, what was the climax of the Eucharistic Prayer in this celebration? Why? Overall, did it feel like the assembly "[joined] with Christ in confessing the great deeds of God and in the offering of Sacrifice" (GIRM 78), or did it feel like just the priest's prayer? What made it feel that way?

About Liturgical Music

Evaluating the Preparation of Gifts and the Eucharistic Prayer: The preparation of gifts is a bridge between the Liturgy of the Word and the Liturgy of the Eucharist. Though it is secondary to these two main parts of the Mass, it still requires some careful preparation. Because the liturgical action during this time is relatively simple with very little to no spoken audible text, the music often takes the focal lead. This is an appropriate time for the choir to exercise its ministry by singing a hymn on its own. However, the music here still must serve the liturgical action and cannot delay the flow of the Mass. The text should also relate to the celebration of the day or liturgical season.

The Eucharistic Prayer, on the other hand, is the "center and high point of the entire celebration" (GIRM 78). The ritual music here is critical to the assembly's ritual action of offering praise to the Father through Christ. Here are some points to observe as you evaluate the liturgical music for the Eucharistic Prayer: Did the assembly sing all three Eucharistic Prayer acclamations (Holy, Mystery of Faith, Great Amen)? Did the assembly know the music? Did they sing confidently? Did the musical setting of the acclamations match the feel of the liturgical season? Did the Great Amen feel "Great"?

SPIRITUALITY

GOSPEL ACCLAMATION
John 13:34

R︎. Alleluia, alleluia.
I gave you a new commandment, says the Lord:
love one another as I have loved you.
R︎. Alleluia, alleluia.

Gospel   Luke 6:27-38; L81C

Jesus said to his disciples:
"To you who hear I say,
    love your enemies, do good to those who
        hate you,
    bless those who curse you, pray for those
        who mistreat you.
To the person who strikes you on one cheek,
    offer the other one as well,
    and from the person who takes your cloak,
        do not withhold even your tunic.
Give to everyone who asks of you,
    and from the one who takes what is yours
        do not demand it back.
Do to others as you would have them do to
    you.
For if you love those who love you,
    what credit is that to you?
Even sinners love those who love them.
And if you do good to those who do good to
        you,
    what credit is that to you?
Even sinners do the same.
If you lend money to those from whom you
        expect repayment,
    what credit is that to you?
Even sinners lend to sinners,
    and get back the same amount.
But rather, love your enemies and do good
        to them,
    and lend expecting nothing back;
    then your reward will be great
    and you will be children of the Most High,
    for he himself is kind to the ungrateful
        and the wicked.
Be merciful, just as your Father is merciful.

"Stop judging and you will not be judged.
Stop condemning and you will not be
    condemned.
Forgive and you will be forgiven.
Give, and gifts will be given to you;
    a good measure, packed together, shaken
        down, and overflowing,
    will be poured into your lap.
For the measure with which you measure
    will in return be measured out to you."

Reflecting on the Gospel

A classic device when children are called upon to share something is to have one divide it and the other choose which half is hers. This can happen with a piece of cake, cookie, pizza, or other food. But it can also happen with other items as well. Rarely does one child say to the other, "You can have it all." The purpose of the device is to share something in an equitable manner. And perhaps this works for children. It sometimes works for adults too!

The advice Jesus gives in today's gospel couldn't be more different. He is calling us to a higher standard. It's as though we are asked to divvy up the treat and instead we say, "You can have it all."

Even more, the way of sharing a cookie between children might assume they are friendly. But Jesus speaks here of "enemies." This is an entirely different category. Jesus assumes his ancient listeners have enemies, and that is something that transcends culture and time. Enemies are not limited to the ancient world!

Christians are to love their enemies, blessing them and praying for them. The Christian standard is one higher than what we could expect from the world with its transactional view of relationships. As Jesus himself notes, it's fairly easy to love those who love us, and to do good to those who do good to us. But it's another thing entirely to love those who are our enemies, to pray for them and to bless them.

We Christians are to be this way because God is this way. God is "kind to the ungrateful and the wicked." Should we be any different? We are to be merciful as the Father is merciful. And here we see in our own time the example of mercy given to us by Pope Francis. It is said that the word "mercy" is the hermeneutical key to his papacy. It is the way to understand and make sense of his actions. Pope Francis chose mercy because mercy is of God, and acting in this way demonstrates that we are followers of his son, Jesus.

Living the Paschal Mystery

When faced with the extraordinary demands of the gospel outlined in today's reading, one person said, "How can I do that? I'd end up with nothing?" Then we look to the example of Jesus who enfleshed the words he preached. Jesus himself loved his enemies and prayed for those who persecuted him. In the Gospel of Luke we will hear Jesus from the cross pray for their forgiveness. What did he end up with? Nothing: he died on a cross. But of course we know the rest of the story. God raised him from the dead. Only by Jesus giving himself completely and without reservation to the point of death is he ultimately raised up to glory with the Father. The words that form the conclusion of today's gospel are especially apropos. "Forgive and you will be forgiven. . . . For the measure with which you measure / will in return be measured out to you." We forgive others not so much for their sake but for our own.

Focusing the Gospel

Key words and phrases: [L]ove your enemies

To the point: In today's gospel Jesus tells us twice, "[L]ove your enemies." This statement is nestled into a longer list of moral injunctions. We could say, however, that this phrase, "love your enemies," encompasses all the others and also points the way to emulating God's love. God does not love only those who are worthy or good. God loves everyone simply because of their very existence. And so are we called to love as well. Our enemies could be one specific person with whom we have a feud, or it could be a group of people that we see (even if it is subconsciously) as "other" than ourselves and therefore not worthy of our concern. No matter how we might encounter "enemies" Jesus' command remains the same, love them with the mercy, forgiveness, and compassion of God.

Connecting the Gospel

to the first reading: In the first reading from First Samuel we have an example par excellence of one man loving his enemy. David is pursued by King Saul. In his jealousy, Saul fears that David wants the throne for himself. Bent on killing David, Saul takes three thousand of his best warriors into the wilderness area where he hears David is hiding. Through the work of the Lord it is David, not Saul, who comes upon his enemy unawares. David finds Saul asleep with a spear stuck into the ground at his head, while all of his warriors slumber around him. And yet, with a clear opportunity to end his life of hiding and running from Saul, he does the king no harm. Our reading ends with David (now safely separated from Saul by a hilltop) telling the king, "The LORD will reward each man for his justice and faithfulness."

to experience: Is there a contentious relationship in your life where you can follow David's example and refuse to pick up the spear?

Connecting the Responsorial Psalm

to the readings: In the gospel Jesus tells us to be "merciful, just as your Father is merciful." And how would we define God's mercy? Today's psalm paints a picture for us. Our God is "slow to anger and abounding in kindness." No wrongdoing can put us beyond the reach of God, who "pardons all your iniquities," removing them "[a]s far as the east is from the west." We cannot give to our brothers and sisters what we have not received ourselves. Let us immerse ourselves in the infinite mercy of our God—only then will we be able to offer it to others.

to psalmist preparation: It is only in acknowledging our sins that we experience the gracious mercy of God. As you prepare to proclaim this psalm, lauding God's abundant mercy, call to mind a time when you experienced forgiveness—either from a person in your life, or from God. What did it feel like to know your sin had been wiped away and your wrongdoing was forgotten?

PROMPTS FOR FAITH-SHARING

In the first reading, David refuses to do harm to his enemy when he comes upon Saul unprotected. Where in your own life are you being called to choose peace and mercy over bitterness and revenge?

_____

_____

_____

In the second reading, St. Paul tells us that we will bear the image of the heavenly man, Jesus, just as we have born the image of the earthly man, Adam. How might we, as individuals and as a parish, conform ourselves more perfectly to the image of Christ, the one who loves without counting the cost?

_____

_____

_____

How does your family and/or parish follow Jesus' command to "bless those who curse you, pray for those who mistreat you"?

_____

_____

_____

In the gospel we are told, "Give, and gifts will be given to you." When have you experienced in your own life generosity begetting abundance?

_____

_____

_____

Model Penitential Act

Presider: In today's gospel we hear the Golden Rule, "Do to others as you would have them do to you." We pause now to consider the times we have not lived up to this rule . . . [*pause*]

Lord Jesus, you call us to love our enemies: Lord, have mercy.
Christ Jesus, show us the way of mercy and compassion: Christ, have mercy.
Lord Jesus, you are the Son of the Most High: Lord, have mercy.

Homily Points

• As human beings we are often caught up in the question of fairness. We want to be fair to our children, our students, our employees, our neighbors. . . . And we want others to be fair to us. In the gospel today Jesus tells us to love without limit, to go beyond being fair, for "if you love those who love you, / what credit is that to you?" As Christians we are called to radically trust in the power of love beyond what is fair.

• When we love the way Jesus loves we might be surprised at what happens. But then again we might not. People continue to be people no matter our actions. Is this reason to stop? No. St. Teresa of Calcutta inscribed a poem on the wall of her children's house called "Paradoxical Commandments" by Dr. Kent M. Keith. It begins, "People are illogical, unreasonable, and self-centered. Love them anyway."

• As Christians we are tasked with being Christ-bearers in the world. To love as Jesus himself loves. We are to respond to hate with compassion, empathy, and mercy. We are to lend to others expecting nothing in return. We are to forgive others, even as the "other" persecutes and tortures us. Adopting this way of living is not easy. Perhaps this week we might begin by taking one area in our lives where we have been focused on fairness, on loving others with the same amount of love they show us, and instead strive to personify the abundant, illogical, joyful love of Christ.

Model Universal Prayer (Prayer of the Faithful)

Presider: Confident in God's mercy and compassion, let us present our needs to the Lord.

Response: Lord, hear our prayer.

That the church be a sign of unity and reconciliation . . .

That the prosperous nations of the world share their resources and gifts with nations in need . . .

That those who are enslaved by bitterness and thoughts of revenge receive the grace to grant forgiveness . . .

That all of us here grow in our vocation to show the merciful, compassionate love of Christ to all we encounter . . .

Presider: Gracious God, you call us to emulate your way of love. Grant our prayers that we may trust in your grace as we travel this holy way. We ask this through Jesus Christ, our Lord. Amen.

COLLECT

Let us pray.

Pause for silent prayer

Grant, we pray, almighty God,
that, always pondering spiritual things,
we may carry out in both word and deed
that which is pleasing to you.
Through our Lord Jesus Christ, your Son,
who lives and reigns with you in the unity
of the Holy Spirit,
one God, for ever and ever. **Amen.**

FIRST READING

1 Sam 26:2, 7-9, 12-13, 22-23

In those days, Saul went down to the
desert of Ziph
with three thousand picked men of Israel,
to search for David in the desert of Ziph.
So David and Abishai went among Saul's
soldiers by night
and found Saul lying asleep within the
barricade,
with his spear thrust into the ground at
his head
and Abner and his men sleeping around
him.

Abishai whispered to David:
"God has delivered your enemy into
your grasp this day.
Let me nail him to the ground with one
thrust of the spear;
I will not need a second thrust!"
But David said to Abishai, "Do not harm
him,
for who can lay hands on the LORD's
anointed and remain unpunished?"
So David took the spear and the water jug
from their place at Saul's head,
and they got away without anyone's
seeing or knowing or awakening.
All remained asleep,
because the LORD had put them into a
deep slumber.

Going across to an opposite slope,
David stood on a remote hilltop
at a great distance from Abner, son of
Ner, and the troops.
He said: "Here is the king's spear.
Let an attendant come over to get it.
The LORD will reward each man for his
justice and faithfulness.
Today, though the LORD delivered you into
my grasp,
I would not harm the LORD's anointed."

RESPONSORIAL PSALM

Ps 103:1-2, 3-4, 8, 10, 12-13

R̯. (8a) The Lord is kind and merciful.

Bless the Lᴏʀᴅ, O my soul;
  and all my being, bless his holy name.
Bless the Lᴏʀᴅ, O my soul,
  and forget not all his benefits.

R̯. The Lord is kind and merciful.

He pardons all your iniquities,
  heals all your ills.
He redeems your life from destruction,
  crowns you with kindness and
    compassion.

R̯. The Lord is kind and merciful.

Merciful and gracious is the Lᴏʀᴅ,
  slow to anger and abounding in
    kindness.
Not according to our sins does he deal
    with us,
  nor does he requite us according to our
    crimes.

R̯. The Lord is kind and merciful.

As far as the east is from the west,
  so far has he put our transgressions
    from us.
As a father has compassion on his
    children,
  so the Lᴏʀᴅ has compassion on those
    who fear him.

R̯. The Lord is kind and merciful.

SECOND READING

1 Cor 15:45-49

Brothers and sisters:
It is written, *The first man, Adam, became
    a living being,*
  the last Adam a life-giving spirit.
But the spiritual was not first;
  rather the natural and then the spiritual.
The first man was from the earth, earthly;
  the second man, from heaven.
As was the earthly one, so also are the
    earthly,
  and as is the heavenly one, so also are
    the heavenly.
Just as we have borne the image of the
    earthly one,
  we shall also bear the image of the
    heavenly one.

About Liturgy

Observing the Communion Rite: The communion rite is often where the liturgical flow and logistics of a Mass may fall apart or lag. The communion rite begins with the Lord's Prayer and continues through the end of the prayer after Communion. Because there is so much movement of ministers and people during this time, you will want to plan the "choreography" and placement of ministers with careful attention to your specific liturgical space. Then all liturgical ministers assisting during this time need to know and rehearse their movements and tasks. This includes not only the clergy who are assisting at the altar but also servers, extraordinary ministers of Holy Communion, ushers, sacristans, and choir members. Here are some specific points to observe during the communion rite as you continue to evaluate each part of your Sunday Mass:

Lord's Prayer: If the Lord's Prayer was sung, did the whole assembly sing it confidently? If it was spoken, was the pacing prayerful?

Sign of Peace: Did you feel that people shared the sign of peace with you genuinely? Did the gesture feel like a ritual sign of peacemaking, reconciliation, and commitment to the Body of Christ, or did it feel simply like a cordial handshake? Was the rite overly lengthened by the priest or other ministers sharing the sign of peace with many people? If so, did the assembly feel engaged during this time, or did the assembly become spectators?

Fraction Rite: Were hosts from the tabernacle used in the fraction rite? Why? Did the rite seem to take too long? If so, why? Did the rite look calm? Chaotic? Organized? Did the priest break the first piece of the Blessed Sacrament in a way that made it look like a dignified ritual for the whole assembly to see? Did the assembly sing the Lamb of God confidently? Did the singing of the Lamb of God begin as the priest broke the first host, and did the singing continue until all the communion vessels were ready?

Communion: After the assembly said, "Lord, I am not worthy . . .," how long did the assembly have to wait before they began processing to the altar? Was the Precious Blood available for the whole assembly? Were there enough communion ministers for the whole assembly so that the procession did not take too long? Did communion ministers have good eye contact with you? Did communion ministers speak clearly and loudly? How did the consecrated host taste? How did the consecrated wine taste? Overall, did the assembly feel united as one body through posture, movement, and song during the entire communion procession, or did it feel like each person's own private time for prayer? Was there a good amount of silence after Communion?

About Liturgical Music

Evaluating the Communion Rite: Music during this time will help to unite the various parts and keep the flow of the ritual prayer moving. Here are a few points to assist in your evaluation of the musical elements of the communion rite:

If the Lord's Prayer was sung, did the whole assembly sing it confidently? After the assembly said, "Lord, I am not worthy . . .," did the communion song begin immediately as the priest received the Sacrament (see GIRM 86)? Was the assembly able to sing the communion song(s) confidently? How many communion songs were sung? Was this the right amount of songs to use for the length of the communion procession? If there was a song of praise after communion, did everyone sing it (see GIRM 88), or was it a song performed by one person or just the choir?

SPIRITUALITY

GOSPEL ACCLAMATION
Philippians 2:15d, 16a

R⃗. Alleluia, alleluia.
Shine like lights in the world
as you hold on to the word of life.
R⃗. Alleluia, alleluia.

Gospel

Luke 6:39-45; L84C

Jesus told his disciples a parable,
  "Can a blind person guide a blind
    person?
Will not both fall into a pit?
No disciple is superior to the
    teacher;
  but when fully trained,
  every disciple will be like his
    teacher.
Why do you notice the splinter in
    your brother's eye,
  but do not perceive the wooden
    beam in your own?
How can you say to your brother,
  'Brother, let me remove that splinter
    in your eye,'
  when you do not even notice the
    wooden beam in your own eye?
You hypocrite! Remove the wooden
    beam from your eye first;
  then you will see clearly
  to remove the splinter in your broth-
    er's eye.

"A good tree does not bear rotten fruit,
  nor does a rotten tree bear good
    fruit.
For every tree is known by its own
    fruit.
For people do not pick figs from
    thornbushes,
  nor do they gather grapes from
    brambles.
A good person out of the store of good-
    ness in his heart produces good,
  but an evil person out of a store of
    evil produces evil;
  for from the fullness of the heart the
    mouth speaks."

Reflecting on the Gospel

We all have words to live by. Maybe they were told to us by parents or grand-parents, or perhaps a teacher or a relative. But we can all recall maxims by which we live. Today's gospel gives us life lessons or words to live by. In fact, if read in isolation, this reading is broader than Christianity. It could readily be accepted by non-Christians too. And such is often the case with life lessons. They are not limited to one religious or denominational outlook.

The life lessons Jesus teaches in this gospel are akin to homespun wisdom rooted in daily life and experience. When we say a project at work is being performed like "the blind leading the blind," we are echoing Jesus' teaching. Though we mean no disrespect to the blind, the metaphor is easily grasped and understood.

And how often have we experienced the nitpicking nag who quickly points out the fault in others while conveniently overlooking his or her own. Jesus' warning about noticing the splinter in another's eye while neglecting the wooden beam in our own captures that sentiment well. Even so, Jesus is more adamant about us removing the beam from our own eye than simply not noticing the splinter in another.

The concluding bit of wisdom is based on lived experience as well. Just as a good tree does not produce bad fruit, so it is with people. "By their fruits you shall know them" is another way to sum this up; "actions speak louder than words" is another. If a person is performing good works, it's likely they are a good person. On the other hand, if a person performs only selfish acts, that, too, is a window into their soul, for as Jesus puts it, "[F]rom the fullness of the heart the mouth speaks." Here the basis on one's fundamental goodness is not whether they believe in Jesus, or even God. It's not whether they go to church or synagogue. And given the time this was written, it's certainly not about praying the rosary or attending First Fridays. Instead, a person's heart is ultimately known by their words and actions. And actions speak louder than words. These are words to live by.

Living the Paschal Mystery

Churchy people can often and easily be caught up in churchy things. What colors are we displaying for the season? What song is most appropriate at this time? What is the second reading and how does it connect to the first? But today we are reminded by Jesus that there are many things broader and perhaps more important than church or even religious identity. We are told not to be hypocritical, finding fault in others while overlooking our own. We are reminded to consider how one acts as an indication of that one's character.

Jesus' teaching and preaching was fundamental to his ministry. He was considered a sage and a prophet. His understanding of human beings moved the crowds. His insight into how we behave versus how we ought to behave, encapsulated in pithy and memorable sayings was profound. And certainly after his death and resurrection his teaching carried new meaning. In light of his undergoing the paschal mystery, he is the Son of God raised to new life. His words are more than homespun wisdom. They are light and life.

Focusing the Gospel

Key words and phrases: every tree is known by its own fruit

To the point: Jesus lived in an agrarian culture where people tilled the soil to provide for themselves and their families. In today's gospel he uses a metaphor that his audience would immediately have understood: "A good tree does not bear rotten fruit, / nor does a rotten tree bear good fruit. / For every tree is known by its own fruit." We might ask, what "fruit" do we bear that marks us as Christians?

Connecting the Gospel

to the first reading: Just as "every tree is known by its own fruit," the writer of Sirach counsels that the true test of a person's heart is in their speech and conversation. The book of Sirach belongs to the category of wisdom literature in the Bible. Uprightness of speech is an important theme in all of wisdom literature. In the book of Proverbs we hear, "Dishonest mouth put away from you, / deceitful lips put far from you" (Prov 4:24; NABRE). Devious and crooked speech might include falsehoods, but gossip and slander are also condemned.

to experience: Survey your own conversation. What percentage of it might you categorize as righteous speech—words that uplift and inspire others? What percentage is crooked or devious—words that put others down or convey anger, hatred or enmity?

Connecting the Responsorial Psalm

to the readings: If slander, gossip, and lying are all speech that places a wedge between the speaker and his or her neighbors and God, what is godly speech? The psalms might be our best guide for speech that uplifts. In Psalm 92 we hear, "It is good to give thanks to the LORD, / to sing praise to your name, Most High." Praise and thanksgiving are not only for the glory of God; these patterns of speech also change the one who is speaking. By focusing on gratitude and praise, one's eyes are further opened to the countless gifts of God and the wonders of creation. Furthermore, the psalmist tells us that the one who is rooted in justice (right relationship with God and others) will "flourish like the palm tree . . . planted in the house of the LORD / shall flourish in the courts of our God. / They shall bear fruit even in old age."

to psalmist preparation: As a cantor, your words within the liturgy lead the people in prayer and praise of God. How might you bring all the other words you speak throughout the week into better alignment with the ones you proclaim in the liturgy?

PROMPTS FOR FAITH-SHARING

The first reading from Sirach warns, "[T]he test of a person is in conversation" (NABRE). What do your own patterns and habits of speech reveal about you and about "the bent" of your heart?

_____

_____

_____

St. Paul urges us to "be firm, steadfast, always fully devoted to the work of the Lord." Where is God calling you to be steadfast at this time?

_____

_____

_____

In the gospel we hear, "[E]very tree is known by its own fruit." In what areas of your life are good fruits being born? Where is your life less fruitful?

_____

_____

_____

Sometimes we are most distressed by the faults of others that we also notice subconsciously in ourselves. Where have you become preoccupied with a "splinter in your brother's eye"? What might this preoccupation tell you about "the wooden beam in your own eye"?

_____

_____

_____

_____

Model Penitential Act

Presider: Jesus tells us today, "A good tree does not bear rotten fruit, / nor does a rotten tree bear good fruit. / For every tree is known by its own fruit." For the times we have failed to produce good fruit we ask for pardon and mercy . . . [*pause*]

Lord Jesus, you conquer sin and death: Lord, have mercy.

Christ Jesus, you are Son of the Most High: Christ, have mercy.

Lord Jesus, you lead us to wisdom: Lord, have mercy.

Homily Points

• On Wednesday we will enter into the season of Lent. As we think about what practice of penance we will embrace it is often easier to come up with penances for our spouse, children, colleagues, or friends than it is for ourselves. Jesus knew the human propensity to point out others' faults. He counsels, "Remove the wooden beam from your eye first; / then you will see clearly / to remove the splinter in your brother's eye." Perhaps this year you might invite a trusted friend or family member to help you in choosing a Lenten practice. Receive feedback with an open mind and then ask God to help you discern what will be the most fruitful practice for you this Lenten season.

• Speech is one of our most precious abilities as humans. Traveling in a foreign country or visiting a neighborhood where one does not speak the language quickly shows us how much we miss out on when we cannot communicate with others. As with all precious gifts, however, there is the possibility of misusing this ability. This week take some time to reflect on how you use speech in your daily life. Perhaps your Lenten practice could include fasting from speech that tears others down, and bestowing words that uplift as a way of giving alms.

• Sometimes we grow weary in the spiritual life. These last few weeks Jesus has called to us through the gospels to do the seemingly impossible: "Be merciful, just as your Father is merciful"; "[L]ove your enemies"; "Give to everyone who asks of you." While we strive to fulfill these commandments, we will often fail. And yet, today St. Paul urges us, "Be firm, steadfast, always fully devoted to the work of the Lord, knowing that in the Lord your labor is not in vain." Let us not become weary by our failures, but continue to trust in Jesus' call to "bear good fruit."

Model Universal Prayer (Prayer of the Faithful)

Presider: Heeding Jesus' call to repentance, we humbly voice our petitions, trusting in God's never-ending mercy.

Response: Lord, hear our prayer.

That the church might bear good fruit for the glory of God . . .

That religious and civic leaders support conditions where all people might grow and flourish . . .

That those in need reap the good fruit of charity, love, and mercy . . .

That all members of our community use their talents and gifts to build up the kingdom of God . . .

Presider: Gracious God, all that we have is a gift from you. May we tend and cultivate these gifts so they might bear abundant fruit for the glory of your name. We ask this through Jesus Christ, our Lord. Amen.

COLLECT

Let us pray.

Pause for silent prayer

Grant us, O Lord, we pray,
that the course of our world
may be directed by your peaceful rule
and that your Church may rejoice,
untroubled in her devotion.
Through our Lord Jesus Christ, your Son,
who lives and reigns with you in the unity
of the Holy Spirit,
one God, for ever and ever. **Amen.**

FIRST READING

Sir 27:4-7

When a sieve is shaken, the husks appear;
so do one's faults when one speaks.
As the test of what the potter molds is in
the furnace,
so in tribulation is the test of the just.
The fruit of a tree shows the care it has
had;
so too does one's speech disclose the
bent of one's mind.
Praise no one before he speaks,
for it is then that people are tested.

RESPONSORIAL PSALM
Ps 92:2-3, 13-14, 15-16

R̊. (cf. 2a) Lord, it is good to give thanks
  to you.

It is good to give thanks to the LORD,
  to sing praise to your name, Most High,
to proclaim your kindness at dawn
  and your faithfulness throughout the
    night.

R̊. Lord, it is good to give thanks to you.

The just one shall flourish like the palm
    tree,
  like a cedar of Lebanon shall he grow.
They that are planted in the house of the
    LORD
  shall flourish in the courts of our God.

R̊. Lord, it is good to give thanks to you.

They shall bear fruit even in old age;
  vigorous and sturdy shall they be,
declaring how just is the Lord,
  my rock, in whom there is no wrong.

R̊. Lord, it is good to give thanks to you.

SECOND READING
1 Cor 15:54-58

Brothers and sisters:
When this which is corruptible clothes
    itself with incorruptibility
  and this which is mortal clothes itself
    with immortality,
  then the word that is written shall come
    about:
  Death is swallowed up in victory.
  Where, O death, is your victory?
  Where, O death, is your sting?
The sting of death is sin,
  and the power of sin is the law.
But thanks be to God who gives us the
    victory
  through our Lord Jesus Christ.

Therefore, my beloved brothers and
    sisters,
  be firm, steadfast, always fully devoted
    to the work of the Lord,
  knowing that in the Lord your labor is
    not in vain.

CATECHESIS

About Liturgy
Observing the Concluding Rites: We come to the last, and possibly most important, part of the Mass. The concluding rites give the Mass its name and, quite literally, its mission: "Go and announce the Gospel of the Lord." Here the faithful are commissioned to evangelize by doing what they have done in the Mass. Out in the world, we welcome the stranger, acknowledge our sins, and give glory for the Father's mercy we have encountered in Christ through the Spirit. Then we listen with the ear of our hearts to God's word, which gives us the lens for recognizing Christ acting in the world and shapes us for mission. We confess our faith, lift up the needs of those who suffer, share our blessings, and, in union with all God's people, praise God and ask God to make us one in Christ. All we have rehearsed in the liturgy of the church we do in our daily lives in the liturgy of the world. This concluding part of the Mass is the beginning of our mission to glorify God by our lives. Here are some points to observe as you evaluate the concluding rites:

Did the announcements come after the prayer after Communion? Were they brief and included only those things that were necessary in order to assist the faithful in doing their mission in the world this week? Was there a second collection? Was it necessary, or is there a better way to ritually attend to the parish's financial stewardship and community's needs? For example, could the second collection have been collected during the preparation of gifts? Were there additional blessings or rituals that were scheduled appropriately so that no single Mass was overburdened with too many additional rites? On more solemn occasions, did the priest use an appropriate solemn (triple) blessing or prayer over the people? Were any part of the dialogues or blessings sung by the priest and people?

About Initiation
Rite of Sending: On this last Sunday before Lent it may be appropriate to celebrate the optional Rite of Sending for those catechumens who are ready to be elected for baptism at Easter. Note that this rite is similar to the Rite of Election, except it does not include the declaration or act of election. Those are the words spoken by the bishop that give your catechumens the promise of baptism at the next Easter Vigil. You will want to find out from your diocesan staff if the catechumens are expected to sign the Book of the Elect prior to coming to the Rite of Election, or if that signing takes place at the Rite of Election itself. Also, if you choose to celebrate the Rite of Sending the godparents typically offer testimony about the catechumen's readiness. However, the godparents do not officially begin their role until the Rite of Election. Therefore, if the godparents are not available for the Rite of Sending the catechumen's sponsor or other community members may give that testimony. Be sure, however, that the godparents are prepared to be present at next week's Rite of Election.

About Liturgical Music
Evaluating the Concluding Rites: There are not many musical elements in this section of the Mass, other than possibly having the ritual dialogues sung or chanted and the concluding song. A note about this song: there are no rubrics or instructions that refer to a concluding song. The expectation is simply that the ministers reverence the altar then leave. Therefore, there is much freedom as to what song, if any, is used at this time. Regardless, the song should still support and enhance the ritual action, even if it is instrumental or sung only by the choir.

MARCH 3, 2019
EIGHTH SUNDAY IN ORDINARY TIME

SEASON OF LENT

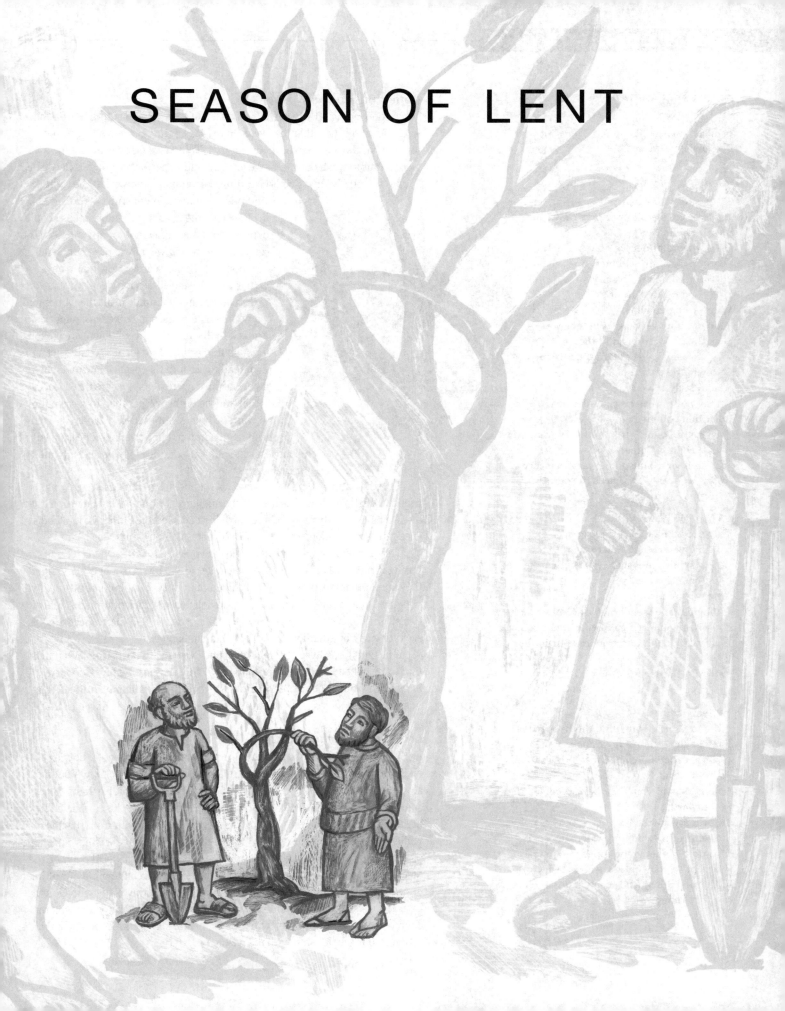

GOSPEL ACCLAMATION
See Ps 95:8

If today you hear his voice,
harden not your hearts.

Gospel   Matt 6:1-6, 16-18; L219

Jesus said to his disciples:
  "Take care not to perform righteous
      deeds
    in order that people may see them;
    otherwise, you will have no
        recompense from your
        heavenly Father.
When you give alms,
    do not blow a trumpet before you,
    as the hypocrites do in the
        synagogues and in the streets
    to win the praise of others.
Amen, I say to you,
    they have received their reward.
But when you give alms,
    do not let your left hand know what your
        right is doing,
    so that your almsgiving may be secret.
And your Father who sees in secret will
        repay you.

"When you pray,
    do not be like the hypocrites,
    who love to stand and pray in the
        synagogues and on street corners
    so that others may see them.
Amen, I say to you,
    they have received their reward.
But when you pray, go to your inner room,
    close the door, and pray to your Father in
        secret.
And your Father who sees in secret will
        repay you.

"When you fast,
    do not look gloomy like the hypocrites.
They neglect their appearance,
    so that they may appear to others to be
        fasting.
Amen, I say to you, they have received their
        reward.
But when you fast,
    anoint your head and wash your face,
    so that you may not appear to be fasting,
    except to your Father who is hidden.
And your Father who sees what is hidden
        will repay you."

See Appendix A, p. 273, for the other readings.

Reflecting on the Gospel

Today, depending on where we live, we'll likely see people with ashes on their foreheads indicating that they've been to Mass. It might seem strange that we do what the gospel exhorts us not to do! When we fast we are not to look gloomy but to wash our faces! We are also told to perform righteous deeds in secret; give alms without letting the left hand know what the right is doing, and pray in an inner room with no audience.

The lesson of the gospel is that our deeds should be done for God the Father, not for anyone else. That is something to which we may aspire, but do our actions match our words? How many of our parishes use envelopes for weekly giving? How many annual funds print the names and amounts of donors, sometimes in categories ranked by the amount given? There are reasons for such things, but they seem to contradict a plain reading of today's gospel. How much has to be stripped away before we are doing deeds solely for the Father rather than to receive the reward of others' admiration? Much as we may hesitate to admit it, our acts of kindness, deeds of righteousness, and alms of sacrifice may be accompanied by a bit of pride.

The exhortation from Jesus today is a reminder that crowds, neighbors, friends, or fellow Christians are not the audience for our works. Indeed, if they are, we have already received a reward. Instead, God the Father is our "audience" and it is He alone that we seek to impress, to put it in those terms.

There is a temptation among religious people to be seen or perceived as "doing it right." Many religious people take care to be seen at church. Perhaps they want others to know they've fulfilled their duty. That kind of attitude was prevalent in antiquity too. But that approach is not sufficient for a disciple of Christ. Our mission is to perform deeds of mercy for God the Father without seeking glory or attention from fellow human beings.

In the end, Jesus lived this mission as he faced death on a cross. What must that have looked like to those around him? Only those cursed by God were hanged on a tree (Deut 21:22-23). But to be true to his calling he fulfilled this mission, and received a reward from God the Father, which is life eternal.

Living the Paschal Mystery

Each year we begin Lent with Ash Wednesday. Though it is not a holy day of obligation, nonetheless, many people attend Mass on this weekday. That fact alone tells us that the day connects with something deep in Christians. The smearing of ashes on our forehead reminds us that we are dust animated by the breath of life, which is the spirit of Christ. When we pass on from this life our bodies will return to the dust from which they came, and we will have the hope of eternal life. Something so elemental, life and death, is the focal point of the liturgy today, especially with the sign of the ashes. We call to mind our ultimate destiny is not to be buried in this earth; rather, our destiny is life with God the Father, and his Son Jesus our Lord, in the Spirit. And perhaps this is why the church begins Lent each year with this elemental sign. It is a fundamental indication of our relationship with the paschal mystery.

Focusing the Gospel

Key words and phrases: Take care not to perform righteous deeds in order that people may see them.

To the point: In Lent we intentionally enter into the practices of prayer, fasting, and almsgiving, and every year as we begin this journey we hear this gospel. Jesus tells us that more is required of us than simply to pray, fast, and give alms. We must also be attentive to our motivation for these actions. Are we embracing righteous deeds so that others might see and laud our righteousness? If so, our actions are empty. They will not change us and they will not change the world. Instead, Jesus invites us to enter into Lent in the secrecy of our hearts. It is there that true transformation occurs—the transformation that will lead to Easter joy.

Model Universal Prayer (Prayer of the Faithful)

Presider: As we enter into this season of Lent, we lift up our prayers to God that our fasting, almsgiving, and prayer might bear abundant fruit.

Response: Lord, hear our prayer.

That the church be a welcome refuge to all who come to her seeking solace, peace, and healing . . .

That leaders throughout the world show sacrificial love and care for those under their leadership . . .

That those in need might benefit from the prayer, fasting and almsgiving of our Lenten practice . . .

That all gathered here encounter the Lord within the secrecy of our hearts this Lent and, transformed by his love, be brought to Easter joy . . .

Presider: Merciful and compassionate God, you call us to return to you with our whole hearts. Hear our prayers this day, that our Lenten prayer, fasting, and almsgiving might bring us ever closer to you. Through Christ our Lord. **Amen.**

About Liturgy

Keeping fonts full: Some churches make it a custom to empty baptismal fonts and holy water stoops during Lent as a way to emphasize a desert-like thirst for God. This may seem like a good idea, but it goes contrary to the nature of Lent: "[By] the recalling of Baptism or the preparation for it, and Penance . . . the church prepares the faithful for the celebration of Easter, while they listen more attentively to God's word and devote more time to prayer. Accordingly . . . more use is to be made of the baptismal features which are part of the Lenten liturgy" (Constitution on the Sacred Liturgy 109).

Instead of removing holy water from your church during this season, or covering up fonts with purple cloth, making the water inaccessible, or replacing the water with sand or rocks, keep your fonts filled with water. Let the constant visual reminder of our baptismal promises inspire greater penitence in the faithful and a deeper thirst for God in our catechumens.

COLLECT

Let us pray.

Pause for silent prayer

Grant, O Lord, that we may begin with holy fasting
this campaign of Christian service,
so that, as we take up battle against spiritual evils,
we may be armed with weapons of self-restraint.
Through our Lord Jesus Christ, your Son,
who lives and reigns with you in the unity of the Holy Spirit,
one God, for ever and ever. **Amen.**

FOR REFLECTION

• How would you live this Lent if you knew it were your last?

• What in your life causes division in your heart and your relationships?

• What actions can you take this Lent to pledge your whole heart to God?

Homily Points

• The apostle Paul assures us in the second reading that "now is a very acceptable time . . . now is the day of salvation." Each year we enter into Lent anew, realizing that in each of our lives there is the need for penance and transformation. Even though Lent comes around every year, there is an urgency to the readings we hear today.

• "Even now . . . return to me with your whole heart," God pleads through the prophet Joel in the first reading. One way to think of sin is that which fragments us. Our Lenten practices of prayer, almsgiving, and fasting are not only acts of penitence, they are also disciplines aimed at bringing us into union with ourselves, our neighbors, and God. With hope, let us embrace the "now" we hear of in the first and second reading. God is always ready to welcome us back to him. Now is the day of salvation.

† SPIRITUALITY

GOSPEL ACCLAMATION
Matt 4:4b

One does not live on bread alone,
but on every word that comes forth from the
mouth of God.

Gospel   Luke 4:1-13; L24C

Filled with the Holy Spirit, Jesus returned from the Jordan
and was led by the Spirit into the
desert for forty days,
to be tempted by the devil.
He ate nothing during those days,
and when they were over he was
hungry.
The devil said to him,
"If you are the Son of God,
command this stone to become bread."
Jesus answered him,
"It is written, *One does not live on bread
alone.*"
Then he took him up and showed him
all the kingdoms of the world in a single
instant.
The devil said to him,
"I shall give to you all this power and glory;
for it has been handed over to me,
and I may give it to whomever I wish.
All this will be yours, if you worship me."
Jesus said to him in reply,
"It is written:
*You shall worship the Lord, your God,
and him alone shall you serve.*"
Then he led him to Jerusalem,
made him stand on the parapet of the
temple, and said to him,
"If you are the Son of God,
throw yourself down from here, for it is
written:
*He will command his angels concern-
ing you, to guard you,*
and:
*With their hands they will support you,
lest you dash your foot against a stone.*"
Jesus said to him in reply,
"It also says,
*You shall not put the Lord, your God, to
the test.*"
When the devil had finished every
temptation,
he departed from him for a time.

Reflecting on the Gospel

Even the devil can quote Scripture! This dismissive line is often declared when one tries to "one-up" another by quoting a familiar Scripture passage to make a point. Simply knowing Scripture does not guarantee one's right relationship with God. One scholar said, "Give me thirty minutes with the Bible and I'll make up any religion you want." So merely citing Scripture does not win the argument. There is much more to it than that.

Luke's version of the temptation of Jesus is more elaborate than the story we find in Mark, which Luke used as a source. In fact, Mark tells the story (if we can even call it that) of the temptation in two verses, whereas Luke uses thirteen (cf. Mark 1:12-13). Luke gives us a dialogue between Jesus and the devil that is completely absent in Mark. To each of the devil's temptations, some supported by Scripture, Jesus retorts with Scripture. The scene is almost one of a theological debating club.

Luke expanded on the story he inherited from Mark to convey theological insights and truths rather than compose a journalist's description of "what really happened." Early church fathers recognized this immediately when they asked how the devil could take Jesus to a place where he could show him all the kingdoms of the world in an instant when no such place exists. The church fathers knew that this story was meant to convey theology, and it was meant to be read metaphorically rather than literally.

By this story Luke tells us a number of things, not least of which is that Jesus was tempted by the devil. And Luke's expansion of the story from what he inherited read more like debating societies than true temptations. They also indicate that even the devil can quote Scripture. In other words, it is not enough merely to know the Scriptures and have the ability to quote them.

As a master storyteller, Luke concludes the episode with three words that set the stage for later drama, namely, that the devil departed from him "for a time." We know that this was not to be the last encounter between the devil and Jesus. This first encounter with its triple temptations ultimately would lead to the Last Supper, the agony in the garden, the passion, and the cross.

Living the Paschal Mystery

Human beings are faced with temptations that concern our well-being (bread), our own power and glory (kingdoms of the world), or the limits of God's power (throwing oneself off the parapet of the temple). Jesus overcame each of these temptations with the power and knowledge of Scripture, and secure in his relationship with God as his son. As Jesus faced such fundamental temptations we shouldn't be surprised by temptation either. However, in Luke's telling there might be a slight disservice to the reader. For our temptations will likely not come in the physical personification of the devil. But we will be tempted, nonetheless, by appeals to our well-being, our own power and glory, and what we would consider the limits of God's power. If we, like Jesus, can be assured of our relationship with God, secure in our filial relationship with the divine, we can overcome temptation as well. Though the devil left Jesus for a time, he did return. And it was then that the ultimate temptation faced Jesus. Then he trusted in God to the point of death, only to be raised up to new life.

Focusing the Gospel

Key words and phrases: Filled with the Holy Spirit, Jesus returned from the Jordan / and was led by the Spirit into the desert for forty days.

To the point: Following his baptism, Jesus is led out into the desert. Though he is without both human company and food he is not lacking comfort and nourishment. Jesus is led by, and filled with, the Holy Spirit. We, too, are called into the desert of Lent. For forty days we embrace fasting, prayer, and alms-giving so as to empty ourselves in order to be filled anew with the abundance of God.

Connecting the Gospel

to the first reading: Today's first reading from Deuteronomy comes at the end of Moses' address to the Israelites before they enter the land of Israel. The people have wandered in the desert for forty years, being formed as the people of God, and now they are on the cusp of a new life. In today's reading Moses details a religious ceremony the people are to observe once they have celebrated the first harvest in the land they have been promised by God. Along with offering a basket of the firstfruits of the harvest they are also to recall the history that has brought them to this point: from refugee, to slave, to free person, to landowner. And in this recounting it is clear that nothing has been earned or gained on its own; it is all pure gift from God. This is the same humility that Jesus embraces in the gospel today. Although he has been declared God's own "beloved Son" at his baptism, he does not exploit this identity. When challenged by the devil to use his power to turn stone into bread or throw himself from the parapet of the temple Jesus refuses. The gifts he has been given by God are not meant to be used for his own gain or to prove his authority; instead they are to be given away for the good of God's people.

to experience: God, the gift-giver, has bestowed on us all that we have. How are we being called to offer the "firstfruits" of these gifts back to God?

Connecting the Responsorial Psalm

to the readings: In the last verses of today's psalm God speaks and says, "He shall call upon me, and I will answer him; / I will be with him in distress." In the gospel today Jesus undergoes his temptation in the desert. For forty days he stays in the desert alone and hungry, and then at the end—when we can imagine his hunger for both food and human contact has become intense—he is visited by the devil. And yet throughout this experience, Jesus isn't alone. Led by and filled with the Holy Spirit he is able to remain resolute in the face of every luring temptation offered by the devil.

to psalmist preparation: Throughout each of our lives there will be desert experiences where we undergo isolation and distress. In those times, the psalmist tells us, God is with us. How have you experienced God in times of distress?

PROMPTS FOR FAITH-SHARING

The first reading from Deuteronomy includes a telling of God's saving action in the history of the Hebrew people. In your life, how have you experienced God's presence in times of distress?

What helps you to remain steadfast in times of temptation?

In the gospel Jesus declares, "One does not live on bread alone." During this Lenten time of fasting, how can you feast on the word and presence of God?

Lent is a time for the whole church, in unity with the catechumens, to go on retreat in preparation for celebrating the sacraments of initiation at Easter. How can you make this season more retreat-like in both the way you live it individually and celebrate it as a parish community?

Model Penitential Act

Presider: In today's gospel Jesus is led out into the desert filled with the Holy Spirit. He remains there for forty days and is tempted by the devil. As we begin these forty days of fasting and prayer we ask for God's grace to sustain us, and for the times we have given into temptation we ask for pardon and mercy . . . [*pause*]

    Confiteor: I confess . . .

Homily Points

• Following his baptism Jesus is led into the desert for forty days of fasting and prayer. Two other heroes of our faith underwent similar experiences. Before receiving the Ten Commandments on Mount Sinai, Moses went without food and water for forty days. The prophet Elijah also fasted for forty days before traveling to Mount Horeb (another name for Mount Sinai), where God came to him as a "light silent sound" (1 Kgs 19:12; NABRE). Moses, Elijah, and Jesus all fast in preparation for an event—for Moses and Elijah it is a particular encounter with God, while for Jesus it is an encounter with temptation. In Lent we fast for both reasons, to prepare for an encounter with God on our holiest feast of the year—the feast of Easter—and also to strengthen us against temptation.

• When the devil tempts Jesus to turn stone into bread, Jesus responds, "It is written, *One does not live on bread alone.*" These words come from the book of Deuteronomy where Moses tells the people, "[God] let you be afflicted with hunger, and then fed you with manna . . . so you might know that it is not by bread alone that people live, but by all that comes forth from the mouth of the Lord" (8:3; NABRE). By taking up the spiritual practice of fasting during Lent we open up space and time within our lives for that which provides us true nourishment.

• Jesus' temptation in the desert reminds us that we are not alone when we face our own temptations. Let us invite God into our experience of temptation, so that filled with the Holy Spirit we might be strengthened to follow the path of holiness.

Model Universal Prayer (Prayer of the Faithful)

Presider: Our God is with us in times of need and so we place our petitions before him.

Response: Lord, hear our prayer.

That all members of the church enter into these forty days of fasting, penance, and almsgiving with fidelity and grace . . .

That leaders of nations resist the temptations of power and wealth . . .

That those overwhelmed by the temptation of addiction be filled with the grace of God and know they are not alone . . .

That all those here, in this time of fasting, might feast on the love and mercy of God . . .

Presider: God of infinite love, you accompany us through distress and anxiety and protect us from temptation and evil. Trusting in your mercy and compassion, we bring you our petitions asking that you hear and grant them through Christ our Lord. **Amen.**

COLLECT
Let us pray.

Pause for silent prayer

Grant, almighty God,
through the yearly observances of holy Lent,
that we may grow in understanding
of the riches hidden in Christ
and by worthy conduct pursue their effects.
Through our Lord Jesus Christ, your Son,
who lives and reigns with you in the unity of the Holy Spirit,
one God, for ever and ever. **Amen.**

FIRST READING
Deut 26:4-10

Moses spoke to the people, saying:
  "The priest shall receive the basket from you
    and shall set it in front of the altar of the Lord, your God.
Then you shall declare before the Lord, your God,
  'My father was a wandering Aramean
    who went down to Egypt with a small household
    and lived there as an alien.
But there he became a nation
    great, strong, and numerous.
When the Egyptians maltreated and oppressed us,
    imposing hard labor upon us,
    we cried to the Lord, the God of our fathers,
    and he heard our cry
    and saw our affliction, our toil, and our oppression.
He brought us out of Egypt
    with his strong hand and outstretched arm,
    with terrifying power, with signs and wonders;
    and bringing us into this country,
    he gave us this land flowing with milk and honey.
Therefore, I have now brought you the firstfruits
    of the products of the soil
    which you, O Lord, have given me.'
And having set them before the Lord, your God,
    you shall bow down in his presence."

RESPONSORIAL PSALM
Ps 91:1-2, 10-11, 12-13, 14-15

℟. (cf. 15b) Be with me, Lord, when I am
in trouble.

You who dwell in the shelter of the Most
High,
who abide in the shadow of the
Almighty,
say to the LORD, "My refuge and fortress,
my God in whom I trust."

℟. Be with me, Lord, when I am in trouble.

No evil shall befall you,
nor shall affliction come near your tent,
for to his angels he has given command
about you,
that they guard you in all your ways.

℟. Be with me, Lord, when I am in trouble.

Upon their hands they shall bear you up,
lest you dash your foot against a stone.
You shall tread upon the asp and the
viper;
you shall trample down the lion and the
dragon.

℟. Be with me, Lord, when I am in trouble.

Because he clings to me, I will deliver him;
I will set him on high because he
acknowledges my name.
He shall call upon me, and I will answer
him;
I will be with him in distress;
I will deliver him and glorify him.

℟. Be with me, Lord, when I am in trouble.

SECOND READING
Rom 10:8-13

See Appendix A, p. 274.

CATECHESIS

About Liturgy
Paschale solemnitatis: A little-known but valuable liturgical document is the 1988 circular letter from the Vatican Congregation for Divine Worship and the Discipline of Sacraments entitled On Preparing and Celebrating the Paschal Feasts (*Paschale Solemnitatis*). This universal document has the same authority as an instruction. It gathers references on Lent, Triduum, and Easter from other liturgical documents and gives guidance and recommendations on how to implement current rubrics and directives. This season would be a good time to read and review this resource.

The section on Lent in this letter begins by quoting the *Ceremonial of Bishops*, an instruction manual for the liturgies celebrated by bishops: "The annual observance of Lent is the special season for the ascent to the holy mountain of Easter" (PS 6; CB 249). This beautiful image recalls the high places we encounter throughout this Lectionary cycle for Lent: the high place where Jesus was tempted by the devil in today's gospel; the mountain where he was transfigured, which we will recall next Sunday; Mount Horeb where Moses encountered the burning bush on the Third Sunday of Lent; and the Mount of Olives where Jesus prayed before his arrest, which we proclaim this Palm Sunday.

Mountains are traditional places where we encounter God's glory. If we reframe the Lenten journey as a slow yet steady climb toward the hill of Golgotha where the ultimate glory of the Father will be revealed in the sacrifice of his Son, we can help our communities connect Lent to the fullness of the paschal mystery that always leads us to the resurrection.

About Initiation
Rite of Election: The period of purification and enlightenment coincides with the season of Lent. During these final weeks of preparation for baptism, the catechumens who will be initiated this Easter participate in "intense spiritual preparation, consisting more in interior reflection than in catechetical instruction" (RCIA 139). For the catechumens, their godparents, and the entire community of the faithful, Lent should be like a five-week retreat. It is not a time for last-minute catechetical sessions to catch up on what they have missed during their catechumenate. Remember that this is an initiation: it is just the *beginning* of their lifelong formation in the Christian way of life. Instead of doing catechesis as usual, trust in the power of the liturgy to catechize and form us. Focus on the liturgies of Lent and on daily prayer, fasting, and works of charity.

About Liturgical Music
Litany of Saints: The circular letter, On Preparing and Celebrating the Paschal Feasts, recommends that on the First Sunday of Lent, "there should be some distinctive elements that underline this important moment; e.g., the entrance procession with litanies of the saints" (PS 23). This is also referenced in the *Ceremonial of Bishops*, which further recommends that "the names of the holy patron or founder and the saints of the local Church may be inserted at the proper places" (261). What a beautiful way not only to begin this holy season of Lent but also to bookend the paschal season by beginning these days in communion with the saints who will accompany the catechumens to the baptismal font at the Easter Vigil. With this in mind, if you choose to sing the Litany of Saints as the entrance chant on this Sunday, use the setting that is sung at the Easter Vigil.

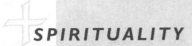

SPIRITUALITY

GOSPEL ACCLAMATION

cf. Matt 17:5

From the shining cloud the Father's voice is
    heard:
This is my beloved Son, hear him.

Gospel   Luke 9:28b-36; L27C

Jesus took Peter, John, and James
    and went up the mountain to
        pray.
While he was praying his face
    changed in appearance
    and his clothing became dazzling
        white.
And behold, two men were convers-
    ing with him, Moses and Elijah,
    who appeared in glory and spoke of
        his exodus
    that he was going to accomplish in
        Jerusalem.
Peter and his companions had been
    overcome by sleep,
    but becoming fully awake,
    they saw his glory and the two men
        standing with him.
As they were about to part from him,
    Peter said to Jesus,
    "Master, it is good that we are here;
    let us make three tents,
    one for you, one for Moses, and one
        for Elijah."
But he did not know what he was
    saying.
While he was still speaking,
    a cloud came and cast a shadow over
        them,
    and they became frightened when
        they entered the cloud.
Then from the cloud came a voice that
    said,
    "This is my chosen Son; listen to
        him."
After the voice had spoken, Jesus was
    found alone.
They fell silent and did not at that time
    tell anyone what they had seen.

Reflecting on the Gospel

For the Second Sunday of Lent the church gives us the reading of the trans-
figuration of Jesus, a story found in the Synoptics but not in the Gospel of John.
Luke tells the story in a way similar to that of Mark, from whom he received it.
Any differences are slight.

The presence of Elijah and Moses indicates Jesus as
the fulfillment of the prophets (Elijah)
and the law (Moses). Only the three
disciples are there to witness this
terrific encounter, and they, too,
are enveloped in the cloud, which
itself is another image from the
Old Testament. In particular,
during the wandering in the
wilderness, the Lord preceded
the Hebrew people by means
of a column of cloud during
the day, and a column of fire at
night (Exod 13:21; cf. Num 9:16-
23). There, too, the cloud covered
the meeting tent, and in doing so
the glory of the Lord filled the place (Exod
40:34-38). Even in the time of Solomon we hear
about the presence of the Lord in a cloud filling
the house of the Lord (1 Kings 8:9-10). Suffice it to say
there are many instances in the Old Testament where the presence of the Lord
is indicated by a cloud, and that is the sense intended here by Luke as well. The
cloud represents the Lord's glory; this is not a story about what happened one
foggy day. Moreover, a voice from the cloud speaks, echoing the message heard
at Jesus' baptism, "This is my chosen Son; listen to him."

More symbolism is present in the face of Jesus changing in appearance and
his clothing becoming "dazzling white." There is so much that is symbolic
and representative of Jesus' glory in this gospel reading that some scholars of
Scripture refer to it as a "displaced resurrection account." In other words, this
was originally a story of a resurrection appearance or a story about the risen
Jesus that was transposed into the narrative of his earthly ministry by Mark
(Matthew and Luke simply followed suit). Whether it is a displaced resurrection
story or not, its Christology is profound, demonstrating that Jesus shares the
glory of the Lord and fulfills the prophets and the law. He is on par with Elijah
and Moses: He is called God's son, to whom we should listen.

Living the Paschal Mystery

As the term itself implies, peak experiences do not come often and they do not
last. But they can become a touchstone, a marker to which we may return mentally and spiritually at various points in our lives. The birth of a child, falling
in love, a special day, or an encounter in nature may all be peak experiences we
want to preserve, remember, and cherish. Perhaps like Peter we want to "build a
tent," or otherwise make a memorial to the event and the person(s) with whom we
shared it. But like the events in today's gospel, as soon as the incident happens, it
seems to end. "After the voice had spoken, Jesus was found alone." The encounter
was over and those who had witnessed it were humbled into silence. The encoun-

ter of the transfiguration informs our own peak experiences. They are a taste of the life that is to come, an eternal peak experience that satisfies all longings.

Focusing the Gospel
Key words and phrases: This is my chosen Son; listen to him.

To the point: For the second time in the Gospel of Luke the voice of God claims Jesus as God's son. The first moment was at his baptism when "the holy Spirit descended upon him in bodily form" (Luke 3:22; NABRE). At that time the voice of God proclaimed, "You are my beloved Son; with you I am well pleased" (NABRE). At the Jordan River the voice from heaven speaks directly to Jesus, but on the mountain where Jesus goes to pray with his closest companions the voice addresses those around Jesus—Peter, James, and John—telling them, "This is my chosen Son; listen to him." These words are addressed to us when we encounter our Lord in the Word and the Eucharist, "Behold, here is Jesus the chosen one, listen to him."

Connecting the Gospel
to the second reading: In St. Paul's letter to the Philippians we hear the promise of what is to come, "He will change our lowly body / to conform with his glorified body / by the power that enables him also / to bring all things into subjection to himself." On the mountain Peter, James, and John see Jesus' "glory" when "his face changed in appearance / and his clothing became dazzling white." We might wonder how this experience of encountering Jesus as he truly is, transfigured in glory, affected them in the life of faith.

to experience: As Christians our ultimate goal is to be Christ-like, to reflect the dazzling glory of Christ in all of our interactions and so to bring honor to God. In our pursuit of this goal the more clearly we see Jesus, the more clearly we see the way to our own transformation in Christ.

Connecting the Responsorial Psalm
to the readings: In Psalm 27 the psalmist yearns for God: "Of you my heart speaks; you my glance seeks." In the gospel, Peter, James, and John encounter God in a whole-body way. They see the face of Jesus transfigured before them, and then, entering into a cloud, they hear the voice of God. The cloud is reminiscent of Moses' meeting with God on Mount Sinai when he received the tablets of the law. As happened with Moses, God's presence envelops Peter, James, and John. Naturally we hear that the disciples "became frightened when they entered the cloud." Yearning for God's presence cannot prepare us for the unfathomable reality of experiencing the living God. And yet we continue to seek God knowing, as St. Augustine said, "Our hearts are restless until they rest in you."

to psalmist preparation: Today's psalm is one of trust and of desire. We know God and yet we yearn to know God more fully. We live in God's kingdom, and yet we long for the complete fulfillment of that kingdom. How do you experience the deep desire to see God's face in your own life?

PROMPTS FOR FAITH-SHARING

Today's psalm encourages us to "[w]ait for the LORD." Where is God asking you to wait and be patient at this time in your life?

_____

_____

_____

_____

What does it mean to you that your "citizenship is in heaven"?

_____

_____

_____

_____

_____

The voice from the cloud tells Peter, James, and John, "This is my chosen Son; listen to him." How do you listen to Jesus in daily life?

_____

_____

_____

_____

In your life, which places of darkness are longing for the light of Christ? How might you lift these places up to the Light?

_____

_____

_____

_____

_____

81

Model Penitential Act

Presider: In today's gospel, Peter, John, and James hear a voice from the cloud saying, "This is my chosen Son; listen to him." For the times we have not listened to the voice of Jesus, our Good Shepherd, we ask for pardon and mercy . . . [*pause*]

  Confiteor: I confess . . .

Homily Points

• Today's readings are filled with imagery of the covenant relationship we have with God. In the first reading God enters into a covenant with Abram. The ritual that cements this covenant might sound odd to us, but was common in Abraham's time. When two parties entered into a treaty or serious agreement they would walk between the bodies of animals, which had been split in two. The animals were a cautionary sign, for if either party broke the treaty they could expect to share the animals' fate. In the covenant between Abram and God, however, only one party walks between the slain animals; the smoking fire pot and the flaming torch represent God, who enters into a covenant of unending fidelity to Abram and his descendants. Even when the human parties of this covenant fail, God remains faithful.

• In the gospel Moses and Elijah appear on the mountain with Jesus and speak "of his exodus / that he was going to accomplish in Jerusalem." With the first exodus, God saves the people of Israel from slavery, forms them as his people, and then delivers them into the Promised Land. With Jesus' exodus (his death and resurrection) we are freed from the slavery of sin, formed as the Body of Christ, and made citizens of the kingdom of God.

• In the second reading St. Paul also reminds us as of the Christian identity that defines us: "[O]ur citizenship is in heaven." As we continue on with our Lenten journey, let us consider how we might show in both word and deed that we are Christ's. Even when we fail, our merciful God invites us to continue living ever deeper into this covenant of love.

Model Universal Prayer (Prayer of the Faithful)

Presider: Like Abraham, our father in faith, we trust God's promises and so dare to voice our petitions.

Response: Lord, hear our prayer.

That the church might be a reflection of the dazzling face of Jesus . . .

That all the nations of the world would extend a welcome to refugees and immigrants within the lands they claim as their own . . .

That those who live in anxiety and fear might know the peace of God that surpasses understanding . . .

That all gathered here would be renewed in faith and filled with courage to go with joy where God calls us to go . . .

Presider: Faithful God, you honor the covenant you have made with your people throughout the world. Trusting in this covenant relationship we ask you to hear our prayers this day and always. Through Christ our Lord. **Amen.**

COLLECT

Let us pray.

Pause for silent prayer

O God, who have commanded us
to listen to your beloved Son,
be pleased, we pray,
to nourish us inwardly by your word,
that, with spiritual sight made pure,
we may rejoice to behold your glory.
Through our Lord Jesus Christ, your Son,
who lives and reigns with you in the unity
    of the Holy Spirit,
one God, for ever and ever. **Amen.**

FIRST READING
Gen 15:5-12, 17-18

The Lord God took Abram outside and
    said,
    "Look up at the sky and count the stars,
        if you can.
Just so," he added, "shall your descendants
    be."
Abram put his faith in the LORD,
    who credited it to him as an act of
        righteousness.

He then said to him,
    "I am the LORD who brought you from
        Ur of the Chaldeans
    to give you this land as a possession."
"O Lord GOD," he asked,
    "how am I to know that I shall possess
        it?"
He answered him,
    "Bring me a three-year-old heifer, a
        three-year-old she-goat,
    a three-year-old ram, a turtledove, and a
        young pigeon."
Abram brought him all these, split them
    in two,
    and placed each half opposite the other;
    but the birds he did not cut up.
Birds of prey swooped down on the
    carcasses,
    but Abram stayed with them.
As the sun was about to set, a trance fell
    upon Abram,
    and a deep, terrifying darkness
        enveloped him.

When the sun had set and it was dark,
    there appeared a smoking fire pot and a
        flaming torch,
    which passed between those pieces.
It was on that occasion that the LORD made
    a covenant with Abram,
    saying: "To your descendants I give this
        land,
    from the Wadi of Egypt to the Great
        River, the Euphrates."

✚ CATECHESIS

RESPONSORIAL PSALM
Ps 27:1, 7-8, 8-9, 13-14

R︎. (1a) The Lord is my light and my
    salvation.

The LORD is my light and my salvation;
    whom should I fear?
The LORD is my life's refuge;
    of whom should I be afraid?

R︎. The Lord is my light and my salvation.

Hear, O LORD, the sound of my call;
    have pity on me, and answer me.
Of you my heart speaks; you my glance
    seeks.

R︎. The Lord is my light and my salvation.

Your presence, O LORD, I seek.
    Hide not your face from me;
do not in anger repel your servant.
    You are my helper: cast me not off.

R︎. The Lord is my light and my salvation.

I believe that I shall see the bounty of the
    LORD
    in the land of the living.
Wait for the LORD with courage;
    be stouthearted, and wait for the LORD.

R︎. The Lord is my light and my salvation.

SECOND READING
Phil 3:17—4:1

Join with others in being imitators of me,
    brothers and sisters,
    and observe those who thus conduct
        themselves
    according to the model you have in us.
For many, as I have often told you
    and now tell you even in tears,
    conduct themselves as enemies of the
        cross of Christ.
Their end is destruction.
Their God is their stomach;
    their glory is in their "shame."
Their minds are occupied with earthly
    things.
But our citizenship is in heaven,
    and from it we also await a savior, the
        Lord Jesus Christ.
He will change our lowly body
    to conform with his glorified body
    by the power that enables him also
    to bring all things into subjection to
        himself.

Therefore, my brothers and sisters,
    whom I love and long for, my joy and
        crown,
    in this way stand firm in the Lord.

or Phil 3:20—4:1, see Appendix A, p. 274.

About Liturgy
Darkness and light: In today's readings we see the image of darkness as the place where God's shining glory is revealed. In Genesis, once the sun had set and it was dark, the smoking fire pot and the flaming torch represented God who made the covenant with Abram. In the gospel, the disciples were afraid to enter the cloud, which had cast a shadow over them, yet it was from this cloud where the voice was heard: "This is my chosen Son."

The circular letter, On Preparing and Celebrating the Paschal Feasts, recommends that "catechesis on the paschal mystery and the sacraments should be given a special place in the Sunday homilies" (PS 12). Today's image of darkness leading to light gives homilists an opportunity to focus on baptism and on the mercy of God. For example, you can help the assembly understand better the purpose for the church's rubric that the Easter Vigil begin in darkness only after sundown, or the baptismal symbol of the Easter candle as the Light of Christ given to all of us at baptism.

In the liturgy, symbols and symbolic actions express our belief. Therefore, when we say that Christ dispels the darkness of our hearts and minds (Roman Missal, Easter Vigil, 14) as we light the paschal fire at the Easter Vigil, our Christian faith is more clearly visible when the fire we light actually dispels darkness—not a twilight darkness or a darkness we can control with a switch, but one that reflects our fear and confusion as well as our hope and faith in Christ. Like Moses and the disciples today, we are called to enter into the dark places of our human hearts in order to allow Christ's light to shine there. The abiding Light of Christ, present even in our darkest moments, is symbolized by the paschal candle, which we will light from the Easter fire lit in the dark of night. Thus the entire Lenten season, especially the Lenten liturgies for those preparing for baptism, is meant to uncover these dark places and then strengthen the grace that the Spirit has already poured into our hearts.

About Initiation
The role of the faithful: The faithful are the most important ministers of the RCIA because "the initiation of adults is the responsibility of all the baptized" (RCIA 9). Find ways to help all your parishioners take a more active role in the formation and preparation of adults to be baptized.

During Lent, "the faithful should take care to participate in the rites of the scrutinies and presentations and give the elect the example of their own renewal in the spirit of penance, faith, and charity" (RCIA 9.4). The faithful do this primarily through their own practice of prayer, fasting, works of charity, and penitential disciplines. They can also more directly support the elect by intentional prayer. One creative way to do this is to prepare a box for each of your elect with their name on it. Place these boxes in your vestibule, and invite parishioners to write notes of encouragement and prayer for each elect. In these Sundays before Easter, they can place these notes into the boxes. The elect can read these notes during the preparation rites on Holy Saturday.

About Liturgical Music
Use of instruments: In the circular letter, On Preparing and Celebrating the Paschal Feasts, there is an unusual directive: "[M]usical instruments may be played only to give necessary support to the singing" (PS 17). Most parishes have not followed this directive for good reasons. However, we can still strive to incorporate the principle behind the directive, which is to focus more intensely on what is fundamentally necessary to be a disciple—trust in Christ and in the Body of Christ.

MARCH 17, 2019
SECOND SUNDAY OF LENT

GOSPEL ACCLAMATION
Ps 84:5

Blessed are those who dwell in your house,
    O Lord;
they never cease to praise you.

Gospel   Matt 1:16, 18-21, 24a; L543

Jacob was the father of Joseph, the husband
    of Mary.
Of her was born Jesus who is called the
    Christ.

Now this is how the birth of Jesus Christ
    came about.
When his mother Mary was betrothed to
    Joseph,
    but before they lived together,
    she was found with child through the
        Holy Spirit.
Joseph her husband, since he was a righ-
    teous man,
    yet unwilling to expose her to shame,
    decided to divorce her quietly.
Such was his intention when, behold,
    the angel of the Lord appeared to him in
        a dream and said,
    "Joseph, son of David,
    do not be afraid to take Mary your wife
        into your home.
For it is through the Holy Spirit
    that this child has been conceived in her.
She will bear a son and you are to name him
    Jesus,
    because he will save his people from their
        sins."
When Joseph awoke,
    he did as the angel of the Lord had com-
        manded him
    and took his wife into his home.

or Luke 2:41-51a in Appendix A, p. 274.

See Appendix A., p. 275, for the other readings.

Reflecting on the Gospel

Scandals of the political, gossipy, and celebrity type are often in the news. We know from our own experience that our lives sometimes have scandals, embarrassments, and fodder for gossip. How we love to talk about people who are down on their luck, made a mistake, or are facing hard times. Maybe talking about others makes us feel better about ourselves. The underlying attitude is that at least we're not in their situation, facing their troubles.

We can also consider the "holy family" and "Joseph the Most Chaste Spouse" of Mary to have had an idyllic home, a perfect family. But today's gospel reading from Matthew tells us otherwise. Joseph and Mary were betrothed (engaged) and Mary was found to be pregnant "by the Holy Spirit." Can we imagine the talk of the town if such a thing happened today? Who would believe that kind of story? Two thousand years and a major world religion later we do not stop to think about the shame and scandal that would have been the reaction to Mary's pregnancy. The shame was not only upon her but also Joseph and her family, and certainly upon her child, Jesus. Even later anti-Christian legends tell of Mary being impregnated by a Roman soldier, not the Holy Spirit. If those stories have survived for so long, what must have been said at the time Mary was pregnant?

The gospel tells us that since Joseph was a "righteous man," meaning one who stood upright in the eyes of God by following the law of Moses, he did not want to expose Mary to shame. Exposing her to shame is a euphemistic way of saying exposing her to the law, which required adulterers to be stoned (Deut 22:21-23). Joseph's solution was a quiet divorce. In other words, Joseph would end the betrothal (engagement) before the wedding day.

At that point God intervened by communicating with Joseph in a dream via an angel, assuring him that he should go forward with the marriage. Mary's story was sincere and true. It was through the Holy Spirit that this child was conceived. Joseph acts accordingly and takes Mary into his home as his wife. After that we scarcely hear anything else about Joseph. He is righteous, never speaking a word, but following God's will. His noble decision was likely seen as anything but that in his time. We might look around our own world, nation, and neighborhood. Where are the Josephs today? Those noble, righteous, often silent individuals sheltering those who would otherwise be exposed to shame.

Living the Paschal Mystery

Family life can sometimes seem like an endless onslaught of responsibilities for caring for others and providing for them. And it doesn't necessarily end when the children reach early (or later!) adulthood. In fact, some in the so-called sandwich generation may find themselves caring for both children and parents. Our celebration of St. Joseph today is a good reminder that family life is sacred. Joseph welcomed Mary into his home and they lived together as a family. They didn't live at a synagogue or temple, and certainly not a church (as there were none then). They were in many ways a typical family with family issues. Yet Joseph was rearing a child that was not his own. Mary's story of being with child by the Holy Spirit was enough to drive Joseph to divorce, but he was guided away from that by a dream. The Holy Family did not live a perfect idyllic life. Quite likely they faced gossip, slander, and perhaps even insults. They would not have been perceived in their time as a model family. And yet, we celebrate them not because they lived without scandal, but precisely the opposite. They lived through scandal and gossip in a righteous way. On this feast of St. Joseph, let's imagine his life not reduced to a plastic holy card, but one lived in the complexity and moral ambiguity of adulthood.

Focusing the Gospel

Key words and phrases: Joseph her husband . . . was a righteous man

To the point: Within the trio of the Holy Family, St. Joseph is the one most often overlooked, and so we pause today to celebrate the protection, support, and love with which he lived out his vocation as a righteous man and as husband to Mary and foster-father of Jesus. We see his righteousness as he listens to the angel's message with faith and then welcomes Mary and the miraculous baby she bears into his home. May we seek to follow the model of Joseph, the husband of Mary, in his fidelity, love, and trust.

Model Penitential Act

Presider: Today we honor St. Joseph, and remember his model of love and fidelity within the holy family. As we enter into this celebration let us pause to remember the times we have not embodied this same love . . . [*pause*]

Lord Jesus, you are the son of David: Lord, have mercy.
Christ Jesus, your kingdom endures forever: Christ, have mercy.
Lord Jesus, you teach us to call God "Father": Lord, have mercy.

Model Universal Prayer (Prayer of the Faithful)

Presider: Along with St. Joseph, patron of the universal church, we lift up our prayers to God.

Response: Lord, hear our prayer.

That all members of the church strive to live with the perseverance, compassion, and fidelity of St. Joseph . . .

That workers throughout the world might have meaningful employment and a just wage . . .

That foster and adoptive parents find solace, strength and joy in the example of St. Joseph . . .

That each of us here encounter and welcome Christ within the people who share our homes and workplaces . . .

Presider: Gracious God, you called St. Joseph to be the husband of Mary and the foster father of Jesus. Hear our prayers that we might emulate his model of love and faithfulness. Through Christ our Lord. **Amen.**

About Liturgy

A saint for dreamers and doers: Have you noticed that St. Joseph says nothing in Scripture? Rather, what he created with his hands as a carpenter and did with his feet as a protector of his family proclaimed his faith in God. Perhaps that is why much of our iconography for Joseph depicts him carrying, holding, moving, making, and building.

Yet Joseph is also the patron of dreamers, those who see visions others can't and hear God's voice in their dreams. Like Joseph, our work as liturgists, musicians, presiders, and liturgical ministers is both artistic and functional. It requires dreaming and doing, discernment and follow-through. Joseph does both and thus is more an artisan and craftsperson than an impractical daydreamer or detached worker. Let us rekindle our commitment to be dreamers *and* doers of the Gospel in the work and art of liturgy.

COLLECT
Let us pray.

Pause for silent prayer

Grant, we pray, almighty God,
that by Saint Joseph's intercession
your Church may constantly watch over
the unfolding of the mysteries of human
    salvation,
whose beginnings you entrusted to his
    faithful care.
Through our Lord Jesus Christ, your Son,
who lives and reigns with you in the unity
    of the Holy Spirit,
one God, for ever and ever. **Amen.**

FOR REFLECTION

• St. Paul tells us we are to follow the example of Abraham, "father of us all." On this feast of St. Joseph, foster father of Jesus, who in your life has "fathered" you in faith?

• As we seek to emulate St. Joseph, how do you offer Jesus a place to dwell in your own life?

Homily Points

• In the Gospel of Matthew, it is Joseph instead of Mary who is visited by an angel bringing the news of Jesus' conception by the Holy Spirit. It is Joseph who must give his *fiat*, his "yes" to the wondrous plan of God. Unlike the annunciation to Mary, we don't hear Joseph's response to the angel. Instead of words, Joseph responds with actions by immediately doing "as the angel of the Lord had commanded him." Joseph shows us a model of love in action.

• In the first reading, the prophet Nathan speaks to Joseph's ancestor David, asking on God's behalf, "Is it you who would build me a house to dwell in?" (NABRE). Instead, God proclaims that there is one who is to come who will "build a house for my name." In the gospel we see Joseph, the carpenter, welcoming Mary (and the baby in her womb) into his own house. He offers them a place to dwell in safety and comfort.

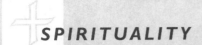

SPIRITUALITY

GOSPEL ACCLAMATION
Matt 4:17

Repent, says the Lord;
the kingdom of heaven is at hand.

Gospel Luke 13:1-9; L30C

Some people told Jesus about the
    Galileans
  whose blood Pilate had mingled
      with the blood of their
      sacrifices.
Jesus said to them in reply,
  "Do you think that because
      these Galileans suffered in
      this way
  they were greater sinners than
      all other Galileans?
By no means!
But I tell you, if you do not
    repent,
  you will all perish as they did!
Or those eighteen people who were killed
  when the tower at Siloam fell on
      them—
  do you think they were more guilty
  than everyone else who lived in
      Jerusalem?
By no means!
But I tell you, if you do not repent,
  you will all perish as they did!"

And he told them this parable:
  "There once was a person who had a fig
      tree planted in his orchard,
  and when he came in search of fruit on
      it but found none,
  he said to the gardener,
  'For three years now I have come in
      search of fruit on this fig tree
  but have found none.
So cut it down.
Why should it exhaust the soil?'
He said to him in reply,
  'Sir, leave it for this year also,
  and I shall cultivate the ground around
      it and fertilize it;
  it may bear fruit in the future.
If not you can cut it down.'"

*Year A readings may be used, see Appendix A,
pp. 276–77.*

Reflecting on the Gospel

Human beings have an innate drive to find causation, a reason for things and events happening. This generally works well and helps us devise systems and ways of doing things that are safer and more productive. For example, automobile accident rates have been going down for years, measured by deaths per million miles driven. We design cars and trucks to be safer, based on research and testing. Though there might be an accident, it is far more likely that a human being will survive due to better engineering, design, etc. And yet, when an accident happens we still look for reasons, for example, excessive speed of the vehicle, or perhaps the driver was impaired by alcohol, lack of sleep, or something else. We seek to explain reasons for events, especially accidents.

In the ancient world, and perhaps even our own, many accidents or tragic events were explained by appeal to the gods, or God. It was understood that bad things happened to bad people; in other words, if something bad happened to someone, it's because that someone did something bad. Good people lived lives that were blessed and filled with good things. A tragedy or accident nearly guaranteed that the victim was somehow at fault, had reaped the tragic remuneration for what he had sown. Much of the Old Testament, especially the Torah, provides the underpinnings for this view. But there are other books, for example, Job, that question it.

At the time of Jesus, when a tragic event happened at Siloam or when Pilate desecrated Jewish blood, the popular idea was that these people somehow had it coming. They must have done something bad for which they were punished. Jesus, however, interprets these events differently. He does not see this as a just punishment for some hidden sin. Instead, he tells those who are self-righteous in their smugness that the same will happen to them unless they repent. The period of time they have between witnessing the tragedy that befell others and the unknown time of their own death is a time for repentance. And the parable Jesus gives them underlines this point. The parable also subtly informs the audience that they have not been producing the fruit of good works. They have been given a limited amount of time to repent, but if that doesn't happen they, too, will be cut down like the barren fig tree, like those who suffered the tragedy at Siloam or desecration at the hands of Pilate. The message of today's gospel can be summarized in one simple word: Repent!

Living the Paschal Mystery

A tragic and untimely death has a way of focusing our attention. Unfortunately, when we lose someone dear suddenly we become painfully aware of how short our life is, how precious are the days that we have been given. Too often our lives are occupied with simple tasks rather than profound meaning. There are daily chores to do, people who rely on us to do our part. But today's gospel reminds us that the time we are given is short and may come to a conclusion quickly and without warning. The time we have on this earth is for repentance and subsequently for doing the will of God. When we see tragedy strike others it can be easy for some to explain away the circumstances to poor decision making on their part, or plain bad luck. We might even become a bit proud at our own more fortunate and prudent decision making, not recognizing the many close calls we have certainly faced. But the time we are given is not for smugness or pride. Tragedy can befall any of us without warning. The gospel is a call for us to appreciate the limited time we have on earth, to respond generously to the needs of others, and to walk humbly.

Focusing the Gospel

Key words and phrases: if you do not repent, / you will all perish

To the point: When Jesus tells the crowds that they must repent lest they perish, he is speaking of a spiritual death rather than a physical one. After all, the first part of the gospel is denying the all-too-human belief that bad things only happen to bad people. Instead, we are called to focus on the fruitfulness of our own fig trees. Have we been cultivating and fertilizing the soil of our lives so that we might bear good fruit in the kingdom of God?

Connecting the Gospel

to the second reading: A tone of warning continues in the second reading from St. Paul's first letter to the Corinthians. Paul warns the community at Corinth against the scourge of overconfidence: "[W]hoever thinks he is standing secure / should take care not to fall." In the gospel reading we are not told whom Jesus is talking to. But we can assume that whatever the demographics of this particular crowd, Jesus is intent upon warning them against complacency and self-righteousness. The parable of the barren fig tree invited them—as it invites us today—to consider whether we are bearing good fruit or merely exhausting the soil.

to experience: Each year during the season of Lent we heed the gospel call to repent. This season helps to protect against the overconfidence that St. Paul warns of. Instead of spending our spiritual lives in a self-satisfied bubble, we are called to place them under a microscope and to see where we are in need of God's grace and forgiveness.

Connecting the Responsorial Psalm

to the readings: While the gospel and the second reading call us to repentance, the psalm reminds us of the response we can expect from God. The psalmist assures us that we have a God who "pardons all [our] iniquities, / heals all [our] ills." His compassion and mercy are infinite and unfathomable for "[a]s far as the east is from the west, / so far has he removed our sins from us" (NABRE). We can depend on the mercy of God because we have witnessed it throughout history. The psalmist reminds us, "He has made known his ways to Moses, / and his deeds to the children of Israel." In the first reading, God speaks to Moses from the burning bush and tells him, "I have witnessed the affliction of my people in Egypt / and have heard their cry of complaint against their slave drivers, / so I know well what they are suffering." Our God is a God of empathy. Just as God entered into the suffering of the Israelites in bondage in Egypt, he enters into the bondage and suffering we experience when our lives are touched by sin. The psalmist's message reminds us to heed the warnings of Jesus and St. Paul with complete trust in God's love, mercy, and forgiveness.

to psalmist preparation: In the readings for this Third Sunday of Lent it is your role to proclaim the good news of God's never-ending mercy and compassion. How have you experienced this mercy in your own life?

PROMPTS FOR FAITH-SHARING

God calls Moses by name and Moses answers, "Here I am." How have you experienced God's call in your own life? What has been your response?

God identifies himself to Moses as the "the God of your ancestors" (NABRE). We know God throughout history and also within our own lives of faith. How does your family and/or community pass on faith to younger generations?

St. Paul admonishes us, "Do not grumble." What situations in your life are met with grumbling? How might you greet them a different way?

Jesus gives us the parable of the barren fig tree. Where in your life, family, or parish is there a lack of fruit being borne? How might you cultivate the ground to encourage fruitfulness?

Model Penitential Act

Presider: In our first reading, God appears to Moses from a burning bush and gives him a mission to lead his people to freedom. As we prepare to enter into this liturgy, let us pause to consider how God might be calling to us this day, and to ask for mercy and pardon for the times we have not responded to this call . . . [*pause*]

Confiteor: I confess . . .

Homily Points

• In the second reading, St. Paul tells the Corinthians, "I do not want you to be unaware . . . that our ancestors were all under the cloud / and all passed through the sea." Paul raises a theme that is common throughout both the Bible and the liturgy. As Christians we are to consider ourselves as having participated in each of the great historical moments that we commemorate. Each time we come to the table of the Lord at Mass we are participating in the Last Supper, death, and resurrection of Jesus.

• Today when we read the familiar story of Moses at the burning bush we can place ourselves within that narrative. God calls from the bush, "Moses, Moses." There is a pattern in the Bible that whenever someone's name is called twice, his or her life is about to change forever. And Moses' life does change. He is called from being a shepherd in the wilderness of Egypt to shepherding the Hebrew people by leading them out of slavery and into the freedom of God.

• Just as with Moses, God also has a plan for each of our lives. Even if this plan is not as grand as challenging a powerful political figure to gain freedom for an entire nation, it is a call for us to collaborate in building the kingdom of God on earth—a kingdom where all are cared for and where peace, love, and hope prevail. Listen. Do you hear God calling your name?

Model Universal Prayer (Prayer of the Faithful)

Presider: Jesus calls us to repentance and conversion and so, trusting in the God of redemption, we bring our needs before the Lord.

Response: Lord, hear our prayer.

That the church bear abundant fruit throughout the world . . .

That all the nations of the world come together to end human trafficking and slavery . . .

That all those who experience calamities and trauma know the healing love of God and the support of a compassionate community . . .

That all those gathered in this place might hear God calling them by name and have the courage to answer, "Here I am, Lord" . . .

Presider: God of compassion and mercy, no matter how far we wander from your love you are always ready to welcome us home. Hear these prayers that, as we continue this Lenten journey, we are brought ever closer to you. Through Christ our Lord. **Amen.**

COLLECT

Let us pray.

Pause for silent prayer

O God, author of every mercy and of all
    goodness,
who in fasting, prayer and almsgiving
have shown us a remedy for sin,
look graciously on this confession of our
    lowliness,
that we, who are bowed down by our
    conscience,
may always be lifted up by your mercy.
Through our Lord Jesus Christ, your Son,
who lives and reigns with you in the unity
    of the Holy Spirit,
one God, for ever and ever. **Amen.**

FIRST READING

Exod 3:1-8a, 13-15

Moses was tending the flock of his father-
    in-law Jethro,
    the priest of Midian.
Leading the flock across the desert, he
    came to Horeb,
    the mountain of God.
There an angel of the LORD appeared to
    Moses in fire
    flaming out of a bush.
As he looked on, he was surprised to see
    that the bush,
    though on fire, was not consumed.
So Moses decided,
    "I must go over to look at this
        remarkable sight,
    and see why the bush is not burned."

When the LORD saw him coming over to
    look at it more closely,
    God called out to him from the bush,
        "Moses! Moses!"
He answered, "Here I am."
God said, "Come no nearer!
Remove the sandals from your feet,
    for the place where you stand is holy
        ground.
I am the God of your fathers," he
    continued,
    "the God of Abraham, the God of Isaac,
        the God of Jacob."
Moses hid his face, for he was afraid to
    look at God.
But the LORD said,
    "I have witnessed the affliction of my
        people in Egypt
    and have heard their cry of complaint
        against their slave drivers,
    so I know well what they are suffering.
Therefore I have come down to rescue
    them
    from the hands of the Egyptians

and lead them out of that land into a
   good and spacious land,
   a land flowing with milk and honey."

Moses said to God, "But when I go to the
      Israelites
   and say to them, 'The God of your
      fathers has sent me to you,'
   if they ask me, 'What is his name?'
      what am I to tell them?"
God replied, "I am who am."
Then he added, "This is what you shall tell
      the Israelites:
   I AM sent me to you."

God spoke further to Moses, "Thus shall
      you say to the Israelites:
   The LORD, the God of your fathers,
   the God of Abraham, the God of Isaac,
      the God of Jacob,
   has sent me to you.

"This is my name forever;
   thus am I to be remembered through all
      generations."

RESPONSORIAL PSALM
Ps 103:1-2, 3-4, 6-7, 8, 11

R̸. (8a) The Lord is kind and merciful.

Bless the LORD, O my soul;
   and all my being, bless his holy name.
Bless the LORD, O my soul,
   and forget not all his benefits.

R̸. The Lord is kind and merciful.

He pardons all your iniquities,
   heals all your ills.
He redeems your life from destruction,
   crowns you with kindness and
      compassion.

R̸. The Lord is kind and merciful.

The LORD secures justice
   and the rights of all the oppressed.
He has made known his ways to Moses,
   and his deeds to the children of Israel.

R̸. The Lord is kind and merciful.

Merciful and gracious is the LORD,
   slow to anger and abounding in
      kindness.
For as the heavens are high above the
      earth,
   so surpassing is his kindness toward
      those who fear him.

R̸. The Lord is kind and merciful.

SECOND READING
1 Cor 10:1-6, 10-12

See Appendix A, p. 275.

About Liturgy

Repentance: Sometimes we might think that the suffering a person experiences is caused by God because of their sinfulness. Somehow, God is punishing them. Although the readings today at first might sound that way, a careful reading of them shows exactly the opposite. We hear the Lord say, "I have witnessed the affliction of my people in Egypt / and have heard their cry of complaint against their slave drivers, / so I know well what they are suffering. / Therefore I have come down to rescue them" (Exod 3:7-8). God wants to save us from our suffering. The one who is the source of all goodness can never desire harm to come upon his own children.

Yet, suffering is a reality because it is the nature of being human. We who have been saved by Christ by baptism are not immune to human suffering. However, the difference that our baptism makes is that we are aware that we have been given the promise of God's mercy. Therefore, we live always in hope and in constant repentance for when we have doubted in God's merciful love.

Today is a good opportunity to reflect on the second form of the penitential act that may be unfamiliar to most assemblies. This second form is a brief dialogue between presider and people.

Priest: Lord, we have sinned against you; Lord, have mercy.
People: Lord, have mercy.
Priest: Lord, show us your mercy and love.
People: And grant us your salvation.

This dialogue is a succinct summary of what we believe about repentance and God's mercy. Forgiveness and mercy are not rewards for being repentant. Rather, God desires to forgive us and ever awaits that moment when we turn to God with hearts open to his mercy.

About Initiation

Scrutinies: Today and the next two Sundays call for the celebration of the scrutinies if you have elect present in your assembly. Remember three important points about these rituals. First, you must use the readings for Year A even though we are in Year C of the Lectionary. Second, all three scrutinies are required. If your elect miss one or two of these scrutinies for a serious reason, and they cannot be rescheduled, you must request dispensation from your bishop. See RCIA 20. Third, the scrutinies cannot be combined with the presentations of the Creed and the Lord's Prayer because each ritual has readings assigned specifically to it.

About Liturgical Music

Suggestions: Today should be filled with songs of God's mercy. Look especially for text that reflects the need for our repentance and turning (conversion) of our hearts to God, from whom we receive the fullness of mercy. One suggestion is "Attende, Domine," which is a simple yet accessible chant. Although many resources have an English translation of this text, the Latin text and melody of the refrain are easy enough to be memorable. The verses can be sung by a schola or cantor. Another suggestion is *Psallite*'s "Those Who Love me, I Will Deliver." The refrain text is, "Those who love me, I will deliver; those who know my name, I will protect. When you call me, I will answer you, I will be with you who know my name." This connects to today's first reading in which God loves us so much as to reveal his own name to us. This is a God who is present to us and ready to save us as soon as we turn toward the one who has called us each by name.

GOSPEL ACCLAMATION
John 1:14ab

The Word of God became flesh and made his
    dwelling among us;
and we saw his glory.

Gospel Luke 1:26-38; L545

The angel Gabriel was sent from God
    to a town of Galilee called Nazareth,
    to a virgin betrothed to a man named
        Joseph,
    of the house of David,
    and the virgin's name was Mary.
And coming to her, he said,
    "Hail, full of grace! The Lord is with
        you."
But she was greatly troubled at what was
        said
    and pondered what sort of greeting
        this might be.
Then the angel said to her,
    "Do not be afraid, Mary,
    for you have found favor with God.
Behold, you will conceive in your womb
        and bear a son,
    and you shall name him Jesus.
He will be great and will be called Son of
        the Most High,
    and the Lord God will give him the
        throne of David his father,
    and he will rule over the house of
        Jacob forever,
    and of his Kingdom there will be no
        end."

Continued in Appendix A, p. 278.

See Appendix A, p. 278, for the other readings.

Reflecting on the Gospel

The story of the annunciation, set in Nazareth, with the angel Gabriel and his greeting that forms the basis of the first lines of the Hail Mary prayer, Mary's *fiat* ("May it be done to me") and more are all packed into this short thirteen-verse story told by Luke. There is no other evangelist who relates this event. And no other New Testament author even references it. The later stories, artistic depictions, legends, and lore surrounding the annunciation ultimately find their source in today's gospel. The Gospel of Matthew, as we read earlier, has a different story about Joseph and Mary living separately as a betrothed couple, not in Nazareth but Bethlehem, when Joseph discovers that Mary is pregnant. In Matthew there is no annunciation, only Joseph's dream in which he is assured that he can take her as his wife. So even though we are in the liturgical year when we read Luke, we also read him today because he's the only evangelist to tell us the story of the annunciation. Liturgically, this feast is nine months prior to Christmas, the feast of the Nativity, when we celebrate the birth of Jesus.

It is significant that we hear about this event from Luke's pen as he is the evangelist who tells us more stories about women than any other evangelist. And here we have not only Mary, but Elizabeth, her cousin. Mary displays the attitude of a proper disciple. She listens to the word of God spoken through Gabriel. Her response is a simple but profound, "May it be done to me according to your word." She knows that nothing is impossible for God. There were stories in the Scriptures about women becoming pregnant in older age, like Sarah, Abraham's wife. Mary learns that Elizabeth, thought to be barren, will also have a child. But Mary herself is young and betrothed to Joseph. She, too, will have a child. Here Luke and Matthew have in common the idea that Mary was a virgin when she conceived. And this is a theological point echoed even in the Qur'an (chap. 19). In this way Luke draws attention to Jesus' identity as "Son of God," for he was born of a virgin. Ultimately, this is a theological, rather than a biological, truth. For the Gospel of Mark, the Gospel of John, the apostle Paul, and other New Testament authors also claim Jesus as "Son of God" without saying anything about Mary's virginity. Today we focus on the theological significance of the annunciation because the story is more about theology than biology.

Living the Paschal Mystery

If an angel were to appear to us and tell us what to do, it would be much easier to follow God's will for our lives. But such an appearance is unlikely. Instead, we are left to meander through life making a series of choices, most if not all of which seem like a good idea at the time. But with reflection, some of our choices might not seem to have been all that good! How we wish for an angel to show us the way!

Adult Christianity demands that we are open to God and God's will for our lives. But our discernment of his will is especially important. To become attuned to the spirit of God at work in our lives we would do well to be aware of God's presence in the quotidian aspects of our routine. God breaks into our daily routine not according to our schedule, but his. When Gabriel broke into Mary's world it was with good news, an announcement of her bearing a child, the Son of God, and that his kingdom would be everlasting. We do not need to wait until Jesus returns to live in this kingdom. We can do it now, and by so doing we help usher in his everlasting reign.

Focusing the Gospel

Key words and phrases: Hail, full of grace! The Lord is with you.

To the point: These words are familiar to us as the opening line of the Hail Mary. Mary is not only a model of discipleship, she is also a model of what the Lord would like to do for each of us. Jesus longs to make his home in us as well. We, too, are called to be Christ-bearers in the world. On this day, we honor Mary and we also pray to be like her. Listen for these words in your own life, for the angel wants to tell each of us, "Hail, full of grace! The Lord is with you."

Model Penitential Act

Presider: On this feast of the Annunciation we celebrate Mary's response to the angel that made Jesus' birth possible: "May it be done to me according to your word." For the times we have not lived up to the example of Mary's free and generous collaboration with God we ask for pardon and healing . . . [*pause*]

Lord Jesus, you were born of the Virgin Mary: Lord, have mercy.

Christ Jesus, you are Emmanuel, God with us: Christ, have mercy.

Lord Jesus, you are the Son of God: Lord, have mercy.

Model Universal Prayer (Prayer of the Faithful)

Presider: Through the intercession of Mary, the Mother of God, we offer our prayers to the Lord.

Response: Lord, hear our prayer.

That all members of the church might receive the gifts of God with the joy and humility of Mary . . .

That leaders in governments throughout the world do all within their power to protect life in the womb . . .

That all married couples who experience infertility, miscarriage, and stillbirth be comforted and their dreams of a family brought to fruition . . .

That all of us here follow the model of Mary, our Mother, and proclaim to God, "May it be done to me according to your word" . . .

Presider: Most High God, you sent your only son to be born of the Virgin Mary through the power of the Holy Spirit. Hear these prayers that we might emulate Mary's trust in your power and generous collaboration in your plan. We ask this through Christ our Lord. **Amen.**

About Liturgy

To Jesus through Mary: The phrase "To Jesus through Mary" is often heard among those with great devotion to the Blessed Virgin Mary. This saying is attributed to St. Louis de Montfort, although many earlier saints and spiritual writers also expressed this deep connection between Jesus to Mary and Mary to us. More recently, St. John Paul II had promoted St. Louis's spirituality that focused on consecrating one's entire life to Mary in order to be in closer union with Christ. (John Paul II's coat of arms used a motto inspired by St. Louis's own writings on true devotion to Mary.)

Today's solemnity is a good reminder that any true Christian devotion must always have as its goal and focus closer union to Christ. The incarnation of God through a human, no matter how holy or revered the human, is foremost Christocentric, and authentic Marian devotion must be as well.

Therefore, resist any urge to add Marian devotional practices or songs to the Mass today. The rosary or the Hail Mary find their rightful place as prayerful preparation for Mass so that the faithful may give their complete focus and praise to Christ alone.

COLLECT

Let us pray.

Pause for silent prayer

O God, who willed that your Word
should take on the reality of human flesh
in the womb of the Virgin Mary,
grant, we pray,
that we, who confess our Redeemer to be God
    and man,
may merit to become partakers even in his
    divine nature.
Who lives and reigns with you in the unity of
    the Holy Spirit,
one God, for ever and ever. **Amen.**

FOR REFLECTION

• The angel proclaims, "[N]othing will be impossible for God." Where in your life do you need this reminder of God's power?

• Our God is a great gift-giver. How might you follow the example of Mary in saying yes to the gifts God is offering to you?

Homily Points

• The secular definition of "annunciation" is simply "the announcement of something." In today's gospel there are two announcements made. There is the announcement of the angel that Mary will conceive and bear a son, the Son of God; and also Mary's announcement, "Behold, I am the handmaid of the Lord. / May it be done to me according to your word."

• These announcements are of equal importance because our God respects free will. He desires a relationship in love with us, his creatures, but love is not love if it is coerced. And so the annunciation to Mary requires Mary's announcement back in order to bear fruit. And Mary responds freely, "May it be done to me according to your word."

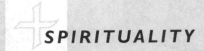

SPIRITUALITY

GOSPEL ACCLAMATION
Luke 15:18

I will get up and go to my Father and shall say
to him:
Father, I have sinned against heaven and against
you.

Gospel   Luke 15:1-3, 11-32; L33C

Tax collectors and sinners were
    all drawing near to listen to
    Jesus,
    but the Pharisees and scribes
        began to complain, saying,
    "This man welcomes sinners and
        eats with them."
So to them Jesus addressed this
    parable:
"A man had two sons, and the younger
    son said to his father,
    'Father give me the share of your estate
        that should come to me.'
So the father divided the property between
    them.
After a few days, the younger son collected
    all his belongings
    and set off to a distant country
    where he squandered his inheritance on
        a life of dissipation.
When he had freely spent everything,
    a severe famine struck that country,
    and he found himself in dire need.
So he hired himself out to one of the local
    citizens
    who sent him to his farm to tend the
        swine.
And he longed to eat his fill of the pods on
    which the swine fed,
    but nobody gave him any.
Coming to his senses he thought,
    'How many of my father's hired workers
    have more than enough food to eat,
    but here am I, dying from hunger.
I shall get up and go to my father and I
    shall say to him,
    "Father, I have sinned against heaven
        and against you.

Continued in Appendix A, p. 279.

*Year A readings may be used, see Appendix A,
pp. 280–81.*

Reflecting on the Gospel

Oftentimes we hear today's gospel referred to as the story of the Prodigal Son. But this might be a bit of a misnomer. Even the New American Bible has a different title for this story, calling it the "lost son." The term "prodigal" means "wastefully extravagant," as in, "My vacation spending this summer was especially prodigal, as I was having a good time after working so hard during the previous year." The word has a different etymology from "prodigy," which means "one endowed with exceptional abilities," although sometimes preachers conflate the meaning of the two terms. So when we refer to the Prodigal Son it might be worth the time to clarify what we actually mean by the term prodigal!

But ultimately the story is not so much about the lost or prodigal son. It's not even so much about his brother, though we could call it the story of the two sons. In reality, the story is about the loving father, how the father is a personification of God, and the kind of love God has for us. The story is sometimes interpreted so that the sons represent Gentile (lost) and Jewish (favored) identities. In this, the Gentiles have lost their way and lived generally wanton lives of decadence, whereas Jews have followed the wishes of God. But in the end both sons, Gentile and Jew, receive the same reward.

In today's telling, the story is often interpreted more literally, or at least personally, as referring to a wayward person who has ultimately been redeemed. The story is particularly meaningful to many who have lived lives of regret or shame, only to feel the loving embrace of God, a community of hope, a family, or even church upon turning away from their wayward lifestyle.

One of the advantages of a story like this is that it has so many possible interpretations. And this story is told only by Luke. Without him we would know nothing of the Prodigal Son, and certainly nothing of the many works of art inspired by the parable, such as Rembrandt's "Return of the Prodigal Son." There is no sole or singular point to this story. The parable is polyvalent and ought to make us ponder it, as the church has done for centuries.

Living the Paschal Mystery

Redemption and forgiveness are powerful themes, and they are articulated in today's gospel in a particularly dramatic way. These themes are also favorites of Luke, who uses the term "forgiveness [of sins]" more than any other New Testament author. The apostle Paul, for example, never says the word "forgiveness." (And perhaps he should have, as it's a much easier concept to grasp than "justification"!) Luke is a master storyteller, he crafts a brief but memorable narrative here. The characters are stock: we probably know people like the sons in today's gospel. Do we know people like the father? Would *we* react like the father? *Do* we react like the father? Though we might or might not have lost wayward children, there are many opportunities to express mercy and loving kindness, and share reconciliation and forgiveness with another. When we behave in this way, we are acting like the father, acting in a way that God acts. Perhaps this is why Pope Francis chose the theme "mercy" for his pontificate. As we learn in today's gospel, mercy is a fundamental expression of God and God's character. Mercy is not merely for God alone: mercy is worthy of emulation.

Focusing the Gospel

Key words and phrases: While he was still a long way off, / his father caught sight of him, and was filled with compassion.

To the point: In our gospel Jesus gives us a parable illustrating the abundant mercy of God. The father in the parable respects his son's freedom. He gives him the inheritance he requests and lets him go. But he never stops watching for this son to return home. And when he does catch sight of his wayward son, the father does not wait for the son to complete his journey or to speak the words of contrition he had so carefully practiced. It's as if Jesus wants to tell us that we need only turn toward God for our merciful father to run out to meet us and usher us home.

Connecting the Gospel

to the second reading: The apostle Paul's words in his second letter to the Corinthians are a perfect partner to the gospel of the Prodigal Son and the forgiving father. St. Paul counsels us to "be reconciled to God." Not only are we called to personal reconciliation but also to become messengers of this reconciliation to the entire world. God waits and watches for each one of us individually, and also for the world as a whole to come to our senses just as the prodigal did and realize who we truly are, beloved daughters and sons of God.

to experience: We are halfway through with our Lenten journey. How have you experienced reconciliation so far with God and with others? What areas in your life are still in need of God's healing touch and redeeming embrace?

Connecting the Responsorial Psalm

to the readings: We might imagine Psalm 34 as the song of one who has been redeemed and saved. In fact, it could be the psalm of the prodigal returned to dignity and joy as a child of God. The psalmist sings, "Look to him that you may be radiant with joy, / and your faces may not blush with shame." Our God wants nothing more than to find the lost and to save the sinner. Just before the parable of the Prodigal Son in Luke's gospel, Jesus tells of the shepherd who searches for his lost sheep. He ends this parable by saying, "[T]here will be more joy in heaven over one sinner who repents than over ninety-nine righteous people who have no need of repentance" (NABRE). Sometimes this is a difficult teaching to accept, especially for those of us who identify more with the older brother in the parable of the Prodigal Son. The truth is, each and every one of us is in need of repentance. In experiencing our need for forgiveness, we can share in the joy of the prodigal returned fully to his father's embrace.

to psalmist preparation: In Psalm 34 we hear the line, "Glorify the Lord with me, / and let us together extol his name." Reflect on your ministry of leading the people of God in prayer. How do you invite the assembly to pray with you?

PROMPTS FOR FAITH-SHARING

The psalmist tells us, "Look to [God] that you may be radiant with joy, / and your faces may not blush with shame." Where do you feel shame or guilt over past transgressions? How might you give these emotions to the Lord?

St. Paul tells us we are entrusted with the "message of reconciliation." How does your parish carry out the ministry of reconciliation within the wider community?

Which figure in the parable of the Prodigal Son do you identify with the most at this point in your faith journey: the prodigal, the older son, or forgiving father? Why?

At this halfway point in our Lenten journey, how have you been living the spiritual practices of prayer, fasting, and almsgiving? Is there anything you would like to do differently for the second half of Lent?

Model Penitential Act

Presider: In today's gospel we hear the familiar parable of the Prodigal Son. As we prepare to enter into this celebration, let us pause to consider the times we have wandered far from God and to ask for pardon and healing . . . [*pause*]

   Confiteor: I confess . . .

Homily Points

• In the parable from today's gospel it is easy to focus on the characters of the two sons. We can relate with the younger son, mired in sin, who realizes his need for repentance, or with the older son who is so focused on comparing his behavior with his brother's that he is unable to appreciate the love his father continues to gift him with. But what happens if we turn our attention instead to the father?

• Everything changes when we consider the father as the protagonist of the parable today. Instead of the shame of the younger son or the bitterness of the elder one taking center stage, our attention is focused on the tender love of the father who yearns for his children to be close to him. In fact, it is the remembrance of his father's love and care for his servants, which leads the younger son to repentance. And hopefully it will be the father's gentle invitation to join the celebration that will induce the older son to be reconciled to father and brother alike.

• Pope Francis wrote in his apostolic exhortation, *Evangelii Gaudium,* "God never tires of forgiving us; we are the ones who tire of seeking his mercy." We are human and sinful. And it is disheartening when we fall into sin (sometimes the same one) again and again. And yet our God continues to watch and wait for us to "come to ourselves," as the young son did, and return to him. Let us pray for perseverance in the way of repentance this Lent.

Model Universal Prayer (Prayer of the Faithful)

Presider: Trusting in the compassionate mercy of our heavenly Father we lift our prayers and needs to God.

Response: Lord, hear our prayer.

That the church be a beacon of mercy to all people, especially those on the margins of society . . .

That nations at war be reconciled . . .

That families experiencing conflict and division encounter the healing touch of God . . .

That all gathered here might receive the grace to emulate the love of the forgiving father who welcomes his son with open arms . . .

Presider: Merciful God, you constantly wait and watch for your children to return to you. Hear our prayers that we might be reconciled to you and to each other. We ask this through Christ our Lord. **Amen.**

About Liturgy

Examination of conscience: Today's familiar gospel reading of the Prodigal Son—though many would rightly rename it the "Prodigal Father" for his abundant compassion—gives us an opportunity to look at how we examine our conscience. Many of us will recall from our childhood our preparations for making a good confession by going through some kind of list of questions that helped us see where we had failed to live up to our baptism. Such lists can be very useful when preparing for the sacrament

COLLECT

Let us pray.

Pause for silent prayer

O God, who through your Word
reconcile the human race to yourself in a
   wonderful way,
grant, we pray,
that with prompt devotion and eager faith
the Christian people may hasten
toward the solemn celebrations to come.
Through our Lord Jesus Christ, your Son,
who lives and reigns with you in the unity
   of the Holy Spirit,
one God, for ever and ever. **Amen.**

FIRST READING

Josh 5:9a, 10-12

The LORD said to Joshua,
   "Today I have removed the reproach of
      Egypt from you."

While the Israelites were encamped at
      Gilgal on the plains of Jericho,
   they celebrated the Passover
   on the evening of the fourteenth of the
      month.
On the day after the Passover,
   they ate of the produce of the land
   in the form of unleavened cakes and
      parched grain.
On that same day after the Passover,
   on which they ate of the produce of the
      land, the manna ceased.
No longer was there manna for the
      Israelites,
   who that year ate of the yield of the
      land of Canaan.

RESPONSORIAL PSALM
Ps 34:2-3, 4-5, 6-7

℟. (9a) Taste and see the goodness of the
    Lord.

I will bless the LORD at all times;
    his praise shall be ever in my mouth.
Let my soul glory in the LORD;
    the lowly will hear me and be glad.

℟. Taste and see the goodness of the Lord.

Glorify the LORD with me,
    let us together extol his name.
I sought the LORD, and he answered me
    and delivered me from all my fears.

℟. Taste and see the goodness of the Lord.

Look to him that you may be radiant with
        joy,
    and your faces may not blush with
            shame.
When the poor one called out, the LORD
        heard,
    and from all his distress he saved him.

℟. Taste and see the goodness of the Lord.

SECOND READING
2 Cor 5:17-21

Brothers and sisters:
Whoever is in Christ is a new creation:
    the old things have passed away;
    behold, new things have come.
And all this is from God,
    who has reconciled us to himself
            through Christ
    and given us the ministry of
            reconciliation,
    namely, God was reconciling the world
            to himself in Christ,
    not counting their trespasses against
            them
    and entrusting to us the message of
            reconciliation.
So we are ambassadors for Christ,
    as if God were appealing through us.
We implore you on behalf of Christ,
    be reconciled to God.
For our sake he made him to be sin who
        did not know sin,
    so that we might become the
            righteousness of God in him.

of reconciliation. In fact, the church gives us several examples of an examination of conscience, which you can find in appendix III of the Rite of Penance. The purpose of these is to help us examine our life in the light of God's word.

However, the church also invites us to do a daily examination of conscience. We see this embedded in the liturgy of Compline, or Night Prayer, which is part of the Liturgy of the Hours. It is the final liturgy before sleeping that we pray either individually or communally.

At the beginning of Night Prayer we are invited to spend some moments examining our conscience. Some use the Ignatian discipline of the *examen*. A simple structure for this has five steps: 1) recall God's presence; 2) look back on the day and give thanks; 3) pay attention to your feelings, whether positive or negative; 4) reflect more deeply on one part of your day that God may be calling you to examine more closely; and 5) give thanks again to God in hope for more opportunities to encounter Christ in our daily lives.

Finally, every Eucharist we celebrate invites us into an examination of conscience. At the beginning of the penitential rite the presider calls us to acknowledge our sin in order to prepare ourselves for the sacred mysteries. Then follows a brief silence during which we examine our hearts.

When we practice a daily, weekly, and sacramental examination of our lives, we will be participating in Christ's ministry of reconciliation and will be ambassadors of his constant mercy.

About Initiation
Sacrament of Reconciliation: Baptized adults who are preparing for Reception into the Full Communion of the Catholic Church or for the celebration of confirmation and Eucharist are encouraged to celebrate the sacrament of reconciliation. This would take place at a time prior to and distinct from the celebrations of reception or confirmation and Eucharist. Whether or not they do partake of the sacrament of reconciliation, they should be strongly encouraged to participate in your parish's Lenten penitential liturgies.

Note that catechumens cannot celebrate the sacrament of reconciliation; however, they can certainly participate in your parish's penitential liturgies.

About Liturgical Music
Rejoice!: We come to the midway point of Lent and Laetare ("Rejoice") Sunday. We get the name for this Sunday from the entrance antiphon: "Rejoice, Jerusalem, and all who love her. / Be joyful, all who were in mourning; / exult and be satisfied at her consoling breast" (Isa 66:10-11). Like Gaudete Sunday in Advent, today is a little break from the austerity of Lent. Therefore, the circular letter, On Preparing and Celebrating the Paschal Feasts, states that on this Sunday, and on solemnities and feasts, "musical instruments may be played" (PS 25).

One delightful piece to consider as an entrance antiphon is *Psallite*'s "Rejoice, Rejoice, All You Who Love Jerusalem!" The refrain melody borrows from Handel's *Messiah*, but one need not be a coloratura soprano to sing it! Another *Psallite* piece that would be excellent for Communion is "Come, Come to the Banquet." The text reflects the "prodigal" father's plea to his older son, "Come to banquet: all that I have is yours."

✚ SPIRITUALITY

GOSPEL ACCLAMATION
Joel 2:12-13

Even now, says the Lord,
return to me with your whole heart;
for I am gracious and merciful.

Gospel   John 8:1-11; L36C

Jesus went to the Mount of Olives.
But early in the morning he arrived
    again in the temple area,
    and all the people started coming to him,
    and he sat down and taught them.
Then the scribes and the Pharisees
    brought a woman
    who had been caught in adultery
    and made her stand in the middle.
They said to him,
    "Teacher, this woman was caught
    in the very act of committing adultery.
Now in the law, Moses commanded us to
    stone such women.
So what do you say?"
They said this to test him,
    so that they could have some charge to
    bring against him.
Jesus bent down and began to write on
    the ground with his finger.
But when they continued asking him,
    he straightened up and said to them,
    "Let the one among you who is without
    sin
    be the first to throw a stone at her."
Again he bent down and wrote on the
    ground.
And in response, they went away one by
    one,
    beginning with the elders.
So he was left alone with the woman be-
    fore him.
Then Jesus straightened up and said to her,
    "Woman, where are they?
Has no one condemned you?"
She replied, "No one, sir."
Then Jesus said, "Neither do I condemn
    you.
Go, and from now on do not sin any more."

Year A readings may be used, see Appendix A,
p. 283.

Reflecting on the Gospel

Although liturgically we are reading from the Gospel of Luke, Cycle C, today we read from John. But interestingly, this story is not in the earliest or best manuscripts of the Gospel of John. In fact, many later manuscripts place this story in the Gospel of Luke, effectively between Luke 21:38 and 22:1, or after the last chapter of the gospel. And other manuscripts have this story not in John 8 (where we find it in the canon) but following John 7:36. Of course, none of this detracts from the story being canonical and inspired Scripture. But it's good to keep in mind the varied history and manuscript difficulties with the story. The notes in the New American Bible explain more.

Part of the reason we pay attention to the problematic background of the story is that it gives us an insight into the early church that produced the text. There was a time in church history, a few centuries after Jesus' death and resurrection, that some Christians did not believe in forgiveness of sin after one's baptism. As a result, many Christians were delaying baptism until well after their "sinning years" were over, effectively delaying baptism until one's deathbed! But that can be a difficult time to predict. Other Christians were proclaiming what was perceived to be a more libertine attitude, namely, that one could be forgiven for sins even after one was baptized. Recall that part of the difficulty was that the Letter to the Hebrews states quite clearly, "If we sin deliberately after receiving knowledge of the truth, there no longer remains sacrifice for sins but a fearful prospect of judgment and a flaming fire that is going to consume the adversaries" (Heb 10:26-27; NABRE; cf. Heb 10:26-31). Further, Tertullian argued against any forgiveness of sins after baptism.

In the face of such internal church disputes comes this story about Jesus. That is to say, it was about the time that the church was engaging in the debate about forgiveness of sins that the story of Jesus forgiving the woman caught in adultery began to appear in early manuscripts. It's as though the church recalled an episode from Jesus' life, or told a story about how Jesus might approach the issue. And now, of course, we have the sacrament of reconciliation. The history of the sacrament of reconciliation is beyond the purview of this brief essay. But the story in today's gospel seems to have been a prominent post in the journey of how the church went from Jesus' personal ministry to the sacrament of reconciliation we have today.

Living the Paschal Mystery

Forgiveness is not an easy thing to express; it is not an easy thing to do. We see from Jesus' own ministry, from the experience of the early church, and probably our own past experiences how quickly we exclude others, setting apart and separating them. But Jesus' ministry, and by extension, the church's own ministry, is about inclusion through reconciliation. Jesus proclaims the forgiveness of sins, even undergoing a baptism of forgiveness. By his ministry those on the margins, those who have been condemned, are brought back and welcomed into the fold. The disciples of Jesus carry this ministry forward into the world. And like the time of Jesus, this ministry moves forward even when there are forces present who prefer exclusion. The question on the WWJD bracelet, "What would Jesus do?" is particularly appropriate here. Jesus did not condemn. Neither should we. Jesus forgave. So should we.

Focusing the Gospel

Key words and phrases: Let the one among you who is without sin / be the first to throw a stone at her.

To the point: It is so much easier to point out other people's sins than to confront our own. Jesus reminds us in the gospel today that when our focus shifts to another's sinfulness we need to refocus our attention. Following Jesus' challenge, "Let the one among you who is without sin / be the first to throw a stone at her," the crowd slowly dissipates. Finally the woman is left with the only one who *is* without sin, Jesus himself. But instead of hurling vicious words or any other projectiles intent on hurting, Jesus offers the woman forgiveness. As in all things, Jesus shows us the way. We are called to love our neighbors, not to condemn them.

Connecting the Gospel

to the first and second readings: In the first reading from the prophet Isaiah, God proclaims words of hope and redemption, saying, "[S]ee, I am doing something new! / Now it springs forth, do you not perceive it?" In the second reading, St. Paul also emphasizes the newness of his life in Christ: "[F]orgetting what lies behind / but straining forward to what lies ahead, / I continue my pursuit toward the goal." Our God is not rigid and predictable, but creative and uncontained. And this is how Jesus reveals him to be. In the gospel reading Jesus invites the adulterous woman to new life through forgiveness. Her sin is removed and she can look forward with hope, instead of remaining mired in her sin and forever marked by condemnation.

to experience: The God of newness offers each of us a fresh beginning as well. We are invited in every moment to step into the freedom of Christ and to leave our past sins behind.

Connecting the Responsorial Psalm

to the readings: Psalm 126 recalls the joy the people of Israel felt when their exile in Babylon ended and they were allowed to return to their homeland. After fifty years in captivity the people returned to Israel to begin the long difficult work of rebuilding their cities, temple, and lives as a free people. This is the time that Isaiah speaks of in the first reading. God is doing something new by delivering God's people from Babylon. Restoring the Babylonian captives is compared to God's action in saving the people from slavery in Egypt when God opened "a way in the sea / and a path in the mighty waters." The theme is clear. Our God longs to save the downcast, brokenhearted, enslaved, and marginalized, whether this is an entire people or a woman accused of adultery and threatened with capital punishment.

to psalmist preparation: Today's psalm is a powerful message of hope in despair. Consider a person in your life who needs this message. Proclaim this psalm as if you were singing directly to this person.

PROMPTS FOR FAITH-SHARING

In the reading from Isaiah, God proclaims, "[S]ee, I am doing something new!" Where do you see God's action in your life, family, or parish bringing about something new?

_____

_____

_____

_____

St. Paul writes to the Philippians, "I have accepted the loss of all things / and I consider them so much rubbish, / that I may gain Christ." How has your practice of fasting been this Lent? How has it enriched or affected your relationship with God and others?

_____

_____

_____

_____

How does your parish extend forgiveness to those who have committed a public sin?

_____

_____

_____

_____

Jesus gives us a model of mercy in today's gospel. How have you experienced giving and receiving mercy in your own life of faith?

_____

_____

_____

_____

Model Penitential Act

Presider: In today's gospel Jesus tells the accusers of the adulterous woman, "Let the one among you who is without sin / be the first to throw a stone at her." For the times we have cast stones of accusation and condemnation at our brothers and sisters let us ask for God's mercy and forgiveness . . . [*pause*]

    Confiteor: I confess . . .

Homily Points

• We are nearing the end of Lent. Next week will be Palm Sunday and together we will read the account of Jesus' passion and death. In his letter to the Philippians, St. Paul tells us that he counts everything else in his life as "loss" compared to "the supreme good of knowing Christ Jesus my Lord." Throughout this time of Lenten fasting, our intention has been to loosen the hold material things have over us. By removing indulgences of food, drink, and possessions, we are able to focus on what gives our life direction and purpose, our relationship with Jesus.

• Now as we come closer to Palm Sunday and the beginning of Holy Week, instead of waning, our spiritual practices of prayer, fasting, and almsgiving become even more intense. Our desire in these holiest days of the year that will soon be upon us is to be "conformed to [Jesus'] death," as St. Paul urges us.

• In today's gospel Jesus takes a potential act of violence (the stoning of the adulterous woman) and turns it into a moment of encounter and forgiveness. Jesus' death is another transformational moment. Within the violence of the crucifixion, Jesus' infinite love transforms the violence into the ultimate reconciliation of humanity and divinity. In longing to be conformed to Jesus' death, we are asking for the grace to become the light that is stronger than darkness, the love that is stronger than hatred, the life that is stronger than death. Let us persevere in our Lenten practices confident that the God of life will bring us to Easter joy.

Model Universal Prayer (Prayer of the Faithful)

Presider: Let us raise our prayers up to the God of mercy and compassion.

Response: Lord, hear our prayer.

That the church be a beacon of forgiveness and redemption for those condemned by society . . .

That leaders of nations enact laws that balance mercy and justice . . .

That those who have been sentenced to death within our criminal justice systems might know the Lord of life and be spared capital punishment . . .

That all of us gathered here be given the grace to forgive those who have wronged us . . .

Presider: God of infinite kindness, who redeems sinners and restores captives, hear our prayers that we might be led to Easter joy. We ask this through Christ our Lord. **Amen.**

COLLECT
Let us pray.

Pause for silent prayer

By your help, we beseech you, Lord our God,
may we walk eagerly in that same charity
with which, out of love for the world,
your Son handed himself over to death.
Through our Lord Jesus Christ, your Son,
who lives and reigns with you in the unity of the Holy Spirit,
one God, for ever and ever. **Amen.**

FIRST READING
Isa 43:16-21

Thus says the LORD,
   who opens a way in the sea
   and a path in the mighty waters,
who leads out chariots and horsemen,
   a powerful army,
till they lie prostrate together, never to rise,
   snuffed out and quenched like a wick.
Remember not the events of the past,
   the things of long ago consider not;
see, I am doing something new!
   Now it springs forth, do you not perceive it?
In the desert I make a way,
   in the wasteland, rivers.
Wild beasts honor me,
   jackals and ostriches,
for I put water in the desert
   and rivers in the wasteland
   for my chosen people to drink,
the people whom I formed for myself,
   that they might announce my praise.

RESPONSORIAL PSALM
Ps 126:1-2, 2-3, 4-5, 6

℞. (3) The Lord has done great things for us; we are filled with joy.

When the LORD brought back the captives of Zion,
   we were like men dreaming.
Then our mouth was filled with laughter,
   and our tongue with rejoicing.

℞. The Lord has done great things for us; we are filled with joy.

Then they said among the nations,
   "The LORD has done great things for them."
The LORD has done great things for us;
   we are glad indeed.

℞. The Lord has done great things for us; we are filled with joy.

Restore our fortunes, O Lᴏʀᴅ,
   like the torrents in the southern desert.
Those that sow in tears
   shall reap rejoicing.

R℣. The Lord has done great things for us;
   we are filled with joy.

Although they go forth weeping,
   carrying the seed to be sown,
they shall come back rejoicing,
   carrying their sheaves.

R℣. The Lord has done great things for us;
   we are filled with joy.

SECOND READING
Phil 3:8-14

Brothers and sisters:
I consider everything as a loss
   because of the supreme good of
      knowing Christ Jesus my Lord.
For his sake I have accepted the loss of all
     things
   and I consider them so much rubbish,
   that I may gain Christ and be found in
     him,
   not having any righteousness of my
     own based on the law
   but that which comes through faith in
     Christ,
   the righteousness from God,
   depending on faith to know him and the
     power of his resurrection
   and the sharing of his sufferings by being
     conformed to his death,
   if somehow I may attain the
     resurrection from the dead.

It is not that I have already taken hold of it
   or have already attained perfect maturity,
   but I continue my pursuit in hope that I
     may possess it,
   since I have indeed been taken
     possession of by Christ Jesus.
Brothers and sisters, I for my part
   do not consider myself to have taken
     possession.
Just one thing: forgetting what lies behind
   but straining forward to what lies
     ahead,
   I continue my pursuit toward the goal,
   the prize of God's upward calling, in
     Christ Jesus.

About Liturgy

Misery and mercy meet: In his lecture on the Gospel of John, St. Augustine beautifully describes the moment in today's gospel story when the woman and Jesus were left alone. Augustine said, *Relicti sunt duo: misera et misericordia* (Two were left: misery and mercy) (Tract 33.5). When we hear this gospel passage we often focus on the woman's sin, which is certainly serious. Yet she is not the only sinner in this story. The scribes and Pharisees were guilty of pride and anger disguised as religious piety, directed not only toward the woman but also Jesus, whom they hoped to ensnare. Although one could say that Jesus did not condemn the scribes and Pharisees for their sin, neither did Jesus offer them a word of forgiveness as he gave to the woman. Perhaps this is because the scribes and Pharisees had not recognized their own misery in the face of mercy, whereas the woman, dragged half naked into the streets to endure public scrutiny, had no choice but to stand silently in her misery.

Every time we pray the Lord's Prayer, particularly when we say, "Forgive us our trespasses as we forgive those who trespass against us," we are given the opportunity to bring our misery before the Father, whose name is mercy. How often though do we say these words without careful attention and intention, without hearing them as a call to offer mercy as much as a plea for it?

As we pray the Lord's Prayer this week let us be even more attentive to the meaning of the words we pray so that we too might learn to act with mercy when we encounter another's misery, and thus sin no longer.

About Initiation

Presentation of the Lord's Prayer: During the Fifth Week of Lent the community of the faithful present the Lord's Prayer to the elect who will be baptized this Easter. (See RCIA 178–84.) This presentation is celebrated outside of the Sunday Mass either at a liturgy of the word or a weekday Mass. This is because the presentation has assigned readings that must be used in place of the readings for the Mass of the day. In particular, the gospel reading comes from Matthew 6:9-13 in which Jesus teaches his disciples to pray and gives them the words we use today as the Our Father. Note that the presentation is oral. No scroll or piece of paper with the prayer is given to the elect during the presentation itself. Rather, the text is handed on orally and received orally.

If the elect are unable to participate in a parish weekday Mass schedule a gathering with a group from the parish that will already be meeting that week, or plan this for the weekly parish Lenten gathering, such as your Friday soup supper or Stations of the Cross. This presentation might even work as part of your parish communal reconciliation liturgy.

About Liturgical Music

Singing the Lord's Prayer: The Lord's Prayer is a communal prayer that all recite together. Many communities are already familiar with the chant melody of the English words set by Robert Snow, found in the Roman Missal. Fewer communities will be able to sing the Latin text with its corresponding chant also found in the missal. Other communities have incorporated a metrical setting of the Lord's Prayer. Many composers have provided such settings that we can choose from. However, the priority is always that the assembly be able to participate in this venerable prayer. If they are unfamiliar with the musical setting you have chosen, it is better that it be spoken so that all might participate.

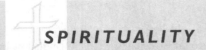

SPIRITUALITY

GOSPEL ACCLAMATION
Phil 2:8-9

Christ became obedient to the point of death,
even death on a cross.
Because of this, God greatly exalted him
and bestowed on him the name which is above
    every name.

Gospel at the Procession with Palms
Luke 19:28-40; L37C

Jesus proceeded on his journey
    up to Jerusalem.
As he drew near to Bethphage
    and Bethany
  at the place called the Mount
    of Olives,
  he sent two of his disciples.
He said, "Go into the village op-
    posite you,
  and as you enter it you will
    find a colt tethered
  on which no one has ever sat.
Untie it and bring it here.
And if anyone should ask you,
  'Why are you untying it?'
  you will answer,
  'The Master has need of it.'"
So those who had been sent went off
  and found everything just as he had
    told them.
And as they were untying the colt, its
    owners said to them,
  "Why are you untying this colt?"
They answered,
  "The Master has need of it."
So they brought it to Jesus,
  threw their cloaks over the colt,
  and helped Jesus to mount.
As he rode along,
  the people were spreading their cloaks
    on the road;
  and now as he was approaching the
    slope of the Mount of Olives,
  the whole multitude of his disciples
  began to praise God aloud with joy
  for all the mighty deeds they had seen.

Continued in Appendix A, p. 284.

Gospel at Mass   Luke 22:14–23:56; L38ABC
or Luke 23:1-49 *in Appendix A, pp. 284–87.*

Reflecting on the Gospel

We are fickle creatures. We can experience happiness to the point of being ecstatic one minute and sink to the depths of despair the next. We can sing the praises of somebody now that we will despise later. There are certainly reasons for the changes in our emotions and attitudes, but there can be no dispute that our emotions and attitudes change, and sometimes quickly so.

The church attempts to capture and express this fickleness in the liturgy today when we enter with palm branches singing songs of praise, only to cry out in unison moments later during the gospel, "Crucify him! Crucify him!"

Luke's version of the passion of Jesus has several unique characteristics when compared especially with his Marcan source. For example, Luke gives us the episode of the back-and-forth between Pilate and Herod that is absent in all other gospels. Some scholars see that Luke's Christology bears even on the relationship between these two rulers, who, unwittingly through their encounter with Christ, "became friends that very day, / even though they had been enemies formerly." It's as though Christ has the power to bring friendship even among those who are seeking to have him executed.

The power of Christ is also on display in this gospel when Jesus prays from the cross, "Father, forgive them." The distinctly Lucan theme of forgiveness is on Jesus' lips at the moment before his death. And the mercy of Jesus extends even to a criminal, which Luke relates to us in an exchange between them. Again, no other evangelist tells this story. The other evangelists simply narrate that two criminals were crucified along with Jesus.

The profundity of these two chapters (or even only one if the parish reads the shorter reading) is something that we reflect upon year after year. We will not exhaust this story. It will exhaust us, and we shall return to it to gain insight, understanding, and strength. The grand themes that Luke employed in his gospel are on full display here: mercy and forgiveness.

Let's soak up the gospel today and try to keep our fickleness in check. Let's wave palm branches and sing songs of praise without losing ourselves in a call to "Crucify him! Crucify him!" But even if, and perhaps when, we do, we know that forgiveness awaits from a merciful God.

Living the Paschal Mystery

Perhaps the liturgical expression of palm branches followed by shouts of crucifixion has something in common with our spiritual life. When are the moments we are ecstatic? When are our palm branch and singing moments? What causes those moments? Are we caught up with the crowd? Are we praising the Messiah, or the things we want the Messiah to do? Are we caught up in expectations, or ready to be a disciple, which literally means "to follow"?

It's much easier to sing somebody's praise when we think that person will live up to our expectations. But what happens when they do not? What happens when there is another path to follow?

The moments in our spiritual life when we cry, "Crucify him! Crucify him!" are not likely to be "high praise" moments. Crucifixions happen by our negligence and our selfishness. We crucify when we destroy, uproot, tear down, or otherwise extinguish life and that which is life-giving. And often we don't realize it until it's too late. But we believe in a God who brings life from death, even when we cause the death. And that is the ultimate paschal mystery.

Focusing the Gospel

Key words and phrases: This is my body, which will be given for you; / do this in memory of me.

To the point: Before the pain and horror of Good Friday, Jesus gives his disciples the key to understand what will happen to him when he celebrates the Passover with them for one last time. Though it will take on the guise of a terrible act of violence, the crucifixion will be a gift of Jesus in his totality for the salvation of the world. It is the physical enacting of Jesus' words over the bread and wine, "This is my body, [this is my blood,] which will be given for you." As we read the passion today let us remember the mystery we are celebrating. Jesus died, but that is not the end of the story. The sorrow of Palm Sunday leads to the overflowing joy of Easter.

Connecting the Gospel

to the first reading: Isaiah also speaks of gift: "The Lord GOD has given me / a well-trained tongue." And Isaiah uses this well-trained tongue to preach a word to the weary. The words of Isaiah continue to chasten and comfort us when world-weariness infects our souls. Isaiah also gives his "back to those who beat [him], / [his] cheeks to those who plucked [his] beard." Just as Jesus freely gives his body and blood in the crucifixion, Isaiah's gift of his back and cheeks to his tormentors free him from their tyranny.

to experience: We often feel that we have no control in our lives. When tragedy strikes in the form of illness, the death of a loved one, or being wronged, we can become bitter and fearful. But what would happen if we followed the example of Isaiah and Jesus? Can we make a gift of what is being demanded of us?

Connecting the Responsorial Psalm

to the readings: The psalm today is Psalm 22, which begins, "My God, my God, why have you abandoned me?" Jesus speaks these words from the cross in both the gospels of Mark and Matthew. We can see from the verses we sing today, however, that the first line of the psalm does not dictate the rest. Though the psalmist begins with this cry of despair, soon he sings, "You who fear the LORD, praise him; / all you descendants of Jacob, give glory to him." In the account of the passion that we read in Luke's gospel, Jesus does not become despondent. Instead, from the cross we hear him say, just before he takes his final breath, "Father, into your hands I commend my spirit."

to psalmist preparation: Despair and hope live side by side in Psalm 22. The first verses bespeak the most terrible suffering. But the last verses give glory to God who does not "stay far off" when trouble comes (NABRE). To be a disciple, one must follow Jesus to Calvary. Are you ready?

PROMPTS FOR FAITH-SHARING

The prophet Isaiah tells us, "The Lord GOD has given me / a well-trained tongue, / that I might know how to speak to the weary / a word that will rouse them." Who are the weary in your parish or community? What word do they need to hear?

St. Paul records an early hymn to Christ in his letter to the Philippians, lauding the one who "emptied himself." What spiritual practice helps you to empty yourself so as to make room for Jesus?

At the beginning of today's gospel we hear Luke's account of the Last Supper, when Jesus gives his body and blood, his entire self, to us. How do you experience Jesus' presence in the Eucharist?

How will you set aside your regular routine these next eight days to enter into Holy Week?

Model Penitential Act

Presider: On this feast of Palm Sunday we read from St. Paul's letter to the Philippians the ancient hymn of Jesus' glory. The Son of God emptied himself and became obedient unto death, death on a cross. Let us pause now to empty ourselves so there might be room within us for the Lord of Life to dwell . . . [*pause*]

   Confiteor: I confess . . .

Homily Points

• In last week's second reading St. Paul urged us to be conformed to the death of Christ, and today we come face to face with that death. In it Jesus once again shows us the way. Jesus shows us the way of generosity. At the Last Supper Jesus tells his disciples (then and now) that his death will be a total and complete gift of self. For what more is body and blood than a way of saying "all of me." Jesus holds nothing back.

• Jesus shows us the way of nonviolence. When the crowd approaches to arrest Jesus, his followers react by drawing a sword and cutting off the ear of a servant of the high priest. Jesus' response is swift. He tells them unequivocally, "Stop, no more of this!" and heals the servant's ear. Jesus does not meet violence with violence. He meets harm with healing and hatred with love. So must we, if wish to be called his disciples.

• Jesus shows us the way of compassion. Even as he is being nailed to the cross Jesus prays, "Father, forgive them, they know not what they do." In his own physical pain and suffering, Jesus' concern is for the spiritual welfare of his executioners. No physical pain can compare to the spiritual agony of being far from God. In the Gospel of Luke, Jesus gives us the parables of the Lost Sheep, Lost Coin, and Lost (Prodigal) Son in quick succession. The common feature of these parables? God never stops seeking the lost. Neither does Jesus, and upon the cross he finds one more lost child, the thief who asks for forgiveness and is promised paradise. May we be conformed to the way of the cross, the way of generosity, nonviolence, and compassion.

Model Universal Prayer (Prayer of the Faithful)

Presider: Clinging to God, our shelter and strength, we make our needs known.

Response: Lord, hear our prayer.

That the pope, bishops, priests, deacons, and lay ministers of the church might recommit themselves to serving the poor and outcast within society . . .

That nations of the world embrace the nonviolence of Jesus who said, "Stop, no more of this!" at the maiming of the high priest's servant . . .

That political prisoners and victims of torture be strengthened and comforted by the passion of Jesus, the Lord of life . . .

That all those gathered here might enter into this holiest of weeks with fidelity and love . . .

Presider: Life-giving God, you are the light in our darkness. Be our strength as we journey with Jesus through his passion and death into the glory of Easter. We ask this through Christ our Lord. **Amen.**

COLLECT

Let us pray.

Pause for silent prayer

Almighty ever-living God,
who as an example of humility for the
   human race to follow
caused our Savior to take flesh and submit
   to the Cross,
graciously grant that we may heed his
   lesson of patient suffering
and so merit a share in his Resurrection.
Who lives and reigns with you in the unity
   of the Holy Spirit,
one God, for ever and ever. **Amen.**

FIRST READING

Isa 50:4-7

The Lord GOD has given me
   a well-trained tongue,
that I might know how to speak to the
   weary
   a word that will rouse them.
Morning after morning
   he opens my ear that I may hear;
and I have not rebelled,
   have not turned back.
I gave my back to those who beat me,
   my cheeks to those who plucked my
      beard;
my face I did not shield
   from buffets and spitting.

The Lord GOD is my help,
   therefore I am not disgraced;
I have set my face like flint,
   knowing that I shall not be put to
      shame.

RESPONSORIAL PSALM

Ps 22:8-9, 17-18, 19-20, 23-24

R̸. (2a) My God, my God, why have you
   abandoned me?

All who see me scoff at me;
   they mock me with parted lips, they
      wag their heads:
"He relied on the LORD; let him deliver him,
   let him rescue him, if he loves him."

R̸. My God, my God, why have you
   abandoned me?

Indeed, many dogs surround me,
　　a pack of evildoers closes in upon me;
they have pierced my hands and my feet;
　　I can count all my bones.

R̸. My God, my God, why have you
　　abandoned me?

They divide my garments among them,
　　and for my vesture they cast lots.
But you, O LORD, be not far from me;
　　O my help, hasten to aid me.

R̸. My God, my God, why have you
　　abandoned me?

I will proclaim your name to my brethren;
　　in the midst of the assembly I will
　　　　praise you:
"You who fear the LORD, praise him;
　　all you descendants of Jacob, give glory
　　　　to him;
　　revere him, all you descendants of
　　　　Israel!"

R̸. My God, my God, why have you
　　abandoned me?

SECOND READING
Phil 2:6-11

Christ Jesus, though he was in the form
　　of God,
　　did not regard equality with God
　　something to be grasped.
Rather, he emptied himself,
　　taking the form of a slave,
　　coming in human likeness;
　　and found human in appearance,
　　he humbled himself,
　　becoming obedient to the point of
　　　　death,
　　even death on a cross.
Because of this, God greatly exalted him
　　and bestowed on him the name
　　which is above every name,
　　that at the name of Jesus
　　every knee should bend,
　　of those in heaven and on earth and
　　　　under the earth,
　　and every tongue confess that
Jesus Christ is Lord,
　　to the glory of God the Father.

About Liturgy

Proclamation of the Passion: Holy Week is unlike any other week of the year for Christians. All our usual routines that attempt to satisfy our need for convenience and efficiency take a back seat to the lavish "waste" of our rituals this week. The extravagance of these days has no other purpose than to immerse us fully into the meaning of paschal mystery, which is inexhaustible. In that light, let us look at the proclamation of the passion, which is proclaimed today and again on Good Friday.

The first clue that this proclamation is different from other Sundays is this rubric in the Roman Missal: "The narrative of the Lord's Passion is read without candles and without incense, with no greeting or signing of the book" (Palm Sunday 21). The absence of the usual signs of honor we give to the gospel call our attention to what truly is required in order to reverence the presence of Christ in the gospel, that is, our full attention, heart, soul, and strength, to hearing and doing the Word in our lives.

Second, the normative posture for the assembly to hear the gospel is standing. This is no different even for longer readings. If we are to give our full attention, our bodies must also be *at* attention, which is standing. Those who are too weak to remain standing for the entirety of the gospel should be given the option to be seated if they find it necessary. However, that invitation to sit should be presented as the pastoral exception for those who need it and not the normative posture for all in the assembly.

Finally, the passion reading cuts to the heart of the paschal mystery: the cross. Those who offer this proclamation given only twice a year should be among the best lectors of the parish. Ideally, the deacon or priest who leads the proclamation has rehearsed this gospel carefully as well.

A caution about enacting the gospel reading: although it is popular to dramatize this reading, the primary ritual action is proclamation and listening. Acting out the scenes of the gospel tends to distract from the primary ritual action and runs the risk of historicizing text that is meant to be *anamnetic*, that is, a memorial of a past event whose reality is fully present now.

About Initiation

Preparation rites: On Holy Saturday the elect refrain from their usual routine and spend time in prayer and reflection. RCIA 185–205 gives a possible outline for this time of preparation. Be sure to remind your elect and their godparents of these preparation rites and the schedule for the liturgies this week.

About Liturgical Music

Suggestions: Instead of putting extra energy into a choral anthem or other special musical hymn for this Sunday, consider keeping the music simple and concentrating more effort into presenting the gospel proclamation of the passion as a sung proclamation. Any proclamation of the gospel can be sung using chant tones provided in the Roman Missal. But especially today and Good Friday that option should be considered in order to highlight the unique solemnity of the liturgies of Holy Week. GIA Publications has a collection of the four passion gospels set to the traditional Vatican chants.

For simple yet beautiful assembly antiphons, look to *Psallite*'s "Hosanna, Hosanna, Hosanna in the Highest" and "If I Must Drink the Cup" (*Sacred Song*). The latter would be perfect as a gospel refrain for Communion, recalling Jesus' own prayer in today's passion reading. Also, Alexander Means's stirring text, "What Wondrous Love Is This?" set to WONDROUS LOVE is an excellent hymn that should be used throughout the liturgies of this week.

EASTER
TRIDUUM

How many exclaim: What a joy it would be to behold his face; even his clothing, or merely his sandals! Yet, in the Eucharist, He is the one you see, He is the one your hands touch, He is the one who becomes one flesh with you.

—John Chrysostom, *Homily on Matthew* 80 (PG 58.743)

Reflecting on the Triduum

The "Triduum," these three sacred days are unlike any other in the liturgical year for the Christian. They carry forward an echo of faith from centuries ago and then ripple through the year with their profound theological significance. The three days are not a reenactment of events from two thousand years ago, but they make the effects of that event present in our lives today. The Triduum is a touchstone of faith to which we return year after year.

On these three days we commemorate essential and everlasting elements of our incarnational spirituality, celebrating the death and resurrection of the author of life, the Word made flesh. This is too much for one liturgy or even one day. The movements of the sacred events take place over three days so that we may enter more fully into the mysteries we celebrate.

Holy Thursday commemorates the sign of service that Jesus gave us on that night of the Last Supper. He who came not to be served but to serve is our master who set an example for us. If the master served, we too must serve. Service is a constitutive element of following the one who served to the point of giving his life. Tragic themes of betrayal by a friend, a shared meal with the knowledge of betrayal, and the lure of money make this commemoration haunting in its near universal applicability.

On Good Friday we witness the cross; there is no eucharistic prayer, but only a significant Liturgy of the Word followed by Communion. As Christians have done for centuries, we pray for the world and for many other things. The prayers of intercession are accompanied by dramatic action and even movement. This day is unlike any other, and we leave the service in silence, alone with our thoughts.

After sunset on Saturday it's as though we cannot contain the Easter joy we know will be ours and we celebrate the resurrection. Readings of promise and salvation are punctuated by psalms of praise and exaltation. Easter lilies, lights, fire, bells, a Gloria—all signify that our Lord has risen, never to be subject to death again. Life has been transformed and will never be the same now that we have this existential promise of eternity with Christ.

The Triduum is too much for one liturgy or even one day. We are given three days to enter into this profound ancient mystery. Let's give ourselves the gift of not only preparing others for this experience, but undergoing it ourselves too.

Living the Paschal Mystery

The Triduum could be said to be the ultimate commemoration of the paschal mystery. In dramatic fashion, the Author of life is handed over to death by a friend for a few pieces of silver. Anyone who has been betrayed by another knows the hurt, pain, and loss of that experience, which is felt by the psalmist who says, "Even my trusted friend / who ate my bread, / has raised his heel against me" (Ps 41:10; NABRE). This psalm is quoted in the Gospel of John (13:18), and is certainly apropos. In addition to betrayal, we experience a sham trial, rigged "justice" that sends an innocent person to death. It is not too much of a leap to imagine those on death row today who have been exonerated because of DNA evidence. Unfortunately the condemnation of the innocent or not guilty is with us even today. The Triduum we celebrate is not only the paschal mystery that Jesus underwent, but it is being lived out in our midst today when people are betrayed and others sent to death. It's easy to look at Jesus as an unfortunate victim of betrayal and swift justice. But his experience should cause us to see all those who face similar action. When we do nothing, or cheer for vengeance, we are like those in the crowd on these days. The paschal mystery did not happen only once two millennia ago. It continues today. With eyes of faith we can see, and we have hope for an eternal future where God's justice truly reigns.

TRIDUUM

"Triduum" is an odd-sounding word that comes from the Latin term for "three days." These most sacred days begin Holy Thursday evening through Friday evening (day one), include Friday evening through Saturday evening (day two), and conclude with the Easter Vigil and Easter Sunday (day three). We recall that though the modern world (like the ancient Romans) starts a day at midnight, the Jewish day starts at sundown. (And a day for the ancient Greeks started at sunrise!)

These "three days" are the most sacred of the year. And the pinnacle liturgical celebration of the Triduum is the Easter Vigil (General Norms for the Liturgical Year and the Calendar 19). Parishes sometimes begin this only an hour after sundown. It's as though the church can't wait to celebrate Easter.

SOLEMN PASCHAL FAST

Even though Lent officially ends with the Holy Thursday liturgy, that does not mean our Lenten fast ends too. Rather, the church keeps a solemn paschal fast on Good Friday and we are encouraged to keep it on Saturday as well, in anticipation of Communion at the Easter Vigil. Only then is our fast complete and the Easter season begun. "But the paschal fast must be kept sacrosanct. It should be celebrated everywhere on Good Friday, and where possible should be prolonged through Holy Saturday so that the faithful may attain the joys of Easter Sunday with uplifted and receptive minds" (Constitution on the Sacred Liturgy 110).

GOSPEL ACCLAMATION
John 13:34

I give you a new commandment, says the Lord:
love one another as I have loved you.

Gospel   John 13:1-15; L39ABC

Before the feast of Passover, Jesus knew
    that his hour had come
  to pass from this world to the
    Father.
He loved his own in the world
    and he loved them to the
    end.
The devil had already in-
    duced Judas, son of
    Simon the Iscariot, to
    hand him over.
So, during supper,
  fully aware that the Father had put
    everything into his power
  and that he had come from God and
    was returning to God,
  he rose from supper and took off his
    outer garments.
He took a towel and tied it around his
    waist.
Then he poured water into a basin
  and began to wash the disciples' feet
  and dry them with the towel around his
    waist.
He came to Simon Peter, who said to him,
  "Master, are you going to wash my
    feet?"
Jesus answered and said to him,
  "What I am doing, you do not
    understand now,
  but you will understand later."
Peter said to him, "You will never wash
    my feet."
Jesus answered him,
  "Unless I wash you, you will have no
    inheritance with me."
Simon Peter said to him,
  "Master, then not only my feet, but my
    hands and head as well."
Jesus said to him,
  "Whoever has bathed has no need
    except to have his feet washed,
  for he is clean all over;
  so you are clean, but not all."

Continued in Appendix A, p. 288.
See Appendix A, p. 288, for the other readings.

Reflecting on the Gospel and Living the Paschal Mystery

Key words and phrases: washed their feet; as I have done for you, you
should also do

To the point: This evening as we celebrate the institution of the Eucharist,
we listen to the sole gospel that does not include that story! The Last Supper
in the Gospel of John is not the story of the Passover meal, for John situates
the Last Supper on the night before Passover, as the
opening verses of this evening's gospel reading
indicate. Recall that the Gospel of John gives
us the eloquent and sophisticated bread of
life discourse in chapter 6, which effectively
theologizes about the Eucharist. No Passover
meal is needed at the Last Supper, especially
when we consider that for this gospel,
Jesus is understood to be the Lamb of God.
Upon seeing Jesus for the first time, John
the Baptist cried out, "Behold, the Lamb of
God" (John 1:36; NABRE). And we shall see
that the crucifixion takes place on the day
of preparation, when the lambs are being
slaughtered in *preparation* for Passover
later that night.
So the Last Supper for the Gospel of
John is not about Eucharist as much as ser-
vice. Jesus the master becomes the servant of his disciples, thus giving them an
example. Jesus overturns the role of master so that the master is the one who
serves, not the one who is served. By so doing, Jesus exemplifies a core message
of the gospel, and core message of his own identity. If we are to follow Jesus,
we, too, must become servants. There will never be a time when we are content
to sit back, relax, and be served. Instead, we are the ones who serve, in imitation
of Jesus, our master, and the one true servant of God.

To ponder and pray: Service is a constitutive element of discipleship. Without service, it is nearly impossible to be a disciple of Jesus, for to be a disciple
is to be a follower, which is what the term disciple means. And since Jesus the
master became the servant of others we, too, have a duty and an obligation to
do the same if we are to bear the name "disciple." Without service, we are mere
admirers of Jesus.

Liturgically, the Eucharist is where we come to be fed so that we might continue this service in the name of Jesus. Bread broken and shared becomes an apt
metaphor for our lives of service in which we, like the master, become broken
and shared, food for others.

The sign Jesus instituted to represent this service was the washing of the
feet. And according to early church fathers, this "sacrament" of washing the
feet was carried on for many decades, if not centuries, before the church officially declared there to be only seven sacraments, with a capital "S." But at
the liturgy today we reenact this powerful sign. We only need to consider how
powerful a sign it really is when we look to the reaction caused by Pope Francis
washing the feet of inmates in 2013, some of whom were beyond the strict
bounds of what the then rubrics (rules) permitted, including Muslims, nonbe-
lievers, and women. The Holy Father officially changed the rubrics in 2016 to in-

clude the option of washing women's feet in this liturgy. The example of Jesus echoes down through the ages, giving us a clarion call to service.

Model Penitential Act

Presider: In the washing of his disciples' feet, Jesus has given us a model of humility and service. As he has done, so we are to do. Let us pause to ask forgiveness for the times we have failed to serve God and one another . . . [*pause*]

Lord Jesus, you are the Lamb of God: Lord, have mercy.
Christ Jesus, you give your body and blood for the life of the world: Christ, have mercy.
Lord Jesus, you show us the way of love: Lord, have mercy.

Model Universal Prayer (Prayer of the Faithful)

Presider: On this holy night we lift our prayers and petitions up to the Lord.

Response: Lord, hear our prayer.

That all members of the church might be strengthened and sanctified by this celebration of our most sacred feast: the Holy Triduum . . .

That all the peoples of the world might know the tender, compassionate, and saving love of Christ . . .

That those preparing for baptism, confirmation, and first communion might be ever more configured to the person of Christ and welcomed lovingly into his body, the church . . .

That all gathered here might follow the model of Jesus in washing the feet of our friends and enemies in humility and love . . .

Presider: Saving God, you have called us to yourself through the witness of Jesus, your son. Hear our prayers that we might celebrate these holy days with reverence and fidelity. Through Christ our Lord. **Amen.**

About Liturgy

Memorial: In the Triduum, we remember the past events of our salvation and keep memorial of the Lord crucified, buried, and risen. Memorial, however, is not the same as going back in time. Memorial is anamnetic. We recall the past event in our present reality so as to remember and reconnect to the future hope that is already here in Christ today.

In the liturgy, if we try to re-create the past or pretend to be characters from it, we step out of the *kairos* of the heavenly liturgy and into the *chronos* of human time. On this first day of the Triduum, we might be tempted to reconstruct the past by decorating the church as if it were the Upper Room, or by inviting twelve men to represent the twelve disciples in the washing of the feet, or by re-creating the garden of Gethsemane for the reposition of the Blessed Sacrament at the end of Mass.

Instead, focus on the primary symbols of assembly: word and altar. Imagine how you can help the assembly participate fully and encounter the mystery of Christ who is active and present today.

FOR REFLECTION

• In today's gospel Jesus tells Peter, "Unless I wash you, you will have no inheritance with me." How has serving or being served affected your understanding of being a Christian?

• We are told, "He loved his own in the world and he loved them to the end." How do you experience Jesus' love in your life?

Homily Points

• In the first two readings today we hear about remembrance. The Hebrew people are to remember every year the Passover of the Lord when the angel of death passes over the houses marked by the blood of the lamb, and the people are led to freedom through the Red Sea. In celebrating the Passover, the Jewish people render the events of the past present so that each one of them can say, I was there when the angel of death passed over. I was there at the crossing of the Red Sea.

• And so it is with us. Two thousand years after the Last Supper we are also present there. In our churches as we gather for the Eucharist whenever it is celebrated, we are present with Jesus and his disciples at the table when Jesus first said these precious words, "This is my body . . . [this is] my blood." We can say, I was there.

GOSPEL ACCLAMATION
Phil 2:8-9

Christ became obedient to the point of death,
even death on a cross.
Because of this, God greatly exalted him
and bestowed on him the name which is above
    every other name.

Gospel   John 18:1–19:42; L40ABC

Jesus went out with his disciples across
    the Kidron valley
    to where there was a garden,
    into which he and his disciples entered.
Judas his betrayer also knew the place,
    because Jesus had often met there
        with his disciples.
So Judas got a band of soldiers and
    guards
    from the chief priests and the
        Pharisees
    and went there with lanterns, torches,
        and weapons.
Jesus, knowing everything that was going
    to happen to him,
    went out and said to them, "Whom are
        you looking for?"
They answered him, "Jesus the Nazorean."
He said to them, "I AM."
Judas his betrayer was also with them.
When he said to them, "I AM,"
    they turned away and fell to the ground.
So he again asked them,
    "Whom are you looking for?"
They said, "Jesus the Nazorean."
Jesus answered,
    "I told you that I AM.
So if you are looking for me, let these
    men go."
This was to fulfill what he had said,
    "I have not lost any of those you gave me."
Then Simon Peter, who had a sword,
    drew it,
    struck the high priest's slave, and cut
        off his right ear.
The slave's name was Malchus.
Jesus said to Peter,
    "Put your sword into its scabbard.
Shall I not drink the cup that the Father
    gave me?"

Continued in Appendix A, pp. 289–90.
See Appendix A, p. 291, for the other readings.

Reflecting on the Gospel and Living the Paschal Mystery
Key words and phrases: I AM; Crucify him; Jesus the Nazarene, the King of
the Jews

To the point: On this day, the only one in the liturgical year without a Mass,
we have two pivotal chapters from the Gospel of John. We feast on
the Word before consuming Communion. And the feast is rich.
The evangelist has been called simply, "the theologian" and that
is precisely because of his profound insight into the person of
Jesus, and Jesus' relationship with the Father. In today's gospel
we hear the dramatic story of the trial and ultimate crucifixion of Jesus, though even with the scourging and
mockery it does not seem to be much of a "passion." In
the Gospel of John, the moment of crucifixion
is the ultimate "lifting up," "glorification,"
and "exaltation" of Jesus that has been prefigured and predicted throughout the story.
Jesus knew everything that was to happen to
him. Even so, it is Pilate, rather than Jesus, who displays
fear. The evangelist does not dwell on how physically
painful was the experience for Jesus, and the preacher is
advised to do the same. The story instead is imbued with
theological and christological depth, posing questions
about Jesus' identity ("Where are you from?") and even the
nature of truth itself, as Pilate infamously asks, "What
is truth?" Yet the entire affair is a grand fulfillment of
Scripture foreseen by Jesus himself, as well as the
prophets.
Irony is replete in this gospel where the
crowds claim they have no king but Caesar and
thereby demand the death of the author of life. Pilate's inscription over the cross, written in mockery, is absolutely true. Jesus is a king; yet his kingdom is not of this world. Pilate claims to
have power over life and death but does not know truth. The disciples who have
been with Jesus throughout his ministry seek first to fight with a sword only
to scatter moments later. Then, when Peter is faced with temptation, the simple
yet profound question as to whether he knows Jesus, he melts like wax under a
flame of inquisition. The public humiliation of Jesus on the cross is in reality
his victory, as foretold by Scripture. The ways of the world are being upended.

To ponder and pray: Rather than a play to be reenacted, the Gospel of John
gives us the eternal Word, sacred Scripture, on which to gnaw. It is good for us
to ponder this lengthy reading and the profound insights it displays. Each Good
Friday we read this passion narrative culminating in the death but ultimate exaltation of Jesus. Jesus is the eternal Word made flesh, because God so loved the
world. And yet the world does not respond in kind. Instead, the world executes
the Word made flesh. Perfect love made incarnate is killed on a cross by us who
prefer a king like Caesar to the author of life who comes to serve. When faced
with love we crush it underfoot claiming not to know, "What is truth?" But now
we have the opportunity to reflect on this drama that happened not only two
millennia ago, but each and every day. When we encounter the lowly and downtrodden, those who are trampled underfoot by the state, or religious authorities,

or any system, what is our response? Do we argue away our responsibility, claiming like Peter not to know Jesus in our midst? Or are we like Pilate and engage in philosophical speculation and shuck responsibility? The death and exaltation of Jesus should cause us to reexamine our values. To follow the master, to be a disciple, is to follow the example of service. And that service pours itself out for another to the point of ultimate exhaustion and self-sacrifice, which is itself our glory.

About Liturgy

The Holy Cross: On this second day of the Triduum we turn our full gaze toward the Cross. Just as we adored the Blessed Sacrament the night before, on this night, we behold and adore the wood on which hung the Savior of the world.

This showing of the cross at the liturgy of the passion of the Lord can take two forms. In the first form, the covered cross in the sanctuary is gradually unveiled by the priest as a deacon or the choir sings an acclamation. In the second form, the priest or deacon processes the veiled cross from the door of the church through the assembly to the sanctuary, stopping at various points to unveil a portion of the cross. The one carrying the cross leads the sung acclamation. Note that this second form parallels the stational procession with the paschal candle that will take place the following night at the Easter Vigil.

The Roman Missal directs that there be only one cross offered for adoration. Also, at the end of the liturgy the cross remains in the church with four lit candles so that people may stay to pray before it.

COLLECT
Let us pray.

Remember your mercies, O Lord,
and with your eternal protection sanctify your
   servants,
for whom Christ your Son,
by the shedding of his Blood,
established the Paschal Mystery.
Who lives and reigns for ever and ever.
Amen.

or:

O God, who by the Passion of Christ your
   Son, our Lord,
abolished the death inherited from ancient sin
by every succeeding generation,
grant that just as, being conformed to him,
we have borne by the law of nature
the image of the man of earth,
so by the sanctification of grace
we may bear the image of the Man of heaven.
Through Christ our Lord.
Amen.

FOR REFLECTION

• On Good Friday we pause at this moment when Jesus breathes his last and is placed in the tomb. How do you keep the stillness of Good Friday?

Homily Points

• A few days before his crucifixion Jesus gives his disciples a new and cryptic parable, "[U]nless a grain of wheat falls to the ground and dies, it remains just a grain of wheat; but if it dies, it produces much fruit" (John 12:24; NABRE). And now as we are gathered around the foot of the cross we look on as the grain falls to the ground and dies.

• There is a stillness to Good Friday. All the earth witnesses the death of the grain of wheat. And all the earth holds its breath in anticipation of the fruit it will bear.

Gospel Luke 24:1-12; L41ABC

At daybreak on the first day of the week
  the women who had come from Gali-
      lee with Jesus
  took the spices they had prepared
  and went to the tomb.
They found the stone rolled away
      from the tomb;
  but when they entered,
  they did not find the body of
      the Lord Jesus.
While they were puzzling over
    this, behold,
  two men in dazzling garments
      appeared to them.
They were terrified and bowed
      their faces to the ground.
They said to them,
  "Why do you seek the living
      one among the dead?
He is not here, but he has been
      raised.
Remember what he said to
      you while he was still in
      Galilee,
  that the Son of Man must be
      handed over to sinners
  and be crucified, and rise on the
      third day."
And they remembered his words.
Then they returned from the tomb
  and announced all these things to the
      eleven
  and to all the others.
The women were Mary Magdalene,
    Joanna, and Mary the mother of
    James;
  the others who accompanied them
      also told this to the apostles,
  but their story seemed like nonsense
  and they did not believe them.
But Peter got up and ran to the tomb,
  bent down, and saw the burial cloths
      alone;
  then he went home amazed at what
      had happened.

*See Appendix A, pp. 292–97, for the other
readings.*

Reflecting on the Gospel and Living the Paschal Mystery

Key words and phrases: [Empty] tomb, daybreak, women, Mary Magdalene

To the point: Easter morning was a time of confusion. The women who had come with Jesus from Galilee only a few days earlier were now prepared to anoint his crucified, dead body. But they would find instead an empty tomb and two men. Though Luke says they were in dazzling garments, and that has been understood to mean angels, he clearly calls them "men." Matthew, on the other hand, tells his readers that there was an angel who came down from heaven to roll away the stone and then speak to the women, for the guards were struck with fear (Matt 28:1-5). But this is one instance where Matthew has the better story, simply in terms of clearing up any perceived anomalies. Were the men really angels? How was the stone rolled away? Why were there no guards? These are all questions one might rightly ask after reading Luke's account. But in the end Luke's account was not written to convince an unbeliever, but to give "certainty" to the faith of the believer (Luke 1:1-4; NABRE).

The confusion experienced by those early disciples is perhaps something of the confusion we might have upon reading the various narratives of Easter morning. Each evangelist tells the tale with certain differences. Ultimately, each is convinced that Jesus rose from the dead to eternal life.

Despite Jesus' having foretold this event, it seems to have taken the disciples and his friends by surprise. They were not expecting a resurrection after all. Interestingly too, the women are the first to find the empty tomb, and among them, Mary Magdalene. Luke, who is the one evangelist to tell us more stories about women than any other, is also the one to tell us the most about Mary Magdalene. In the first three verses of chapter 8, Luke related how the women from Galilee were providing for Jesus and his followers out of their resources. The women seem to have been wealthy, and this might explain how Jesus and the Twelve could have travelled throughout Galilee during his ministry seemingly without a way to make money. They were being supported by these rich women! Luke also tells us how the women witnessed the events of the crucifixion (Luke 23:49) and saw where his body was laid (Luke 23:55). It should be no surprise then that in Luke's telling it was the women (rather than the disciples) who came upon the empty tomb first. This is why church fathers referred to Mary Magdalene as *apostola apostolorum* (apostle to the apostles). Out of the confusion of Easter morning, Mary Magdalene and her female companions were the first to preach the good news.

To ponder and pray: The ways of God are not our ways. How often do we make plans, have expectations, and firm ideas only to have them dashed? With hindsight we can see more clearly that perhaps our understanding of a situation was not entirely complete. We lacked a critical piece of information or a crucial perspective. This might be something similar to what happened with the disciples and the women who followed Jesus from Galilee. The first to make sense of the empty tomb were the women, and it's likely because they had accompanied Jesus throughout this time. Not only that, they witnessed the crucifixion and the deposition of the body. They returned after Passover to perform a kind of ministry and their expectations were shattered. Soon they "remembered his words" and ran to announce the good news to the eleven and the others. On this Easter morning let us sit before the empty tomb, ponder his words, then go out to announce the good news. In so doing, we will follow the example of the earliest apostles, the women followers of Jesus.

Model Universal Prayer (Prayer of the Faithful)

Presider: With Easter joy we lift up our prayers to the God of light and life.

Response: Lord, hear our prayer.

That the church embody the good news of the gospel that life is stronger than death, light is stronger than darkness, and love is stronger than hatred . . .

That all the peoples of the world be drawn together in peace and communion . . .

That those who have been baptized this night might know the light and love of Jesus alive within them, now and always . . .

That all gathered here, renewed in our baptismal promises, might go forward to be light which brightens the darkness of our world . . .

Presider: God of everlasting life and light, throughout history you have led your people from darkness to light, from death to life, from despair to joy. Hear our prayers on this holy night that we might proclaim the good news of the resurrection with our lives. Through Christ our Lord. **Amen.**

About Liturgy

Why darkness matters: One of the most important directives to come from the restoration of the Triduum liturgies is that the entire Easter Vigil must take place after nightfall (Roman Missal, Easter Vigil 3). Prior to this, it was not uncommon for parishes to celebrate the Easter Vigil on Holy Saturday morning. Imagine lighting the paschal fire in the bright of day, proclaiming how the light of Christ has dispelled the darkness! No wonder so many parishes have become content with tiny paschal fires. When darkness doesn't matter, neither does the fire.

Today, most parishes wait until the evening. However many of these will still begin their vigil while daylight remains on the horizon. Though it may technically be nightfall, the intent of the lighting of the paschal fire is clear. We must show fully by our symbols how the light of Christ has dispelled not just partial darkness but the complete and overwhelming darkness of death, a darkness we cannot control.

The exact time for total darkness depends on your location. So check your local sunset timetables. Also turn off any unnecessary exterior lights near the place of your paschal fire.

Let us pray.

Pause for silent prayer

O God, who make this most sacred night radiant with the glory of the Lord's Resurrection, stir up in your Church a spirit of adoption, so that, renewed in body and mind, we may render you undivided service. Through our Lord Jesus Christ, your Son, who lives and reigns with you in the unity of the Holy Spirit, one God, for ever and ever. **Amen.**

FOR REFLECTION

• "Why do you seek the living one among the dead?" the men in dazzling garments ask. How is God calling you to new life and to embrace the good news of the resurrection?

• Lent is over and the Easter season of joy and celebration has begun. How will you keep this season?

Homily Points

• Tonight we gather to sit vigil and hear the story of salvation proclaimed anew. From the seven days of creation, to the crossing of the Red Sea, to the voices of the prophets, we listen to the greatest love story ever told. God, who created the world and proclaimed it good, continues to redeem and restore it when darkness, death, and despair threaten to destroy everything.

• The waters of baptism are blessed tonight after we hear St. Paul tell us, "Are you unaware that we who were baptized into Christ Jesus / were baptized into his death?" This hardly seems to be the triumphant proclamation of Easter, until we hear the words of the mysterious men at the empty tomb who ask the women, "Why do you seek the living one among the dead? / He is not here, but he has been raised." Death does not have the last word. We are baptized into the death of Christ and so rise with him in the light of the resurrection. Alleluia!

GOSPEL ACCLAMATION
cf. 1 Cor 5:7b-8a

R⁊. Alleluia, alleluia.
Christ, our paschal lamb, has been sacrificed;
let us then feast with joy in the Lord.
R⁊. Alleluia, alleluia.

Gospel

John 20:1-9; L42ABC

On the first day of the week,
Mary of Magdala came to the tomb
early in the morning,
while it was still dark,
and saw the stone removed from
the tomb.
So she ran and went to Simon Peter
and to the other disciple whom
Jesus loved, and told them,
"They have taken the Lord from
the tomb,
and we don't know where they
put him."
So Peter and the other disciple
went out and came to the
tomb.
They both ran, but the other dis-
ciple ran faster than Peter
and arrived at the tomb first;
he bent down and saw the burial
cloths there, but did not go in.
When Simon Peter arrived after him,
he went into the tomb and saw the
burial cloths there,
and the cloth that had covered his
head,
not with the burial cloths but rolled
up in a separate place.
Then the other disciple also went in,
the one who had arrived at the tomb
first,
and he saw and believed.
For they did not yet understand the
Scripture
that he had to rise from the dead.

or

Luke 24:1-12; L41C *in Appendix A, p. 298,*

or, at an afternoon or evening Mass
Luke 24:13-35; L46 *in Appendix A, p. 298.*

See Appendix A, p. 299, for the other readings.

Reflecting on the Gospel and Living the Paschal Mystery

Key words and phrases: Mary of Magdala, rise from the dead, [empty] tomb, disciple whom Jesus loved

To the point: The Fourth Gospel gives us many takes on the stories about the life and ministry of Jesus. Now with the story of the discovery of the empty tomb we have another story. Though Luke tells us that Mary Magdalene (in the Gospel of John: Mary of Magdala) and other women were the first to encounter the empty tomb, that story also had two men "in dazzling garments" speaking to the women. In John's account Mary seems to be alone, and upon finding the stone turned away, she runs to Simon Peter and the disciple whom Jesus loved. We need to read further in the gospel than what we hear in today's liturgy to find out more about Mary's role on that morning. The gospel reading for today is content to have Mary fetch Peter and the other disciple. We hear no more about her.

And though Luke tells us in one verse, which happens to be missing from many ancient manuscripts, that Peter found the tomb empty, John tells us that he was accompanied by the disciple whom Jesus loved. And it is he, this latter disciple, who is the first to believe, even though neither he nor Peter at that time understood the Scripture about rising from the dead. So this becomes something of a model of faith. We, like the beloved disciple, believe before we understand completely. Upon believing, we spend the rest of our lives contemplating the mystery of faith. And like the Beloved Disciple we are led to faith by another, in this case Mary of Magdala. She is the one who indicates that the stone was rolled away. She points to something that needs to be explored, investigated. And once the Beloved Disciple has that encounter the response is faith.

To ponder and pray: How often do we say yes before completely understanding the ramifications of our assent? How often does something simply feel right and we dive in before we have a complete picture of what's at stake? That might happen upon falling in love, having a child, or making another sort of life commitment. Once made, these decisions and commitments alter the course of our lives.

In the case of the Beloved Disciple, once he encountered the empty tomb he believed even before he understood. It's quite likely that he spent the rest of his life pondering the events of Jesus' life, death, and ultimate resurrection, drawing connections between the Scriptures and what he had witnessed. The entirety of Jesus is something we can never fully comprehend or understand, much like we can never fully comprehend or understand any human being. At the center of each is mystery.

On this Easter Day, let us sit with Simon Peter and the Beloved Disciple in the empty tomb, having been drawn there by Mary. Let us ponder the meaning of this extraordinary event and believe. We have the rest of our lives to unpack and better understand what that entails.

Model Penitential Act

Presider: Christ is risen, alleluia! We gather together on this feast of life that is stronger than death and ask the Lord to bring light to the darkness within us. . . [*pause*]

   Lord Jesus, you rose from the tomb, conquering death forever: Lord, have mercy.
   Christ Jesus, you call us to proclaim the Good News to everyone we meet: Christ, have mercy.
   Lord Jesus, you reign at the right hand of God: Lord, have mercy.

Model Universal Prayer (Prayer of the Faithful)

Presider: On this day of joy, we dare to bring our needs and petitions to the God of everlasting life.

Response: Lord, hear our prayer.

That the leaders of the church be examples of faith and hope for all those who doubt . . .

That the world be renewed by the light and life of Christ . . .

That all those who were baptized at the Easter Vigil experience the abundant life of the risen Lord . . .

That all gathered here be strengthened in our baptismal vocation to proclaim Christ to everyone we meet . . .

Presider: God of light and life, you called us by name and washed us clean in the waters of baptism. May we grow more Christlike with each day. We ask this through your son Jesus, our Lord. **Amen.**

About Liturgy

Endings and beginnings: Triduum doesn't end after the Easter Vigil or even after the Masses on Easter Sunday. The three days of the Triduum are counted from nightfall on Thursday to nightfall on Friday (day 1); nightfall Friday to nightfall Saturday (day 2); and nightfall Saturday to nightfall Sunday (day 3). Thus, the General Norms of the Liturgical Year and the Calendar says that the Triduum ends with evening prayer on Easter Sunday (19).

You will probably be exhausted by the time Easter Sunday comes, and having one more liturgy to prepare really isn't feasible. But consider giving your parishioners a simplified Evening Prayer outline to use at home on Sunday night to end the Triduum. This can be as simple as giving them the words of Psalm 118, a brief Scripture reading, and the text for the *Magnificat*. When people gather for Easter dinner at home on this day, they can use this to conclude the three days in a simple but prayerful way.

Easter Sunday also begins the Easter Octave, eight days of solemnities that extend the joy of Easter Sunday. Be sure to highlight the special nature of these daily Masses of the octave.

COLLECT
Let us pray.

Pause for silent prayer

O God, who on this day,
through your Only Begotten Son,
have conquered death
and unlocked for us the path to eternity,
grant, we pray, that we who keep
the solemnity of the Lord's Resurrection
may, through the renewal brought by your Spirit,
rise up in the light of life.
Through our Lord Jesus Christ, your Son,
who lives and reigns with you in the unity of
   the Holy Spirit,
one God, for ever and ever. **Amen.**

FOR REFLECTION

• At the empty tomb the Beloved Disciple believes but does not yet understand. What mysteries of faith do you lack understanding of? How might God be calling you to strengthen your belief?

• How are you being called to live deeper into this mystery of life coming from death?

Homily Points

• Peter and the Beloved Disciple race to the tomb and once they arrive find it empty except for the burial cloths. These trappings of death lie in the tomb but the body they swaddled is nowhere to be found. These mysterious happenings hint that the story of Jesus' life is not over, but the disciples "[do] not yet understand the Scripture / that he had to rise from the dead." Today we gather with cries of "Alleluia, he is risen!" But the question remains for us, do we, even now, nearly two thousand years after the event, understand the rising from the dead?

• Surely, it defies understanding. How can one who has been confirmed dead and lain within a tomb for three days be "raised"? How can life return stronger than death? And yet, we are resurrection people, called to proclaim the death and resurrection of Christ in our words, actions, and very being. If we truly believe in this audacious event it changes everything.

SEASON OF EASTER

SPIRITUALITY

GOSPEL ACCLAMATION
John 20:29

R⁊. Alleluia, alleluia.
You believe in me, Thomas, because you have
    seen me, says the Lord;
blessed are those who have not seen me, but still
    believe!
R⁊. Alleluia, alleluia.

Gospel   John 20:19-31; L45C

On the evening of that first day of the
    week,
    when the doors were locked, where
        the disciples were,
    for fear of the Jews,
    Jesus came and stood in their midst
    and said to them, "Peace be with
        you."
When he had said this, he showed them
    his hands and his side.
The disciples rejoiced when they saw
    the Lord.
Jesus said to them again, "Peace be
    with you.
As the Father has sent me, so I send you."
And when he had said this, he breathed
    on them and said to them,
    "Receive the Holy Spirit.
Whose sins you forgive are forgiven them,
    and whose sins you retain are retained."

Thomas, called Didymus, one of the
    Twelve,
    was not with them when Jesus came.
So the other disciples said to him, "We
    have seen the Lord."
But he said to them,
    "Unless I see the mark of the nails in
        his hands
    and put my finger into the nailmarks
    and put my hand into his side, I will
        not believe."

Now a week later his disciples were again
    inside
    and Thomas was with them.
Jesus came, although the doors were locked,
    and stood in their midst and said,
        "Peace be with you."

Continued in Appendix A, p. 299.

Reflecting on the Gospel

The Second Sunday of Easter, which the church calls Divine Mercy Sunday, is punctuated by a reading from John, the conclusion of that gospel. Of course, if we open our Bibles we will see that there is another chapter (John 21) that follows this conclusion (John 20:30-31), but that chapter is usually referred to as an epilogue, as it was written later by another author. Indeed, simply reading the closing verses of today's gospel gives one the sense that the story is over, the gospel is complete. Thomas makes a christological claim *par excellence*, addressing Jesus as, "My Lord and my God!" With that, the gospel rightfully and elegantly comes to a close. How strange it is that there is yet another chapter! Yes, that's the epilogue.

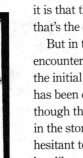

But in today's gospel reading Thomas encounters the risen Christ the week after the initial resurrection appearance. He has been called "doubting Thomas," even though the word "doubt" does not appear in the story. Still, it's clear Thomas was hesitant to believe. More than one preacher has likened Thomas's attitude to a "show me" skepticism. His belief is conditioned on physically inspecting the risen Christ. And yet, the story does not say that when given the opportunity Thomas actually probed the nail marks or put his hand in Jesus' side. Instead, upon encountering the risen Christ he immediately proclaims, "My Lord and my God!" What the reader has known from the opening verses of the gospel—"In the beginning was the Word, / and the Word was with God, / and the Word was God. . . . And the Word became flesh" (John 1:1, 14; NABRE)—is effectively proclaimed by a human being, Thomas. Then Jesus appropriately has the last word, and the gospel concludes with two verses from the author.

Moreover, it is significant that Roman historians tell us that the emperor Domitian (r. 81–96) gave himself the title, "Dominus et Deus" (Lord and God; cf. Suetonius, Domitian 13.2). If the author of the Gospel of John knew about this imperial claim, he would be effectively undermining it by showing that Jesus is the true Lord and God. The Gospel of John has a profound Christology. The closing verses of chapter 20 give us some indication as to why.

Living the Paschal Mystery

In the Fourth Gospel, knowledge of Jesus as the Son of God, the Word made flesh, is fundamental to being a disciple. In some ways, belief is as important as another commandment in the Gospel of John: love. This axis of belief and love informs our identity as disciples as well. In many ways it is a fine summation of the Christian life, bypassing other terms like "righteousness," "Trinity," and other theologically sophisticated words. Once we believe in the Son of God and love one another as he loves us, our life is complete. We then unfold this relationship day after day, week after week, month after month, and year after year. Neither "belief" nor "love" know fulfillment. There is always more, there is always a frontier, a horizon we never reach. As human beings we can never achieve perfect belief or perfect love. But the pursuit of both is lifelong. On this Second Sunday of Easter when we encounter divine mercy, we recall the simplicity yet profundity of the gospel message: Believe and love.

Focusing the Gospel

Key words and phrases: Peace be with you.

To the point: In our gospel passage today Jesus speaks the words "Peace be with you" three times. When we hear the word "peace," we often think of it as the absence of war or conflict, but the meaning of *shalom* (the Hebrew word for peace) denotes the presence of something instead of an absence. To offer someone peace in Jesus' time meant to wish him or her a completeness and fullness of life. Earlier in John's gospel Jesus proclaims that he has come that we "might have life and have it more abundantly" (10:10; NABRE). Despite the locks the disciples had placed upon the door, Jesus enters the room in which they are barricaded and says to them, "Peace be with you." Their fear cannot keep him away. Once again he stands before them, offering them abundant life.

Connecting the Gospel

to the first reading: Throughout the Easter season we read the Acts of the Apostles, the story of the early church. In today's first reading we hear of the fruitfulness of the apostle's evangelizing mission in which many men and women are added to their number and people are cured, but also of the persecution they undergo when they are put in jail. But just as Jesus passes through locked doors unimpeded, the apostles cannot be contained by a jail cell. The angel of the Lord opens the prison doors and leads them out.

to experience: Fear, anger, and jealousy are no match for the love, peace, and mercy of God. God's spirit of love and peace breaks down barriers and calls us to true communion with one another.

Connecting the Responsorial Psalm

to the readings: As we did on Easter Sunday, again we hear the triumphant chant of Psalm 118. The psalm begins with a litany whose response is "His mercy endures forever." In the gospel we see that God's mercy indeed endures forever, even beyond the grave and the end of earthly life. Jesus returns to his disciples and the first words he speaks to them are, "Peace be with you." This might not have been the greeting they expected. During Jesus' passion and crucifixion Peter had denied knowing him three times, and we only hear of one man, the unnamed Beloved Disciple who is present at the foot of the cross. But far from anger or bitterness, Jesus greets his closest followers with joy and love. "Peace be with you." And thus redeemed, Jesus invites them to become instruments of mercy, "Whose sins you forgive are forgiven them, / and whose sins you retain are retained."

to psalmist preparation: Today is a day of exultation. In the death and resurrection of Jesus, the paschal mystery, we have been offered everlasting life and freedom from sin. The divine mercy of our God is the balm our broken world desperately craves. As you lead the assembly in prayer today, pray for mercy to cover the earth.

PROMPTS FOR FAITH-SHARING

In today's first reading the apostles carry on the work of Jesus, performing signs and wonders as the Holy Spirit enables them. We are also called to carry on Jesus' work. How do you proclaim the good news of the resurrection in your everyday life?

_____

_____

_____

_____

Jesus tells the disciples, "Peace be with you," three times in today's gospel. Where in your life are you in need of the peace of the Lord?

_____

_____

_____

_____

How do you offer peace to others through your words and actions?

_____

_____

_____

_____

We are offered mercy and also instructed to offer it to others. Who is in need of mercy in your life? How might you offer them this gift?

_____

_____

_____

_____

Model Rite for the Blessing and Sprinkling of Water

Presider: In the waters of baptism we have been buried with Christ, the one who tells St. John in Revelation, "I am the first and the last, the one who lives." May this water remind us of the life that conquers death . . . [*pause*]

[*continue with* The Roman Missal, *Appendix II*]

Homily Points

• Today is not only the Second Sunday of Easter but also the completion of the octave of Easter and the feast of Divine Mercy. In the year 2000, St. Pope John Paul II established this feast. On the first anniversary of the founding of Divine Mercy Sunday, John Paul II recalled, "Jesus said to St. Faustina one day: 'Humanity will never find peace until it turns with trust to Divine Mercy.' Divine Mercy! This is the Easter gift that the Church receives from the risen Christ and offers to humanity."

• Jesus enters the room where the apostles are hiding in fear and offers them peace, the peace of God that surpasses understanding (Phil 4:7). And then he gives them a commission, "Receive the Holy Spirit. / Whose sins you forgive are forgiven them, / and whose sins you retain are retained." The apostles are not offered peace merely for themselves. In receiving this peace they are in turn to bear peace to others.

• In the spiritual life every action begins with God's initiative. God speaks and we listen. God gives a gift and we receive it. Only after God's action can we form a response. On Divine Mercy Sunday we must celebrate this twofold movement. God offers us Divine Mercy, which we are invited to receive and then pass on to others. Individually in our lives and collectively as the church, the Body of Christ, we experience mercy as a transformational gift from God. Now it's our job to offer it to humanity.

Model Universal Prayer (Prayer of the Faithful)

Presider: Jesus greets the disciples gathered in the upper room, "Peace be with you." In confidence we pray for the peace of the Lord.

Response: Lord, hear our prayer.

That the church might have the resources to deal with conflict in grace . . .

That leaders of the world band together to forge lasting peace . . .

That refugees from war-torn countries find welcome, shelter, and safety in their new homes . . .

That all of us gathered here know the peace of the Lord that banishes all fear . . .

Presider: God of mercy and love, you call us to live in harmony with one another. Show us the path of peace. We offer our prayers through Christ our Lord. **Amen.**

COLLECT

Let us pray.

Pause for silent prayer

God of everlasting mercy,
who in the very recurrence of the paschal feast
kindle the faith of the people you have made your own,
increase, we pray, the grace you have bestowed,
that all may grasp and rightly understand
in what font they have been washed,
by whose Spirit they have been reborn,
by whose Blood they have been redeemed.
Through our Lord Jesus Christ, your Son,
who lives and reigns with you in the unity of the Holy Spirit,
one God, for ever and ever. **Amen.**

FIRST READING

Acts 5:12-16

Many signs and wonders were done among the people
at the hands of the apostles.
They were all together in Solomon's portico.
None of the others dared to join them, but the people esteemed them.
Yet more than ever, believers in the Lord, great numbers of men and women,
were added to them.
Thus they even carried the sick out into the streets
and laid them on cots and mats
so that when Peter came by,
at least his shadow might fall on one or another of them.
A large number of people from the towns in the vicinity of Jerusalem also gathered,
bringing the sick and those disturbed by unclean spirits,
and they were all cured.

RESPONSORIAL PSALM

Ps 118:2-4, 13-15, 22-24

R̸. (1) Give thanks to the Lord for he is good, his love is everlasting.
or:
R̸. Alleluia.

Let the house of Israel say,
"His mercy endures forever."
Let the house of Aaron say,
"His mercy endures forever."
Let those who fear the LORD say,
"His mercy endures forever."

R̸. Give thanks to the Lord for he is good, his love is everlasting.
or:
R̸. Alleluia.

I was hard pressed and was falling,
  but the LORD helped me.
My strength and my courage is the LORD,
  and he has been my savior.
The joyful shout of victory
  in the tents of the just.

R̸. Give thanks to the Lord for he is good,
  his love is everlasting.
    or:
R̸. Alleluia.

The stone which the builders rejected
  has become the cornerstone.
By the LORD has this been done;
  it is wonderful in our eyes.
This is the day the LORD has made;
  let us be glad and rejoice in it.

R̸. Give thanks to the Lord for he is good,
  his love is everlasting.
    or:
R̸. Alleluia.

SECOND READING
Rev 1:9-11a, 12-13, 17-19

I, John, your brother, who share with you
  the distress, the kingdom, and the
    endurance we have in Jesus,
  found myself on the island called
    Patmos
  because I proclaimed God's word and
    gave testimony to Jesus.
I was caught up in spirit on the Lord's day
  and heard behind me a voice as loud as
    a trumpet, which said,
  "Write on a scroll what you see."
Then I turned to see whose voice it was
  that spoke to me,
  and when I turned, I saw seven gold
    lampstands
  and in the midst of the lampstands one
    like a son of man,
  wearing an ankle-length robe, with a
    gold sash around his chest.

When I caught sight of him, I fell down at
  his feet as though dead.
He touched me with his right hand and
  said, "Do not be afraid.
I am the first and the last, the one who
  lives.
Once I was dead, but now I am alive
  forever and ever.
I hold the keys to death and the
  netherworld.
Write down, therefore, what you have
  seen,
  and what is happening, and what will
    happen afterwards."

CATECHESIS

About Liturgy

Putting on our "mystagoggles": In all three cycles of the Lectionary, the Second Sunday of Easter presents to us this gospel passage from John that recalls Thomas's conversion from skeptical doubter to professor of faith. I can think of no other non-thematic Sunday that has the same gospel every year. What might this mean?

I think the key is Jesus' final statement: "Blessed are those who have not seen and have believed" (John 20:29). He's talking about *us*! This is a blessing specifically for *us*! None of the disciples who walked with Jesus are as blessed as we who have never seen him face to face. This is the blessing of faith—to believe not with our eyes but with our heart. When you love a person completely and know that you are completely loved, everything looks different. The sky is bluer, the daylight clearer, even the people you meet on the street seem friendlier. Is it because the world has changed? No, you have changed. You've been given a new way of seeing so that you see all creation as God sees it—blessed. You've been given mystagoggles!

The church teaches that during the period of mystagogy, the newly baptized "derive a new perception of the faith, of the Church, and of the world" out of their experience of the sacraments, and this new way of seeing "increases as it is lived" (RCIA 245). The neophytes, fresh from the font, can't help but see Christ everywhere, just as newlyweds can see and think of only their beloved. But for us who may not be so fresh in our faith, our "mystagoggles" might have clouded, and we sound more like Thomas the skeptic than Thomas the believer.

The Easter season is a time for all of us with the neophytes to train our eyes to see the world sacramentally. When we put on our "mystagoggles," every meal is the supper of the Lord, every wound is the brand mark of Christ, and every moment of doubt is an invitation to cry in faith, "My Lord and my God!"

About Initiation

Postbaptismal catechesis: The catechesis that takes place during this period of mystagogy is unlike the catechesis during the catechumenate in that "its main setting is the so-called Masses for neophytes, that is, the Sunday Masses of the Easter season" (RCIA 247). Let the Sunday Masses this Easter season be the primary gathering for your neophytes and their godparents, and be sure that these Masses are the best of the year, for they are how the neophytes are catechized to live as new "Christs" in the world.

About Liturgical Music

Easter's long tail: The first few weeks of the Easter season revel in the joy of the Resurrection. These weeks are a bit like the temporary high you feel from a mountaintop experience. As the season progresses, that joy is transformed into a more constant and steadfast call to witness and mission into the world driven by the Spirit. As you prepare your music and music ministers, keep in mind that the Triduum was not the final objective for all your liturgical efforts this year. Rather, it was the summit that now propels us toward Pentecost and beyond. Help your music ministers keep their focus toward that goal so that the energy you inspired from them in the Triduum keeps building throughout the weeks of Easter.

A delightful antiphon to use for Communion today is *Psallite*'s "Put Your Hand Here, Thomas." Pairing these words with the act of sharing in the Body and Blood of Christ deepens our view of whom we are receiving and what we are called to do in faith.

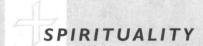

SPIRITUALITY

GOSPEL ACCLAMATION

℟. Alleluia, alleluia.
Christ is risen, creator of all;
he has shown pity on all people.
℟. Alleluia, alleluia.

Gospel John 21:1-19; L48C

At that time, Jesus revealed himself
    again to his disciples at the Sea of
    Tiberias.
He revealed himself in this way.
Together were Simon Peter, Thomas
    called Didymus,
    Nathanael from Cana in Galilee,
    Zebedee's sons, and two others of his
    disciples.
Simon Peter said to them, "I am going
    fishing."
They said to him, "We also will come
    with you."
So they went out and got into the boat,
    but that night they caught nothing.
When it was already dawn, Jesus was
    standing on the shore;
    but the disciples did not realize that it
    was Jesus.
Jesus said to them, "Children, have you
    caught anything to eat?"
They answered him, "No."
So he said to them, "Cast the net over the
    right side of the boat
    and you will find something."
So they cast it, and were not able to pull
    it in
    because of the number of fish.
So the disciple whom Jesus loved said to
    Peter, "It is the Lord."
When Simon Peter heard that it was the
    Lord,
    he tucked in his garment, for he was
        lightly clad,
    and jumped into the sea.
The other disciples came in the boat,
    for they were not far from shore, only
        about a hundred yards,
    dragging the net with the fish.

Continued in Appendix A, p. 300.

or John 21:1-14

Reflecting on the Gospel

Last week we read from the conclusion of John's gospel. Today we read from the epilogue, the chapter that follows the conclusion. Scholars refer to John 21 as the epilogue in part because it is markedly different from the preceding chapters in some vocabulary and in style. In fact, it is so different that it was likely written by a different author to address, in part, realities that had emerged in the decades following the initial composition of the gospel.

Today's reading incorporates two stories: one of the appearance on the seashore, followed by another of the rehabilitation of Peter. The Beloved Disciple, who remains nameless, is the first to recognize Jesus with the proclamation, "It is the Lord" (John 21:7). This is an echo of the discovery of the empty tomb when, even though Peter was the first to go into the empty tomb, the Beloved Disciple "saw and believed" (John 20:8; NABRE). The Beloved Disciple is portrayed as the true model of discipleship. And he does not appear in any other gospel!

Another nod to earlier stories in the Gospel of John includes the mention of a "charcoal fire," as that is the place where Peter denied Jesus three times (John 18:18; NABRE). The presence of a charcoal fire here sets the stage, narratively speaking, for his threefold rehabilitation. Three times Jesus asks Peter, "Do you love me?" and three times Peter responds affirmatively. This three-time inquisition is quite obviously a retort to Peter's threefold denial during the passion. After the Beloved Disciple died, the Johannine community—for whom the Beloved Disciple was a model of discipleship—was coming to recognize their role in the greater Christian world, which was led (at least figuratively) by Peter. But the last story we heard about Peter was his denial of Christ. Thus, the epilogue, the additional chapter following the conclusion, tells the story of Peter's rehabilitation. Peter represents the larger Christian community. Though he denied Jesus, unlike the Beloved Disciple who was the ideal, Peter was effectively forgiven and placed in a leadership role. Thus in the Christian imagination, Peter represents the ideals and realities of discipleship. No Christian community is an island unto itself. Even leaders can stumble; when they do they can be forgiven by Jesus himself. Such is the power of the risen Christ.

Living the Paschal Mystery

Sometimes it's easy to imagine the saints and disciples as those who had it all figured out. But today's gospel reminds us otherwise. Even now, a time after the resurrection, the disciples are fishing. They do not seem to be about the business of preaching or teaching. Instead, they have gone back to what they were doing before they met Jesus. One nameless disciple recognizes Jesus and his proclamation causes Peter to jump into the water and swim to the seashore to meet Jesus. Jesus does not harangue or scold Peter for the weakness he showed during the passion. Instead, Jesus asks him three times whether he loves him. And three times Peter says yes, though clearly becoming a bit agitated. But in so doing, Jesus rehabilitates Peter and gives each subsequent Christian the hope and promise of rehabilitation when we fall short too. The saints and disciples were real human beings with faults and shortcomings. Jesus did not choose perfect human beings. Rather, he chose disciples, those who would follow him. And he chose us too. Our task is to follow. When we fall short Jesus will be there for us too.

Focusing the Gospel

Key words and phrases: Do you love me?; Feed my lambs

To the point: Jesus asks Peter three times, "Do you love me?" Each time Peter answers him in the affirmative, Jesus gives him an action in which to show his love: feed my lambs, tend my sheep, feed my sheep. Next Sunday (commonly known as Good Shepherd Sunday) we will read from chapter 10 of John's gospel where Jesus proclaims, "I am the good shepherd." Now Jesus calls on Peter to continue his work. He might have denied Jesus three times during the passion, but now, in his proclamations of love, Peter is called to serve Jesus by serving those Jesus loved, by feeding and tending the lambs of the Good Shepherd.

Connecting the Gospel

to the first reading: Peter is true to his word. In the first reading from the Acts of the Apostles we hear yet another instance of his care and ministry to the early church. Peter feeds Jesus' "sheep" by witnessing to them about the good news of Jesus of Nazareth who has been exalted at the right hand of God "as leader and savior / to grant Israel repentance and forgiveness of sins." In his fear Peter might have denied Jesus three times during the passion, but now he gladly undergoes persecution, even flogging. He and his companions accept this treatment by "rejoicing that they had been found worthy / to suffer dishonor for the sake of the name."

to experience: Jesus asks us, "Do you love me?" He invites us to continue his work of caring for and tending the flock of the Lord. How do you tend Jesus' lambs? How do you feed his sheep?

Connecting the Responsorial Psalm

to the readings: There is a temptation in the spiritual life to believe that if we do everything right we will escape hardship and suffering. And yet, we know from experience that this is simply not true. Through no fault of our own, calamity strikes. Today the psalmist reminds us to cling to God when we pass through these moments of despair and darkness: "O Lord, you brought me up from the netherworld; / you preserved me from among those going down into the pit." In the gospel we witness the journey from one state to another. The disciples go from catching nothing all night to filling their nets with such an abundance of fish they fear they might burst. And then, confronted by the Lord of life, Peter's threefold expression of love redeems him from his earlier threefold denial and liberates him from the fear of following in the footsteps of the risen Lord.

to psalmist preparation: We believe in a God who journeys with us through darkness and despair and who will not abandon us in times of trial and suffering. How do you hold onto this hope in your own life?

PROMPTS FOR FAITH-SHARING

In the first reading the apostles, led by Peter, tell the authorities, "We must obey God rather than men." Has there been a time in your life where you needed to take a stand for God's law? How did you find the strength to do so?

Today's psalm proclaims, "O Lord, you brought me up from the netherworld; / you preserved me from among those going down into the pit." What sustains your faith in times of despair?

What groups of people are missing in your parish community? How might the parish become more welcoming for all?

Who are the lambs that Jesus has given you to tend and feed? How do you serve them?

Model Rite for the Blessing and Sprinkling of Water

Presider: In today's gospel, Simon Peter recognizes the risen Lord on the shores of the Sea of Galilee and immediately jumps from his boat into the water. May this sprinkling rite symbolize our own desire to be close to Jesus . . . [*pause*]

> [*continue with* The Roman Missal, *Appendix II*]

Homily Points

• Much has been made of the number 153 in the gospel passage we read from today about the miraculous catch of fish that was so great the disciples were not able to haul the net in, instead dragging it to shore. And yet, the net held. Of all of the theories surrounding what this number might mean, the most popular is from St. Jerome who postulates that at the time of the gospel writing it was believed there were precisely 153 species of fish in the world.

• By including all 153 within the net we see the radical inclusivity of the new covenant. All the people of the world are invited into the net of the church. And even if it seems like this "net" might burst, it will hold; we need not fear inviting everyone.

• There is a tremendous difference between ministering out of fear and ministering out of abundance. A community that ministers from fear will find excuses for why certain people (whether individuals or entire classes and races) cannot be included within its walls. They fear that such diversity will stress the "net" beyond its limits. And yet today we hear that our fears have no place within the expansive vision of God. This net was meant to hold every kind of fish, every kind of person. Today let us pause to consider who is welcome and who is not in our community, in our family, our parish. As Christians, we are all called to carry on the ministry of Christ and today he shows us the way. Out of love, along with St. Peter, we are called to feed Jesus' lambs and to tend his sheep. All of his lambs. All of his sheep.

Model Universal Prayer (Prayer of the Faithful)

Presider: Confident that God provides for all our needs, we lift up our prayers to the Lord.

Response: Lord, hear our prayer.

That the church show her love for God by tenderly feeding and tending Jesus' flock . . .

That all peoples of the world know the love of God who calls them by name and invites them to abundant life . . .

That all those who are persecuted for their religious beliefs find sanctuary and protection . . .

That all gathered here have the strength to follow the law of God when it conflicts with human laws . . .

Presider: Gracious God, you sustain us in life and provide us with everything we need. Help us to trust in your loving care. We ask this through Christ our Lord. **Amen.**

COLLECT
Let us pray.

Pause for silent prayer

May your people exult for ever, O God,
in renewed youthfulness of spirit,
so that, rejoicing now in the restored glory
    of our adoption,
we may look forward in confident hope
to the rejoicing of the day of resurrection.
Through our Lord Jesus Christ, your Son,
who lives and reigns with you in the unity
    of the Holy Spirit,
one God, for ever and ever. **Amen.**

FIRST READING
Acts 5:27-32, 40b-41

When the captain and the court officers had
    brought the apostles in
  and made them stand before the
    Sanhedrin,
  the high priest questioned them,
  "We gave you strict orders, did we not,
  to stop teaching in that name?
Yet you have filled Jerusalem with your
    teaching
  and want to bring this man's blood
    upon us."
But Peter and the apostles said in reply,
  "We must obey God rather than men.
The God of our ancestors raised Jesus,
  though you had him killed by hanging
    him on a tree.
God exalted him at his right hand as
    leader and savior
  to grant Israel repentance and
    forgiveness of sins.
We are witnesses of these things,
  as is the Holy Spirit whom God has given
    to those who obey him."

The Sanhedrin ordered the apostles
  to stop speaking in the name of Jesus,
    and dismissed them.
So they left the presence of the Sanhedrin,
  rejoicing that they had been found
    worthy
  to suffer dishonor for the sake of the
    name.

RESPONSORIAL PSALM
Ps 30:2, 4, 5-6, 11-12, 13

R̸. (2a) I will praise you, Lord, for you
    have rescued me.
  or
R̸. Alleluia.

I will extol you, O LORD, for you drew me
    clear
  and did not let my enemies rejoice over
    me.

O LORD, you brought me up from the
    netherworld;
  you preserved me from among those
    going down into the pit.

R℣. I will praise you, Lord, for you have
    rescued me.
or
R℣. Alleluia.

Sing praise to the LORD, you his faithful
    ones,
  and give thanks to his holy name.
For his anger lasts but a moment;
  a lifetime, his good will.
At nightfall, weeping enters in,
  but with the dawn, rejoicing.

R℣. I will praise you, Lord, for you have
    rescued me.
or
R℣. Alleluia.

Hear, O LORD, and have pity on me;
  O LORD, be my helper.
You changed my mourning into dancing;
  O LORD, my God, forever will I give you
    thanks.

R℣. I will praise you, Lord, for you have
    rescued me.
or
R℣. Alleluia.

SECOND READING
Rev 5:11-14

I, John, looked and heard the voices of
    many angels
  who surrounded the throne
  and the living creatures and the elders.
They were countless in number, and they
    cried out in a loud voice:
    "Worthy is the Lamb that was
      slain
      to receive power and riches,
        wisdom and strength,
        honor and glory and blessing."
Then I heard every creature in heaven and
    on earth
  and under the earth and in the sea,
  everything in the universe, cry out:
    "To the one who sits on the throne
      and to the Lamb
      be blessing and honor, glory and
        might,
      forever and ever."
The four living creatures answered,
    "Amen,"
  and the elders fell down and worshiped.

About Liturgy

Companions at table: How many of your most significant moments in life have taken place at a meal? There's something about sharing food and drink that enables us to share our innermost selves as well with the others at that table. In the same vein, how difficult it is to spend even one moment at a meal with someone who has hurt you.

How remarkable then is this breakfast at the seashore! Over a charcoal fire with a piece of fish and a bit of bread, the risen Christ reveals his true self to the one who betrayed him. Instead of resentful words that reprimand, Jesus gives to Peter words of mercy and trust: "Feed my lambs." Christ does not keep score; there is no logbook in heaven recording our every sin. There is only an empty seat at Jesus' table waiting for us to sit down and be fed, forgiven, and sent once again.

This is what we mean by being companions at the Lord's table. We are those who break bread with one another. Recognizing that all of us are sinners before God, we share our brokenness and the brokenness of the world with Christ and with one another at the altar. In return Christ takes these broken pieces of our lives and mends them together, multiplying them into an abundance of blessing for those in need of mercy. In grateful response to this healing, we say "Amen" to the cup of sacrifice and the new covenant, a sharing in the Blood of Christ that will lead us where we might not want to go. Yet we do not go alone. Our companions around the heavenly and earthly altars go with us.

Pope Francis said, "All family life is a 'shepherding' in mercy. Each of us, by our love and care, leaves a mark on the life of others" (*Amoris Laetitia* 322). In our homes, there is a table where every day, over a bit of bread, we have the opportunity to shepherd and feed our companions in mercy, forgiveness, courage, and love.

About Initiation

Found worthy to suffer: In the period of the catechumenate, the RCIA says that the formation of catechumens in the discipline of living as part of the Christian community will lead them to "experience divisions and separations" because "the Lord in whom they believe is a sign of contradiction" (RCIA 75.2). As the neophytes continue on their mystagogical journey, today might be a good opportunity to help them reflect on how they may have been "found worthy / to suffer dishonor for the sake of the name" (Acts 5:41) and how their sharing in the Eucharist with the faithful strengthen and encourage them even in moments of discord.

About Liturgical Music

Singing during Communion: Music ministers serve as an example for the assembly when they are seen singing in procession to share in Communion. Be sure that as your music ministers come forward to share in the Eucharist, the music and singing continue. This will require that the music you choose for Communion is familiar and accessible enough for the assembly to take the lead even when the choir is not standing in their usual place singing. It also means that the assembly may need to sing *a cappella* for a few moments while your accompanist and instrumentalists share in Communion as well.

To help the assembly take the musical lead, choose songs that have simple refrains that can be repeated several times, as with Taizé refrains. One such refrain is *Psallite*'s "If You Love Me, Feed My Lambs," which has two different textual versions for this Sunday.

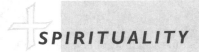

SPIRITUALITY

GOSPEL ACCLAMATION
John 10:14

R✒. Alleluia, alleluia.
I am the good shepherd, says the Lord;
I know my sheep, and mine know me.
R✒. Alleluia, alleluia.

Gospel

John 10:27-30; L51C

Jesus said:
"My sheep hear my voice;
   I know them, and they follow me.
I give them eternal life, and they shall
      never perish.
No one can take them out of my hand.
My Father, who has given them to me,
      is greater than all,
   and no one can take them out of the
         Father's hand.
The Father and I are one."

Reflecting on the Gospel

Though we are in Cycle C (the Gospel of Luke), today we have another reading from the Gospel of John. Each week since Easter we have read from this gospel. Today we read not about a resurrection appearance but instead we hear about the familiar, comforting image of Jesus as the Good Shepherd. We are his sheep who hear his voice and respond by following him. Of course, to follow means to be a disciple, so the image of a shepherd and his sheep is especially apt.

Pope Francis seems to find this image instructive as well. He speaks of the role of bishops and priests to be shepherds (for that is the meaning of the Latin term *pastor*). Pope Francis says that the shepherd must have the "smell of the sheep." Such an image is certainly vivid, graphic, and leaves little to the imagination. It conjures up one who is uncomfortably close to the sheep. But that is essentially the model of the Good Shepherd, and one to be emulated by those who serve.

Not only do we follow the Good Shepherd upon hearing his voice, but we learn that the Good Shepherd gives eternal life.

The symbolism is profound and perhaps even more so because the snippet we read today is so short. The meaning of the words should not be lost in their brevity. The relationship of the sheep to the shepherd is dependent upon the Father and Jesus. The Father has given the sheep to Jesus. No one can take them from the Father or the Son, for the Father and the Son are one. Again, the theological sophistication and the high Christology are worthy of meditation.

Given the symbolism, the task of the sheep is pure and simple, to follow Jesus, to be a disciple. The task of the Father and the Son is not to lose the sheep, or perhaps not to give them up to those who might try to pry open their hands.

Our task, therefore, is no more difficult than following Jesus. To do that we must be attentive to his voice.

Living the Paschal Mystery

It would be easy to follow Jesus if he were physically present here upon the earth, healing the sick and curing the lame. Who wouldn't leave everything to do that? But it's much more difficult to be attentive to the voice of Jesus after the resurrection. And that is precisely what this gospel passage requires of us. We are to listen closely amidst the noise and sound of our world and discern the voice of the Good Shepherd. What is he calling us to do? Where does he want us to go? We would like to follow him, but how to hear his voice?

When we speak do we sound more like we are echoing the gospel or syndicated TV or radio shows? Are we following Christ, attuned to his voice in Scripture? Or are we more closely attuned to the culture, knowing the voice of the more popular media? How we speak and how we act may tell us more about who we are ultimately following. On this Fourth Sunday of Easter it is good to pause and reflect on our path. Whose voice do we follow?

Focusing the Gospel

Key words and phrases: No one can take them out of my hand.

To the point: John's gospel gives us the beloved image of Jesus, the Good Shepherd, who calls his sheep by name and leads them in safety along the pathways of life. In today's gospel passage we hear only a fraction of Jesus' discourse on the Good Shepherd, and yet we are told what is most essential, we are united to Jesus in an unbreakable bond of love. Jesus proclaims, "No one can take [my sheep] out of my hand." In the spiritual life we are called to attune our ears to the voice of our Good Shepherd showing us the way, and to fear not; nothing can separate us from the love of God.

Connecting the Gospel

to the second readings: In the second reading from Revelation we are given a vision of "a great multitude, / which no one could count, / from every nation, race, people, and tongue." It is revealed that this multitude is comprised of the ones who have "survived the time of great distress" and "washed their robes / and made them white in the blood of the Lamb." The early church encountered grave persecution. From the martyrdom of nearly all of the apostles (tradition tells us only John died of old age on the island of Patmos) to the violent campaigns of the Roman government intent on ending the fledgling religion, many would have cause to doubt Jesus' statement that "[n]o one can take them out of my hand." And yet, as the apostle Paul stated in his First Letter to the Corinthians, "O death, where is your victory?" (15:55; NABRE). Our Good Shepherd gives us eternal life. Even death itself cannot separate us from him.

to experience: In joy and in despair we can rely on the voice of the Good Shepherd to lead us.

Connecting the Responsorial Psalm

to the readings: Psalm 100 is an invitation to come before the Lord with joy and thanksgiving knowing who we truly are, "[God's] people, the flock he tends." This simple psalm speaks to our self-understanding as a community dedicated to the Lord. We are not individuals intent on our own personal salvation, but a group of disciples that listens to the Lord in community and comes before him (together) with joy and thanksgiving. The beautiful diversity of the "multitude" in Revelation reveals this to us. Among them are counted "every nation, race, people, and tongue," and yet they sing out in one voice to their God. So may we worship, in one voice, unified in our diversity.

to psalmist preparation: Your voice in song calls the community to come before the Lord with joy and to know they are the flock of God. How do you experience and rejoice in your parish community?

PROMPTS FOR FAITH-SHARING

Psalm 100 tells us we are "[God's] people, the flock he tends." How is your parish community a unified flock, led by the Good Shepherd? How can you strive to embrace even greater unity?

How do you listen for the voice of the Good Shepherd in your daily life?

How is Jesus, the Good Shepherd, calling you to follow him at this moment in your life?

Good Shepherd Sunday is a traditional time to pray for vocations to serve the church. What are some ways you can grow in your vocation, whether to marriage, holy orders, religious life, or single life, over the coming year?

Model Rite for the Blessing and Sprinkling of Water

Presider: In the waters of baptism we entered the church, the sheepfold of the Lord. May this water remind us of the joy of that day and strengthen us in our baptismal promises . . . [*pause*]

  [*continue with* The Roman Missal, *Appendix II]*

Homily Points

• In the gospel today we are given a condensed model of the spiritual life. It involves listening and knowing and following. The sheep of the Good Shepherd listen to his voice. Unlike the voice of strangers, the sheep listen and respond to the voice of their shepherd. They are attuned to his tone and the rhythm of his speech. They find a home within his words. We who belong to the flock of the Lord might ask, how well do we know this voice? How much time do we spend listening to it with love each day? How might we build a home with the Word of God?

• Whether we recognize it or not we are deeply known by this Shepherd. Indeed, he knows us better than we know ourselves. In this knowing there is no shame. We are recognized for who we are as beloved children of God. And we are called to become even more authentically ourselves. The Good Shepherd knows us and calls us by name. Are there pieces of yourself you are still trying to hide from God? It is no use. The psalmist tells us, "My very self you know" (Psalm 139:14; NABRE). Take time to experience yourself as deeply known (and deeply loved) by the Lord of life.

• Only after we have listened to the voice of the Good Shepherd and heard him call us by name can we then follow him. Theologian Sofia Cavalletti wrote, "It is only in love, and not in fear, that one may have a moral life worthy of the name" (*The Religious Potential of the Child*). God does not crave our fearful submission but our loving and joyful collaboration in building the kingdom of God. May we listen, know, and follow.

Model Universal Prayer (Prayer of the Faithful)

Presider: We follow Jesus, the Good Shepherd, who calls us by name and cares for us tenderly, and so we lift up our needs with gratitude and confidence.

Response: Lord, hear our prayer.

That the church be sustained and buoyed through an increase in vocations to the religious life and holy orders . . .

That every nation of the world might hear the voice of the Good Shepherd calling in their native language, "Come, follow me" . . .

That those who are spiritually lost and seeking meaning in life would encounter leaders and guides to show them the way . . .

That all gathered here be strengthened in our own vocation, whether to marriage, the single life, religious life, or holy orders . . .

Presider: Heavenly Father, we are your people, the flock that you shepherd. Hear our prayers that we might listen for your voice and follow you always. We ask in the name of Jesus, the Good Shepherd. **Amen.**

COLLECT

Let us pray.

Pause for silent prayer

Almighty ever-living God,
lead us to a share in the joys of heaven,
so that the humble flock may reach
where the brave Shepherd has gone before.
Who lives and reigns with you in the unity
    of the Holy Spirit,
one God, for ever and ever. **Amen.**

FIRST READING
Acts 13:14, 43-52

Paul and Barnabas continued on from
    Perga
  and reached Antioch in Pisidia.
On the sabbath they entered the
    synagogue and took their seats.
Many Jews and worshipers who were
    converts to Judaism
  followed Paul and Barnabas, who spoke
    to them
  and urged them to remain faithful to the
    grace of God.

On the following sabbath almost the whole
    city gathered
  to hear the word of the Lord.
When the Jews saw the crowds, they were
    filled with jealousy
  and with violent abuse contradicted
    what Paul said.
Both Paul and Barnabas spoke out boldly
    and said,
  "It was necessary that the word of God
    be spoken to you first,
  but since you reject it
  and condemn yourselves as unworthy
    of eternal life,
  we now turn to the Gentiles.
For so the Lord has commanded us,
  I have made you a light to the Gentiles,
  that you may be an instrument of
    salvation
  to the ends of the earth."

The Gentiles were delighted when they
    heard this
  and glorified the word of the Lord.
All who were destined for eternal life came
    to believe,
  and the word of the Lord continued to
    spread
  through the whole region.
The Jews, however, incited the women of
    prominence who were worshipers
  and the leading men of the city,
  stirred up a persecution against Paul
    and Barnabas,
  and expelled them from their territory.

So they shook the dust from their feet in
protest against them,
and went to Iconium.
The disciples were filled with joy and the
Holy Spirit.

RESPONSORIAL PSALM
Ps 100:1-2, 3, 5

R̸. (3c) We are his people, the sheep of his
flock.
or
R̸. Alleluia.

Sing joyfully to the LORD, all you lands;
serve the LORD with gladness;
come before him with joyful song.

R̸. We are his people, the sheep of his
flock.
or
R̸. Alleluia.

Know that the LORD is God;
he made us, his we are;
his people, the flock he tends.

R̸. We are his people, the sheep of his
flock.
or
R̸. Alleluia.

The LORD is good:
his kindness endures forever,
and his faithfulness, to all generations.

R̸. We are his people, the sheep of his
flock.
or
R̸. Alleluia.

SECOND READING
Rev 7:9, 14b-17

See Appendix A, p. 300.

About Liturgy

Vocations: One layer of meaning that has been given to this Fourth Sunday of Easter is that of vocations, especially to ordained ministries and religious life. This is a laudable lens through which to see the image of Christ, the Good Shepherd. However, it is not the only way we should understand vocation.

Pope Benedict XVI described a broader understanding of vocation in a greeting he gave to a parish council at a church in Rome administered by the Vocationist Fathers: "Every person carries within himself a project of God, a personal vocation, a personal idea of God on what he is required to do in history to build his Church. . . . And the priest's role is above all to reawaken this awareness, to help the individual discover his personal vocation, God's task for each one of us" (March 25, 2007).

As you prepare the liturgies for this day, certainly connect the image of the Good Shepherd to all who shepherd the church, and include prayers for vocations to the priesthood, diaconate, and religious life. But also help your assemblies understand that all of us are called to a vocation and have a specific role to play in the mission of Christ in whatever state of life we are in. Also include prayers for those called to the vocations of spouses, widows, and single persons.

We are God's people: In *Called to Participate: Theological, Ritual, and Social Perspectives* (Liturgical Press), liturgist and theologian Mark Searle wrote: "The Church community is less a network of friends than it is, in Parker Palmer's striking phrase, 'a company of strangers.' This 'company of strangers' will often have little in common beyond our common humanity and the Spirit poured into our hearts in baptism" (75).

True parish communities in which evangelization and radical hospitality are practiced will be a mix of people who are different. If everyone we know in our parish looks and sounds and talks and acts the same way as we do, we might not be reflecting as clearly as we can the people of God who come "from every nation, race, people, and tongue" (Rev 7:9). If that is the case, it is a call for us to seek out those who are missing from the flock. And you might not have to go to the ends of the earth to find them. They may even be sitting in another part of the church. All we have to do is make an effort to go and meet them.

About Liturgical Music

Singing in a language not our own: If the heavenly gathering of God's people includes those from every nation and tongue, it would be well for us to begin learning some music that reflects the diversity of God's people so that we'll be ready for the heavenly choir! In our increasingly diverse neighborhoods, this would not be difficult to do. We simply have to seek out those who have different roots than we do and spend time listening to their story and their song. If your parish has a Mass in a different language from yours, make an effort to participate in it even if you don't understand the language. Simply being present in the other's community gatherings will speak more about your care for them than if you learned their language but never spent time with them.

Many English-language hymnals today include at least a few songs in other languages. One beautiful and simple song in Spanish that fits nicely with today's readings is *"Pues Si Vivimos* / When We Are Living" with text by Robert Escamilla (*Sacred Song*).

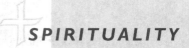

SPIRITUALITY

GOSPEL ACCLAMATION
John 13:34

℟. Alleluia, alleluia.
I give you a new commandment, says the Lord:
love one another as I have loved you.
℟. Alleluia, alleluia.

Gospel

John 13:31-33a, 34-35; L54C

When Judas had left them, Jesus said,
 "Now is the Son of Man glorified,
  and God is glorified in him.
If God is glorified in him,
 God will also glorify him in himself,
 and God will glorify him at once.
My children, I will be with you only a
  little while longer.
I give you a new commandment: love
  one another.
As I have loved you, so you also should
  love one another.
This is how all will know that you are
  my disciples,
 if you have love for one another."

Reflecting on the Gospel

We continue reading from the Gospel of John during the Easter season. This evangelist has unique things to say about Jesus, and he relates stories about Jesus not found anywhere else. Our gospel reading for today is a case in point. Other gospels have Jesus saying, "Love your neighbor" (Matt 19:19; Mark 12:31; Luke 10:27; NABRE), or even, "Love your enemies" (Matt 5:44; Luke 6:27; NABRE). But today we hear the simple but profound command to "love one another," which presumes that there are others in the community. In cases where semantics can open a debate about "who is my neighbor?" or how precisely we "love" an "enemy," the command to love one another is straightforward and leaves little room for negotiation or explanation. Further, it is a command related to "one another," which means those in the Christian community closest to us. In some senses it harkens to family, and the relationships we have with one another as family. It's nearly a plea for siblings to do more than "get along" but to actually "love one another."

But Jesus goes further, pointing to the example he gave them as a model for love: "As I have loved you, so you also should love one another." In a few chapters, we will see that includes laying down his life for them. The disciples will be known by their love for one another. Our own displays of charity and acts of love will mark us as Christian.

To love one another is challenging. It can be easier and more convenient to go to church, or to sit in one's room and pray. But love requires action and some doing. As is often said, "Love is a verb." The image of a family comes to mind again as it can be easier to love those on the outside or the margins. But what about those most familiar to us? We know their foibles, idiosyncrasies, annoying tics, and habits. We have a history with them. Yet, we are called, perhaps even reminded, to love one another.

For the Fourth Gospel, all ethical commands of Jesus may be summed up in this one command to love. Other than some references that seem to reflect the Ten Commandments (don't steal, lie, covet) the Gospel of John has one overriding exhortation: Love.

Living the Paschal Mystery

Ghandi is reported to have said: "I love your Christ, but your Christians are not like Christ." From this we might be fairly sure that the Christians he encountered were not living up to the ideal reflected in today's gospel. That is certainly unfortunate. But what image of Christianity do we present by our actions? By our love? Do we love like Jesus did, to the point of laying down our life?

It can be easier to be consumed with external rituals or internal theological debates. But Jesus' command today is simply to love. In its simplicity, it is exceptionally difficult. Love knows no bounds. Love does not say, "That's enough." Love puts the needs of the other ahead of our own. And in our global society we see that vast numbers of people have more needs than we do. Where to begin? It is our life's calling as a disciple of Jesus to follow him in the way of love. It's been said that a great journey begins with a single step. So we love one another and in doing so we become more devoted disciples of Christ.

Focusing the Gospel

Key words and phrases: As I have loved you, so you also should love one another.

To the point: Jesus prefaces this new commandment to his disciples by telling them, "I will be with you only a little while longer." Speaking at the Last Supper, Jesus prepares his disciples for what is to come. Soon Jesus will not be with them in the tangible way they are used to. They will no longer be able to walk with him in person or to ask him their questions and hear an answer with their ears. They are moving into a new time of discipleship, a time that will require more from them. In this time to come they are to love one another as Jesus has loved them. And soon, Jesus will show them just what that love looks like when he lays down his life.

Connecting the Gospel

to the first reading: Although in some places the Acts of the Apostles presents an idyllic picture of the early church, the first communities of Christians were not without their disagreements. One of the first of these was about how to admit Gentiles to the church, and whether they must first undergo a process of Jewish conversion, that is, be circumcised and follow Jewish dietary laws. In the first reading, Paul, the apostle to the Gentiles, shares with the Jewish Christian communities "how [God] had opened the door of faith to the Gentiles." This time of transition where the Jewish Christians welcomed Gentiles must have been difficult at times, and yet, the church survived and thrived by following the commandment Jesus gave to his closest friends on the night before he died, "[L]ove one another."

to experience: Only in love are we able to form the Body of Christ. Only in love are we given the grace to find unity in our diversity and to worship God as one.

Connecting the Responsorial Psalm

to the readings: Just as modern authors and poets enjoy word play, so, too, did the psalmists of ancient Israel. Though it's hard to tell in English, in Hebrew, today's psalm is an acrostic in which the first word of each line begins with the letter of the alphabet in alphabetical order: *aleph, bet, gimel, dalet,* etc. There are about a dozen alphabetic acrostic psalms in the Bible. The verses we pray with today center around the theme of God's mercy and goodness, as well as the glory of his reign. In the second reading from Revelation we see an image of God's kingdom where "there shall be no more death or mourning, wailing or pain." Even as we await the fulfillment of this kingdom, we can continue to build it every day when we follow the new commandment Jesus gave, "As I have loved you, so you also should love one another."

to psalmist preparation: We belong to the glorious reign of God when we love with the self-giving love of Christ. How do you embody this love? Where in your life is God asking you to love with more intention?

PROMPTS FOR FAITH-SHARING

In the first reading, Barnabas and Paul minister to the fledgling Christian communities through prayer, fasting, and proclaiming the Good News. How do you support others in faith?

_____

_____

_____

_____

Jesus gives us a new commandment: "[L]ove one another." How do you show love for the people closest to you?

_____

_____

_____

_____

When in your life have you needed to make a conscious decision to act out of love? What helped you make this decision?

_____

_____

_____

_____

Jesus says we will be recognized as his disciples by how we love each other. How loving is your parish community? What issues are you currently dealing with that might require an extra outpouring of love and charity?

_____

_____

_____

_____

_____

Model Rite for the Blessing and Sprinkling of Water

Presider: In the waters of baptism we are washed clean of original sin and filled with the grace and love of God. May this water renew our hearts and spirits to be signs of God's love and life on the earth . . . [*pause*]

    [*continue with* The Roman Missal, *Appendix II*]

Homily Points

• In today's gospel Jesus gets to the point very quickly: Love one another as I have loved you. In all things, Jesus leads by example and so when we ask ourselves, "How did Jesus love?" many images come to mind. We see Jesus healing the blind and lame. We see him touching lepers and blessing children. We hear him telling the woman caught in adultery, "Neither do I condemn you" (John 8:11; NABRE). And we see his arms stretched wide on the cross, submitting to a criminal's death.

• Jesus' entire life, not just his death, was a continual outpouring of self for others. Jesus loved with his presence, and he continues to love us this way. We experience his presence when we come to the Word of God, seek him out in prayer, and encounter his Body and Blood in the Eucharist.

• Jesus gives this new commandment at the Last Supper. His disciples have travelled with him for several years now. They have witnessed him loving everyone he has encountered. And hopefully these images of Jesus' love are seared into their memories because this new commandment asks them to continue the work of bringing Christ's love to the world. St. Teresa of Ávila wrote a famous prayer called "Christ has no body." In it she tells us, "Christ has no body but yours, / no hands, no feet on earth but yours, / yours are the eyes with which he looks / compassion on the world." The mantle has been passed to us. Now we are the ones who are given this mission: "As I have loved you, so you also should love one another."

Model Universal Prayer (Prayer of the Faithful)

Presider: Jesus gives us a new commandment, to love one another as he has loved us. Let us pray for the self-giving, compassionate love of Jesus to transform the world.

Response: Lord, hear our prayer.

That the church might stand with the persecuted throughout the world and be a voice of hope for the time when God "will wipe every tear from their eyes" . . .

That people throughout the world, especially those in power, embrace Jesus' way of selfless giving and love . . .

That those in need of love, especially the orphaned, abandoned and imprisoned, experience Christ's care and compassion through the actions of those they encounter . . .

That all gathered here be strengthened to act as Christ's body on earth, to be "the hands with which he blesses all the world" and "the feet with which he walks to do good" . . .

Presider: God of unending love, you call us to be a people after your own heart. Hear our prayers that we might witness to your love throughout the earth. In the name of Jesus we pray. **Amen.**

COLLECT

Let us pray.

Pause for silent prayer

Almighty ever-living God,
constantly accomplish the Paschal
    Mystery within us,
that those you were pleased to make new
    in Holy Baptism
may, under your protective care, bear
    much fruit
and come to the joys of life eternal.
Through our Lord Jesus Christ, your Son,
who lives and reigns with you in the unity
    of the Holy Spirit,
one God, for ever and ever. **Amen.**

FIRST READING

Acts 14:21-27

After Paul and Barnabas had proclaimed
    the good news to that city
    and made a considerable number of
        disciples,
    they returned to Lystra and to Iconium
        and to Antioch.
They strengthened the spirits of the
    disciples
    and exhorted them to persevere in the
        faith, saying,
"It is necessary for us to undergo many
    hardships
to enter the kingdom of God."
They appointed elders for them in each
    church and,
    with prayer and fasting, commended
        them to the Lord
in whom they had put their faith.
Then they traveled through Pisidia and
    reached Pamphylia.
After proclaiming the word at Perga they
    went down to Attalia.
From there they sailed to Antioch,
    where they had been commended to the
        grace of God
    for the work they had now
        accomplished.
And when they arrived, they called the
    church together
    and reported what God had done with
        them
    and how he had opened the door of
        faith to the Gentiles.

RESPONSORIAL PSALM

Ps 145:8-9, 10-11, 12-13

Ry. (cf. 1) I will praise your name forever,
    my king and my God.

or

Ry. Alleluia.

The Lord is gracious and merciful,
    slow to anger and of great kindness.
The Lord is good to all
    and compassionate toward all his
        works.
R/. I will praise your name forever, my
        king and my God.
    or
R/. Alleluia.

Let all your works give you thanks,
    O Lord,
    and let your faithful ones bless you.
Let them discourse of the glory of your
        kingdom
    and speak of your might.
R/. I will praise your name forever, my
        king and my God.
    or
R/. Alleluia.

Let them make known your might to the
        children of Adam,
    and the glorious splendor of your
        kingdom.
Your kingdom is a kingdom for all ages,
    and your dominion endures through all
        generations.
R/. I will praise your name forever, my
        king and my God.
    or
R/. Alleluia.

SECOND READING
Rev 21:1-5a

Then I, John, saw a new heaven and a new
        earth.
The former heaven and the former earth
        had passed away,
    and the sea was no more.
I also saw the holy city, a new Jerusalem,
    coming down out of heaven from God,
    prepared as a bride adorned for her
        husband.
I heard a loud voice from the throne
        saying,
    "Behold, God's dwelling is with the
        human race.
He will dwell with them and they will be
        his people
    and God himself will always be with
        them as their God.
He will wipe every tear from their eyes,
    and there shall be no more death or
        mourning, wailing or pain,
    for the old order has passed away."

The One who sat on the throne said,
    "Behold, I make all things new."

About Liturgy

Proof of discipleship: If you pay attention to Catholic websites, social media, or maybe even your diocesan newspaper, it probably doesn't take long for you to find mean-spirited comments about fellow Christians who hold different viewpoints than the writer's. Reading these articles and comments might lead one to believe that the proof of discipleship is measured by one's level of orthodoxy, obedience, liberalism, or whatever measuring stick you like.

However, today's gospel reminds us that the proof of discipleship is not how right we are but how loving we are. If we are to follow Jesus' commandment to love one another as he has loved us, there can be no room in our language or in our hearts for such meanness.

How then should we prepare ourselves to be witnesses for the gospel when we encounter others who may disagree with us? Let us look at how Paul and Barnabas helped the earliest Christian disciples. They strengthened the spirits of the disciples. They encouraged them to persevere in faith. They recognized their hardships. They discerned good leaders to help them, and they all prayed and fasted. Did this guarantee harmony and agreement? Not really. But it did prove to all that they were followers of Christ.

When we encounter discord among our fellow Christians, let us remember that our primary objective is to love as Jesus loved us. That requires an ongoing, gradual relationship that recognizes the dignity of each person and sees them as our brother or sister in Christ.

About Initiation

Glorifying God: Today's gospel reflects the final command we receive at every Eucharist: "Go in peace, glorifying the Lord by your lives." The neophytes had been training to be witnesses to Christ through their words and deeds all during their catechumenate. As they continue to be visible signs in our midst of the new life we receive in Christ, invite some of them who are comfortable to share their testimony of how Christ has loved them. They can do this either as a brief reflection during Mass, a written testimony included in the parish bulletin, or as a short video on the website.

About Liturgical Music

Suggestions: There are so many excellent songs that express today's gospel command to love. It is always good to return to those with solid texts taken from Scripture and our tradition. One example of this is the text of *Ubi caritas* from the Mass of the Lord's Supper. Settings of this include: "Where Charity and Love Prevail" translated by Omer Westendorf and set by Paul Benoit, OSB (WLP), and "Ubi Caritas" by Bob Hurd (OCP). A good option for the preparation of gifts is "Christians, Let Us Love One Another" with text by Claudia Foltz, SNJM, and Armand Nigro, SJ, set to PICARDY (OCP). Another piece that connects back to the Holy Thursday *mandatum* is "So You Must Do" by Marty Haugen (GIA). For Communion, look to *Psallite*'s "A New Commandment I Give to You" (*Sacred Song*). A contemporary song that would work well for the dismissal is "With This Bread" by Kate Cuddy (GIA).

As you choose music for this Sunday, keep some of these selections in mind as well for the liturgies of matrimony in your parish. These texts give us a deeper understanding of Christian love and can enhance your wedding repertoire with songs that build upon spousal love to become a vocation of love for others.

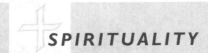

SPIRITUALITY

GOSPEL ACCLAMATION
John 14:23

℟. Alleluia, alleluia.
Whoever loves me will keep my word, says the Lord,
and my Father will love him and we will come to him.
℟. Alleluia, alleluia.

Gospel

John 14:23-29; L57C

Jesus said to his disciples:
   "Whoever loves me will keep my
      word,
   and my Father will love him,
   and we will come to him and
      make our dwelling with him.
Whoever does not love me does not
      keep my words;
   yet the word you hear is not mine
   but that of the Father who sent
      me.

"I have told you this while I am with
      you.
The Advocate, the Holy Spirit,
   whom the Father will send in my
      name,
   will teach you everything
   and remind you of all that I told you.
Peace I leave with you; my peace I give
      to you.
Not as the world gives do I give it to
      you.
Do not let your hearts be troubled or
      afraid.
You heard me tell you,
   'I am going away and I will come
      back to you.'
If you loved me,
   you would rejoice that I am going to
      the Father;
   for the Father is greater than I.
And now I have told you this before it
      happens,
   so that when it happens you may
      believe."

Reflecting on the Gospel

Our reading today continues to be from the Gospel of John, and interestingly it's from Jesus' Last Supper discourse. So even though we are in the Easter season, we hearken back to the Last Supper for words of wisdom from Jesus. And these words are appropriate as we approach the conclusion of the Easter season at Pentecost, the feast of the giving of the Holy Spirit, which we will celebrate in two weeks. But here Jesus tells the disciples forthrightly that the Father will send the Holy Spirit, the Advocate, in Jesus' name. The role of the Spirit is to teach the disciples, and to remind them of what Jesus said. The Spirit then is a gift of the Father. This gift was given not only to that generation of Christians but to us too. We have that same Advocate to teach us and the other followers of Jesus. But that is not the only gift we receive.

A gift of Jesus given to the disciples is peace, but Jesus is quick to say that it's not the peace given by the world, but that given by Jesus. The world's peace can be understood as the absence of war, or a cessation of hostilities. Others interpret it as the peace gained by domination of subject peoples. And in Jesus' time and place we recall that the Romans were the occupying power. A generation after Jesus the city of Jerusalem with its temple would be destroyed by Rome. At the conclusion of that campaign the Romans would say they pacified Judea! The death, destruction, slaughter, fire, and pillaging of Jerusalem and its temple meant for the Romans that the land was at peace! So, no, Jesus' peace is not like that given by the world, given by the Romans.

The peace Jesus gives is an interior wholeness, to be at peace with oneself and the world around us. The inner disposition of a disciple is one of peace, not aggression; peace, rather than anger; peace, not hostility; peace, rather than anxiety; peace, not pursuit of ill-gotten gain. The life of a disciple is marked by the gift of peace given by Jesus.

Living the Paschal Mystery

How many of us live lives of peace? And by peace do we mean absence of strife? Or the peace that Christ gives? The peace that Christ gives is not only for those disciples in the New Testament, it is for us. The relationship we have with Christ means that we do not look to outside forces or external sources for validation. Our worth and sense of self is not measured by a job, position, house, children, family, retirement plan, or the praise of others. Instead, our peace and well-being come from Christ himself. That peace and security can never be taken away. We are no longer subject to the whims of others, the hazards of the world, or the vagaries of passing fancies. Regardless of our condition in life, we have something fundamental at our core that is a gift. Let us rest in the knowledge that we have been given the gift of peace that comes from Christ himself.

Focusing the Gospel

Key words and phrases: Peace I leave with you; my peace I give you.

To the point: Just as we read on the Second Sunday of Easter, Jesus again offers the disciples peace. The gospel we hear today is actually taken from earlier in the Gospel of John, during the Last Supper discourse. These closest friends of Jesus are about to be shaken completely in faith. They will see the man they have come to know as the Lord die on a cross. But before these calamities take place Jesus gives them one final gift, peace, and not just a general feeling of peace, but the very peace of Christ. When he sees them for the first time after the resurrection in the Upper Room where they are huddled due to fear, Jesus offers this gift again, "Peace be with you." Jesus had told his friends, "Do not let your hearts be troubled or afraid." This is a difficult lesson to learn, but Jesus never tires of offering his peace to us.

Connecting the Gospel

to the first reading: In the Acts of the Apostles the early church continues to ponder and discern the process for Gentiles to join the new Christian faith. Paul and Barnabas go to Jerusalem to discuss with the apostles if circumcision should be required for Gentile Christians. Led by Peter and James, the council comes to a decision that circumcision will not be required and writes a letter to the Gentile churches. In it they express concern that these matters have disturbed the Gentiles' peace of mind and clarify that they do not want to place any undue burden upon them.

to experience: When our rules for worship or faith place burdens upon others we are called to step back and discern if this is truly the will of Jesus, the Prince of Peace.

Connecting the Responsorial Psalm

to the readings: In Psalm 67 we hear the cry, "May the peoples praise you, O God; / may all the peoples praise you!" And in the first and second reading we see this exclamation coming true. In the Acts of the Apostles, Gentiles receive the good news of Jesus' death and resurrection and are brought into the early church along with their Jewish brothers and sisters. In the second reading from Revelation we are given a vision of the holy city, Jerusalem, becoming a beacon for the world that all nations may "walk by its light" (21:24). Our faith has never been a treasure to hoard and stow away. It is to be shared with all nations and peoples.

to psalmist preparation: This psalm begins, "May God have pity on us and bless us; / may he let his face shine upon us." After asking for blessing from the Lord it also expresses the desire that all the peoples of the world might bless the Lord in return. How do you experience blessing in your life? What or who blesses you? What or whom do you bless?

PROMPTS FOR FAITH-SHARING

In the Acts of the Apostles we see the Jewish leaders of the early church reaching out to the Gentile members of the community. Within your own church community are there groups that seem at odds with each other? How might they be invited to reach out to one another in peace?

_____

_____

_____

_____

In the reading from Revelation we hear of a city that needs no sun or moon for it is lit by the glory of the Lord. What are the places in your life that need to be touched by the Lord's light?

_____

_____

_____

_____

How do you experience the peace of Christ in your daily life?

_____

_____

_____

_____

Jesus tells us, "Do not let your hearts be troubled or afraid." What troubles your heart at this moment? How might you entrust this fear to God?

_____

_____

_____

_____

Model Rite for the Blessing and Sprinkling of Water

Presider: Through the waters of Baptism we are given new life in the Spirit of God. May this sprinkling rite renew us in joy, hope, and love . . . [*pause*]

    [*continue with* The Roman Missal, *Appendix II*]

Homily Points

• In the Last Supper discourse of John's gospel Jesus carefully prepares the disciples for the time when he will no longer be with them in the way they are used to. His physical presence in the human body they are accustomed to might be gone, but he wants them to know in no uncertain terms that he will still dwell with them through his word, his peace, and the Holy Spirit.

• We live in the time of waiting—the time after Jesus' ascension to the Father but before the fulfillment of the kingdom of God where God will be "all in all" (1 Cor 15:28; NABRE) and "every tear" will be wiped away as we heard in last week's reading from Revelation. In this time of waiting and building the kingdom of God Jesus reassures us as well that he will dwell with us always, even when we can't see him.

• Our lives as disciples require that we cultivate these gifts of the Lord. That we love his word with our whole heart, mind, soul, and self. That we take time to experience and receive Jesus' peace so that we might share it with others. That we know the Holy Spirit through prayer and worship. The first Easter season when Jesus appeared to his disciples after his resurrection was a time of joy and a time of transition. Jesus knew his disciples would need time to integrate this new reality. And so it is with us. We have experienced the great fast of Lent, the solemnity of the Holy Triduum, and the overwhelming joy of Easter. Now we are given time to integrate these new spiritual insights into our own life before we return to the routine rhythm of Ordinary Time. How will your life be different after encountering Jesus in his word, peace, and Spirit anew?

Model Universal Prayer (Prayer of the Faithful)

Presider: Jesus tells us, "Do not let your hearts be troubled or afraid" and so with confidence in God's love and care we bring our needs before the Lord.

Response: Lord, hear our prayer.

That the church may trust in the Advocate, the Holy Spirit, to lead her now and always . . .

That nations might walk in the light of the Lamb of God . . .

That those who are burdened by anxiety and depression know the peace of the Lord . . .

That all gathered here today be strengthened in our love of Jesus and our fidelity to his word . . .

Presider: God of peace, you sent your only son to dwell among us and to teach us your ways. Hear our prayers that we might become instruments of his peace. Through Christ our Lord. **Amen.**

COLLECT

Let us pray.

Pause for silent prayer

Grant, almighty God,
    that we may celebrate with heartfelt
        devotion these days of joy,
which we keep in honor of the risen Lord,
and that what we relive in remembrance
we may always hold to in what we do.
Through our Lord Jesus Christ, your Son,
who lives and reigns with you in the unity
    of the Holy Spirit,
one God, for ever and ever. **Amen.**

FIRST READING
Acts 15:1-2, 22-29

Some who had come down from Judea were
    instructing the brothers,
    "Unless you are circumcised according
        to the Mosaic practice,
    you cannot be saved."
Because there arose no little dissension
    and debate
    by Paul and Barnabas with them,
    it was decided that Paul, Barnabas, and
        some of the others
    should go up to Jerusalem to the
        apostles and elders
    about this question.

The apostles and elders, in agreement
    with the whole church,
    decided to choose representatives
    and to send them to Antioch with Paul
        and Barnabas.
The ones chosen were Judas, who was
    called Barsabbas,
    and Silas, leaders among the brothers.
This is the letter delivered by them:

"The apostles and the elders, your brothers,
    to the brothers in Antioch, Syria, and
        Cilicia
    of Gentile origin: greetings.
Since we have heard that some of our
    number
    who went out without any mandate
        from us
    have upset you with their teachings
    and disturbed your peace of mind,
    we have with one accord decided to
        choose representatives
    and to send them to you along with our
        beloved Barnabas and Paul,
    who have dedicated their lives to the
        name of our Lord Jesus Christ.
So we are sending Judas and Silas
    who will also convey this same message
        by word of mouth:
    'It is the decision of the Holy Spirit and
        of us

not to place on you any burden beyond
    these necessities,
namely, to abstain from meat sacrificed
    to idols,
from blood, from meats of strangled
    animals,
and from unlawful marriage.
If you keep free of these,
    you will be doing what is right. Farewell.'"

RESPONSORIAL PSALM

Ps 67:2-3, 5, 6, 8

℟. (4) O God, let all the nations praise you!
or
℟. Alleluia.

May God have pity on us and bless us;
    may he let his face shine upon us.
So may your way be known upon earth;
    among all nations, your salvation.

℟. O God, let all the nations praise you!
or
℟. Alleluia.

May the nations be glad and exult
    because you rule the peoples in equity;
    the nations on the earth you guide.

℟. O God, let all the nations praise you!
or
℟. Alleluia.

May the peoples praise you, O God;
    may all the peoples praise you!
May God bless us,
    and may all the ends of the earth fear
      him!

℟. O God, let all the nations praise you!
or
℟. Alleluia.

SECOND READING

Rev 21:10-14, 22-23

See Appendix A, p. 301.

CATECHESIS

About Liturgy

The temple where the Spirit dwells: Today's reading from Revelation gives us an opportunity to contemplate the symbol of the parish church as a sign of Christ's presence. For this we look to the Rite of Dedication of a Church:

"Christ became the true and perfect temple of the New Covenant and gathered together a people to be his own. This holy people . . . is the Church, that is, the temple of God built of living stones, where the Father is worshiped in spirit and in truth. Rightly, then, from early times 'church' has also been the name given to the building in which the Christian community gathers" (1). Here we see that the church is first the people assembled to give praise to God. Second, it is the building in which the people gather. *Ekklesia* is the Greek word for the Hebrew *qahal:* it describes a group of people who are summoned or convoked, set apart for a purpose.

What is the purpose of this gathering of the people called the church? Again, we look to the Rite of Dedication: "May we open our hearts and minds to receive his word with faith; may our fellowship born in the one font of baptism and sustained at the one table of the Lord, become the one temple of his Spirit, as we gather round his altar in love" (30). By hearing and receiving God's word and in unity through font and table, we become the temple of the Spirit made visible around the altar. What makes the church building holy is not so much the prayers and anointings over the stone and wood but the love and unity that is visible and shared among its members, most especially with those who have been left out.

This week look deeper into the history of your parish church. When was it dedicated? Why was it given the name it bears? Look also to the neighborhood. Who is missing from the neighborhood among your Sunday assemblies? What are some ways to help them know this building called the church belongs to them?

About Initiation

No greater burden: Today's reading from Acts gives us this line: "It is the decision of the Holy Spirit and of us / not to place on you any burden beyond these necessities" (Acts 15:28). This is echoed in the introductory notes for the Rite of Reception of Baptized Christians into the Full Communion of the Catholic Church: "The rite is so arranged that no greater burden than necessary is required for the establishment of communion and unity" (RCIA 473). This means that those who have been baptized in another ecclesial community whose baptism is recognized as valid are to be treated with the dignity of God's chosen ones. What is primary is their baptism in Christ; secondary is their ecclesial affiliation. Therefore, those who are ready to renew their baptismal promises and make a profession of faith in the Catholic Church should do so as soon as possible (see RCIA 476). We need not wait until the next Easter Vigil to establish their full communion with the Catholic Church.

About Liturgical Music

Singing us home: Theologian Timothy Matovina has said: "The church is holy not just because all are welcome. The church is holy because all belong." Two songs that express clearly that church is first the people of God called to be a home for all God's children are "All Are Welcome" by Marty Haugen and "A Place Called Home" with text by Michael Joncas set to FINLANDIA, both from GIA. This latter was written as a response to the need to welcome immigrants and refugees into our communities.

MAY 26, 2019
SIXTH SUNDAY OF EASTER

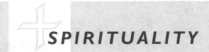

SPIRITUALITY

GOSPEL ACCLAMATION
Matt 28:19a, 20b

R̸. Alleluia, alleluia.
Go and teach all nations, says the Lord;
I am with you always, until the end of the world.
R̸. Alleluia, alleluia.

Gospel

Luke 24:46-53; L58C

Jesus said to his disciples:
 "Thus it is written that the
  Christ would suffer
 and rise from the dead on
  the third day
 and that repentance, for the
  forgiveness of sins,
 would be preached in his
  name
 to all the nations, beginning
  from Jerusalem.
You are witnesses of these
  things.
And behold I am sending the promise
  of my Father upon you;
 but stay in the city
 until you are clothed with power
  from on high."

Then he led them out as far as
  Bethany,
 raised his hands, and blessed them.
As he blessed them he parted from
  them
 and was taken up to heaven.
They did him homage
 and then returned to Jerusalem with
  great joy,
 and they were continually in the
  temple praising God.

Reflecting on the Gospel

Beginnings and endings are important. Sometimes we even ritualize those events, such as with baptism and funerals. But there are other important beginnings and endings throughout our lives too. Today's reading is from the end of the Gospel of Luke. It ends where it began, in the Jerusalem temple. It's as though Luke is telling us that all has come full circle. And immediately prior to the disciples being in the temple, they had been brought out to Bethany, a village on the slope of the Mount of Olives, about a mile and a half from ancient Jerusalem. There at Bethany they witnessed for the final time the visible, risen Christ. And that is the fundamental definition of the ascension, the going up to the heavens; it is the final leave-taking of Jesus before his assembled followers. After this, the risen Lord will no longer appear as he did.

Importantly, we are reading today from the Gospel of Luke, where the ascension of Jesus takes place on Easter Sunday evening. Later, when Luke writes the Acts of the Apostles, he says that the ascension took place forty days after Easter (Acts 1:9-11). But in the Acts of the Apostles Luke is also telling us the story of Pentecost, a Jewish feast celebrated fifty days after Passover, which we do not hear about in the gospel. So that might be part of the reason Luke gives us the extended time frame in Acts, because it brings the narrative forward to Pentecost.

Luke is keen to indicate both in the gospel and in Acts that there was a time when the resurrection appearances to the disciples came to an end. After that time Jesus would be known in the "breaking of the bread" (Luke 24:35; NABRE).

So, according the Gospel of Luke, the story has come full circle. What began in the temple with the appearance to Zechariah (Luke 1:9) has now been completed. The disciples are left praising God in the temple for the wondrous works God has done in and through Jesus. No longer will they witness the risen Christ, but from now on, they know him in the breaking of the bread.

Living the Paschal Mystery

So many of us Christians long to have witnessed Christ. Why does he not appear anymore? Where is he now? These are questions the ascension is meant to answer. Jesus has ascended to his glory with the Father. The time of his appearance has been completed. And now, as we will learn in Acts, the gift of the Spirit has been given to us. Moreover, as we learn in the last chapter of Luke, we now come to know Jesus in the breaking of the bread.

The ascension, then, is not so much about a physically present Jesus floating up and up into the clouds as it is a theologically sophisticated concept proclaiming his eternal presence with the Father in glory. When we take this image too literally we miss the theological truth it attempts to convey. As we live the paschal mystery we are reminded that rising with Christ is rising to new life, no longer to be subject to death. Rising with Christ is rising to glory with the Father. This is much more profound and sophisticated than flying through the sky without wings.

Focusing the Gospel

Key words and phrases: You are witnesses of these things.

To the point: Before ascending to his Father, Jesus commissions the disciples to take the seed of faith that has been planted in Israel and to bring it to the whole world. They are to proclaim the good news that God became man, was crucified, died, and then rose again on the third day and now offers his very light and life to us. This light and life comes to us through "repentance, for the forgiveness of sins." Let us pause to consider for a moment where this good news has spread in the two thousand years since the disciples saw the risen Lord ascend into heaven. Where has the good news found you?

Connecting the Gospel

to the first reading: The first reading and the gospel for today tell the same story by the same author, but with slightly different details. Both contain the central theme of witness. Jesus tells the disciples in the Gospel of Luke, "You are witnesses of these things." In the Acts of the Apostles he instructs them, "[Y]ou will be my witnesses in Jerusalem, / throughout Judea and Samaria, / and to the ends of the earth." A witness is someone who has seen an event and gives testimony about it. For the disciples it is not enough that they have been the firsthand witnesses to the ministry, death, and resurrection of Jesus. They need one more thing to carry out their mission: "power from on high."

to experience: Only through the grace of God are we able to accomplish the tasks we are given. In the Holy Spirit the disciples of today are also able to witness to the risen Lord, even without the firsthand experiences of the original disciples.

Connecting the Responsorial Psalm

to the readings: Once again the psalm for today calls for all the peoples of the world to "clap your hands, / shout to God with cries of gladness." For the Lord is not Lord of Israel alone, but of "all the earth." Today's readings from the New Testament confirm this as well. Jesus wishes for the redemption of the cross to spread to "the ends of the earth." The saving action that has taken place in a particular time and place is actually meant for all times, all places, and all peoples.

to psalmist preparation: In the psalm today we are given the image, "God mounts his throne amid shouts of joy; / the LORD, amid trumpet blasts." Today's feast of the Ascension calls for joy, even though it marks a transition from Christ's earthly ministry to his reign at the right hand of God. This transition ushers in a new time when Jesus, no longer limited in time and space, is present to us always and everywhere. How do you experience the risen Lord in your life? Can you cultivate even more joy in this relationship?

PROMPTS FOR FAITH-SHARING

In the Acts of the Apostles, the two men in white ask the disciples, "[W]hy are you standing there looking at the sky?" Where have you been looking for Jesus in your life?

_____

_____

_____

Jesus calls his disciples to witness "to the ends of the earth." What places are "the ends of the earth" for you? What people are the most difficult for you to contemplate witnessing the love of Jesus to?

_____

_____

_____

In what areas of your life are you in need of "power from on high" in order to persevere and be successful?

_____

_____

_____

The Gospel of Luke ends where it began, in the temple in Jerusalem. Often our lives seem cyclical. Where and when did your spiritual journey begin? Where is the journey taking you now?

_____

_____

_____

Model Rite for the Blessing and Sprinkling of Water

Presider: Jesus tells us today, "[Y]ou will be my witnesses in Jerusalem, / throughout Judea and Samaria, / and to the ends of the earth." May this water sprinkled over us strengthen our resolve to witness to the love of Jesus in all aspects of our lives . . . [*pause*]

[*continue with* The Roman Missal, *Appendix II*]

Homily Points

• In today's reading from the Acts of the Apostles we hear many phrases that echo to us from the women's experience at the empty tomb in Luke's gospel. In both instances we have two men in white who show up to ask the onlookers questions. The women, who are staring in disbelief at the place where they expected to find Jesus' body, are asked, "Why do you seek the living one among the dead?" At the scene of the ascension, we hear these men asking the disciples, who are still looking at the place where Jesus disappeared, "Men of Galilee, / why are you standing there looking at the sky?"

• In both cases the women at the tomb and the disciples who have just witnessed the ascension are looking in the wrong place for Jesus. Their attention is turned in the wrong direction. For the women it is in the direction of death and grief. They were certain they would find the body of their Lord and friend within the tomb and would be able to minister to him and prepare his body for burial. But he is not to be found among the dead. He is alive! The disciples are also looking in the wrong direction. Jesus is not in the sky. He is with them in a different way. Now they will meet him in the breaking of the bread. They will meet him when they minister to each other. They will meet him in prayer.

• And so in our lives we might ask the same question. Where are we looking for Jesus? Do we look for him only within the confines of our parish church? Or do we look for him among the poor and lonely, in the Eucharist, and all those we meet?

Model Universal Prayer (Prayer of the Faithful)

Presider: Jesus calls us to be witnesses to the ends of the earth. Let us pray for the wisdom, knowledge, and fidelity to fulfill this call.

Response: Lord, hear our prayer.

That the church faithfully pass on all that she has been taught by Christ . . .

That the good news of Jesus' life, death, and resurrection be known throughout all the nations of the earth . . .

That those in desperate need of the hope, love, and peace of Christ encounter preachers of the good news . . .

That all gathered here be enlightened and strengthened by the Holy Spirit to carry out the work given to us by Jesus . . .

Presider: Good and gracious God, you sent us your Son so that we might know and love you. Grant our prayers that we would continue to spread the good news of Jesus Christ to the ends of the earth, through the power of the Holy Spirit. We ask this through Jesus, our Lord. **Amen.**

COLLECT

Let us pray.

Pause for silent prayer

Gladden us with holy joys, almighty God,
and make us rejoice with devout
thanksgiving,
for the Ascension of Christ your Son
is our exaltation,
and, where the Head has gone before in
glory,
the Body is called to follow in hope.
Through our Lord Jesus Christ, your Son,
who lives and reigns with you in the unity
of the Holy Spirit,
one God, for ever and ever. **Amen.**

or

Grant, we pray, almighty God,
that we, who believe that your Only
Begotten Son, our Redeemer,
ascended this day to the heavens,
may in spirit dwell already in heavenly
realms.
Who lives and reigns with you in the unity
of the Holy Spirit,
one God, for ever and ever. **Amen.**

FIRST READING

Acts 1:1-11

In the first book, Theophilus,
    I dealt with all that Jesus did and taught
    until the day he was taken up,
    after giving instructions through the
        Holy Spirit
    to the apostles whom he had chosen.
He presented himself alive to them
    by many proofs after he had suffered,
    appearing to them during forty days
    and speaking about the kingdom of God.
While meeting with them,
    he enjoined them not to depart from
        Jerusalem,
    but to wait for "the promise of the
        Father
    about which you have heard me speak;
    for John baptized with water,
    but in a few days you will be baptized
        with the Holy Spirit."

When they had gathered together they
        asked him,
    "Lord, are you at this time going to
        restore the kingdom to Israel?"
He answered them, "It is not for you to
        know the times or seasons
    that the Father has established by his
        own authority.
But you will receive power when the Holy
        Spirit comes upon you,
    and you will be my witnesses in
        Jerusalem,

throughout Judea and Samaria,
and to the ends of the earth."
When he had said this, as they were
looking on,
he was lifted up, and a cloud took him
from their sight.
While they were looking intently at the
sky as he was going,
suddenly two men dressed in white
garments stood beside them.
They said, "Men of Galilee,
why are you standing there looking at
the sky?
This Jesus who has been taken up from
you into heaven
will return in the same way as you have
seen him going into heaven."

RESPONSORIAL PSALM
Ps 47:2-3, 6-7, 8-9

R℣. (6) God mounts his throne to shouts of
joy: a blare of trumpets for the Lord.
or:
R℣. Alleluia.

All you peoples, clap your hands,
shout to God with cries of gladness,
for the LORD, the Most High, the awesome,
is the great king over all the earth.

R℣. God mounts his throne to shouts of joy:
a blare of trumpets for the Lord.
or:
R℣. Alleluia.

God mounts his throne amid shouts of joy;
the LORD, amid trumpet blasts.
Sing praise to God, sing praise;
sing praise to our king, sing praise.

R℣. God mounts his throne to shouts of joy:
a blare of trumpets for the Lord.
or:
R℣. Alleluia.

For king of all the earth is God;
sing hymns of praise.
God reigns over the nations,
God sits upon his holy throne.

R℣. God mounts his throne to shouts of joy:
a blare of trumpets for the Lord.
or:
R℣. Alleluia.

SECOND READING
Eph 1:17-23

or Heb 9:24-28; 10:19-23

See Appendix A, p. 301.

About Liturgy

Commissioned to go: One unique aspect of Luke's gospel account of the ascension is that Jesus "raised his hands, and blessed them" (Luke 24:50), that is, he blessed the disciples. Every Sunday the same gesture is made over us at the end of the Mass when the priest raises his hands over the assembly, blesses us, and he or the deacon dismisses us to "[g]o and announce the Gospel of the Lord." The word "mass" is taken from this very ritual of sending in which, at one point, the words of dismissal were *Ite, missa est,* meaning "Go, she [the church] has been sent."

In the ascension, what is primary is not so much *where* Jesus went but where Jesus sends *us.* We are sent to "be [Christ's] witnesses in Jerusalem, / throughout Judea and Samaria, / and to the ends of the earth" (Acts 1:8). Imagine that! Every time we celebrate the Mass, we are given a mission to go as far as we can beyond our neighborhoods and familiar places, beyond our comfort zones and our own preferences, needs, and biases, to announce what we have seen, heard, touched, tasted, and known—that Jesus has conquered death by death, so we need not be afraid any longer to lay down our lives for one another.

Yet, sometimes the dismissal is seen as a welcome end to what might have been a less than life-giving ritual and our final "Thanks be to God" takes on a sense of relief rather than readiness for the work that continues in the world. If we find that our assembly is lacking in its sense of mission, let us look to the other parts of the Mass to see where we can better emphasize the liturgical rhythm of gathering and sending.

As we begin the days awaiting the memorial of the coming of the Spirit upon the disciples, let us pray that the Spirit will also rekindle the flame of Christ's mission in our hearts this day.

About Initiation

Dismissing catechumens: Once unbaptized adults have entered the order of catechumens, they are "kindly dismissed before the liturgy of the eucharist begins" whenever they are present at Mass (RCIA 75.3). Some RCIA teams avoid dismissing catechumens from the Eucharist for fear of seeming inhospitable. This negative feeling may come from a misunderstanding of the meaning of the dismissal.

Each member of the church is given a mission. Those in the order of the faithful are sent at the end of Mass to "[g]o and announce the Gospel of the Lord." Those in the order of catechumens are sent at the end of the Liturgy of the Word to "share their joy and spiritual experiences" (RCIA 67).

The reason catechumens are dismissed before the Liturgy of the Eucharist is not because they cannot yet share in Communion but because their "order" has a specific mission—to share what they have heard in the Word. Once they enter the order of the baptized, their mission will include the priestly duty to pray the prayers of the faithful (the Creed, universal prayer, and the eucharistic prayer), to share in the Body and Blood of Christ, and to go be that presence of Christ in the world.

About Liturgical Music

Songs of sending: Two beautiful hymns will help put the mission of the church on the lips of the assembly today: first, "To Be Your Presence" with text by Delores Dufner, OSB, set to ENGELBERG; second, "The Church of Christ in Every Age" with text by Fred Pratt Green, set to PROSPECT (both in *Sacred Song*). An alternative to a dismissal song is an *ostinato* refrain sung after Communion that anticipates the coming of the Spirit, such as Paul Page's "Come, Spirit, Come" (WLP).

MAY 30 (Thursday) or JUNE 2, 2019
THE ASCENSION OF THE LORD

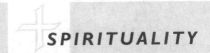

SPIRITUALITY

GOSPEL ACCLAMATION
cf. John 14:18

R̸. Alleluia, alleluia.
I will not leave you orphans, says the Lord.
I will come back to you, and your hearts will
    rejoice.
R̸. Alleluia, alleluia.

Gospel   John 17:20-26; L61C

Lifting up his eyes to heaven, Jesus
    prayed, saying:
"Holy Father, I pray not only for
    them,
but also for those who will believe
    in me through their word,
so that they may all be one,
as you, Father, are in me and I in
    you,
that they also may be in us,
that the world may believe that you
    sent me.
And I have given them the glory you
    gave me,
so that they may be one, as we are one,
I in them and you in me,
that they may be brought to perfection
    as one,
that the world may know that you sent
    me,
and that you loved them even as you
    loved me.
Father, they are your gift to me.
I wish that where I am they also may be
    with me,
that they may see my glory that you
    gave me,
because you loved me before the foun-
    dation of the world.
Righteous Father, the world also does not
    know you,
but I know you, and they know that you
    sent me.
I made known to them your name and I
    will make it known,
that the love with which you loved me
    may be in them and I in them."

Reflecting on the Gospel

There is a joke among Scripture scholars that if you ask Jesus in the Gospel of John how he's doing, he'll take three chapters to say that he and the Father are just fine. That's certainly a stretch, but today's gospel reading from John gives us an insight into where that joke comes from.

All joking aside, the Christology conveyed in this gospel is essentially theology, for Jesus and the Father are one, as is repeated several times in these few verses. But the image of unity does not stop with the Father and Son. For in Jesus' prayer he is sure to include his followers, not only his living, breathing disciples at the time, but all those who will

"believe in me through their word." That is, he is praying for us today. And he is praying for us that we all might be one. Unfortunately, we only need to look out on the street corners of our towns, villages, and cities to see that we are not one in Christ. There are many, many denominations split by creedal statements, theological beliefs, doctrinal beliefs, ethical practices, treatment and role of women, gender differences, sexual orientation, care for the earth, and more. Sadly, Jesus' prayer has not yet been realized. And we know from the Johannine literature (Gospel of John, 1 John, 2 John, and 3 John) that the early community faced ruptures and schisms too. So that reality is not new to us, or new to the Reformation in the sixteenth century. As long as there have been Christians there has been disunity.

Still, Jesus prays for our unity just the same. A critical theme, then, in these few verses is unity: unity of the Father and Son, and of the Son in believers.

There is a juxtaposition, too, between the believers who know Jesus and the world that does not know him. One goal is that when believers—Christians—are one, the world will know that the Father sent Jesus. So if we Christians want the world to believe, we might start with reconciling ourselves to one another. According to the words of Jesus in this gospel, Christian unity will cause the world to know Christ.

Living the Paschal Mystery

It's so easy for us to spot differences. Our brains are made to do just that. Rather than know every possible way to make a counterfeit dollar bill, we instead know the true dollar bill. Then, when we find a dollar with something amiss we can label it a counterfeit. Spotting differences saves our mental energy for more important things. But it's good to be aware that sometimes our snap judgments or inclination to find the difference is not always required. In fact, sometimes it is better (and it takes more energy) to find what's common. And perhaps if we did that with our Christian brothers and sisters we'd be more apt to find occasions of agreement, or reconciliation. In so doing, we would be working toward Christian unity. And unity does not mean sameness or even similarity. There can be differences in unity. Jesus does not pray for us to be the same. He prays for us to be one, as he and the Father are one. Today, let's be more mindful about finding common ground than finding difference. By doing so, we just might be realizing the prayer of Jesus.

Focusing the Gospel

Key words and phrases: that they may be brought to perfection as one

To the point: We are not saved on our own, but as the community of the Body of Christ. Jesus prays for the unity of his followers. Not only the ones immediately in front of him but for the followers that will stretch throughout the centuries as one unbroken family of the people of God. It seems that in this prayer Jesus asks for the impossible. As humans, our sinfulness keeps us both from perfection and from complete unity with one another. Luckily, Jesus is not asking that we be perfect or unified through our own efforts alone. Instead he prays to God for that which makes all things possible, "that the love with which you loved me / may be in them and I in them."

Connecting the Gospel

to the first and second readings: In the Acts of the Apostles we see a scene dominated by division and enmity. Stephen becomes the first martyr to follow in the footsteps of Jesus. He is brought before the Sanhedrin and is ultimately stoned. Before he dies, however, Stephen's last words echo those of Jesus on the cross, "Lord, do not hold this sin against them." Only through the perfect love of God is Stephen able to hope for unity with his assailants. Despite their mortal violence against him, his words of forgiveness leave the door open for reconciliation. Today we also come to the end of the book of Revelation, which we have been reading throughout the Easter season. Within this reading we receive a clue about what will bring us to the fulfillment of God's kingdom and Jesus' hope for unity: our own desire. Jesus invites us, "Let the one who thirsts come forward, / and the one who wants it receive the gift of life-giving water."

to experience: How much do we long for the unity that Jesus prays for in the gospel? Do we long for it so much we are willing to follow the example of Stephen and pray for the forgiveness of those who wound, hurt, and persecute us?

Connecting the Responsorial Psalm

to the readings: Psalm 97 presents a picture of Israel worshiping among other nations who serve other gods. In this day and age idols are not foreign gods, but whatever we let rule our lives in place of the God of love. Chaos and division reign when our primary devotion is to money, power, fame, drugs, alcohol, or any other *thing*. The unity that Jesus prays for can only come about when these addictions and desires are submitted to God. When our primary devotion is to the "Most High over all the earth" we will find peace and unity.

to psalmist preparation: Where are false idols disturbing the peace and unity of your own life? How might you reject these idols in favor of the God of "justice and right"?

PROMPTS FOR FAITH-SHARING

In the Acts of the Apostles Stephen prays for his executioners shortly before dying. Jesus has instructed us to pray for our enemies (see Matt 5:44). Who are you being called to pray for?

In today's gospel Jesus prays for those who will become followers through the word of the disciples. In your life of faith, whose "word" helped lead you to belief?

Jesus also prays for unity among his followers. Where do you see division in your local Christian community? How might you work for unity?

When have you experienced unity with other Christian denominations? How did this experience come about?

143

Model Rite for the Blessing and Sprinkling of Water

Presider: In baptism we are born into the universal church, the Body of Christ. May the sprinkling of this water strengthen us in unity with one another and with Christians throughout the world . . . [*pause*]

　　[*continue with* The Roman Missal, *Appendix II*]

Homily Points

• Jesus begins his prayer in today's gospel by praying not only for the disciples who are with him, but also for "those who will believe in me through their word, / so that they may all be one." Let us pause together to consider the web of connections that have led from that moment in time to this one. How many people in how many different places and times have continued to pass on the word of Jesus so that it might come to us today? And when did our specific family first hear the word of Jesus? Was it in a foreign country, many centuries ago, or just recently within the very community you find yourself now sitting?

• We might also consider the many people who underwent persecutions in order for this word to come to us today. In the Acts of the Apostles we hear of the first martyr, St. Stephen. Even today, people continue to give their lives as a consequence of sharing the word of Jesus. And yet, in the book of Revelation we are given hope. The Jesus who prayed for his disciples in the Upper Room in Jerusalem is also "the Alpha and the Omega, the first and the last, / the beginning and the end."

• And this Jesus continues to pray for us and for all of the people in the future who will hear his word through our lips. We are now threads on the web of good news reaching out to cover all space and all time. Who will God bring to us to preach the Word? We are given a part to play in bringing about the full unity and breadth of the kingdom of God.

Model Universal Prayer (Prayer of the Faithful)

Presider: Jesus prays in today's gospel that his followers might be unified as he and the Father are unified. Let us join our voices to Jesus' as we offer up our petitions.

Response: Lord, hear our prayer.

That the church reach out in love and fraternity to other Christian denominations and work for the unity of all Christians . . .

That leaders of nations join together to work for the well-being of all the world's people . . .

That those who are homebound find comfort in the love of their community who are unified with them in prayer . . .

That all gathered here might take on the work of peacemaking and conflict resolution as we seek to build up the unity of the people of God . . .

Presider: God of all creation, you call us to live in harmony and love. Hear our prayers that we might be signs of your unity throughout the earth. In the name of Jesus Christ our Lord. **Amen.**

COLLECT

Let us pray.

Pause for silent prayer

Graciously hear our supplications, O Lord,
so that we, who believe that the Savior of
　　the human race
is with you in your glory,
may experience, as he promised,
until the end of the world,
his abiding presence among us.
Who lives and reigns with you in the unity
　　of the Holy Spirit,
one God, for ever and ever. **Amen.**

FIRST READING
Acts 7:55-60

Stephen, filled with the Holy Spirit,
　　looked up intently to heaven and saw
　　　　the glory of God
　　and Jesus standing at the right hand of
　　　　God,
　　and Stephen said, "Behold, I see the
　　　　heavens opened
　　and the Son of Man standing at the
　　　　right hand of God."
But they cried out in a loud voice,
　　covered their ears, and rushed upon him
　　　　together.
They threw him out of the city, and began
　　to stone him.
The witnesses laid down their cloaks
　　at the feet of a young man named Saul.
As they were stoning Stephen, he called
　　out,
　　"Lord Jesus, receive my spirit."
Then he fell to his knees and cried out in a
　　loud voice,
　　"Lord, do not hold this sin against
　　　　them";
　　and when he said this, he fell asleep.

RESPONSORIAL PSALM
Ps 97:1-2, 6-7, 9

℟. (1a and 9a) The Lord is king, the most
　　high over all the earth.
　　or
℟. Alleluia.

The LORD is king; let the earth rejoice;
　　let the many islands be glad.
Justice and judgment are the foundation
　　of his throne.

℟. The Lord is king, the most high over all
　　the earth.
　　or
℟. Alleluia.

The heavens proclaim his justice,
   and all peoples see his glory.
All gods are prostrate before him.

R̸. The Lord is king, the most high over all
      the earth.
   or
R̸. Alleluia.

You, O Lᴏʀᴅ, are the Most High over all
      the earth,
   exalted far above all gods.

R̸. The Lord is king, the most high over all
      the earth.
   or
R̸. Alleluia.

SECOND READING
Rev 22:12-14, 16-17, 20

I, John, heard a voice saying to me:
   "Behold, I am coming soon.
I bring with me the recompense I will give
      to each
   according to his deeds.
I am the Alpha and the Omega, the first
      and the last,
   the beginning and the end."

Blessed are they who wash their robes
   so as to have the right to the tree of life
   and enter the city through its gates.

"I, Jesus, sent my angel to give you this
      testimony for the churches.
I am the root and offspring of David,
   the bright morning star."

The Spirit and the bride say, "Come."
Let the hearer say, "Come."
Let the one who thirsts come forward,
   and the one who wants it receive the gift
      of life-giving water.

The one who gives this testimony says,
   "Yes, I am coming soon."
Amen! Come, Lord Jesus!

About Liturgy

Hearing as the beginning of prayer: Notice how in the account of Stephen's martyrdom, those who were about to stone him "covered their ears" (Acts 7:57). What agitated this mob to kill Stephen was his long discourse before the Sanhedrin and the high priest recounting how God's people time and time again refused to hear the voice of God. Stephen's testimony before his accusers ends with this charge: "You stiff-necked people, uncircumcised in heart and ears, you always oppose the holy Spirit; you are just like your ancestors" (Acts 7:51; NABRE). His murderers would hear no more of this, and rushed upon him in anger.

Hearing in Judeo-Christian tradition is closely tied to obedience. The great *Shema* prayer from Deuteronomy 6, "Hear, O Israel! . . . you shall love the Lᴏʀᴅ, your God . . . Take to heart these words" (NABRE), is an example of the close connection between "hearing" and "obeying." *Shema* connotes more than simply perceiving sounds; it implies hearing the meaning behind the words so deeply that it changes our hearts and moves us to respond in obedience. Recall how often Jesus referred to hearing as the beginning of conversion, especially after a parable or teaching, for example, "Whoever has ears ought to hear," concluding the parable of the Sower (Matt 13:9; NABRE).

Those who do the word of God are those who have first heard it and allowed it into their hearts. The mob that killed Stephen closed their ears and their hearts to the word.

As we pray this week, in common in the liturgy and in our own private prayers, let us commit to first *hearing* what God has to say so that when we open our lips, our words may become a response to the Spirit we have heard in our hearts that leads us to embody that same Word by our lives.

About Liturgical Music

Singing our unity: The very act of singing itself is a lesson in unity. Specifically, it teaches us three things. First, we cannot sing together unless we breathe together. We must, in a literal sense, *conspire* with one another in order to make the song a reality. Second, we cannot make music together unless we submit our individual preferences to the common good of singing the song. Communal singing is a group effort, not an individual action done in the same room with others. Finally, we cannot make something beautiful unless we give up something of ourselves for the sake of the other. We open our mouths to give up our breath. We allow ourselves to be vulnerable by offering our voice, as imperfect as it might be. We humble ourselves by remembering the song is not about me but about us and who God has called us to be—one voice singing with the breath of the Spirit.

This week let us listen to one another as we sing that we may breathe together and sacrifice ourselves for the sake of becoming one body in Christ.

Suggestions: A lovely and profound hymn text appropriate for today's focus on unity is Fred Pratt Green's "One in Christ, We Meet Together" (Hope Publishing). This is set to HYFRYDOL. This could serve as an entrance chant or a dismissal song at the end of Mass.

SPIRITUALITY

GOSPEL ACCLAMATION

℟. Alleluia, alleluia.
Come, Holy Spirit, fill the hearts of your faithful
and kindle in them the fire of your love.
℟. Alleluia, alleluia.

Gospel   John 14:15-16, 23b-26; L63C

Jesus said to his disciples:
   "If you love me, you will keep my
      commandments.
And I will ask the Father,
   and he will give you another Advo-
      cate to be with you always.

"Whoever loves me will keep my word,
   and my Father will love him,
   and we will come to him and make
      our dwelling with him.
Those who do not love me do not keep
   my words;
   yet the word you hear is not mine
   but that of the Father who sent me.

"I have told you this while I am with
   you.
The Advocate, the Holy Spirit whom the
   Father will send in my name,
   will teach you everything
   and remind you of all that I told you."

or John 20:19-23

On the evening of that first day of the
      week,
   when the doors were locked, where the
      disciples were,
   for fear of the Jews,
   Jesus came and stood in their midst
   and said to them, "Peace be with you."
When he had said this, he showed them his
      hands and his side.
The disciples rejoiced when they saw the
      Lord.
Jesus said to them again, "Peace be with
   you.
As the Father has sent me, so I send you."
And when he had said this, he breathed on
      them and said to them,
   "Receive the Holy Spirit.
Whose sins you forgive are forgiven them,
   and whose sins you retain are retained."

Reflecting on the Gospel

We are now about fifty days, or seven weeks, from Easter. To be clear, Pentecost was a Jewish feast of the springtime, also known as the Feast of Weeks, or the Feast of the New Harvest or even the Feast of New Wine. Because it comes about fifty days (Lev 23:16) after the feast of Passover it was also called Pentecost (which means "fifty" in Greek). The Acts of the Apostles tell us that it was on the Jewish Feast of Pentecost that the apostles were emboldened by the Spirit to preach to Israel, assembled in Jerusalem for the feast. Thus, Luke precedes the story of Peter (as representing the Twelve) and his preaching, with the outpouring of the Spirit, thereby emboldening the Twelve so.

But today we read from the Gospel of John, which seems not to know anything about the feast of Pentecost and the emboldened Peter preaching. Instead, the story we have in John takes place on Easter Sunday when the risen Christ appears to the disciples (save Thomas, which we shall learn later) to give them the Spirit and the gift of peace. Upon receiving the gift of the Spirit, the disciples are emboldened not to preach (as Luke would have it) but to forgive sins. Though Jesus conquered the cosmic power of sin on the cross, it is the role of the disciples to forgive individual sins, almost as a clean-up operation after the major victory has been won.

Though this power to forgive sins has been traditionally understood to be the sacrament of reconciliation, this should not stop modern followers of Jesus (disciples) from forgiving others. In other words, forgiveness is not limited to sacramental ritual. Forgiveness has a power to unleash one held by some wrongdoing. We need think only about our own friends and families. How often do we forgive someone who has wronged us? How often do we seek forgiveness when we've wronged another? Those tasks belong to the disciples of Jesus per his handing on of the Spirit after Easter. We can certainly forgive and seek forgiveness without taking anything away from the sacrament of reconciliation.

Living the Paschal Mystery

The paschal mystery calls us to die to ourselves so we might be lifted up by and with Christ. One way we die to ourselves is to seek forgiveness when we do something wrong. Simply asking for forgiveness is a sign of humility, and it is something not often done. Not only are we to ask for forgiveness, but we are to forgive when someone wrongs us. Rather than hold a grudge our role as disciples is to forgive, in imitation of Jesus who set the example for us. If he can forgive those who wronged him, how much more must we forgive those who wrong us. To be a disciple requires nothing less. An admirer will certainly respect and praise the forgiveness Jesus effects, but a follower will seek to do the same, and forgive. As disciples, followers of Jesus, let us forgive as he forgave.

Focusing the Gospel

Key words and phrases: As the Father has sent me, so I send you.

To the point: We come to the end of the Easter season and we are given a mission. After being formed anew in the life and light of Jesus' death and resurrection we are to go forth as Jesus did in his ministry. Jesus sends us out into the world to be with people. To feed the hungry, comfort the outcast, touch the sick and lame, and everywhere proclaim the redemptive love of God.

Connecting the Gospel

to the first and second readings: In the gospel, Jesus gives the gift of the Holy Spirit by breathing on the disciples. In the first and second readings we see the effects of this gift. In the first reading, the apostles proclaim "the mighty acts of God" to "Jews from every nation under heaven," and yet, through the power of the Holy Spirit each person hears the message in their own native language. In the second reading we hear a listing of the many different gifts the Holy Spirit confers upon us. From these two readings we see that the Spirit's work is universal and also particular. The Spirit works within the community to draw people from every nation together in praising God. But the Spirit also works within us individually by giving gifts that are to be used to build up the kingdom of God. The action of the Holy Spirit enables the followers of Jesus to carry on Jesus' mission, "As the Father has sent me, so I send you."

to experience: It is difficult not to compare the gifts we recognize in ourselves with the gifts we see in others. St. Paul reminds us that all gifts come from the same source, God. Instead of comparing our abilities and talents to those around us, let us focus on how we can use our gifts for the good of all.

Connecting the Responsorial Psalm

to the readings: In the readings today there are many allusions to the first two chapters of Genesis and the creation of the world. The "strong driving wind" that fills the Upper Room where the apostles are gathered is reminiscent of the "mighty wind" that swept over the waters on the first day of creation. And Jesus breathing on the disciples parallels the action of God who "blew into [Adam's] nostrils the breath of life" (Gen 2:7; NABRE). It is no surprise then that our psalm today speaks of creation too: "When you send forth your spirit, they are created, / and you renew the face of the earth." The God of creation continues to create. By ushering in the time of our redemption through his death and resurrection, Jesus' breath imparts new life that is stronger than death upon his followers.

to psalmist preparation: Where do you notice the creative and renewing work of God in your own life? Where is the Spirit at work within you?

PROMPTS FOR FAITH-SHARING

In the Acts of the Apostles the gift of the Holy Spirit allows the apostles to communicate to people from many different countries. Have you ever experienced the Mass in a foreign language? What was this experience like?

In the psalm we pray for the Holy Spirit to renew the face of the earth. In your community where is there the need of renewal? How might you be a part of the renewing work of the Spirit?

In the First Letter to the Corinthians St. Paul lists the gifts of the Holy Spirit: wisdom, knowledge, faith, healing, mighty deeds, prophecy, discernment, tongues, interpretation of tongues. Which gift do you feel the most comfortable with? Which gift discomforts or challenges you?

In the gospel reading we find one of the scriptural sources for the sacrament of reconciliation. What was your first experience of reconciliation like? Was it positive or negative? Have you celebrated reconciliation recently? If not, what is holding you back?

147

Model Rite for the Blessing and Sprinkling of Water

Presider: On the Third Sunday of Advent we heard John the Baptist proclaim that the one who was to come would baptize with the Holy Spirit and with fire. And now on the Feast of Pentecost we see this come true. In baptism we are baptized into the life of the Holy Spirit. May this water rekindle the fire of the Holy Spirit within us . . . *[pause]*
> *[continue with* The Roman Missal, *Appendix II]*

Homily Points

• In the second chapter of Genesis God creates man from the dust of the earth and brings him to life by blowing into his nostrils. And so Adam comes alive with the very breath of God. God's breath is all that distinguishes Adam from the lifeless clay. In today's psalm we hear, "If you take away their breath, they perish / and return to their dust." The breath of God is an apt metaphor for the spiritual life. Without breath we die within minutes, and yet how often are we actually aware of this essential bodily function?

• In today's gospel Jesus appears to the disciples on the evening of Easter Sunday and breathes on them. In the four gospels we hear about breathing four times. Each of the synoptic gospels records how Jesus "breathed his last" upon the cross (see Matt 27:50, Mark 15:37, Luke 23:46). The Gospel of John, instead of recording the last breath of Jesus before death, records the first breath the disciples receive of resurrected life. Within this breath we witness a kind of new creation. Jesus confers the life that cannot be overcome.

• Today concludes our paschal feast that began fifty days ago on Easter Sunday. Our liturgical calendar invites us to enter into times of fasting and feasting and also into Ordinary Time, where we live and grow in our faith. Perhaps this Ordinary Time will be a good opportunity to heighten our awareness of the breath of God sustaining us in every moment. On this feast of Pentecost we pray for the Spirit of God, the breath of life, to renew the face of the earth and to renew us.

Model Universal Prayer (Prayer of the Faithful)

Presider: Emboldened by the Holy Spirit we bring our prayers before the Lord.

Response: Lord, hear our prayer.

That the church proclaim the joy of the gospel to people of every language . . .

That the earth be protected and renewed by our constant care and tending . . .

That all those who are confirmed on this feast of Pentecost be filled with the breath of Christ . . .

That all those gathered here might receive an abundance of spiritual gifts and be led by the Holy Spirit to use them for the building of the Kingdom of God . . .

Presider: God of creation, you sent your Holy Spirit upon the apostles as tongues of fire. Hear our prayers that our hearts may be set on fire by this same Spirit so that we might spread your love throughout the earth. We ask this through Jesus' name. **Amen.**

COLLECT

Let us pray.

Pause for silent prayer

O God, who by the mystery of today's
> great feast
sanctify your whole Church in every
> people and nation,
pour out, we pray, the gifts of the Holy Spirit
across the face of the earth
and, with the divine grace that was at work
when the Gospel was first proclaimed,
fill now once more the hearts of believers.
Through our Lord Jesus Christ, your Son,
who lives and reigns with you in the unity
> of the Holy Spirit,
one God, for ever and ever. **Amen.**

FIRST READING

Acts 2:1-11

When the time for Pentecost was fulfilled,
> they were all in one place together.
And suddenly there came from the sky
> a noise like a strong driving wind,
> and it filled the entire house in which
> they were.
Then there appeared to them tongues as
> of fire,
> which parted and came to rest on each
> one of them.
And they were all filled with the Holy Spirit
> and began to speak in different tongues,
> as the Spirit enabled them to proclaim.

Now there were devout Jews from every
> nation under heaven staying in
> Jerusalem.
At this sound, they gathered in a large
> crowd,
> but they were confused
> because each one heard them speaking
> in his own language.
They were astounded, and in amazement
> they asked,
> "Are not all these people who are
> speaking Galileans?
Then how does each of us hear them in
> his native language?
We are Parthians, Medes, and Elamites,
> inhabitants of Mesopotamia, Judea and
> Cappadocia,
> Pontus and Asia, Phrygia and
> Pamphylia,
> Egypt and the districts of Libya near
> Cyrene,
> as well as travelers from Rome,
> both Jews and converts to Judaism,
> Cretans and Arabs,
> yet we hear them speaking in our own
> tongues
> of the mighty acts of God."

RESPONSORIAL PSALM
Ps 104:1, 24, 29-30, 31, 34

℟. (cf. 30) Lord, send out your Spirit, and
    renew the face of the earth.
    or:
℟. Alleluia.

Bless the LORD, O my soul!
    O LORD, my God, you are great indeed!
How manifold are your works, O LORD!
    The earth is full of your creatures.

℟. Lord, send out your Spirit, and renew
    the face of the earth.
    or:
℟. Alleluia.

If you take away their breath, they perish
    and return to their dust.
When you send forth your spirit, they are
    created,
    and you renew the face of the earth.

℟. Lord, send out your Spirit, and renew
    the face of the earth.
    or:
℟. Alleluia.

May the glory of the LORD endure forever;
    may the LORD be glad in his works!
Pleasing to him be my theme;
    I will be glad in the LORD.

℟. Lord, send out your Spirit, and renew
    the face of the earth.
    or:
℟. Alleluia.

SECOND READING
Rom 8:8-17

or
1 Cor 12:3b-7, 12-13

SEQUENCE

See Appendix A, p. 302.

About Liturgy
A second wind: Hopefully, by the time we get to Pentecost we have not exhausted ourselves so much during the seven weeks plus one day of the Easter season. But even if you're feeling relief more than rejuvenation on this day, you can still find simple ways to catch a second wind of the Spirit from Easter. Here are some ideas:

Wear red: If you're the presider, that's easy. But even beyond liturgical vestments, find a way to add a touch of red to your clothing—in a pendant, or socks, with a tie, or shoes. As you go about your day, you will be a walking reminder to yourself and others that the Spirit dwells among us.

Remember and give thanks for your godparents: If your baptismal or confirmation godparents are still around, contact them and thank them for the gift of their faith. If you are a godparent, connect with your companion and let them know you are praying for them.

Make every breath count: A beautiful image from today's reading from the Gospel of John is Jesus breathing on his disciples and blessing them with his words. Pay special attention to the words you share with others today. Make every word you give a blessing upon them.

Remember the neophytes: Invite the neophytes of your parish to be part of the entrance procession, and, if possible, have them wear their baptismal garments. This reminds us that the fullness of the Spirit's presence is found in these "new plants" who have been brought to new life by the saving breath of God.

About Initiation
Celebrating with the neophytes: Easter Vigil seemed so long ago, fifty days, to be exact. Are your neophytes still front and center in the focus of the parish as we all continue to deepen our grasp of the paschal mystery in our lives (see RCIA 244)? Even if the neophytes have been overshadowed by the many other celebrations and important occasions of this time of year, you can still rekindle your parish's care and concern for them during these days near Pentecost. A simple way to do this is just to plan a party. RCIA 249 says, "[S]ome sort of celebration should be held at the end of the Easter season near Pentecost Sunday." It might even be as easy as hosting coffee and donuts after Sunday Mass and making sure the neophytes and their godparents are present and greeted by the parishioners. Also invite those who were baptized at last year's Easter Vigil to be part of this celebration, too.

About Liturgical Music
Suggestions: There is an abundance of music that refers to the Holy Spirit that you can find in any of your liturgical music resources. Other kinds of texts to seek out include those that speak of mission, baptism, and forgiveness. One such example is "Church of God, Elect and Glorious" with text by James Siddon (Hope Publishing). This text works well set to either NETTLETON or HYFRYDOL. Also look for ways to reprise the music from the entire Easter season. For example, including the Litany of the Saints in some way at today's Mass provides a beautiful thread from First Sunday of Lent (when you might have used the Litany of the Saints as an entrance chant), to the Easter Vigil when we sang the litany as the elect processed to the font, to this last day of the paschal feasts.

Finally, don't forget to plan for the Pentecost sequence. This is a hymn that precedes the gospel acclamation Alleluia. Several settings of the text can be found in your hymnals. Consider using one that all the assembly can sing together.

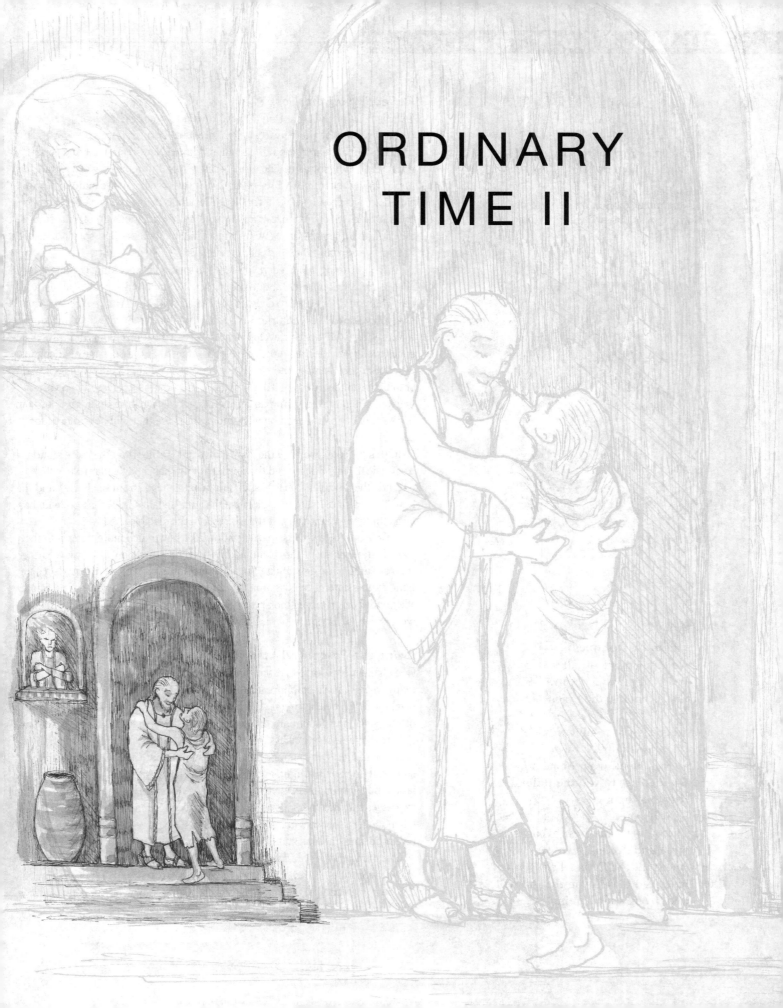

ORDINARY
TIME II

✠ SPIRITUALITY

GOSPEL ACCLAMATION
Cf. Rev 1:8

℞. Alleluia, alleluia.
Glory to the Father, the Son, and the Holy Spirit;
to God who is, who was, and who is to come.
℞. Alleluia, alleluia.

Gospel

John 16:12-15; L166C

Jesus said to his disciples:
　"I have much more to tell you, but
　　you cannot bear it now.
But when he comes, the Spirit
　of truth,
　he will guide you to all truth.
He will not speak on his own,
　but he will speak what he hears,
　and will declare to you the things
　　that are coming.
He will glorify me,
　because he will take from what is
　　mine and declare it to you.
Everything that the Father has is mine;
　for this reason I told you that he will
　　take from what is mine
　and declare it to you."

Reflecting on the Gospel

On this feast of the Most Holy Trinity we read from the Gospel of John. Some modern readers of the New Testament are often surprised that the word "Trinity" does not appear in the Bible at all, not in the New Testament and certainly not in the Old Testament. The term "Trinity" is a Latin-based word from *trinitas*, meaning the number three or a triad. It can also mean the state of being threefold, or triple. It's a term that later Christian theologians, particularly in the patristic era, coined to talk about God, and the relationship of Father, Son, and Spirit. So, though the New Testament has many texts that speak of God the Father, the Son, and the Spirit, it never refers to them as Trinity.

Today's reading is one such where Jesus the Son is speaking, making reference to the Spirit of truth and to the Father. As such, this is one of many texts that church fathers used to develop the theology of the Trinity. And that theology developed over centuries with many roadblocks, hurdles, and missteps, but also many advances, developments, and clarifications along the way. One conclusion from the theological developments is that the doctrine of the Trinity is sophisticated, subtle, and worthy of reflection. There is a dynamic relationship between the three "persons" of the Trinity that is expressed in a variety of ways in different scriptural passages. Today's passage from John gives us some of the subtlety of the relationship among the three that will be explored for centuries.

In this passage, we have the "Spirit of truth" rather than the more standard or classical, Holy Spirit. And the Spirit of truth has a particular role, which is to guide the disciples to truth, speaking what is heard from the Father and the Son. The Spirit of truth also glorifies the Son. He takes from the Son, who has everything the Father has, and declares it to the disciples.

This is only a four-verse passage! Consider how much more there is in the New Testament about the relationship between Father, Son, and Spirit! Rather than a mathematical formula to be explained and known, the Trinity is a shorthand expression for the dynamic relationship between Father, Son, and Spirit. We ponder this relationship and we will never exhaust it. We drink from the wellsprings of Scripture, which never run dry.

Living the Paschal Mystery

One challenge we have in discussing the Trinity is that we've been given so many images and metaphors for it. For example, it's been said that St. Patrick used the shamrock, a three-leafed clover, to teach the natives about Trinity. But of course God is more than three leaves, and each "person of the Trinity" has a more dynamic relationship than leaves on a shamrock. Some church fathers used the image of the sun for the Trinity, saying that the Father was like the sun itself, the Son the light, and the Spirit the heat. All three are in dynamic relation, but the sun itself is primary. This is a better image than a shamrock, but expresses the three persons as inanimate objects. Something similar happens when modern thinkers imagine the Trinity as the three modes of water in a liquid, solid, and gaseous state, but all at once!

The many images of Trinity and each of them incomplete in one way or another contribute to a fundamental challenge in discussing Trinity. Ultimately, it is best to go back to Scripture itself, and let that inform our understanding, which we do today by reading from the Gospel of John.

Focusing the Gospel

Key words and phrases: Everything that the Father has is mine; / for this reason I told you that [the Spirit of truth] will take from what is mine / and declare it to you.

To the point: In this one verse from today's gospel we see the interplay of the three persons of the Trinity. The Son has received everything from the Father, and the Spirit communicates the fullness of Father and Son. Within God there is a relationship among Father, Son, and Holy Spirit that can be seen as a complete outpouring from one to the other. We, who have been created in the image and likeness of God, are invited into this community of complete gift of self. In emptying ourselves, we are filled with the love of Father, Son, and Holy Spirit.

Connecting the Gospel

to the first and second readings: In the book of Proverbs we are introduced to the figure of "Lady Wisdom." In our first reading, Wisdom sings a hymn of self-revelation. Over the centuries theologians have seen this figure as both Jesus and the Holy Spirit. In this hymn we see the beginning of understanding that even before creation God lived in relationship. Wisdom tells us, "The LORD possessed me, the beginning of his ways, / the forerunner of his prodigies of long ago." The relationship between God, the creator, and Wisdom is one of joy: "I was his delight day by day, / playing before him all the while, / playing on the surface of his earth." In the gospel passage for today Jesus explains the relationship of Father, Son, and Holy Spirit as a complete knowing. In Proverbs we see it as complete joy. In the second reading from St. Paul's letter to the Romans we hear how we are connected to this dynamic. The love of Father and Son are poured into one another, but also "poured out into our hearts/ through the Holy Spirit that has been given to us."

to experience: To receive more fully the love of the triune God we make space by taking on the work of spiritual housekeeping. Greed, anger, hatred, apathy—what can be removed from our lives to make more room for God's love?

Connecting the Responsorial Psalm

to the readings: Delving into the mystery of the Trinity increases our wonder in life. Mysteries, such as that of the Trinity, are not problems to be solved or questions with one clear distinct answer that our human minds can grasp as they might a number. Rather, theological mysteries invite us into a deeper relationship with the One who calls us into being. In today's psalm we see this wonder in God's mysterious ways. After witnessing the beauty of creation the psalmist asks, "[W]hat is man that you should be mindful of him, / or the son of man that you should care for him?"

to psalmist preparation: God invites us into the outpouring of love between Father, Son, and Holy Spirit. Such an invitation inspires wonder, awe, and even incredulity at times. What in your life fills you with wonder and awe in the presence of God?

PROMPTS FOR FAITH-SHARING

In the psalm we hear the psalmist marvel at the works of creation. When have you experienced wonder and awe in nature?

St. Paul tells us today that we can boast in our affliction because "affliction produces endurance." When have you experienced affliction in your life that, looking back on, you can see made you stronger?

In your prayer, which member of the Trinity do you address the most often? Why do you think this is?

How has your understanding of the Trinity grown throughout your life?

Model Penitential Act

Presider: As we prepare to celebrate this feast of the Holy Trinity, let us pray for the grace to always listen to the call and counsel of God the Father, God the Son, and God the Holy Spirit . . . [*pause*]

Lord Jesus, you are the wisdom of God: Lord, have mercy.

Christ Jesus, you are the second person of the Holy Trinity: Christ, have mercy.

Lord Jesus, you call us to listen to the Spirit of Truth: Lord, have mercy.

Homily Points

• God, within God's own nature, is relationship. We believe in one God of three persons, the Father, the Son, and the Holy Spirit. Is it any surprise then that we, who are created in the image and likeness of God, are so hardwired for relationship? After birth, a baby who is given food and shelter but does not receive loving human interaction will fail to develop normally. From the very beginning of our lives, our relationships are our greatest joy and also can cause us the deepest sorrow.

• In the readings for today we hear how God lives out this triune relationship. In Proverbs, Wisdom is personified—identified later with both Jesus and the Holy Spirit—and brings joy to God, the creator. Wisdom is God's companion and delight. In the second reading, the Holy Spirit conveys the love between Father and Son, just as in the gospel the Spirit gives truth. Could this combination of joy, love, and truth serve as a blueprint for our own relationships?

• All relationships require celebration. In our world where so much revolves around transactions, we need time in relationships where we simply enjoy the other. We know, too, that all relationships require love, whether it is the relationship between spouses, parents and children, friends, or coworkers. Within the Trinity, love is dynamic and constantly outpouring. Relationships also demand truth, especially an authentic sharing of oneself with the other. From the very beginning of our lives within the womb we have experienced relationship—the relationship with God and the relationship with other humans. On this feast of the Holy Trinity let us rededicate ourselves to living out these relationships in joy, love, and truth.

Model Universal Prayer (Prayer of the Faithful)

Presider: In the gospel, Jesus tells the disciples of the Spirit of truth who will "guide [them] to all truth." Confident in the Spirit's guidance we lift up our prayers for ourselves and for our world.

Response: Lord, hear our prayer.

That those entrusted with leadership in the church diligently seek for and proclaim the truth . . .

That the world might know the self-giving love of the Father, Son, and Holy Spirit that is constantly poured out on all . . .

That those who suffer from broken relationships experience God's healing . . .

That all of us gathered here would follow the Spirit of truth in our daily decisions . . .

Presider: Triune God, you give us everything we need. Hear our prayers that we might be signs of your generous and gracious care in our world. Through Christ our Lord. Amen.

COLLECT

Let us pray.

Pause for silent prayer

God our Father, who by sending into the world
    the Word of truth and the Spirit of
    sanctification
made known to the human race your
    wondrous mystery,
grant us, we pray, that in professing the
    true faith,
we may acknowledge the Trinity of
    eternal glory
and adore your Unity, powerful in majesty.
Through our Lord Jesus Christ, your Son,
who lives and reigns with you in the unity
    of the Holy Spirit,
one God, for ever and ever. **Amen.**

FIRST READING

Prov 8:22-31

Thus says the wisdom of God:
"The LORD possessed me, the beginning of
    his ways,
    the forerunner of his prodigies of long
        ago;
from of old I was poured forth,
    at the first, before the earth.
When there were no depths I was brought
    forth,
    when there were no fountains or springs
        of water;
before the mountains were settled into
    place,
    before the hills, I was brought forth;
while as yet the earth and fields were not
    made,
    nor the first clods of the world.

"When the Lord established the heavens
    I was there,
    when he marked out the vault over the
        face of the deep;
when he made firm the skies above,
    when he fixed fast the foundations of
        the earth;
when he set for the sea its limit,
    so that the waters should not transgress
        his command;
then was I beside him as his craftsman,
    and I was his delight day by day,
playing before him all the while,
    playing on the surface of his earth;
    and I found delight in the human race."

RESPONSORIAL PSALM

Ps 8:4-5, 6-7, 8-9

℟. (2a) O Lord, our God, how wonderful
your name in all the earth!

When I behold your heavens, the work of
your fingers,
the moon and the stars which you set in
place—
what is man that you should be mindful
of him,
or the son of man that you should care
for him?

℟. O Lord, our God, how wonderful your
name in all the earth!

You have made him little less than the
angels,
and crowned him with glory and honor.
You have given him rule over the works of
your hands,
putting all things under his feet.

℟. O Lord, our God, how wonderful your
name in all the earth!

All sheep and oxen,
yes, and the beasts of the field,
the birds of the air, the fishes of the sea,
and whatever swims the paths of the
seas.

℟. O Lord, our God, how wonderful your
name in all the earth!

SECOND READING

Rom 5:1-5

Brothers and sisters:
Therefore, since we have been justified by
faith,
we have peace with God through our
Lord Jesus Christ,
through whom we have gained access
by faith
to this grace in which we stand,
and we boast in hope of the glory of God.
Not only that, but we even boast of our
afflictions,
knowing that affliction produces
endurance,
and endurance, proven character,
and proven character, hope,
and hope does not disappoint,
because the love of God has been
poured out into our hearts
through the Holy Spirit that has been
given to us.

About Liturgy

Join in the dance: In the fourth century, the Cappadocian Fathers developed a systematic theological connection between the Father, Son, and Holy Spirit. Their focus on the dynamic relationship among the divine persons led them to a description of the Trinity that was more an action than a definition. The interdependency and ongoing mutual self-giving in love of the divine persons not only made the Trinity One but also clarified each person as individuals. Their intimate relationship is a permeation of self, one with the other, but without any kind of confusion or blurring of self.

All this sounds quite complex! Perhaps a better image inspired by the Cappadocian Fathers to describe the dynamism of this divine relationship is a group dance. One word used to describe this dynamic communion of persons is *perichoresis*, translated by some as a circle dance. Each person contributes to a part of the dance and has a specific role in the choreography, but the entire group together and what they do together make up the dance. The partners pull and push against one another, not in resistance or by force but in support and unity. The dance is in constant motion, and the dancers are always focused on the other and not themselves. Moreover, the circle is never closed; the joy and unity of the dance and the dancers draw others into the circle to become part of the dance too.

Our celebration of the Trinity today gives us a moment to look at how we embody the open and intimate dynamism of the Trinity in our relationships with one another, especially in the ritual steps of the liturgy. Do our processions look like a joyful movement of gathering and sending? Can people feel connected to one another in the liturgy, or are there physical, psychological, or spiritual barriers that keep people inwardly focused on themselves or separated by status, distance, or disability? Do outsiders feel drawn in, and do they find a space ready and waiting for them so they can feel at home and part of the dance of the Trinity?

About Liturgical Music

Suggestions: Today's first reading, especially, reflects the dynamic movement of the Trinity as our vibrant, joyful source of life. How can one not delight in the image of the wisdom of God playing on the surface of the earth? Highlight this animated, life-giving aspect of the Trinity, and don't limit yourself to just using doctrinal statements set to music.

Jennifer Kerr Budziak's adaptation of Cecil Alexander's famous text of St. Patrick's Breastplate, "I Bind Unto Myself Today" (GIA), is one example of a charming, dance-like song that would be delightful during the preparation of gifts or even during the communion procession. Another such song is the Shaker melody and text by Sydney Carter, "Lord of the Dance" (Hope Publishing). The text recalls the first reading and God's abiding presence throughout all history and the Trinity's constant invitation to join in the dance.

Whatever songs you choose for today, look carefully at the text. Many hymns written with the three persons of the Trinity in mind will focus one stanza on the Father, another on the Son, and a third on the Spirit. Be sure that you sing all the necessary stanzas so as to keep the Trinity's union intact!

✝ SPIRITUALITY

GOSPEL ACCLAMATION
John 6:51

℟. Alleluia, alleluia.
I am the living bread that came down from heaven,
says the Lord; / whoever eats this bread will live
    forever.
℟. Alleluia, alleluia.

Gospel

Luke 9:11b-17; L169C

Jesus spoke to the crowds about
    the kingdom of God,
    and he healed those who
        needed to be cured.
As the day was drawing to a
        close,
    the Twelve approached him
        and said,
"Dismiss the crowd
    so that they can go to the sur-
        rounding villages and farms
    and find lodging and provisions;
    for we are in a deserted place here."
He said to them, "Give them some food
    yourselves."
They replied, "Five loaves and two fish
    are all we have,
    unless we ourselves go and buy food
        for all these people."
Now the men there numbered about
    five thousand.
Then he said to his disciples,
    "Have them sit down in groups of
        about fifty."
They did so and made them all sit down.
Then taking the five loaves and the two
    fish,
    and looking up to heaven,
    he said the blessing over them, broke
        them,
    and gave them to the disciples to set
        before the crowd.
They all ate and were satisfied.
And when the leftover fragments were
    picked up,
    they filled twelve wicker baskets.

Reflecting on the Gospel

"*Mange, mange!*" the Italian grandmother said to her grandchild. The plate of homemade pasta was too good to simply sit there untouched. The grandmother encouraged the child to "eat, eat!" And so the grandchild did and soon there was nothing left but some stray noodles. It brought a smile to both faces.

The feast of the Most Holy Body and Blood of Christ has its historical roots in thirteenth-century Belgium but it is celebrated worldwide today. Our reading comes from the Gospel of Luke. Though we might expect Luke's account of the institution of the Eucharist at the Last Supper, we have, instead, the multiplication of the loaves. But of course, this episode is laden with eucharistic overtones, especially in the verbs used: taking, blessed, broke, and gave. These are the verbs used at the Last Supper, and the verbs we use today in our eucharistic liturgy. So even though we are not reading from the Last Supper, eucharistic theology is baked into the story of the multiplication of the loaves.

Recall that the evangelist Luke portrayed Jesus as an infant lying in a manger. The word manger is often misunderstood as a cozy, comfy place to set a sleeping baby. But a manger is actually a "feed-trough," as the root word, *mange*, indicates. It's the place from which the animals eat. Narratively speaking, Luke is showing that from infancy Jesus, placed in the feed-trough, is food for the world. In the concluding chapter of the Gospel of Luke, on the road to Emmaus the disciples will learn that after the resurrection they come to know Jesus in the breaking of the bread. And in the Acts of the Apostles, too, the apostle Paul is shown celebrating a meal with the breaking of the bread (Acts 27:35). So this eucharistic theology is not limited to the Last Supper. It permeates the Gospel of Luke and his Acts of the Apostles. How appropriate that we read from his gospel today, on the feast of the Body and Blood of Christ. We feast on the body of Jesus, food for the world. *Mange, mange!*

Living the Paschal Mystery

It's said by Christians that Jesus is food for the world. This reflects the eucharistic theology that is the core of Christian spirituality. Jesus himself is the bread broken and shared. This is prefigured by Luke when the infant Jesus lies in the manger. Though we consider often the paschal mystery, the Eucharist itself is the food for our journey to the paschal mystery. Jesus himself comes to us as the Bread of Life, food for the world, and satisfaction for the hungry. Now, after the resurrection, after his many appearances to his disciples, we come to know him in the breaking of the bread. The breaking implies, and even foreshadows, the paschal mystery. The bread is not merely admired, but it is broken as Jesus himself is broken for us during the passion and death. In so doing, he becomes food for us, life-giving sustenance as we embark on the path to follow him.

Focusing the Gospel

Key words and phrases: Give them some food yourselves.

To the point: Jesus commands the bewildered disciples to feed the crowd of over five thousand. They reply, "Five loaves and two fish are all we have." The disciples are forgetting something, however. They also have the Bread of Life within their midst. The feeding of the five thousand comes immediately after the Twelve have returned from their first apostolic mission to proclaim the kingdom of God and heal the sick (Luke 9:1-6). Entrusted with a share in Jesus' saving work, the Twelve still do not comprehend the breadth of their mission. With Jesus there is no need to fear scarcity. The five loaves and two fish are enough to feed the hungry crowd with twelve baskets left over.

Connecting the Gospel

to the first and second readings: On this feast of Corpus Christi, it almost seems as if the first and second readings relate more readily to the Eucharist than the gospel reading from Luke. In Genesis, Abram is blessed by Melchizedek, "Priest of God Most High," who "takes bread and wine" as part of the ceremony. In Paul's first letter to the Corinthians we have the earliest reference to Christian Eucharist! In all three of today's readings we see a similar pattern. Food—bread and wine, loaves and fishes—are taken, a blessing is said, and something is given. Abram gives a tenth of all he has to Melchizedek; the disciples distribute the five loaves and two fish to the crowd; and Jesus gives his own Body and Blood to his friends.

to experience: Jesus calls us each to the eucharistic feast where the bread and wine are taken, blessed, and shared. In this same way we, as the Body of Christ, are to experience ourselves as chosen, blessed, and shared.

Connecting the Responsorial Psalm

to the readings: "You are a priest forever, in the line of Melchizedek." When this psalm was first composed, hundreds of years before Jesus was born, it proclaimed the priesthood of the king of Israel. As Christians, we recognize in these words a prefiguring of Christ. When this psalm refrain is chanted we see the image of Christ, our high priest, presiding over the first Eucharist at the Last Supper and presiding still at every altar throughout the world where the words are said, "This is my Body. This is my Blood."

to psalmist preparation: Within our eucharistic celebration Christ is present in the bread and wine, in the Word, in the gathered assembly and in the priest who acts *in persona Christi* as he consecrates the bread and the wine to become the Body and Blood of our Lord. As a cantor you serve the priesthood of the people of God by leading them in prayer and song. As you prepare this week, consider how you exercise your own priesthood. How are you called to bless others and share with them the Body of Christ?

PROMPTS FOR FAITH-SHARING

Jesus tells the disciples, "Give them some food yourselves," when they ask him to dismiss the hungry crowd. How does Jesus call you to feed those who experience hunger, whether physical or spiritual?

How do you see the eucharistic pattern of taking, blessing, breaking, and giving in your own life? How have you been chosen, blessed, and shared with others?

At first, in the feeding of the five thousand, the disciples react out of fear of scarcity, but Jesus abundantly provides. What resource in your life provokes this fear of scarcity? Is there a way you might see Jesus' abundant care in this experience?

In the Eucharist we experience Jesus present in the bread and wine, the Word of God, the priest who acts *in persona Christi* in the consecration of the Eucharist, and the gathered assembly singing and praying. Which of these communicates Christ's presence to you most strongly? Why?

Model Penitential Act

Presider: On this feast of Corpus Christi, we recall in a particular way Jesus' gift of his whole self to us in the Eucharist. As we begin this celebration let us pause to prepare ourselves to receive the Body and Blood of our Lord . . . [*pause*]

Lord Jesus, you are the bread of life: Lord, have mercy.

Christ Jesus, you are the wine of salvation: Christ, have mercy.

Lord Jesus, you are high priest forever: Lord, have mercy.

Homily Points

• Today we honor the gift of Christ's Body and Blood. In the second reading we hear the earliest account of the Last Supper in the New Testament. The words that Jesus speaks are the same words we hear spoken over the bread and the wine at every eucharistic celebration: "This is my Body . . . [This is] my Blood . . . Do this in memory of me."

• Our remembering is not a passive action recalling an event, which took place many centuries ago. Instead, it is a dynamic living of this past event in the present moment. Here, in this church, Jesus is present to us once more in the bread and the wine, his Body and Blood. Jesus gives himself to us completely. We might pause to ask ourselves, how present are we to Jesus? How willing are we to completely give ourselves to him?

• Unlike baptism and confirmation, the Eucharist isn't a sacrament we experience only once. Again and again we are called to this table to be with Jesus who desperately wants to be with us, to nourish us and strengthen us on this journey of faith. In a sermon given to catechumens on the feast of Pentecost, St. Augustine said of the Eucharist, "Become what you see, and receive what you are." The Body and Blood of Christ are not only to be adored, they are to be received with love and with the fervent prayer that we might become what we receive, the Body and Blood of Christ completely poured out for others.

Model Universal Prayer (Prayer of the Faithful)

Presider: Christ, our high priest, offers us his Body and Blood in the eucharistic feast. In thanksgiving for this great gift, we, in turn, offer up all that we are to God as we pray for our needs and the needs of our world.

Response: Lord, hear our prayer.

That all members of the church would heed the words of Jesus, "Give them some food yourselves" and seek to alleviate spiritual and physical hunger throughout the world . . .

That Christian denominations around the world be led into unity by Jesus, our high priest . . .

That all those who experience hunger, especially children and vulnerable adults, be provided for out of the earth's abundant resources . . .

That all of us gathered here might be strengthened and nourished by the Body and Blood of Christ . . .

Presider: God of infinite love, you sent your only Son to dwell among us and to give us the gift of his very self in bread and wine. Hear our prayers, that in receiving him we might become his healing presence to all those we meet. We ask this through Christ, our Lord. Amen.

RESPONSORIAL PSALM

Ps 110:1, 2, 3, 4

R⍭. (4b) You are a priest forever, in the line of Melchizedek.

The LORD said to my Lord: "Sit at my right hand
    till I make your enemies your footstool."

R⍭. You are a priest forever, in the line of Melchizedek.

The scepter of your power the LORD will stretch forth from Zion:
    "Rule in the midst of your enemies."

R⍭. You are a priest forever, in the line of Melchizedek.

"Yours is princely power in the day of your birth, in holy splendor;
    before the daystar, like the dew, I have begotten you."

R⍭. You are a priest forever, in the line of Melchizedek.

The LORD has sworn, and he will not repent:
    "You are a priest forever, according to the order of Melchizedek."

R⍭. You are a priest forever, in the line of Melchizedek.

SECOND READING

1 Cor 11:23-26

Brothers and sisters:
I received from the Lord what I also
    handed on to you,
    that the Lord Jesus, on the night he was handed over,
    took bread, and, after he had given thanks,
    broke it and said, "This is my body that is for you.
Do this in remembrance of me."
In the same way also the cup, after supper, saying,
    "This cup is the new covenant in my blood.
Do this, as often as you drink it, in remembrance of me."
For as often as you eat this bread and drink the cup,
    you proclaim the death of the Lord until he comes.

OPTIONAL SEQUENCE

See Appendix A, p. 303.

About Liturgy

Hosts from the tabernacle at Mass: One of the least-followed instructions of the Roman Missal is this: "It is most desirable that the faithful, just as the Priest himself is bound to do, receive the Lord's Body from hosts consecrated at the same Mass . . . so that even by means of the signs Communion may stand out more clearly as a participation in the sacrifice actually being celebrated" (General Instruction of the Roman Missal 85). This directive was first stated in the Constitution on the Sacred Liturgy (55), promulgated in 1963, and has been present in the Roman Missal ever since.

Yet, go to almost any Mass and you will see someone approach the tabernacle to retrieve hosts to be distributed to the assembly. The reasons they give for doing this have nothing to do with running out of hosts consecrated at that Mass. The practice is simply done because of old habits from preconciliar days, ignorance, or in some cases, because that's what they were taught to do.

Some proponents argue that the hosts at the altar and those in the tabernacle are one and the same Lord. That is certainly true, although it is not the primary issue.

First, the hosts reserved in the tabernacle are for the purpose of adoration and Communion to the dying and the sick unable to be present at Mass. There is no provision in any current liturgical document that allows for the assembly to normatively receive Communion from the hosts in the tabernacle during Mass.

Second and more importantly, the assembly's participation in the sacrifice of Christ stands out more clearly when they receive the hosts consecrated by the Holy Spirit through the Eucharistic Prayer they just prayed together with the priest. Sharing in the Eucharist at Mass is not simply about receiving the Body of Christ but about participating in what Christ did, that is, his sacrifice of praise to the Father through the giving of his life.

About Initiation

The Eucharistic Prayer: Although they are not yet able to share in Communion, the baptized who are preparing to be received or to celebrate the sacraments of confirmation and Eucharist are not dismissed from the Mass as are the catechumens. This is because their participation in Christ's sacrifice is embodied in their praying of the Eucharistic Prayer. The General Instruction of the Roman Missal says that "the meaning of this Prayer is that the whole congregation of the faithful joins with Christ in confessing the great deeds of God and in the offering of Sacrifice" (78). The baptized are full members of the faithful by their baptism. Thus, they are called to pray the prayers reserved for the faithful, of which the Eucharistic Prayer is primary.

About Liturgical Music

Ostinato refrains: Ideally, the assembly should be able to sing the communion song fully even as they are processing to the altar to share in the Body and Blood of Christ. A hymnal or even projected music on a screen can still be difficult to manage while one is walking. Here, short, memorable ostinato refrains that are repeated like a mantra can be helpful.

One common song used for Communion is Taize's "Eat This Bread" (GIA). Another song that is similar in style is *Psallite*'s "This Is My Body" (*Sacred Song*). The repeated antiphon is, "This is my body, given for you. This is my blood, poured out for you. Do this and remember me; do this and remember me." The choir, cantor, or schola has verses using the words from Psalm 23 that can be sung in alternation with the refrain or as a countermelody.

JUNE 23, 2019

THE MOST HOLY BODY AND BLOOD OF CHRIST (CORPUS CHRISTI)

GOSPEL ACCLAMATION
cf. Luke 1:76

℟. Alleluia, alleluia.
You, child, will be called prophet of the Most
    High,
for you will go before the Lord to prepare his
    way.
℟. Alleluia, alleluia.

Gospel   Luke 1:57-66, 80; L587

When the time arrived for Elizabeth
    to have her child
    she gave birth to a son.
Her neighbors and relatives heard
    that the Lord had shown his
        great mercy toward her,
    and they rejoiced with her.
When they came on the
        eighth day to circumcise
        the child,
    they were going to call him
        Zechariah after his
        father,
    but his mother said in reply,
    "No. He will be called John."
But they answered her,
    "There is no one among your
        relatives who has this name."
So they made signs, asking his father
    what he wished him to be called.
He asked for a tablet and wrote, "John
    is his name,"
    and all were amazed.
Immediately his mouth was opened, his
    tongue freed,
    and he spoke blessing God.
Then fear came upon all their
    neighbors,
    and all these matters were discussed
    throughout the hill country of Judea.
All who heard these things took them
    to heart, saying,
    "What, then, will this child be?"
For surely the hand of the Lord was
    with him.

The child grew and became strong in
    spirit,
    and he was in the desert until the day
    of his manifestation to Israel.

See Appendix A, p. 304, for the other readings.

Reflecting on the Gospel

Luke is the only evangelist to give us the story of John the Baptist's birth. And the way Luke tells it, John the Baptist and Jesus were cousins: their mothers were sisters. No other evangelist or New Testament author makes that connection. For Luke, other signs accompany the birth of John, demonstrating that the "hand of the Lord was with him." We recall how Zechariah, his father, doubted that Elizabeth would become pregnant, and he was subsequently struck dumb. That condition remained until he had the chance to ratify the name Elizabeth had chosen for the infant. Only then is Zechariah's "tongue freed" and he immediately blesses God.

These wondrous signs demonstrate clearly for Luke's audience that John will be something spectacular. Born six months prior to his cousin Jesus, John will prepare the way for the Son of God.

Luke has a particular concern for women as many of his stories throughout the gospel and the Acts of the Apostles demonstrate. The fact that Elizabeth is the one to name him John, when others wanted to name him Zechariah after his father, is significant. Not following Elizabeth's direction, her neighbors and relatives turn to Zechariah to get his input. He, of course, confirms Elizabeth's decision and the boy is named John, a heretofore-unknown family name. As Elizabeth plays a major role in the naming of John, so Mary will play a similar role for Jesus when he is born. In her case the angel tells her that "you shall name him Jesus" (Luke 1:31; NABRE). Thus the mothers are instrumental in each case, demonstrating how critical women are in Luke's gospel.

The role of women in the lives of John the Baptist and Jesus should come as no surprise. Though not the focus of our attention in many cases, it's clear that Luke is sure to draw our eyes to these critical female relationships throughout his gospel. To borrow a phrase, Mary and Elizabeth were each the hand that rocked the cradle. Their input and influence made John and Jesus the men they became, standing up to injustice and preaching the reign of God. On this celebration of the birth of John the Baptist it is appropriate to look to Elizabeth and her relative Mary to ponder the role and importance of women in the life of this great saint, the forerunner of Christ.

Living the Paschal Mystery

The birth of a child is the cause for joy. New life springing into the world gives hope. There is possibility and tremendous potential when each person is born. We might ponder who or what she will become, how her life will influence others. Will this child be a leader or more of a follower? What are the exhilarations or sad events she will experience? How will he deal with success or disappointment?

It's likely that Elizabeth wondered about her child in a similar way, especially given the extraordinary events that surrounded his birth. Not only Elizabeth's child, but each new human life is special and to be treasured, as we know. New life is an expression of the paschal mystery, giving meaning and joy to our lives. We seek to create a loving, caring environment for each human being so every person can grow into their full potential.

Focusing the Gospel

Key words and phrases: surely the hand of the Lord was with him

To the point: From the moment of his conception John was given a role in salvation history: point to Jesus. Even in the womb he witnessed to Christ's presence by leaping when Mary, bearing Jesus, drew near. After his birth we are told, "The child grew and became strong in spirit, / and he was in the desert until the day / of his manifestation to Israel." John's ministry throughout his life can be a model for us. Whether working actively, or in quiet recollection, John's whole life heralded the presence of Jesus to all those around him.

Model Penitential Act

Presider: On this feast of the Nativity of John the Baptist we celebrate this saint's complete and total devotion to God. For the times that our devotion has faltered we ask for pardon and forgiveness . . . [*pause*]

   Lord Jesus, you are the savior of the world: Lord, have mercy.
   Christ Jesus, you call us to repentance: Christ, have mercy.
   Lord Jesus, you are the light of the nations: Lord, have mercy.

Model Universal Prayer (Prayer of the Faithful)

Presider: Through the intercession of John the Baptist we lift up our prayers to the Lord.

Response: Lord, hear our prayer.

That the church, following the example of John the Baptist, constantly point to Jesus, the light of the world . . .

That leaders of nations embrace humble servant leadership . . .

That pregnant women and their unborn children receive necessary healthcare and support . . .

That this church community might help all of its young people discern God's call in their life . . .

Presider: God of salvation, you called John the Baptist to herald the coming of your Son. Hear our prayers that we might continue to proclaim the good news in everything we do. We ask this through Christ our Lord. Amen.

About Liturgy

A sacredness of a person's name: Today's readings give us an opportunity to reflect on our names. Many older Catholics grew up during a time when children's names looked like the litany of saints. Today, however, parents are more open to a greater variety of names for their children, so that many popular names today have no historical Christian connection to a saint or virtue.

   Some may lament this trend in giving non-Christian-specific names to children. Although church teaching praises the practice of giving one's child the name of a saint, the actual law does not require it for baptism or confirmation. Canon 855 of the Code of Canon Law simply states that the name should not be "foreign to Christian sensibility." The *Catechism of the Catholic Church* goes further and describes the holiness of a person's given name this way: "Everyone's name is sacred. The name is the icon of the person. It demands respect as a sign of the dignity of the one who bears it" (2158).

   In all our rites and interactions with one another, let us honor each person's given name with respect and reverence.

COLLECT

Let us pray.

Pause for silent prayer

O God, who raised up Saint John the Baptist
to make ready a nation fit for Christ the
      Lord,
give your people, we pray,
the grace of spiritual joys
and direct the hearts of all the faithful
into the way of salvation and peace.
Through our Lord Jesus Christ, your Son,
who lives and reigns with you in the unity
      of the Holy Spirit,
one God, for ever and ever. **Amen**.

FOR REFLECTION

• At John's birth the people gathered wonder, "What, then, will this child be?" How have you experienced God's evolving call in your own life?

• As John grew he was "in the desert." How do you experience "desert times" of reflection and contemplation in your own life?

Homily Points

• In the Gospel of Luke we are given two birth stories in close succession, the birth of John the Baptist and six months later, the birth of Jesus. Though both are born to the same extended Jewish family these births are quite different.

• Elizabeth births John surrounded by her family and community. As a priest, John's father, Zechariah, has standing in the religious community, and so his circumcision and naming carry some import as evidenced by the discussion over John's name.

• Jesus' birth takes place far from family, community, and even human company as he is born in a place where animals are kept.

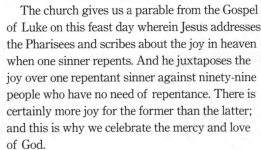

GOSPEL ACCLAMATION
Matt 11:29ab

R̸. Alleluia, alleluia.
Take my yoke upon you, says the Lord;
and learn from me, for I am meek and humble
    of heart.
R̸. Alleluia, alleluia.

or

John 10:14

R̸. Alleluia, alleluia.
I am the good shepherd says the
    Lord,
I know my sheep, and mine
    know me.
R̸. Alleluia, alleluia.

Gospel

Luke 15:3-7; L172C

**Jesus addressed this par-
    able to the Pharisees
    and scribes:
"What man among you
    having a hundred
    sheep and losing one
    of them
would not leave the
    ninety-nine in the
    desert
and go after the lost one until
    he finds it?
And when he does find it,
    he sets it on his shoulders with great
        joy
and, upon his arrival home,
he calls together his friends and
    neighbors and says to them,
'Rejoice with me because I have
    found my lost sheep.'
I tell you, in just the same way
    there will be more joy in heaven over
        one sinner who repents
than over ninety-nine righteous
        people
who have no need of repentance."**

See Appendix A, p. 305, for the other readings.

Reflecting on the Gospel

On this feast of the Most Sacred Heart of Jesus we might encounter artwork that represents graphically a heart, sometimes wrapped in thorns or topped by a cross. Younger people might wince at such a depiction, wondering what precisely we are celebrating. Historically, this feast has been one of the most popular devotions in Catholicism, with roots deep into the eleventh century. A devotion to the heart of Jesus is meant to express a devotion to the love of God, or the mercy of Christ. The graphic portrayal of a physical heart might not capture that sense today, but it is what we celebrate nonetheless.

The church gives us a parable from the Gospel of Luke on this feast day wherein Jesus addresses the Pharisees and scribes about the joy in heaven when one sinner repents. And he juxtaposes the joy over one repentant sinner against ninety-nine people who have no need of repentance. There is certainly more joy for the former than the latter; and this is why we celebrate the mercy and love of God.

When Jesus preaches good news, we might ask ourselves, "Who thinks it's good news and why?" This parable gives us one answer. The news of salvation is good for the repentant sinner. There is forgiveness, mercy, and redemption. And once that offer is accepted, all heaven rejoices mightily. On the other hand, for those who consider them-selves righteous and do not repent there is not the same joy in heaven. These people do not seek forgiveness, mercy, or redemption because they do not sense that they need to repent of anything.

So the good news is "good" precisely for those who repent and experience the mercy of God. Redemption is a possibility, and God is ready to welcome the lost. For this quality of the divine, we celebrate the "Sacred Heart," the mercy and tenderness of our God.

So where do we find ourselves today? With the ninety-nine? Or are we the lost sheep? When lost, we know that mercy awaits, and for that, there is great rejoicing.

Living the Paschal Mystery

How many of us have it all figured out? How many of us have a plan and exe-cute it flawlessly? Or, how do we present ourselves to friends and family? There is a natural human tendency to put the best face on things, to present a pleasant disposition, to act as though all is fine. But in reality each of us has been lost at some point and perhaps even now. When we experience that sensation of being lost, it is then that we are invited to undergo a death of sorts so that we might rise to new life. Not every plan is executed flawlessly. Ultimately we are not in control. By following our own designs it is likely that we will end up at a dead end, or walking in circles. It's then that we can turn matters over to the divine, recognizing that God will raise us up to new life. When we repent of our own self-righteousness and embrace the role of lost sheep, there we will find rejoic-ing in heaven for we will have died to ourselves to live with the eternal one. It is then that we experience the mercy of God, the Sacred Heart.

Focusing the Gospel

Key words and phrases: What man among you . . .

To the point: Jesus offers the parable of the Lost Sheep in response to the grumbling of the Pharisees and scribes over his hospitality to sinners. Jesus begins with a question, "What man among you having a hundred sheep and losing one of them / would not leave the ninety-nine in the desert / and go after the lost one until he finds it?" The scribes and Pharisees are invited to put themselves in the shoes of the shepherd. If the shepherd would so labor for one lost sheep, how much more does God labor and rejoice to find one who is lost?

Model Penitential Act

Presider: Today we celebrate the love and compassion of Jesus' Sacred Heart. Let us acknowledge our sins before the Lord and so prepare to receive his infinite mercy . . . [*pause*]

Lord Jesus, you are the Good Shepherd who seeks the lost: Lord, have mercy.
Christ Jesus, you came to show sinners the way: Christ, have mercy.
Lord Jesus, you invite us to live within your Sacred Heart: Lord, have mercy.

Model Universal Prayer (Prayer of the Faithful)

Presider: Confident in God's mercy, we lift up our prayers through the intercession of the Sacred Heart of Jesus.

Response: Lord, hear our prayer.

That the church be a welcome refuge for sinners and a place of healing and joy . . .

That all people of the world might know the compassionate and merciful love of God who never ceases to seek the lost . . .

That those who experience crushing grief, despair, anxiety, and depression find comfort and strength within the Sacred Heart of Jesus . . .

That all gathered here might follow the example of Jesus, our Good Shepherd, and offer fellowship, hospitality, and welcome to those on the outskirts of society . . .

Presider: Merciful Father, you sent your Son to reveal to all people the depths of your love for us. Hear our prayers that we might find shelter within this merciful love and become shelter for others. We ask this in the name of Jesus, Our Lord. Amen.

About Liturgy

Creed: When asked what Christians believe, we tend to think of the Creed. As we pray the Creed today on this solemnity, let us remember that faith is a relationship with the person of Christ, through whose heart we are called to love one another. As the post-communion prayer for this day says so well, "make us fervent with the fire of holy love, / so that, drawn always to your Son, / we may learn to see him in our neighbor."

COLLECT

Let us pray.

Grant, we pray, almighty God,
that we, who glory in the Heart of your
    beloved Son
and recall the wonders of his love for us,
may be made worthy to receive
an overflowing measure of grace
from that fount of heavenly gifts.
Through our Lord Jesus Christ, your Son,
who lives and reigns with you in the unity of
    the Holy Spirit,
one God, for ever and ever. **Amen.**

or:

O God, who in the Heart of your Son,
wounded by our sins,
bestow on us in mercy
the boundless treasures of your love,
grant, we pray,
that, in paying him the homage of our devotion,
we may also offer worthy reparation.
Through our Lord Jesus Christ, your Son,
who lives and reigns with you in the unity of
    the Holy Spirit,
one God, for ever and ever. **Amen.**

FOR REFLECTION

• On the feast of the Sacred Heart of Jesus we remember the Lord's infinite mercy. How have you experienced this mercy in your own life?

• Our gospel reading today is the familiar parable of the Lost Sheep. Who are the "lost" in your community? How might you be called to embody Jesus' Sacred Heart to them?

Homily Points

• There are many images we use to relate to God: Father, Mother, Creator, Redeemer, King. . . . None, of course, is perfect or complete, but each may help us to draw closer to the mystery of God. In the passages we read today, it is revealed that God is an attentive, loving, shepherd. In the prophecy from Ezekiel, God proclaims, "The lost I will seek out, / the strayed I will bring back, / the injured I will bind up, the sick I will heal."

R︋. Alleluia, alleluia.
You are Peter and upon this rock I will build my
    Church,
and the gates of the netherworld shall not
    prevail against it.
R︋. Alleluia, alleluia.

Gospel

Matt 16:13-19; L591

When Jesus went into the
    region of Caesarea
    Philippi
he asked his
    disciples,
"Who do people
    say that the
    Son of Man
    is?"
They replied, "Some
    say John the Bap-
    tist, others Elijah,
    still others Jeremiah or one
    of the prophets."
He said to them, "But who do you say
    that I am?"
Simon Peter said in reply,
    "You are the Christ, the Son of the
    living God."
Jesus said to him in reply, "Blessed are
    you, Simon son of Jonah.
For flesh and blood has not revealed
    this to you, but my heavenly
    Father.
And so I say to you, you are Peter,
    and upon this rock I will build my
    Church,
    and the gates of the netherworld
    shall not prevail against it.
I will give you the keys to the Kingdom
    of heaven.
Whatever you bind on earth shall be
    bound in heaven;
    and whatever you loose on earth
    shall be loosed in heaven."

See Appendix A, p. 306, for the other readings.

Reflecting on the Gospel

Peter and Paul were quite different people. Depending on which gospel we read, Peter was with Jesus from nearly the beginning of his ministry while Paul never knew or witnessed the historical Jesus. Peter denied knowing Jesus three times before being rehabilitated in a resurrection appearance when Jesus asked him three times, "Do you love me?" Paul never denied Jesus, but certainly persecuted him by persecuting the disciples and encountered the risen Christ only once in "a vision" on the road to Damascus. Peter evangelized the Jews and seemed content to stay with many of the other apostles in Jerusalem for several years after the resurrection. Paul saw the wider implications of the Christ-event and began evangelizing Gentiles, referring to himself as an "apostle" even though he was not one of the Twelve. After coming to an agreement at the Council of Jerusalem (Acts 15), Peter and Paul sparred with one another in Antioch as each had understood the ramifications of the council differently. Their parting ways in that important ancient city, where the disciples were first called Christians, is the last time the New Testament says they were together. All in all they might have spent less than three weeks of their lives together, and yet in martyrdom they are linked as founders of the church in Rome, even though neither was the first Christian in the Eternal City. This is a good reminder that there is more than one way to be a saint, or even live out a relationship with Christ.

In today's gospel we hear Peter's proclamation par excellence: "You are the Christ, the Son of the living God." And Jesus in reply refers to Peter—or perhaps his confession—as the rock on which he will build the church. Thus Peter becomes the de facto leader of the Twelve, though Paul will step in after the resurrection to play a critical role as well. As Peter and Paul had different but authentic responses to Christ we, too, will have our own response to what Christ calls us to be and to do. Peter was not Paul; Paul was not Peter. Each lived their response in their own way, and not even agreeing with each other all or perhaps even much of the time. Such is the life of the Christian disciple. United by Christ, we live our own response to his call, sometimes bumping heads along the way, but always united by something stronger.

Living the Paschal Mystery

On this feast of the saints Peter and Paul we might step back to consider our own response to Christ's call. Peter's confession of Jesus as the Messiah, Son of the Living God, became the cornerstone of the church. Paul's response on the road to Damascus turned him from a persecutor to a disciple, and ultimately, apostle to the Gentiles. Each died to a past way of life and opened themselves to new possibilities by their faith in Christ. Peter overcame his denial of Jesus and Paul overcame his persecution, but both did so only with the grace of God. Though neither could likely foresee their eventual martyrdom in Rome, the capital of the empire, each pursued what they knew to be true to the end. May we like Peter and Paul find the grace to pursue our own path of discipleship, remaining true to the end, no matter where that might lead.

Focusing the Gospel

Key words and phrases: But who do you say that I am?

To the point: Jesus' line of questioning goes from the general to the personal. After asking the disciples, "Who do people say that the Son of Man is?" he asks them directly, "But who do you say that I am?" The Christian faith requires from us both a communal and an individual response. Today we celebrate the witnesses of two foundational Christian saints, Peter and Paul. Their relationship to Jesus, response to his call, and mission in the early church were each different from the other's, and yet, in concert they helped to establish the universal church that we know today. Just as we celebrate the differences of Peter and Paul we are called to foster our own unique relationships with the Lord. Jesus calls us by name and asks us in this moment in our lives, "Who do *you* say that I am?"

Model Penitential Act

Presider: On this feast of Saints Peter and Paul we remember these two who gave everything for the Lord and his people. As we enter into this celebration let us call to mind the times we have not lived up to their example . . . [*pause*]

Lord Jesus, you are the Messiah, the Son of the Living God: Lord, have mercy.

Christ Jesus, you redeem sinners and offer salvation to all: Christ, have mercy.

Lord Jesus, you called Saints Peter and Paul to proclaim the good news to the Jews and the Gentiles: Lord, have mercy.

Model Universal Prayer (Prayer of the Faithful)

Presider: In their lives and in their deaths Saints Peter and Paul dedicated themselves to Jesus Christ and his people. Together with them, we offer our prayers to God.

Response: Lord, hear our prayer.

That, through the intercession of St. Peter and St. Paul, the church continue to bring the good news of Jesus Christ to all corners of the world . . .

That all nations ensure freedom of religion for their people . . .

That those who experience religious persecution be strengthened, comforted, and protected . . .

That all gathered here follow in the footsteps of St. Peter and St. Paul by serving Jesus with love and fidelity . . .

Presider: God of faithfulness, through your saints Peter and Paul you give us an example of lives poured out as a libation for others. Hear our prayers that we might give of ourselves with the same generosity and abandon. We pray through Jesus Christ our Lord. Amen.

About Liturgy

True Christian community: Parker Palmer, noted educator and author, says that true community is committing to sit down at dinner next to the person you dislike the most. And when they get up to leave, someone worse takes their place.

We can't know for sure what Peter and Paul's relationship was like, but we know that it wasn't always pleasant, and it got downright nasty at times. Yet, Christian iconography rarely shows one without the other. Although they may have spent no more than a few weeks together, their commitment to the gospel became a crucial element upon which the church was built.

COLLECT
Let us pray.

Pause for silent prayer

O God, who on the Solemnity of the Apostles Peter and Paul
give us the noble and holy joy of this day,
grant, we pray, that your Church
may in all things follow the teaching
of those through whom she received
the beginnings of right religion.
Through our Lord Jesus Christ, your Son,
who lives and reigns with you in the unity of the Holy Spirit,
one God, for ever and ever. **Amen.**

FOR REFLECTION

• St. Peter and St. Paul answered Jesus' call to mission through their own unique gifts and talents. Which God-given gifts are you being called to use for the good of Jesus and his church?

• In his second letter to Timothy St. Paul says, "I have competed well; I have finished the race." Which aspects of the spiritual life require the most effort from you?

• At this point in your journey of faith how do you answer the question of Jesus, "Who do you say that I am?"

Homily Points

• Sts. Peter and Paul are spiritual giants in our faith. Together they continued the work of Jesus in establishing his church throughout the Eastern Mediterranean. The successor of St. Peter continues to lead and shape our Catholic Church whereas the epistles of St. Paul form nearly one quarter of the New Testament.

• And yet, both of these men were also sinners. Today on their feast day, let us not only stand back in awe at the good work they were able to accomplish, but let us also rejoice in the God who works with sinful humanity to bring life to the world.

GOSPEL ACCLAMATION

1 Sam 3:9; John 6:68c

R⁊. Alleluia, alleluia.
Speak, Lord, your servant is listening;
you have he words of everlasting life.
R⁊. Alleluia, alleluia.

Gospel   Luke 9:51-62; L99C

When the days for Jesus' being taken up
     were fulfilled,
  he resolutely determined to journey
       to Jerusalem,
  and he sent messengers ahead of
       him.
On the way they entered a Samaritan
     village
  to prepare for his reception there,
  but they would not welcome him
  because the destination of his jour-
       ney was Jerusalem.
When the disciples James and John saw this
     they asked,
  "Lord, do you want us to call down fire
       from heaven
  to consume them?"
Jesus turned and rebuked them, and they
     journeyed to another village.

As they were proceeding on their journey
     someone said to him,
  "I will follow you wherever you go."
Jesus answered him,
  "Foxes have dens and birds of the sky
       have nests,
  but the Son of Man has nowhere to rest
       his head."

And to another he said, "Follow me."
But he replied, "Lord, let me go first and
     bury my father."
But he answered him, "Let the dead bury
     their dead.
But you, go and proclaim the kingdom of
     God."
And another said, "I will follow you, Lord,
  but first let me say farewell to my family
       at home."
To him Jesus said, "No one who sets a hand
     to the plow
  and looks to what was left behind is fit
       for the kingdom of God."

Reflecting on the Gospel

Now we are in the midst of summer. July is around the corner and we are fully within Ordinary Time. Today's gospel begins with the journey to Jerusalem, a section of the gospel that scholars call the major insertion, stretching from Luke 9:51 to 18:14. In this section, Luke departs from his Markan source and uses material from other sources. Some of the most cherished stories about Jesus are found in this journey to Jerusalem section of the Gospel of Luke, which we begin reading today.

Jesus "resolutely determined" to make his way to Jerusalem, where the reader knows what fate awaits him. Still, Jesus is not shy; he does not lack courage. The Greek that is translated into English as "resolutely determined" literally means "he set his face." There is no turning back.

Three examples of "would-be disciples" illustrate the point that there is no turning back for the life of a true disciple. The first would-be disciple is told that discipleship means a life of following, without even a place to rest one's head. The second has unfinished business, the burying of the dead; yet a life of discipleship still comes first. And the third wants to say good-bye, but here, too, a life of discipleship comes first. The image is stark. Once one puts their hand to the plow there is no turning back; there is no wistful glance at what was left behind. Instead, the disciple, like Jesus himself, must "set his face" toward Jerusalem and pursue that end with a single-minded devotion. This ideal may seem unattainable but it is the call of the disciple nevertheless. Jesus himself sets the example.

And when hospitality is not found along the journey, the immediate desire of the disciples is "to call down fire"! That is not an appropriate response, as the rebuke from Jesus makes clear. There is much to learn on the journey to Jerusalem. Luke's Jesus has many parables to teach, many examples to give, and some rebukes to issue. The conclusion of this ministry will end with the cross, the ultimate example of single-minded devotion that does not look back.

Living the Paschal Mystery

We are a great geographical distance, foreign language, and culture, and about twenty centuries removed from the time and place of Jesus. We do not have the opportunity to follow him literally throughout Judea and Samaria, and we never did. He spoke Aramaic, so we would not understand him if we heard him. We have stories about him, his followers, and his would-be followers. From them we learn lessons and seek to apply them to ourselves in our own situation.

Jesus knows where his ministry will end: Jerusalem, not only a city but a metaphor for the paschal mystery where he will face his passion, death, and resurrection. It is for this reason that he "sets his face" to Jerusalem. Where do we set our face? What is our ultimate destiny? From what will we not look back to see what we have left behind? May we set our face toward our own Jerusalem and a journey with Christ, at the conclusion of which we will experience the paschal mystery. The journey is worthy of the effort. There is no turning back.

Focusing the Gospel

Key words and phrases: When the days for Jesus' being taken up were fulfilled, he resolutely determined to journey to Jerusalem

To the point: In today's gospel reading we reach a turning point in Jesus' ministry. Jesus begins his final travel toward Jerusalem that will ultimately end in his death and resurrection. We might expect this moment to take place near the end of Luke's gospel. Actually, we still have ten more chapters in Luke before Jesus even enters Jerusalem. We could say a full *half* of Jesus' ministry takes place on the road to Jerusalem. In the second part of today's gospel Jesus encounters three "would-be disciples." His responses to them may seem harsh. But Jesus knows that this journey he has undertaken will require determination and perseverance. Being a disciple of Jesus demands the same.

Connecting the Gospel

to the first reading: The total commitment Jesus demands of those who would be citizens of the kingdom of God is illustrated in our first reading about Elijah and Elisha. Elijah symbolically passes the mantle of his prophecy to Elisha by throwing his cloak upon Elisha as he plows a field with twelve yoke of oxen. Elisha accepts this commission by destroying the vestiges of his previous life. He slaughters the oxen, burns the plowing equipment to cook the meat, and then feeds "the people." Perhaps this crowd is comprised of all those he has known and loved.

to experience: For Elisha there is no going back. His encounter with Elijah has radically changed the trajectory of his life. What have been the moments in your life that have marked definitive turning points?

Connecting the Responsorial Psalm

to the readings: In the gospel and the first reading following the path of God seems difficult. It demands giving up home and livelihood. Psalm 16 reminds us, however, of the delight that is found when one responds to Jesus' call. The psalmist sings, "I set the Lord ever before me . . . You will show me the path to life, / fullness of joys in your presence." Seldom will modern followers find the need to answer Jesus' call by destroying the tools of their previous profession as Elijah did, and yet the path of discipleship requires sacrifice. To follow the Lord of life we are called to give up all that does not lead to our greatest flourishing.

to psalmist preparation: In our daily life we encounter Jesus' call to follow him. Each moment is a new opportunity to respond out of love and fidelity. This week, consider how the Lord is calling you in small and large events to follow him.

PROMPTS FOR FAITH-SHARING

In today's psalm we hear the psalmist proclaim, "You will show me the path to life, / fullness of joys in your presence." When have you experienced particular joy in the life of discipleship?

Following Jesus often requires less of a physical shift and more of an internal one. St. Paul tells us the whole law is encapsulated in the commandment, "You shall love your neighbor as yourself." How are you being called to follow Jesus more closely by embracing this commandment in your daily life?

Jesus gives us an example of perseverance by resolutely turning his face toward Jerusalem. What areas in your life require perseverance and determination right now?

What have been turning points in your life when you experienced Jesus' call and responded to it?

Model Penitential Act

Presider: Jesus calls us to follow him. For the times we have wavered in our calling to be disciples we ask for pardon and forgiveness . . . [*pause*]

Lord Jesus, you teach us the way of perseverance: Lord, have mercy.

Christ Jesus, you show us the way of faithfulness: Christ, have mercy.

Lord Jesus, you call us to follow you in humility and love: Lord, have mercy.

Homily Points

• In the first "call" stories in the Gospel of Luke from chapter 5 we see Simon, James, John, and Levi get up and "leave everything" to follow Jesus (5:11, 28). In today's reading from chapter 9 of Luke's gospel we hear of three different accounts where three different people either ask to follow Jesus or are called to follow Jesus and for each there is a condition. The first tells Jesus, "I will follow you wherever you go." Jesus replies, "[T]he Son of Man has nowhere to rest his head." Perhaps he is warning this would-be disciple that if he wishes to become a disciple because of the anticipated destination. Jesus has no acclaim, wealth, or stability to share.

• The second is called but asks to first go and bury his father. Jesus replies, "Let the dead bury their dead. / But you, go and proclaim the kingdom of God." In Judaism burying the dead is an important act of service. This man would especially be expected to bury his father and perform the religious rites surrounding burial. Jesus' response is shocking therefore, but the message comes through clearly: Let nothing, not even a commitment to bury the dead, distract you from proclaiming the kingdom of God.

• The third assures Jesus, "I will follow you, Lord, / but first let me say farewell to my family." Again, this is a reasonable request from a person steeped in a tradition that teaches children to respect their father and mother. But Jesus sees something else, perhaps an excuse or a hesitation, because he answers, "No one who sets a hand to the plow / and looks to what was left behind is fit for the kingdom of God." In these calls we see the urgency and importance of Jesus' mission. The kingdom of God, this kingdom of light, life, and love must be our primary objective.

Model Universal Prayer (Prayer of the Faithful)

Presider: The Lord of life calls us to follow him. In faith may we turn our lives over to him in deed and prayer.

Response: Lord, hear our prayer.

That the church be blessed with good and faithful leaders who answer the calling of the Lord, "Follow me" . . .

That world leaders persevere in seeking a solution for homelessness among their populations . . .

That those who are seeking for meaning, fulfillment, and purpose within their lives be led by Jesus to use their gifts for the good of others . . .

That all of us here be given the gift of discernment in following Jesus wherever he leads . . .

Presider: God of the humble and small, you sent your Son, Jesus Christ, to guide us in the ways of faithfulness and fidelity. Hear our prayers that we might follow him in all ways, all the days of our lives. We ask this through Christ, our Lord. Amen.

COLLECT

Let us pray.

Pause for silent prayer

O God, who through the grace of adoption
chose us to be children of light,
grant, we pray,
that we may not be wrapped in the
    darkness of error
but always be seen to stand in the bright
    light of truth.
Through our Lord Jesus Christ, your Son,
who lives and reigns with you in the unity
    of the Holy Spirit,
one God, for ever and ever. **Amen.**

FIRST READING

1 Kgs 19:16b, 19-21

The LORD said to Elijah:
    "You shall anoint Elisha, son of
        Shaphat of Abel-meholah,
    as prophet to succeed you."

Elijah set out and came upon Elisha, son
    of Shaphat,
    as he was plowing with twelve yoke of
        oxen;
    he was following the twelfth.
Elijah went over to him and threw his
    cloak over him.
Elisha left the oxen, ran after Elijah,
    and said,
    "Please, let me kiss my father and
        mother goodbye,
    and I will follow you."
Elijah answered, "Go back!
Have I done anything to you?"
Elisha left him and, taking the yoke of
    oxen, slaughtered them;
    he used the plowing equipment for fuel
        to boil their flesh,
    and gave it to his people to eat.
Then Elisha left and followed Elijah as his
    attendant.

RESPONSORIAL PSALM

Ps 16:1-2, 5, 7-8, 9-10, 11

R̸. (cf. 5a) You are my inheritance, O Lord.

Keep me, O God, for in you I take refuge;
   I say to the LORD, "My Lord are you.
O LORD, my allotted portion and my cup,
   you it is who hold fast my lot."

R̸. You are my inheritance, O Lord.

I bless the LORD who counsels me;
   even in the night my heart exhorts me.
I set the LORD ever before me;
   with him at my right hand I shall not be
     disturbed.

R̸. You are my inheritance, O Lord.

Therefore my heart is glad and my soul
   rejoices,
   my body, too, abides in confidence
because you will not abandon my soul to
   the netherworld,
   nor will you suffer your faithful one to
     undergo corruption.

R̸. You are my inheritance, O Lord.

You will show me the path to life,
   fullness of joys in your presence,
   the delights at your right hand forever.

R̸. You are my inheritance, O Lord.

SECOND READING

Gal 5:1, 13-18

Brothers and sisters:
For freedom Christ set us free;
   so stand firm and do not submit again
     to the yoke of slavery.

For you were called for freedom, brothers
   and sisters.
But do not use this freedom
   as an opportunity for the flesh;
   rather, serve one another through love.
For the whole law is fulfilled in one
   statement,
   namely, *You shall love your neighbor as
     yourself.*
But if you go on biting and devouring one
   another,
   beware that you are not consumed by
     one another.

I say, then: live by the Spirit
   and you will certainly not gratify the
     desire of the flesh.
For the flesh has desires against the Spirit,
   and the Spirit against the flesh;
   these are opposed to each other,
   so that you may not do what you want.
But if you are guided by the Spirit, you
   are not under the law.

About Liturgy

Single-mindedness: Over the next several weeks, let us reexamine various parts of the Mass and review our own practices. Today's readings challenge us to follow Christ and never turn back to our old ways. This resolute single-mindedness reminds us of one of the beatitudes: "Blessed are the clean of heart, / for they will see God" (Matt 5:8; NABRE). Some translations phrase this as "Blessed are the single-minded of heart."

In our liturgy, how do we practice single-mindedness, that attitude of prayer that is completely focused upon God without ignoring God present also in those around us? How do we integrate what we may label as distractions but are actually windows for seeing God?

The opening action of the liturgy is one way to nurture this communal focus. We gather not of our own will but because God has called us. *Qahal*, a Hebrew word meaning "convoked" or "summoned," is translated into Greek as *ekklesia*, the "church." We do not choose whom God summons; we can only embrace them and love them as ourselves. Thus, as we gather, let us not neglect to greet one another as companions in Christ, for Christ is present when the church prays and sings.

The first official action in the Mass of this summoned assembly is their gathering in formal procession. Here diverse individuals become one voice and one body ready to give praise to one God.

It would be much more efficient if we just began the Mass with everyone in place. But in the liturgy's wisdom, we must process from one place to another, move from an old way of life to a new, always looking forward, never looking back, as we seek together to follow Christ.

About Initiation

Members of the household of Christ: Sometimes people lament the length of the RCIA process and worry that inquirers and catechumens might get discouraged at how long it takes to become part of the church. For some, complete conversion to Christ does and should take time, but becoming a member of the household of Christ does not. The Rite of Christian Initiation says that those who have celebrated the Rite of Acceptance into the Order of Catechumens are "now part of the household of Christ" (RCIA 47). As catechumens, they have an official role and status in the Catholic Church. We can encourage catechumens who feel that initiation takes too long by letting them know that they belong to Christ already. The rest of the process is a gift of time to deepen their incorporation into that body of Christ.

About Liturgical Music

How to choose an entrance song: Lots of liturgy-planning resources provide a listing of appropriate songs for each Sunday. These listings help give music ministers ideas for songs they might not have thought of. However, one should not simply pick and choose music from a list without giving some careful thought on whether or not a specific piece works for that specific assembly. Here are some things to consider as you look through music ideas for entrance songs.

Does the song fulfill the purpose of the ritual action, that is, does it "open the celebration, foster the unity of those who have been gathered, introduce their thoughts to the mystery of the liturgical season or festivity, and accompany the procession of the priest and ministers" (GIRM 47)? Do the people know the song, and are they able to sing it well so that they may feel united with one another? Does it set an appropriate tone for that season or feast day? Does it have strong text that comes from an approved source?

JUNE 30, 2019
THIRTEENTH SUNDAY
IN ORDINARY TIME

✦ SPIRITUALITY

GOSPEL ACCLAMATION
Col 3:15a, 16a

℟. Alleluia, alleluia.
Let the peace of Christ control your hearts;
let the word of Christ dwell in you richly.
℟. Alleluia, alleluia.

Gospel   Luke 10:1-12, 17-20; L102C

At that time the Lord appointed sev-
    enty-two others
  whom he sent ahead of him in pairs
  to every town and place he in-
    tended to visit.
He said to them,
  "The harvest is abundant but the
    laborers are few;
  so ask the master of the harvest
  to send out laborers for his harvest.
Go on your way;
  behold, I am sending you like lambs
    among wolves.
Carry no money bag, no sack, no
    sandals;
  and greet no one along the way.
Into whatever house you enter, first say,
  'Peace to this household.'
If a peaceful person lives there,
  your peace will rest on him;
  but if not, it will return to you.
Stay in the same house and eat and
    drink what is offered to you,
  for the laborer deserves his payment.
Do not move about from one house to
    another.
Whatever town you enter and they wel-
    come you,
  eat what is set before you,
  cure the sick in it and say to them,
  'The kingdom of God is at hand for
    you.'
Whatever town you enter and they do
    not receive you,
  go out into the streets and say,
  'The dust of your town that clings to
    our feet,
  even that we shake off against you.'

Continued in Appendix A, p. 307,

or Luke 10:1-9, in Appendix A, p. 307.

Reflecting on the Gospel

How many people can play on a team? Baseball uses nine players on defense and one at a time on offense, with the possibility of other players on base. But teams are much larger than that. For example, it's not enough to have only nine players. There needs to be more in case some are injured, or to give others a rest. A baseball team with only one pitcher will not win many games in a row. Teams need back-up players. And what about football? Each team has eleven players on the field at a time. But there are offensive, defensive, and special teams squads. The players on a college football team number more than a hundred. In the NFL, teams may have fifty-three players, but only forty-five can suit up for a game.

During the ministry of Jesus there were many on the team as well: crowds, disciples, apostles, and a special few. In the Gospel of Matthew, there are only twelve disciples, and they were also the twelve apostles (Matt 10:1-2). But Luke has a much more expansive view of discipleship. In fact, in Acts, he invents a feminine form of the word to mention Tabitha, a female disciple (9:36). And in today's gospel we have the mission of the seventy-two! In Luke there were many, many disciples. Nearly anyone could be on the team!

And this simple lesson gives us great hope today. According to Luke, men, women, the Twelve, the seventy-two, and many more were in a special relationship with Jesus, chosen to follow him and chosen also to be sent by him. In this gospel there were not such tight boundaries around who could or could not be a disciple. Instead, the situation seems to have been more fluid or dynamic. And that's likely a more accurate reflection of the situation around Jesus' earthly ministry. It would also seem to reflect our lives more accurately too, with dynamic, fluid relationships.

Aside from this story in Luke we never hear about the seventy-two again. But surely these people were likely some of the early evangelizers after the resurrection. It all gives us a brief inkling into the situation of the early church. Though it might be easier to imagine the Twelve with Peter at the head, knowing who is "on the team" and who isn't, today's gospel reading invites us to consider a much more complex picture.

Living the Paschal Mystery

Many of us like to draw boundaries, establishing membership and determining limits. But life is not often like that. Our lived realities are much more complex, and perhaps that's part of the reason we seek to create order! The mission of the seventy-two gives us a peek into the greater apostolic ministry of Jesus. He was content to *send* (the word "apostle" means "one sent") more than the twelve on mission. And the seventy-two are not specifically called disciples or apostles, though they are certainly sent. They go to the places Jesus intends to visit. We might ask ourselves who are the "seventy-two" today? And are we part of that large group sent to places where Jesus intends to visit? Just because we are not part of the Twelve does not mean we don't have a mission. These seventy-two were critical to the ministry of Jesus. They prepared the way for him. In looking to a New Testament example of our call in life, there is something worthy of emulation here.

Focusing the Gospel

Key words and phrases: the Lord appointed seventy-two others / whom he sent ahead of him in pairs

To the point: Jesus continues on the road to Jerusalem by sending missionaries ahead of him to prepare the way. Much like John the Baptist at the beginning of Luke's gospel, these seventy-two disciples are to proclaim, "The kingdom of God is at hand" and to call the people, communally and individually, to repentance. This account of the mission of the seventy-two reveals to us Jesus' method in ministry. He calls others to help him in spreading the good news of God's kingdom and he sends them to minister in pairs. The Christian mission is not to be undertaken as a solitary endeavor. If Jesus continually called on others to help him establish the kingdom of God, how much more do we, modern-day disciples, need to rely on co-laborers in ministry?

Connecting the Gospel

to the first reading: In last week's gospel we heard of a Samaritan village that would not welcome Jesus because his final destination was Jerusalem. This week as well, Jesus' disciples are sent on ahead of Jesus to "every town and place he intended to visit." Jesus acknowledges that they might find welcome or they might not, but everywhere they venture they are first to say, "Peace to this household." The first reading from Isaiah is a hymn to Jerusalem, Jesus' final destination and the place of his death and resurrection. The prophet Isaiah, speaking after the exile into Babylon, reassures the people that Jerusalem will again be their "comfort." This sacred ground, which has seen such ruin and such glory, will once again nurture the people of God.

to experience: In Jerusalem throughout history and in the life of Jesus we see the paschal mystery made manifest. Death leads to new life. Are there broken places in your own life that are ready to be reborn?

Connecting the Responsorial Psalm

to the readings: In the gospel Jesus sends his disciples out on mission with a list of what they are not to take: "no money bag, no sack, no sandals." In fact they will be "like lambs among wolves." But this is no reason for distress. The psalmist sings a hymn to God's strength and deliverance: "Come and see the works of God, / his tremendous deeds among the children of Adam." Though the disciples are sent without material possessions, they go with the love of God whose "enemies cringe" before his "great strength" (NABRE).

to psalmist preparation: In the life of faith we are at times asked to do the seemingly impossible. To love people who do not show love for us. To continue working on a task that seems doomed to failure. To wake up every morning and recommit ourselves to our own ongoing conversion in the ways of Christ. No matter how daunting our daily mission may be, we are not alone. The God of all love, compassion, and strength is with us. How do you proclaim this good news with your life?

PROMPTS FOR FAITH-SHARING

The seventy-two are sent out to proclaim, "The kingdom of God is at hand." What do these words mean to you?

_____

_____

_____

_____

Jesus sends the disciples out in pairs. Do you have a companion on the journey of faith? How does it change ministry when it is done in a team setting?

_____

_____

_____

_____

The disciples are to greet each house they enter by saying, "Peace to this household." How do you offer peace to those you visit?

_____

_____

_____

_____

Jesus tells the disciples, "The harvest is abundant but the laborers are few." How do we experience this lack of laborers in our own time?

_____

_____

_____

_____

Model Penitential Act

Presider: As modern day disciples Jesus sends us out, like the seventy-two, to proclaim the good news of God's kingdom. Let us pause for a moment to pray for the strength, humility, and grace needed to fulfill this mission . . . [*pause*]

Lord Jesus, you invite us to labor in building the kingdom of God: Lord, have mercy.
Christ Jesus, you are the source of peace: Christ, have mercy.
Lord Jesus, you call all people to yourself: Lord, have mercy.

Homily Points

• Seventy-two disciples are sent out along the road to Jerusalem, to all the places Jesus intends to visit on this last journey of his earthly life. The disciples are given a message to proclaim and they are to proclaim it whether the communities they enter are receptive to them or not: "The kingdom of God is at hand." There is an urgency to their task and because of this Jesus tells them to not be encumbered by material things. They are to bring "no money bag, no sack, no sandals" and even more than that they are to "greet no one along the way." Nothing must dissuade them from this mission, the mission of announcing the kingdom of God.

• The people of that time (much like the people of this time) were caught up in waiting for the kingdom of God to arrive. They longed for the time when there would be no more war, illness, hunger, oppression, hatred, or enmity, and all would live in peace and abundance. The message to them and to us is that this kingdom is already here. All it requires is for us to claim our places as citizens of the kingdom of God.

• What would the world be like if we all truly believed the bold proclamation of Jesus that the kingdom of God is at hand? We are kingdom people and when we act as kingdom people, just as the saints throughout history have shown us, the kingdom breaks out all around us. The hungry are fed, the grieving are comforted, and building lasting peace becomes more important than preparing for war. This urgent message proclaimed by the disciples on the road to Jerusalem is passed on to us today. The kingdom of God is at hand.

Model Universal Prayer (Prayer of the Faithful)

Presider: In today's gospel, Jesus sends out the seventy-two to proclaim, "The kingdom of God is at hand." Let us pray for the seed of God's kingdom to continue to take root in the world.

Response: Lord, hear our prayer.

That missionaries of the church proclaim the kingdom of God to all they meet while also listening to, learning from, and growing alongside the people they serve . . .

That God's kingdom of justice, peace, and mercy continue to grow throughout the world . . .

That those who live in the darkness of sin might hear the good news that the kingdom of God is at hand and receive the grace to labor for this kingdom . . .

That all gathered here proclaim in our words and actions the joy inherent in the kingdom of God . . .

Presider: God of abundance, you sent your son Jesus to reveal to us the fullness of life in your kingdom. Hear our prayers that we might labor to build up the kingdom of God in all that we say and do. Through Jesus Christ, our Lord. Amen.

COLLECT

Let us pray.

Pause for silent prayer

O God, who in the abasement of your Son
have raised up a fallen world,
fill your faithful with holy joy,
for on those you have rescued from slavery
  to sin
you bestow eternal gladness.
Through our Lord Jesus Christ, your Son,
who lives and reigns with you in the unity
  of the Holy Spirit,
one God, for ever and ever. **Amen.**

FIRST READING
Isa 66:10-14c

Thus says the LORD:
Rejoice with Jerusalem and be glad
  because of her,
  all you who love her;
exult, exult with her,
  all you who were mourning over her!
Oh, that you may suck fully
  of the milk of her comfort,
that you may nurse with delight
  at her abundant breasts!
  For thus says the LORD:
Lo, I will spread prosperity over Jerusalem
  like a river,
  and the wealth of the nations like an
    overflowing torrent.
As nurslings, you shall be carried in her
    arms,
  and fondled in her lap;
as a mother comforts her child,
  so will I comfort you;
  in Jerusalem you shall find your
    comfort.

When you see this, your heart shall rejoice
  and your bodies flourish like the grass;
the LORD's power shall be known to his
  servants.

RESPONSORIAL PSALM
Ps 66:1-3, 4-5, 6-7, 16, 20

R℣. (1) Let all the earth cry out to God with joy.

Shout joyfully to God, all the earth,
    sing praise to the glory of his name;
    proclaim his glorious praise.
Say to God, "How tremendous are your
    deeds!"

R℣. Let all the earth cry out to God with joy.

"Let all on earth worship and sing praise
    to you,
    sing praise to your name!"
Come and see the works of God,
    his tremendous deeds among the
        children of Adam.

R℣. Let all the earth cry out to God with joy.

He has changed the sea into dry land;
    through the river they passed on foot;
    therefore let us rejoice in him.
He rules by his might forever.

R℣. Let all the earth cry out to God with joy.

Hear now, all you who fear God,
    while I declare what he has done for me.
Blessed be God who refused me not
    my prayer or his kindness!

R℣. Let all the earth cry out to God with joy.

SECOND READING
Gal 6:14-18

Brothers and sisters:
May I never boast except in the cross of
    our Lord Jesus Christ,
    through which the world has been
        crucified to me,
    and I to the world.
For neither does circumcision mean
    anything, nor does uncircumcision,
    but only a new creation.
Peace and mercy be to all who follow this
    rule
    and to the Israel of God.

From now on, let no one make troubles
    for me;
    for I bear the marks of Jesus on my
        body.

The grace of our Lord Jesus Christ be
    with your spirit,
    brothers and sisters. Amen.

About Liturgy

Go, you are sent: Last week we looked at the opening of the Mass and the ritual action of gathering. This week, let us examine the very last part of the Mass and what some may call the most important part of the Mass itself: the dismissal.

Our word "Mass" comes from the Latin text of the Mass's final dialogue, *Ite, missa est.* Some liturgical scholars have translated this as, "Go forth, the Mass is completed." Others have interpreted it as, "Go forth, the assembly is dismissed." No matter the exact definition of *missa*, the meaning is clear. The grace we have received and shared in the eucharistic action cannot remain here. It must go forth, and it can only do so through us and our actions in our daily lives. The General Instruction of the Roman Missal says the purpose of the dismissal is "so that each may go back to doing good works, praising and blessing God" (90).

Next the GIRM says that the priest and deacon kiss the altar. Then all the ministers make a profound bow to the altar. There is no mention of a concluding procession nor of a song to accompany that procession. It is simply presumed that there is some kind of leave-taking by the ministers.

The abrupt quality of the instructions and rubrics here give us a sense of the urgency of the dismissal. Go, now! You are sent. Take only what you have been given here, and give it away freely to all you meet this week. Then come back next Sunday rejoicing and giving thanks for all God has done.

About Initiation

Dismissal of catechumens: Although the catechumens are not present for the assembly's dismissal at the end of Mass, they, too, are sent on mission. The catechumens' dismissal takes place at every Mass after the homily and before the Creed. The Rite of Christian Initiation of Adults provides a brief ritual dialogue for this dismissal at number 67. More importantly, the rubrics found just before the dialogue give us the purpose for the catechumens' dismissal. They are sent to "share their joy and spiritual experience." Like the baptized who remain in the Mass and are dismissed at the end of it, the catechumens also are sent to proclaim what they have heard and to share what they have been given.

About Liturgical Music

How to choose a dismissal song: You may be surprised to discover that there are no instructions or directives regarding singing a closing song at Mass. In contrast to the lengthy description it provides for the entrance song, the General Instruction of the Roman Missal mentions no such song for the end of Mass. This gives music ministers much freedom in choice, but one that still requires forethought.

The United States bishops recommend that if a closing song is sung, its conclusion coincides with the end of the ministers' recessional from the sanctuary (see Sing to the Lord 199). No instructions have been given as to the choice of text, but it seems appropriate that the song's text reflects the season and intention of the dismissal.

If a song of praise has been sung after Communion, perhaps an instrumental may be more suitable for the end of Mass. It might also be an opportunity for the choir to sing on their own as the assembly departs. During Lent and other simpler liturgies, you might consider having the assembly leave in silence.

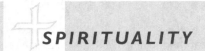

SPIRITUALITY

R/. Alleluia, alleluia.
Your words, Lord, are Spirit and life;
you have the words of everlasting life.
R/. Alleluia, alleluia.

Gospel

Luke 10:25-37; L105C

There was a scholar of the law
　　who stood up to test Jesus
　　and said,
　"Teacher, what must I do to
　　　inherit eternal life?"
Jesus said to him, "What is writ-
　　ten in the law?
How do you read it?"
He said in reply,
　"You shall love the Lord, your God,
　with all your heart,
　with all your being,
　with all your strength,
　and with all your mind,
　and your neighbor as
　　yourself."
He replied to him, "You have
　　answered correctly;
　do this and you will live."

But because he wished to justify him-
　　self, he said to Jesus,
　"And who is my neighbor?"
Jesus replied,
　"A man fell victim to robbers
　as he went down from Jerusalem to
　　Jericho.
They stripped and beat him and went
　　off leaving him half-dead.
A priest happened to be going down
　　that road,
　but when he saw him, he passed by
　　on the opposite side.
Likewise a Levite came to the place,
　and when he saw him, he passed by
　　on the opposite side.

Continued in Appendix A, p. 307.

Reflecting on the Gospel

Luke introduces the parable of the Good Samaritan with a story found in Matthew and Mark, namely, a scholar of the law correctly summing up the law as loving God and loving one's neighbor. In the other gospels the story effectively ends and another teaching is introduced. But Luke tells us that the scholar wanted "to justify himself" and so to clarify who is his neighbor. Rather than answer straightforwardly, Jesus poses a story with which we are familiar. The priest and the Levite, both upright privileged people considered favored by God, leave the unfortunate man in the ditch. Only the Samaritan, one of a group of people generally despised by many Jewish people of the time, offered any assistance. And it was no mere prayer or well-wish. He went out of his way, cared for the victim, bandaged him, carried him, and paid for his stay at the equivalent of a hotel. With that, Jesus asks the scholar which of the three was the neighbor to the man in the ditch? The scholar of the law in reply does not even use the word Samaritan, but says, "The one who treated him with mercy."

Though the question is about "neighbor," mercy is the keyword in this gospel. The scholar was likely predisposed to believe that the priest or the Levite would be a neighbor, by acting mercifully. But it was the person the scholar did not expect who acted in that way. When the scholar asks, "And who is my neighbor?" the answer could rightfully be said, "The one who treated him with mercy." When one is in the ditch needing help, who is neighbor? More important than role or station, privilege or power, is the capacity and the willingness to be merciful and to receive mercy. Without mercy, the person in the ditch dies. One reading of Jesus' story might be that we are the person in the ditch. We should be open to receive acts of mercy no matter where they come from, or who performs them. Those who act in this way are neighbor, much more so than those we might otherwise expect. As Jesus continues to do, he creates upheaval in our worldview by a simple story that causes us to reconsider our priorities and prejudices.

Living the Paschal Mystery

Sometimes those who need to be helped want help on their own terms. But today's gospel is a reminder that to those in the ditch, help may come from the most unforeseen or even unimaginable people. When we place limitations on even such things as who might lend us help or assistance, we might not be open to the mercy of God, which is extended in a variety of ways. Though this parable of the Good Samaritan is often read to mean we should be neighborly and act mercifully, it can also be read in a way so that we are open to receive mercy and kindness from others, no matter who they might be. Jesus invites us to move beyond ourselves in moments of crisis and to be open to mercy from wherever it might come. In doing so, we die to our own preconceived notions and live anew with an openness broader than we had before. For if we in the ditch are not willing to see the Samaritan as a neighbor, and accept his act of mercy, we will surely die in that same ditch.

Focusing the Gospel

Key words and phrases: You shall love the Lord, your God, / with all your heart, / with all your being, / with all your strength, / and with all your mind, / and your neighbor as yourself.

To the point: Everything in Judaism and Christianity can be reduced to this one essential statement: Love God and love your neighbor. And yet, the life-changing nature of this teaching to love God and love your neighbor as yourself is only discovered in the interpretation. In the parable of the Good Samaritan, the priest and the Levite pass by the man left for dead. Obviously, they did not recognize him as "neighbor." The Samaritan, acting with mercy, interprets this ancient Jewish commandment with the full abundance of the God of love.

Connecting the Gospel

to the first reading: The reading from Deuteronomy confirms the model of discipleship Jesus gives us in the parable of the Good Samaritan. The writer tells us that you can only keep the commandments and statutes of God when "you return to the LORD, your God, / with all your heart and all your soul." The Samaritan gives not only of his time and energy but also of his material resources to care for the stranger he finds on the side of the road half-dead. His response begins when, seeing the robbers' victim, he is "moved with compassion." Unlike the Levite and the priest, the Samaritan allows himself to fully encounter the person in front of him in need.

to experience: Sometimes our lives become compartmentalized. In some ways this is good. We want our work to stay at work and our family life to take priority at home. But spirituality is not meant to be one of many facets of life that sits apart from the others. Instead of Christianity being something we do on Sunday morning, it is a way of *being*. As the first reading and the gospel show us, it is a way of being fully for God.

Connecting the Responsorial Psalm

to the readings: In the responsorial psalm we can hear the plea of the robbers' victim on the side of the road: "I am afflicted and in pain; / let your saving help, O God, protect me." And if this was the prayer of the man left for dead, it is answered. But perhaps not in the way he expected.

to psalmist preparation: We are not told if the victim in the parable of the Good Samaritan is conscious, but if he was we can imagine his hope and excitement on seeing first a priest and then a Levite coming toward him on the road. We can also imagine his crushing disappointment as these men turned away from him. Being neglected by his own people, what must the victim's thoughts have been when he spied the Samaritan coming toward him? Did he still have hope or was he fearful? How would you feel if you saw your enemy coming toward you while you lay helplessly in a ditch? Jesus tells a parable to expand our vision of "neighbor." Both the Samaritan and the robbers' victim must look past external labels to recognize the neighbor within each other.

PROMPTS FOR FAITH-SHARING

Jesus confronts his Jewish audience by making a Samaritan the hero of his story. What groups within your life do you have a hard time believing well of? What happens if you imagine a member of this group as taking the place of the Samaritan in this parable?

The scholar of the law tries to get out of the commandment of God on a technicality. Love my neighbor, but who is my neighbor? Are there places in the life of faith where you are tempted to limit God and God's mercy? Are there some people you believe are outside the realm of God's mercy?

Jesus tells the scholar of the law, "Go and do likewise," after relaying the parable of the Samaritan's care for the robbers' victim. Who are the people in your community who are left on the side of the road isolated, wounded, and alone. How might you begin to be a neighbor to these people?

The man in the ditch must accept the help of the Samaritan in order to find relief. When have you received help from unexpected or even shocking sources?

Model Penitential Act

Presider: In today's gospel Jesus lifts up the example of the Samaritan who acts with mercy and commands us to "Go and do likewise." Let us pause to remember the times we have not treated others as neighbor . . . [*pause*]

> Lord Jesus, you welcome outcasts and sinners: Lord, have mercy.
> Christ Jesus, you lift up outsiders as models of discipleship: Christ, have mercy.
> Lord Jesus, you show us the way of love: Lord, have mercy.

Homily Points

• Today we hear the central teaching of Judaism and Christianity encapsulated in one sentence: Love God and love neighbor. As Rabbi Hillel stated shortly before the time of Jesus, "What is hateful to yourself, do not do to your fellow man. That is the whole Torah; the rest is just commentary." We are called to be a people rooted and grounded in the love of God who also extend that love to all we meet. The scholar of the law in today's gospel who asks Jesus, "Who is my neighbor?" does not yet understand this teaching. His faithfulness to God has penetrated his mind, for he can recite the teachings of his faith, but they have not transformed his heart.

• In St. Paul's letter to the Colossians we find the source of the Samaritan's compassion in an early Christian hymn: "For in him all the fullness was pleased to dwell, / and through him to reconcile all things for him." In Christ there is no division between races, religions, genders, or political parties. Instead, Christ, encompassing the fullness of creation, brings all together in unity. The Samaritan knows this. Instead of seeing only a Jewish man, the Samaritan sees a fellow human being. He sees his neighbor.

• Within our communities it is much easier to see the divisions rather than the similarities. This is because our human minds are primed to sort and identify. And the way we do this is by finding that which is different from the rest. Jesus invites us into a new worldview, one where we look for commonalities and celebrate unity. In this worldview we are all beloved children of God, and we are all neighbors.

Model Universal Prayer (Prayer of the Faithful)

Presider: Jesus calls us to recognize each person we encounter as our neighbor. With compassion we lift up our needs and the needs of others to the Lord.

Response: Lord, hear our prayer.

That the church recognize and lift up the loving deeds of all people of good will . . .

That wars and divisions cease as people look on each other with empathy . . .

That victims of crimes and all those who feel forgotten and abandoned experience the love of God and the care of their fellow human beings . . .

That all gathered here might know the law of God written on our hearts and live it with integrity . . .

Presider: God of all people, you call us to live your law by loving you and loving others. Hear our prayers that we might embody your compassion in the world. We ask this through Jesus Christ, our brother. Amen.

COLLECT
Let us pray.

Pause for silent prayer

O God, who show the light of your truth
to those who go astray,
so that they may return to the right path,
give all who for the faith they profess
are accounted Christians
the grace to reject whatever is contrary to
  the name of Christ
and to strive after all that does it honor.
Through our Lord Jesus Christ, your Son,
who lives and reigns with you in the unity
  of the Holy Spirit,
one God, for ever and ever. **Amen.**

FIRST READING
Deut 30:10-14

Moses said to the people:
  "If only you would heed the voice of the
    LORD, your God,
  and keep his commandments and
    statutes
    that are written in this book of the law,
  when you return to the LORD, your God,
  with all your heart and all your soul.

"For this command that I enjoin on you
    today
  is not too mysterious and remote for
    you.
It is not up in the sky, that you should say,
  'Who will go up in the sky to get it for
    us
  and tell us of it, that we may carry it
    out?'
Nor is it across the sea, that you should
    say,
  'Who will cross the sea to get it for us
  and tell us of it, that we may carry it
    out?'
No, it is something very near to you,
  already in your mouths and in your
    hearts;
  you have only to carry it out."

RESPONSORIAL PSALM
Ps 69:14, 17, 30-31, 33-34, 36, 37

℟. (cf. 33) Turn to the Lord in your need,
  and you will live.

I pray to you, O LORD,
  for the time of your favor, O God!
In your great kindness answer me
  with your constant help.
Answer me, O LORD, for bounteous is your
    kindness:
  in your great mercy turn toward me.

℟. Turn to the Lord in your need, and you
  will live.

I am afflicted and in pain;
    let your saving help, O God, protect me.
I will praise the name of God in song,
    and I will glorify him with
        thanksgiving.

Rȳ. Turn to the Lord in your need, and you
    will live.

"See, you lowly ones, and be glad;
    you who seek God, may your hearts
        revive!
For the LORD hears the poor,
    and his own who are in bonds he spurns
        not."

Rȳ. Turn to the Lord in your need, and you
    will live.

For God will save Zion
    and rebuild the cities of Judah.
The descendants of his servants shall
        inherit it,
    and those who love his name shall
        inhabit it.

Rȳ. Turn to the Lord in your need, and you
    will live.

or

RESPONSORIAL PSALM
Ps 19:8, 9, 10, 11

See Appendix A, p. 307.

SECOND READING
Col 1:15-20

Christ Jesus is the image of the invisible
        God,
    the firstborn of all creation.
For in him were created all things in
        heaven and on earth,
    the visible and the invisible,
    whether thrones or dominions or
        principalities or powers;
    all things were created through him and
        for him.
He is before all things,
    and in him all things hold together.
He is the head of the body, the church.
He is the beginning, the firstborn from the
        dead,
    that in all things he himself might be
        preeminent.
For in him all the fullness was pleased to
        dwell,
    and through him to reconcile all things
        for him,
    making peace by the blood of his cross
    through him, whether those on earth or
        those in heaven.

About Liturgy

Effective strategies for hospitality: In today's gospel, the question posed by the scholar, "And who is my neighbor?" gives us an opportunity to look at how we might answer this question based on our practice of hospitality at the Mass.

Like many good intentions, hospitality can become relegated to a committee or group of people who become responsible for hospitality on behalf of the parish. Thus we get hospitality committees, or we have announcements that go something like, "Hospitality is provided after Mass today by the Knights of Columbus." Can you hear how strange that might sound to a visitor, as if being welcoming is a scheduled event or fulfilled by a specific group?

When we approach hospitality this way, we can often get the notion that we have "done hospitality" if the priest asks all the visitors to stand up at some point during Mass "so we can welcome them." That may convey a sense of welcome to the visitors. However, if that were all they experienced as hospitality, and no one actually spoke to them or engaged them in personal conversation, one would doubt they would actually feel they belonged.

Hospitality is not a task we can check off a to-do list. It's not something that is scheduled. Hospitality is the attitude we take when we are going about our ordinary routine and we come across a stranger along the roadside who needs our attention. Hospitality is not welcoming people into *our* home but treating them as though this place is *their* home and they belong here and have a voice here. Hospitality then is everyone's responsibility, offered at all times, for the sake of acknowledging that the stranger is actually our neighbor. Here are some simple actions that you can encourage parishioners to take to cultivate an attitude of hospitality.

Ask parishioners to sit in the middle of the pew so that people who arrive after them have a place ready and waiting. When a person sits by you, say hello, shake their hand, and introduce yourself to them. Don't wait to be prompted to welcome them. Be sure greeters and other ministers standing in the vestibule before or after Mass are not clustered in groups of people they know. They should be searching out the newcomer and actively looking to talk to people they don't know.

About Liturgical Music

How to choose a psalm setting: Today's assigned readings give us the unusual occurrence in Ordinary Time of having two different responsorial psalms to choose from—Psalm 69 or Psalm 19. Although *Living Liturgy* is focusing on Psalm 69, this gives us an opportunity to explore how to select an appropriate psalm setting for an assembly.

The responsorial psalm is meant to help the assembly "perceive the word of God speaking in the psalms and to turn these psalms into the prayer of the church" (*Lectionary for Mass* 19). The Lectionary provides two ways to sing the psalms, with preference given to the first: 1) antiphonally as a dialogue between cantor and people; or 2) straight through like a hymn sung by cantor alone or by all the people.

Emphasizing the importance of the people's participation in singing the psalm, the Lectionary encourages us to use every means available to foster the people's singing of the psalms. To this end, select the setting that your assembly knows best and can almost sing by heart. When no such setting is available for your assembly, the Lectionary also provides seasonal psalms and refrains (Lectionary 173–74) that may be used if the assembly is more familiar with a setting of a different psalm than the one assigned for the day.

JULY 14, 2019
FIFTEENTH SUNDAY
IN ORDINARY TIME

✟ SPIRITUALITY

GOSPEL ACCLAMATION
cf. Luke 8:15

R̸. Alleluia, alleluia.
Blessed are they who have kept the word with a
     generous heart
and yield a harvest through perseverance.
R̸. Alleluia, alleluia.

Gospel

Luke 10:38-42; L108C

**Jesus entered a village
     where a woman whose name
          was Martha welcomed
          him.
She had a sister named Mary
     who sat beside the Lord at
          his feet listening to him
          speak.
Martha, burdened with much
     serving, came to him and
     said,
     "Lord, do you not care
     that my sister has left me by
          myself to do the serving?
Tell her to help me."
The Lord said to her in reply,
     "Martha, Martha, you are anx-
          ious and worried about many
          things.
There is need of only one thing.
Mary has chosen the better part
     and it will not be taken from her."**

Reflecting on the Gospel

The Martha and Mary story in Luke is so familiar many people refer to them-selves as either a "Martha," meaning they are good at or even prefer working in the kitchen, or a "Mary," meaning they do not worry about such things. Indeed this gospel has been quoted so often and used to support so many various un-derstandings of ministry, household chores, the role of women, and more, that it is good to simply step back and read the words, or listen carefully when they are proclaimed.

Ultimately, it is the last verse that causes many to perk up or question their own priorities. Is it really the better part to sit and visit, leaving others to do the serving? What if the Marthas of the world stopped working in the kitchen, leaving the Marys and even Jesus himself without a meal!

At its worst, some use this passage to reinforce traditional domestic roles of women and men, with women doing the serving and men doing the reclining, visiting, and eating. Sometimes the read-ing is also used to claim that religious life (priesthood/sisterhood) is "better" than the lay state. But such facile readings do not do justice to the short story in Luke. In fact, they turn the moral of the story on its head.

Primarily, it is significant that Jesus is interacting with two women. One, Mary, is seated at his feet, listening to his instruction as a disciple, though she is not called that here. The other, Martha, is "bur-dened with much serving" in attempting to prepare a meal for Jesus. Jesus tells Martha in effect that the proper service for a disciple in this situation is to listen to Jesus. It is not to fret about serving meals.

Luke will make this point again in Acts of the Apostles, when the apostles are too busy serving at table to be attentive to God's word and to prayer. To free themselves up for prayer and reading the word, the apostles appoint seven to serve at table, as "deacons." The deacons then do just that. They see to the needs of the Hebrew-speaking and Greek-speaking Christians, so that the apostles can devote themselves entirely to their ministry.

The gospel reading today is not about the role of women, or the clerical/reli-gious state versus the laity. Instead, the story demonstrates that the proper role of a disciple is attentiveness to Jesus and his word.

Living the Paschal Mystery

It is so easy for us to be consumed by activities, checking boxes, crossing items off lists. There can be a great satisfaction in acting this way and a tremendous sense of accomplishment. But we hear a different message with other priorities today. Rather than busy ourselves or stir ourselves into a frenzy, it is the proper role of a disciple to listen to Jesus' instruction. And this does not mean become a priest or sister. Instead, it can mean to spend time in prayer, or with Scripture, coming to know the person of Jesus in a better way. This activity is critical for any disciple. And the example we have today is that of a woman. Luke is clear in presenting Jesus as giving pride of place to the disciple who listens to his instruction. Let us go and do the same.

Focusing the Gospel

Key words and phrases: Martha, Martha, you are anxious and worried about many things. / There is need of only one thing.

To the point: In the Bible we hear of seven people who are called by name twice: Abraham, Jacob, Moses, Samuel, Martha, Simon, and Saul. Some of these calls come in extraordinary circumstances. An angel stops Abraham's hand just as he is about to offer his son Isaac in sacrifice. Moses hears God's voice from a burning bush. Saul is thrown down on the road to Damascus in search of Christians to persecute. Martha's calling, however, takes place within the confines of everyday life as she and her sister Mary offer hospitality to an itinerant preacher, Jesus of Nazareth. Just as Moses is called away from shepherding his father-in-law's flock and hiding in the desert, and Saul is turned back from his pursuit of Christians, Martha is called from her anxieties and worries. Only without these burdens clouding her vision can she see the man who sits before her. He is the Word of God. The only hospitality he desires is for people to sit at his feet and listen.

Connecting the Gospel

to the first reading: Abraham and Sarah also offer hospitality to three mysterious visitors. Christians see these men as representing the triune God, though the Old Testament text says, "The LORD appeared to Abraham." Abraham's response seems much like Martha's. He eagerly invites the men to pause in their travel and rest awhile with him. He rushes about asking for Sarah to make bread and choosing a calf for one of his servants to butcher and prepare. Finally, he joins the men under the tree and waits on them while they eat. Abraham, like Martha, focuses on taking care of the physical needs of his guests. Unlike Martha, Abraham doesn't seem upset or worried about it—but then, he also has Sarah and his servant helping him with the work!

to experience: Hospitality was a revered part of the ancient culture of Abraham and even Jesus' time. It was important to offer food, drink, and rest in a desert or wilderness region, lest a traveler perish. As Christians we are invited into this hospitality, not for fear of death, but because we recognize Jesus within each and every person we welcome.

Connecting the Responsorial Psalm

to the readings: Our verses from Psalm 15 for today are in response to a question: "LORD, who may abide in your tent? / Who may dwell on your holy mountain?" (15:1; NABRE). In the first reading and the gospel, Abraham, Sarah, Mary, and Martha all have an intimate encounter with God where they offer hospitality to the Lord. In a way they are "abiding in God's tent." The psalmist tells us that those who are upright, truthful, and just are the ones who will dwell with the Lord.

to psalmist preparation: We, also, are invited to abide with God. How do you put the traits of uprightness, truthfulness, justice into practice in your own life?

PROMPTS FOR FAITH-SHARING

In our readings we see Abraham and Sarah, Mary and Martha caring for the needs of a visitor. How do you practice hospitality in your own life?

If Jesus were speaking to you, what burdens and anxieties would he tell you to let go of?

When someone's name is called twice in the Bible his/her life is about to change forever. Have you experienced a moment in your life where you felt God calling you to something new?

How might you find more time in your daily life to sit at Jesus' feet and listen?

Model Penitential Act

Presider: In today's gospel Jesus gently calls Martha away from her many burdens and anxieties to encounter him with the peace and devotion of her sister Mary. For the times our burdens and anxieties have clouded us to the presence of the Lord we pause to ask for forgiveness . . . [*pause*]

> Lord Jesus, you are the source of peace: Lord, have mercy.
> Christ Jesus, you are the Word of God: Christ, have mercy.
> Lord Jesus, you call us to everlasting life: Lord, have mercy.

Homily Points

• Jesus, the Word of God, is invited into the home of Mary and Martha. While Martha bustles about, preoccupied with the demands of hosting, Mary sits at Jesus' feet and listens. Martha is concerned with Jesus' human needs for comfort, food, and hospitality. And these are important, but they are not Jesus' only needs, nor his most important. As the Word of God, Jesus desires to be heard. In John's gospel, Jesus tells the bewildered disciples, "My food is to do the will of the one who sent me and to finish his work" (4:34; NABRE). Jesus came into the world to proclaim the kingdom of God and Mary sits and listens.

• Martha also serves the Word of God. But instead of finding the peace of Mary, she is overcome by her work. She cannot hear the voice of Jesus when her mind is overflowing with recriminations and complaints against Mary! Jesus tells her, "Martha, Martha, you are anxious and worried about many things. / There is need of only one thing." And what is this one thing? Jesus, himself. The Word of God, spoken aloud, desperately desiring to be heard.

• In our lives there will always be much to do. We have tasks that demand our time and attention: houses to clean, children to feed and clothe, work to do. And yet, present among us is the Word of God, calling out to us amidst all the chaos. Like Martha, Jesus invites us to put down our burdens and choose the one thing—to know the peace and joy of Mary, sitting at the feet of the Lord and listening to the Word of God.

Model Universal Prayer (Prayer of the Faithful)

Presider: Through the intercession of St. Mary and St. Martha let us bring our needs before the Lord.

Response: Lord, hear our prayer.

That the church embrace the charisms of Mary and Martha in contemplation and in active service . . .

That societies all over the world support education opportunities for all of their people regardless of gender, race, or class . . .

That those who are overcome by burdens and anxieties hear the voice of the Lord inviting them to rest in his love . . .

That all gathered here might find time everyday to listen in contemplative silence to Jesus and his life-giving Word . . .

Presider: God of all, you rejoiced when Mary sat at the feet of your Son, Jesus, and listened to him. Hear our prayers that we might follow her example of devotion and contemplation. We ask this through Christ our Lord. Amen.

COLLECT
Let us pray.

Pause for silent prayer

Show favor, O Lord, to your servants
and mercifully increase the gifts of your
    grace,
that, made fervent in hope, faith and
    charity,
they may be ever watchful in keeping your
    commands.
Through our Lord Jesus Christ, your Son,
who lives and reigns with you in the unity
    of the Holy Spirit,
one God, for ever and ever. **Amen.**

FIRST READING
Gen 18:1-10a

The LORD appeared to Abraham by the
    terebinth of Mamre,
    as he sat in the entrance of his tent,
    while the day was growing hot.
Looking up, Abraham saw three men
    standing nearby.
When he saw them, he ran from the
    entrance of the tent to greet them;
    and bowing to the ground, he said:
"Sir, if I may ask you this favor,
    please do not go on past your servant.
Let some water be brought, that you may
    bathe your feet,
    and then rest yourselves under the tree.
Now that you have come this close to your
    servant,
    let me bring you a little food, that you
      may refresh yourselves;
    and afterward you may go on your
      way."
The men replied, "Very well, do as you
    have said."

Abraham hastened into the tent and told
    Sarah,
"Quick, three measures of fine flour!
    Knead it and make rolls."
He ran to the herd, picked out a tender,
    choice steer,
    and gave it to a servant, who quickly
      prepared it.
Then Abraham got some curds and milk,
    as well as the steer that had been
      prepared,
    and set these before the three men;
    and he waited on them under the tree
      while they ate.

They asked Abraham, "Where is your
    wife Sarah?"
He replied, "There in the tent."
One of them said, "I will surely return to
    you about this time next year,
    and Sarah will then have a son."

RESPONSORIAL PSALM
Ps 15:2-3, 3-4, 5

℟. (1a) He who does justice will live in the
    presence of the Lord.

One who walks blamelessly and does
    justice;
  who thinks the truth in his heart
  and slanders not with his tongue.

℟. He who does justice will live in the
    presence of the Lord.

Who harms not his fellow man,
  nor takes up a reproach against his
    neighbor;
by whom the reprobate is despised,
  while he honors those who fear the
    LORD.

℟. He who does justice will live in the
    presence of the Lord.

Who lends not his money at usury
  and accepts no bribe against the
    innocent.
One who does these things
  shall never be disturbed.

℟. He who does justice will live in the
    presence of the Lord.

SECOND READING
Col 1:24-28

Brothers and sisters:
Now I rejoice in my sufferings for your
  sake,
  and in my flesh I am filling up
what is lacking in the afflictions of
  Christ
on behalf of his body, which is the
  church,
of which I am a minister
in accordance with God's stewardship
  given to me
to bring to completion for you the word
  of God,
the mystery hidden from ages and from
  generations past.
But now it has been manifested to his holy
  ones,
to whom God chose to make known the
  riches of the glory
of this mystery among the Gentiles;
it is Christ in you, the hope for glory.
It is he whom we proclaim,
  admonishing everyone and teaching
    everyone with all wisdom,
that we may present everyone perfect
  in Christ.

About Liturgy

Praying through the details: A question that many liturgists and liturgical ministers have is how to pray at Mass when they have so many things to worry about in doing their ministry. Presiders and liturgists, especially, have a tough job being in charge of the entire liturgical flow of a Mass while still appearing, as some of the old liturgical rubrics said, "as if to pray." Surely, Martha must be the patron saint of liturgists!

Unfortunately, Martha often gets placed in a bad light for her attention to detail and focus on the tasks at hand. Yet if we didn't have any Marthas, what would become of the liturgy, much less dinner?

Even as we might try to avoid being overly focused on small things and sustaining an unhealthy anxiety over things we cannot control, we can also revel in remembering that it was Martha, not Mary, who made the highest statement of faith in Jesus at the side of her brother's tomb: "Yes, Lord. I have come to believe that you are the Messiah, the Son of God, the one who is coming into the world" (John 11:27; NABRE). When faced with ultimate crisis, Martha was prepared to place her faith in Jesus. If you worry about worrying as you do your ministry, here are some ideas that might help.

Be prepared as much as you can be before Mass. Use the days before Mass to prepare, rehearse, check, and double-check every small detail you are responsible for. On the day of Mass, take some time for yourself to pray. As you arrive at church, commit to giving your attention to the person right in front of you, for in them, you are entertaining angels. Then once the Mass begins, become the Martha not of the table but of the tomb, putting all your trust in Jesus.

About Initiation

Your parish is your RCIA team: Most RCIA coordinators wish they had a bigger team, more sponsors, or more people to help with catechesis and other tasks for RCIA gatherings. We certainly need to continually invite more people to participate directly in the work of initiation. However, we also need to recall that the responsibility of the initiation of adults belongs to all the faithful, not just the pastor or the RCIA team. Your parishioners, by their ordinary encounters with the catechumens and candidates at Mass and at other parish gatherings, will be your most effective team members. Don't wait for your parishioners to get involved with RCIA. Bring your catechumens and candidates to where your parishioners are already so all the faithful can exercise their role of being members of the RCIA team.

About Liturgical Music

How to choose a preparation of gifts song: The Liturgy of the Eucharist begins with the preparation of gifts. The song that is sung during this time is meant to accompany the ritual action of processing the gifts of bread and wine to the altar and of collecting other gifts for the poor and the church. Therefore, the length of the song you choose needs to match the logistics of your particular church and local custom.

The norms for the text follow the same guidelines given for the entrance song (see GIRM 48). However, you have more freedom in terms of the song's themes.

Although this part of the Mass is important, it is secondary to the ritual action that follows it, namely, the Eucharistic Prayer and the Communion Rite. Whatever music you select here, whether sung by the assembly or choir or instrumental, should not overshadow the highpoint of the Mass.

JULY 21, 2019
SIXTEENTH SUNDAY
IN ORDINARY TIME

✠ SPIRITUALITY

GOSPEL ACCLAMATION
Rom 8:15bc

℞. Alleluia, alleluia.
You have received a Spirit of adoption,
through which we cry, Abba, Father.
℞. Alleluia, alleluia.

Gospel

Luke 11:1-13; L111C

**Jesus was praying in a certain place,
and when he had finished,
one of his disciples said to him,
"Lord, teach us to pray just as
John taught his disciples."
He said to them, "When you
pray, say:
Father, hallowed be your
name,
your kingdom come.
Give us each day our daily
bread
and forgive us our sins
for we ourselves forgive everyone in debt to us,
and do not subject us to the final
test."**

**And he said to them, "Suppose one of
you has a friend
to whom he goes at midnight and says,
'Friend, lend me three loaves of bread,
for a friend of mine has arrived at
my house from a journey
and I have nothing to offer him,'
and he says in reply from within,
'Do not bother me; the door has already been locked
and my children and I are already in
bed.
I cannot get up to give you anything.'
I tell you,
if he does not get up to give the
visitor the loaves
because of their friendship,
he will get up to give him whatever
he needs
because of his persistence.**

Continued in Appendix A, p. 308.

Reflecting on the Gospel

The Our Father prayer is something we likely learned as children, perhaps one of the first memorized or rote prayers we acquired. So, today's gospel and its version of the prayer might strike us as a bit odd. It's not the version we find in Matthew, which is much closer to the version we have memorized and recite at Mass. Instead, Luke's version has some elements that might be closer to the words uttered by Jesus himself. The Lukan version is certainly shorter and does not seem to have undergone the Matthean expansion from apparent liturgical use. Luke's version also begins dramatically with the direct address, "Father," rather than the more communal, "*Our* Father." The two petitions about the Father (three in Matthew) are shorter in Luke too, "hallowed be *your* name, / *your* kingdom come." But there are elements in Matthew that point to the words of Jesus too. For it seems a favorite Lukan theme, "forgive us our sins" overcame the original, "forgive us our debts" that Matthew preserves.

In the end, this short prayer of Jesus addressed directly to the Father likely offended sensibilities of the time. This was not the mere recitation of a psalm; this was not a lengthy sacrifice of praise and thanksgiving; this was not rooted in prophets, Moses, or the Law. This was the prayer of Jesus given to his disciples. And in just one generation the curt address was expanded as we find in Matthew. And some of the imagery, "forgive debts" was changed by Luke to conform more closely to his theological outlook of "forgive sins." And yet, this prayer is not found in Mark, John, or anywhere else in the New Testament. Only Luke and Matthew give us their respective versions. Still, they are so similar—their differences can be understood and explained—that scholars believe we have here something very close to the words of the historical Jesus when he taught his disciples this prayer.

Next time we rush through this memorized prayer at Mass or another occasion, it might be good to set ourselves in the context of Jesus and his disciples, imagining receiving this prayer and his instruction. Let's consider the words we are praying and the worldview they depict. Ultimately, the prayer constitutes a way of life and disposition much deeper than mere prattle.

Living the Paschal Mystery

Jesus was no mere myth as were the ancient Greek and Roman gods and goddesses. He was a human being who walked the face of the earth, as even pagan historians relate. The Christian claim is not merely that Jesus existed, but that he was the Son of God, the Incarnate Word of God. But his existence as a human being on this earth is something that nearly every single noteworthy scholar admits.

Part of his time on earth consisted of prayer and teaching, and this prayer known as the Our Father or the Lord's Prayer is something that scholars can attribute to the Jesus of history with great certainty. As Luke has it, the prayer includes an injunction to keep us from the final test. The astute reader immediately thinks of Jesus and his coming passion. Later in the gospel, Jesus will pray that the cup pass him by, for such a passion and death is the desire of no one, not even Jesus. But his prayer has strengthened him for such a moment. After this final test he will be raised to new life in paradise eternally. Such a future awaits us too when we will ultimately live the paschal mystery *par excellence*.

Focusing the Gospel

Key words and phrases: Lord, teach us to pray.

To the point: In Luke's gospel we see Jesus at prayer many times. He prays at his baptism, after healing people, before choosing the twelve disciples, and before feeding the five thousand, to name only a few. Those closest to him in the gospel have witnessed his life of prayer, and you can sense their desire to have what Jesus has in the request, "Lord, teach us to pray." Jesus' response is the beloved words of the Our Father and several teachings on prayer: pray persistently and constantly and trust God to give you what you need. In our life of faith we are called to pray at all times. Sometimes these prayers are the traditional words passed down through generations of faith, but other times they are our own unique communication. Just like the disciples in today's gospel, let us trustingly request of Jesus, "Lord, teach us to pray."

Connecting the Gospel

to the first reading: In the first reading from Genesis we see Abraham at prayer with God. Far from how we might imagine conversing with God (kneeling, head bowed, alone) Abraham stands before the Lord, draws near, and begins a frank discussion over the requisite number of righteous people who must be in Sodom and Gomorrah for God to agree not to destroy the city. As Jesus instructs in today's gospel, Abraham's prayer is certainly persistent. He questions God six times, slowly moving the number of righteous people required from fifty to ten. At one point Abraham exclaims, "See how I am presuming to speak to my Lord, / though I am but dust and ashes!" Jesus wants us to have this same boldness in approaching God the Father in prayer.

to experience: In prayer we give God thanks and praise, but we are also invited to converse with God freely about our needs, anxieties, frustrations, and even our anger. Nothing is out of bounds when it comes to prayer. All that is required is that, like Abraham, we show up, draw near, and share what's in our heart.

Connecting the Responsorial Psalm

to the readings: The psalmist sings, "[F]orsake not the work of your hands." In prayer we demonstrate our belief in God's faithfulness. We reach out, asking for what we need, giving thanks and praise, because we believe in a God who loves us and desires only our good. Even in times when our faith is shaken or when we are struggling in the spiritual life, we enter into prayer relying on the God who "is with me to the end." The psalms themselves show us that we can come to God in every circumstance. Whether we approach him in hope or despair, joy or grief, love or anger, God is there.

to psalmist preparation: As a cantor, your ministry draws the people of God to pray through song. How do you experience your role as being a prayer leader in your community? As a prayer leader, how would you like to nourish and deepen your own prayer life?

PROMPTS FOR FAITH-SHARING

In today's gospel we are given the beginnings of the Our Father, our most treasured prayer. Say the Our Father slowly. Which line stands out to you? Why?

Jesus tells us, "[A]sk and you will receive." How have you experienced God answering prayer?

In the movie, *Shadowlands,* about Christian author C. S. Lewis, there is a well-known quote about prayer: "It doesn't change God—it changes me." How have you been changed by prayer?

How do you pray at this time in your faith journey? Alone or with others? Spontaneously or by reciting the prayers of the church? How is Jesus calling you to deepen your prayer life?

183

Model Penitential Act

Presider: In today's gospel the disciples approach Jesus with a simple request, "Lord, teach us to pray." Let us pause to prepare ourselves to be present to God in prayer . . . [*pause*]

Lord Jesus, you teach us to call God, "Father": Lord, have mercy.

Christ Jesus, you intercede for us at God's right hand: Christ, have mercy.

Lord Jesus, you show us how to pray without ceasing: Lord, have mercy.

Homily Points

• The disciples ask Jesus, "[T]each us to pray." And Jesus complies with the words of the Our Father and instructions on prayer. But the real school of prayer is observing the place prayer held in Jesus' earthly life. Throughout the gospels Jesus prays publicly and privately, in front of crowds and in the intimate group of his closest disciples. He prays from the very beginning of his public ministry, marked with his baptism by John in the Jordan (Luke 3:21-22), to his last breath on the cross when he commends his spirit to his Father (23:46). And it is with a prayer that he ascends into heaven after his resurrection (Luke 24:50-53).

• What do we learn from Jesus' prayer? More than an action, prayer is a way of being, a way of living out a relationship with his Father. Because of this, Jesus can pray in all situations—in thanksgiving, blessing, or even deep grief as he prays in Gethsemane for the cup to pass him by. Jesus tells us, "[A]sk and you will receive," and yet it seems as though this Gethsemane prayer wasn't answered. Jesus did undergo "the final test" even as he taught his disciples to pray for God to deliver them from it.

• We have all known the experience of feeling as though our prayers have gone unanswered. In the movie *Shadowlands*, about Christian author C. S. Lewis, there is a line spoken by Lewis's character: "I pray because the need flows out of me all the time—waking and sleeping. . . . It doesn't change God—it changes me." Seen this way, prayer is a tool of our own transformation. God didn't stop the crucifixion, and yet, through his complete love of God and gift of himself, Jesus could not remain dead. He rose. In prayer we enter into the paschal mystery. May it lead us to new life, too.

Model Universal Prayer (Prayer of the Faithful)

Presider: Jesus tells us, "[A]sk and you will receive." With confidence and trust we bring our prayers before the Lord.

Response: Lord, hear our prayer.

That all members of the church grow and deepen in their relationship with God through prayer . . .

That the world might continue to be transformed into the kingdom of God where love, peace, and hope reign . . .

That those who suffer from hunger and poverty have their daily needs provided for . . .

That all gathered here might persistently intercede for those on the outskirts and margins of our community . . .

Presider: God of mercy, you sent your Son Jesus to teach us to pray. Hear these petitions that we might learn how to pray without ceasing. We ask this through Christ, our Lord. Amen.

COLLECT

Let us pray.

Pause for silent prayer

O God, protector of those who hope in you,
without whom nothing has firm
    foundation, nothing is holy,
bestow in abundance your mercy upon us
and grant that, with you as our ruler and
    guide,
we may use the good things that pass
in such a way as to hold fast even now
to those that ever endure.
Through our Lord Jesus Christ, your Son,
who lives and reigns with you in the unity
    of the Holy Spirit,
one God, for ever and ever. **Amen.**

FIRST READING

Gen 18:20-32

In those days, the LORD said: "The outcry
    against Sodom and Gomorrah is so
    great,
    and their sin so grave,
    that I must go down and see whether or
    not their actions
    fully correspond to the cry against them
    that comes to me.
I mean to find out."

While Abraham's visitors walked on
    farther toward Sodom,
    the LORD remained standing before
    Abraham.
Then Abraham drew nearer and said:
    "Will you sweep away the innocent with
    the guilty?
Suppose there were fifty innocent people
    in the city;
    would you wipe out the place, rather
    than spare it
    for the sake of the fifty innocent people
    within it?
Far be it from you to do such a thing,
    to make the innocent die with the guilty
    so that the innocent and the guilty
    would be treated alike!
Should not the judge of all the world act
    with justice?"
The LORD replied,
    "If I find fifty innocent people in the
    city of Sodom,
    I will spare the whole place for their sake."
Abraham spoke up again:
    "See how I am presuming to speak to
    my Lord,
    though I am but dust and ashes!
What if there are five less than fifty
    innocent people?
Will you destroy the whole city because of
    those five?"
He answered, "I will not destroy it, if I find
    forty-five there."
But Abraham persisted, saying, "What if
    only forty are found there?"

He replied, "I will forbear doing it for the sake of the forty."
Then Abraham said, "Let not my Lord grow impatient if I go on.
What if only thirty are found there?"
He replied, "I will forbear doing it if I can find but thirty there."
Still Abraham went on,
"Since I have thus dared to speak to my Lord,
what if there are no more than twenty?"
The LORD answered, "I will not destroy it, for the sake of the twenty."
But he still persisted:
"Please, let not my Lord grow angry if I speak up this last time.
What if there are at least ten there?"
He replied, "For the sake of those ten, I will not destroy it."

RESPONSORIAL PSALM
Ps 138:1-2, 2-3, 6-7, 7-8

R︎. (3a) Lord, on the day I called for help, you answered me.

I will give thanks to you, O LORD, with all my heart,
    for you have heard the words of my mouth;
    in the presence of the angels I will sing your praise;
I will worship at your holy temple
    and give thanks to your name.

R︎. Lord, on the day I called for help, you answered me.

Because of your kindness and your truth;
    for you have made great above all things
    your name and your promise.
When I called you answered me;
    you built up strength within me.

R︎. Lord, on the day I called for help, you answered me.

The LORD is exalted, yet the lowly he sees,
    and the proud he knows from afar.
Though I walk amid distress, you preserve me;
    against the anger of my enemies you raise your hand.

R︎. Lord, on the day I called for help, you answered me.

Your right hand saves me.
    The LORD will complete what he has done for me;
your kindness, O LORD, endures forever;
    forsake not the work of your hands.

R︎. Lord, on the day I called for help, you answered me.

SECOND READING
Col 2:12-14

See Appendix A, p. 308.

About Liturgy

The Lord's Prayer: In the years leading up to the 2011 promulgation of the new English translation of the Mass, one thing was a common concern: that the words of the Lord's Prayer not be changed. Although the words remain the same, how we pray this prayer varies greatly from parish to parish, and even from Mass to Mass.

One variation is in the gestures of the assembly during the prayer. The rubrics in the Roman Missal say that the priest extends his hands as he leads the prayer. However, the ritual text gives no prescribed gesture for the people to make as they pray the Lord's Prayer. The United States bishops have determined that they would give no specific directive regarding this issue. Thus, in some communities, the custom is to hold their neighbors' hands during this prayer. Others have chosen to extend their hands as the priest does. Still others keep their hands lowered or folded.

Should there be uniformity in gesture in this prayer that expresses our unity? The answer is unclear. However, where unity can certainly be fostered, beyond gestures, is the way in which the prayer is prayed. The preferred form is singing by the entire assembly. The communal praying of the Lord's Prayer can never be replaced by a solo performance of it, no matter how stirring the rendition. Nor should a musical setting known only by a portion of the assembly be used. If the prayer is to be sung, then the best option for most assemblies will be the chant setting found in the Roman Missal.

About Initiation

Knocking on doors at the Rite of Acceptance: In some places, parishes have incorporated a custom of asking inquirers to knock on the doors of the church at the beginning of the Rite of Acceptance, explaining that it signifies the inquirers' desire to enter the church. However, this action is nowhere in the official rite, and it distorts the meaning of the rite itself. Forcing inquirers to knock on the church doors actually shows the church as passive, waiting for inquirers to come to them instead of going out to draw others to Christ through the work of evangelization.

The rite's intention is to show the dual action of God's call through Christian witness and the inquirers' response to that call by following the gospel. Thus, the rubrics state that a group of the faithful go outside to meet the inquirers and their sponsors (RCIA 48) in order to bring them over the threshold of the church doors to hear the word of God.

About Liturgical Music

Repeating music: As music ministers, our primary job is to assist and enhance the assembly's voice as it sings the acclamations, responses, and hymns of the Mass. To do our job well, we need to rehearse the music ahead of time. In the course of the week we might sing through a particular song five or six times: several times during rehearsal, once before Mass, and once during Mass. The assembly, however, typically only gets one chance to sing that song that week. Thus, music ministers will get bored with a piece of music five times quicker than the assembly. Let us remember that repeating the same song over several weeks helps us do our job well because it helps the assembly learn that song. Recall that the community's unrehearsed singing "is the primary song of the liturgy" (Sing to the Lord 28).

JULY 28, 2019
SEVENTEENTH SUNDAY IN ORDINARY TIME

✝ SPIRITUALITY

GOSPEL ACCLAMATION
Matt 5:3

℟. Alleluia, alleluia.
Blessed are the poor in spirit,
for theirs is the kingdom of heaven.
℟. Alleluia, alleluia.

Gospel Luke 12:13-21; L114C

Someone in the crowd said to
    Jesus,
  "Teacher, tell my brother to
      share the inheritance with
      me."
He replied to him,
  "Friend, who appointed
      me as your judge and
      arbitrator?"
Then he said to the crowd,
  "Take care to guard
      against all greed,
  for though one may be rich,
  one's life does not consist of
      possessions."

Then he told them a parable.
"There was a rich man whose land pro-
    duced a bountiful harvest.
He asked himself, 'What shall I do,
  for I do not have space to store my
      harvest?'
And he said, 'This is what I shall do:
  I shall tear down my barns and build
      larger ones.
There I shall store all my grain and
    other goods
  and I shall say to myself, "Now as for
      you,
  you have so many good things stored
      up for many years,
  rest, eat, drink, be merry!"'
But God said to him,
  'You fool, this night your life will be
      demanded of you;
  and the things you have prepared, to
      whom will they belong?'
Thus will it be for all who store up
    treasure for themselves
  but are not rich in what matters to
      God."

Reflecting on the Gospel

Many of us know and are familiar with Jesus' teachings. But what would we consider to be among the most popular topics that Jesus addressed? Or another question we might ask is, what are the most popular topics we hear about today in churches? Are the two related? Do the priorities of Jesus and his preaching align with preaching we hear at the parish? Interestingly, some of the issues Jesus addressed more than others were about money and the right use of it. Rarely did he address issues concerning buildings of worship, parish schools, sexuality, LGBT, or even contraception. Jesus preached often about how people use their money. And today's gospel is a case, or rather two cases, in point.

The first story is about someone who wants his share of the inheritance. Rather than get in the middle of that quagmire (Jesus seems to have been wise not to step into that battle!), he gives a quick aphorism that's appropriate for Christian and non-Christian alike, "[O]ne's life does not consist of possessions." In fact, this teaching reflects certain schools of Greek philosophy, and even modern common sense.

The second story is called the parable of the rich fool. Indeed, God himself addresses the rich man as "You fool," for he spent his time on earth acquiring a bountiful harvest, a "treasure for himself." But that very night he will die, not "rich in what matters to God." Here it is clear that bountiful harvests, storehouses, and great material blessings are not what matters to God. Other gospel passages from Luke will make clear what does matter to God. In this reading we learn *via negativa*, by a negative way, what does not.

The parable calls us to reconsider our own harvests and storehouses. What are we acquiring and for what purpose? "[O]ne's life does not consist of possessions." It's a lesson so clear and fundamental that we need to be reminded of it again and again.

Parish preaching would do well to echo themes introduced by Jesus himself. All other ancillary but related issues will then naturally fall in line. But how we spend our money says a great deal about us as human beings. Our values, priorities, and interests are all expressed by the way we spend money.

Living the Paschal Mystery

The reading from Luke invites us to take stock of our lives from a different perspective. When God calls us from this life, what will we have left? The old adage, "you can't take it with you," comes to mind. No matter what physical things or possessions we acquire here on earth we take nothing with us after we die. Put another way, our lives are not our possessions. A monthly checking account statement or credit card bill can become a moment of prayer. Our spending reflects our priorities.

It behooves us to step back from a desire to acquire and ask ourselves why. What is the purpose of our possessions? Rather than become rich in the eyes of the world, it is better to become rich in what matters to God. When we lift up the lowly, feed the hungry, and forgive sins of others we acquire riches in what matters to God. We have no ledger sheet or checking account to track this behavior. Instead, it flows from our identity as Christians, living a spirituality of the paschal mystery.

Focusing the Gospel

Key words and phrases: Take care to guard against all greed.

To the point: Merriam-Webster's dictionary defines greed as "a selfish and excessive desire for more of something than is needed." We see this greed played out in today's gospel with the rich man who finds himself with such a bountiful harvest he cannot possibly use it all. Instead of sharing this bounty with others or putting it to some good use, he decides to tear down his current barn to build an even bigger one to hold the excess. If we are not careful, the desire for more can take over every aspect of our lives, because no *thing* will satisfy our deepest hunger. Only God can do that. As St. Augustine said, "Our hearts are restless until they can find rest in you."

Connecting the Gospel

to the first reading: In the reading from Ecclesiastes, Qoheleth laments, "For what profit comes to man from all the toil and anxiety of heart / with which he has labored under the sun?" His answer? Only "sorrow and grief." For the wise and knowledgeable face the same fate as the foolish (2:16), so what point is there in life? Reading through Ecclesiastes, we might ask ourselves, where is the good news here? If all is vanity, where is our sure foundation and a treasure that will last? The answer comes to us in the gospel. Our lives are meaningful when they belong to God. When we are rich in God we have all we need.

to experience: As Qoheleth tells us and as the rich fool in the gospel discovers, human lives are unpredictable. All things fade away, including those that we cling to like a life preserver: health, beauty, money . . . . Instead of placing our hope and trust in what is transitory, our lives become secure only when we turn to the one who is truly unchanging: our triune God.

Connecting the Responsorial Psalm

to the readings: Following Qoheleth's line of thought, the psalmist too reflects on the transitory nature of life. We are the creatures who will turn "back to dust," our lives as fragile and as fleeting as the grass, "which at dawn springs up anew, / but by evening wilts and fades." When considered in light of human limitations, it indeed seems to be vanity to toil for that which will pass away. Saint Paul urges us to put away "the parts of you that are earthly" in order to enter into the life of Christ. We are mortals, made in the image and likeness of God, the eternal one, called by Jesus to become "rich in what matters to God."

to psalmist preparation: The final verse of today's psalm points to this true richness when we are bathed in the kindness, joy, and gladness of a life steeped in God's gracious care. Where do you find this richness in your life?

PROMPTS FOR FAITH-SHARING

Which activities in your life fall into the category of "vanity of vanities"? How might you exchange some of these meaningless pursuits for more fulfilling work?

Our finances can tell us a lot about our priorities in life. When you look at your monthly expenses is your spending in line with what is most important to you? What about what is most important to Jesus?

Where in your life are you "rich in what matters to God"?

Where is there excess in your life? How might God be calling you to share that excess with others?

Model Penitential Act

Presider: In today's gospel Jesus counsels, "Take care to guard against all greed, / for though one may be rich, / one's life does not consist of possessions." For the times we have prioritized wealth, power, and possessions over the kingdom of God, let us pause to ask for pardon and mercy . . . [*pause*]

Lord Jesus, you fulfill the deepest longings of our hearts: Lord, have mercy.

Christ Jesus, you invite us to store up treasure in heaven: Christ, have mercy.

Lord Jesus, you shepherd us to everlasting life: Lord, have mercy.

Homily Points

• Today's gospel challenges us to consider one central question, what (or where) is our treasure? For the rich man in the parable the answer is obvious. His treasure is the stability provided by a bounteous harvest. He even builds a storehouse for this treasure (new and larger barns), and once it is safely tucked away tells himself, "Now as for you, / you have so many good things stored up for many years, / rest, eat, drink, be merry!" The stability he thinks he has found is an illusion, however, because life is fragile and uncertain.

• It is natural for human beings to seek stability and control. We want to know that we have enough to provide for our needs and the needs of our families. But at what point do we begin to place all of our faith and hope in material goods, instead of in God, the only true constant in life? And when can we truly say, enough is enough? Greed is a sickness of the spirit that constantly goads us to acquire more and more. The things we seek will never fill the deepest longings of our hearts, and, as long as wealth or power, fame, or beauty is our aim, we will never be satisfied.

• Jesus offers us another way. A few verses after this gospel reading he tells the disciples to focus on the "inexhaustible treasure in heaven that no thief can reach nor moth destroy. For where your treasure is, there also will your heart be" (12:33-34; NABRE). Where do you store your treasure? Where do you keep your heart?

Model Universal Prayer (Prayer of the Faithful)

Presider: Jesus calls us to become rich in what matters to God. Humbly, we turn to God in prayer and lift up our needs and the needs of our world.

Response: Lord, hear our prayer.

That the church might be transparent in matters of finance and dedicate resources to caring for the poor . . .

That those who control a disproportionate amount of the world's resources might use their leadership and power for justice so that all may have what they need . . .

That those who have devoted themselves to the empty pursuit of wealth and power know the fulfillment found in Jesus' path of service and generosity . . .

That all gathered here listen for the voice of our Good Shepherd calling us to become rich in what matters to God . . .

Presider: God of life, you sent your son to lead us to you, our true treasure and source of all peace. Hear our prayers that we might be freed from the desire to always have more, and instead invest our time and resources in building the kingdom of God. We ask this through Christ, our Lord. Amen.

COLLECT

Let us pray.

Pause for silent prayer

Draw near to your servants, O Lord,
and answer their prayers with unceasing kindness,
that, for those who glory in you as their Creator and guide,
you may restore what you have created
and keep safe what you have restored.
Through our Lord Jesus Christ, your Son,
who lives and reigns with you in the unity of the Holy Spirit,
one God, for ever and ever. **Amen.**

FIRST READING

Eccl 1:2; 2:21-23

Vanity of vanities, says Qoheleth,
vanity of vanities! All things are vanity!

Here is one who has labored with wisdom and knowledge and skill,
and yet to another who has not labored over it,
he must leave property.
This also is vanity and a great misfortune.
For what profit comes to man from all the toil and anxiety of heart
with which he has labored under the sun?
All his days sorrow and grief are his occupation;
even at night his mind is not at rest.
This also is vanity.

RESPONSORIAL PSALM

Ps 90:3-4, 5-6, 12-13, 14 and 17

R̸. (8) If today you hear his voice, harden not your hearts.

You turn man back to dust,
saying, "Return, O children of men."
For a thousand years in your sight
are as yesterday, now that it is past,
or as a watch of the night.

R̸. If today you hear his voice, harden not your hearts.

You make an end of them in their sleep;
the next morning they are like the changing grass,
which at dawn springs up anew,
but by evening wilts and fades.

R̸. If today you hear his voice, harden not your hearts.

Teach us to number our days aright,
    that we may gain wisdom of heart.
Return, O Lᴏʀᴅ! How long?
    Have pity on your servants!

℞. If today you hear his voice, harden not
    your hearts.

Fill us at daybreak with your kindness,
    that we may shout for joy and gladness
        all our days.
And may the gracious care of the Lᴏʀᴅ
    our God be ours;
    prosper the work of our hands for us!
    Prosper the work of our hands!

℞. If today you hear his voice, harden not
    your hearts.

SECOND READING
Col 3:1-5, 9-11

Brothers and sisters:
If you were raised with Christ, seek what
    is above,
    where Christ is seated at the right hand
        of God.
Think of what is above, not of what is on
    earth.
For you have died,
    and your life is hidden with Christ in
        God.
When Christ your life appears,
    then you too will appear with him in
        glory.

Put to death, then, the parts of you that
    are earthly:
    immorality, impurity, passion, evil
        desire,
    and the greed that is idolatry.
Stop lying to one another,
    since you have taken off the old self
        with its practices
    and have put on the new self,
    which is being renewed, for knowledge,
    in the image of its creator.
Here there is not Greek and Jew,
    circumcision and uncircumcision,
    barbarian, Scythian, slave, free;
    but Christ is all and in all.

About Liturgy

The collection at Mass: The collection taken up during Mass is an ancient tradition with its roots in the early church. Originally, the people brought forward bread and wine from their own homes to be used for the Eucharist. They also presented goods from their possessions—foods they harvested, livestock from their farms, household items from their own storeroom. These would be distributed by the deacons to those in need in the community as well as given for the material needs of the church.

Today, the people still ritually present bread and wine, though not usually from their own home. Also, the gifts for the poor and the church are now given in the form of money.

Taking up a collection has significant meaning for what we do at the Eucharist. Giving money at Mass is not, as some might treat it, a measure of one's satisfaction with the liturgy or with the church in general. Our Christian sacrifice cannot be some vague theoretical idea. We have to give something of ourselves that is a real sacrifice—something we would rather not give up. For most of us today, that's money. Beyond simply being a way to help the parish pay its bills, the collection is one way we bring ourselves—"the work of human hands" along with the "fruit of the earth"—to the altar. That's why the collection is brought forward with the bread and wine we use at Mass. The money we put in the basket helps the church do the mission of Christ not only by keeping the lights on but also by funding the activities and people of the church who help the poor, teach the faith, prepare the liturgy, visit the sick, and more.

Finally, giving money at Mass is also a way we express our trust in God. We give the fruit of our own labor back to God, acknowledging that every good gift we have been given comes first from God.

The most appropriate time to take up a collection is at the preparation of gifts. If a second collection must be taken, do this during this time as well instead of after Communion where it can disrupt the ritual flow of the communion rite. Once the collection has been brought forward, it is placed in another suitable and secure location away from the altar (see GIRM 73). Another option that works well is to invite the assembly to come forward to the altar to place their gifts at baskets located there. Once all have come forward, the baskets are gathered and the bread and wine are brought to the altar.

About Liturgical Music

Music suggestions: Today's readings are powerful challenges for us to trust completely in God's care. Three songs help express this call. First, *Psallite*'s "Do Not Store Up Earthly Treasures" (*Sacred Song*) is a creative adaptation of J. S. Bach's hymn tune WACHET AUF (commonly found in hymnals as "Wake, O Wake, and Sleep No Longer"). The *Psallite* version is intended to be sung a cappella but can also be accompanied by any familiar arrangement of the hymn tune. The second is David Haas's "Seek First the Kingdom" (GIA). The text of its spirited refrain is, "Seek first the kingdom of God and good will come to you! Where your treasure lies is where your heart will be! Seek first the kingdom! Come and follow me!" Finally, any setting of St. Ignatius of Loyola's *Suscipe* prayer fits well. Two of the more familiar settings are John Foley's "Take, Lord, Receive" (OCP) and Dan Schutte's "These Alone Are Enough" (OCP).

SPIRITUALITY

GOSPEL ACCLAMATION
Matt 24:42a, 44

℟. Alleluia, alleluia.
Stay awake and be ready!
For you do not know on what day your Lord will
   come.
℟. Alleluia, alleluia.

Gospel   Luke 12:32-48; L117C

Jesus said to his disciples:
   "Do not be afraid any longer, little
      flock,
   for your Father is pleased to give
      you the kingdom.
Sell your belongings and give alms.
Provide money bags for yourselves
   that do not wear out,
   an inexhaustible treasure in heaven
   that no thief can reach nor moth
      destroy.
For where your treasure is, there also
   will your heart be.

"Gird your loins and light your lamps
   and be like servants who await
      their master's return from a
      wedding,
   ready to open immediately when he
      comes and knocks.
Blessed are those servants
   whom the master finds vigilant on
      his arrival.
Amen, I say to you, he will gird
   himself,
   have them recline at table, and pro-
      ceed to wait on them.
And should he come in the second or
   third watch
   and find them prepared in this way,
   blessed are those servants.
Be sure of this:
   if the master of the house had
      known the hour
   when the thief was coming,
   he would not have let his house be
      broken into.

Continued in Appendix A, p. 308,

or Luke 12:35-40 in Appendix A, p. 308.

Reflecting on the Gospel

As we continue our Ordinary Time journey with Jesus to Jerusalem we hear more parables and teachings, laden with ancient imagery. As we are familiar with the expression, "Gird your loins," many in the pew may not know exactly what that means. Though it has the sense "brace yourself," it literally means something like "tighten your pants." That image, coupled with "light your lamps" and "be like servants who await their master's return," and even "recline at table" tells us we are in the ancient world, in a culture quite removed from our own. But despite these images and the imaginary cultural bridge we must cross, we can certainly gain a sense of what is meant by these teachings. Some simply prefer to focus on the line "be prepared, for at an hour you do not expect, / the Son of Man will come," shedding all ancient and other imagery.

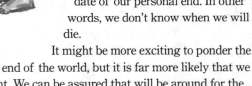

When we reduce the teaching to this essential element, it becomes easier to grasp the message, which is not solely about the end times. Instead, the exhortation to be prepared applies to each of us as we do not know the time, place, or date of our personal end. In other words, we don't know when we will die.

It might be more exciting to ponder the end of the world, but it is far more likely that we will not be around for that event. We can be assured that will be around for the end of *our own* world. And for that we should be prepared spiritually.

This might not be such a happy or pleasant message on an August weekend in the midst of Ordinary Time. But perhaps this is a good time to hear it. When summer plans are winding down and attention is turning to the start of the school year, we ask ourselves if we are ready for the coming of the Son of Man. Or, are we deluding ourselves in thinking that day will never come? When it does, it comes like a thief in the night. Brace yourself!

Living the Paschal Mystery

There will come a time for each of us to pass on from this life. In all likelihood it's not a topic we discuss much. Most of us live our lives in anticipation of future events, making plans, and carrying on our way. Especially now in the modern world when the science of medicine and the pace of technology has improved day-to-day life a great deal, it seems there is nothing we cannot solve. And yet, tragedy still strikes. Death and loss come. There is the pain of losing someone we love. And at that point we might imagine all we wish we had said or expressed.

The gospel passage today reminds us that we all will ultimately face our own end. But the paschal mystery tells us that after death there is new life. It is not the same, but it will be transformed. Even so, our current life can end in a moment, coming "like a thief in the night." We are advised to be on guard, to watch, to act in a way that we will be ready for that day. Where is our treasure? There too is our heart.

Focusing the Gospel

Key words and phrases: You also must be prepared, for at an hour you do not expect, / the Son of Man will come.

To the point: In our church year we have two great seasons of preparation: Advent and Lent. In these times we prepare our hearts and minds, as well as our homes and families, to celebrate the feasts of Christmas and Easter. Though preparation can take on a penitential overtone, it is also filled with joy as a foretaste of the celebration to come. In our gospel today, Jesus counsels his disciples to be vigilant in preparation for the coming of the Son of Man. Whether we meet Jesus at the end of time or at the end of our earthly lives, we do not know the hour or the day when this will occur. May our preparation be intentional and constant, but also joyful as we look forward to an eternity with God.

Connecting the Gospel

to the second reading: The second reading from the Letter to the Hebrews focuses on the person of Abraham. Not knowing what lay ahead of him, Abraham followed God's call to leave his home and family to enter into a new land, which God would show him. Even when it seemed as if God's promises of a land of his own and descendants could not be fulfilled Abraham remained steadfast, "for he thought that the one who had made the promise was trustworthy." Jesus has promised that he will return for us, that he is preparing a place for us. Do we also hold the one who has made this promise to be trustworthy?

to experience: We can take Abraham as our model in faith as we wait for the fulfillment of God's promises. For a time when there will be no more war, sickness, death, or grief, for the time when God will be "all in all" (1 Cor 15:28; NABRE).

Connecting the Responsorial Psalm

to the readings: To be like the servants in today's gospel requires not only vigilance but also extreme patience. The servants do not know when their master will return. If he is delayed will they grow tired of watching for him? Will they begin to lose hope that he is returning at all? The psalmist lifts up today the necessity of "wait[ing] for the Lord." We know that God's ways are not our ways, nor God's thoughts our thoughts (Isa 55:8). And yet it is difficult to have patience when we feel like it is time for the Lord to show up and intervene. The psalmist reassures us, "See, the eyes of the Lord are upon those who fear him, / upon those who hope for his kindness." As we live in this time of waiting and preparation for the fullness of the kingdom of God, it might be easy to grow weary and to give up hope. But we come from generations upon generations of God's people who despite hardship and persecution continued to "[wait] for the Lord." We are called to do the same.

to psalmist preparation: Patience is a muscle that grows stronger with use. Where is God calling on you to wait upon him?

PROMPTS FOR FAITH-SHARING

St. Paul lifts up for us Abraham, our father in faith, as a role model for our own trust in God. Who are the spiritual ancestors who have built up your faith?

Abraham goes forth from his homeland and family to a new land God will reveal to him. Has there been a time in your life when you left all that you knew to embark on a different path? What sustained you through that experience?

We do not know the hour or the day when the Son of Man will come or when we will go to meet the Son of Man. How are you exercising vigilance in preparation for this moment?

Jesus tells us, "Gird your loins and light your lamps." How might we spiritually respond to these commands?

CELEBRATION

Model Penitential Act

Presider: Jesus counsels us, "be prepared, for at an hour you do not expect, / the Son of Man will come." Let us pause to prepare our hearts and minds to welcome Jesus . . . [*pause*]

Lord Jesus, you are Son of God and Son of Man: Lord, have mercy.

Christ Jesus, you have gone on ahead to prepare a place for us: Christ, have mercy.

Lord Jesus, you point the way to everlasting life: Lord, have mercy.

Homily Points

• The themes of preparation, waiting, and hope are woven throughout today's readings. The first reading from the book of Wisdom hearkens back to the first Passover when the people of God, enslaved in Egypt, ate their meal of lamb and unleavened bread with hope in God's power to save them. The psalmist tells us to "[wait] for the Lord." In the gospel Jesus admonishes the disciples, "You . . . must be prepared." And in the second reading from the Letter to the Hebrews we hear of how it all began with the covenant God established with Abraham.

• In the figure of Abraham we can see both where we have been and where we are going. God promised Abraham land and descendants, and Abraham lived to see both promises brought to fulfillment, though perhaps on a smaller scale than he might have wished. Near the end of his life Abraham acquires a field and a cave in the land of Canaan as a burial plot for his wife Sarah. He also lives to see his son Isaac married to Rebekah. Through the many ups and downs of his life, Abraham does not lose hope in God's promises for, the Letter to the Hebrews tells us, "[H]e was looking forward to the city with foundations, / whose architect and maker is God." Abraham trusted in the vision of God, even when he himself could not see how it could possibly come about.

• St. Paul reminds us that from Abraham came "descendants as numerous as the stars in the sky / and as countless as the sands on the seashore." From one wandering nomad in the land of Israel has come forth the people of God spread throughout the world and throughout generations. We count ourselves as members of this family. Like Abraham, we look to the future when God's kingdom of peace and justice will come to fulfillment. We might not know when this will come about but we will continue preparing for it, because we believe that the one who has made this promise is trustworthy.

Model Universal Prayer (Prayer of the Faithful)

Presider: Let us bring our prayers to the Lord that we might always vigilantly be about the work of building the kingdom of God.

Response: Lord, hear our prayer.

That the church be a shining light, constantly in service to God and people . . .

That leaders of the world see themselves as servants of their people . . .

That those who are nearing death be consoled and supported in their transition from earthly life . . .

That those gathered here might joyfully prepare our hearts and minds for the day we meet the Son of Man face to face . . .

Presider: God of salvation, we joyfully await the fulfillment of your kingdom. Hear our prayers that we might never tire of the work you have given us to do. We ask this through Christ, our Lord. Amen.

COLLECT

Let us pray.

Pause for silent prayer

Almighty ever-living God,
whom, taught by the Holy Spirit,
we dare to call our Father,
bring, we pray, to perfection in our hearts
the spirit of adoption as your sons and
    daughters,
that we may merit to enter into the
    inheritance
which you have promised.
Through our Lord Jesus Christ, your Son,
who lives and reigns with you in the unity
    of the Holy Spirit,
one God, for ever and ever. **Amen.**

FIRST READING

Wis 18:6-9

The night of the passover was known
    beforehand to our fathers,
    that, with sure knowledge of the oaths
      in which they put their faith,
    they might have courage.
Your people awaited the salvation of the
    just
    and the destruction of their foes.
For when you punished our adversaries,
    in this you glorified us whom you had
      summoned.
For in secret the holy children of the good
    were offering sacrifice
    and putting into effect with one accord
      the divine institution.

RESPONSORIAL PSALM

Ps 33:1, 12, 18-19, 20-22

℟. (12b) Blessed the people the Lord has chosen to be his own.

Exult, you just, in the LORD;
  praise from the upright is fitting.
Blessed the nation whose God is the LORD,
  the people he has chosen for his own inheritance.

℟. Blessed the people the Lord has chosen to be his own.

See, the eyes of the LORD are upon those who fear him,
  upon those who hope for his kindness,
to deliver them from death
  and preserve them in spite of famine.

℟. Blessed the people the Lord has chosen to be his own.

Our soul waits for the LORD,
  who is our help and our shield.
May your kindness, O LORD, be upon us
  who have put our hope in you.

℟. Blessed the people the Lord has chosen to be his own.

SECOND READING

Heb 11:1-2, 8-19

Brothers and sisters:
Faith is the realization of what is hoped for
  and evidence of things not seen.
Because of it the ancients were well attested.

By faith Abraham obeyed when he was
  called to go out to a place
  that he was to receive as an inheritance;
  he went out, not knowing where he was
    to go.
By faith he sojourned in the promised land
  as in a foreign country,
  dwelling in tents with Isaac and Jacob,
    heirs of the same promise;
  for he was looking forward to the city
    with foundations,
  whose architect and maker is God.
By faith he received power to generate,
  even though he was past the normal age
  —and Sarah herself was sterile—
  for he thought that the one who had
    made the promise was trustworthy.

Continued in Appendix A, p. 309,

or Heb 11:1-2, 8-12.

About Liturgy

Children's Liturgy of the Word: This is a good time to read or reread the Directory for Masses with Children, issued by the then-called Congregation for Divine Worship in 1973. The document explores principles for children who have not yet reached preadolescence, generally considered the pre-teen years. Chapter 2 looks specifically at Masses for adults at which children are present. A parish's Sunday Masses will typically fall under the norms listed in that chapter.

In chapter 2, the document emphasizes the importance of the witness of adult believers upon the faith life of children. The presence of children in the assembly, in turn, also benefits the faith life of adults. This is why the directory foresees that, within such Masses where most are adults, the norm is for children to remain within the assembly to participate in the Mass alongside adults. Paragraph 17 states that we should take great care to ensure that children can participate fully even with adults. Thus, the presider can speak to the children directly during the introduction to the Mass or at the end and within the homily itself. The children may also participate in some of the ministries and tasks of the Mass.

It might be surprising to learn that paragraph 17 envisions that the dismissal of children to celebrate a separate Liturgy of the Word just for them should be an occasional occurrence and not one celebrated every Sunday at the parish Masses.

Children learn how to pray and participate in the Mass by imitating what they see and hear adults do. It would actually be detrimental to children if most of their experience of the Sunday Mass is only with other children. If you are currently celebrating a separate Liturgy of the Word for children every Sunday at the parish Mass, you might review your reasons for doing so and consider if there are more benefits to the children and the adults if all celebrated the Liturgy of the Word together on a regular basis.

About Initiation

Everyone has a year-round RCIA: If you have Sunday Mass at your parish every week, you have a year-round RCIA. The process for preparing adults for initiation is not a program for a small group of people with a start and end date. It is initiation into Christ by incorporation into the Christian community. Therefore, if your community gathers on a regular basis to do what Christians do, such as Sunday Mass, you have something right now that will help form a seeker to live the Christian way of life. So stop telling inquirers to "come back in September when RCIA classes begin." Just invite them to your next Sunday Mass.

About Liturgical Music

Being ritual ready: Music ministers have a huge influence on the ritual flow of a liturgy. That is, they contribute to the pace of the liturgical action and can drag it, rush it, or make it just right at each moment of the liturgy.

A primary place where this happens is in acclamations and responses preceded by an invitation, for example, the Eucharistic Prayer acclamations. The presider's words lead directly into the people's sung response. Any kind of delay in beginning the music at these moments clouds the dialogic nature of this prayer. Consider shortening, or even omitting altogether, lengthy musical introductions for these acclamations.

Another place is when an acclamation accompanies a ritual action, such as the Lamb of God or the Communion of the priest. In all these cases, music ministers need to be aware and ready so that the assembly is singing at just the right time.

AUGUST 11, 2019

NINETEENTH SUNDAY IN ORDINARY TIME

GOSPEL ACCLAMATION

R̸. Alleluia, alleluia.
Mary is taken up to heaven;
a chorus of angels exults.
R̸. Alleluia, alleluia.

Gospel

Luke 1:39-56; L622

Mary set out
   and traveled to the hill country in haste
   to a town of Judah,
   where she entered the house of
      Zechariah
   and greeted Elizabeth.
When Elizabeth heard Mary's
      greeting,
   the infant leaped in her womb,
   and Elizabeth, filled with the
      Holy Spirit,
   cried out in a loud voice and said,
"Blessed are you among women,
   and blessed is the fruit of your womb.
And how does this happen to me,
   that the mother of my Lord should
      come to me?
For at the moment the sound of your
      greeting reached my ears,
   the infant in my womb leaped for joy.
Blessed are you who believed
   that what was spoken to you by the
      Lord
   would be fulfilled."

And Mary said:

"My soul proclaims the greatness of
      the Lord;
   my spirit rejoices in God my Savior
   for he has looked with favor on his
      lowly servant.
From this day all generations will call
      me blessed:
   the Almighty has done great things
      for me,
   and holy is his Name.
He has mercy on those who fear him
   in every generation.
He has shown the strength of his arm,
   and has scattered the proud in their
      conceit.

Continued in Appendix A, p. 310.

See Appendix A, p. 310, for the other readings.

Reflecting on the Gospel

The feast of the Assumption, like all Marian feasts, says more about Jesus than it does about Mary. Marian feasts are fundamentally christological, expressing something foundational about Christ and the power of the incarnation and resurrection. With respect to the assumption, the church has long maintained, at least since the fourth century, a belief that Mary was taken up to heaven after her earthly life. The Eastern Church typically refers to this as the *dormition* (or sleeping) of Mary, expressing the belief that she did not die but slept, and then was taken up to heaven. The Roman Catholic Church refers to this as the *assumption*. Whether or not Mary actually died has never been dogmatically defined. However, in an act of papal infallibility, Pope Pius XII dogmatically proclaimed the assumption as a matter of faith in 1950. It might seem odd that nineteen hundred years after the assumption it was proclaimed dogmatically, but again, it says more about Christ than about Mary. Ultimately, it is the power of Christ and his resurrection that prevented Mary's body from seeing decay.

Some believe that this dogma was proclaimed in 1950, shortly after World War II as so many millions had been killed in that war and in World War I that had shortly preceded it. With the value of human life apparently so cheapened, this dogma would underscore its sanctity, especially that of the body.

The reading that the church uses to celebrate this feast is Mary's *Magnificat*. She proclaims this upon meeting her relative Elizabeth. The *Magnificat* is a canticle that sets the stage for the gospel's themes. It sounds notes that will be reverberating throughout the gospel and in Acts. God lifts up the lowly and throws down the mighty. He fills the hungry with good things and turns the rich away empty. A great reversal is underway and the social order will be overturned. If this was Mary's theological outlook before Jesus was born, imagine the lessons he learned from her as a mother. Mary is no shrinking violet. She has been called the first disciple for good reason. The power of Christ's resurrection extended to her in life and death.

Living the Paschal Mystery

As we consider the life and death (or dormition) of Mary we recall that she witnessed the paschal mystery and lived it in her own way. She who said yes at the annunciation, who proclaimed her canticle to Elizabeth, and who gave birth to Jesus also witnessed his passion, death, resurrection, and the handing on of the Spirit at Pentecost according to Luke. We are reminded that as her life was full of grace, so are our lives. The power of the resurrection is celebrated in Mary's life but it is also present in our own. The pain, loss, grief, and even death that we experience will be brought to new life by Christ. As Mary listened to the word of God and gave birth to it, may we too listen attentively and bring to bear the word of God in our own world. When we raise up the lowly, fill the hungry with good things, we are bringing about the kingdom of God imagined by Mary, the first disciple. Her destiny is our own, which is a cause of celebration.

Focusing the Gospel

Key words and phrases: he has looked upon his lowly servant

To the point: Mary begins her hymn to God by identifying herself with the lowly. She knows the God of Israel and how he has a habit of choosing the small and unassuming to do his greatest work. So it is no surprise that he chose a young woman from Nazareth to be to the Mother of God. On this feast of the Assumption we celebrate Mary's entrance into heaven following her death. God honors Mary in death as he did in life by preserving her body, the first tabernacle of the Lord.

Model Penitential Act

Presider: On this feast of the Assumption we celebrate the life and death of Mary, the Mother of God, and her assumption, body and soul, into heaven. Let us pause to ask that we might also completely give our lives to God . . . [*pause*]

Lord Jesus, you are Son of God and son of Mary: Lord, have mercy.

Christ Jesus, you are the Messiah, the anointed one: Christ, have mercy.

Lord Jesus, you are the resurrection and the life: Lord, have mercy.

Model Universal Prayer (Prayer of the Faithful)

Presider: We offer our prayers to God through the intercession of the Blessed Virgin Mary who identified herself with the lowly.

Response: Lord, hear our prayer.

That the leaders of the church follow the example of Mary and be a prophetic voice for the poor . . .

That people all over the world know the compassionate love of the Mother of God . . .

That those who hunger might be filled . . .

That all gathered here might lead lives that proclaim the greatness of God . . .

Presider: God of justice, you chose Mary to be the mother of your Son. Hear our prayers that we might meditate on the precious words of her *Magnificat* and bring them to fruition in our own lives. We ask this through Christ, our Lord. Amen.

About Liturgy

The **Magnificat:** Preparing the liturgy for Marian feasts can always be a bit challenging. How do you appropriately give honor to the Blessed Virgin Mary while rightfully keeping the focus on Christ? Today's gospel text gives us a good model to follow.

In Luke's account of the visitation between Elizabeth and Mary, we hear two familiar canticles: Elizabeth's blessing from which developed the Hail Mary; and Mary's *Magnificat*. Mary's own focus in her song is on God's faithfulness and on what God has done.

The *Magnificat* holds a special place in the liturgical life of the church. It is the gospel canticle that is typically sung at Evening Prayer for the Liturgy of the Hours every day. It is also the prayer that we, too, hope to embody in our life of praise and trust in God's will for us.

Use a familiar setting of the *Magnificat* today. It would be very appropriate as a song of praise after Communion or as an entrance song. Also reflect on the canticle's text as part of the homily for this day.

FOR REFLECTION

• In St. Paul's first letter to the Corinthians we are told that Jesus will destroy all enemies, even death. How does it change your life, knowing death is not the end?

• When Mary and Elizabeth meet, Elizabeth recognizes Jesus present within Mary. What relationships in your life foster your understanding of Jesus present within you?

• Mary's canticle of praise to God reads as a manifesto on justice. How are you called to serve the God of Mary who fills the hungry and lifts up the lowly?

Homily Points

• In our gospel today, Elizabeth proclaims who Mary is: Mother of the Lord, and blessed among all people. Mary's words to the angel, "May it be done to me according to your word," at the annunciation changed her entire life. Elizabeth's greeting confirms what has occurred. She recognizes the mystery of the incarnation in their midst.

• Mary's words, her canticle of praise, proclaim who God is: the merciful One who disperses the arrogant and lifts up the lowly. Mary doesn't know the end of the story when she meets with Elizabeth. But she trusts the God she loves. This is a God who keeps his promises. This is a God worthy of all honor and praise.

✝ SPIRITUALITY

R⍭. Alleluia, alleluia.
My sheep hear my voice, says the Lord;
I know them, and they follow me.
R⍭. Alleluia, alleluia.

Gospel

Luke 12:49-53; L120C

Jesus said to his disciples:
  "I have come to set the earth
    on fire,
  and how I wish it were already
    blazing!
There is a baptism with which I
    must be baptized,
  and how great is my anguish
    until it is accomplished!
Do you think that I have come to es-
    tablish peace on the earth?
No, I tell you, but rather
    division.
From now on a household of
    five will be divided,
  three against two and two
    against three;
  a father will be divided against his
    son
  and a son against his father,
  a mother against her daughter
  and a daughter against her mother,
  a mother-in-law against her
    daughter-in-law
  and a daughter-in-law against her
    mother-in-law."

Reflecting on the Gospel

Christians are so familiar with "peace on earth" as a tagline of Christianity that today's gospel can be something of a shock to the system. The angels sang, "[P]eace to those on whom his favor rests" (Luke 2:14; NABRE), and the cry of the crowds upon Jesus' entry into Jerusalem will be "Blessed is the king who comes in the name of the Lord. / Peace in heaven and glory in the highest" (Luke 19:38; NABRE). So it sounds strange today to hear Jesus saying that he is *not* bringing peace but division.

But then, upon a closer reading of the Gospel of Luke we do hear inklings of this theme. As an infant, Jesus is said by Simeon to be "destined for the fall and rise of many in Israel" (Luke 2:34; NABRE). Simeon continues by saying that Mary will be pierced with a sword (Luke 2:35). Moreover, early Christianity was perceived by the Romans and others as we would consider a cult today. No self-respecting Roman wanted their children to be caught up in this Judean "superstition" as they called it. And those who became Christian often pulled away from their families, forming new bonds with other Christians, whom they considered a new family. So given that background, the idea that Jesus brought division might be seen in a different light. The peace that the Christians experienced was with one another, not the peace the world gives. And that peace might have come at the price of family divisions who did not understand this new way of life.

Of course, Christianity has been so domesticated today, with the culture empowering it and supporting it, that we have little experiential sense of what the early Christians encountered simply to be Christian. Any perceived impingement of religious freedom in the Western world today can scarcely be compared to what the first generations of Christians experienced, or Christians in the Middle East or Africa today, when some were and are being executed for their faith.

Though we share many common elements of our faith with those who have gone before us, the divisions they experienced in the early years seem distant. Still, when we take seriously the gospel message and live it boldly, we may be shunned or avoided by those we considered friends or family.

Living the Paschal Mystery

Paradoxically, the peace that Jesus brings comes served with division. It's as though the poison is within the antidote. Living as a disciple of Jesus means that we will lose company with some, perhaps even family and friends. Disciples are no mere "go along to get along" kind of people. Faith in Christ, service of the poor, and working for justice are essential elements of discipleship. Others may have a vested interest in the status quo, and do not want things overturned or upended. But for a serious follower of Christ, for a disciple who follows in the footsteps of Jesus, opposition can be expected. Jesus himself lost his life in a confrontation with evil. Many of his followers down to the present day have lost their lives as well, or faced imprisonment, persecution, and hostility. "Good news" preached to the poor, the outcast, and the downtrodden, can sound eerily like sedition or revolution. When we stand on the side of the persecuted and marginalized we should not be surprised to face persecution and marginalization ourselves.

Focusing the Gospel

Key words and phrases: Do you think that I have come to establish peace on the earth? / No, I tell you, but rather division.

To the point: How do we reconcile today's gospel with Jesus, the Prince of Peace? Human beings, with our God-given free will, are able to accept or reject peace in whatever form it comes to us. We see this in the time of Jesus and throughout the past two thousand years. Jesus' proclamation of the kingdom of God where the poor and the humble are blessed and the rich and powerful are turned away has often been rejected and met with resistance. Jesus proclaimed the reign of God and this reign challenged people, especially those in power. However, when Jesus himself met with resistance, even resistance up to death on a cross, he responded with nonviolence, forgiveness, and love. On our journey of faith we will meet resistance too when we challenge the status quo. May our response be that of Jesus, the Prince of Peace.

Connecting the Gospel

to the first and second readings: The prophet Jeremiah also caused division in his own day. Speaking to the king and the temple elite in Jerusalem, Jeremiah urged the people to surrender to the Babylonian army attacking Judea. This was not a popular message. Jeremiah's fidelity to God's message landed him in prison and then in the pit of mud we hear of today. What gave Jeremiah and Jesus the strength to continue on in the face of imprisonment, torture, and even death? In the Letter to the Hebrews we hear, "For the sake of the joy that lay before him / he endured the cross, despising its shame."

to experience: What gives us the strength to carry on in times of struggle? It is the belief that life is stronger than death, light is stronger than darkness, and love is stronger than hatred.

Connecting the Responsorial Psalm

to the readings: The psalmist appears to have physically or metaphorically shared the experience of Jeremiah, sinking into the mud at the bottom of a cistern. And just as Jeremiah is drawn out of the cistern before perishing, the psalmist has also experienced God's saving action, for this is the Lord who "drew me out of the pit of destruction, / out of the mud of the swamp." In all three of today's readings and within the psalm we see that the spiritual life is not easy. One must undergo the cross in order to arrive at the resurrection.

to psalmist preparation: In the psalms we see extremes of emotion, from despair to joy and everything in between. And in the midst of our human volatility, we can say that our God is the rock that "made firm my steps. / And he put a new song into my mouth." Where, in your life, are you in need of the steady foundation of God? When you look with the eyes of faith, can you see God, the bedrock of life, supporting you?

PROMPTS FOR FAITH-SHARING

Like Jeremiah, when in life have you taken an unpopular position because you felt it was the right thing to do? Where did you find the fortitude and perseverance to remain firm in your conviction?

The Letter to the Hebrews speaks of the "great . . . cloud of witnesses" that surrounds us. How do you experience this cloud of witnesses in the life of faith?

Similar to the words of Jesus in the gospel, St. Catherine of Siena is quoted as saying, "Be who God meant you to be and you will set the world on fire." How is God calling you right now to be more faithful to who you are truly meant to be?

Where do you see division within your family, parish, or community? Where is Jesus within this division?

Model Penitential Act

Presider: Today Jesus proclaims, "I have come to set the earth on fire, / and how I wish it were already blazing!" For the times we have failed to burn with the brilliance of God's love, let us ask for pardon and mercy . . . [*pause*]

Lord Jesus, you stand with the persecuted and outcast: Lord, have mercy.

Christ Jesus, you baptize with fire and the Holy Spirit: Christ, have mercy.

Lord Jesus, you are the Prince of Peace: Lord, have mercy.

Homily Points

• In today's gospel Jesus exclaims, "I have come to set the earth on fire, / and how I wish it were already blazing!" We see fire in so many of the signs and symbols of our church: the candles that we light at the altar and ambo, the sanctuary lamp lit whenever Jesus is present in the tabernacle, the Easter fire that lights the paschal candle, which in turn lights our own individual candles and the candle of each newly baptized member of our church. Flame marks all of the significant moments in our life of faith, and often the everyday moments too, as we light a candle to pray at home, to enjoy a family meal, or to blow out on a birthday cake.

• And this makes sense. Jesus tells us in John's gospel, "I am the light of the world" (8:12; NABRE), and in Matthew's gospel he commissions us to act as people of flame, saying: "You are the light of the world" (5:14; NABRE). Why does Jesus use fire imagery so much? What does fire do? Fire transforms: what is cold becomes hot, what is hard becomes soft, what is dirty is purified, what is hidden in darkness becomes illuminated for all to see.

• In Jesus' life we see these moments of transformation taking place as he ministers to the people he meets on the dusty roads of ancient Israel. And now it is our turn. We are called into this mission of Jesus to set the world on fire. But how? At World Youth Day 2000, Pope John Paul II paraphrased a famous quote of St. Catherine of Siena, "If you are what you should be, you will set the whole world ablaze!" Nothing more, nothing less: Be who God dreams you to be.

Model Universal Prayer (Prayer of the Faithful)

Presider: With trust in God's mercy and belief in his faithfulness, we bring our prayers before the Lord.

Response: Lord, hear our prayer.

That Christians throughout the world come together in unity to serve the Lord of life and to care for the human family . . .

That leaders of nations be endowed with skills to peacefully resolve conflicts within their societies . . .

That those who experience persecution due to religious belief might dwell in safety and in freedom to practice their faith . . .

That all gathered here be strengthened to stand firmly in faith in the face of division . . .

Presider: God of creation, you call us to yourself and invite us to be prophets of peace and justice. Hear our prayers that we might serve you in righteousness and truth. We ask this through Jesus Christ, our Lord. Amen.

COLLECT

Let us pray.

Pause for silent prayer

O God, who have prepared for those who
    love you
good things which no eye can see,
fill our hearts, we pray, with the warmth
    of your love,
so that, loving you in all things and above
    all things,
we may attain your promises,
which surpass every human desire.
Through our Lord Jesus Christ, your Son,
who lives and reigns with you in the unity
    of the Holy Spirit,
one God, for ever and ever. **Amen.**

FIRST READING
Jer 38:4-6, 8-10

In those days, the princes said to the king:
    "Jeremiah ought to be put to death;
      he is demoralizing the soldiers who are
          left in this city,
      and all the people, by speaking such
          things to them;
      he is not interested in the welfare of our
          people,
      but in their ruin."
King Zedekiah answered: "He is in your
      power";
    for the king could do nothing with them.
And so they took Jeremiah
    and threw him into the cistern of Prince
      Malchiah,
    which was in the quarters of the guard,
    letting him down with ropes.
There was no water in the cistern, only
      mud,
    and Jeremiah sank into the mud.

Ebed-melech, a court official,
    went there from the palace and said to
      him:
    "My lord king,
    these men have been at fault
    in all they have done to the prophet
      Jeremiah,
    casting him into the cistern.
He will die of famine on the spot,
    for there is no more food in the city."
Then the king ordered Ebed-melech the
      Cushite
    to take three men along with him,
    and draw the prophet Jeremiah out of
      the cistern before he should die.

RESPONSORIAL PSALM

Ps 40:2, 3, 4, 18

R℣. (14b) Lord, come to my aid!

I have waited, waited for the LORD,
    and he stooped toward me.

R℣. Lord, come to my aid!

The LORD heard my cry.
He drew me out of the pit of destruction,
    out of the mud of the swamp;
he set my feet upon a crag;
    he made firm my steps.

R℣. Lord, come to my aid!

And he put a new song into my mouth,
    a hymn to our God.
Many shall look on in awe
    and trust in the LORD.

R℣. Lord, come to my aid!

Though I am afflicted and poor,
    yet the LORD thinks of me.
You are my help and my deliverer;
    O my God, hold not back!

R℣. Lord, come to my aid!

SECOND READING

Heb 12:1-4

Brothers and sisters:
Since we are surrounded by so great a
    cloud of witnesses,
    let us rid ourselves of every burden and
        sin that clings to us
    and persevere in running the race that
        lies before us
    while keeping our eyes fixed on Jesus,
    the leader and perfecter of faith.
For the sake of the joy that lay before him
    he endured the cross, despising its
        shame,
    and has taken his seat at the right of
        the throne of God.
Consider how he endured such opposition
    from sinners,
    in order that you may not grow weary
        and lose heart.
In your struggle against sin
    you have not yet resisted to the point of
        shedding blood.

About Liturgy

The Sign of Peace: Who doesn't like the good feeling that comes with being part of a community? However, Christian community must go deeper than good feelings. The heart of our faith, Jesus, requires that we lay down our lives even for those who would hate us—even for those whom we do not love or like. For God does not save individuals one by one: God saves a people. What we express in the sharing of the Body and Blood of Christ is not a "me-and-Jesus" relationship, for we cannot be a eucharistic people without dying to our own needs, preferences, likes, and dislikes. And our faith cannot be swayed by our ever-changing feelings toward others. Only a faith that is grounded in the faith of Christ will be able to transcend our selfish need for what feels good in order to seek the good of others, even if it means our own suffering.

In the sign of peace, we rehearse having this mind of Christ and showing that sacrificial kind of love. The rubrics of the Roman Missal say that this sign "expresses peace, communion, and charity" (128). For it to be an authentic sign, we must seek daily to share peace with those with whom we have not been peaceful. If we are to show that our sharing in Communion is credible, then we must seek the ones we have harmed, the ones we have judged, and the ones whom we think are unworthy of God's love, and offer a sign of reconciliation with them. If we cannot see the stranger, the foreigner, the outcast, and sinner as one with us and in need of God's mercy just as we are, then our sign of peace is not a sign of charity but an empty sign.

On this day when the gospel discomforts the comfortable, help the assembly remember the meaning of the sign of peace and how it prepares our hearts to authentically share in the Eucharist.

About Initiation

RCIA is not a small faith community: RCIA teams often note how close-knit the RCIA community becomes. As the catechumens and candidates with their sponsors gather each week with the RCIA team to break open the word and deepen their faith, there truly is a sense of community that is rarely found in other parish groups. This is both a blessing and a curse, for the purpose of RCIA is not to create community but to initiate people into Christ. The people Christ gathers often will not be people we get along with. Yet to be Christian means to see them as our sister and brother anyway and to love them as Christ loves them. How will your RCIA process form seekers into this kind of community?

About Liturgical Music

Mass by musical style: What does it say about the unity of the church if we separate and promote each Mass by its unique musical and liturgical style? Saturday night is cantor-only; mid-morning Sunday is the family Mass; late-morning is the traditional organ Mass; Sunday night is the youth praise-band Mass; and early Sunday morning is the quiet Mass. Here we have commodified Sunday Mass and encouraged parishioners to find the style that fits their comfort level.

Sunday must train us to be the household of God in which we gather with a wide variety of people with their own preferences. Let us "keep in mind that to live and worship in community often demands a personal sacrifice. All must be willing to share likes and dislikes with others whose ideas and experiences may be quite unlike [our] own" (Music in Catholic Worship 17).

AUGUST 18, 2019
TWENTIETH SUNDAY
IN ORDINARY TIME

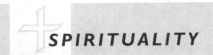

SPIRITUALITY

GOSPEL ACCLAMATION
John 14:6

R̸. Alleluia, alleluia.
I am the way, the truth and the life, says the
    Lord;
no one comes to the Father, except through me.
R̸. Alleluia, alleluia.

Gospel

Luke 13:22-30; L123C

**Jesus passed through towns and villages,
    teaching as he went and making his
        way to Jerusalem.
Someone asked him,
    "Lord, will only a few people be
        saved?"
He answered them,
    "Strive to enter through the narrow
        gate,
    for many, I tell you, will attempt to
        enter
    but will not be strong enough.
After the master of the house has arisen
        and locked the door,
    then will you stand outside knocking
        and saying,
    'Lord, open the door for us.'
He will say to you in reply,
    'I do not know where you are from.'
And you will say,
    'We ate and drank in your company
        and you taught in our streets.'
Then he will say to you,
    'I do not know where you are from.
    Depart from me, all you evildoers!'
And there will be wailing and grinding of
        teeth
    when you see Abraham, Isaac, and Jacob
    and all the prophets in the kingdom of
        God
    and you yourselves cast out.
And people will come from the east and
        the west
    and from the north and the south
    and will recline at table in the kingdom
        of God.
For behold, some are last who will be first,
    and some are first who will be last."**

Reflecting on the Gospel

Nobody likes disappointment. Dealing with it can be a difficult lesson that many of us learn in childhood, and some still struggle to learn as adults! We can avoid disappointment in a number of ways including being prepared, having proper expectations, and knowing a given situation. When we employ these strategies our chances for disappointment diminish. For example, we don't expect a friend who is chronically late to be punctual. It's a matter of managing expectations.

Today's gospel gives us a somewhat troubling story of those who were undoubtedly disappointed. Can we imagine standing, knocking on the door to the house only to be told by the master, "I do not know where you are from"? or even more, "Depart from me, all you evildoers!" Yet this is precisely the story Jesus tells someone who asks whether only a few will be saved. Matthew (7:21-23; 25:31-46) tells a similar story and we are thereby reminded that simply knowing the Lord is not enough to be saved. Jesus exhorts the man to enter through the narrow door. And what is more, he is advised not to wait too late, for there will come a time when the master will lock the door.

This passage and others in the gospels like it remind us of an uncomfortable, and perhaps even disappointing, truth. The effective answer to the man's question about salvation is that many will attempt it but not be able. And some of those who know the Lord, who ate and drank in his company, are those who will be shut out. Such a message is far from the feel good, open wide, broad path to salvation that we might imagine. And the warning to those who know the Lord should fall squarely on us.

Still, those who will be saved may not be those who expect it, for in an echo of Mary's canticle and earlier Lucan themes, there will be a reversal of fortune. "[S]ome are last who will be first, / and some are first who will be last." Moreover, salvation is not limited to a particular group of people as they will come from all directions to recline at table in the kingdom of God.

Are we open to disappointment? Or do we need to be prepared, manage our expectations, and know the given situation? Salvation is for all; many attempt to enter but are not strong enough. Even those who know the Lord are not guaranteed salvation.

Living the Paschal Mystery

A relationship with Christ is not an insurance policy whereby we pay our premiums and expect to receive a settlement when needed. This relationship with the Son of God is not so transactional that we do x, y, and z and Jesus in return grants salvation. If such were the case we would be effectively earning our own salvation by our works. But salvation is a free gift, undeserved, no matter how much we might feel we deserve it.

The master locks the door on the evildoers, barring entry to them. The frightening thing is that some of those locked out know the Lord. Would they consider themselves evildoers? Not likely.

Where are we in this story? Are we striving to enter through the narrow door? Are we waiting until later before we make up our minds? When will the door be shut, not in some apocalyptic sense, but when we come to the end of our own personal life? There will be a reversal of fortune. Let us be prepared and manage our expectations lest we be disappointed.

Focusing the Gospel

Key words and phrases: And people will come from the east and the west / and from the north and the south / and will recline at table in the kingdom of God.

To the point: In today's gospel we hear a paradox. Jesus urges his followers to "enter through the narrow gate," but this constricted entrance leads to an abundant gathering that includes people from the four corners of the world. All people are welcome in the kingdom of God. Not because of their lineage, race, gender, or ancestors, but because they have followed the narrow way of peace and love: the way of Christ.

Connecting the Gospel

to the first reading: The first reading comes from the end of the book of the prophet Isaiah. In the gospel Jesus is travelling to Jerusalem to offer himself on the cross as a complete self-gift to humanity and to God. Isaiah shares a vision of others coming to Jerusalem as well. God is gathering "nations of every language" to see God's glory. In Jerusalem, at the house of the Lord they will present their grain, and also themselves "as an offering to the LORD."

to experience: Jesus and Isaiah paint a picture of God's kingdom where all of creation is at home. These words would have challenged the people who originally heard them, and should challenge us today. We are not necessarily members of this kingdom because of the religion we identify with or our observance of the sacraments. Jesus points to the "narrow gate" that leads to this kingdom. Perhaps it is narrow because of all of the things that can bar our entry like fear, hatred, and pride. To enter into this kingdom that welcomes all people, we must also know radical hospitality. We can enter into the kingdom of God only if we can delight in the others who are also welcome there.

Connecting the Responsorial Psalm

to the readings: The paradox we saw in the gospel reading is also present in the psalm. This shortest of all psalms calls for nothing less than every nation and person to extol and praise the Lord. Even as a young nation, Israel knew their God was not only theirs alone, but also desired to gather all nations, all people together in unity. Jesus shares this vision, reminding the people of his own ancestry, and reminding us today that the kingdom is not ours alone. It does not belong to just one nation, one religion, or one race. The kingdom of God is as expansive as God's mercy and faithfulness.

to psalmist preparation: As you prepare to sing this Sunday's psalm, pause to consider how your community welcomes in those who are outside of its familiar borders. How do you show hospitality in your ministry and in your life as a Christian?

PROMPTS FOR FAITH-SHARING

The prophet Isaiah shares a vision of peoples of all nations and tongues converging on Jerusalem as an offering to the Lord. What place does Jerusalem hold in your journey of faith?

The Letter to the Hebrews says, "[D]o not disdain the discipline of the Lord." How have you experienced the Lord's discipline? What place does discipline have in your spiritual life?

Jesus tells the people, "Strive to enter through the narrow gate." What do you think he is referring to? Where in your life do you find the "narrow gate"?

How does your family or parish welcome the stranger in your midst? How do you make room in your life for those that are different from you?

Model Penitential Act

Presider: In today's gospel, Jesus urges us to "[s]trive to enter through the narrow gate." For the times we have chosen what is easy instead of what is right let us pause to ask for pardon and mercy . . . [*pause*]

> Lord Jesus, you show us the narrow way of righteousness: Lord, have mercy.
> Christ Jesus, you gather all nations and all peoples to yourself: Christ, have mercy.
> Lord Jesus, you lead the humble to the kingdom of God: Lord, have mercy.

Homily Points

• In the gospel Jesus continues on the road to Jerusalem. He is now about halfway through the journey that he began in chapter 9 of Luke's gospel. Along the way Jesus meets Samaritans, women, men, children, Pharisees, scholars, people who are lame, people who suffer from leprosy, people who are blind, a rich official, and tax collectors. To each of these diverse groups, Jesus proclaims the same message: the kingdom of God is at hand. In all that he does Jesus speaks the kingdom and lives the kingdom.

• Today's gospel gives us another vision of what this kingdom is about. The way to enter is "narrow," but inside the kingdom we will find people from every race, nation, and tongue. We might be surprised about who we don't find, however. Jesus issues the warning that some of those who knock on the door and tell the Lord, "We ate and drank in your company and you taught in our streets," will not find welcome inside the kingdom of God. Instead the master of the kingdom will say, "I do not know where you are from."

• Entry to the kingdom does not depend on physical proximity to Jesus. Even those who spend their lives in the church, eating and drinking at the table of the Lord, cannot stop there, passively living a faith that demands much more from us, our very selves. In order to enter the kingdom we must be *from* the kingdom. Our words and actions must proclaim this kingdom as Jesus' did. Can we be found among the poor, vulnerable, and lost? Do we offer welcome and hospitality to all that we meet? We are called to be kingdom people. Where are you from?

Model Universal Prayer (Prayer of the Faithful)

Presider: With faith in God's mercy and fidelity, we bring our prayers before the Lord.

Response: Lord, hear our prayer.

That the church be a sign and symbol of the inclusivity of the kingdom of God . . .

That nations of the world come together to provide for the needs of refugees and those who are displaced from their homes by natural disasters . . .

That those who experience racism, prejudice, and bias in daily life have their inherent dignity and worth as children of God recognized by all they encounter . . .

That all gathered here would have the strength to embrace the radical hospitality of the kingdom of God and to live as kingdom people . . .

Presider: Faithful and merciful God, you call all people to yourself. Hear our prayers that we might build communities of welcome and refuge. We ask this in the name of Jesus, our Lord. Amen.

RESPONSORIAL PSALM
Ps 117:1, 2

℟. (Mark 16:15) Go out to all the world
and tell the Good News.
or
℟. Alleluia.

Praise the Lord, all you nations;
glorify him, all you peoples!

℟. Go out to all the world and tell the
Good News.
or
℟. Alleluia.

For steadfast is his kindness toward us,
and the fidelity of the Lord endures
forever.

℟. Go out to all the world and tell the
Good News.
or
℟. Alleluia.

SECOND READING
Heb 12:5-7, 11-13

Brothers and sisters,
You have forgotten the exhortation
addressed to you as children:
"My son, do not disdain the discipline
of the Lord
or lose heart when reproved by him;
for whom the Lord loves, he disciplines;
he scourges every son he
acknowledges."
Endure your trials as "discipline";
God treats you as sons.
For what "son" is there whom his father
does not discipline?
At the time,
all discipline seems a cause not for joy
but for pain,
yet later it brings the peaceful fruit of
righteousness
to those who are trained by it.

So strengthen your drooping hands and
your weak knees.
Make straight paths for your feet,
that what is lame may not be disjointed
but healed.

About Liturgy

Communion procession: What would happen if, in Communion, we took literally Jesus' prophecy in today's gospel that the last will be first and the first will be last? That's just what Roger Cardinal Mahony wanted to do in his own envisioning of what Sunday Mass might be like in the Archdiocese of Los Angeles if the entirety of the assembly made the sharing of Communion more than just lining up to receive the Body and Blood of Christ.

In his pastoral letter on the liturgy, "Gather Faithfully Together" (1997), Cardinal Mahony described a community that desired to understand and reflect better what it meant for the Body of Christ, the church, to receive the Body of Christ in the Eucharist. That need led to exploring a practice that would replace an individualistic approach to sharing Communion with one in which the communal procession helped foster unity among the people and restore a sense of wonder and thanksgiving in the Eucharist.

The cardinal described a communion procession in which the first to come forward down the aisle toward the altar were not those seated in the front pews but those in the very back of the church. Imagine everyone in the assembly surrounded by the members of the Body of Christ singing together as they come forward to share in the Body of Christ. Imagine being aware not just of the people sitting by you but those who stay in the back whom you might never see, who may feel too self-conscious or unworthy, or who, for whatever reason, had a difficult time choosing to be at Mass that day but made it nonetheless. Can we deepen our understanding of the mystery of the Eucharist even more if we make one simple change to the way we come forward to the altar at Communion?

About Initiation

Rite of Acceptance: Today would be an appropriate time to celebrate the Rite of Acceptance, especially in light of the first reading's image of the gathering of all the nations to the holy mountain of God. Even if you do not have any possible persons to celebrate this rite, mark the day in your parish's calendar and schedule a possible rite for one of the main Masses so that you and all your parish will be prepared just in case the Spirit sends you a seeker who is ready to begin learning the gospel way of life.

About Liturgical Music

Intercultural liturgy: Every parish will find within its neighborhood a diversity of cultures. This is simply a reality, if not today, then within the next few years. In liturgical music, we can describe this as a spectrum. On one end we have what can be called a "diversity" phase, expressed in the use of multilingual music and reflecting an understanding of community from the head, focusing solely on language. In the middle of this spectrum, we have an "inclusion" phase expressed by multicultural music reflecting a desire to understand with the heart. In addition to language, here we begin to incorporate the cultural rhythms, instruments, and musical styles of different cultures within our common repertoire. The other end of the spectrum is a "communion" phase expressed by intercultural liturgy reflecting a desire for unity through our shared culture. Here we long for a spiritual communion that recognizes one another as family members, equal in leadership and say in the good of the community and how it prays together.

Wherever your parish is on this spectrum, you will be heeding the psalm's message of going out to the world to tell the Good News if you continue to attend to the needs of those who are different from you.

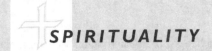

SPIRITUALITY

GOSPEL ACCLAMATION
Matt 11:29ab

℟. Alleluia, alleluia.
Take my yoke upon you, says the Lord;
and learn from me, for I am meek and humble
    of heart.
℟. Alleluia, alleluia.

Gospel Luke 14:1, 7-14; L126C

On a sabbath Jesus went to dine
    at the home of one of the lead-
        ing Pharisees,
    and the people there were ob-
        serving him carefully.

He told a parable to those who had
        been invited,
    noticing how they were choosing the
        places of honor at the table.
"When you are invited by someone to a
        wedding banquet,
    do not recline at table in the place of
        honor.
A more distinguished guest than you
        may have been invited by him,
    and the host who invited both of you
        may approach you and say,
    'Give your place to this man,'
    and then you would proceed with
        embarrassment
    to take the lowest place.
Rather, when you are invited,
    go and take the lowest place
    so that when the host comes to you
        he may say,
    'My friend, move up to a higher
        position.'
Then you will enjoy the esteem of your
        companions at the table.
For everyone who exalts himself will
        be humbled,
    but the one who humbles himself will
        be exalted."

Continued in Appendix A, p. 310.

Reflecting on the Gospel

Who doesn't love a good dinner party?! Great food, excellent company, good wine, and lively conversation. Jesus certainly enjoyed himself at such events and was considered by some to be a glutton and a drunkard (Matt 11:19)!

In today's gospel Jesus is being hosted by a leading Pharisee. This was likely an extravagant event and certainly wasn't Jesus' first or last such dinner.

The first piece of advice Jesus gives is hardly unique to Christianity or even rooted in his identity as Son of God. Instead, it's practical advice reminiscent of Greek philosophers and good Jewish etiquette. In fact, it sounds much like modern-day Miss Manners! The aphorism, "[E]veryone who exalts himself will be humbled, / but the one who humbles himself will be exalted," will be repeated later in the gospel (Luke 18:14).

The second piece of advice culminating in a promise to be "repaid at the resurrection of the righteous" is rooted more in religious identity and a belief that there would even be a resurrection of the righteous. To receive such an invitation, Jesus implores his host to invite "the poor, the crippled, the lame, the blind." In other words, invite those people who cannot reciprocate. By so doing, God himself will reciprocate on their behalf!

So we have two lessons from today's reading: humble oneself and serve those who cannot reciprocate. There is certainly more to the entire gospel message than that, but it is an excellent place to start. Moreover, both can be done in imitation of Jesus himself, who truly humbled himself and served us, we who cannot truly reciprocate.

Living the Paschal Mystery

Our liturgies, prayers, Catholic culture, and more do much to promote a high Christology and rightly so. But a gospel reading like the one we have today reminds us that Jesus was a human being who attended dinner parties, told stories at such parties, and even offered sage advice. One modern teacher made the point that in the Gospel of Luke there are so many meals that Jesus attends that one can eat one's way through the story! Is it no wonder then, that by the conclusion of this gospel the disciples come to know Jesus through the breaking of the bread? And this is the way the risen Christ is made known to believers ever since. Each meal, and even the liturgical Eucharist, is a foreshadowing of the heavenly banquet. Let's tap into this aspect of Christ, the one who enjoyed a good dinner party, to learn from him about the life that awaits us.

Focusing the Gospel

Key words and phrases: For everyone who exalts himself will be humbled, but the one who humbles himself will be exalted.

To the point: We are told in the gospel today that Jesus tells a parable. It's actually less of a parable and more of a saying, one that has become very famous but not necessarily very well followed: "[E]veryone who exalts himself will be humbled, but the one who humbles himself will be exalted." The key is not what one does, but who one is. A humble person naturally chooses the lowest position, not wishing to draw attention to herself. Sometimes this leads to acclaim. Sometimes it just means that the humble are not as visible as those who would like to be exalted. Even if the world does not notice the humble, we know that God's eye is trained upon them, as ours should be.

Connecting the Gospel

to the first reading: In some ways Jesus is echoing the words of the writer of Sirach (Ben Sira) from two hundred years before Jesus' birth: "Humble yourself the more, the greater you are." Both Jesus and Ben Sira seem to offer this advice in a pragmatic way. By embracing humility you will be exalted. By making yourself small you will be great. Merriam-Webster's dictionary defines humility as "freedom from pride or arrogance." Whereas pride and arrogance are shackles that imprison and weigh one down, humility allows a person to be filled with something other than himself, to be filled with God.

to experience: In the gospel reading Jesus speaks as a wisdom teacher, offering sage advice for living well. As Christians we take as our example Jesus, the Son of God, who humbled himself to become human and even die on a cross. Jesus shows us the way of humility. May we follow him.

Connecting the Responsorial Psalm

to the readings: In the gospel Jesus describes a banquet that might have been very different from the dinner he is attending at the home of one of the most prominent Pharisees. The banquet he envisions is populated not with the distinguished and honored but with those who are too often invisible in society: "the poor, the crippled, the lame, the blind." Could this be an image of the heavenly banquet table? The psalmist sings of a God who is "father of orphans and the defender of widows," who "gives a home to the forsaken, / he leads forth prisoners to prosperity."

to psalmist preparation: The words of Jesus in the gospel and the psalmist are ones that challenge us to rethink our priorities and beliefs. In God's eyes, the people who are pushed to the margins of society like the homeless, those addicted to drugs and alcohol, prisoners are loved, precious, and worthy of the kingdom of God. Do we invite them to our banquet tables?

PROMPTS FOR FAITH-SHARING

The first reading comes from the Wisdom book, Sirach, whose author is intent on lifting up the Jewish wisdom tradition in a world increasingly influenced by Greek philosophy. What sources of wisdom do you turn to in your life?

Today's psalm encourages, "The just rejoice and exult before God . . . Sing to God, chant praise to his name; / whose name is the Lord." What place does joy and rejoicing hold in your spiritual life?

How have you experienced Jesus' saying, "[E]veryone who exalts himself will be humbled, but the one who humbles himself will be exalted," to be true?

In your parish community how are you following Jesus' command, "[W]hen you hold a banquet, / invite the poor, the crippled, the lame, the blind"? How are you being called to live into this more?

Model Penitential Act

Presider: In today's gospel Jesus cautions, "everyone who exalts himself will be humbled, but the one who humbles himself will be exalted." Let us pause to remember the times we have sought favor in the eyes of the world and shunned the path of humility . . . [*pause*]

Lord Jesus, you are the host of the heavenly banquet: Lord, have mercy.

Christ Jesus, you save the outcast and the lost: Christ, have mercy.

Lord Jesus, you show us the way of humility: Lord, have mercy.

Homily Points

• The first reading from Sirach ends with the line, "[A]n attentive ear is the joy of the wise." In today's gospel Jesus offers us two pieces of wisdom to incorporate into our lives: Be humble. Be hospitable.

• Being humble requires trust and contentment. When we are fearful of being overlooked or anxious about how we are perceived, we begin to grasp at "exaltation." We want people to recognize us and laud our accomplishments. And if they don't, we try to force them to. Jesus knows that when we strive after the world's approval it will never satisfy us. But when we let go of this desire—when we are free from the prisons of pride and arrogance, when we stop grasping at acceptance and recognition—we can finally know the peace of God.

• Jesus' second teaching is on hospitality, but not the hospitality of offering welcome to friends and family. The radical hospitality of Jesus is being open to "the other," the ones who are not regularly seen at our tables. This is a difficult teaching. To break bread together requires a certain level of trust and comfort. Jesus is not asking us to be unsafe, but he is challenging us to do more than donate to charitable causes. We are called to personal contact with those on the outskirts of society, to sit down and eat a meal with the patrons of a homeless shelter instead of remaining in the kitchen preparing food. When we follow the paths of humility and hospitality, not only do we serve others, we are changed by our actions. Be humble. Be hospitable. As in all things, Jesus offers us these maxims as the way to "life in the full" (see John 10:10). Sirach tells us, "[A]n attentive ear is the joy of the wise." Are we listening?

Model Universal Prayer (Prayer of the Faithful)

Presider: With humility and trust we bring our prayers before the Lord.

Response: Lord, hear our prayer.

That the church be in alignment with the humble, vulnerable, and needy of the world . . .

That all the people of the world might yearn for the wisdom of God and seek the path of humility . . .

That the poor, crippled, lame, and blind, whom Jesus speaks of in today's gospel, be met with a banquet of love, dignity, and welcome wherever they go . . .

That all gathered here might find ways to offer radical hospitality to those on the margins of society, especially the homeless, those who suffer from drug and alcohol addiction, and prisoners . . .

Presider: God of the humble and the outcast, you call us to build your kingdom here on earth. Hear our prayers that we might be living signs of your love and care to all we meet. We ask this through Christ, our Lord. Amen.

COLLECT
Let us pray.

Pause for silent prayer

God of might, giver of every good gift,
put into our hearts the love of your name,
so that, by deepening our sense of
    reverence,
you may nurture in us what is good
and, by your watchful care,
keep safe what you have nurtured.
Through our Lord Jesus Christ, your Son,
who lives and reigns with you in the unity
    of the Holy Spirit,
one God, for ever and ever. **Amen.**

FIRST READING
Sir 3:17-18, 20, 28-29

My child, conduct your affairs with
    humility,
    and you will be loved more than a giver
    of gifts.
Humble yourself the more, the greater
    you are,
    and you will find favor with God.
What is too sublime for you, seek not,
    into things beyond your strength search
    not.
The mind of a sage appreciates proverbs,
    and an attentive ear is the joy of the
    wise.
Water quenches a flaming fire,
    and alms atone for sins.

RESPONSORIAL PSALM
Ps 68:4-5, 6-7, 10-11

R⁒. (cf. 11b) God, in your goodness, you
    have made a home for the poor.

The just rejoice and exult before God;
    they are glad and rejoice.
Sing to God, chant praise to his name;
    whose name is the LORD.

R⁒. God, in your goodness, you have made
    a home for the poor.

The father of orphans and the defender of
    widows
    is God in his holy dwelling.
God gives a home to the forsaken;
    he leads forth prisoners to prosperity.

R⁒. God, in your goodness, you have made
    a home for the poor.

A bountiful rain you showered down, O
    God, upon your inheritance;
you restored the land when it
    languished;
your flock settled in it;
    in your goodness, O God, you provided
    it for the needy.

R⁒. God, in your goodness, you have made
    a home for the poor.

SECOND READING
Heb 12:18-19, 22-24a

Brothers and sisters:
You have not approached that which could
    be touched
    and a blazing fire and gloomy darkness
    and storm and a trumpet blast
    and a voice speaking words such that
        those who heard
    begged that no message be further
        addressed to them.
No, you have approached Mount Zion
    and the city of the living God, the
        heavenly Jerusalem,
    and countless angels in festal gathering,
    and the assembly of the firstborn
        enrolled in heaven,
    and God the judge of all,
    and the spirits of the just made perfect,
    and Jesus, the mediator of a new
        covenant,
    and the sprinkled blood that speaks
        more eloquently than that of Abel.

About Liturgy

Making the church a home for the poor: There is a Catholic parish in the poorest neighborhood of San Francisco that opens its doors every weekday at 6:00 a.m. to welcome about 150 of its unhoused neighbors who have spent the night on the streets and give them a secure place for a few hours of rest. They call it "sacred sleep." A neighboring Episcopal church does the same for about 75 of its unhoused community members.

These women and men—some with mental health issues, others addicted to drugs, all of them rejected in one way or another by family, friends, and our society—sleep on the pews in the back two-thirds of the churches. At the Catholic church, the parishioners gather for Mass at 12:15 p.m. each weekday and they celebrate the Eucharist in the front part of the church as their neighbors sleep behind them. After Mass, some parishioners stay to share a meal with their unhoused neighbors and offer them material and spiritual support.

This work, called the Gubbio Project, strives to provide a beautiful and safe place for people to rest, cultivate true community and shared responsibility between people of the gospel and the least among them, and attend to the real and immediate needs of their unhoused neighbors.

Not every church can open its doors every day to the same radical extent as these two communities. But every parish can do something to bring beauty, safety, support, and care to the poorest of its own neighborhoods. For what we proclaim in liturgy must be lived out in our daily lives if our Sunday Eucharist is to be authentic and credible.

About Initiation

Reserved places of honor: The only liturgical document to prescribe places of honor for members of the assembly is the Rite of Christian Initiation of Adults when it refers to the neophytes and their godparents during the period of mystagogy and post-baptismal catechesis. The RCIA gives no mention of where catechumens, candidates, and their sponsors should be seated during the periods of preparation and formation. They could sit wherever they desire. Ideally, they would not be clustered all together but seated throughout the church so that they can interact with more members of the community.

About Liturgical Music

Who is the principle music minister? Music ministers might imagine that the music director, the cantor, or the organist is the principle minister of music. Some choir members may see themselves as the ones who provide music for the liturgy. In many ways these are true. But two references in our liturgical documents give us a different way of understanding who the primary music ministers in our assemblies are.

First, Liturgical Music Today says, "The entire worshiping assembly exercises a ministry of music" (63). Second, Sing to the Lord states that the congregation's unrehearsed community singing "is the primary song of the Liturgy" (28).

When music ministers remember that the people are the primary music makers, they can begin to understand better their role in supporting and enhancing the primary song of the liturgy.

One very easy way to remind everyone of this is to pay attention to how you invite the assembly to take on its role as primary music minister. For example, instead of saying to the assembly, "Join us in singing the opening song," say instead, "Let us sing together . . ."

SEPTEMBER 1, 2019
TWENTY-SECOND SUNDAY
IN ORDINARY TIME

✠ SPIRITUALITY

GOSPEL ACCLAMATION
Ps 119:135

℟. Alleluia, alleluia.
Let your face shine upon your servant;
and teach me your laws.
℟. Alleluia, alleluia.

Gospel   Luke 14:25-33; L129C

Great crowds were traveling with Jesus,
and he turned and addressed them,
"If anyone comes to me without hating his father and
mother,
wife and children, brothers and
sisters,
and even his own life,
he cannot be my disciple.
Whoever does not carry his
own cross and come after me
cannot be my disciple.
Which of you wishing to construct a
tower
does not first sit down and calculate
the cost
to see if there is enough for its
completion?
Otherwise, after laying the foundation
and finding himself unable to finish the
work
the onlookers should laugh at him and
say,
'This one began to build but did not
have the resources to finish.'
Or what king marching into battle would
not first sit down
and decide whether with ten thousand
troops
he can successfully oppose another
king
advancing upon him with twenty thousand troops?
But if not, while he is still far away,
he will send a delegation to ask for
peace terms.
In the same way,
anyone of you who does not renounce
all his possessions
cannot be my disciple."

Reflecting on the Gospel

Hyperbole and exaggeration can be effective rhetorical tools. They are used by almost everyone at some point. Even the fictitious news announcer Kent Brockman from the Simpsons said, "Ladies and gentlemen, I've been to Vietnam, Iraq, and Afghanistan, and I can say without hyperbole that this is a million times worse than all of them put together."

Of course, it's easy to spot hyperbole and we don't take it literally. But sometimes it's easy to miss this rhetorical tool when it's on the lips of Jesus in the Scriptures. A good rule of thumb is to see how the early Christians understood a passage in question. For example, Jesus advises his listeners in another story that "if your eye causes you to sin, tear it out" (Matt 18:9; NABRE)! But early, as well as later Christians, did not take that literally. The passage is rhetorical hyperbole. Something similar is at work in today's gospel passage when Jesus says that no one coming to him "without hating his father and mother, / wife and children, brothers and sisters, / and even his own life" can be a disciple. Rather than try to twist ourselves into knots over that quote, it's best to recognize it for what it is: rhetorical hyperbole. Even one of the concluding thoughts about renouncing all possessions is hyperbolic. Part of the reason we know this is by reading other passages in Luke in which Jesus' women followers provide for Jesus and the disciples from their means (Luke 8:1-3). So even Jesus did not expect his own followers to take this advice about renouncing all possessions literally. If they had, he would not have had such a widespread support network in Judea and Galilee.

Jesus is an effective preacher: he used the rhetorical tools of hyperbole and exaggeration to make his point. This can be a challenge for us if we want to take literally each and every saying of his in the New Testament. But gratefully we are part of a long line of believers, a large family of faith. And we can look to ancient Christians to see that they recognized this as hyperbole too.

In the end, what Jesus demands is a wholehearted, complete commitment, without distraction. And that's no exaggeration.

Living the Paschal Mystery

Discipleship is a lifelong process, often called a journey. We learn things along the way, likely starting out resolutely as Jesus does on his own journey to Je-rusalem. During this lifelong process we encounter different ways of looking at reality, new insights, challenging statements, and more. The metaphor of a journey is especially apt as we never stay still, nor does our environment or the people around us. We are all growing in knowledge, understanding, and experi-ence with former ways of understanding giving way to the new.

Developmentally, human beings tend to grow from a place of literalism to understanding the broader picture. Children can be told not to touch the stove, but as they mature they internalize the lesson and take care around a hot stove.

Discipleship follows a similar path. We tend to be more literal in the early stages of a relationship with Christ, but as we mature we see the deeper meaning of his injunctions and exhortations. Let us continue on this path to an adult relationship with Christ.

Focusing the Gospel

Key words and phrases: Whoever does not carry his own cross and come after me / cannot be my disciple.

To the point: This phrase appears in all three of the Synoptic Gospels: Matthew (10:38, 16:24) and Luke (9:23, 14:27) repeat it twice, and Mark once (8:34). It's hard to imagine the pre-crucifixion Jesus uttering these words. What would they have meant to the crowd that was following him? Looking back from two thousand years after the event, we know Jesus is on his way to Jerusalem where he will literally carry his own cross and then be crucified upon it. The spiritual life requires struggle and sacrifice. But we also know the end of the story: life everlasting.

Connecting the Gospel

to the first and second readings: The sayings in today's gospel are demanding. Following Jesus requires single-minded dedication. The book of Wisdom reminds us how difficult it can be to follow the dictates of God. The author asks, "[W]ho can conceive what the LORD intends?" Interpreting biblical texts requires an expansive mind. We cannot focus on one line in the Bible to the exclusion of everything else. Otherwise, lines like, "If anyone comes to me without hating his father and mother, / wife and children, brothers and sisters, / and even his own life, / he cannot be my disciple," could lead us to renounce the wisdom of Jesus completely. In the second reading St. Paul writes to Philemon requesting that Philemon receive back his former (possibly runaway) slave with love and equality, "that you might have him back for ever, / no longer as a slave / but more than a slave, a brother, / beloved especially to me, but even more so to you, / as a man and in the Lord."

to experience: We know that the basis of Christianity is love: love of God and love of others. Interpreted through this lens today's shocking gospel helps us to put our lives in perspective. Jesus, the source of love and peace, must be at the center of all that we do.

Connecting the Responsorial Psalm

to the readings: Today's psalm also reminds us to put our lives in perspective. To us, our days and years upon the earth might stretch out, but in the vast expanse of the history of salvation they are less than the blink of an eye. The psalmist prays, "Teach us to number our days aright, / that we may gain wisdom of heart." Though fleeting, our earthly lives are not futile. We are given a work to do. Jesus urges us to take up our cross and follow him, while the psalmist asks God to "prosper the work of our hands!"

to psalmist preparation: In the assembly of the faithful, your work of leading the community in song and prayer is service to the people of God. How might you pray this week for God to "prosper" your ministry and to bless the work of your hands?

PROMPTS FOR FAITH-SHARING

The writer of the book of Wisdom asks, "[W]ho can conceive what the LORD intends?" If you could ask God one question, what would it be?

The psalmist prays twice, "[P]rosper the work of our hands!" Of the many things you do, what work or labor would you like to ask God's blessing on?

What cross are you being asked to carry right now? Are there crosses you have been struggling with that are not yours to carry?

The last line of today's gospel asks us to renounce our possessions in order to be Jesus' disciples. Is there a possession that does not lead to fullness of life that God might be calling for you to renounce?

Model Penitential Act

Presider: Today's gospel challenges us to be faithful disciples of Jesus. For the times we have put other things before our commitment to Christ let us pause to ask for pardon and mercy . . . [*pause*]

Lord Jesus, you call us to fidelity in discipleship: Lord, have mercy.

Christ Jesus, you gift us with your Holy Spirit so we might know your ways: Christ, have mercy.

Lord Jesus, you are the Wisdom of God: Lord, have mercy.

Homily Points

• This is the second time in Luke's gospel that Jesus has told his would-be followers that if they wish to be his disciples they must take up their crosses and follow him. We, who wear crosses around our necks and place them in prominent places in our churches and homes, are probably not shocked by this statement. How might Jesus' original audience have felt when these words came out of his mouth? In Jesus' day the cross was a tool of torture and execution used by the Roman Empire to punish and make examples of those who would dare to defy its might. To carry your cross would be to constantly bear the weight of that which would ultimately kill you. And this is just what Jesus does. Knowing that his current path is leading him to Jerusalem and the crucifixion, he takes it anyway.

• What does this saying mean for us today? Fortunately, many of us will never face martyrdom for our beliefs. However, there are many ways of pouring out our lives for others. In *The Sound of Music*, the mother superior counsels Maria, the wayward postulant, to discern which path in life, marriage or sisterhood, "will need / all the love you can give / every day of your life / for as long as you live."

• For us today, the cross is not so much a symbol of violence or brutality, but of the complete and total gift of self that Jesus completes on Calvary. On the cross, just as he did with every moment of his life, Jesus pours out all the love he can give. He invites us to do the same, "Take up your cross and follow me."

Model Universal Prayer (Prayer of the Faithful)

Presider: Trusting in God's wisdom and love, let us bring our prayers before the Lord.

Response: Lord, hear our prayer.

That those in church leadership renew their commitment to complete fidelity to Christ and, with the help of the Holy Spirit, guide their communities with love . . .

That all peoples of the world might have meaningful work and adequate resources of food, water, and shelter . . .

That those who are victims of human trafficking be freed from their captors and receive support in healing and rebuilding their lives . . .

That all gathered here be strengthened to answer Jesus' call to take up our crosses and follow him . . .

Presider: God of wisdom, your ways are beyond our comprehension. Hear our prayers, that we might place our trust in you and dedicate our lives to building your kingdom. We ask this through Christ our Lord. Amen.

COLLECT

Let us pray.

Pause for silent prayer

O God, by whom we are redeemed and
    receive adoption,
look graciously upon your beloved sons
    and daughters,
that those who believe in Christ
may receive true freedom
and an everlasting inheritance.
Through our Lord Jesus Christ, your Son,
who lives and reigns with you in the unity
    of the Holy Spirit,
one God, for ever and ever. **Amen.**

FIRST READING

Wis 9:13-18b

Who can know God's counsel,
    or who can conceive what the LORD
        intends?
For the deliberations of mortals are timid,
    and unsure are our plans.
For the corruptible body burdens the soul
    and the earthen shelter weighs down
        the mind that has many concerns.
And scarce do we guess the things on
    earth,
    and what is within our grasp we find
      with difficulty;
    but when things are in heaven, who can
      search them out?
Or who ever knew your counsel, except
    you had given wisdom
and sent your holy spirit from on high?
And thus were the paths of those on earth
    made straight.

RESPONSORIAL PSALM

Ps 90:3-4, 5-6, 12-13, 14 and 17

R̸. (1) In every age, O Lord, you have been
    our refuge.

You turn man back to dust,
    saying, "Return, O children of men."
For a thousand years in your sight
    are as yesterday, now that it is past,
    or as a watch of the night.

R̸. In every age, O Lord, you have been
    our refuge.

You make an end of them in their sleep;
    the next morning they are like the
      changing grass,
which at dawn springs up anew,
    but by evening wilts and fades.

R̸. In every age, O Lord, you have been
    our refuge.

Teach us to number our days aright,
   that we may gain wisdom of heart.
Return, O Lord! How long?
   Have pity on your servants!

℞. In every age, O Lord, you have been
   our refuge.

Fill us at daybreak with your kindness,
   that we may shout for joy and gladness
      all our days.
And may the gracious care of the Lord
   our God be ours;
   prosper the work of our hands for us!
   Prosper the work of our hands!

℞. In every age, O Lord, you have been
   our refuge.

SECOND READING
Phlm 9-10, 12-17

I, Paul, an old man,
   and now also a prisoner for Christ Jesus,
   urge you on behalf of my child
      Onesimus,
   whose father I have become in my
      imprisonment;
   I am sending him, that is, my own heart,
      back to you.
I should have liked to retain him for
      myself,
   so that he might serve me on your
      behalf
   in my imprisonment for the gospel,
   but I did not want to do anything
      without your consent,
   so that the good you do might not be
      forced but voluntary.
Perhaps this is why he was away from you
      for a while,
   that you might have him back forever,
   no longer as a slave
   but more than a slave, a brother,
   beloved especially to me, but even more
      so to you,
   as a man and in the Lord.
So if you regard me as a partner, welcome
      him as you would me.

CATECHESIS

About Liturgy
Evaluating liturgical ministers: Ministry is a call that comes with great responsibility. One should not treat ministry as a right but as a duty if given the privilege of being called.

Yet, how often do we allow liturgical ministers to serve in a ministry although they have not shown the necessary competence, desire to improve, or commitment to fulfill the requirements of their ministry? Why are we content with poor or only passable liturgical ministers? Shouldn't we desire excellence in the work we each do for the benefit of the assembly? Contrary to common practice, it is perfectly appropriate—and sometimes necessary—to ask a volunteer to step down from a ministry if she has not committed herself to the disciplines of growing into excellence in ministry.

However, before we do that, we need to ensure that we have put into place processes for fostering excellence in those who answer the call to serve. This requires good discernment throughout the process of recruiting, training, forming, and evaluating liturgical ministers.

A good process informs volunteers up front of the specific characteristics, talents, disciplines, and attitudes necessary for each liturgical ministry. Better yet, instead of making ministry an open invitation, have your best current liturgical ministers seek out possible new ministers in your community whom they recognize as having the gifts needed for that ministry. Then ask them to discern with those persons if they might have a genuine call to serve.

A good process also includes ongoing training, even for veteran ministers, and regular evaluations throughout the year. Think of these as opportunities for mutual discernment with the ministers. Help them reflect on how well they are serving the assembly, where their strengths are, where they need improvement, or where else they might serve the assembly better.

About Initiation
Rite of Acceptance or Rite of Welcome: Because of the gospel's focus on discipleship, today is a good day to celebrate a Rite of Acceptance into the Order of Catechumens or a Rite of Welcoming Candidates. Although in the United States there is a combined rite available that joins these two rituals together into one liturgy, it is best to keep them separate for the sake of clarity. Instead of using the combined rite, celebrate each rite at different Masses or on different days.

About Liturgical Music
Introducing new music: Introducing new music to the assembly takes a bit of strategic planning if your assembly is to embrace it as its own. This is especially true if the music is for a critical moment of assembly singing, such as the entrance song, eucharistic prayer acclamations, or communion song.

Several weeks before you want the assembly to sing the new piece in the Mass, play the song as an instrumental for the prelude, preparation of gifts, or postlude. The next week, sing the song with the choir alone as a prelude or, if appropriate, at the preparation of gifts. The following week, invite the assembly to listen to the song before Mass and start to teach it to them, but do not include it within the Mass yet. If needed, teach the song again to the assembly before Mass the next week. Once the assembly has heard the song over several weeks and has rehearsed singing it a few more weeks, then schedule the song for use with the Mass.

This process works well if you plan to introduce a new Mass setting or seasonal song for Advent later this year.

✠ SPIRITUALITY

GOSPEL ACCLAMATION
2 Cor 5:19

R℔. Alleluia, alleluia.
God was reconciling the world to himself in
    Christ
and entrusting to us the message of
    reconciliation.
R℔. Alleluia, alleluia.

Gospel   Luke 15:1-32; L132C

Tax collectors and sinners were all
    drawing near to listen to Jesus,
  but the Pharisees and scribes began
      to complain, saying,
  "This man welcomes sinners and
      eats with them."
So to them he addressed this parable.
"What man among you having a hun-
      dred sheep and losing one of
      them
  would not leave the ninety-nine in
      the desert
  and go after the lost one until
      he finds it?
And when he does find it,
  he sets it on his shoulders
      with great joy
  and, upon his arrival home,
  he calls together his friends and
      neighbors and says to them,
  'Rejoice with me because I have
      found my lost sheep.'
I tell you, in just the same way
  there will be more joy in heaven over
      one sinner who repents
  than over ninety-nine righteous people
  who have no need of repentance.

"Or what woman having ten coins and
      losing one
  would not light a lamp and sweep the
      house,
  searching carefully until she finds it?

Continued in Appendix A, p. 311,

or Luke 15:1-10.

Reflecting on the Gospel

Our reading today is one of the most memorable of Jesus' parables and it's told only in the Gospel of Luke. It is the parable of the Prodigal Son, or the two sons, or perhaps more appropriately, the story of the mercy of the father. This short story has been the subject matter of innumerable artistic works, including paintings by some of the world's masters.

Since the story is a parable, it has many possible meanings. Each listener may have something different that speaks to them in the parable. But one meaning which would have been clear to the early Christians is that the two sons can represent Gentiles and Jews. The younger son, the one who spends his share of the inheritance on wanton living, is certainly representative of the Gentiles for it reflects the attitudes that many Jews had of the Gentiles of the day. The Gentiles, not having the Mosaic Law, had a different moral code than Jews. Because there was not a monolithic moral code among non-Jews, Gentiles were perceived by Jews as more libertine.

On the other hand, the Jews had Mosaic Law, which, in the parable, could be said to be the wishes of the father or God the Father. They kept the Mosaic Law and served God for many years without disobeying, as the parable indicates. But God rejoices when the hedonistic Gentile repents while offering nothing for the observant Jews? So although the story on its face is about two sons and their father, there is a deeper meaning with respect to the Gentiles and Jews of the apostolic era.

The moral of the story, the mercy of the father, is echoed throughout the gospel in other parables such as the payment of day laborers, who all receive the same wage even though some worked all day and others only an hour. These parables tell us about God's mercy, which does not follow strict justice. The love, care, and concern that our Father shows for his creation is superabundant. How do we react when faced with this overwhelming generosity? Are we repentant, ready to be received by this mercy? Or are we despondent, questioning why mercy is given so freely to others, thinking we might not have received our "rightful" share?

Living the Paschal Mystery

Mercy is a keyword in the gospel today even though it does not appear in the text. But mercy is the motivating force behind the father's actions, and the experience of the younger son who has been forgiven. Only when the younger son has "hit bottom," so to speak, does he awaken to the notion of returning to his father's home, where he hopes to be a hired hand. And that part of the story is an accurate reflection of human nature. Often, before we seek repentance and ask forgiveness we must hit bottom. The younger son was not interested in repentance when he had plenty of money and resources! Only when he was feeding the pigs and desirous of their food did the realization strike him.

And so it may be with us. We must die to our own pride, self-assurance, and resources, recognizing that all is a gift of the Father. The son did not earn this money on his own. Perhaps it is only when we hit bottom with the recognition that all is the Father's, not our own, will we be ready to return to the embrace of mercy, and live a new life of reconciliation.

Focusing the Gospel

Key words and phrases: [N]ow we must celebrate and rejoice, / because your brother was dead and has come to life again; / he was lost and has been found.

To the point: Jesus tells the grumbling Pharisees and scribes three parables and each follows a similar pattern. There is loss, search, finding, and finally rejoicing. In our human condition it is easy to focus on the first few moments. Whether it's our keys, an overdue library book, or a child in the supermarket, we lose, search, and hopefully find on a daily basis. How often do we celebrate these findings though? This seems to be an important point that Jesus tries to convey to the self-righteous religious leaders of his day who were not pleased with Jesus' association with sinners. The lost being found demands a public celebration because their straying hurt not only them but also the entire community. In rejoicing the community is rebuilt and healed.

Connecting the Gospel

to the second reading: In the first letter to Timothy, St. Paul describes himself as "the foremost" of sinners, given an abundance of mercy and grace so that "Christ Jesus might display all his patience as an example / for those who would come to believe in him for everlasting life." If the parables from today's gospel illustrate God's mercy, Paul's conversion-story concretizes it. Stopped in his tracks on the way to Damascus where he is intending to arrest followers of the Way, and "bring them back to Jerusalem in chains" (Acts 9:2; NABRE), Paul hears a voice that changes his life forever. Instead of condemning this man who is bent on violently destroying his followers, the risen Lord invites Paul to become a pillar of the early church.

to experience: We see the parables of mercy lived out in the lives of men and women who have had their lives changed by an experience of the living God. Although, like the apostle Paul's, some conversions are flashy and life altering, more often than not they are slow and subtle. Throughout our lives, Jesus continually calls us to return to him, to follow him more closely, to be found.

Connecting the Responsorial Psalm

to the readings: Psalm 51 is a fitting response to the first reading from Exodus where the people, having grown weary of waiting for Moses to return from Mount Sinai, construct a golden calf to worship. God laments to Moses, "They have soon turned aside from the way I pointed out to them." Such is life. We, inconstant creatures who are easily distracted and wearied, stumble and fall. And yet, like the psalmist, we are surrounded by the "merciful love" and "abundant compassion" of a God who never ceases to seek the lost and restore the sinner (v. 3; NABRE).

to psalmist preparation: This week consider how you have experienced God's "merciful love" and "abundant compassion" in your own life. Where do you most need God's renewing touch right now?

PROMPTS FOR FAITH-SHARING

Today's psalm reminds us of Lent, especially in the line, "Thoroughly wash me from my guilt / and of my sin cleanse me." How do you attend to repentance and reconciliation in Ordinary Time?

In the second reading we hear, "This saying is trustworthy and deserves full acceptance: / Christ Jesus came into the world to save sinners." Is this statement a cornerstone of your own faith? How does it affect your ministry and mission as a disciple?

In the parable of the Prodigal Son, which character do you empathize with the most: the younger son who returns, the father who waits, or the older son outside the celebration? What is the message for you today in this parable?

Who are the lost in your family and/or faith community? How is God calling you to seek them?

213

Model Penitential Act

Presider: In today's gospel, Jesus tells three parables of the lost being found. Let us pause to remember the times we have strayed far from God . . . [*pause*]

Lord Jesus, you search tirelessly for the lost: Lord, have mercy.

Christ Jesus, you came into the world to save sinners: Christ, have mercy.

Lord Jesus, you reveal the infinite compassion of God: Lord, have mercy.

Homily Points

• The scribes and the Pharisees are not happy. He whom the crowds follow, who multiplies loaves and fishes, and who heals those with infirmities also eats with tax collectors and sinners. In response to their grumblings, Jesus tells three parables of three things lost and found: a sheep, a coin, a son. In each parable the joy of finding is so great it must be shared with others. The shepherd and the woman invite their friends and neighbors to rejoice with them, while the father of the prodigal son slaughters the fattened calf and puts on a banquet with music and dancing.

• There are many layers to these parables to be explored, but one of them is certainly the joy of finding. The shepherd wastes no time scolding his sheep, and the father of the prodigal won't even let his son complete his apology before he clothes him in a fine robe and new sandals. Jesus answers the scribes' and the Pharisees' self-righteous stinginess with abundant welcome. The tax collectors and sinners are not to be turned away from Jesus' table; they are the very reason he is here. St. Paul says in today's second reading, "This saying is trustworthy and deserves full acceptance: / Christ Jesus came into the world to save sinners."

• There is a lesson here for us, especially those of us who find our place in the pews every Sunday and holy day. Are we prone to grumbling too when we see those who drop in once or twice a year join us at the table of the Lord? Does our community practice the hospitality of Jesus who welcomed all with joy, love, and compassion? If we call ourselves Christian we must take on the path of Jesus: seek the lost and welcome the sinner.

Model Universal Prayer (Prayer of the Faithful)

Presider: Confident in God's mercy to the lost and the sinful we bring our needs before the Lord.

Response: Lord, hear our prayer.

That the church embrace its mission to serve as a field hospital for wounded and weary souls . . .

That nations come together in peace and fellowship to provide for the needs of the poor, the powerless, and the vulnerable . . .

That those who have wandered far from the loving hand of God come to know the Lord who constantly seeks them . . .

That all gathered here might create a community of hospitality where sinners find welcome and the lost are called home . . .

Presider: God of compassion and mercy, you never cease to search for your wayward children or tire of gathering them to yourself. Hear our prayers that we might join you in seeking the lost and rejoicing when they are found. We ask this through Jesus Christ our Lord. Amen.

COLLECT

Let us pray.

Pause for silent prayer

Look upon us, O God,
Creator and ruler of all things,
and, that we may feel the working of your
    mercy,
grant that we may serve you with all our
    heart.
Through our Lord Jesus Christ, your Son,
who lives and reigns with you in the unity
    of the Holy Spirit,
one God, for ever and ever. **Amen.**

FIRST READING

Exod 32:7-11, 13-14

The LORD said to Moses,
    "Go down at once to your people,
    whom you brought out of the land of
        Egypt,
    for they have become depraved.
They have soon turned aside from the way
        I pointed out to them,
    making for themselves a molten calf
        and worshiping it,
    sacrificing to it and crying out,
    'This is your God, O Israel,
    who brought you out of the land of
        Egypt!'
I see how stiff-necked this people is,"
        continued the LORD to Moses.
"Let me alone, then,
    that my wrath may blaze up against
        them to consume them.
Then I will make of you a great nation."

But Moses implored the Lord, his God,
        saying,
    "Why, O LORD, should your wrath blaze
        up against your own people,
    whom you brought out of the land of
        Egypt
    with such great power and with so
        strong a hand?
Remember your servants Abraham, Isaac,
        and Israel,
    and how you swore to them by your
        own self, saying,
    'I will make your descendants as
        numerous as the stars in the sky;
    and all this land that I promised,
    I will give your descendants as their
        perpetual heritage.'"
So the LORD relented in the punishment
    he had threatened to inflict on his
        people.

RESPONSORIAL PSALM

Ps 51:3-4, 12-13, 17, 19

R̊. (Luke 15:18) I will rise and go to my father.

Have mercy on me, O God, in your goodness;
  in the greatness of your compassion wipe out my offense.
Thoroughly wash me from my guilt and of my sin cleanse me.

R̊. I will rise and go to my father.

A clean heart create for me, O God,
  and a steadfast spirit renew within me.
Cast me not out from your presence,
  and your Holy Spirit take not from me.

R̊. I will rise and go to my father.

O Lord, open my lips,
  and my mouth shall proclaim your praise.
My sacrifice, O God, is a contrite spirit;
  a heart contrite and humbled, O God, you will not spurn.

R̊. I will rise and go to my father.

SECOND READING

1 Tim 1:12-17

Beloved:
I am grateful to him who has strengthened me, Christ Jesus our Lord,
  because he considered me trustworthy in appointing me to the ministry.
I was once a blasphemer and a persecutor and arrogant,
  but I have been mercifully treated because I acted out of ignorance in my unbelief.
Indeed, the grace of our Lord has been abundant,
  along with the faith and love that are in Christ Jesus.
This saying is trustworthy and deserves full acceptance:
  Christ Jesus came into the world to save sinners.
Of these I am the foremost.
But for that reason I was mercifully treated,
  so that in me, as the foremost,
  Christ Jesus might display all his patience as an example
  for those who would come to believe in him for everlasting life.
To the king of ages, incorruptible, invisible, the only God,
  honor and glory forever and ever. Amen.

About Liturgy

Penitential Act invocations: The third form of the penitential act gives us the opportunity to choose from a variety of invocations for the threefold litany: "Lord/Christ, have mercy" or "Kyrie/Christe, eleison." Appendix VI of the Roman Missal includes several sample invocations. On occasion, you might want to compose your own invocations incorporating some of the images from the day's Scriptures.

A main principle to keep in mind when writing invocations for the penitential act is that the focus here is always on God's mercy in Christ and not on our sinfulness. The priest's invitation that opens the penitential act indicates that the acknowledgement of our sin, and not its forgiveness, is what makes us ready to celebrate the sacred mysteries. We place ourselves in right relationship before God by acknowledging that before the glory of God, none of us is without need of mercy.

Therefore, the invocations in the third form of the penitential act are invocations to Christ, not petitions for forgiveness. Look at the samples given in the Roman Missal. All of these have Christ as the subject, and the emphasis is on what Christ has done.

If you decide to write your own invocations, avoid wording such as, "For the times we have sinned, Lord, have mercy." Instead, keep Christ as the subject. Here are some examples using images from today's gospel: "You are the Good Shepherd who sought out the lost sheep. Lord, have mercy." "You prepare a feast, rejoicing over the sinner who repents. Christ, have mercy." "You will run to meet us when we return home to you. Lord, have mercy."

About Initiation

Reconciliation for baptized candidates: In the Rite of Christian Initiation of Adults, baptized but uncatechized candidates are to be prepared during their formation to celebrate the sacrament of penance (see RCIA 408). Ideally, they would participate in penitential celebrations with the rest of the faithful, doing an examination of conscience and discerning their need for the sacrament. Especially during penitential times of the liturgical year, such as Advent or Lent, they should be prepared and encouraged to celebrate reconciliation along with the rest of the parish.

Catechumens cannot yet celebrate penance until after their baptism. However, they can join the faithful in participating in other penitential disciplines.

About Liturgical Music

Lamb of God: In addition to the third form of the penitential act, the Lamb of God is another litany of praise for God's mercy in Christ. Unlike the penitential act, the singing or recitation of the Lamb of God does not stand as a ritual by itself but rather accompanies the ritual action of breaking the eucharistic bread for Communion.

Because it accompanies this ritual, the singing of the Lamb of God should begin as the priest breaks the first host. This requires music directors to be attentive during the sign of peace and accompanists to be flexible with the musical introduction, shortening or lengthening it as needed, so that the singing of the cantor's first invocation begins at the appropriate moment. (Remember that in the third edition of the Roman Missal, the only invocation allowed is "Lamb of God.")

Although neither the rubrics nor the General Instruction of the Roman Missal indicate the exact number of times the litany should be repeated, it is traditionally repeated at least three times. The rubrics do indicate that the litany should be repeated as many times as necessary to accompany the fractioning, with the final response always being "Grant us peace" (GIRM 83; Roman Missal 130).

SEPTEMBER 15, 2019
TWENTY-FOURTH SUNDAY IN ORDINARY TIME

✝ SPIRITUALITY

GOSPEL ACCLAMATION
cf. 2 Cor 8:9

℟. Alleluia, alleluia.
Though our Lord Jesus Christ was rich, he
    became poor,
so that by his poverty you might become rich.
℟. Alleluia, alleluia.

Gospel

Luke 16:1-13; L135C

Jesus said to his disciples,
    "A rich man had a steward
    who was reported to him for
        squandering his property.
He summoned him and said,
    'What is this I hear about you?
Prepare a full account of your
        stewardship,
    because you can no longer be
        my steward.'
The steward said to himself,
    'What shall I do,
    now that my master is taking
        the position of steward away
        from me?
I am not strong enough to dig and I am
        ashamed to beg.
I know what I shall do so that,
    when I am removed from the
        stewardship,
    they may welcome me into their
        homes.'
He called in his master's debtors one
        by one.
To the first he said,
    'How much do you owe my master?'
He replied, 'One hundred measures of
        olive oil.'
He said to him, 'Here is your promis-
        sory note.
Sit down and quickly write one for fifty.'
Then to another the steward said, 'And
        you, how much do you owe?'
He replied, 'One hundred kors of wheat.'

Continued in Appendix A, p. 312,

or Luke 16:10-13.

Reflecting on the Gospel

Have you ever heard a story and wondered what exactly was its point? It's almost like not quite understanding a joke, and then asking for an explanation. Sometimes our wondering about the point of a story can happen listening to children, but it can also happen in a boardroom! Few times will a brave soul step up and ask, "How does that apply?" or "And what does that mean?"

Today's parable is a case in point. It has puzzled interpreters for centuries. Part of the problem is that Luke appends to the parable a number of other sayings that attempt to explain it, but which create more difficulties. At least as the New American Bible presents it, the parable ends with this phrase, "And the master commended that dishonest steward for acting prudently." What follows is Jesus' commentary, which some misunderstand as somehow encouraging dishonest behavior! But there is more going on than a facile reading might indicate.

In antiquity, a steward functioned as the agent of the master or lord of the estate with the power to hire, fire, enter into contracts, etc. The steward kept the books and received some payment for himself by charging interest. The loan note indicated the amount to be paid back, not the amount borrowed. In essence, the amount to be paid back included the interest, and that extra money was for the steward. So in the parable, when the steward writes down the note, he is effectively giving up *his own share* of the money owed, 25 percent in one case, 50 percent in the other. The rich man will still receive what is his due in full. So the parable is not about encouraging dishonesty, but rather, the right use of money and resources, which itself is a favorite Lukan theme. It is certainly true that the steward is dishonest, as we learn at the opening verse. And it is for this reason that he is being released. But his writing down of the debt is a crafty way for him to use his own resources (the money owed to him) to curry favor with others.

In fact, this chapter of the Gospel of Luke will have a number of stories reflecting this theme of money. We will read another next week. The right use of wealth was foreshadowed even in last week's story of the prodigal son.

Luke is the only evangelist to tell this parable of the Dishonest Steward. It is rooted firmly in the ancient world; discerning the likely meaning is much like deciphering a puzzle. Rather than a quick, easy read it's important to understand something of the context of the ancient world so as to more appropriately apply its lesson.

Living the Paschal Mystery

Jesus has more to say about money and how we use it than nearly any other ethical or moral matter in the gospels. And Luke the evangelist gives us more of these sayings, parables, and teachings than any other evangelist. Though the steward is being released from his position due to some dishonesty, he now acts in a shrewd way to leverage his remaining resources. He understands quickly that the money in the ledger due to him is better utilized currying favor than being handed over to the master. The master, upon realizing this, does not condemn him for stealing, for after all he was not stealing. Instead, the master admires him.

We are advised to be as cunning and creative as this steward. It would be a misreading and a sure misunderstanding to imagine Jesus is encouraging dishonesty. Instead, with our own resources we are to be creative, using wealth for a greater good.

Focusing the Gospel

Key words and phrases: No servant can serve two masters.

To the point: Today's gospel reading includes the parable of the Dishonest Steward as well as collected sayings of Jesus related to prudence, trustworthiness, and wealth. The passage concludes, "You cannot serve both God and mammon." Mammon is usually translated as "wealth," "riches," or even "that in which one trusts." As in all things, Jesus points to the true source of riches and wealth, the only one completely worthy of trust, the eternal God.

Connecting the Gospel

to the first reading: The sixteenth chapter of the Gospel of Luke, which we read from this Sunday and the next, is focused on the proper use of wealth and the unjust distribution of goods between the very rich and the very poor. This chapter is complemented perfectly by the prophet Amos who was called from the southern kingdom of Judah to prophesy against the northern kingdom of Israel. And what was Israel's most prominent offense? The callous mistreatment of the poor by the rich. In today's reading, Amos lists off the crimes of the wealthy Israelites who cheat the poor and then proclaims, "The LORD has sworn by the pride of Jacob: / Never will I forget a thing they have done!"

to experience: This Sunday we are given the warning that we cannot serve both God and earthly riches. We must choose one or the other. Are we willing to use our wealth and resources wisely and prudently in service of others?

Connecting the Responsorial Psalm

to the readings: Amos's emphasis on care of the poor is echoed in Psalm 113. Not only is God "High above all nations," but he also "raises up the lowly from the dust; / from the dunghill he lifts up the poor / to seat them with princes, / with the princes of his own people." Though today's gospel reading does not focus specifically on the plight of the poor, as next Sunday's will, we can see within it the roots of economic prudence. Wealth and riches can enslave a person who entrusts himself entirely to them. Instead, with God as the true master, wealth can take up its proper post, as a gift to be shared with others, especially those most in need.

to psalmist preparation: Today's psalm is good news for all who identify with, befriend, or care for the poor. To proclaim this psalm well, you must live it. How do you relate to the poor within your community?

PROMPTS FOR FAITH-SHARING

The prophet Amos was tasked with calling the Israelites back to right living by caring for the poor. In our time, who are the prophets who call us to share our resources with others?

How does your family and/or parish engage in advocating for the poor and vulnerable in society? How might you be called to do more?

Today's parable of the Dishonest Steward is difficult to interpret. What action of the steward's do you think Jesus is upholding as a model for us?

Jesus tells us that a servant can serve only one master. In our culture what other "masters" demand to be served? How do you keep your focus on God?

Model Penitential Act

Presider: In today's gospel Jesus exhorts us, "No servant can serve two masters." For the times we have placed other interests above God let us pause to ask forgiveness . . . [*pause*]

> Lord Jesus, you call us to be trustworthy and honest in all matters large and small: Lord, have mercy.
>
> Christ Jesus, you mediate for us at the right hand of God: Christ, have mercy.
>
> Lord Jesus, you gave yourself as a ransom for all: Lord, have mercy.

Homily Points

• This week and next our gospel readings come from the sixteenth chapter of Luke. The bulk of this chapter is taken up with two parables: the parable of the Dishonest Steward and the parable of the Rich Man and Lazarus. Both of these parables begin with the character of a "rich man." In between the parables we hear a reason for this focus on wealth, "The Pharisees, who loved money, heard all these things and sneered at him" (16:14; NABRE). Just as with the parables of the Lost Sheep, Lost Coin, and Prodigal Son from last Sunday's gospel, Jesus has an audience in mind for these parables about riches.

• The final verse of today's gospel is the most searing indictment of these Pharisees in his audience, "No servant can serve two masters. / He will either hate one and love the other, / or be devoted to one and despise the other. / You cannot serve both God and mammon." What do these words mean for us? Within our culture it is considered an acceptable goal to amass wealth for oneself and one's family. In some ways it can be seen as foolhardy *not* to take as much as one can for oneself. Jesus shows us another way.

• We are to be devoted to only one master, God. Through the self-revelation of Jesus we begin to know what this master asks of us. Over and over again in his actions and his words we see Jesus place the highest value on communion between people and God. Jesus restores the sinner, seeks the lost, and shares table fellowship with people from all walks of life. Far from being interested in amassing things, Jesus preaches for us to store up treasure in heaven where neither moth nor decay destroy. This is the only treasure that lasts. This is the only treasure that satisfies.

Model Universal Prayer (Prayer of the Faithful)

Presider: With thanksgiving and trust we hand over to God all of our needs and petitions.

Response: Lord, hear our prayer.

That the church be a wise and prudent steward of financial and spiritual wealth in service to all God's people . . .

That all people of the world commit themselves to faithful stewardship of the earth's natural resources . . .

That those who are enslaved to the pursuit of money and power find freedom and peace in the one whose "yoke is easy and burden light" . . .

That everyone gathered here strive for honesty and trustworthiness in all matters, large and small . . .

Presider: God of Creation, you are the giver of all good gifts. Hear our prayers that we might be good and faithful stewards to the resources you have entrusted to us. We ask this through Christ our Lord. Amen.

COLLECT

Let us pray.

Pause for silent prayer

O God, who founded all the commands of
    your sacred Law
upon love of you and of our neighbor,
grant that, by keeping your precepts,
we may merit to attain eternal life.
Through our Lord Jesus Christ, your Son,
who lives and reigns with you in the unity
    of the Holy Spirit,
one God, for ever and ever. **Amen.**

FIRST READING

Amos 8:4-7

Hear this, you who trample upon the
    needy
    and destroy the poor of the land!
"When will the new moon be over," you
    ask,
    "that we may sell our grain,
    and the sabbath, that we may display
      the wheat?
We will diminish the ephah,
    add to the shekel,
    and fix our scales for cheating!
We will buy the lowly for silver,
    and the poor for a pair of sandals;
    even the refuse of the wheat we will
      sell!"
The LORD has sworn by the pride of Jacob:
    Never will I forget a thing they have
      done!

RESPONSORIAL PSALM

Ps 113:1-2, 4-6, 7-8

℟. (cf. 1a, 7b) Praise the Lord, who lifts up
    the poor.
    or
℟. Alleluia.

Praise, you servants of the LORD,
    praise the name of the LORD.
Blessed be the name of the LORD
    both now and forever.

℟. Praise the Lord, who lifts up the poor.
    or
℟. Alleluia.

High above all nations is the LORD;
    above the heavens is his glory.
Who is like the LORD, our God, who is
      enthroned on high
    and looks upon the heavens and the
      earth below?

℟. Praise the Lord, who lifts up the poor.
    or
℟. Alleluia.

He raises up the lowly from the dust;
    from the dunghill he lifts up the poor
to seat them with princes,
    with the princes of his own people.

R℣. Praise the Lord, who lifts up the poor.
    or
R℣. Alleluia.

SECOND READING
1 Tim 2:1-8

Beloved:
First of all, I ask that supplications,
    prayers,
    petitions, and thanksgivings be offered
        for everyone,
    for kings and for all in authority,
    that we may lead a quiet and tranquil
        life
in all devotion and dignity.
This is good and pleasing to God our
    savior,
    who wills everyone to be saved
    and to come to knowledge of the truth.
        For there is one God.
        There is also one mediator between God
            and men,
        the man Christ Jesus,
        who gave himself as ransom for all.
This was the testimony at the proper time.
For this I was appointed preacher and
    apostle
    —I am speaking the truth, I am not
        lying—,
    teacher of the Gentiles in faith and
        truth.

It is my wish, then, that in every place the
    men should pray,
    lifting up holy hands, without anger
        or argument.

✝ CATECHESIS

About Liturgy

Can a person serve multiple ministries?: Within the same Mass, can a lector also serve as a communion minister or a choir member proclaim one of the readings? According to a liturgical principle from the Constitution on the Sacred Liturgy, not really. That principle states: "In liturgical celebrations each person, minister, or layman who has an office to perform, should carry out all and only those parts which pertain to his office by the nature of the rite and the norms of the liturgy" (28).

Many parishes do not really think of the roles of liturgical ministers, other than the priest or deacon, as "offices." Thus, many parishes allow people to serve in more than one ministry during a liturgy.

However, a central goal of the Second Vatican Council was to distribute the liturgical roles as widely as possible among the assembly to show more clearly the various members of the Body of Christ working together to do the action of the liturgy. This shows the hierarchical nature of the liturgy. In other words, each member of the body has a role to play. Thus, each member of the body is necessary. It also shows dignity to each member when we allow each person to do their proper role and we don't let others usurp it.

There will be times when this cannot be avoided because not enough trained persons are available. But those emergencies should not become our normative practice.

About Initiation

Apostolic witness: We often think that catechesis for initiation consists of learning only the doctrines and teachings of the church. However, a complete catechesis requires that catechumens live the Word they have heard by the witness of their lives. Thus, part of discerning the readiness of catechumens for baptism is knowing if they have learned "how to work actively with others to spread the Gospel and build up the Church by the witness of their lives and by professing their faith" (RCIA 75.4). Or as the bishop will inquire of their godparents in the Rite of Election, "Have they responded to [God's] word and begun to walk in God's presence?" Even before their baptism, they must show themselves to be credible witnesses to the Gospel.

About Liturgical Music

Copyright laws: Part of being just and honest as a music minister is to follow the copyright laws of your country. When we ignore these laws, we are essentially stealing. These regulations are in place to protect the rights of composers and performers and to give them just compensation for the work they have produced.

Before you make a photocopy of a song, share an electronic file of sheet music, or upload a recording from the internet to your own website, know first whether you have the right to do so. Unless a piece of music and its arrangement are specifically labeled "public domain," you must typically purchase a license from the copyright holder to make or share copies of that song.

You cannot make copies of music for your choir members even if your parish has legally purchased a copy of the octavo or accompaniment books. You must purchase a copy for each choir member. Even if you have a reprint license for assembly editions of the music (melody and/or text of a song), making copies of sheet music with chords, harmonies, or keyboard accompaniment falls under a separate license.

Printed worship aids, music or text projected on a screen, and digital or physical recordings of music your choir performs also require a copyright license from the copyright holder.

Always contact the publisher of the song if you are unsure of your permission for using the music. Not doing so can legally jeopardize your entire parish.

SEPTEMBER 22, 2019
TWENTY-FIFTH SUNDAY
IN ORDINARY TIME

✛ SPIRITUALITY

GOSPEL ACCLAMATION
cf. 2 Cor 8:9

℟. Alleluia, alleluia.
Though our Lord Jesus Christ was rich, he
　　became poor,
so that by his poverty you might become rich.
℟. Alleluia, alleluia.

Gospel

Luke 16:19-31; L138C

Jesus said to the Pharisees:
　"There was a rich man who dressed
　　in purple garments and fine
　　linen
　and dined sumptuously each day.
And lying at his door was a poor
　man named Lazarus, covered
　　with sores,
　who would gladly have eaten his fill
　　of the scraps
　that fell from the rich man's table.
Dogs even used to come and lick his
　sores.
When the poor man died,
　he was carried away by angels to the
　　bosom of Abraham.
The rich man also died and was buried,
　and from the netherworld, where he
　　was in torment,
　he raised his eyes and saw Abraham
　　far off
　and Lazarus at his side.
And he cried out, 'Father Abraham,
　have pity on me.
Send Lazarus to dip the tip of his fin-
　ger in water and cool my tongue,
　for I am suffering torment in these
　　flames.'
Abraham replied,
　'My child, remember that you
　　received
　what was good during your lifetime
　while Lazarus likewise received what
　　was bad;
　but now he is comforted here,
　　whereas you are tormented.

Continued in Appendix A, p. 312.

Reflecting on the Gospel

As we continue to journey with Jesus to Jerusalem we hear another parable unique to Luke: the story of the Rich Man and Lazarus. This parable develops many themes in the gospel, including the right use of money from last week, and also the reversal of the social order that has been foretold in Mary's canticle: he has lifted up the lowly and sent the rich away empty.

We should find this story troubling for a number of reasons, not least of which is that those of us in the developed world are likely the rich man, dressed in fine clothes and eating well while there is a Lazarus effectively at our doorstep who needs our help. When examined from a global perspective, most human beings live on meager amounts each day. Most of the wealth in the world has been localized, and even if we are not part of the infamous "1 percent" we are likely among the top 25 percent globally. Indeed the annual median wage globally is about $10,000. So if we are looking to place ourselves in this parable, the person of the rich man is likely where we belong, generally enjoying the good things of this world while others go without, or go with less. The line on Abraham's lips sounds the toll of doom: "My child, remember that you received / what was good during your lifetime / while Lazarus likewise received what was bad; / but now he is comforted here, whereas you are tormented." A reversal is in order!

The message that Jesus preached was good news for those on the outside of power, privilege, and wealth. Those who enjoyed such things put him to death!

In the nether world, the rich man cries out for someone to warn his brothers. But the message of caring for one's neighbor is spread liberally throughout the Law and Prophets. In a telling sign, which foreshadows the situation of the early Christians, Abraham says ominously that people will not learn even if someone rises from the dead.

The lesson is difficult and likely hits home now that globalization means someone an ocean away is our neighbor. While we may no longer see a poor Lazarus literally at our doorstep, he is there nonetheless, and can be seen with television, radio, internet, and other modern means of communication. But it would be a mistake to believe that the only Lazaruses are an ocean away. There may be a Lazarus picking vegetables for meager wages and no health care nearby. There may be a Lazarus working in unsafe conditions creating the latest technological device. And there is certainly a Lazarus overlooked by systems, institutions, and even churches. What is our response? We have been told by the Law, the Prophets, and even by someone who rose from the dead to care for them.

Living the Paschal Mystery

For many, Christianity has become a comfortable societal institution. Parishioners and church members attend Mass regularly, build community with others in their geographical boundary, and might even send their children to the parish school. Today's gospel is a reminder that Jesus did not found parishes. The basis of one's salvation is not parish membership, but how we treat the poor and disenfranchised among us. And now that our world has become flat, we are so interconnected that nearly the entire globe is our neighbor. Our responsibility to one another has increased exponentially. No longer are we concerned merely with our neighborhood, parish, or school, but we are concerned with a much broader spectrum. The moral life includes decisions we make while shopping, hiring labor, or disposing of waste. With today's reading, we are called to let go of any narrow vision we might have of "neighbor" and see the Lazarus figures before us both locally and worldwide.

Focusing the Gospel

Key words and phrases: There was a rich man . . . And lying at his door was a poor man named Lazarus.

To the point: Where most parables deal with everyday objects and stock characters like farmers, travelers, or a woman baking bread, today's parable, the Rich Man and Lazarus, is distinctive in that it contains two first names. The rich man could be any person enjoying an extravagant lifestyle while others suffer but the poor man is *Lazarus* and when he dies he is carried to the bosom of *Abraham.* We're not given many details about Lazarus's life other than his poverty, his hunger, and his illness (sores). We don't know if Lazarus lived an upright life, how he came to his current state in life, or if he had any friends or family. But we are given a name. This man, lying at the rich man's door, is not just a poor person, a person in need, he is Lazarus. Perhaps if the rich man had crossed the chasm of social class that separated him and Lazarus in their earthly life he wouldn't have found himself staring across an even greater chasm in eternity. Who are the ones in need at your door? Do you know their names?

Connecting the Gospel

to the first and second readings: As in last Sunday's first reading, the prophet Amos condemns the rich who show no care and compassion for their neighbors in need. The ones that Amos berates are not only rich but one could say, obscenely wealthy, lying on "beds of ivory," and drinking "wine from bowls." The rich man who ignores Lazarus would be at home in their company with his "sumptuous" dining and fine linen clothing. In many ways the role of the prophet is to point out the nature of God, especially when the behavior of people is not in line with the Creator in whose image and likeness they were made.

to experience: In all three readings today, Amos, Jesus, and St. Paul challenge us to think not merely as humans, intent upon our own comfort, but with the compassion and love of God. Jesus tells us, "[L]ove your neighbor as yourself" (Mark 12:31; NABRE). When we love this way we cannot be content to simply enjoy the riches we have, because when others are poor and suffering, so are we.

Connecting the Responsorial Psalm

to the readings: Psalm 147 reads almost like a litany recounting the deeds of the Lord. These actions on God's part turn the world upside down: prisoners are freed, the blind can see, the lowly are raised up, and the most vulnerable are protected. In the first reading and the gospel, Amos and Jesus condemn those who profit from the status quo—the ones who lounge on ivory couches and dine at sumptuous feasts while their neighbors suffer in poverty.

to psalmist preparation: As God's children we are called to act as God acts. How does your lifestyle oppress others, especially in ways you don't intend? How might you become more like the God of today's psalm, intent upon caring for the vulnerable?

Model Penitential Act

Presider: Today Jesus tells us the parable of the rich man and Lazarus. For the times we have ignored the hungry and destitute at our door, let us pause to ask for mercy and forgiveness . . . [*pause*]

Lord Jesus, you call us to love our neighbor as ourselves: Lord, have mercy.

Christ Jesus, you show us the way of light and life: Christ, have mercy.

Lord Jesus, you embody the compassion and love of God: Lord, have mercy.

Homily Points

• We can find a companion for today's gospel of the Rich Man and Lazarus in Pope Francis's apostolic exhortation, *Evangelii Gaudium.* In it, Pope Francis states, "there is an inseparable bond between our faith and the poor" (48). Just as Pope Francis minces no words, neither does Jesus. As followers of Christ, we cannot ignore the poor on our doorstep. When we build a chasm to separate ourselves from their suffering, this chasm in turn separates us from God. In our life of faith, concern for the poor needs to be just as central as prayers before meals and Sunday Mass.

• And yet, for those of us who live in the developed world, enjoying an outsized proportion of the world's resources, concern for the poor can be easily pushed to the side. Pope Francis writes, "Almost without being aware of it, we end up being incapable of feeling compassion at the outcry of the poor . . . the culture of prosperity deadens us" (54).

• And so, the question becomes, how do we come back alive to the needs of others? Perhaps one of the places to start is through the example of today's gospel. The poor man has a name, Lazarus. We care for people when we know them. Do you know the names of the people in need in your community, in your neighborhood? When you visit other countries do you take the time to see the places hidden away from tourists' eyes? Let us take up Pope Francis's challenge not only to know the poor but to learn from them: "This is why I want a Church which is poor and for the poor. They have much to teach us . . . in their difficulties they know the suffering of Christ. We need to let ourselves be evangelized by them" (198).

Model Universal Prayer (Prayer of the Faithful)

Presider: Knowing the God of infinite justice and mercy, we offer up our prayers to the Lord.

Response: Lord, hear our prayer.

That parishes and dioceses around the world use their resources to care for the poor and neglected . . .

That nations that are rich in resources generously share with those in need . . .

That all people experiencing devastating poverty might find comfort and support within their communities . . .

That all gathered here might see their brothers and sisters in need with the eyes of God and in compassion and care reach out with love and kindness . . .

Presider: God of the poor and the outcast, you sustain and care for every human life. Hear our prayers that we might reach out from our abundance to share with all those in need. We ask this through Christ our Lord. Amen.

COLLECT

Let us pray.

Pause for silent prayer

O God, who manifest your almighty power
above all by pardoning and showing
    mercy,
bestow, we pray, your grace abundantly
    upon us
and make those hastening to attain your
    promises
heirs to the treasures of heaven.
Through our Lord Jesus Christ, your Son,
who lives and reigns with you in the unity
    of the Holy Spirit,
one God, for ever and ever. **Amen.**

FIRST READING

Amos 6:1a, 4-7

Thus says the LORD, the God of hosts:
Woe to the complacent in Zion!
Lying upon beds of ivory,
    stretched comfortably on their couches,
they eat lambs taken from the flock,
    and calves from the stall!
Improvising to the music of the harp,
    like David, they devise their own
        accompaniment.
They drink wine from bowls
    and anoint themselves with the best oils;
    yet they are not made ill by the collapse
        of Joseph!
Therefore, now they shall be the first to go
    into exile,
    and their wanton revelry shall be done
        away with.

RESPONSORIAL PSALM

Ps 146:7, 8-9, 9-10

℞. (1b) Praise the Lord, my soul!
or
℞. Alleluia.

Blessed is he who keeps faith forever,
    secures justice for the oppressed,
    gives food to the hungry.
The LORD sets captives free.

℞. Praise the Lord, my soul!
or
℞. Alleluia.

The LORD gives sight to the blind.
    The LORD raises up those who were
        bowed down.
The LORD loves the just.
    The LORD protects strangers.

℞. Praise the Lord, my soul!
or
℞. Alleluia.

The fatherless and the widow he sustains,
    but the way of the wicked he thwarts.
The Lord shall reign forever;
    your God, O Zion, through all
        generations. Alleluia.

R. Praise the Lord, my soul!
    or
R. Alleluia.

SECOND READING
1 Tim 6:11-16

But you, man of God, pursue righteousness,
    devotion, faith, love, patience, and
        gentleness.
Compete well for the faith.
Lay hold of eternal life, to which you were
    called
    when you made the noble confession in
        the presence of many witnesses.
I charge you before God, who gives life to
    all things,
    and before Christ Jesus,
    who gave testimony under Pontius
        Pilate for the noble confession,
    to keep the commandment without stain
        or reproach
    until the appearance of our Lord Jesus
        Christ
    that the blessed and only ruler
    will make manifest at the proper time,
    the King of kings and Lord of lords,
    who alone has immortality, who dwells
        in unapproachable light,
    and whom no human being has seen or
        can see.
To him be honor and eternal power. Amen.

CATECHESIS

About Liturgy

Does liturgy have anything to with justice?: Today's readings are a clear reminder that the way we treat those in need will be the criterion by which we will be judged on the last day. Yet, some will still claim that the celebration of the Eucharist is disconnected from our works of justice. They will say that the Mass is their one-hour retreat from the world and its concerns. Or they will complain if the homily mentions too much of the current events and issues of the day, wondering why we have to "politicize" the Mass.

Our Christian faith is certainly not partisan in its politics, but it *is* political in that the gospel critiques the *polis*, that is, the structures we uphold in our society. So much Scripture focuses not on spiritual, mystical realms but on the concrete ways we operate as a society and use our resources in this world for the good of those who are poor.

We cannot separate praising God and doing justice. We praise God *by* doing justice: "Go in peace, glorifying the Lord by your life." We do justice *by* praising God: "Lift up your hearts. . . . It is right and just." On this Sunday, let us remember the words of St. John Paul II and of the Catechism:

"We cannot delude ourselves: by our mutual love and, in particular, by our concern for those in need we will be recognized as true followers of Christ. This will be the criterion by which the authenticity of our Eucharistic celebrations is judged (*Mane Nobiscum Domine* 28).

"The Eucharist commits us to the poor. To receive in truth the Body and Blood of Christ given up for us, we must recognize Christ in the poorest, his brethren" (*Catechism of the Catholic Church* 1397).

About Liturgical Music

***Song of Farewell and* In paradisum:** The final commendation of a funeral is the ritual in which the gathered assembly says its final farewell before the body is brought to the place for burial or interment. In the final commendation, there are two important musical rituals that connect to today's gospel reading.

The first significant musical moment is singing the Song of Farewell. The text of this song includes the line, "May angels lead you to the bosom of Abraham," quoting directly from verse 22 of today's Gospel of Luke.

The Song of Farewell is a stand-alone ritual, meaning that the singing itself, like the Gloria, is the primary liturgical action and does not accompany any other ritual action, although there is the option that the body be incensed during the song. The Order of Christian Funerals calls this song, "the climax of the rite of final commendation" (147). Therefore, it should be sung by the entire assembly.

The second significant musical moment comes at the procession to the place of committal. Although the funeral rite allows for any suitable song, the traditional Latin text that accompanies this procession is the *In paradisum*, or "In paradise." Here is one English translation of this short refrain found in the Order of Christian Funerals: "May choirs of angels welcome you and lead you to the bosom of Abraham; and where Lazarus is poor no longer may you find eternal rest" (176B).

As we recall Lazarus and the rich man today, let us also remember that at the end of our lives as Christians, we hope that our compassion for those in need in this life will make us worthy to be with Lazarus at Abraham's side.

✢ SPIRITUALITY

GOSPEL ACCLAMATION
1 Pet 1:25

℟. Alleluia, alleluia.
The word of the Lord remains forever.
This is the word that has been proclaimed to you.
℟. Alleluia, alleluia.

Gospel

Luke 17:5-10; L141C

The apostles said to the
    Lord, "Increase our
    faith."
The Lord replied,
    "If you have faith the
        size of a mustard
        seed,
    you would say to this
        mulberry tree,
    'Be uprooted and
        planted in the sea,'
    and it would obey
        you.

"Who among you would say to
    your servant
    who has just come in from plowing or
        tending sheep in the field,
    'Come here immediately and take
        your place at table'?
Would he not rather say to him,
    'Prepare something for me to eat.
Put on your apron and wait on me
    while I eat and drink.
You may eat and drink when I am
    finished'?
Is he grateful to that servant because
    he did what was commanded?
So should it be with you.
When you have done all you have been
    commanded,
    say, 'We are unprofitable servants;
    we have done what we were obliged
        to do.'"

Reflecting on the Gospel

Philosophers and thinkers debate the meaning of justice and charity. Justice is often considered the doing or giving what is owed to another, for example, money, labor, or some other arrangement. On the other hand, charity is the gift one gives expecting nothing in return. A philosophical parlor game centers around the definition of charity. Can an act be considered charity if the doer expects a thank you? Or does the expectation of an expression of gratitude annul the act of charity, which is given expecting *nothing* in return?

The disciples have a simple request of Jesus today: "Increase our faith." How many of us have made the same request? But what did the disciples mean by it? And what would we mean by it? Further, what is the point of the request?

In another example of hyperbole, Jesus responds by saying that if their faith was the size of a mustard seed (about the size of a sesame seed) they would be able to move trees. Now, nobody, not even Jesus, moved trees. Significantly, there are other gospels where the claim is that they could with faith the size of a mustard seed move *mountains* (Mark 11:23; Matt 17:20). But apparently Luke thought that was hyperbole taken too far. For in this gospel the extent of faith is moving only trees. Mountains are not mentioned. Nevertheless, the point is simply that they have little faith, not even that the size of a mustard seed.

Jesus continues his lesson with a demonstration of the proper attitude of a servant who does what he is told expecting nothing, not even gratitude, in return. That attitude, striking for us today, is proper for discipleship.

So the disciples' query about increasing their faith brings a mild rebuke from Jesus, stating that their faith is smaller than the size of a mustard seed. Even so, they should simply carry out their mission without expecting even a thank you.

This "tough love" approach to discipleship may seem at odds with the Jesus that has been portrayed in much of the gospel. It's as though he is sure to put the disciples in their place so they turn their attention away from their own wants, desires, and requests, and on to carrying out the mission of Jesus. This is the true call of discipleship, to serve the master rather than oneself. And upon offering and completing that service, to have no expectations at all, not even a thank you.

This is a tall order. How many of us, upon performing an act of kindness, no matter how small, appreciate a word of gratitude. In fact, many of us likely expect that. But the story we have today presents a different standard. It would be good for us to reevaluate our role in this relationship. We are mere servants, carrying out the wishes of the Lord. When complete, we are happy simply to have done his bidding.

Living the Paschal Mystery

Today's gospel reminds us of the place disciples have before the Lord. Jesus uses an image from the ancient world about servants and a master. Such an image can be problematic today, but it reflects the worldview of antiquity. We, as disciples, are advised to do what we are told, follow directions, and carry out what we are obliged to do. Such an image does not leave much room for self-agency, or self-determination, other than to align oneself with the Lord. And this is why the image has some challenges as we bring it to the modern world. And yet, doing the will of the Father is precisely the role of the disciple, the follower. Our task is to discern that will in our world and to carry it out, expecting nothing in return. We die to our own wants, needs, and desires, noble as they might be, such as an increase in faith. Instead, we follow the direction set for us, using our gifts, talents, and abilities in such a way that there is not even the expectation of a thank you.

Focusing the Gospel

Key words and phrases: Increase our faith.

To the point: What is faith? The Letter to the Hebrews defines it as, "the realization of what is hoped for and evidence of things not seen" (11:1; NABRE). The disciples continue to follow Jesus on the road to Jerusalem, the path that will end in his death and resurrection. We might wonder what are the disciples hoping for at this moment when they ask Jesus, "Increase our faith"? Do they harbor a desire for Jesus to be the kind of Messiah who will lead them in a military revolt that will free Israel from the oppression of the Romans? Are they expecting a triumphant continuation of Jesus' life and ministry that might include earthly power and authority? Jesus has already chided the disciples once, calling them, "you of little faith" (Luke 12:28; NABRE). Their request for Jesus to increase their faith seems reasonable. Perhaps Jesus' abrupt response points to the disciples' need to reevaluate what they are hoping for.

Connecting the Gospel

to the first reading: The book of Habakkuk contains a dialogue between God and the prophet. The prophet, frustrated with violence and injustice, cries out to God in reproach, "How long, O Lord? I cry for help / but you do not listen!" God responds with reassurance, urging patience and trust in God's help, "if it delays, wait for it, / it will surely come, it will not be late."

to experience: Faith requires perseverance, especially in times of distress and suffering. In these moments, we believe in the God of justice who does not will that which is evil, but continues to work for the good of all.

Connecting the Responsorial Psalm

to the readings: Today's gospel, and the gospels of the following two Sundays all touch on the concept of faith. While the disciples' request for the Lord to increase their faith meets with a harsh response, next Sunday the leper who returns to thank Jesus will have his faith upheld as the reason for his salvation. Jesus also praises the faith of the persistent widow in the gospel the week following. In Psalm 95 we are given a metaphor for faith, "For he is our God, / and we are the people he shepherds, the flock he guides." Sheep are known for their complete and total trust in their shepherd.

to psalmist preparation: Sheep follow their shepherd because they know him or her. While their sight and depth perception is a bit limited, sheep have excellent hearing and the sound of their voice is the primary way they recognize their shepherd. A stranger using the same words or sounds will not be able to effectively call a herd of sheep, only their shepherd's voice will be successful. How do you hone your ear to be attentive to the voice of the Lord?

PROMPTS FOR FAITH-SHARING

The prophet Habakkuk, living in a time of violence and injustice, cries out to God, "How long, O Lord? I cry for help / but you do not listen!" In the world today, what are the dire situations that cause you to cry out to God?

_____

_____

_____

In Psalm 95 we are given the image of our relationship with God as that of a shepherd and sheep. Sheep recognize and follow their shepherd by listening to his or her voice. How do you cultivate deep listening to the voice of the Good Shepherd?

_____

_____

_____

St. Paul urges Timothy, "[S]tir into flame / the gift of God that you have through the imposition of my hands." What are the spiritual practices that help you to keep the flame of faith alive?

_____

_____

_____

The disciples implore Jesus, "Increase our faith." If faith is "the realization of what is hoped for and evidence of things not seen" (Heb 11:1), what is it that you are hoping for? What unseen realities are you convinced of being true?

_____

_____

_____

_____

Model Penitential Act

Presider: In today's gospel the disciples come to Jesus with a request, "Increase our faith." Let us echo this prayer of the disciples as we pause to remember the times our faith has failed us . . . [*pause*]

Lord Jesus, you are the Son of God: Lord, have mercy.

Christ Jesus, you show us the way of service and humility: Christ, have mercy.

Lord Jesus, you have given us your Spirit of love, power, and self-control: Lord, have mercy.

Homily Points

• In today's second reading Paul exhorts Timothy, "[S]tir into flame / the gift of God that you have through the imposition of my hands." Another biblical translation renders this verse, "Rekindle the gift of God within you." Paul reminds Timothy of who he is called to be, a disciple filled with the powerful spirit of love and self-control, one who testifies to Jesus, the Son of God, and who is ready to bear his share of hardship for the gospel. And how will Timothy become this? He must enkindle or stir into flame the gift of God within.

• Fires need constant tending: the coals must be stirred when the flames die out, new wood must be placed in a way that allows air to pass through, and sometimes our very own breath is required to urge a reluctant fire to spring to life. And so it is with the gift of God within. This flame must be stirred, nurtured, protected from rain and draughts, and also relished and enjoyed. The gift of God within, the spirit of power, love, and self-control animates our living to allow us to be a place of welcome, safety, and warmth for others.

• There are times that it might seem like the flame has gone out, when we are tired, grief-stricken, lost, and confused. In those times, maybe we can think of God blowing on the coals to bring the flame to life again, just as God blew life into the lungs of Adam. As Paul reminds Timothy, may we also remember who we are called to be—flames of God's love bringing light and warmth to the world.

Model Universal Prayer (Prayer of the Faithful)

Presider: With faith in the infinite mercy and complete justice of our God we lift up our prayers.

Response: Lord, hear our prayer.

That the church might remain faithful to the will of God in the spirit of the humble and unworthy servant . . .

That leaders of the world come together to remedy injustices and work for peace . . .

That those suffering from a crisis of faith come to know and trust in the voice of the Good Shepherd . . .

That all gathered here might rekindle the flame of faith in order to live our lives with courage and love . . .

Presider: Faithful God, in you we live and move and have our being. Hear our prayers that with increased faith we might humbly serve you and our neighbor. We ask this through Jesus our Lord. Amen.

COLLECT

Let us pray.

Pause for silent prayer

Almighty ever-living God,
who in the abundance of your kindness
surpass the merits and the desires of
    those who entreat you,
pour out your mercy upon us
to pardon what conscience dreads
and to give what prayer does not dare to
    ask.
Through our Lord Jesus Christ, your Son,
who lives and reigns with you in the unity
    of the Holy Spirit,
one God, for ever and ever. **Amen.**

FIRST READING
Hab 1:2-3; 2:2-4

How long, O Lord? I cry for help
    but you do not listen!
I cry out to you, "Violence!"
    but you do not intervene.
Why do you let me see ruin;
    why must I look at misery?
Destruction and violence are before me;
    there is strife, and clamorous discord.
Then the Lord answered me and said:
    Write down the vision clearly upon the
        tablets,
    so that one can read it readily.
For the vision still has its time,
    presses on to fulfillment, and will not
        disappoint;
if it delays, wait for it,
    it will surely come, it will not be late.
The rash one has no integrity;
    but the just one, because of his faith,
        shall live.

RESPONSORIAL PSALM

Ps 95:1-2, 6-7, 8-9

R̸. (8) If today you hear his voice, harden not your hearts.

Come, let us sing joyfully to the LORD;
    let us acclaim the Rock of our salvation.
Let us come into his presence with
    thanksgiving;
    let us joyfully sing psalms to him.

R̸. If today you hear his voice, harden not your hearts.

Come, let us bow down in worship;
    let us kneel before the LORD who made us.
For he is our God,
    and we are the people he shepherds, the
        flock he guides.

R̸. If today you hear his voice, harden not your hearts.

Oh, that today you would hear his voice:
    "Harden not your hearts as at Meribah,
    as in the day of Massah in the desert,
where your fathers tempted me;
    they tested me though they had seen
        my works."

R̸. If today you hear his voice, harden not your hearts.

SECOND READING

2 Tim 1:6-8, 13-14

Beloved:
I remind you to stir into flame
    the gift of God that you have through the
        imposition of my hands.
For God did not give us a spirit of
    cowardice
    but rather of power and love and
        self-control.
So do not be ashamed of your testimony
    to our Lord,
    nor of me, a prisoner for his sake;
    but bear your share of hardship for the
        gospel
    with the strength that comes from God.

Take as your norm the sound words that
    you heard from me,
    in the faith and love that are in Christ
        Jesus.
Guard this rich trust with the help of the
    Holy Spirit
    that dwells within us.

About Liturgy

Commissioning liturgical ministers: We live as disciples not for recognition but simply because it is what our faith in Christ demands. The gift of faith is all we need in order to accomplish what we are obliged to do as followers of Christ. It does not mean discipleship will be easy; it simply means that we are not alone. We have the Word to guide us, the sacraments to nourish us, and one another to be companions in service.

Today may be an appropriate day to acknowledge, bless, and commission liturgical ministers who have been preparing for service to the worshiping assembly. The Book of Blessings has a rite in chapter 61 for blessing readers (lectors), and in chapter 62, a rite for blessing altar servers, sacristans, musicians, and ushers. The structure of these blessings is quite simple. After the homily, suggested intercessions are incorporated into the usual intercessions of the Mass. In place of the concluding prayer of the intercessions, the pastor or another priest (or a deacon outside of Mass) prays the blessing over the liturgical ministers. The texts for these prayers are different enough that the blessing of readers should take place at a separate liturgy from the blessing of the other ministers.

Extraordinary ministers of Holy Communion have a completely different and more complex ritual for their blessing. Those who serve in this ministry must be authorized and commissioned by the local bishop or his delegate, who is usually the parish pastor, since the bishop must give faculties to extraordinary ministers in order to assist the church's ordinary ministers of Communion, that is, priests, deacons, and instituted acolytes.

After the homily, the candidates for this ministry are presented to the assembly. The pastor questions them regarding their resolve to undertake the duties of this office. Next, all stand as the pastor prays the blessing over the candidates. The ritual ends with the intercessions and a concluding prayer. At the preparation of gifts, the newly commissioned extraordinary ministers bring forward the bread and wine.

About Liturgical Music

Applause at the end of Mass: Often, the assembly is so moved by a Mass that they applaud at the end of the closing song, or, perhaps, after a particularly inspiring homily or other piece of music. Although we don't want to encourage adulation of anyone other than God, we can understand how the Holy Spirit can move hearts so deeply that we naturally want to express our thanksgiving and gratitude. In Western culture, we often show this through applause.

We can never anticipate when the Spirit will touch people's hearts deeply, and we certainly don't want to stifle the movement of the Spirit. In those moments of true communal praise for the work of the Spirit in the liturgy, we can let our thanksgiving rise in whatever way is natural for the assembly to express it.

Where this response can become problematic is when the assembly applauds at the end of Mass out of habit, regardless of how moving the liturgy was. In this case, your pastoral staff might discern how to address this with some gentle catechesis. The goal is not to chastise but to help parishioners understand that the work of the liturgy is a common work shared by all the members of the assembly.

When the assembly applauds at the end of Mass, one nonverbal way music ministers can help with catechesis is simply to applaud the assembly right back, clearly indicating that the gratitude is shared by all and is rightly credited to the goodness of God at work in the assembly.

OCTOBER 6, 2019
TWENTY-SEVENTH SUNDAY IN ORDINARY TIME

✠ SPIRITUALITY

GOSPEL ACCLAMATION
1 Thess 5:18

R̸. Alleluia, alleluia.
In all circumstances, give thanks,
for this is the will of God for you in Christ Jesus.
R̸. Alleluia, alleluia.

Gospel

Luke 17:11-19; L144C

As Jesus continued his journey to Jerusalem,
  he traveled through Samaria and Galilee.
As he was entering a village, ten lepers met him.
They stood at a distance from him
  and raised their voices, saying,
  "Jesus, Master! Have pity on us!"
And when he saw them, he said,
  "Go show yourselves to the priests."
As they were going they were cleansed.
And one of them, realizing he had been healed,
  returned, glorifying God in a loud voice;
  and he fell at the feet of Jesus and thanked him.
He was a Samaritan.
Jesus said in reply,
  "Ten were cleansed, were they not?
Where are the other nine?
Has none but this foreigner returned to give thanks to God?"
Then he said to him, "Stand up and go;
  your faith has saved you."

Reflecting on the Gospel

Expressing gratitude is essential for positive, healthy relationships. Many of the Psalms are prayers of gratitude. And of course the word "Eucharist" means "thanksgiving," essentially giving gratitude. A pithy rhyme sums it up best in exhorting us to cultivate an "attitude of gratitude."

Today Luke reminds us that Jesus is continuing his long journey to Jerusalem, now through Samaria and Galilee. We recall that Jesus is a Galilean for whom the Samaritans were considered foreigners. The most famous Samaritan is probably the character in one of Jesus' parables known as the Good Samaritan, who offers care and comfort to the man left for dead in the ditch. That such mercy and kindness were performed by a foreigner rather than a priest or Levite would have been shocking. Today we have not a fictional Samaritan but a Samaritan leper who interacted with Jesus, along with nine other lepers.

Of course, the challenge is that the Samaritan was the only one of the ten who, upon being healed, went back to thank Jesus. Jesus himself seems to be surprised that no one but the foreigner, the Samaritan, expressed gratitude. Even Jesus could be surprised. And even Jesus appreciated a word of thanks.

Then, the Samaritan is sent on his way with the knowledge that his faith saved him.

Among many lessons we learn in this short story is the power and importance of saying thank you, as well as the fact that salvation is extended even to the foreigner. We try to instill an "attitude of gratitude" in children, when we teach them to write thank-you notes after birthday parties, graduations, and even weddings. The lack of a thank you says much about the one who received the gift. An expression of gratitude comes from a place in the heart that recognizes the kindness done for another and acknowledges it, not because it's required, but because it is an authentic expression of one's thoughts and feelings. Though we instill this lesson in children, we hope it becomes internalized by the time they grow to adulthood. When it's not internalized it can be a bit surprising, as Jesus himself expresses: "Ten were cleansed, were they not? / Where are the other nine?"

Today let's make a point to express thanks to someone, cultivating an "attitude of gratitude."

Living the Paschal Mystery

Saying thank you is much more than polite manners. When we express thanks we are forging and strengthening personal bonds. Whether it be a phone call, a handwritten note, or even a text, acknowledging an action or gift with a word of thanks does as much if not more for the receiver of the gift as the giver. There are so many occasions in our daily life to express gratitude that it can become something of a prayer, punctuating our day. Our ancient forebears in faith knew this quite well. The Psalms give voice to much of this attitude, as does the eucharistic prayer itself, "Let us give thanks to the Lord our God."

This week, let's consider the opportunities we have to say thank you. In so doing, we echo our forebears in faith and our eternal Eucharist; and we likewise spread gratitude throughout the world.

Focusing the Gospel
Key words and phrases: Jesus, Master!

To the point: On the road to Jerusalem, Jesus meets ten lepers who call out to him, "Jesus, Master!" At the time of Jesus, people afflicted with skin diseases were quarantined from others to ensure that their disease would not spread. While keeping their distance the lepers attract Jesus' attention with their shouts. They call him, "Master!" Jesus' reputation as a healer must have preceded him. These lepers recognize Jesus' mastery over disease, which flees at the touch of his hand or even at a word from his mouth. In this healing, Jesus does more than restore the lepers' bodies to health, he also restores them back to their families, friends, and communities, whom they may now approach, touch, and share life with again.

Connecting the Gospel
to the first and second readings: In today's readings we have two healings from leprosy. The prophet Elisha heals Namaan the Aramean in the first reading. In the gospel, Jesus restores ten lepers to health, but only one, a Samaritan, returns to express gratitude and to glorify God. In both instances the one who is "other" and foreign is held to us as an example of faith. In his second letter to Timothy, St. Paul alludes to his imprisonment by saying, "I am suffering, / even to the point of chains." He continues, "But the word of God is not chained." We witness the freedom of the word of God—spoken by Elisha, enfleshed in Jesus—in the first reading and the gospel.

to experience: God's abounding kindness cannot be controlled. At times, we may be tempted to define who is inside or outside of the kingdom of God, but this is not our place. God's unchained word offers healing and wholeness to all.

Connecting the Responsorial Psalm
to the readings: The opening phrase of Psalm 98 expresses the joy of Namaan and the Samaritan leper freed from their illnesses, "Sing to the LORD a new song, / for he has done wondrous deeds." For both of these men, their skin diseases defined their lives for a time. Now that they have been "made clean" a new life can begin and, not only a new life of health, but also a new life in covenant with the God of Israel, the God of Jesus.

to psalmist preparation: We believe in and proclaim a God who is always ready to heal, forgive, and redeem. When we experience this healing and redemption in our own lives we are thrust into a new way of being, which requires new behaviors from us. To sing "a new song" to the Lord we must step out from what is familiar into a new creativity in our relationship with God. Where is God calling you to newness of life?

PROMPTS FOR FAITH-SHARING

Today's psalm enjoins us to "[s]ing to the LORD a new song." If you were to choose one song that symbolizes your spiritual journey at this point in your life, what would it be?

Speaking from prison St. Paul tells Timothy, "[T]he word of God is not chained." How have you experienced the word of God, alive and free, in your life? How do you bring this word to others?

In today's gospel one of the ten lepers returns to "give thanks to God" for being healed. How do you give thanks to God for blessings received?

How do you practice an "attitude of gratitude" in your daily life?

Model Penitential Act

Presider: In today's gospel ten lepers cry out to Jesus, "Jesus, Master! Have pity on us!" Let us pause for a moment to bring our own brokenness before the Lord and to ask for mercy and healing . . . [*pause*]

Lord Jesus, you restore the sick to health and the broken to wholeness: Lord, have mercy.

Christ Jesus, you are the Word of God unchained: Christ, have mercy.

Lord Jesus, your faithfulness extends to every generation: Lord, have mercy.

Homily Points

• In the opening chapters of the Gospel of Luke we are told again and again that this child that is being born is a gift for the entire world, not just for one particular family, religion, or nation. The angel proclaims to the shepherds in the fields of Bethlehem, "I proclaim to you good news of great joy that will be for all the people" (2:10; NABRE). In the temple Simeon prophesies that this child is "a light for revelation to the Gentiles, / and glory for your people Israel" (2:32; NABRE). This is not a new theme for the people of Israel. Today's psalm speaks of "the ends of the earth" seeing "the salvation by our God," and in the first reading Namaan the Aramean is healed of leprosy and vows to "no longer make burnt offerings or sacrifices to any other god except the Lord."

• In the gospel, it is the Samaritan among the ten lepers who returns to give thanks and glory to God. Jesus continually stretches his followers' understanding of who is included within the kingdom of God. He eats with sinners and tax collectors. He heals the daughter of the Syrophoenician woman and the servant of the Roman centurion. He upholds a Samaritan as the hero within a parable about how to love our neighbors, and today he tells the man who returns to give thanks, "[Y]our faith has saved you."

• In our lives of faith, how do we interact with people of differing nationalities, races, and religious beliefs? In the Second Vatican Council document, *Nostra Aetate*, we hear, "The Catholic Church rejects nothing of what is true and holy" in other religions. Can we look with the eyes of Christ and recognize the holy and the true in those who are different from us? Jesus certainly does.

Model Universal Prayer (Prayer of the Faithful)

Presider: With hearts full of thanksgiving we bring our prayers before the Lord.

Response: Lord, hear our prayer.

That the church throughout the world might continually offer praise and thanksgiving to God, the giver of all good gifts . . .

That leaders of the world extend welcome to refugees, immigrants, and visitors from foreign lands . . .

That those who are isolated from family, friends, and community due to illness or disease be surrounded by care and compassion . . .

That all gathered here might bring our brokenness to the Lord and experience healing and mercy . . .

Presider: God of healing, you desire for each of your children to have fullness of life. Hear our prayers that we might be signs of your love and compassion to all people. We ask this through Jesus, our Lord. Amen.

COLLECT

Let us pray.

Pause for silent prayer

May your grace, O Lord, we pray,
at all times go before us and follow after
and make us always determined
to carry out good works.
Through our Lord Jesus Christ, your Son,
who lives and reigns with you in the unity
　　　of the Holy Spirit,
one God, for ever and ever. **Amen.**

FIRST READING
2 Kgs 5:14-17

Naaman went down and plunged into the
　　　Jordan seven times
　　　at the word of Elisha, the man of God.
His flesh became again like the flesh of a
　　　little child,
　　　and he was clean of his leprosy.

Naaman returned with his whole retinue
　　　to the man of God.
On his arrival he stood before Elisha and
　　　said,
　　　"Now I know that there is no God in all
　　　　　the earth,
　　　except in Israel.
Please accept a gift from your servant."

Elisha replied, "As the Lord lives whom
　　　I serve, I will not take it";
　　　and despite Naaman's urging, he still
　　　　　refused.
Naaman said: "If you will not accept,
　　　please let me, your servant, have two
　　　　　mule-loads of earth,
　　　for I will no longer offer holocaust or
　　　　　sacrifice
　　　to any other god except to the LORD."

RESPONSORIAL PSALM
Ps 98:1, 2-3, 3-4

℟. (cf. 2b) The Lord has revealed to the
nations his saving power.

Sing to the LORD a new song,
　for he has done wondrous deeds;
his right hand has won victory for him,
　his holy arm.

℟. The Lord has revealed to the nations
his saving power.

The LORD has made his salvation known:
　in the sight of the nations he has
　　revealed his justice.
He has remembered his kindness and his
　faithfulness
　toward the house of Israel.

℟. The Lord has revealed to the nations
his saving power.

All the ends of the earth have seen
　the salvation by our God.
Sing joyfully to the LORD, all you lands:
　break into song; sing praise.

℟. The Lord has revealed to the nations
his saving power.

SECOND READING
2 Tim 2:8-13

Beloved:
Remember Jesus Christ, raised from the
　dead, a descendant of David:
　such is my gospel, for which I am
　　suffering,
　even to the point of chains, like a
　　criminal.
But the word of God is not chained.
Therefore, I bear with everything for the
　sake of those who are chosen,
　so that they too may obtain the
　　salvation that is in Christ Jesus,
　together with eternal glory.
This saying is trustworthy:
　If we have died with him
　　we shall also live with him;
　if we persevere
　　we shall also reign with him.
　But if we deny him
　　he will deny us.
　If we are unfaithful
　　he remains faithful,
　　for he cannot deny himself.

About Liturgy

Pastoral care of the sick: Today's readings about the miraculous curing of those who are sick can be a good opportunity for the homilist to reflect on the mystery of illness and healing. If appropriate and the assembly has prepared for it, you might also consider celebrating the sacrament of anointing of the sick within the Mass today.

In all of the prayers and liturgical texts concerning the pastoral care of the sick, the church stresses the importance of those who suffer from illness. Unlike our society that measures the worth of a person by their power or by what they can achieve, those who are sick, by their very weakness, are visible signs of the mystery of Christ's suffering and resurrection. In their very bodies, they carry both the wounds of Christ and the promise of salvation.

As we pray for the sick and for their recovery, we understand that the Christian approach to healing is not primarily about bodily restoration—although that is always our hope. The healing that Christ gives is a restoration of the one who is sick back into the assembly of the faithful. Illness, no matter how minor, isolates us in some way from our family, friends, and the community. We are unable to do the things we normally do when we are well. Especially when we are very sick, we cannot join with the assembly to give thanks in the celebration of the Eucharist.

When the church remembers the sick, and especially when it gathers with them in prayer, the sick are spiritually reconnected to the assembly. When they are gathered in the midst of the assembly, their very presence gives praise to God even before their bodies are healed. For Christians, the very purpose of healing—whether or not the body recovers—is always thanksgiving to God, for that is the primary work of the body of Christ.

About Initiation

Eucharistic prayer: Unlike catechumens, baptized candidates preparing for confirmation and Eucharist or for reception into the communion of the Catholic Church stay for the entire Mass, even though they cannot yet share in Communion. By their baptism, they are members of the order of the faithful. This means, they have the right and duty to pray the prayers of the faithful, which are the Creed, the universal prayer (general intercessions), and the eucharistic prayer. In response to the gift of their baptism, they, with all the baptized, are called to offer with Christ their sacrifice of praise and thanksgiving. The eucharistic prayer, embodied by a life of sacrifice, is the premier way all the baptized offer their thanksgiving to God.

About Liturgical Music

Song of praise: One of the most misunderstood moments in the Mass is the time after Communion. The General Instruction of the Roman Missal says that when the distribution of Communion has ended, there may be silence, or "if desired, a psalm or other canticle of praise or a hymn may also be sung by the whole congregation" (88).

The time after Communion is not meant for a meditation song sung by a soloist or the choir alone. It's not the time to feature a performance by the school children. If a song is sung after Communion, it is a song praising God sung by the entire assembly together. Having been healed by the Body and Blood of Christ, we must together give our thanks to God for so great a gift.

✝ SPIRITUALITY

GOSPEL ACCLAMATION
Heb 4:12

R̊. Alleluia, alleluia.
The word of God is living and effective,
discerning reflections and thoughts of the heart.
R̊. Alleluia, alleluia.

Gospel

Luke 18:1-8; L147C

Jesus told his disciples a parable
about the necessity for them
to pray always without becoming weary.
He said, "There was a judge in a
certain town
who neither feared God nor respected any human being.
And a widow in that town used to
come to him and say,
'Render a just decision for me
against my adversary.'
For a long time the judge was
unwilling, but eventually he
thought,
'While it is true that I neither
fear God nor respect any human
being,
because this widow keeps bothering me
I shall deliver a just decision for her
lest she finally come and strike me.'"
The Lord said, "Pay attention to what the
dishonest judge says.
Will not God then secure the rights of his
chosen ones
who call out to him day and night?
Will he be slow to answer them?
I tell you, he will see to it that justice is
done for them speedily.
But when the Son of Man comes, will he
find faith on earth?"

Reflecting on the Gospel

"Are we there yet? Are we there yet?" Persistent questioning bordering on bothering behavior is something with which we are all too familiar. Children have a knack for this, especially at an inquisitive age. But office drama can bring it out too, as well as adult family relationships. This is something Jesus was familiar with as well, as today's parable demonstrates.

In the parable, the judge is named "unjust." He is willing to (and likely has) perverted justice in cases before him, which is a clear violation of Mosaic Law. The point of naming him as an unjust judge is to make clear that his decision is for sale, whether to the widow (who likely has little money) or to her adversary. The judge is willing to make a decision in her favor simply to get rid of her, regardless of the merits of the case.

If an unjust judge is willing to do what is right simply to get rid of a persistent nag, how much more will a loving Father in heaven do what is right? This simple but profound insight forms the core of the message today.

Then, the gospel ends on a puzzling note, "But when the Son of Man comes, will he find faith on earth?" The story opens with the necessity to pray always, but concludes with a question about faith. It's as though the song started in a major key but ends on a minor. This is no mere "throwaway" line, but is something significant and even vital to interpreting the parable.

Luke writes at a time when Jesus' expected return has been delayed, thus the injunction "to pray always without becoming weary." Perhaps Luke himself is aware of some in his own generation who have given up on this expected return of Jesus, and gone back to a former way of life. This might be the reason, too, for the explanation of the parable on Jesus' lips: "Will he be slow to answer them? / I tell you, he will see to it that justice is done for them speedily." The ceaseless praying is about justice, not necessarily Christ's return. And then the story ends on a wistful note, wondering whether, when the Son of Man ultimately does return, he will find faith. Or will it be that the disciples have effectively abandoned the injunction to pray always and thereby lost their faith? This question, pertinent as it was nearly two thousand years ago, is applicable still.

Living the Paschal Mystery

It can be so difficult to be patient. Lessons we learned or attempted to learn in childhood are still with us as adults. Opportunities to learn patience abound! One clever prayer, inspired by St. Francis of Assisi, reads: "Lord, grant me patience . . . NOW!"

Early Christians, and maybe even modern, grew impatient with the delayed Parousia, the promised coming of Christ. Some Christians eventually abandoned this hope and therefore abandoned their discipleship. Luke's gospel is a reminder that disciples are "to pray always." And not only that, but to do so "without becoming weary." That may seem like a tall order, equivalent to telling a child on a long drive to "sit patiently; we'll be there soon enough." Yet, that's the exhortation we receive, along with a final question wondering whether the Son of Man will find faith when he returns. This, too, in a nod to the children in the car, might be the equivalent of, "I wonder if there will be ice cream for children who were quiet the entire way?" The issues that concerned the early church concern us. When will Jesus return? How long will this be? Is he slow to answer? The response is that we continue praying, doing justice, and God will act when he does.

Focusing the Gospel

Key words and phrases: Jesus told his disciples a parable / about the necessity for them to pray always without becoming weary.

To the point: What does it mean to pray and particularly to "pray always"? The widow in today's gospel continues to bring her petition to the judge, even when she has no reason to believe he will hear and answer her. Jesus presupposes that this relationship in prayer will require effort and persistence when he warns the disciples against "becoming weary." As in all relationships, sometimes communication is easy and at other times it might seem nearly impossible. In our relationship with God we are called to persevere even when it seems like our prayers are not being heard, much less answered. Unlike the widow, our Judge cares for us deeply and constantly works for our good.

Connecting the Gospel

to the first reading: In the book of Exodus Moses stands on the top of a hill with hands raised as Joshua engages the Amalekites in battle below. Throughout the day, as his arms grow weak, he is supported by Aaron and Hur. At this time in the story of the Exodus, the people have been delivered from slavery in Egypt into the freedom and desolation of the desert. Here they face new challenges. Where will they find water? What about food? In each instance God provides, first sweetening the bitter water at Marah and then providing quail and manna for the people every morning. Now the people face a new threat from the attacking Amalekites and once again they are assured that God is with them. Each answer to prayer builds up the relationship between God and God's people.

to experience: We no longer subscribe to the belief that God gives us power to vanquish our enemies in battle. Prayer is not a tool that we use to bend God's will to our own. Rather it is the other way around. Through prayer, we are changed, and change is often painful and tiring. Prayer demands spiritual perseverance. As Moses requires the support of Aaron and Hur to keep his hands upright, we also need the support of our community of faith to carry us in prayer when our strength is depleted.

Connecting the Responsorial Psalm

to the readings: There is only one reason to bring our needs, desires, and cares to the Lord in prayer: we believe in God's goodness and mercy. Indeed, the one we cry out to in prayer "neither slumbers nor sleeps," but "guard[s] [our] coming and [our] going, / both now and forever." From our ancestors in faith like Moses, Aaron, Hur, the disciples, St. Paul, and Timothy, we can learn to walk in the way of prayerful trust.

to psalmist preparation: Today's psalm is indeed good news. Our God is faithful. His protective love surrounds us at all times. How does this knowledge of God's care for you affect your daily life? What areas of struggle is God calling you to place in his hands?

PROMPTS FOR FAITH-SHARING

Aaron and Hur hold up Moses' arms as he prays for Joshua. Who supports your prayer life?

How do you understand the line from today's psalm, "The LORD will guard your coming and your going"?

In today's second reading St. Paul urges Timothy to "be persistent whether it is convenient or inconvenient." Where is God calling you to persistence right now in your spiritual life?

The gospel writer tells us the moral being illustrated in today's parable: we are to "pray always without becoming weary." How do you follow Jesus' command to pray always?

Model Penitential Act

Presider: In today's gospel Jesus calls us to persevere in prayer. Confident in God's mercy, let us lift up the broken places in our lives and ask for forgiveness and healing . . . [*pause*]

Lord Jesus, you call us to constant prayer: Lord, have mercy.

Christ Jesus, you are our help in times of trouble: Christ, have mercy.

Lord Jesus, you are the just One who will judge the living and the dead: Lord, have mercy.

Homily Points

• Some biblical scholars have viewed the second letter of St. Paul to Timothy as a farewell letter from the imprisoned apostle to his dearest and closest collaborator. In it, Paul encourages and exhorts Timothy to continue on with the mission of preaching the good news of Jesus Christ. In today's second reading Paul is clear: "[P]roclaim the word; / be persistent whether it is convenient or inconvenient." We see examples of this very persistence in today's first reading and gospel: Moses, with the help of Aaron and Hur, keeps his hands raised throughout the daylong battle with Amalek; the widow in Jesus' parable continues to pester the unfeeling judge to render justice for her.

• In a life of faith persistence is an important virtue to foster. Oftentimes we are called to be faithful even when we cannot see that our efforts are making any difference. We might embrace a new practice of prayer and continue on for weeks without seeing fruits in the way we interact with others or go about our day. We might take on a new ministry and devote time and energy to it only to become discouraged when it doesn't seem to be successful.

• In these times when we are tempted to give up it is helpful to "step back and take a long view," as Bishop Ken Untener wrote in his well-known prayer inspired by Archbishop Oscar Romero. He counsels, "We accomplish in our lifetime only a tiny fraction of the magnificent enterprise that is God's work. Nothing we do is complete, which is a way of saying that the Kingdom always lies beyond us." Let us pray always for the persistence to continue building this magnificent kingdom, even when the reality of it lies beyond us.

Model Universal Prayer (Prayer of the Faithful)

Presider: In today's gospel Jesus tells a parable to illustrate the necessity to pray always. With persistence and faith let us bring our needs before the Lord.

Response: Lord, hear our prayer.

That the leaders of the church might dedicate themselves to constant prayer . . .

That Christians throughout the world follow the widow's example in today's parable and persist in praying for the needs of the poor and the persecuted . . .

That those who are vulnerable within society receive the support necessary to live lives of purpose and meaning . . .

That all gathered here might help each other in leading lives devoted to prayer and worship . . .

Presider: God of love, you hear the cries of your people. You know our needs before we even voice them. Hear our intercessions this day that we might never cease to come to you in prayer, knowing you hear and answer us through Jesus Christ, our Lord. Amen.

COLLECT

Let us pray.

Pause for silent prayer

Almighty ever-living God,
grant that we may always conform our
will to yours
and serve your majesty in sincerity of
heart.
Through our Lord Jesus Christ, your Son,
who lives and reigns with you in the unity
of the Holy Spirit,
one God, for ever and ever. **Amen.**

FIRST READING

Exod 17:8-13

In those days, Amalek came and waged
war against Israel.
Moses, therefore, said to Joshua,
"Pick out certain men,
and tomorrow go out and engage
Amalek in battle.
I will be standing on top of the hill
with the staff of God in my hand."
So Joshua did as Moses told him:
he engaged Amalek in battle
after Moses had climbed to the top of
the hill with Aaron and Hur.
As long as Moses kept his hands raised
up,
Israel had the better of the fight,
but when he let his hands rest,
Amalek had the better of the fight.
Moses' hands, however, grew tired;
so they put a rock in place for him to
sit on.
Meanwhile Aaron and Hur supported his
hands,
one on one side and one on the other,
so that his hands remained steady till
sunset.
And Joshua mowed down Amalek and his
people
with the edge of the sword.

RESPONSORIAL PSALM

Ps 121:1-2, 3-4, 5-6, 7-8

R. (cf. 2) Our help is from the Lord, who
made heaven and earth.

I lift up my eyes toward the mountains;
whence shall help come to me?
My help is from the LORD,
who made heaven and earth.

R. Our help is from the Lord, who made
heaven and earth.

May he not suffer your foot to slip;
    may he slumber not who guards you:
indeed he neither slumbers nor sleeps,
    the guardian of Israel.

R℣. Our help is from the Lord, who made
    heaven and earth.

The LORD is your guardian; the LORD is
    your shade;
    he is beside you at your right hand.
The sun shall not harm you by day,
    nor the moon by night.

R℣. Our help is from the Lord, who made
    heaven and earth.

The LORD will guard you from all evil;
    he will guard your life.
The LORD will guard your coming and
    your going,
    both now and forever.

R℣. Our help is from the Lord, who made
    heaven and earth.

SECOND READING
2 Tim 3:14–4:2

Beloved:
Remain faithful to what you have learned
    and believed,
    because you know from whom you
        learned it,
    and that from infancy you have known
        the sacred Scriptures,
    which are capable of giving you
        wisdom for salvation
    through faith in Christ Jesus.
All Scripture is inspired by God
    and is useful for teaching, for refutation,
        for correction,
    and for training in righteousness,
    so that one who belongs to God may be
        competent,
    equipped for every good work.

I charge you in the presence of God and of
    Christ Jesus,
    who will judge the living and the dead,
    and by his appearing and his kingly
        power:
    proclaim the word;
    be persistent whether it is convenient or
        inconvenient;
    convince, reprimand, encourage through
        all patience and teaching.

About Liturgy

The Liturgy of the Hours: The rhythm of the church's liturgical cycle is one way we learn perseverance in prayer and how to pray always. Sunday is the heart of our week, with the Easter Triduum being the heart and highpoint of the liturgical year. This rhythm of prayer of the church is actually the constant prayer of Christ, who "continues his priestly work through his Church. The Church, by celebrating the Eucharist and by other means, especially the celebration of the divine office, is ceaselessly engaged in praising the Lord and interceding for the salvation of the entire world" (Constitution on the Sacred Liturgy 83). The main scriptural texts for the Divine Office are the Psalms, which were also the daily prayers of Jesus himself.

The Divine Office, also called the Liturgy of the Hours, is the official daily prayer of the church. The schedule of prayer for the Liturgy of the Hours pervades the entire day and night in order to sanctify the entire day to God. However, the two principal hours are Morning and Evening Prayer. The daily Office turns on the hinges of these two liturgies (89).

In Morning Prayer, the church gives thanks to God for the rising sun symbolizing the promise of Christ's resurrection. In Evening Prayer, we place the work we have done into the merciful hands of God and give thanks for all the blessings God has done for us through the course of our day.

Although daily Mass is a venerable tradition, the practice of consecrating the day to God through the celebration of the Liturgy of the Hours deepens our encounter with Christ, with whom we sing the psalms and canticles in ceaseless praise of God's blessings.

About Initiation

How long does RCIA take?: That's a common question many seekers might have when they come to us asking for baptism, reception, or the other sacraments of initiation. We might be tempted to show them the schedule of gatherings and to ease their anxiety by promising them initiation by a specific date on the calendar. But this is a disservice not only to the process of initiation but also to the good of the seeker.

The work of initiation belongs to the Holy Spirit. And the goal of the Spirit is not a person's completion of a course of study but their complete conversion of heart to the Father through Christ. Ultimately, this is about falling in love, and how long that takes cannot be predetermined.

About Liturgical Music

Song suggestions: Today's responsorial psalm (Psalm 121) gives us an opportunity to explore various settings that could be used not only as the psalm response but also for other parts of the Mass. Two in particular should be considered.

First, *Psallite*'s "Our Help Shall Come from the Lord" (*Sacred Song*) has a delightful and lilting refrain for the assembly that can be sung as a round. The verses are unmetered chant; however, the refrain alone might be very appropriate as a song of praise after Communion or even as a sending-forth song at the end of Mass leading into an instrumental improvisation.

The second is Tony Alonso's "I Will Lift My Eyes" (GIA), which combines the refrain of today's psalm with some of the writings of Thomas Merton. The rhythm and mood are steadfast, emphasizing the trust we are called to have in God though we may not know where God is leading us. This would be a wonderful song for the communion procession today.

OCTOBER 20, 2019
TWENTY-NINTH SUNDAY IN ORDINARY TIME

✠ SPIRITUALITY

GOSPEL ACCLAMATION
2 Cor 5:19

℟. Alleluia, alleluia.
God was reconciling the world to himself in Christ,
and entrusting to us the message of salvation.
℟. Alleluia, alleluia.

Gospel

Luke 18:9-14; L150C

Jesus addressed this parable
to those who were con-
vinced of their own
righteousness
and despised everyone else.
"Two people went up to the
temple area to pray;
one was a Pharisee and the
other was a tax collector.
The Pharisee took up his position and spoke this prayer
to himself,
'O God, I thank you that I am not like
the rest of humanity—
greedy, dishonest, adulterous—or
even like this tax collector.
I fast twice a week, and I pay tithes on
my whole income.'
But the tax collector stood off at a
distance
and would not even raise his eyes to
heaven
but beat his breast and prayed,
'O God, be merciful to me a sinner.'
I tell you, the latter went home justified,
not the former;
for whoever exalts himself will be
humbled,
and the one who humbles himself will
be exalted."

Reflecting on the Gospel

On this Thirtieth Sunday in Ordinary Time, the last Sunday of October, we come to the conclusion of the Lukan material on the journey to Jerusalem, also known as the "major insertion" from Luke 9:51 through 18:14. We began reading from this section in June, on the Thirteenth Sunday in Ordinary Time! So we've been with Luke's special material for some time and we remain on the journey to Jerusalem with Jesus even after this week.

The parable today strikes one's conscience with the desire most if not all Christians have to "be right with God." This desire animated the Jewish people of Jesus' time too, and it continues to be a goal of many religious people regardless of faith or denomination. But Jesus' parable penetrates deeply into the attitudes that often lie below the surface. And for the Pharisee in the parable, his attitudes were on full display. He prays in thanksgiving that he is not like "the rest of humanity" (quite a broad stroke!) or "even like this tax collector." The Pharisee has justified himself before God by following the rules, obeying Mosaic Law, doing "what God wants" as he understands it. On the other hand, the tax collector approaches God with sincere humility, admitting his sinfulness. For that, he, rather than the Pharisee, is justified, or "right with God."

We are not the authors of our own salvation. Nothing we do or accomplish will achieve a right relationship with God other than admitting we are sinners and asking for God's mercy. A fundamental temptation for religious people the world over is to fall into the false notion that by our actions we make ourselves pleasing to God. The good deeds we do, attending Mass, keeping holy days, praying the rosary or other special prayers, being active at the parish are all well and good. But none by itself or in combination with the others will put us in a right relationship with God. Only by acknowledging our own shortfalls without excuse and by simply relying on the mercy of God will we be placed upright before God. There is a reversal at work as the concluding line of the gospel indicates: "whoever exalts himself will be humbled, / and the one who humbles himself will be exalted."

Living the Paschal Mystery

The Christian life and the entire paschal mystery is a reversal of the norms, standards, and structures of the world. We do not need to look far in our world to see those who seek to exalt themselves. We too are likely part of that group from time to time if we are honest with ourselves. Each of us has a bit of the Pharisee's attitude. Today's parable tells us that we are to identify with the tax collector, the one who comes humbly before God confessing himself to be a sinner. Only by humbling oneself will exaltation come. And those who seek exaltation will be humbled. This echoes a theme announced by Mary's canticle in the opening chapter of the gospel. "He has thrown down the rulers from their thrones / but lifted up the lowly" (Luke 1:52).

Jesus, too, will be humbled to the point of death on the cross, and subsequently exalted to heaven. This fundamental reversal is an essential Christian message, and it can be difficult to absorb. In our modern world (and in the ancient) the proud are exalted, the humble are brought low. But we proclaim the Good News. The lowly will be exalted and the proud will be brought low. It is the paschal mystery.

Focusing the Gospel

Key words and phrases: O God, be merciful to me a sinner.

To the point: The words of the Pharisee and the tax collector provide an interesting contrast in prayer. The Pharisee is intent upon listing off his many attributes and even though he does this under the guise of giving God thanks for his many virtues, we get the sense that his prayer is about *him*, not about God. The tax collector's prayer is simple. He calls God "merciful" and identifies himself as a "sinner." Despite his lowly standing in the religious community, this tax collector, whose job requires him to collude with the Roman oppressors, has a relationship with the living God, the Merciful One. This is what sends him home justified, while the Pharisee, too full of himself to have room for God's mercy, leaves empty.

Connecting the Gospel

to the second reading: St. Paul's words to Timothy in some ways could be likened to the prayer of the Pharisee in the gospel parable. St. Paul writes, "I have competed well; I have finished the race; / I have kept the faith." But whereas the Pharisee is self-satisfied and content with his own righteousness, Paul is focused on the larger picture that all might come to salvation in Jesus. He gives credit to Jesus for the strength afforded him in his ministry to the Gentiles. Paul even prays that the failure of some to stand by him when he was arrested "not be held against them."

to experience: It is not the Pharisee's recognition of his own good works like fasting and tithing, and abstention from bad ones like greed, dishonesty, and adultery, that leads him to be the villain in this parable. Instead, it is the way his pride separates him from his fellow human being and from God that makes him the villain. Prayer should be an act of unity, not of exclusion.

Connecting the Responsorial Psalm

to the readings: The psalmist sings, "The Lord is close to the brokenhearted; / and those who are crushed in spirit he saves." We see this illustrated in Jesus' parable. The tax collector, who knows his sin, beats his breast, and stands "off at a distance," is restored to right relationship with God. Despite this we should not whitewash the tax collector's sins. As Jewish New Testament scholar Amy-Jill Levine writes, this tax collector "is probably rich, an agent of Rome, and, as a tax collector, has likely shown no mercy to others" (*Short Stories by Jesus*). We can assume he is in very real need of the mercy he asks for in the temple. And it is granted to him, for, as the psalmist knows, "The Lord redeems the lives of his servants; / and no one incurs guilt who takes refuge in him."

to psalmist preparation: We believe in a God of perfect justice and perfect mercy. Where in your life are you in need of God's justice? Where do you experience God's mercy?

PROMPTS FOR FAITH-SHARING

The author of Sirach tells us, "Give to the Most High as he has given to you" (35:12; NABRE). What are the most precious gifts you have received from the Lord? How are you using these gifts to build God's kingdom?

The psalmist sings, "The Lord is close to the brokenhearted; / and those who are crushed in spirit he saves." How have you experienced God's presence in times of extreme grief and sorrow?

Nearing the end of his letter to Timothy, St. Paul writes, "I have competed well; I have finished the race; / I have kept the faith." Does this metaphor of the spiritual life as a race speak to you? Why or why not?

If Jesus were to tell the parable of the Pharisee and the Tax Collector in your community, which characters would he use to illustrate his point about the humble and the proud? Who is given spiritual status in your community and who is looked down on?

Model Penitential Act

Presider: In the gospel parable of the Pharisee and the tax collector, the Pharisee is too focused on his own merits to accept God's mercy. For the times that pride has separated us from the love of God let us pause to ask for pardon and forgiveness . . . [*pause*]

Lord Jesus, you exalt the humble and humble the exalted: Lord, have mercy.

Christ Jesus, you call us to repentance: Christ, have mercy.

Lord Jesus, you redeem the souls of sinners and heal the brokenhearted: Lord, have mercy.

Homily Points

• There is a famous Zen Buddhist story about a man of import who goes to visit a spiritual master asking to be taught. The master suggests they begin by sharing a cup of tea. He fills his visitor's cup, but continues to pour even as the tea spills over the top and onto the table. When his visitor protests, the master tells him, "You are like this cup. You are so full of your own ideas and opinions there is no room for teaching. Come back when your cup is empty."

• And so it is with the Pharisee within our parable today. As he takes his position in the temple we are told he "spoke this prayer to himself." Even though he begins with the words, "O God," it does seem indeed that he is mostly talking to himself. With self-satisfied contentment he lists off his own merits. The only mention of anyone other than himself is to draw a comparison between his own righteousness and the depravity of the tax collector. In the words of Jesus from Matthew's gospel, it seems that this Pharisee has already received his reward (6:1-18), the reward of feeling superior to others. The tax collector's prayer is a perfect foil for the Pharisee's bragging. His words are simple and direct, "O God, be merciful to me a sinner." He has a single focus on the mercy of God.

• Today's parable presents a challenge to us. Do we dare to place ourselves in the company of the tax collector, the public sinner? There is a temptation to mask our own sinfulness and to hide it under layers of propriety and self-righteousness. This is not what Jesus would have us do. He longs to be with us—wounds and warts and all. Can we empty our cups and invite him in?

Model Universal Prayer (Prayer of the Faithful)

Presider: With humble hearts let us bring our prayers before the Lord.

Response: Lord, hear our prayer.

That the church throughout the world be a sanctuary and spiritual home for repentant sinners and those in search of mercy . . .

That leaders of nations humbly seek to serve their people without care for political and personal gain . . .

That those who are nearing the end of life receive the compassionate care and spiritual support they need . . .

That all gathered here embrace a life of humble prayer and self-less service . . .

Presider: God of compassion, you are near to the brokenhearted and those whose spirits are crushed. Hear our prayers that we might bring your love to all those in need. We ask this through Jesus Christ, our Lord. Amen.

COLLECT

Let us pray.

Pause for silent prayer

Almighty ever-living God,
increase our faith, hope and charity,
and make us love what you command,
so that we may merit what you promise.
Through our Lord Jesus Christ, your Son,
who lives and reigns with you in the unity
    of the Holy Spirit,
one God, for ever and ever. **Amen.**

FIRST READING

Sir 35:12-14, 16-18

The Lord is a God of justice,
    who knows no favorites.
Though not unduly partial toward the
        weak,
    yet he hears the cry of the oppressed.
The Lord is not deaf to the wail of the
        orphan,
    nor to the widow when she pours out
        her complaint.
The one who serves God willingly is
        heard;
    his petition reaches the heavens.
The prayer of the lowly pierces the clouds;
    it does not rest till it reaches its goal,
nor will it withdraw till the Most High
        responds,
    judges justly and affirms the right,
and the Lord will not delay.

RESPONSORIAL PSALM

Ps 34:2-3, 17-18, 19, 23

℞. (7a) The Lord hears the cry of the poor.

I will bless the Lord at all times;
    his praise shall be ever in my mouth.
Let my soul glory in the Lord;
    the lowly will hear me and be glad.

℞. The Lord hears the cry of the poor.

The Lord confronts the evildoers,
    to destroy remembrance of them from
        the earth.
When the just cry out, the Lord hears
        them,
    and from all their distress he rescues
        them.

℞. The Lord hears the cry of the poor.

The Lord is close to the brokenhearted;
    and those who are crushed in spirit he
        saves.
The Lord redeems the lives of his
        servants;
    no one incurs guilt who takes refuge in
        him.

R℣. The Lord hears the cry of the poor.

SECOND READING
2 Tim 4:6-8, 16-18

Beloved:
I am already being poured out like a
        libation,
    and the time of my departure is at
        hand.
I have competed well; I have finished the
        race;
    I have kept the faith.
From now on the crown of righteousness
        awaits me,
    which the Lord, the just judge,
    will award to me on that day, and not
        only to me,
    but to all who have longed for his
        appearance.

At my first defense no one appeared on
        my behalf,
    but everyone deserted me.
May it not be held against them!
But the Lord stood by me and gave me
        strength,
    so that through me the proclamation
        might be completed
    and all the Gentiles might hear it.
And I was rescued from the lion's mouth.
The Lord will rescue me from every evil
        threat
    and will bring me safe to his heavenly
        kingdom.
To him be glory forever and ever. Amen.

About Liturgy

That kind of liturgist: Shortly after I started my first job as a liturgist, I was invited by one of the parish groups to give a talk on liturgy at their monthly meeting. They wanted to begin the meeting with an adapted Morning Prayer from the Liturgy of the Hours, which they would prepare, and asked if I would lead the singing. I was more than happy to and looked forward to speaking with them. Fresh out of graduate school, this would be my first chance to put my shiny new liturgy degree to work helping people know how to do liturgy well.

The day of the talk came and I arrived early. The group leader gave me a copy of the script for the prayer they prepared, and I was horrified! Everything was wrong. The psalm was in the wrong place, the dialogues weren't right, and they had chosen a gospel reading instead of one from the Old Testament or the epistles.

I couldn't have them go through with this, not on my watch! I stormed right up to the leaders and demanded that they revise the script. They could see how upset I was and graciously indulged me. It was a flurry of activity in the sacristy during that half hour before prayer as they looked for a different reading and informed the nervous lector, crossed out lines and drew arrows in the script for the presider showing the new order of prayers, and rewrote dialogues to my satisfaction. I was pleased knowing I had saved the liturgy that day. What would they have done if I had not corrected them?

They would have prayed just fine, in fact. The Spirit would have been just as present and powerful without my intervention. Most importantly, they would have felt loved and respected and not scolded like children. I would have learned humility and felt awe and wonder at the goodness and passion of God's people. Instead, that day, I just felt smug and loved the liturgy more than I loved the people called to do the liturgy.

It would be years later before I truly understood what I had done that day, and the realization gave me the gift of remorse, which has helped me try to be more humble. Every day since I have done penance for being *that* kind of liturgist. Each day I pray, "O God, be merciful to me a sinner."

About Liturgical Music

Transparent ministry: Most music ministers really want to support and assist the assembly. They get that their job is to enhance the singing and not overpower the song of the assembly. Yet sometimes, our habits get the best of us, and our efforts actually impede our goal. Here are some things to watch for as you strive to make yourselves transparent and humble music ministers.

Use the microphone only when the assembly needs you to: if you're the cantor or song leader, during songs, acclamations, and psalm refrains that the assembly knows well, back off of the mic. Better yet, let the assembly sing them without you.

Louder isn't always more supportive: if the assembly is tentative in their singing, your singing or playing louder won't always help them. When cantors, choirs, and musicians sing or play louder, especially through amplification, to try to get the assembly singing more confidently, the assembly will often just sit back and let you do the singing for them. When the assembly can hear themselves, then they will actually sing better. Teach music *a cappella* and, on occasion, sing refrains or even entire songs without accompaniment.

GOSPEL ACCLAMATION
Matt 11:28

℟. Alleluia, alleluia.
Come to me, all you who labor and are burdened,
and I will give you rest, says the Lord.
℟. Alleluia, alleluia.

Gospel

Matt 5:1-12a; L667

When Jesus saw the crowds, he
    went up the mountain,
    and after he had sat down, his
        disciples came to him.
He began to teach them, saying:

"Blessed are the poor in spirit,
    for theirs is the Kingdom of
        heaven.
Blessed are they who mourn,
    for they will be comforted.
Blessed are the meek,
    for they will inherit the
        land.
Blessed are they who hunger
    and thirst for righteousness,
    for they will be satisfied.
Blessed are the merciful,
    for they will be shown mercy.
Blessed are the clean of heart,
    for they will see God.
Blessed are the peacemakers,
    for they will be called children of
        God.
Blessed are they who are persecuted
    for the sake of righteousness,
    for theirs is the Kingdom of
        heaven.
Blessed are you when they insult you
    and persecute you
    and utter every kind of evil against
        you falsely because of me.
Rejoice and be glad,
    for your reward will be great in
        heaven."

See Appendix A., p. 313, for the other readings.

Reflecting on the Gospel

On this feast of All Saints the church gives us the Beatitudes of the Gospel of Matthew, sometimes called a "self-portrait" of Jesus. We sometimes wonder what a life of Christ would look like in a different age or culture, or from different perspectives. For this we have the saints. Each saint takes as a keynote the life and mission of Jesus, then plays this song in his or her own time and place as one expression of the Christian life. St. Francis of Assisi shows how this is done in thirteenth-century Italy. St. Ignatius of Loyola shows how this is done in Reformation Spain. Mother Teresa shows how this is done in the late twentieth century. Our task is to play this song as well in our own time and place.

The gospel begins with Jesus ascending a mountain, taking his seat, and issuing these Beatitudes in a clear echo of the Sinai covenant when God himself issued the Law to Moses. It's as though Matthew is saying this teaching of Jesus is the (new) law. It enjoys pride of place.

In fact, chapters 5 through 7 are referred to as the Sermon on the Mount, opened by the Beatitudes. But it is the entire three chapters that might be considered the new "law" for the disciples.

The nine Beatitudes that Matthew gives us are translated into English as "Blessed," but they could just as easily be translated as "Happy" as in "Happy are the poor in spirit." These Beatitudes express a different way of approaching the world. The poor in spirit in Jesus' day were certainly not considered "blessed" or "happy," but for Jesus theirs was the kingdom of heaven. For Jesus, those mourning would be comforted and the meek would inherit the earth. A reversal was in order to be brought about by God himself. The kingdoms of this world do not alleviate all poverty and mourning. But God will! This doesn't mean we don't work to alleviate suffering, poverty, and the like, but it will happen once and for all with God himself as king.

The example of the saints shows us what the Christian life, the self-portrait of Jesus, looks like throughout history. We have many examples. Now let's go do this ourselves, live the Beatitudes in our time and place.

Living the Paschal Mystery

As the Beatitudes are often considered a self-portrait of Jesus, we might apply them to ourselves as disciples too. The disciples, like Jesus himself, are those who hunger and thirst for righteousness; they are merciful, clean of heart, and peacemakers. In a sense, the Beatitudes are our mission statement. Though God will bring about his kingdom in the end, that does not excuse us from doing the work of justice or bringing about peace. Paul VI showed the close link between the two when he said, "If you want peace, work for justice" (World Day of Peace, 1972). We believe in both the "already" and the "not yet" of salvation. There will be a time when justice and peace rule, but we are not there yet. So we, like the many disciples and saints who have come before us, work toward it, knowing that only God can ultimately bring it about to completion.

Focusing the Gospel
Key words and phrases: Blessed

To the point: Merriam-Webster's dictionary has two definitions for blessed. If used as an adjective "blessed" means "made holy, consecrated." If used as a noun the definition is "those who live with God in heaven." For today's feast both definitions fit. The saints lived consecrated lives that gave glory to God. From heaven they continue to illumine the way for their fellow human beings. May we look to their blessedness as we embrace our own.

Model Rite for the Blessing and Sprinkling of Water
Presider: In the waters of Baptism we have been washed clean and sealed as Christ's own. May this water remind us of our blessedness and inspire us to follow in the footsteps of the saints . . . [pause]
    [continue with The Roman Missal, Appendix II]

Model Universal Prayer (Prayer of the Faithful)
Presider: Together with all holy men and women throughout the ages we lift up our needs and the needs of our world to our loving God.

Response: Lord, hear our prayer.

That the church be a beacon of blessing within the darkness and chaos of the world . . .

That all people come to know the blessedness, happiness, and beauty of living a life faithful to the beatitudes . . .

That all those oppressed by grief and persecution might find hope and comfort . . .

That all gathered here, inspired by the lives of the saints, might persevere in the life of faith . . .

Presider: Holy God, throughout the ages you have called holy men, women, and children to live lives of peace, beauty, and blessing. Hear our prayers that we might answer your call to holiness within our own lives. We ask this through Christ our Lord. Amen.

About Liturgy
Saints among us: Our church walls are filled with images of the saints, and almost every parish has statues, icons, murals, banners, or windows depicting their stories. The saints are all around us! Use your parish church and the surrounding grounds to help people get to know the holy women and men of our faith.

Highlight these places with flowers, fabrics, or extra candles. Point them out in the homily, and tell the stories behind them. Focus especially on your parish's or diocese's patron saint. If your parish is preparing an altar of the dead (see "About Liturgy" for November 2), consider also preparing an altar of the saints where parishioners can bring in holy cards, small statues, icons, or other images of their favorite saint.

Today is an appropriate day to sing the Litany of the Saints, especially as the entrance song or during the preparation of gifts. Another place to consider using the Litany is in place of the intercessions. In the appendix of the Rite of Baptism, there is a Litany of the Saints that is used for solemn intercessions. Be sure to include your parish's saint and other saints important to your local area.

FOR REFLECTION

• In the second reading from the first letter of St. John we read, "Beloved, we are God's children now." What implication does this have for your spirituality?

• Today we read from the Beatitudes, one of the most famous passages in all Scripture. Which Beatitude do you find most challenging? How might you seek to live this Beatitude in your own life?

• On this feast of All Saints, what saint have you found particularly inspiring in your journey of faith?

Homily Points
• The Beatitudes are often translated using the words "blessed" or "happy." Dominican sister Carla Mae Streeter proposes another word we could substitute: "beautiful." She says, "What moves us is the beauty of someone's life" (*Foundations of Spirituality*, 2012). This is particularly true when we look at the stories of the saints. Each contains beauty that calls to us.

• Within this beauty we see the face of God revealed in new ways. Each saint's life could be considered one facet of an infinite diamond. As we celebrate the saints we remember that this is what we are called to as well. To lead lives of beauty, happiness, blessedness and to show the face of God to all those we meet.

GOSPEL ACCLAMATION
See John 6:40

This is the will of my Father, says the Lord,
that everyone who sees the Son and believes in
    him
may have eternal life.

Gospel

John 6:37-40; L668

Jesus said to the crowds:
"Everything that the Father gives me
        will come to me,
    and I will not reject anyone who
            comes to me,
        because I came down from heaven
            not to do my own will
        but the will of the one who sent me.
And this is the will of the one who sent
        me,
    that I should not lose anything of
            what he gave me,
    but that I should raise it on the last
            day.
For this is the will of my Father,
    that everyone who sees the Son and
            believes in him
    may have eternal life,
    and I shall raise him on the last day."

See Appendix A., p. 314, for the other readings.

Additional reading choices are in the Lectionary
*for Mass (L668) or those given in the Masses for
the Dead (L1011–1016).*

Reflecting on the Gospel

Yesterday we celebrated the feast of All Saints, those heroes of the faith who have gone before us as exemplars, and there are thousands! These are the ones who have been "officially" proclaimed by the church as saints. But we know there are many more saints than those. Even the apostle Paul (himself a saint) addressed his letters to the "saints" in the various locales to which he wrote. The term does not mean a "holy roller," but instead it means one who is set apart for service to God. Those who did this exceptionally well are recognized by the church, but as noted above there are many who live lives of service to God but are not given the formal title of "saint."

In this latter category are likely those members of our family who have gone before us in faith: all our parents, grandparents, and even great-grandparents with all of their siblings and extended families as well may fall into this category. Christianity is a faith that is passed down through storytelling, one person telling another about what God has done in Christ. Many of these stories are in the Bible, but after two thousand years we have many more stories of heroic figures of faith to tell. And these heroes of faith extend to those we have known and loved.

The gospel reading from John reminds us that Jesus does not reject anyone who comes to him. Nor does he lose anything given to him. Rather, on the last day he will raise it up. This hope of eternal life and reconnecting with those we love who have gone before us is an essential element of Christian faith. We have this hope precisely because Jesus himself rose from the dead and promised he would do the same for those who come to him.

On this day of commemoration of all the faithful departed, let us celebrate their lives by sharing stories of faith, enkindling in us that Christian hope which inspires.

Living the Paschal Mystery

As the weather is turning colder and we approach the winter season, it seems an apt time to recall those who have gone before us. All lived lives of Christian hope built on the promise of Jesus to raise them up on the last day. This is our hope too, inspired by that same promise. And there will be Christians who come after us who might be remembering us too. We are in a long line of disciples who believe in Jesus, the one sent by the Father. And with that belief comes eternal life. Our own personal death is not the end, and Jesus' own death was not the end for him. Resurrection and new life await. This is not a restoration of the old, but something new and transformative when we will all be united in him, generations past and those still to come. This is the paschal mystery where dying leads to new life. One end leads to a beginning, and the tomb opens to the resurrection. At this time of year, when darkness and cold increase, our Christian hope in eternal life remains resilient.

Focusing the Gospel

Key words and phrases: I will not reject anyone who comes to me.

To the point: In our short gospel today, three times Jesus proclaims his radical hospitality to all who sincerely seek him. The number three in the Bible is a symbol of completeness. In our God and in his Son we see a complete commitment to raising the souls of the faithful departed. In the uncertainty of existence, and certainty of death, we can rest in the knowledge that with God there is always abundant life.

Model Penitential Act

Presider: As we gather together to commemorate the souls of all the faithful departed, let us pause to remember the times our own faith has wavered and to ask for pardon and healing . . . [*pause*]

    Lord Jesus, you came to do the will of the Father: Lord, have mercy.

    Christ Jesus, you welcome all who come to you: Christ, have mercy.

    Lord Jesus, you are the Lord of everlasting life: Lord, have mercy.

Model Universal Prayer (Prayer of the Faithful)

Presider: United with our brothers and sisters who have fallen asleep in the hope of the resurrection, let us lift up our prayers to the Lord.

Response: Lord, hear our prayer.

That, strengthened by the faith of countless disciples throughout the ages, the church might grow in holiness and fidelity to the Lord's will . . .

That nations throughout the world be guided by the wisdom of their ancestors in caring for the earth . . .

That those grieving the loss of a loved one may be comforted by the Lord of everlasting life . . .

That all gathered here might extend the radical hospitality of Jesus to all those we meet . . .

Presider: God of eternal life, you desire to raise all souls to the abundance of heaven. Hear our prayers that we, and all people, might lead lives of holiness and peace. We ask this through Christ our Lord. Amen.

About Liturgy

Altar of the dead: On November 1st and 2nd in Mexico, families remember their beloved dead by preparing an *altarcito de los muertos* (little altar of the dead) in their homes. There they place photos of their deceased loved ones and decorate the table with candles, crosses, marigolds, and other flowers. Often, they include some of their loved ones' favorite foods and drinks. They also add colorful fabrics, paper cutouts, and sugar candies in the shape of skulls and skeletons. These are not meant to be macabre images but are ways to say, "O Death, where is your sting?" Thus, these days of *Dia de los Muertos* are joyful times for spending with family and friends, telling the stories of our loved ones, and once again making space for their memory.

Some Catholic churches help their Mexican communities continue this tradition by building *altarcitos* in a church or parish hall alcove. Throughout November, they invite parishioners to add the photos of their loved ones to the altar. Sometimes they begin and end the month with some kind of prayer at the *altarcito* in memory of the dead.

COLLECT (from the first Mass)
Let us pray.

Pause for silent prayer

Listen kindly to our prayers, O Lord,
and, as our faith in your Son,
raised from the dead, is deepened,
so may our hope of resurrection for your
    departed servants
also find new strength.
Through our Lord Jesus Christ, your Son,
who lives and reigns with you in the unity of
    the Holy Spirit,
one God, for ever and ever. **Amen.**

FOR REFLECTION

• What is a treasured story of faith within your family?

• What cultural, family, or religious traditions shape your celebration of the feast of All Souls' Day?

• Even in the event of the death of a loved one, how do you experience the God of abundant life?

Homily Points

• Today's gospel comes from the bread of life discourse in John's gospel where Jesus tells his disciples, "I am the bread of life; whoever comes to me will never hunger, and whoever believes in me will never thirst" (6:35; NABRE). In the Eucharist, by which we receive Jesus, the Bread of Life, we are united again with the loved ones who have gone before us. This bread, which sustained them, now sustains us.

• On All Souls' Day we celebrate the relationship we continue to have with past generations. They form links on a chain leading back to the time of Christ, to the people who stood with him on the shores of the Sea of Galilee and asked, "Sir, give us this bread always" (6:34; NABRE). Generations upon generations have echoed this prayer and, nourished by the bread of life, we are strengthened to form our link on the chain of faith.

✝ SPIRITUALITY

GOSPEL ACCLAMATION
John 3:16

℟. Alleluia, alleluia.
God so loved the world that he gave his only Son,
so that everyone who believes in him might have
    eternal life.
℟. Alleluia, alleluia.

Gospel   Luke 19:1-10; L153C

At that time, Jesus came to
    Jericho and intended to pass
    through the town.
Now a man there named
    Zacchaeus,
  who was a chief tax collector
      and also a wealthy man,
  was seeking to see who Jesus
      was;
  but he could not see him be-
      cause of the crowd,
  for he was short in stature.
So he ran ahead and climbed a
    sycamore tree in order to see Jesus,
  who was about to pass that way.
When he reached the place, Jesus looked
    up and said,
  "Zacchaeus, come down quickly,
  for today I must stay at your house."
And he came down quickly and received
    him with joy.
When they all saw this, they began to
    grumble, saying,
  "He has gone to stay at the house of a
      sinner."
But Zacchaeus stood there and said to the
    Lord,
  "Behold, half of my possessions, Lord,
      I shall give to the poor,
  and if I have extorted anything from
      anyone
  I shall repay it four times over."
And Jesus said to him,
  "Today salvation has come to this
      house
  because this man too is a descendant
      of Abraham.
For the Son of Man has come to seek
    and to save what was lost."

Reflecting on the Gospel

Crowds are difficult places to be for many of us, especially those of short stature! Even at relatively tame events like a city parade, the hustle and bustle and bumps and jolts can be challenging, and that's before we see anything. With our example of a parade, sometimes parents will raise children up on their shoulders to give them a better glimpse. Zacchaeus seems to have had a similar idea when he decided to climb a sycamore tree to have a better view. Though a tax collector and a very wealthy man, Jesus chose to stay with him.

What follows develops a major Lukan theme: the right use of wealth. We recall the many other stories in Luke's gospel that touch on this theme as well: the Prodigal Son, the Rich Man and Lazarus, and the Dishonest Steward, to name a few. These were parables. The story of Zacchaeus is about Jesus and his interaction with the wealthy tax collector. Interestingly, he does not tell him to sell his possessions and give them all to the poor. That commandment is reserved for only one person, a lover of money whose sole love prevented him from following Jesus (Luke 18:18-23). No, Zacchaeus does not receive that command. He tells Jesus that he will give half of his possessions to the poor. Moreover, any extortion will be paid back four times over. With that, he is right with the Lord. So the story is about the right use of wealth, in this case, up to half of his money for the poor, making amends for any unsavory activity in his business, and paying four times anything he might have extorted.

The question naturally comes to us, how do we use our wealth? How have we gained it? Are we willing to make amends if some of our resources were ill-gotten? Such amends are much more than merely paying a fine as a part of doing business. Zacchaeus offers up to four times the amount extorted if such a thing happened.

In the end, this "sinner," for he is a tax collector, is willing to use his money rightly, and for that he has salvation. We too can examine how we use our money, resources, and wealth. Is it for the building up of other people or for our own self-hording or indulgence? Our own salvation may hang in the balance.

Living the Paschal Mystery

The right use of money has been a perennial challenge for Christians and many others. We are not in the "rat race" to enrich ourselves but we undoubtedly want to provide for our families and give them the care and concern that leads to a healthy, productive life. Yet we hear injunctions to give to the poor, in one case to sell everything and give it to the poor! Luke's admonition in today's story is not that every Christian disciple sell everything and give it to the poor. That command was for one person, for whom wealth had become a true obstacle to following Jesus. Rather, each disciple is required to use wealth and money rightly. What that looks like will be as different as each person. But ultimately, we are not disciples of money. We are disciples of Christ. And nobody can serve two masters. Perhaps one question we might ask ourselves today is: Do we serve money, or does our money serve us? In Zacchaeus's case, his wealth served him. He was master over his wealth and was willing to give away a substantial portion. What are we willing to give away to serve the Lord. Is there anything we serve rather than him?

Focusing the Gospel

Key words and phrases: Zacchaeus . . . was seeking to see who Jesus was.

To the point: In the gospel we hear that both Zacchaeus and Jesus share something in common. They are both "seekers." In the beginning of this gospel passage we are told that Zacchaeus is "seeking to see who Jesus was" and at the end Jesus discloses that he is in fact the one who has "come to seek / and to save what was lost." To seek requires effort and an ability to be open to what one might find. Jesus and Zacchaeus are both rewarded in their seeking. Their search ends with joy and communion.

Connecting the Gospel

to the first reading: When Jesus enters Jericho his plan is to "pass through the town." Upon seeing Zacchaeus perched in the sycamore, however, this plan changes, and Jesus tells this man who is a wealthy, chief tax collector, "[C]ome down quickly, / for today I must stay at your house." The crowd surrounding Jesus is surprised and dismayed. Why would this man who has profited from his collaboration with a foreign, oppressive government be rewarded with a personal invitation from Jesus? Who is this God who seeks the lost? The author of the book of Wisdom names him the "Ruler and Lover of souls." This divine ruler and lover can "loathe nothing" he has made, and "overlook[s] sins for the sake of repentance" (NABRE).

to experience: As with the parable of the Prodigal Son we are left with the question, can we be happy at the repentance and forgiveness of a sinner? If not, we are not fit for the kingdom of God as revealed by our first reading and gospel today.

Connecting the Responsorial Psalm

to the readings: Psalm 145 is written as an acrostic, with each verse beginning with a successive letter of the Hebrew alphabet. Its theme covers the "greatness and goodness of God." How fitting, therefore, that it uses every letter available to praise that which is limitless and infinite. As first-century Jews, both Jesus and Zacchaeus would have grown up with the words of the psalms citing God's grandeur and mercy. While the crowd surrounding Jesus is aghast at his decision to stay with such a well-known sinner, it makes sense when we remember that this is the Lord who is "gracious and merciful, / slow to anger and of great kindness," who is "faithful in all his words, / and holy in all his works."

to psalmist preparation: Sometimes it seems that we are at a loss for words when we think about God. This week, take some time to try and write your own acrostic of praise. Beginning with each letter of the alphabet write a statement about the God who has been with you even from your mother's womb, the one who seeks the lost, and shows sinners the way.

PROMPTS FOR FAITH-SHARING

The book of Wisdom names God the "Ruler and Lover of souls." Other than Father, Son, and Holy Spirit, what name for God are you most drawn to at this point in your spiritual journey?

St. Paul tells the Thessalonians, "We always pray for you, / that our God may make you worthy of his calling / and powerfully bring to fulfillment every good purpose / and every effort of faith." How does your family and/or parish practice intercessory prayer?

In the gospel, Zacchaeus climbs a sycamore tree because he is "seeking to see . . . Jesus." What helps you to see Jesus clearly?

How would you answer the question, Do I serve money or does my money serve me?

Model Penitential Act

Presider: In today's gospel, Zacchaeus, a tax collector and a sinner, climbs a sycamore tree so he can see Jesus. Let us pause to prepare ourselves to encounter the Lord in Word and sacrament today . . . [*pause*]

Lord Jesus, you came to seek and save the lost: Lord, have mercy.

Christ Jesus, you are Son of Man and Son of God: Christ, have mercy.

Lord Jesus, you are trustworthy in all your words and loving in all your works: Lord, have mercy.

Homily Points

• In today's gospel you could say that there are three distinct characters: Zacchaeus, Jesus, and the crowd. "[S]eeking to see . . . Jesus," Zacchaeus runs ahead of the crowd to perch on the limb of a sycamore tree. Instead of a stationary group of bystanders watching Jesus make his way through the streets of Jericho, this is a mobile crowd following Jesus on his journey to Jerusalem. Even though they are walking with Jesus and surrounding him they don't seem to know who he is. But they think they know. When Jesus looks up and sees Zacchaeus perched on a limb, he stops, and calls the man by name and tells him, "[T]oday I must stay at your house," and the crowd is outraged.

• Zacchaeus climbs down from the tree and receives Jesus with joy. But the others, the ones who have been traveling with Jesus, grumble. Somewhere along their journey they've stopped seeking to see who Jesus is, and they've started expecting him to be who they want him to be. And that isn't someone who calls sinners by name and goes to dine with them.

• This moment in Jericho with Zacchaeus and the crowd is the last occurrence in Luke's gospel before Jesus enters Jerusalem on the eve of his passion, death, and resurrection, and so the revelation he offers to Zacchaeus and the crowd is all the more striking. He tells them that "the Son of Man has come to seek / and to save what was lost." And this is indeed good news, but only for those who are willing to identify with "the lost." And so today, we might ask ourselves, where do we stand? Are we most comfortable among the crowd surrounding Jesus, shrouded in our false confidence that we know the identity of the Son of Man and who he would welcome into his company? Or do we dare to go out on the limb of the sycamore tree with Zacchaeus and seek to see who Jesus really is?

Model Universal Prayer (Prayer of the Faithful)

Presider: With humble spirits and contrite hearts let us bring our prayers before the Lord.

Response: Lord, hear our prayer.

That leaders of the church seek to use resources and wealth for the good of those in need . . .

That the world be filled with the grace of God bringing all of creation to the fulfillment of God's plan of salvation . . .

That those who are weighed down by sin would come to know Jesus, the compassionate One, who came to seek the lost . . .

That all gathered here might continue to seek to see Jesus and to follow him in all we do . . .

Presider: God of creation, lover and ruler of souls, you never cease to seek the lost and sinful. Hear our prayers that we might give our burdens to you so as to live in the joy and peace of your friendship. We ask this through Jesus Christ our Lord. Amen.

COLLECT

Let us pray.

Pause for silent prayer

Almighty and merciful God,
by whose gift your faithful offer you
right and praiseworthy service,
grant, we pray,
that we may hasten without stumbling
to receive the things you have promised.
Through our Lord Jesus Christ, your Son,
who lives and reigns with you in the unity
    of the Holy Spirit,
one God, for ever and ever. **Amen.**

FIRST READING

Wis 11:22–12:2

Before the LORD the whole universe is as a
        grain from a balance
    or a drop of morning dew come down
        upon the earth.
But you have mercy on all, because you
        can do all things;
    and you overlook people's sins that they
        may repent.
For you love all things that are
    and loathe nothing that you have made;
    for what you hated, you would not have
        fashioned.
And how could a thing remain, unless you
        willed it;
    or be preserved, had it not been called
        forth by you?
But you spare all things, because they are
        yours,
    O LORD and lover of souls,
    for your imperishable spirit is in all
        things!
Therefore you rebuke offenders little by
        little,
    warn them and remind them of the sins
        they are committing,
    that they may abandon their wickedness
        and believe in you, O LORD!

RESPONSORIAL PSALM

Ps 145:1-2, 8-9, 10-11, 13, 14

℟. (cf. 1) I will praise your name forever,
        my king and my God.

I will extol you, O my God and King,
    and I will bless your name forever and
        ever.
Every day will I bless you,
    and I will praise your name forever and
        ever.

℟. I will praise your name forever, my
        king and my God.

The Lord is gracious and merciful,
   slow to anger and of great kindness.
The Lord is good to all
   and compassionate toward all his
      works.

R̸. I will praise your name forever, my
   king and my God.

Let all your works give you thanks, O
   Lord,
   and let your faithful ones bless you.
Let them discourse of the glory of your
   kingdom
   and speak of your might.

R̸. I will praise your name forever, my
   king and my God.

The Lord is faithful in all his words
   and holy in all his works.
The Lord lifts up all who are falling
   and raises up all who are bowed down.

R̸. I will praise your name forever, my
   king and my God.

SECOND READING
2 Thess 1:11—2:2

Brothers and sisters:
We always pray for you,
   that our God may make you worthy of
      his calling
   and powerfully bring to fulfillment
      every good purpose
   and every effort of faith,
   that the name of our Lord Jesus may be
      glorified in you,
   and you in him,
   in accord with the grace of our God and
      Lord Jesus Christ.

We ask you, brothers and sisters,
   with regard to the coming of our Lord
      Jesus Christ
   and our assembling with him,
   not to be shaken out of your minds
      suddenly, or to be alarmed
   either by a "spirit," or by an oral
      statement,
   or by a letter allegedly from us
   to the effect that the day of the Lord is
      at hand.

About Liturgy

Your collection is an act of justice: If it is true that where your treasure lies, there also your heart will be, then how we disburse money from the weekly collection can be seen as an act of justice. We discussed the history and ritual meaning of the collection in the section on liturgy for the Eighteenth Sunday in Ordinary Time, but what might today's gospel tell us about how to use the collection to show our own conversion of heart?

Churches depend greatly on the weekly collection to cover internal costs. They need to pay just wages to its employees, take care of bills, purchase equipment and supplies, and invest in programs that help parishioners grow in their faith.

Many churches also depend on collections to help them directly serve those in need. Daily, people come to its doors looking for food, clothing, housing, or some other assistance, and parishes have many programs designed specifically for works of service. How can the ritual action of the collection be more clearly connected to a parish's ministry to those in need?

Some parishes have prepared a list of charitable organizations, both local and abroad, to whom they will give a percentage of each week's collection. Before the preparation of gifts begins, the presider or another commentator makes an announcement, such as, "Ten percent of this week's collection will go to the Downtown Women's Shelter, a local organization where abused women and their children can find a place of safety and long-term help. Thank you for your generosity." A similar statement can be included in the bulletin and parish website.

This is not a second collection but an intentional way a parish can include monetary support for those in need into both their parish budget and ritual practice.

About Initiation

Should catechumens pay?: Should catechumens pay to go through the RCIA process, just as some parishes require registration fees for infant baptism classes? It seems completely against the intent of the church's call to evangelize to make people pay to hear and learn to follow the gospel. Therefore, there should not be fees associated with RCIA. However, part of formation for living the Christian way of life is learning to sacrifice, especially on behalf of those in need. Although catechumens are dismissed at Mass before the collection is taken up, you might consider asking them to contribute to the parish's ministry to the poor as part of their formation. They could prepare their donation ahead of time and give it to their sponsor at Mass to be placed into the collection basket for them.

About Liturgical Music

Suggestions: There aren't many songs about Zacchaeus that aren't more appropriate for a children's liturgy. But *Psallite* provides us with one beautiful setting that identifies the main point of today's gospel: today salvation has come to this house. In "Salvation Has Come to This House" (*Sacred Song*), the assembly is given a stately refrain with verses that employ Psalm 16. This would be a perfect processional song for Communion.

A song that does not mention Zacchaeus by name but reflects well his story is Tom Booth's "You Stand Knocking" (OCP). One verse says, "You spoke my name, and took my hand, and called me friend. Such faithful love, so undeserved, a heart transformed."

NOVEMBER 3, 2019
THIRTY-FIRST SUNDAY
IN ORDINARY TIME

✠ SPIRITUALITY

GOSPEL ACCLAMATION
Rev 1:5a, 6b

℟. Alleluia, alleluia.
Jesus Christ is the firstborn of the dead;
to him be glory and power, forever and
    ever.
℟. Alleluia, alleluia.

Gospel   Luke 20:27-38; L156C

Some Sadducees, those who deny
    that there is a resurrection,
came forward and put this ques-
    tion to Jesus, saying,
"Teacher, Moses wrote for us,
*If someone's brother dies leav-
    ing a wife but no child,*
*his brother must take the wife
and raise up descendants for his
    brother.*
Now there were seven brothers;
    the first married a woman but
        died childless.
Then the second and the third married
    her,
    and likewise all the seven died childless.
Finally the woman also died.
Now at the resurrection whose wife will
    that woman be?
For all seven had been married to her."
Jesus said to them,
    "The children of this age marry and
        remarry;
    but those who are deemed worthy to at-
        tain to the coming age
    and to the resurrection of the dead
    neither marry nor are given in marriage.
They can no longer die,
    for they are like angels;
    and they are the children of God
    because they are the ones who will rise.
That the dead will rise
    even Moses made known in the passage
        about the bush,
    when he called out 'Lord,'
    the God of Abraham, the God of Isaac,
        and the God of Jacob;
    and he is not God of the dead, but of the
        living,
    for to him all are alive."

or Luke 20:27, 34-38 *in Appendix A, p. 315.*

Reflecting on the Gospel

Theological sophistication is on display today when Jesus responds to the de-
rogatory question about resurrection. While Jesus is in the Jerusalem temple
after making his lengthy journey, he faces a question from a powerful party of
religious leaders. The Sadducees did not accept resurrection, as they focused
squarely on Mosaic Law, the first five books of the Bible. And in those books
the word resurrection is not mentioned. Instead,
it's a term more closely associated with the book
of Daniel or even 2 Maccabees, which were not
accepted by the Sadducees as authoritative.
So the question the Sadducees pose to Jesus is
meant to illustrate how ridiculous the concept of
resurrection is. This is a good reminder that not
all Jews of Jesus' day had similar beliefs. There
were differences in understanding and applying
Jewish faith, much as there are differences among
Jews today. And for that matter, there are doctrinal differences between Christians today too!

But this question allows Jesus the chance to
correct their misunderstanding, using Mosaic
Law, something they would have accepted as
authoritative. Jesus' words indicate that there is
no marriage in the afterlife, thereby undercutting
the foundation of their question. His response also indicates that resurrection
was not for all, but only those who are deemed worthy. This, too, reflects a common understanding at that time by those who believed in resurrection. They
held that only the just were raised as a reward for their right conduct. In later
centuries Christians wondered whether the unjust would be raised too, if only
to be punished eternally. But that is not the question Jesus faced. For him, the
question was a literal understanding of resurrection to such a degree that it
involved marriage in the afterlife. Jesus continues his counterargument by citing
Mosaic Law and the words of Moses, who spoke of the God of Abraham, Isaac,
and Jacob, all of whom died centuries before Moses.

As God is the God of the living, Abraham, Isaac, and Jacob must be alive.
This is a clever twist on a familiar passage, and it demonstrates the theological
sophistication of this Jew from the backwaters of Galilee. He was in Jerusalem
now, arguing with the learned in the temple. His audience was likely growing,
and after this encounter so too was the opposition he faced.

Living the Paschal Mystery

Today's gospel is one of the few stories where we hear Jesus' thoughts on the
question of resurrection. Of course, one of the reasons it's so interesting is that
we know he will experience resurrection after a humiliating public death less
than a week later. Though resurrection is a central element of Christian faith, it
continues to be debated through the centuries. Even the apostle Paul had issues
with preaching the resurrection, as the longest chapter in any of his letters (1
Cor 15) deals entirely with the topic, while some of the Pastoral Letters indicate
that other Christians continued to misunderstand resurrection. And the Apostolic Fathers also address the issue, as do many others in every century including our own.

What do we believe about resurrection? How does this central element of our belief animate our daily life? How is our life different because of this promise? We proclaim the paschal mystery: suffering and death ultimately lead to joy and new life.

Focusing the Gospel

Key words and phrases: [H]e is not God of the dead, but of the living, / for to him all are alive.

To the point: The Sadducees pose a ridiculous scenario to Jesus in the hopes it will trip him up. But Jesus cuts through to the heart of their question about the resurrection of the dead. Do we really believe that God has authority over life and death and the ability to bring life *from* death? Jesus is about to live his certainty in the resurrection by submitting to death. He knows, as he tells the Sadducees, that God is God of the living—there is no death in him.

Connecting the Gospel

to the first reading: Jesus is not alone in believing in the resurrection of the dead. In the first reading from the second book of Maccabees we hear of the martyrdom of a mother and her seven sons. Rather than profane their ancestral beliefs, the brothers willingly submit to execution, each first stating complete trust that "the King of the world will raise us up to live again forever." The question of resurrection is one that divided the two main Jewish religious groups of Jesus' day, the Sadducees and the Pharisees. In his teaching and his preaching Jesus seems to offer a challenge and an invitation to everyone he meets. He calls the tax collectors to repentance, the self-righteous to humility, and the complacent to continue to delve into the mystery of God.

to experience: In a sermon St. Augustine famously said, "We are talking about God. What wonder is it that you do not understand? If you do understand, then it is not God." Our faith in God is not about perfect understanding or knowledge, but about radical trust in the king of the universe, the God of the living.

Connecting the Responsorial Psalm

to the readings: The first and the second readings present communities facing distress and persecution. At the time of the Maccabees, the second century BC, the Israelites were under the rule of the Seleucid Empire, whose brutal leader, Antiochus, plays a role in the torture and execution of the seven brothers and their mother from today's first reading. In his second letter to the Thessalonians, St. Paul mentions the persecutions and trials this community has undergone. He also alludes to his own safety when he asks the Thessalonians to pray "that we may be delivered from perverse and wicked people." Sandwiched in the middle of these two readings, today's psalm is fittingly a prayer for rescue from persecution. While the psalmist implores the Lord, "Hear, O LORD, a just suit; / attend to my outcry," this plea is balanced by deep trust. The psalm ends, "But I in justice shall behold your face; / on waking I shall be content in your presence."

to psalmist preparation: When have you most needed the Lord's strength and faithfulness to continue on in the face of life's trials?

PROMPTS FOR FAITH-SHARING

The second book of Maccabees lifts up the seven sons and their mother as models of faith and trust in God's authority over life and death. Which saints have inspired you with their belief (even unto death) in God's power to bring life from death?

Psalm 17 is a prayer for deliverance from persecution. How have you experienced persecution in your life? What gave you the strength to continue on?

In the second letter to the Thessalonians St. Paul prays for God to "encourage your hearts and strengthen them in every good deed and word." What kind of encouragement is your heart in need of at this time?

Jesus tells us in the gospel that God "is not God of the dead, but of the living, / for to him all are alive." How do you experience this in your own life of faith?

Model Penitential Act

Presider: In today's gospel some Sadducees question Jesus about the resurrection. Jesus tells them God "is not God of the dead, but of the living, / for to him all are alive." In thanksgiving for this gift of everlasting life, let us pause to prepare ourselves to enter into these sacred mysteries . . . [*pause*]

Lord Jesus, you lay down your life to take it up again: Lord, have mercy.

Christ Jesus, you are the King of the universe: Christ, have mercy.

Lord Jesus, you strengthen and guard us: Lord, have mercy.

Homily Points

• The Sadducees and the Pharisees were the major sects in Judaism at the time of Jesus. In Luke's gospel we've heard a lot about the Pharisees and most of it hasn't been positive. They accuse Jesus of blasphemy, complain when he eats with sinners, and reproach him for breaking the law when he heals on the Sabbath. Jesus in turn paints the Pharisees as hypocrites and lovers of money. By contrast, we read about the Sadducees only once. With this inequality of attention, it may come as a surprise that the Pharisees enjoyed the support of common people, like the fishermen and townspeople that Jesus spent most of his time with, while the aristocratic Sadducees weren't very popular.

• The Sadducees don't seem to take any notice of Jesus until the very end of his life when he is in Jerusalem where they are. They begin to worry he will start a revolt against their own authority and against the Roman Empire. In the gospel passage today, the Sadducees aren't concerned about the implications of marriage and the resurrection. Their intent is to undermine Jesus' message. They want to expose the improbably absurd notion of life after death.

• But Jesus will not be deterred. Throughout his ministry Jesus calls people away from the boxes in which they have placed God. He preaches and reveals a God beyond human comprehension. In the Sadducees and the Pharisees, Jesus is talking to the religious people of his day, the ones who faithfully visited the temple and studied in the synagogue. The ones who felt they had the most claim on Judaism of the time. There is a lesson here for us. Like the Sadducees do we try to control God, or to claim that we understand who God is and what God can do? If so, Jesus tells us, "Look again."

Model Universal Prayer (Prayer of the Faithful)

Presider: With trust in the God of life let us offer our prayers to the Lord.

Response: Lord, hear our prayer.

That persecuted Christians throughout the world find safe harbor and be granted the grace to forgive their persecutors . . .

That leaders of nations come together to advance the right of religious freedom for all people . . .

That those who grieve might be comforted by the Lord of everlasting life . . .

That all gathered might be renewed in our commitment to follow Jesus with fidelity, trust, and joy . . .

Presider: God of abundance, you desire to gift all people with life everlasting. Hear our prayers that we might proclaim your love to all the world. We ask this through Christ our Lord. Amen.

COLLECT

Let us pray.

Pause for silent prayer

Almighty and merciful God,
graciously keep from us all adversity,
so that, unhindered in mind and body
     alike,
we may pursue in freedom of heart
the things that are yours.
Through our Lord Jesus Christ, your Son,
who lives and reigns with you in the unity
     of the Holy Spirit,
one God, for ever and ever. **Amen.**

FIRST READING 2 Macc 7:1-2, 9-14

It happened that seven brothers with their
     mother were arrested
     and tortured with whips and scourges
          by the king,
     to force them to eat pork in violation of
          God's law.
One of the brothers, speaking for the
     others, said:
     "What do you expect to achieve by
          questioning us?
We are ready to die rather than transgress
     the laws of our ancestors."

At the point of death he said:
     "You accursed fiend, you are depriving
          us of this present life,
     but the King of the world will raise us
          up to live again forever.
It is for his laws that we are dying."

After him the third suffered their cruel
     sport.
He put out his tongue at once when told
     to do so,
     and bravely held out his hands, as he
          spoke these noble words:
     "It was from Heaven that I received these;
     for the sake of his laws I disdain them;
     from him I hope to receive them again."
Even the king and his attendants marveled
     at the young man's courage,
     because he regarded his sufferings as
          nothing.

After he had died,
     they tortured and maltreated the fourth
          brother in the same way.
When he was near death, he said,
     "It is my choice to die at the hands of men
     with the hope God gives of being raised
          up by him;
     but for you, there will be no resurrection
          to life."

RESPONSORIAL PSALM
Ps 17:1, 5-6, 8, 15

℟. (15b) Lord, when your glory appears,
  my joy will be full.

Hear, O LORD, a just suit;
  attend to my outcry;
  hearken to my prayer from lips without
    deceit.

℟. Lord, when your glory appears, my joy
  will be full.

My steps have been steadfast in your
    paths,
  my feet have not faltered.
I call upon you, for you will answer me,
    O God;
  incline your ear to me; hear my word.

℟. Lord, when your glory appears, my joy
  will be full.

Keep me as the apple of your eye,
  hide me in the shadow of your wings.
But I in justice shall behold your face;
  on waking I shall be content in your
    presence.

℟. Lord, when your glory appears, my joy
  will be full.

SECOND READING
2 Thess 2:16–3:5

Brothers and sisters:
May our Lord Jesus Christ himself and
    God our Father,
  who has loved us and given us
    everlasting encouragement
  and good hope through his grace,
  encourage your hearts and strengthen
    them in every good deed and word.

Finally, brothers and sisters, pray for us,
  so that the word of the Lord may speed
    forward and be glorified,
  as it did among you,
  and that we may be delivered from
    perverse and wicked people,
  for not all have faith.
But the Lord is faithful;
  he will strengthen you and guard you
    from the evil one.
We are confident of you in the Lord that
    what we instruct you,
  you are doing and will continue to do.
May the Lord direct your hearts to the love
    of God
  and to the endurance of Christ.

About Liturgy

Liturgical gymnastics: The hypothetical and hyperbolic situation posed by the Sadducees in today's gospel reminds me of some people who take liturgical rubrics a bit too far. Like the Sadducees, they focus on the letter of the law and miss the spirit of it entirely.

We see this quite often in concerns about the Eucharist and the consecrated host and wine. For example, in training sessions for extraordinary ministers of Holy Communion, I often hear questions like, "What if I drop the host?" or, "What if the communicant spills some of the wine?" Those who are overly focused on the letter of the law respond with an answer that attends solely to the Body of Christ in the eucharistic species while ignoring completely the Body of Christ in the person of the minister or the communicant. They will give detailed instructions on how to cleanse then purify the spot of carpet where the Precious Blood was spilled, advising communion ministers to create some kind of barrier to ensure that people don't walk over the spot. Or they will recommend that the communion minister pick up the fallen host then take it directly and solemnly to the sacristy where it could be disposed of properly, while leaving the person in line who dropped the host feeling guilty of the gravest of sins.

We absolutely must take care of the sacred gifts of the Eucharist in these kinds of situations. But the very reason we show so much reverence to the Body and Blood of Christ is because Christ was one of us, and through the Eucharist in which we share his Body and Blood, we become one with him. If we bend over backward to follow the letter of the law in order to honor the Body of Christ in the Eucharist while disregarding the spirit of the law that calls us to care for the Body of Christ in the person before us, we have missed the point of the law altogether.

About Initiation

Marriage issues: One of the most painful aspects of the initiation process for some can be helping catechumens and candidates understand the church's teachings on divorce and remarriage. Especially if they may be in need of an annulment, we have a great responsibility to inform them of the canonical requirements early on and to assist them as much as possible in the annulment process.

Just as important is our responsibility to help catechumens and candidates know and see the grace and dignity of the church's teaching on marriage. We cannot focus only on the details of policy and canon law. We must first and foremost express the beauty of what the church teaches about marriage and why it matters to us in our own faith.

About Liturgical Music

Suggestions: Many songs about resurrection and eternal life would be very appropriate today. One song that highlights the image of God as a God of the living and not of the dead is *Psallite*'s "God of Life, God of Hope" (*Sacred Song*). A soloist sings verses from Psalm 105 superimposed over an *ostinato* refrain sung by the assembly. This could work very well as a communion song.

Another song comes from David Haas's collection, *Who Calls You By Name*, Volume 1 (GIA). "God of the Living" was originally composed as a sung refrain for the gospel reading for the Third Scrutiny, the raising of Lazarus. However, this could also be an appropriate and powerful entrance song for today. The chanted verses and higher range need a skilled cantor.

NOVEMBER 10, 2019
THIRTY-SECOND SUNDAY IN ORDINARY TIME

SPIRITUALITY

GOSPEL ACCLAMATION
Luke 21:28

R︮. Alleluia, alleluia.
Stand erect and raise your heads
because your redemption is at hand.
R︮. Alleluia, alleluia.

Gospel

Luke 21:5-19; L159C

While some people were
    speaking about
  how the temple was adorned
      with costly stones and
      votive offerings,
  Jesus said, "All that you see
      here—
  the days will come when there
      will not be left
  a stone upon another stone
      that will not be thrown down."

Then they asked him,
  "Teacher, when will this happen?
And what sign will there be when all
    these things are about to happen?"
He answered,
"See that you not be deceived,
  for many will come in my name,
      saying,
  'I am he,' and 'The time has come.'
Do not follow them!
When you hear of wars and
    insurrections,
  do not be terrified; for such things
      must happen first,
  but it will not immediately be the
      end."
Then he said to them,
  "Nation will rise against nation, and
      kingdom against kingdom.
There will be powerful earthquakes,
    famines, and plagues
  from place to place;
  and awesome sights and mighty signs
      will come from the sky.

Continued in Appendix A, p. 315.

Reflecting on the Gospel

The end of the world is a popular topic among some religious people. Apocalyptic doom, fire and brimstone, death and destruction are hallmarks of the violent end of this earth by these preachers. But as we can see from today's gospel, eschatological fervor has been with us from the time of Jesus and even before. In the decades after Jesus, many claimed to be the Messiah. Some even led certain Jews into rebellion against Rome. But Rome was decisive about striking back. Roman troops led by General Vespasian swept into Judea and Galilee to put down the rebellion. There was a brief pause in the action when the Roman Emperor Nero committed suicide. The year AD 69 saw four emperors, the first three of whom died by suicide or assassination. The fourth was General Vespasian himself, who upon becoming emperor empowered his son Titus as general in his place. Roman troops under his command quickly got back to work and destroyed Jerusalem and its temple.

Many Christians of the time considered these unfolding events a sure sign of the end-times. And yet Christ's return was delayed. Luke wrote his gospel in about the 80s in part to deal with dampened and disappointed apocalyptic fervor. Christians were looking for signs that the end was near, as it had seemed to be so clear. Today's gospel story is Luke's way of addressing this topic. Even though many will come claiming to be a Messiah, and there will be wars and insurrections, it will not be the end.

Perhaps the lesson in all of this is that looking for such signs, discerning the events of our day seeking clues to the end of the world is essentially misguided. After nearly two thousand years of such expectation, we are better off concerning ourselves with helping our neighbors, caring for the sick, and comforting the afflicted. There will always be nation rising against nation and kingdom against kingdom. That is unfortunately the experience of our world. The kingdoms of this age tend to promote war. But Jesus preached a kingdom of God, when God himself will rule, putting an end once and for all to unjust systems, practices, and war itself. Then we will experience an age of peace. This is good news indeed.

Living the Paschal Mystery

The *examen* is a Jesuit practice at the end of the day, when one reviews the day's activities discerning God's presence and looking for his direction in our lives. It can help place one's emotions and experiences in a different perspective, sometimes seeing a bigger picture. Events in daily life may take on new meaning with reflection. What seemed to be a critically important encounter may not have been so critical, whereas a small gesture might become more profound upon reflection.

In today's gospel, the disciples want to know when the end of the world is coming. What signs will they be able to read to discern this important time? Jesus responds with a number of various elements that each generation since has interpreted to be fulfilled in their own time and place.

But perhaps we might experience something of the *examen* and reflect on the events in our own lives to see a bigger picture. Perhaps there is more meaning and more of God's activity in our daily coming and going than we imagine. While it could be more exciting to be on the hunt for clues to Jesus' return, in actuality, nobody knows when that will be! But God is present with us here and now, not only in the apocalyptic future. Let us discern his presence in the quotidian mystery of daily activity, the ebb and flow of our emotions, our existence, and our dying and rising to newness of life.

Focusing the Gospel

Key words and phrases: [D]o not be terrified.

To the point: We began the church year with a gospel much like this one speaking of wars and calamities but with the reassurance also that "when these signs begin to happen, stand erect and raise your heads because your redemption is at hand" (Luke 21:28; NABRE). Again, Jesus gives us comfort in the middle of prophecies of wars, insurrections, earthquakes, famines, and plagues when, in today's gospel, he tells the disciples, "[D]o not be terrified." Although the material world may be passing away, there is a firm foundation underfoot, the compassionate care of God the Father, Son, and Holy Spirit.

Connecting the Gospel

to the first reading: The verses from Malachi in the first reading are among the last of the Old Testament canon. The book of Malachi closes out the prophetic books. Written in the dark times of destruction and exile in the history of Israel, the prophets point to the enduring faithfulness of God. Today's verses reveal God's perfect justice where evil is destroyed through purifying fire and the just are strengthened in the rays of the sun. Light is shed on both, but the results are remarkably different. Today Jesus, in the prophetic tradition, proclaims the light in the darkness. The disciples will undergo persecutions. They will witness nation rising against nation and kingdom against kingdom. But in their persecutions they will be given wisdom to refute their adversaries. And even if they are put to death not a hair on their head will be destroyed.

to experience: At times in the life of faith we will need to remember the words of the prophets. In our broken world nations continue to war with each other, and each year brings its share of natural and manmade disasters. However, as people of faith, we look for the light shining in the darkness, the light that will purify our world from evil and heal us in justice.

Connecting the Responsorial Psalm

to the readings: The psalmist proclaims the justice of God who "comes to rule the earth." We are reminded that the earth is the Lord's from the rivers to the mountains, from the seas to the dry land. Jesus tells the disciples not to fear even when it seems that their world is being shaken at its foundations. God, Creator of the universe, continues to hold them in love even as they experience persecutions, wars, and earthquakes. Even death cannot ultimately touch them, for God is powerful over even death.

to psalmist preparation: Experiencing the beauty and grandeur of creation is a revelation of the Creator. Walking by a river, climbing to the top of a mountain, or witnessing the beauty of a sunset all speak to us of the love of God. This week, find some time to experience God in nature. What do the mountains and rivers, the seas and dry lands tell you about your God?

PROMPTS FOR FAITH-SHARING

Today's psalm calls on creation itself—rivers, mountains, seas, land—to rejoice in God. How have you experienced God in the natural world?

In the second letter to the Thessalonians, St. Paul calls upon the community to imitate his actions. Who has inspired you to imitation in the life of faith: a friend, relative, saint?

The gospel reading ends with Jesus calling the disciples to perseverance. Where in your life are you in need of perseverance at this moment?

Where do you notice God's presence, direction, and activity in your daily life?

Model Penitential Act

Presider: As we near the end of our church year let us pause to remember the Lord's faithfulness in times of joy and times of sorrow . . . [*pause*]

Lord Jesus, you are the source of wisdom and the font of salvation: Lord, have mercy.

Christ Jesus, you are the Prince of Peace: Christ, have mercy.

Lord Jesus, you comfort the afflicted and protect the persecuted: Lord, have mercy.

Homily Points

• As corporal beings, it is easy for us to get caught up in *stuff*. We take comfort in things we can see, touch, hear, and smell. Today's gospel begins with people around Jesus appreciating the beauty of the temple. In architecture we can see what is really important to a community. Just as Europeans in the Middle Ages spent decades and precious resources on their great cathedrals, the people of Jesus' time spent forty-six years constructing the temple, a privileged place to be with God.

• As we look to our own lives, we can name the places that we rely on and appreciate for their beauty and comfort: our homes, churches, schools, government buildings, and national monuments. These structures are good, but not permanent. They can be destroyed by any number of forces, many beyond our control. And yet, Jesus tells us, "[D]o not be terrified." The firm foundation under our feet is not one of wood, concrete, brick, or stone. It is the Lord in which "we live and move and have our being" (Acts 17:28; NABRE).

• As we come to the end of our church year, we can take this time to think about where we place our hope, our time, and our resources. Is there architecture within your interior life that could use some building up? Is God calling you to create more space for prayer, community, and love? Jesus reminds us that these structures alone can never be destroyed.

Model Universal Prayer (Prayer of the Faithful)

Presider: With confidence in God's faithfulness and mercy let us bring our prayers before the Lord.

Response: Lord, hear our prayer.

That the church might be a sign of hope and healing within the chaos of the world . . .

That warring nations turn their attention and care to working for lasting peace . . .

That those who experience terror and fear due to natural and manmade disasters receive physical and spiritual comfort and healing . . .

That all gathered here might lead lives of justice and peace that proclaim the love of God to all we meet . . .

Presider: God of creation, your mercy and justice is revealed in the life, death, and resurrection of your son Jesus Christ. Hear our prayers that we might follow his example in all that we do. We ask this through Christ our Lord. Amen.

COLLECT

Let us pray.

Pause for silent prayer

Grant us, we pray, O Lord our God,
the constant gladness of being devoted
to you,
for it is full and lasting happiness
to serve with constancy
the author of all that is good.
Through our Lord Jesus Christ, your Son,
who lives and reigns with you in the unity
of the Holy Spirit,
one God, for ever and ever. **Amen.**

FIRST READING

Mal 3:19-20a

Lo, the day is coming, blazing like an oven,
when all the proud and all evildoers will
be stubble,
and the day that is coming will set them
on fire,
leaving them neither root nor branch,
says the LORD of hosts.
But for you who fear my name, there will
arise
the sun of justice with its healing rays.

RESPONSORIAL PSALM

Ps 98:5-6, 7-8, 9

R⁄. (cf. 9) The Lord comes to rule the earth with justice.

Sing praise to the LORD with the harp,
    with the harp and melodious song.
With trumpets and the sound of the horn
    sing joyfully before the King, the LORD.

R⁄. The Lord comes to rule the earth with justice.

Let the sea and what fills it resound,
    the world and those who dwell in it;
let the rivers clap their hands,
    the mountains shout with them for joy.

R⁄. The Lord comes to rule the earth with justice.

Before the LORD, for he comes,
    for he comes to rule the earth;
he will rule the world with justice
    and the peoples with equity.

R⁄. The Lord comes to rule the earth with justice.

SECOND READING

2 Thess 3:7-12

Brothers and sisters:
You know how one must imitate us.
For we did not act in a disorderly way
    among you,
    nor did we eat food received free from
    anyone.
On the contrary, in toil and drudgery,
    night and day
    we worked, so as not to burden any of
    you.
Not that we do not have the right.
Rather, we wanted to present ourselves as
    a model for you,
    so that you might imitate us.
In fact, when we were with you,
    we instructed you that if anyone was
      unwilling to work,
    neither should that one eat.
We hear that some are conducting
    themselves among you in a disorderly
    way,
    by not keeping busy but minding the
    business of others.
Such people we instruct and urge in the
    Lord Jesus Christ to work quietly
    and to eat their own food.

About Liturgy

Prophets of doom: Pope Francis famously included in his apostolic exhortation, the Joy of the Gospel (*Evangelii Gaudium*), the term "sourpuss," cautioning that pessimism and defeatism cannot help us proclaim the enduring joy the gospel gives us. As liturgical ministers, we have to take this seriously. When people come to church on Sunday, especially visitors, newcomers, and those seeking a relationship with Christ, we will be the closest thing to the face of God they might see that day. And if our faces look like we just sucked on a lemon, what will that communicate about the joy of our faith?

Jesus gives his listeners the same kind of admonishment in today's gospel when he speaks of pessimism, worry, or fear in the face of persecution, wars, and chaos. Just listening to the news today can make any person feel like sucking a lemon. But for us who proclaim a gospel of life and hope, we must testify by our lives—especially by our words, actions, and faces—that God is not finished with us yet.

As liturgical ministers and leaders, we rehearse this by embodying joy especially when we celebrate the Eucharist. This is not to say that we need to spend the entire Mass with a Pollyanna-ish smile plastered on our face. But it does mean that we should not let nervousness or worry about the things of the liturgy prevent us from showing compassion to the person in front of us who needs our attention.

Boredom and routine can also give us a sourpuss look. So each time you prepare to exercise your ministry on behalf of the assembly, pray for the Spirit to warm your heart with the sun of justice and to kindle the fire of love again in you. Then heed the gospel acclamation verse today: "Stand erect and raise your heads / because your redemption is at hand" (Luke 21:28).

About Initiation

Daily discernment: Catechumens must learn to keep their hopes set on Christ and follow "supernatural inspiration in their deeds" (RCIA 75.2). Essentially this means learning how to do a daily discernment of where they have seen God in their lives and what God is asking them to do. This is the purpose of the Ignatian daily *examen*, a way of praying at the end of each day to learn to follow supernatural inspiration.

There are many ways to do an *examen*, but the five basic parts are 1) be aware of God's presence right now; 2) review the day's events; 3) listen to your feelings; 4) focus on one specific moment from the day, good or bad, and pray about it; 5) ask God to lead you in your actions for tomorrow.

About Liturgical Music

Music minister's examination of conscience: As we come to the end of another liturgical year, we might take this time to do an examination of conscience, reflecting on how well, individually and together, we have served our community as music ministers. Here are some questions that might stir up personal and group reflection, leading to conversion of heart for the following year.

How well have I prepared myself spiritually each week to hear the gospel and participate fully in the Mass with the assembly?

Do I understand the meaning behind the words I sing, and do I strive to believe what I am singing?

How have I grown in faith this past year? Where has my faith become stagnant or weak?

Beyond being part of the choir, will people recognize me as a disciple of Christ by my words and actions?

NOVEMBER 17, 2019
THIRTY-THIRD SUNDAY IN ORDINARY TIME

SPIRITUALITY

GOSPEL ACCLAMATION
Mark 11:9, 10

R⁊. Alleluia, alleluia.
Blessed is he who comes in the name of the
    Lord!
Blessed is the kingdom of our father
    David that is to come!
R⁊. Alleluia, alleluia.

Gospel

Luke 23:35-43; L162C

The rulers sneered at Jesus and
    said,
    "He saved others, let him save
        himself
    if he is the chosen one, the
        Christ of God."
Even the soldiers jeered at him.
As they approached to offer him
    wine they called out,
    "If you are King of the Jews,
        save yourself."
Above him there was an inscription
    that read,
    "This is the King of the Jews."

Now one of the criminals hanging there
    reviled Jesus, saying,
    "Are you not the Christ?
Save yourself and us."
The other, however, rebuking him, said
    in reply,
    "Have you no fear of God,
    for you are subject to the same
        condemnation?
And indeed, we have been condemned
    justly,
    for the sentence we received corre-
        sponds to our crimes,
    but this man has done nothing
        criminal."
Then he said,
    "Jesus, remember me when you come
        into your kingdom."
He replied to him,
    "Amen, I say to you,
    today you will be with me in
        Paradise."

Reflecting on the Gospel

Though we repeat it at church often without thinking, it can be odd to call Jesus, "King." There are not many kings or queens today and those that do exist are usually figureheads. Perhaps the most famous is Queen Elizabeth II. When we call Jesus a king are we equating him in some ways with a figure like Queen Elizabeth II? Or is the queen in some ways equivalent to Jesus? Jesus has many titles in Scripture, one of which is Christ (Messiah, the Anointed), others are Lamb of God, the Alpha and the Omega, Lion of David, Savior, Lord, Son of God, Son of Man, and King. Of course, today's reading tells us that he was given the title "King" by Pilate, or at least by the Romans who crucified him, as they were the ones who would have had the authority and responsibility for placing any sign above the cross.

What is a Christian response to the Romans calling him "king" in such a mocking, derisive way? Christians embraced it and said he was king in a way unlike earthly kings, for his kingdom was not of this world. Even the thieves crucified alongside him encouraged him to save himself if he really is the Anointed One (Christ, Messiah). But again, his kingdom is not of this world. What he does have he offers the repentant thief, "[T]oday you will be with me in Paradise." The true king of a kingdom not of this world offers repentance, forgiveness, and paradise to those who seek it. The suffering encountered in this world will be reversed and overcome in the next. The one dying on a cross is destined for paradise. The authorities of this world are putting to death the king of the kingdom of God. But this king will upend the ways of the world.

We proclaim Jesus as king, but he is no mere figurehead. He rules a kingdom of God where justice reigns, the lowly are raised up, and the mighty brought low. Those who hunger and thirst are satisfied whereas the rich are sent away empty. Is this our king? Are we subjects in this kingdom? Or are we more content being subjects of the kingdoms of this age? Jesus is our king, the crucified, humiliated one whose destiny is paradise. Let us align ourselves with him and all the poor and lowly in the world.

Living the Paschal Mystery

The two thieves on either side of Jesus have remarkably different attitudes toward Jesus. One reviled Jesus, prodding him into saving himself and them. The mockery from the bystanders wasn't enough. Jesus faced mockery from one of his fellow condemned criminals. The other placed faith in Jesus with a simple request to "remember me when you come into your kingdom." That request belies a faith statement that Jesus is a king. What was said in mockery on the cross is true, and the thief knows it. Not only will Jesus remember him, but he promises to be with him in paradise that day. There seems to be no "descent into hell" in Luke's understanding. That very day Jesus and the thief will be in paradise.

Our call is to recognize Jesus' kingship as well, though knowing it is a kingdom not of this world. The paschal mystery gives us hope that upon death Jesus is in paradise without a pit stop along the way. Death leads to new life. And Jesus will bring others with him as they too experience the paschal mystery.

Focusing the Gospel

Key words and phrases: Jesus, remember me when you come into your kingdom.

To the point: In Jesus' final moments on the cross he is surrounded by people calling out, "Save yourself." The rulers, soldiers, and even one of the criminals being crucified at his side repeat this taunt. In their words we might hear an echo of the temptation Jesus underwent at the very beginning of his ministry, when the devil asks him to change rock into bread to sate his hunger, or to throw himself from the parapet of the temple and be saved by angels. Jesus refuses, of course. Our king is not interested in saving himself. Throughout his ministry Jesus multiplies bread and fish to satisfy the needs of others. He heals physical and spiritual maladies. The second criminal understands and makes a request Jesus immediately grants, "Jesus, remember me when you come into your kingdom." Jesus lives a life poured out for others from the very beginning to the very end. Even now our king stands ready, not to save himself, but to save us.

Connecting the Gospel

to the second reading: Today's second reading is taken from St. Paul's letter to the Colossians. In a hymn about the person of Jesus, Paul writes, "For in him all the fullness was pleased to dwell, / and through him to reconcile all things for him, / making peace by the blood of his cross / through him, whether those on earth or those in heaven." In our world of divisions and categorizations, Paul invites us into a vision of Jesus as whole: the one in whom all the fullness was pleased to dwell. The one who takes all into himself and transforms it, reconciles it through the blood of his cross.

to experience: When we proclaim Jesus as king of the entire universe, we proclaim him king in fullness—king of the vulnerable harshness of the cross just as much as he is king in the transcendence of the resurrection.

Connecting the Responsorial Psalm

to the readings: In the first reading David is crowned king of Israel. The people claim him a family member, shepherd, and ruler. David will govern his people and also lead them spiritually. His home is Jerusalem, the seat of the king, and it becomes the place to be close to God when David's son Solomon builds a temple there. In today's psalm Jerusalem is praised as the center of pilgrimage to draw near the Lord. The temple is "the house of the Lord," a place of justice, and a place of thanksgiving.

to psalmist preparation: Unlike the Israelites before the destruction of the temple in the first century, we don't claim a geographical place as the center of our worship. Jesus, the king of the universe, is found in creation, in community, in the Eucharist, in our hearts. Where do you go to draw close to the Lord? Where do you meet your king?

PROMPTS FOR FAITH-SHARING

David is called by God to be a "shepherd" and a "commander." How do you balance authority with service and compassion, as a shepherd might lead his sheep?

Psalm 122 begins "I rejoiced because they said to me, / 'We will go up to the house of the LORD.'" How is your worship of the Lord joyful?

Read the hymn from Colossians (1:15-20) slowly. Which phrase about Jesus speaks to you the loudest at this moment in your life of faith?

On this feast of Christ the King of the Universe, why do you think the church would choose for us to read and meditate on Jesus' crucifixion?

Model Penitential Act

Presider: On this final Sunday of our liturgical year we celebrate the feast of Christ, the King of the Universe. Let us pause to revel in the glory of our God, and the privilege of being one of his children . . . [*pause*]

Lord Jesus, you are the chosen one, the Messiah, the anointed: Lord, have mercy.

Christ Jesus, you are the King of heaven and earth: Christ, have mercy.

Lord Jesus, you desire to reconcile all things and people to yourself: Lord, have mercy.

Homily Points

• On this triumphant feast of Christ, King of the Universe we might be surprised by our gospel reading. While Jesus dies on the cross, the rulers and soldiers shout and taunt, "Save yourself" if you are really the Christ of God. But that is not the kingship of Jesus. Not because he couldn't. Surely the one who healed lepers and fed the five thousand was perfectly capable of climbing down off the cross and walking unharmed through the angry crowd just as he did in Nazareth when his neighbors wanted to throw him off of a cliff. But he doesn't. Jesus' kingship is not about his own glory or power. His kingship is not about saving himself. Instead, in Jesus we witness a life poured out completely, to the last breath, for others.

• As we come to the end of the year in the Northern Hemisphere we see the seasons change. The light grows shorter and the weather colder. Our life follows the patterns of the seasons, and the patterns of the liturgical year. On this feast we proclaim Christ the King, who entered into creation, even to the ultimate brokenness of death. And in Christ, death is transformed. Theologian Sofia Cavalletti writes, "Calvary is not only a brutal, violent act; above all else, it is a tremendous act of love. A tremendous act of violence becomes a tremendous act of love" (*Ways to Nurture the Relationship with God*).

• We end our church year by recalling this tremendous act of love. Jesus, King of the Universe, gives himself completely on the wood of the cross. As we enter into a new year of living and growing in faith, may we keep this paradox of kingship always ahead of us, for at the very beginning of our Christian lives we, too, were anointed priest, prophet, and king. May we come to embrace the kingship of Jesus, a kingship completely poured out for others, transforming death into life, and violence into love.

Model Universal Prayer (Prayer of the Faithful)

Presider: Grateful for our many blessings and confident in God's goodness and mercy, let us bring our prayers before the Lord.

Response: Lord, hear our prayer.

That the church emulate the kingship of Jesus in mercy, charity, and compassion . . .

That the justice and peace of Jesus the King would be known throughout the world . . .

That those who suffer from mental illness, depression, and anxiety be comforted by the love of God, which surpasses understanding . . .

That all gathered here might be strengthened in our resolve to follow and serve Jesus, the King of the Universe . . .

Presider: Saving God, you desire to redeem and consecrate all that you have created. Hear our prayers that we might use our gifts and talents to build your kingdom. We ask this through Christ our Lord. Amen.

COLLECT

Let us pray.

Pause for silent prayer

Almighty ever-living God,
whose will is to restore all things
in your beloved Son, the King of the
    universe,
grant, we pray,
that the whole creation, set free from
    slavery,
may render your majesty service
and ceaselessly proclaim your praise.
Through our Lord Jesus Christ, your Son,
who lives and reigns with you in the unity
    of the Holy Spirit,
one God, for ever and ever. **Amen.**

FIRST READING
2 Sam 5:1-3

In those days, all the tribes of Israel came
    to David in Hebron and said:
    "Here we are, your bone and your flesh.
In days past, when Saul was our king,
    it was you who led the Israelites out and
        brought them back.
And the LORD said to you,
    'You shall shepherd my people Israel
    and shall be commander of Israel.'"
When all the elders of Israel came to
    David in Hebron,
    King David made an agreement with
        them there before the LORD,
    and they anointed him king of Israel.

RESPONSORIAL PSALM
Ps 122:1-2, 3-4, 4-5

℞. (cf. 1) Let us go rejoicing to the house
    of the Lord.

I rejoiced because they said to me,
    "We will go up to the house of the
        LORD."
And now we have set foot
    within your gates, O Jerusalem.

℞. Let us go rejoicing to the house of the
    Lord.

Jerusalem, built as a city
    with compact unity.
To it the tribes go up,
    the tribes of the LORD.

℞. Let us go rejoicing to the house of the
    Lord.

According to the decree for Israel,
    to give thanks to the name of the LORD.
In it are set up judgment seats,
    seats for the house of David.

℞. Let us go rejoicing to the house of the
    Lord.

SECOND READING
Col 1:12-20

Brothers and sisters:
Let us give thanks to the Father,
  who has made you fit to share
  in the inheritance of the holy ones in
      light.
He delivered us from the power of
      darkness
  and transferred us to the kingdom of
      his beloved Son,
  in whom we have redemption, the
      forgiveness of sins.

He is the image of the invisible God,
  the firstborn of all creation.
For in him were created all things in
      heaven and on earth,
  the visible and the invisible,
  whether thrones or dominions or
      principalities or powers;
  all things were created through
      him and for him.
He is before all things,
  and in him all things hold together.
He is the head of the body, the
      church.
He is the beginning, the firstborn
      from the dead,
  that in all things he himself might
      be preeminent.
For in him all the fullness was
      pleased to dwell,
  and through him to reconcile all
      things for him,
  making peace by the blood of his
      cross
  through him, whether those on
      earth or those in heaven.

About Liturgy

Triumphalism: Our rich liturgical tradition is filled with grandeur. Our worship spaces should rightfully elicit feelings of wonder and awe, and our rituals should reflect the best of our gifts we have to offer to our God.

However, there is a great difference between earthly extravagance and divine glory. We can proclaim the victory and triumph of God over death without triumphalism, pomposity, or ostentation. The key to knowing the difference may lie in today's gospel reading.

The kind of king we have in Christ is one who is quite human, suffering the injustices of other humans, and succumbing to the one human trait we all share—death. What made his cross a throne was his compassion for those just as broken—the crowd that reviled him, the mother who wept before him, and the criminals who died with him a criminal's death.

To express the glory and triumph that is rightly Christ's is to take what is broken and to reveal in it that which is royal, holy, and sacred. Our liturgies need not be magnificent in their splendor, erudite and polished to perfection, but they do need to be human and authentic, revealing the best of ourselves in our brokenness.

There is another aspect to the temptation of triumphalism that is even more insidious and can go unnoticed. We can fall into the trap of holding a bias toward one culture, language, style of praying, or genre of music as superior, judging other cultures, languages, styles, and forms as unrefined and less appropriate for worship. The cross, Christ's throne, reminds us that all that is human has been redeemed. Therefore, let us all approach the throne of mercy to receive grace, for the Father has made us all "fit to share / in the inheritance of the holy ones in light" (Col 1:12).

About Initiation

The liturgical year as teacher: The Rite of Christian Initiation of Adults advises that the duration of the catechumenate "should be long enough—several years if necessary—for the conversion and faith of the catechumens to become strong" (RCIA 76). The RCIA does not recommend this simply to give you more time for catechesis with the catechumens. Rather, the RCIA intends that the catechumens' encounter with Christ through the celebration of the liturgical year is how "the Church completes [their] education" (Universal Norms on the Liturgical Year and the Calendar 1). Through the gradual observance of all the Sundays, holy days, feasts, and seasons of the liturgical year, the church "unfolds the whole mystery of Christ" (Constitution on the Sacred Liturgy 102), for it is Christ who teaches us and initiates the catechumens into the mystery of salvation.

About Liturgical Music

Suggestions: A beautiful antiphon for today comes from *Psallite*'s "Christ Laid Down His Life for Us" (*Sacred Song*), which says, "Christ laid down his life for us; so we should do for each other." The verses incorporate parts of the well-known Philippians canticle about Christ emptying himself, taking the form of a slave.

Another piece for this day is the well-known hymn, "Let All Mortal Flesh Keep Silence," set to PICARDY and found in many hymnals. This would be a lovely song for the preparation of gifts.

Because this is the last Sunday before Advent, be sure to enhance the Gloria on this day, using a setting the assembly already knows and loves, but adding more to the instrumentation. Today is also a good day to sing a song of praise with the assembly after Communion. Consider just the refrain of Suzanne Toolan's "Jesus Christ, Yesterday, Today, and Forever" (GIA). Complement this stately hymn with a spirited instrumental for the closing procession.

NOVEMBER 24, 2019
OUR LORD JESUS CHRIST, KING OF THE UNIVERSE

℟. Alleluia, alleluia.
Blessed are you, Father, Lord of heaven and earth;
you have revealed to little ones the mysteries of
    the Kingdom.
℟. Alleluia, alleluia.

Gospel   Matthew 11:25-30; L947.2

At that time Jesus answered:
"I give praise to you, Father, Lord of heaven
    and earth,
    for although you have hidden these things
    from the wise and the learned
    you have revealed them to little ones.
Yes, Father, such has been your gracious
    will.
All things have been handed over to me by
    my Father.
No one knows the Son except the Father,
    and no one knows the Father except the
        Son
    and anyone to whom the Son wishes to
        reveal him.

"Come to me, all you who labor and are
    burdened,
    and I will give you rest.
Take my yoke upon you and learn from me,
    for I am meek and humble of heart;
    and you will find rest for yourselves.
For my yoke is easy, and my burden light."

See Appendix A, p. 315, for the other readings.

Additional reading choices are in the Lectionary
for Mass, *vol. IV, "In Thanksgiving to God," nos.
943–947.*

Reflecting on the Gospel

On this national holiday of Thanksgiving, a uniquely American celebration
of thanks officially promulgated by Abraham Lincoln in the midst of the Civil
War, we hear the words of Jesus from the Gospel of Matthew that sound remarkably like Emma Lazarus's words on the Statue of Liberty. Jesus says in
Matthew, "Come to me, all you who labor and are burdened, / and I will give you
rest," whereas Emma Lazarus has Lady Liberty say, "Give me your tired, your
poor, your huddled masses yearning to breathe free."

Many people in the United States consider this to be a Christian country, but
it has always struggled between the ideal and the real. The Declaration of In-
dependence speaks of the inalienable freedom of all, but it was written by and
endorsed by slaveholders. So the country was founded on Christian values, but
also the injustice of slavery. The Statue of Liberty is a beacon of hope throughout the world, but the United States has not always been a welcoming country.
For example, in 1939 Jewish migrants on the SS *St. Louis* were turned away
from the United States back to Nazi Germany, where many met their end in con-
centration camps.

The United States is a land of high ideals that we do not always meet. But the
ideals remain lofty, nonetheless, so that Martin Luther King Jr. can say he is ready
to redeem the promissory note of freedom that the founding fathers provided.

And there is more work to be done today "in order to form a more perfect
union." If we consider this country to be based on Christian ideals, then perhaps there is no better reading than this from Matthew. Jesus invites all who
labor and are burdened to come to him. He grants rest. He is meek and humble
of heart. If we are his disciples we will imitate his invitation. We will be meek
and humble of heart, providing for the needs of others as is our Christian duty.
We do this not because of who these "others" are but because of who we are as
Christian disciples, followers of Jesus.

Living the Paschal Mystery

The early disciples were given the name "disciple" because it means "follower."
These were the followers of Jesus. They sought to learn from him, to be like
him, and to imitate him. In today's gospel he calls himself meek and humble
of heart, inviting others to himself. For us to be his followers today, it is not
enough to simply attend Mass. It is our duty to learn from him, to be like him,
and to imitate him.

On this Thanksgiving Day when we celebrate as a nation the great bounty
we have, we might consider that nearly all those in America, with the exception of Native Americans, were immigrants to this country. Most came of their
own free will but sadly many did not, including those brought here in bondage.
Most who came here of their own free will found a welcome here, though not all
did. If our country was founded on Christian ideals, it is up to us to carry them
forward and live them out today. Following Jesus means we will welcome the
stranger, invite others to be with us, and assist them with the yoke.

Focusing the Gospel

Key words and phrases: Learn from me, for I am meek and humble of heart

To the point: To embrace thanksgiving is to disabuse oneself of the notion of
self-sufficiency. We are not able to do anything on our own. The coffee we make
in the morning depends on the labor of those who tended the coffee plants and
dried and packaged the beans, on the person who designed the coffee maker,

and the factory workers who labored over it. And ultimately, it all depends on the gifts of God: the rain, sun, earth, and materials for tools provided to us in the natural world. Let us follow the example of Jesus and the childlike and live with profound gratitude for all that we have been given, and in so doing cultivate meek, humble, and Christ-like hearts.

Model Penitential Act

Presider: We gather to give thanks and praise to our God who provides for our every need through his gracious bounty. Let us pause to prepare our hearts and minds to enter into this feast of Thanksgiving . . . [*pause*]

Lord Jesus, you are meek and humble of heart: Lord, have mercy.
Christ Jesus, you are the greatest gift of God: Christ, have mercy.
Lord Jesus, you give rest to the weary: Lord, have mercy.

Model Universal Prayer (Prayer of the Faithful)

Presider: With thanksgiving for our many blessings let us bring our prayers before the Lord.

Response: Lord, hear our prayer.

That the leaders of the church receive strength and wisdom to humbly lead the people of God . . .

That those who enjoy an abundance of the world's resources dedicate time and energy to sharing with those in need . . .

That all those who lack shelter, food, clothing, and water be generously provided for by their friends, neighbors, and communities . . .

That all gathered here might greet each day with gratitude for its many blessings . . .

Presider: God of abundance, you shower us with the gifts of creation, family, and friends. Hear our prayers that nourished by your presence in the Word and the Eucharist, we might go forth to be a blessing in the lives of others. We ask this through Christ our Lord. Amen.

About Liturgy

Teaching people to pray: Many will want to make today's family meal special. Give them the gift of prayer using their own words by teaching them how to create a basic prayer for their meal blessing. Using the following method, entire families can write the prayer together. The prayer leader should have a pen and piece of paper ready.

First, have people call out names or titles for God. These can be common or poetic, such as "Abba" or "Author of Life." The leader writes these down.

Second, ask people to call out loud in a word or short phrase a blessing they have received recently, such as, "good health," "children," or "forgiveness." Write these down.

Third, ask people to say in a word or short phrase what the world needs most today, such as "healing" or "compassion."

The prayer leader then puts these all together, for example:

"Abba and Author of Life, we thank you for good health, children, and forgiveness. We ask you to bless this meal and bless all of us here with healing and compassion. We ask this through Christ our Lord. Amen."

FOR REFLECTION

• How is Jesus calling you to rest from labor and burdens?

• How do you cultivate gratitude every day of the year?

• Over this past liturgical year, what have been the greatest gifts received by you, your family, and your community? How have you responded to these gifts?

Homily Points

• In today's gospel Jesus calls us to be "childlike." When we think of children there are probably many images that run through our heads. But on this feast of Thanksgiving, let's ponder the attitude of the young child that specifically fits our celebration, that of gratitude. When a child prays spontaneously, especially a child age six or younger, the prayer is almost always one of thanksgiving. The litany can be long: "Thank you for my mom, thank you for my dad, thank you for my train set, thank you for the sun . . ."

• Though the items on the list may change, the sentiment is the same: total delight in the bountiful gifts of God. In spiritual terms we could name this orientation to life, wonder and awe, which, fittingly is one of the gifts of the Holy Spirit. On this Thanksgiving Day, what calls you to wonder and awe and fills you with delight?

Readings *(continued)*

The Immaculate Conception of the Blessed Virgin Mary, *December 8, 2018*

Gospel (cont.)
Luke 1:26-38; L689

He will be great and will be called Son of the Most High,
    and the Lord God will give him the throne of David his father,
    and he will rule over the house of Jacob forever,
    and of his Kingdom there will be no end."
But Mary said to the angel,
    "How can this be,
    since I have no relations with a man?"
And the angel said to her in reply,
    "The Holy Spirit will come upon you,
    and the power of the Most High will overshadow you.
Therefore the child to be born
    will be called holy, the Son of God.

And behold, Elizabeth, your relative,
    has also conceived a son in her old age,
    and this is the sixth month for her who was called barren;
    for nothing will be impossible for God."
Mary said, "Behold, I am the handmaid of the Lord.
May it be done to me according to your word."
Then the angel departed from her.

FIRST READING
Gen 3:9-15, 20

After the man, Adam, had eaten of the tree,
    the LORD God called to the man and asked
      him, "Where are you?"
He answered, "I heard you in the garden;
    but I was afraid, because I was naked,
    so I hid myself."
Then he asked, "Who told you that you were
    naked?
You have eaten, then,
    from the tree of which I had forbidden you
      to eat!"
The man replied, "The woman whom you put
    here with me—
    she gave me fruit from the tree, and so I
      ate it."
The LORD God then asked the woman,
    "Why did you do such a thing?"
The woman answered, "The serpent tricked
    me into it, so I ate it."

Then the LORD God said to the serpent:
    "Because you have done this, you shall be
      banned
      from all the animals
      and from all the wild creatures;
    on your belly shall you crawl,
      and dirt shall you eat
      all the days of your life.
I will put enmity between you and the
    woman,
    and between your offspring and hers;
    he will strike at your head,
      while you strike at his heel."

The man called his wife Eve,
    because she became the mother of all the
      living.

RESPONSORIAL PSALM
Ps 98:1, 2-3ab, 3cd-4

℟. (1a) Sing to the Lord a new song, for he has
    done marvelous deeds.

Sing to the LORD a new song,
    for he has done wondrous deeds;
His right hand has won victory for him,
    his holy arm.

℟. Sing to the Lord a new song, for he has
    done marvelous deeds.

The LORD has made his salvation known:
    in the sight of the nations he has revealed
      his justice.
He has remembered his kindness and his
    faithfulness
    toward the house of Israel.

℟. Sing to the Lord a new song, for he has
    done marvelous deeds.

All the ends of the earth have seen
    the salvation by our God.
Sing joyfully to the LORD, all you lands;
    break into song; sing praise.

℟. Sing to the Lord a new song, for he has
    done marvelous deeds.

SECOND READING
Eph 1:3-6, 11-12

Brothers and sisters:
Blessed be the God and Father of our Lord
    Jesus Christ,
    who has blessed us in Christ
    with every spiritual blessing in the heavens,
    as he chose us in him, before the foundation
      of the world,
    to be holy and without blemish before him.
In love he destined us for adoption to himself
    through Jesus Christ,
    in accord with the favor of his will,
    for the praise of the glory of his grace
    that he granted us in the beloved.

In him we were also chosen,
    destined in accord with the purpose of the
      One
    who accomplishes all things according to
      the intention of his will,
    so that we might exist for the praise of his
      glory,
    we who first hoped in Christ.

Gospel (cont.)
Matt 1:1-25; L13ABC

Asaph became the father of Jehoshaphat,
    Jehoshaphat the father of Joram,
    Joram the father of Uzziah.
Uzziah became the father of Jotham,
    Jotham the father of Ahaz,
    Ahaz the father of Hezekiah.
Hezekiah became the father of Manasseh,
    Manasseh the father of Amos,
    Amos the father of Josiah.
Josiah became the father of Jechoniah and his brothers
    at the time of the Babylonian exile.

After the Babylonian exile,
    Jechoniah became the father of Shealtiel,
    Shealtiel the father of Zerubbabel,
    Zerubbabel the father of Abiud.
Abiud became the father of Eliakim,
    Eliakim the father of Azor,
    Azor the father of Zadok.
Zadok became the father of Achim,
    Achim the father of Eliud,
    Eliud the father of Eleazar.
Eleazar became the father of Matthan,
    Matthan the father of Jacob,
    Jacob the father of Joseph, the husband of Mary.
Of her was born Jesus who is called the Christ.

Thus the total number of generations
    from Abraham to David
    is fourteen generations;
    from David to the Babylonian exile,
    fourteen generations;
    from the Babylonian exile to the Christ,
    fourteen generations.

Now this is how the birth of Jesus Christ came about.
When his mother Mary was betrothed to Joseph,
    but before they lived together,
    she was found with child through the Holy Spirit.
Joseph her husband, since he was a righteous man,
    yet unwilling to expose her to shame,
    decided to divorce her quietly.
Such was his intention when, behold,
    the angel of the Lord appeared to him in a dream and said,
    "Joseph, son of David,
    do not be afraid to take Mary your wife into your home.
For it is through the Holy Spirit
    that this child has been conceived in her.
She will bear a son and you are to name him Jesus,
    because he will save his people from their sins."
All this took place to fulfill
    what the Lord had said through the prophet:
        Behold, the virgin shall conceive and bear a son,
        and they shall name him Emmanuel,
    which means "God is with us."
When Joseph awoke,
    he did as the angel of the Lord had commanded him
    and took his wife into his home.
He had no relations with her until she bore a son,
    and he named him Jesus.

or Matt 1:18-25

This is how the birth of Jesus Christ came about.
When his mother Mary was betrothed to Joseph,
    but before they lived together,
    she was found with child through the Holy Spirit.
Joseph her husband, since he was a righteous man,
    yet unwilling to expose her to shame,
    decided to divorce her quietly.
Such was his intention when, behold,
    the angel of the Lord appeared to him in a dream and said,
    "Joseph, son of David,
    do not be afraid to take Mary your wife into your home.
For it is through the Holy Spirit
    that this child has been conceived in her.
She will bear a son and you are to name him Jesus,
    because he will save his people from their sins."
All this took place to fulfill
    what the Lord had said through the prophet:
        Behold, the virgin shall conceive and bear a son,
        and they shall name him Emmanuel,
    which means "God is with us."
When Joseph awoke,
    he did as the angel of the Lord had commanded him
    and took his wife into his home.
He had no relations with her until she bore a son,
    and he named him Jesus.

FIRST READING
Isa 62:1-5

For Zion's sake I will not be silent,
　for Jerusalem's sake I will not be quiet,
until her vindication shines forth like the
　　dawn
　　and her victory like a burning torch.

Nations shall behold your vindication,
　and all the kings your glory;
you shall be called by a new name
　pronounced by the mouth of the LORD.
You shall be a glorious crown in the hand of
　　the LORD,
　a royal diadem held by your God.
No more shall people call you "Forsaken,"
　or your land "Desolate,"
but you shall be called "My Delight,"
　and your land "Espoused."
For the LORD delights in you
　and makes your land his spouse.
As a young man marries a virgin,
　your Builder shall marry you;
and as a bridegroom rejoices in his bride
　so shall your God rejoice in you.

RESPONSORIAL PSALM
Ps 89:4-5, 16-17, 27, 29

R̸. (2a) For ever I will sing the goodness of
　　the Lord.

I have made a covenant with my chosen one,
　I have sworn to David my servant:
forever will I confirm your posterity
　and establish your throne for all
　　generations.

R̸. For ever I will sing the goodness of the
　　Lord.

Blessed the people who know the joyful shout;
　in the light of your countenance, O LORD,
　　they walk.
At your name they rejoice all the day,
　and through your justice they are exalted.

R̸. For ever I will sing the goodness of the
　　Lord.

He shall say of me, "You are my father,
　my God, the rock, my savior."
Forever I will maintain my kindness toward
　him,
　and my covenant with him stands firm.

R̸. For ever I will sing the goodness of the
　　Lord.

SECOND READING
Acts 13:16-17, 22-25

When Paul reached Antioch in Pisidia and
　　entered the synagogue,
　he stood up, motioned with his hand, and
　　said,
　　"Fellow Israelites and you others who are
　　　God-fearing, listen.
The God of this people Israel chose our
　　ancestors
　and exalted the people during their sojourn
　　in the land of Egypt.
With uplifted arm he led them out of it.
Then he removed Saul and raised up David
　　as king;
　of him he testified,
　'I have found David, son of Jesse, a man
　　after my own heart;
　he will carry out my every wish.'
From this man's descendants God, according
　　to his promise,
　has brought to Israel a savior, Jesus.
John heralded his coming by proclaiming a
　　baptism of repentance
　to all the people of Israel;
　and as John was completing his course, he
　　would say,
　'What do you suppose that I am? I am not
　　he.
Behold, one is coming after me;
　I am not worthy to unfasten the sandals of
　　his feet.'"

Gospel (cont.)
Luke 2:1-14; L14ABC

She wrapped him in swaddling clothes and laid him in a manger,
　because there was no room for them in the inn.

Now there were shepherds in that region living in the fields
　and keeping the night watch over their flock.
The angel of the Lord appeared to them
　and the glory of the Lord shone around them,
　and they were struck with great fear.
The angel said to them,
　"Do not be afraid;
　for behold, I proclaim to you good news of great joy
　that will be for all the people.
For today in the city of David
　a savior has been born for you who is Christ and Lord.
And this will be a sign for you:
　you will find an infant wrapped in swaddling clothes
　and lying in a manger."

And suddenly there was a multitude of the heavenly host with the
　angel,
　praising God and saying:
　　"Glory to God in the highest
　　and on earth peace to those on whom his favor rests."

The Nativity of the Lord, *December 25, 2018 (Mass at Midnight)*

FIRST READING
Isa 9:1-6

The people who walked in darkness
  have seen a great light;
upon those who dwelt in the land of gloom
  a light has shone.
You have brought them abundant joy
  and great rejoicing,
as they rejoice before you as at the harvest,
  as people make merry when dividing spoils.
For the yoke that burdened them,
  the pole on their shoulder,
and the rod of their taskmaster
  you have smashed, as on the day of Midian.
For every boot that tramped in battle,
  every cloak rolled in blood,
  will be burned as fuel for flames.
For a child is born to us, a son is given us;
  upon his shoulder dominion rests.
They name him Wonder-Counselor, God-Hero,
  Father-Forever, Prince of Peace.
His dominion is vast
  and forever peaceful,
from David's throne, and over his kingdom,
  which he confirms and sustains
by judgment and justice,
  both now and forever.
The zeal of the LORD of hosts will do this!

RESPONSORIAL PSALM
Ps 96:1-2, 2-3, 11-12, 13

R℣. (Luke 2:11) Today is born our Savior,
  Christ the Lord.

Sing to the LORD a new song;
  sing to the LORD, all you lands.
Sing to the LORD; bless his name.

R℣. Today is born our Savior, Christ the Lord.

Announce his salvation, day after day.
  Tell his glory among the nations;
  among all peoples, his wondrous deeds.

R℣. Today is born our Savior, Christ the Lord.

Let the heavens be glad and the earth rejoice;
  let the sea and what fills it resound;
  let the plains be joyful and all that is in
    them!
Then shall all the trees of the forest exult.

R℣. Today is born our Savior, Christ the Lord.

They shall exult before the LORD, for he
  comes;
  for he comes to rule the earth.
He shall rule the world with justice
  and the peoples with his constancy.

R℣. Today is born our Savior, Christ the Lord.

SECOND READING
Titus 2:11-14

Beloved:
The grace of God has appeared, saving all
  and training us to reject godless ways and
    worldly desires
  and to live temperately, justly, and devoutly
    in this age,
  as we await the blessed hope,
  the appearance of the glory of our great
    God
  and savior Jesus Christ,
who gave himself for us to deliver us from
  all lawlessness
and to cleanse for himself a people as his
  own,
eager to do what is good.

The Nativity of the Lord, *December 25, 2018 (Mass at Dawn)*

FIRST READING
Isa 62:11-12

See, the LORD proclaims
  to the ends of the earth:
say to daughter Zion,
  your savior comes!
Here is his reward with him,
  his recompense before him.
They shall be called the holy people,
  the redeemed of the LORD,
and you shall be called "Frequented,"
  a city that is not forsaken.

RESPONSORIAL PSALM
Ps 97:1, 6, 11-12

R℣. A light will shine on us this day: the Lord
  is born for us.

The LORD is king; let the earth rejoice;
  let the many isles be glad.
The heavens proclaim his justice,
  and all peoples see his glory.

R℣. A light will shine on us this day: the Lord
  is born for us.

Light dawns for the just;
  and gladness, for the upright of heart.
Be glad in the LORD, you just,
  and give thanks to his holy name.

R℣. A light will shine on us this day: the Lord
  is born for us.

SECOND READING
Titus 3:4-7

Beloved:
When the kindness and generous love
  of God our savior appeared,
not because of any righteous deeds we had
  done
  but because of his mercy,
he saved us through the bath of rebirth
  and renewal by the Holy Spirit,
whom he richly poured out on us
  through Jesus Christ our savior,
so that we might be justified by his grace
  and become heirs in hope of eternal life.

Gospel (cont.)
John 1:1-18; L16ABC

And the Word became flesh
and made his dwelling among us,
and we saw his glory,
the glory as of the Father's only Son,
full of grace and truth.
John testified to him and cried out, saying,
"This was he of whom I said,
'The one who is coming after me ranks ahead of me
because he existed before me.'"
From his fullness we have all received,
grace in place of grace,
because while the law was given through Moses,
grace and truth came through Jesus Christ.
No one has ever seen God.
The only Son, God, who is at the Father's side,
has revealed him.

or John 1:1-5, 9-14

In the beginning was the Word,
and the Word was with God,
and the Word was God.
He was in the beginning with God.

All things came to be through him,
and without him nothing came to be.
What came to be through him was life,
and this life was the light of the human race;
the light shines in the darkness,
and the darkness has not overcome it.
The true light, which enlightens everyone,
was coming into the world.
He was in the world,
and the world came to be through him,
but the world did not know him.
He came to what was his own,
but his own people did not accept him.

But to those who did accept him
he gave power to become children of God,
to those who believe in his name,
who were born not by natural generation
nor by human choice nor by a man's decision
but of God.
And the Word became flesh
and made his dwelling among us,
and we saw his glory,
the glory as of the Father's only Son,
full of grace and truth.

FIRST READING
Isa 52:7-10

How beautiful upon the mountains
are the feet of him who brings glad tidings,
announcing peace, bearing good news,
announcing salvation, and saying to Zion,
"Your God is King!"

Hark! Your sentinels raise a cry,
together they shout for joy,
for they see directly, before their eyes,
the LORD restoring Zion.
Break out together in song,
O ruins of Jerusalem!
For the LORD comforts his people,
he redeems Jerusalem.
The LORD has bared his holy arm
in the sight of all the nations;
all the ends of the earth will behold
the salvation of our God.

RESPONSORIAL PSALM
Ps 98:1, 2-3, 3-4, 5-6

R̶. (3c) All the ends of the earth have seen the
saving power of God.

Sing to the LORD a new song,
for he has done wondrous deeds;
his right hand has won victory for him,
his holy arm.

R̶. All the ends of the earth have seen the
saving power of God.

The LORD has made his salvation known:
in the sight of the nations he has revealed
his justice.
He has remembered his kindness and his
faithfulness
toward the house of Israel.

R̶. All the ends of the earth have seen the
saving power of God.

All the ends of the earth have seen
the salvation by our God.
Sing joyfully to the LORD, all you lands;
break into song; sing praise.

R̶. All the ends of the earth have seen the
saving power of God.

Sing praise to the LORD with the harp,
with the harp and melodious song.
With trumpets and the sound of the horn
sing joyfully before the King, the LORD.

R̶. All the ends of the earth have seen the
saving power of God.

SECOND READING
Heb 1:1-6

Brothers and sisters:
In times past, God spoke in partial and
various ways
to our ancestors through the prophets;
in these last days, he has spoken to us
through the Son,
whom he made heir of all things
and through whom he created the universe,
who is the refulgence of his glory,
the very imprint of his being,
and who sustains all things by his
mighty word.
When he had accomplished purification
from sins,
he took his seat at the right hand of the
Majesty on high,
as far superior to the angels
as the name he has inherited is more
excellent than theirs.

For to which of the angels did God ever say:
*You are my son; this day I have begotten
you?*
Or again:
*I will be a father to him, and he shall be a
son to me?*
And again, when he leads the firstborn into
the world, he says:
Let all the angels of God worship him.

Gospel (cont.)

Luke 2:41-52; L17C

When his parents saw him,
   they were astonished,
   and his mother said to him,
   "Son, why have you done this to us?
Your father and I have been looking for you with great anxiety."
And he said to them,
   "Why were you looking for me?
Did you not know that I must be in my Father's house?"
But they did not understand what he said to them.
He went down with them and came to Nazareth,
   and was obedient to them;
   and his mother kept all these things in her heart.
And Jesus advanced in wisdom and age and favor
   before God and man.

FIRST READING

Sir 3:2-6, 12-14

God sets a father in honor over his children;
   a mother's authority he confirms over her
      sons.
Whoever honors his father atones for sins,
   and preserves himself from them.
When he prays, he is heard;
   he stores up riches who reveres his mother.
Whoever honors his father is gladdened by
   children,
   and, when he prays, is heard.
Whoever reveres his father will live a long life;
   he who obeys his father brings comfort to
      his mother.

My son, take care of your father when he is
   old;
   grieve him not as long as he lives.
Even if his mind fail, be considerate of him;
   revile him not all the days of his life;
kindness to a father will not be forgotten,
   firmly planted against the debt of your sins
   —a house raised in justice to you.

RESPONSORIAL PSALM

Ps 128:1-2, 3, 4-5

℞. (cf. 1) Blessed are those who fear the Lord
   and walk in his ways.

Blessed is everyone who fears the LORD,
   who walks in his ways!
For you shall eat the fruit of your handiwork;
   blessed shall you be, and favored.

℞. Blessed are those who fear the Lord and
   walk in his ways.

Your wife shall be like a fruitful vine
   in the recesses of your home;
your children like olive plants
   around your table.

℞. Blessed are those who fear the Lord and
   walk in his ways.

Behold, thus is the man blessed
   who fears the LORD.
The LORD bless you from Zion:
   may you see the prosperity of Jerusalem
   all the days of your life.

℞. Blessed are those who fear the Lord and
   walk in his ways.

SECOND READING

Col 3:12-21

Brothers and sisters:
Put on, as God's chosen ones, holy and
   beloved,
   heartfelt compassion, kindness, humility,
      gentleness, and patience,
   bearing with one another and forgiving one
      another,
   if one has a grievance against another;
   as the Lord has forgiven you, so must you
      also do.
And over all these put on love,
   that is, the bond of perfection.
And let the peace of Christ control your
   hearts,
   the peace into which you were also called in
      one body.
And be thankful.
Let the word of Christ dwell in you richly,
   as in all wisdom you teach and admonish
      one another,
   singing psalms, hymns, and spiritual songs
   with gratitude in your hearts to God.
And whatever you do, in word or in deed,
   do everything in the name of the Lord
      Jesus,
   giving thanks to God the Father through
      him.

Wives, be subordinate to your husbands,
   as is proper in the Lord.
Husbands, love your wives,
   and avoid any bitterness toward them.
Children, obey your parents in everything,
   for this is pleasing to the Lord.
Fathers, do not provoke your children,
   so they may not become discouraged.

or Col 3:12-17

Brothers and sisters:
Put on, as God's chosen ones, holy and beloved,
   heartfelt compassion, kindness, humility,
      gentleness, and patience,
   bearing with one another and forgiving one
      another,
   if one has a grievance against another;
   as the Lord has forgiven you, so must you
      also do.
And over all these put on love,
   that is, the bond of perfection.
And let the peace of Christ control your
   hearts,
   the peace into which you were also called in
      one body.
And be thankful.
Let the word of Christ dwell in you richly,
   as in all wisdom you teach and admonish
      one another,
   singing psalms, hymns, and spiritual songs
   with gratitude in your hearts to God.
And whatever you do, in word or in deed,
   do everything in the name of the Lord
      Jesus,
   giving thanks to God the Father through
      him.

Solemnity of Mary, the Holy Mother of God, *January 1, 2019*

FIRST READING
Num 6:22-27

The Lord said to Moses:
   "Speak to Aaron and his sons and tell them:
   This is how you shall bless the Israelites.
Say to them:
   The Lord bless you and keep you!
   The Lord let his face shine upon
     you, and be gracious to you!
   The Lord look upon you kindly and
     give you peace!
So shall they invoke my name upon the
    Israelites,
   and I will bless them."

RESPONSORIAL PSALM
Ps 67:2-3, 5, 6, 8

R̸. (2a) May God bless us in his mercy.

May God have pity on us and bless us;
   may he let his face shine upon us.
So may your way be known upon earth;
   among all nations, your salvation.

R̸. May God bless us in his mercy.

May the nations be glad and exult
   because you rule the peoples in equity;
   the nations on the earth you guide.

R̸. May God bless us in his mercy.

May the peoples praise you, O God;
   may all the peoples praise you!
May God bless us,
   and may all the ends of the earth fear him!

R̸. May God bless us in his mercy.

SECOND READING
Gal 4:4-7

Brothers and sisters:
When the fullness of time had come, God sent
    his Son,
   born of a woman, born under the law,
   to ransom those under the law,
   so that we might receive adoption as sons.
As proof that you are sons,
   God sent the Spirit of his Son into our
    hearts,
   crying out, "Abba, Father!"
So you are no longer a slave but a son,
   and if a son then also an heir, through God.

The Epiphany of the Lord, *January 6, 2019*

Gospel (cont.)
Matt 2:1-12; L20ABC

Then Herod called the magi secretly
   and ascertained from them the time of the star's appearance.
He sent them to Bethlehem and said,
   "Go and search diligently for the child.
When you have found him, bring me word,
   that I too may go and do him homage."
After their audience with the king they set out.
And behold, the star that they had seen at its rising preceded them,
   until it came and stopped over the place where the child was.
They were overjoyed at seeing the star,
   and on entering the house
   they saw the child with Mary his mother.
They prostrated themselves and did him homage.
Then they opened their treasures
   and offered him gifts of gold, frankincense, and myrrh.
And having been warned in a dream not to return to Herod,
   they departed for their country by another way.

Gospel

Luke 3:15-16, 21-22; L21C

The people were filled with expectation,
and all were asking in their hearts
whether John might be the Christ.
John answered them all, saying,
"I am baptizing you with water,
but one mightier than I is coming.
I am not worthy to loosen the thongs of his sandals.
He will baptize you with the Holy Spirit and fire."

After all the people had been baptized
and Jesus also had been baptized and was praying,
heaven was opened and the Holy Spirit descended upon him
in bodily form like a dove.
And a voice came from heaven,
"You are my beloved Son;
with you I am well pleased."

FIRST READING

Isa 40:1-5, 9-11

Comfort, give comfort to my people,
says your God.
Speak tenderly to Jerusalem, and proclaim
to her
that her service is at an end,
her guilt is expiated;
indeed, she has received from the hand of the
LORD
double for all her sins.

A voice cries out:
In the desert prepare the way of the LORD!
Make straight in the wasteland a highway
for our God!
Every valley shall be filled in,
every mountain and hill shall be made low;
the rugged land shall be made a plain,
the rough country, a broad valley.
Then the glory of the LORD shall be revealed,
and all people shall see it together;
for the mouth of the LORD has spoken.

Go up onto a high mountain,
Zion, herald of glad tidings;
cry out at the top of your voice,
Jerusalem, herald of good news!
Fear not to cry out
and say to the cities of Judah:
Here is your God!
Here comes with power
the Lord GOD,
who rules by a strong arm;
here is his reward with him,
his recompense before him.
Like a shepherd he feeds his flock;
in his arms he gathers the lambs,
carrying them in his bosom,
and leading the ewes with care.

RESPONSORIAL PSALM

Ps 104:1b-2, 3-4, 24-25, 27-28, 29-30

R̥. (1) O bless the Lord, my soul.

O LORD, my God, you are great indeed!
You are clothed with majesty and glory,
robed in light as with a cloak.
You have spread out the heavens like a
tent-cloth.

R̥. O bless the Lord, my soul.

You have constructed your palace upon the
waters.
You make the clouds your chariot;
you travel on the wings of the wind.
You make the winds your messengers,
and flaming fire your ministers.

R̥. O bless the Lord, my soul.

How manifold are your works, O LORD!
In wisdom you have wrought them all—
the earth is full of your creatures;
the sea also, great and wide,
in which are schools without number
of living things both small and great.

R̥. O bless the Lord, my soul.

They look to you to give them food in due
time.
When you give it to them, they gather it;
when you open your hand, they are filled
with good things.

R̥. O bless the Lord, my soul.

If you take away their breath, they perish and
return to the dust.
When you send forth your spirit, they are
created,
and you renew the face of the earth.

R̥. O bless the Lord, my soul.

SECOND READING

Titus 2:11-14; 3:4-7

Beloved:
The grace of God has appeared, saving all
and training us to reject godless ways and
worldly desires
and to live temperately, justly, and devoutly
in this age,
as we await the blessed hope,
the appearance of the glory of our great
God
and savior Jesus Christ,
who gave himself for us to deliver us from
all lawlessness
and to cleanse for himself a people as his
own,
eager to do what is good.
When the kindness and generous love
of God our savior appeared,
not because of any righteous deeds we had
done
but because of his mercy,
he saved us through the bath of rebirth
and renewal by the Holy Spirit,
whom he richly poured out on us
through Jesus Christ our savior,
so that we might be justified by his grace
and become heirs in hope of eternal life.

Gospel (cont.)
Luke 1:1-4; 4:14-21; L69C

He has sent me to proclaim liberty to captives
and recovery of sight to the blind,
to let the oppressed go free,
and to proclaim a year acceptable to the Lord.
Rolling up the scroll, he handed it back to the attendant and sat down,
and the eyes of all in the synagogue looked intently at him.
He said to them,
"Today this Scripture passage is fulfilled in your hearing."

SECOND READING
1 Cor 12:12-30

Brothers and sisters:
As a body is one though it has many parts,
and all the parts of the body, though many,
are one body,
so also Christ.
For in one Spirit we were all baptized into one
body,
whether Jews or Greeks, slaves or free
persons,
and we were all given to drink of one
Spirit.

Now the body is not a single part, but many.
If a foot should say,
"Because I am not a hand I do not belong to
the body,"
it does not for this reason belong any less
to the body.
Or if an ear should say,
"Because I am not an eye I do not belong to
the body,"
it does not for this reason belong any less
to the body.
If the whole body were an eye, where would
the hearing be?
If the whole body were hearing, where would
the sense of smell be?

But as it is, God placed the parts,
each one of them, in the body as he
intended.
If they were all one part, where would the
body be?
But as it is, there are many parts, yet one
body.
The eye cannot say to the hand, "I do not need
you,"
nor again the head to the feet, "I do not
need you."
Indeed, the parts of the body that seem to be
weaker
are all the more necessary,
and those parts of the body that we
consider less honorable
we surround with greater honor,
and our less presentable parts are treated
with greater propriety,
whereas our more presentable parts do not
need this.
But God has so constructed the body
as to give greater honor to a part that is
without it,
so that there may be no division in the
body,
but that the parts may have the same
concern for one another.
If one part suffers, all the parts suffer with it;

if one part is honored, all the parts share
its joy.
Now you are Christ's body, and individually
parts of it.
Some people God has designated in the
church
to be, first, apostles; second, prophets;
third, teachers;
then, mighty deeds;
then gifts of healing, assistance,
administration,
and varieties of tongues.
Are all apostles? Are all prophets? Are all
teachers?
Do all work mighty deeds? Do all have gifts
of healing?
Do all speak in tongues? Do all interpret?

SECOND READING

1 Cor 12:31–13:13

Brothers and sisters:
Strive eagerly for the greatest spiritual gifts.
But I shall show you a still more excellent way.

If I speak in human and angelic tongues,
    but do not have love,
    I am a resounding gong or a clashing cymbal.
And if I have the gift of prophecy,
    and comprehend all mysteries and all
        knowledge;
    if I have all faith so as to move mountains,
    but do not have love, I am nothing.
If I give away everything I own,
    and if I hand my body over so that I may
        boast,
    but do not have love, I gain nothing.

Love is patient, love is kind.
It is not jealous, it is not pompous,
    it is not inflated, it is not rude,
    it does not seek its own interests,
    it is not quick-tempered, it does not brood
        over injury,
    it does not rejoice over wrongdoing
    but rejoices with the truth.
It bears all things, believes all things,
    hopes all things, endures all things.

Love never fails.
If there are prophecies, they will be brought
    to nothing;
    if tongues, they will cease;
    if knowledge, it will be brought to
        nothing.
For we know partially and we prophesy
    partially,
but when the perfect comes, the partial will
    pass away.
When I was a child, I used to talk as a child,
    think as a child, reason as a child;
    when I became a man, I put aside childish
        things.
At present we see indistinctly, as in a mirror,
    but then face to face.
At present I know partially;
    then I shall know fully, as I am fully known.
So faith, hope, love remain, these three;
    but the greatest of these is love.

Gospel (cont.)

Luke 5:1-11; L75C

When Simon Peter saw this, he fell at the knees of Jesus and said,
    "Depart from me, Lord, for I am a sinful man."
For astonishment at the catch of fish they had made seized him
    and all those with him,
    and likewise James and John, the sons of Zebedee,
    who were partners of Simon.
Jesus said to Simon, "Do not be afraid;
    from now on you will be catching men."
When they brought their boats to the shore,
    they left everything and followed him.

SECOND READING

1 Cor 15:1-11

I am reminding you, brothers and sisters,
    of the gospel I preached to you,
    which you indeed received and in which
        you also stand.
Through it you are also being saved,
    if you hold fast to the word I preached to
        you,
    unless you believed in vain.
For I handed on to you as of first importance
    what I also received:
    that Christ died for our sins
        in accordance with the Scriptures;
    that he was buried;
    that he was raised on the third day
        in accordance with the Scriptures;
    that he appeared to Cephas, then to the
        Twelve.

After that, he appeared to more
        than five hundred brothers at once,
    most of whom are still living,
    though some have fallen asleep.
After that he appeared to James,
    then to all the apostles.
Last of all, as to one born abnormally,
    he appeared to me.
For I am the least of the apostles,
    not fit to be called an apostle,
    because I persecuted the church of God.
But by the grace of God I am what I am,
    and his grace to me has not been
        ineffective.
Indeed, I have toiled harder than all of them;
    not I, however, but the grace of God that is
        with me.
Therefore, whether it be I or they,
    so we preach and so you believed.

FIRST READING
Joel 2:12-18

Even now, says the LORD,
    return to me with your whole heart,
    with fasting, and weeping, and mourning;
Rend your hearts, not your garments,
    and return to the LORD, your God.
For gracious and merciful is he,
    slow to anger, rich in kindness,
    and relenting in punishment.
Perhaps he will again relent
    and leave behind him a blessing,
Offerings and libations
    for the LORD, your God.

Blow the trumpet in Zion!
    proclaim a fast,
    call an assembly;
Gather the people,
    notify the congregation;
Assemble the elders,
    gather the children
    and the infants at the breast;
Let the bridegroom quit his room
    and the bride her chamber.
Between the porch and the altar
    let the priests, the ministers of the LORD,
        weep,
And say, "Spare, O LORD, your people,
    and make not your heritage a reproach,
    with the nations ruling over them!
Why should they say among the peoples,
    'Where is their God?'"

Then the LORD was stirred to concern for his
        land
    and took pity on his people.

RESPONSORIAL PSALM
Ps 51:3-4, 5-6ab, 12-13, 14, and 17

℟. (see 3a) Be merciful, O Lord, for we have
    sinned.

Have mercy on me, O God, in your goodness;
    in the greatness of your compassion wipe
        out my offense.
Thoroughly wash me from my guilt
    and of my sin cleanse me.

℟. Be merciful, O Lord, for we have sinned.

For I acknowledge my offense,
    and my sin is before me always:
"Against you only have I sinned,
    and done what is evil in your sight."

℟. Be merciful, O Lord, for we have sinned.

A clean heart create for me, O God,
    and a steadfast spirit renew within me.
Cast me not out from your presence,
    and your Holy Spirit take not from me.

℟. Be merciful, O Lord, for we have sinned.

Give me back the joy of your salvation,
    and a willing spirit sustain in me.
O Lord, open my lips,
    and my mouth shall proclaim your praise.

℟. Be merciful, O Lord, for we have sinned.

SECOND READING
2 Cor 5:20–6:2

Brothers and sisters:
We are ambassadors for Christ,
    as if God were appealing through us.
We implore you on behalf of Christ,
    be reconciled to God.
For our sake he made him to be sin who did
        not know sin,
    so that we might become the righteousness
        of God in him.

Working together, then,
    we appeal to you not to receive the grace of
        God in vain.
For he says:

In an acceptable time I heard you,
    and on the day of salvation I helped you.

Behold, now is a very acceptable time;
    behold, now is the day of salvation.

SECOND READING
Rom 10:8-13

Brothers and sisters:
What does Scripture say?
  The word is near you,
    in your mouth and in your heart
  —that is, the word of faith that we
      preach—,
  for, if you confess with your mouth that
      Jesus is Lord
  and believe in your heart that God raised
      him from the dead,
  you will be saved.
For one believes with the heart and so is
      justified,
  and one confesses with the mouth and so
      is saved.
For the Scripture says,
  No one who believes in him will be put to
      shame.
For there is no distinction between Jew and
      Greek;
  the same Lord is Lord of all,
  enriching all who call upon him.
For "everyone who calls on the name of the
      Lord will be saved."

SECOND READING
Phil 3:20–4:1

Brothers and sisters:
Our citizenship is in heaven,
  and from it we also await a savior, the Lord
      Jesus Christ.
He will change our lowly body
  to conform with his glorified body
  by the power that enables him also
  to bring all things into subjection to
      himself.

Therefore, my brothers and sisters,
  whom I love and long for, my joy and
      crown,
  in this way stand firm in the Lord, beloved.

St. Joseph, Spouse of the Blessed Virgin Mary, *March 19, 2019*

Gospel
Luke 2:41-51a; L543

Each year Jesus' parents went to Jerusalem for the feast of Passover,
  and when he was twelve years old,
    they went up according to festival custom.
After they had completed its days, as they were returning,
  the boy Jesus remained behind in Jerusalem,
    but his parents did not know it.
Thinking that he was in the caravan,
  they journeyed for a day
    and looked for him among their relatives and acquaintances,
  but not finding him,
    they returned to Jerusalem to look for him.
After three days they found him in the temple,
  sitting in the midst of the teachers,
    listening to them and asking them questions,
    and all who heard him were astounded
    at his understanding and his answers.
When his parents saw him,
  they were astonished,
    and his mother said to him,
  "Son, why have you done this to us?
Your father and I have been looking for you with great anxiety."

And he said to them,
    "Why were you looking for me?
Did you not know that I must be in my Father's house?"
But they did not understand what he said to them.
He went down with them and came to Nazareth,
  and was obedient to them.

St. Joseph, Spouse of the Blessed Virgin Mary, *March 19, 2019*

FIRST READING
2 Sam 7:4-5a, 12-14a, 16

The LORD spoke to Nathan and said:
"Go, tell my servant David,
'When your time comes and you rest with
   your ancestors,
I will raise up your heir after you, sprung
   from your loins,
and I will make his kingdom firm.
It is he who shall build a house for my name.
And I will make his royal throne firm forever.
I will be a father to him,
   and he shall be a son to me.
Your house and your kingdom shall endure
   forever before me;
   your throne shall stand firm forever.'"

RESPONSORIAL PSALM
Ps 89:2-3, 4-5, 27 and 29

R̸. (37) The son of David will live for ever.

The promises of the LORD I will sing forever,
   through all generations my mouth will
      proclaim your faithfulness,
For you have said, "My kindness is
   established forever";
   in heaven you have confirmed your
      faithfulness.

R̸. The son of David will live for ever.

"I have made a covenant with my chosen one;
   I have sworn to David my servant:
Forever will I confirm your posterity
   and establish your throne for all
      generations."

R̸. The son of David will live for ever.

"He shall say of me, 'You are my father,
   my God, the Rock, my savior.'
Forever I will maintain my kindness toward
   him,
   and my covenant with him stands firm."

R̸. The son of David will live for ever.

SECOND READING
Rom 4:13, 16-18, 22

Brothers and sisters:
It was not through the law
   that the promise was made to Abraham
      and his descendants
   that he would inherit the world,
   but through the righteousness that comes
      from faith.
For this reason, it depends on faith,
   so that it may be a gift,
   and the promise may be guaranteed to all
      his descendants,
   not to those who only adhere to the law
   but to those who follow the faith of
      Abraham,
   who is the father of all of us, as it is
      written,
   I have made you father of many nations.
He is our father in the sight of God,
   in whom he believed, who gives life to the
      dead
   and calls into being what does not exist.
He believed, hoping against hope,
   that he would become *the father of many
      nations,*
   according to what was said, *Thus shall your
      descendants be.*
That is why *it was credited to him as
   righteousness.*

Third Sunday of Lent, *March 24, 2019*

SECOND READING
1 Cor 10:1-6, 10-12

I do not want you to be unaware, brothers and
   sisters,
   that our ancestors were all under the cloud
   and all passed through the sea,
   and all of them were baptized into Moses
   in the cloud and in the sea.
All ate the same spiritual food,
   and all drank the same spiritual drink,
   for they drank from a spiritual rock that
      followed them,
   and the rock was the Christ.
Yet God was not pleased with most of them,
   for they were struck down in the desert.

These things happened as examples for us,
   so that we might not desire evil things, as
      they did.

Do not grumble as some of them did,
   and suffered death by the destroyer.
These things happened to them as an
      example,
   and they have been written down as a
      warning to us,
   upon whom the end of the ages has come.
Therefore, whoever thinks he is standing
      secure
   should take care not to fall.

Gospel

John 4:5-42; L28A

Jesus came to a town of Samaria called Sychar,
    near the plot of land that Jacob had given to his son Joseph.
Jacob's well was there.
Jesus, tired from his journey, sat down there at the well.
It was about noon.

A woman of Samaria came to draw water.
Jesus said to her,
    "Give me a drink."
His disciples had gone into the town to buy food.
The Samaritan woman said to him,
    "How can you, a Jew, ask me, a Samaritan woman, for a drink?"
—For Jews use nothing in common with Samaritans.—
Jesus answered and said to her,
    "If you knew the gift of God
    and who is saying to you, 'Give me a drink,'
    you would have asked him
    and he would have given you living water."
The woman said to him,
    "Sir, you do not even have a bucket and the cistern is deep;
    where then can you get this living water?
Are you greater than our father Jacob,
    who gave us this cistern and drank from it himself
    with his children and his flocks?"
Jesus answered and said to her,
    "Everyone who drinks this water will be thirsty again;
    but whoever drinks the water I shall give will never thirst;
    the water I shall give will become in him
    a spring of water welling up to eternal life."
The woman said to him,
    "Sir, give me this water, so that I may not be thirsty
    or have to keep coming here to draw water."

Jesus said to her,
    "Go call your husband and come back."
The woman answered and said to him,
    "I do not have a husband."
Jesus answered her,
    "You are right in saying, 'I do not have a husband.'
For you have had five husbands,
    and the one you have now is not your husband.
What you have said is true."
The woman said to him,
    "Sir, I can see that you are a prophet.
Our ancestors worshiped on this mountain;
    but you people say that the place to worship is in Jerusalem."
Jesus said to her,
    "Believe me, woman, the hour is coming
    when you will worship the Father
    neither on this mountain nor in Jerusalem.
You people worship what you do not understand;
    we worship what we understand,
    because salvation is from the Jews.
But the hour is coming, and is now here,
    when true worshipers will worship the Father in Spirit and truth;
    and indeed the Father seeks such people to worship him.
God is Spirit, and those who worship him
    must worship in Spirit and truth."
The woman said to him,

"I know that the Messiah is coming, the one called the Christ;
    when he comes, he will tell us everything."
Jesus said to her,
    "I am he, the one speaking with you."

At that moment his disciples returned,
    and were amazed that he was talking with a woman,
    but still no one said, "What are you looking for?"
    or "Why are you talking with her?"
The woman left her water jar
    and went into the town and said to the people,
    "Come see a man who told me everything I have done.
Could he possibly be the Christ?"
They went out of the town and came to him.
Meanwhile, the disciples urged him, "Rabbi, eat."
But he said to them,
    "I have food to eat of which you do not know."
So the disciples said to one another,
    "Could someone have brought him something to eat?"
Jesus said to them,
    "My food is to do the will of the one who sent me
    and to finish his work.
Do you not say, 'In four months the harvest will be here'?
I tell you, look up and see the fields ripe for the harvest.
The reaper is already receiving payment
    and gathering crops for eternal life,
    so that the sower and reaper can rejoice together.
For here the saying is verified that 'One sows and another reaps.'
I sent you to reap what you have not worked for;
    others have done the work,
    and you are sharing the fruits of their work."

Many of the Samaritans of that town began to believe in him
    because of the word of the woman who testified,
    "He told me everything I have done."
When the Samaritans came to him,
    they invited him to stay with them;
    and he stayed there two days.
Many more began to believe in him because of his word,
    and they said to the woman,
    "We no longer believe because of your word;
    for we have heard for ourselves,
    and we know that this is truly the savior of the world."

or
John 4:5-15, 19b-26, 39a, 40-42; L28A

Jesus came to a town of Samaria called Sychar,
    near the plot of land that Jacob had given to his son Joseph.
Jacob's well was there.
Jesus, tired from his journey, sat down there at the well.
It was about noon.

A woman of Samaria came to draw water.
Jesus said to her,
    "Give me a drink."
His disciples had gone into the town to buy food.
The Samaritan woman said to him,
    "How can you, a Jew, ask me, a Samaritan woman, for a drink?"
—For Jews use nothing in common with Samaritans.—
Jesus answered and said to her,

"If you knew the gift of God
and who is saying to you, 'Give me a drink,'
you would have asked him
and he would have given you living water."
The woman said to him,
"Sir, you do not even have a bucket and the cistern is deep;
where then can you get this living water?
Are you greater than our father Jacob,
who gave us this cistern and drank from it himself
with his children and his flocks?"
Jesus answered and said to her,
"Everyone who drinks this water will be thirsty again;
but whoever drinks the water I shall give will never thirst;
the water I shall give will become in him
a spring of water welling up to eternal life."
The woman said to him,
"Sir, give me this water, so that I may not be thirsty
or have to keep coming here to draw water.

"I can see that you are a prophet.
Our ancestors worshiped on this mountain;
but you people say that the place to worship is in Jerusalem."
Jesus said to her,
"Believe me, woman, the hour is coming
when you will worship the Father

neither on this mountain nor in Jerusalem.
You people worship what you do not understand;
we worship what we understand,
because salvation is from the Jews.
But the hour is coming, and is now here,
when true worshipers will worship the Father in Spirit and truth;
and indeed the Father seeks such people to worship him.
God is Spirit, and those who worship him
must worship in Spirit and truth."
The woman said to him,
"I know that the Messiah is coming, the one called the Christ;
when he comes, he will tell us everything."
Jesus said to her,
"I am he, the one speaking with you."

Many of the Samaritans of that town began to believe in him.
When the Samaritans came to him,
they invited him to stay with them;
and he stayed there two days.
Many more began to believe in him because of his word,
and they said to the woman,
"We no longer believe because of your word;
for we have heard for ourselves,
and we know that this is truly the savior of the world."

FIRST READING
Exod 17:3-7

In those days, in their thirst for water,
the people grumbled against Moses,
saying, "Why did you ever make us leave Egypt?
Was it just to have us die here of thirst
with our children and our livestock?"
So Moses cried out to the LORD,
"What shall I do with this people?
A little more and they will stone me!"
The LORD answered Moses,
"Go over there in front of the people,
along with some of the elders of Israel,
holding in your hand, as you go,
the staff with which you struck the river.
I will be standing there in front of you on the
rock in Horeb.
Strike the rock, and the water will flow from it
for the people to drink."
This Moses did, in the presence of the elders
of Israel.
The place was called Massah and Meribah,
because the Israelites quarreled there
and tested the LORD, saying,
"Is the LORD in our midst or not?"

RESPONSORIAL PSALM
Ps 95:1-2, 6-7, 8-9

R℣. (8) If today you hear his voice, harden not
your hearts.

Come, let us sing joyfully to the LORD;
let us acclaim the Rock of our salvation.
Let us come into his presence with
thanksgiving;
let us joyfully sing psalms to him.

R℣. If today you hear his voice, harden not
your hearts.

Come, let us bow down in worship;
let us kneel before the LORD who made us.
For he is our God,
and we are the people he shepherds, the
flock he guides.

R℣. If today you hear his voice, harden not
your hearts.

Oh, that today you would hear his voice:
"Harden not your hearts as at Meribah,
as in the day of Massah in the desert,
Where your fathers tempted me;
they tested me though they had seen my
works."

R℣. If today you hear his voice, harden not
your hearts.

SECOND READING
Rom 5:1-2, 5-8

Brothers and sisters:
Since we have been justified by faith,
we have peace with God through our Lord
Jesus Christ,
through whom we have gained access by
faith
to this grace in which we stand,
and we boast in hope of the glory of God.

And hope does not disappoint,
because the love of God has been poured
out into our hearts
through the Holy Spirit who has been given
to us.
For Christ, while we were still helpless,
died at the appointed time for the ungodly.
Indeed, only with difficulty does one die for a
just person,
though perhaps for a good person one
might even find courage to die.
But God proves his love for us
in that while we were still sinners Christ
died for us.

Gospel (cont.)
Luke 1:26-38; L545

But Mary said to the angel,
   "How can this be,
   since I have no relations with a man?"
And the angel said to her in reply,
   "The Holy Spirit will come upon you,
   and the power of the Most High will
      overshadow you.
Therefore the child to be born
   will be called holy, the Son of God.
And behold, Elizabeth, your relative,
   has also conceived a son in her old age,
   and this is the sixth month for her who was
      called barren;
   for nothing will be impossible for God."
Mary said, "Behold, I am the handmaid of the
   Lord.
May it be done to me according to your word."
Then the angel departed from her.

FIRST READING
Isa 7:10-14; 8:10

The Lord spoke to Ahaz, saying:
Ask for a sign from the Lord, your God;
   let it be deep as the nether world, or high as
      the sky!
But Ahaz answered,
   "I will not ask! I will not tempt the Lord!"
Then Isaiah said:
   Listen, O house of David!
Is it not enough for you to weary people,
   must you also weary my God?
Therefore the Lord himself will give you this
      sign:
   the virgin shall be with child, and bear a son,
   and shall name him Emmanuel,
   which means "God is with us!"

RESPONSORIAL PSALM
Ps 40:7-8a, 8b-9, 10, 11

R̸. (8a and 9a) Here I am, Lord; I come to do
   your will.

Sacrifice or offering you wished not,
   but ears open to obedience you gave me.
Holocausts and sin-offerings you sought not;
   then said I, "Behold, I come."

R̸. Here I am, Lord; I come to do your will.

"In the written scroll it is prescribed for me,
To do your will, O God, is my delight,
   and your law is within my heart!"

R̸. Here I am, Lord; I come to do your will.

I announced your justice in the vast assembly;
   I did not restrain my lips, as you, O Lord,
      know.

R̸. Here I am, Lord; I come to do your will.

Your justice I kept not hid within my heart;
   your faithfulness and your salvation I have
      spoken of;
I have made no secret of your kindness and
      your truth
   in the vast assembly.

R̸. Here I am, Lord; I come to do your will.

SECOND READING
Heb 10:4-10

Brothers and sisters:
It is impossible that the blood of bulls and
      goats
   takes away sins.
For this reason, when Christ came into the
      world, he said:

   "Sacrifice and offering you did not desire,
      but a body you prepared for me;
   in holocausts and sin offerings you took no
      delight.
   Then I said, 'As is written of me in the scroll,
   behold, I come to do your will, O God.'"

First Christ says, "Sacrifices and offerings,
   holocausts and sin offerings,
   you neither desired nor delighted in."
These are offered according to the law.
Then he says, "Behold, I come to do your will."
He takes away the first to establish the second.
By this "will," we have been consecrated
   through the offering of the Body of Jesus
      Christ once for all.

Gospel (cont.)
Luke 15:1-3, 11-32; L33C

I no longer deserve to be called your son;
    treat me as you would treat one of your hired workers.'"
So he got up and went back to his father.
While he was still a long way off,
    his father caught sight of him, and was filled with compassion.
He ran to his son, embraced him and kissed him.
His son said to him,
    'Father, I have sinned against heaven and against you;
    I no longer deserve to be called your son.'
But his father ordered his servants,
    'Quickly bring the finest robe and put it on him;
    put a ring on his finger and sandals on his feet.
Take the fattened calf and slaughter it.
Then let us celebrate with a feast,
    because this son of mine was dead, and has come to life again;
    he was lost, and has been found.'
Then the celebration began.
Now the older son had been out in the field
    and, on his way back, as he neared the house,
    he heard the sound of music and dancing.
He called one of the servants and asked what this might mean.

The servant said to him,
    'Your brother has returned
    and your father has slaughtered the fattened calf
    because he has him back safe and sound.'
He became angry,
    and when he refused to enter the house,
    his father came out and pleaded with him.
He said to his father in reply,
    'Look, all these years I served you
    and not once did I disobey your orders;
    yet you never gave me even a young goat to feast on with
        my friends.
But when your son returns
    who swallowed up your property with prostitutes,
    for him you slaughter the fattened calf.'
He said to him,
    'My son, you are here with me always;
    everything I have is yours.
But now we must celebrate and rejoice,
    because your brother was dead and has come to life again;
    he was lost and has been found.'"

Gospel

John 9:1-41; L31A

As Jesus passed by he saw a man blind from birth.
His disciples asked him,
    "Rabbi, who sinned, this man or his parents,
    that he was born blind?"
Jesus answered,
    "Neither he nor his parents sinned;
    it is so that the works of God might be made visible through him.
We have to do the works of the one who sent me while it is day.
Night is coming when no one can work.
While I am in the world, I am the light of the world."
When he had said this, he spat on the ground
    and made clay with the saliva,
    and smeared the clay on his eyes, and said to him,
    "Go wash in the Pool of Siloam"—which means Sent—.
So he went and washed, and came back able to see.

His neighbors and those who had seen him earlier as a beggar said,
    "Isn't this the one who used to sit and beg?"
Some said, "It is,"
    but others said, "No, he just looks like him."
He said, "I am."
So they said to him, "How were your eyes opened?"
He replied,
    "The man called Jesus made clay and anointed my eyes
    and told me, 'Go to Siloam and wash.'
So I went there and washed and was able to see."
And they said to him, "Where is he?"
He said, "I don't know."

They brought the one who was once blind to the Pharisees.
Now Jesus had made clay and opened his eyes on a sabbath.
So then the Pharisees also asked him how he was able to see.
He said to them,
    "He put clay on my eyes, and I washed, and now I can see."
So some of the Pharisees said,
    "This man is not from God,
    because he does not keep the sabbath."
But others said,
    "How can a sinful man do such signs?"
And there was a division among them.
So they said to the blind man again,
    "What do you have to say about him,
    since he opened your eyes?"
He said, "He is a prophet."

Now the Jews did not believe
    that he had been blind and gained his sight
    until they summoned the parents of the one who had gained his
        sight.
They asked them,
    "Is this your son, who you say was born blind?
How does he now see?"
His parents answered and said,
    "We know that this is our son and that he was born blind.
We do not know how he sees now,
    nor do we know who opened his eyes.
Ask him, he is of age;
    he can speak for himself."
His parents said this because they were afraid of the Jews,
    for the Jews had already agreed
    that if anyone acknowledged him as the Christ,
    he would be expelled from the synagogue.
For this reason his parents said,
    "He is of age; question him."

So a second time they called the man who had been blind
    and said to him, "Give God the praise!
We know that this man is a sinner."
He replied,
    "If he is a sinner, I do not know.
One thing I do know is that I was blind and now I see."
So they said to him,
    "What did he do to you?
    How did he open your eyes?"
He answered them,
    "I told you already and you did not listen.
Why do you want to hear it again?
Do you want to become his disciples, too?"
They ridiculed him and said,
    "You are that man's disciple;
    we are disciples of Moses!
We know that God spoke to Moses,
    but we do not know where this one is from."
The man answered and said to them,
    "This is what is so amazing,
    that you do not know where he is from, yet he opened my eyes.
We know that God does not listen to sinners,
    but if one is devout and does his will, he listens to him.
It is unheard of that anyone ever opened the eyes of a person born
        blind.
If this man were not from God,
    he would not be able to do anything."
They answered and said to him,
    "You were born totally in sin,
    and are you trying to teach us?"
Then they threw him out.

When Jesus heard that they had thrown him out,
    he found him and said, "Do you believe in the Son of Man?"
He answered and said,
    "Who is he, sir, that I may believe in him?"
Jesus said to him,
    "You have seen him,
    and the one speaking with you is he."
He said,
    "I do believe, Lord," and he worshiped him.
Then Jesus said,
    "I came into this world for judgment,
    so that those who do not see might see,
    and those who do see might become blind."

Some of the Pharisees who were with him heard this
    and said to him, "Surely we are not also blind, are we?"
Jesus said to them,
    "If you were blind, you would have no sin;
    but now you are saying, 'We see,' so your sin remains."

Gospel
John 9:1, 6-9, 13-17, 34-38; L31A

As Jesus passed by he saw a man blind from birth.
He spat on the ground and made clay with the saliva,
and smeared the clay on his eyes, and said to him,
"Go wash in the Pool of Siloam"—which means Sent—.
So he went and washed, and came back able to see.

His neighbors and those who had seen him earlier as a beggar said,
"Isn't this the one who used to sit and beg?"
Some said, "It is,"
but others said, "No, he just looks like him."
He said, "I am."

They brought the one who was once blind to the Pharisees.
Now Jesus had made clay and opened his eyes on a sabbath.
So then the Pharisees also asked him how he was able to see.
He said to them,
"He put clay on my eyes, and I washed, and now I can see."
So some of the Pharisees said,
"This man is not from God,
because he does not keep the sabbath."
But others said,
"How can a sinful man do such signs?"
And there was a division among them.

So they said to the blind man again,
"What do you have to say about him,
since he opened your eyes?"
He said, "He is a prophet."

They answered and said to him,
"You were born totally in sin,
and are you trying to teach us?"
Then they threw him out.

When Jesus heard that they had thrown him out,
he found him and said, "Do you believe in the Son of Man?"
He answered and said,
"Who is he, sir, that I may believe in him?"
Jesus said to him,
"You have seen him,
and the one speaking with you is he."
He said,
"I do believe, Lord," and he worshiped him.

FIRST READING 1 Sam 16:1b, 6-7, 10-13a

The Lord said to Samuel:
"Fill your horn with oil, and be on your way.
I am sending you to Jesse of Bethlehem,
for I have chosen my king from among his
sons."

As Jesse and his sons came to the sacrifice,
Samuel looked at Eliab and thought,
"Surely the Lord's anointed is here before
him."
But the Lord said to Samuel:
"Do not judge from his appearance or from
his lofty stature,
because I have rejected him.
Not as man sees does God see,
because man sees the appearance
but the Lord looks into the heart."
In the same way Jesse presented seven sons
before Samuel,
but Samuel said to Jesse,
"The Lord has not chosen any one of these."
Then Samuel asked Jesse,
"Are these all the sons you have?"
Jesse replied,
"There is still the youngest, who is tending
the sheep."
Samuel said to Jesse,
"Send for him;
we will not begin the sacrificial banquet
until he arrives here."
Jesse sent and had the young man brought to
them.
He was ruddy, a youth handsome to behold
and making a splendid appearance.

The Lord said,
"There—anoint him, for this is the one!"
Then Samuel, with the horn of oil in hand,
anointed David in the presence of his
brothers;
and from that day on, the spirit of the Lord
rushed upon David.

RESPONSORIAL PSALM Ps 23:1-3a, 3b-4, 5, 6

R̸. (1) The Lord is my shepherd; there is nothing I shall want.

The Lord is my shepherd; I shall not want.
In verdant pastures he gives me repose;
beside restful waters he leads me;
he refreshes my soul.

R̸. The Lord is my shepherd; there is nothing
I shall want.

He guides me in right paths
for his name's sake.
Even though I walk in the dark valley
I fear no evil; for you are at my side
with your rod and your staff
that give me courage.

R̸. The Lord is my shepherd; there is nothing
I shall want.

You spread the table before me
in the sight of my foes;
you anoint my head with oil;
my cup overflows.

R̸. The Lord is my shepherd; there is nothing
I shall want.

Only goodness and kindness follow me
all the days of my life;
and I shall dwell in the house of the Lord
for years to come.

R̸. The Lord is my shepherd; there is nothing
I shall want.

SECOND READING
Eph 5:8-14

Brothers and sisters:
You were once darkness,
but now you are light in the Lord.
Live as children of light,
for light produces every kind of goodness
and righteousness and truth.
Try to learn what is pleasing to the Lord.
Take no part in the fruitless works of
darkness;
rather expose them, for it is shameful even
to mention
the things done by them in secret;
but everything exposed by the light
becomes visible,
for everything that becomes visible is light.
Therefore, it says:
"Awake, O sleeper,
and arise from the dead,
and Christ will give you light."

Gospel

John 11:1-45; L34A

Now a man was ill, Lazarus from Bethany,
    the village of Mary and her sister Martha.
Mary was the one who had anointed the Lord with perfumed oil
    and dried his feet with her hair;
    it was her brother Lazarus who was ill.
So the sisters sent word to Jesus saying,
    "Master, the one you love is ill."
When Jesus heard this he said,
    "This illness is not to end in death,
    but is for the glory of God,
    that the Son of God may be glorified through it."
Now Jesus loved Martha and her sister and Lazarus.
So when he heard that he was ill,
    he remained for two days in the place where he was.
Then after this he said to his disciples,
    "Let us go back to Judea."
The disciples said to him,
    "Rabbi, the Jews were just trying to stone you,
    and you want to go back there?"
Jesus answered,
    "Are there not twelve hours in a day?
If one walks during the day, he does not stumble,
    because he sees the light of this world.
But if one walks at night, he stumbles,
    because the light is not in him."
He said this, and then told them,
    "Our friend Lazarus is asleep,
    but I am going to awaken him."
So the disciples said to him,
    "Master, if he is asleep, he will be saved."
But Jesus was talking about his death,
    while they thought that he meant ordinary sleep.
So then Jesus said to them clearly,
    "Lazarus has died.
And I am glad for you that I was not there,
    that you may believe.
Let us go to him."
So Thomas, called Didymus, said to his fellow disciples,
    "Let us also go to die with him."

When Jesus arrived, he found that Lazarus
    had already been in the tomb for four days.
Now Bethany was near Jerusalem, only about two miles away.
And many of the Jews had come to Martha and Mary
    to comfort them about their brother.
When Martha heard that Jesus was coming,
    she went to meet him;
    but Mary sat at home.
Martha said to Jesus,
    "Lord, if you had been here,
    my brother would not have died.
But even now I know that whatever you ask of God,
    God will give you."
Jesus said to her,
    "Your brother will rise."
Martha said to him,
    "I know he will rise,
    in the resurrection on the last day."
Jesus told her,

    "I am the resurrection and the life;
    whoever believes in me, even if he dies, will live,
    and everyone who lives and believes in me will never die.
Do you believe this?"
She said to him, "Yes, Lord.
I have come to believe that you are the Christ, the Son of God,
    the one who is coming into the world."

When she had said this,
    she went and called her sister Mary secretly, saying,
    "The teacher is here and is asking for you."
As soon as she heard this,
    she rose quickly and went to him.
For Jesus had not yet come into the village,
    but was still where Martha had met him.
So when the Jews who were with her in the house comforting her
    saw Mary get up quickly and go out,
    they followed her,
    presuming that she was going to the tomb to weep there.
When Mary came to where Jesus was and saw him,
    she fell at his feet and said to him,
    "Lord, if you had been here,
    my brother would not have died."
When Jesus saw her weeping and the Jews who had come with her
        weeping,
    he became perturbed and deeply troubled, and said,
    "Where have you laid him?"
They said to him, "Sir, come and see."
And Jesus wept.
So the Jews said, "See how he loved him."
But some of them said,
    "Could not the one who opened the eyes of the blind man
    have done something so that this man would not have died?"

So Jesus, perturbed again, came to the tomb.
It was a cave, and a stone lay across it.
Jesus said, "Take away the stone."
Martha, the dead man's sister, said to him,
    "Lord, by now there will be a stench;
    he has been dead for four days."
Jesus said to her,
    "Did I not tell you that if you believe
    you will see the glory of God?"
So they took away the stone.
And Jesus raised his eyes and said,
    "Father, I thank you for hearing me.
I know that you always hear me;
    but because of the crowd here I have said this,
    that they may believe that you sent me."
And when he had said this,
    he cried out in a loud voice,
    "Lazarus, come out!"
The dead man came out,
    tied hand and foot with burial bands,
    and his face was wrapped in a cloth.
So Jesus said to them,
    "Untie him and let him go."

Now many of the Jews who had come to Mary
    and seen what he had done began to believe in him.

Gospel
John 11:3-7, 17, 20-27, 33b-45; L34A

The sisters of Lazarus sent word to Jesus saying,
    "Master, the one you love is ill."
When Jesus heard this he said,
    "This illness is not to end in death,
    but is for the glory of God,
    that the Son of God may be glorified through it."
Now Jesus loved Martha and her sister and Lazarus.
So when he heard that he was ill,
    he remained for two days in the place where he was.
Then after this he said to his disciples,
    "Let us go back to Judea."

When Jesus arrived, he found that Lazarus
    had already been in the tomb for four days.
When Martha heard that Jesus was coming,
    she went to meet him;
    but Mary sat at home.
Martha said to Jesus,
    "Lord, if you had been here,
    my brother would not have died.
But even now I know that whatever you ask of God,
    God will give you."
Jesus said to her,
    "Your brother will rise."
Martha said,
    "I know he will rise,
    in the resurrection on the last day."
Jesus told her,
    "I am the resurrection and the life;
    whoever believes in me, even if he dies, will live,
    and everyone who lives and believes in me will never die.
Do you believe this?"
She said to him, "Yes, Lord.
I have come to believe that you are the Christ, the Son of God,
    the one who is coming into the world."

He became perturbed and deeply troubled, and said,
    "Where have you laid him?"
They said to him, "Sir, come and see."
And Jesus wept.
So the Jews said, "See how he loved him."
But some of them said,
    "Could not the one who opened the eyes of the blind man
    have done something so that this man would not have died?"

So Jesus, perturbed again, came to the tomb.
It was a cave, and a stone lay across it.
Jesus said, "Take away the stone."
Martha, the dead man's sister, said to him,
    "Lord, by now there will be a stench;
    he has been dead for four days."
Jesus said to her,
    "Did I not tell you that if you believe
    you will see the glory of God?"
So they took away the stone.
And Jesus raised his eyes and said,
    "Father, I thank you for hearing me.
I know that you always hear me;
    but because of the crowd here I have said this,
    that they may believe that you sent me."
And when he had said this,
    he cried out in a loud voice,
    "Lazarus, come out!"
The dead man came out,
    tied hand and foot with burial bands,
    and his face was wrapped in a cloth.
So Jesus said to them,
    "Untie him and let him go."

Now many of the Jews who had come to Mary
    and seen what he had done began to believe in him.

FIRST READING
Ezek 37:12-14

Thus says the Lord GOD:
    O my people, I will open your graves
    and have you rise from them,
    and bring you back to the land of Israel.
Then you shall know that I am the LORD,
    when I open your graves and have you rise
        from them,
    O my people!
I will put my spirit in you that you may live,
    and I will settle you upon your land;
    thus you shall know that I am the LORD.
I have promised, and I will do it, says the LORD.

RESPONSORIAL PSALM
Ps 130:1-2, 3-4, 5-6, 7-8

R⁊. (7) With the Lord there is mercy and
    fullness of redemption.

Out of the depths I cry to you, O LORD;
    LORD, hear my voice!
Let your ears be attentive
    to my voice in supplication.
R⁊. With the Lord there is mercy and fullness
    of redemption.

If you, O LORD, mark iniquities,
    LORD, who can stand?
But with you is forgiveness,
    that you may be revered.
R⁊. With the Lord there is mercy and fullness
    of redemption.

I trust in the LORD;
    my soul trusts in his word.
More than sentinels wait for the dawn,
    let Israel wait for the LORD.
R⁊. With the Lord there is mercy and fullness
    of redemption.

For with the LORD is kindness
    and with him is plenteous redemption;
and he will redeem Israel
    from all their iniquities.
R⁊. With the Lord there is mercy and fullness
    of redemption.

SECOND READING
Rom 8:8-11

Brothers and sisters:
Those who are in the flesh cannot please God.
But you are not in the flesh;
    on the contrary, you are in the spirit,
    if only the Spirit of God dwells in you.
Whoever does not have the Spirit of Christ
    does not belong to him.
But if Christ is in you,
    although the body is dead because of sin,
    the spirit is alive because of righteousness.
If the Spirit of the One who raised Jesus from
        the dead dwells in you,
    the One who raised Christ from the dead
    will give life to your mortal bodies also,
    through his Spirit dwelling in you.

Gospel at the Procession with Palms (cont.)
Luke 19:28-40; L37C

They proclaimed:
  "Blessed is the king who comes
    in the name of the Lord.
  Peace in heaven
    and glory in the highest."
Some of the Pharisees in the crowd said to him,
  "Teacher, rebuke your disciples."
He said in reply,
  "I tell you, if they keep silent,
  the stones will cry out!"

Gospel at Mass
Luke 22:14–23:56; L38ABC

When the hour came,
  Jesus took his place at table with the apostles.
He said to them,
  "I have eagerly desired to eat this Passover with you before I suffer,
  for, I tell you, I shall not eat it again
  until there is fulfillment in the kingdom of God."
Then he took a cup, gave thanks, and said,
  "Take this and share it among yourselves;
  for I tell you that from this time on
  I shall not drink of the fruit of the vine
  until the kingdom of God comes."
Then he took the bread, said the blessing,
  broke it, and gave it to them, saying,
  "This is my body, which will be given for you;
  do this in memory of me."
And likewise the cup after they had eaten, saying,
  "This cup is the new covenant in my blood,
  which will be shed for you.

"And yet behold, the hand of the one who is to betray me
  is with me on the table;
  for the Son of Man indeed goes as it has been determined;
  but woe to that man by whom he is betrayed."
And they began to debate among themselves
  who among them would do such a deed.

Then an argument broke out among them
  about which of them should be regarded as the greatest.
He said to them,
  "The kings of the Gentiles lord it over them
  and those in authority over them are addressed as 'Benefactors';
  but among you it shall not be so.
Rather, let the greatest among you be as the youngest,
  and the leader as the servant.
For who is greater:
  the one seated at table or the one who serves?
Is it not the one seated at table?
I am among you as the one who serves.
It is you who have stood by me in my trials;
  and I confer a kingdom on you,
  just as my Father has conferred one on me,
  that you may eat and drink at my table in my kingdom;
  and you will sit on thrones
  judging the twelve tribes of Israel.

"Simon, Simon, behold Satan has demanded
  to sift all of you like wheat,

but I have prayed that your own faith may not fail;
  and once you have turned back,
  you must strengthen your brothers."
He said to him,
  "Lord, I am prepared to go to prison and to die with you."
But he replied,
  "I tell you, Peter, before the cock crows this day,
  you will deny three times that you know me."

He said to them,
  "When I sent you forth without a money bag or a sack or sandals,
  were you in need of anything?"
"No, nothing," they replied.
He said to them,
  "But now one who has a money bag should take it,
  and likewise a sack,
  and one who does not have a sword
  should sell his cloak and buy one.
For I tell you that this Scripture must be fulfilled in me,
  namely, *He was counted among the wicked;*
  and indeed what is written about me is coming to fulfillment."
Then they said,
  "Lord, look, there are two swords here."
But he replied, "It is enough!"

Then going out, he went, as was his custom, to the Mount of Olives,
  and the disciples followed him.
When he arrived at the place he said to them,
  "Pray that you may not undergo the test."
After withdrawing about a stone's throw from them and kneeling,
  he prayed, saying, "Father, if you are willing,
  take this cup away from me;
  still, not my will but yours be done."
And to strengthen him an angel from heaven appeared to him.
He was in such agony and he prayed so fervently
  that his sweat became like drops of blood
  falling on the ground.
When he rose from prayer and returned to his disciples,
  he found them sleeping from grief.
He said to them, "Why are you sleeping?
Get up and pray that you may not undergo the test."

While he was still speaking, a crowd approached
  and in front was one of the Twelve, a man named Judas.
He went up to Jesus to kiss him.
Jesus said to him,
  "Judas, are you betraying the Son of Man with a kiss?"
His disciples realized what was about to happen, and they asked,
  "Lord, shall we strike with a sword?"
And one of them struck the high priest's servant
  and cut off his right ear.
But Jesus said in reply,
  "Stop, no more of this!"
Then he touched the servant's ear and healed him.
And Jesus said to the chief priests and temple guards
  and elders who had come for him,
  "Have you come out as against a robber, with swords and clubs?
Day after day I was with you in the temple area,
  and you did not seize me;
  but this is your hour, the time for the power of darkness."

After arresting him they led him away
  and took him into the house of the high priest;
  Peter was following at a distance.

They lit a fire in the middle of the courtyard and sat around it,
    and Peter sat down with them.
When a maid saw him seated in the light,
    she looked intently at him and said,
    "This man too was with him."
But he denied it saying,
    "Woman, I do not know him."
A short while later someone else saw him and said,
    "You too are one of them";
    but Peter answered, "My friend, I am not."
About an hour later, still another insisted,
    "Assuredly, this man too was with him,
    for he also is a Galilean."
But Peter said,
    "My friend, I do not know what you are talking about."
Just as he was saying this, the cock crowed,
    and the Lord turned and looked at Peter;
    and Peter remembered the word of the Lord,
    how he had said to him,
    "Before the cock crows today, you will deny me three times."
He went out and began to weep bitterly.
The men who held Jesus in custody were ridiculing and beating him.
They blindfolded him and questioned him, saying,
    "Prophesy! Who is it that struck you?"
And they reviled him in saying many other things against him.

When day came the council of elders of the people met,
    both chief priests and scribes,
    and they brought him before their Sanhedrin.
They said, "If you are the Christ, tell us,"
    but he replied to them, "If I tell you, you will not believe,
    and if I question, you will not respond.
But from this time on the Son of Man will be seated
    at the right hand of the power of God."
They all asked, "Are you then the Son of God?"
He replied to them, "You say that I am."
Then they said, "What further need have we for testimony?
We have heard it from his own mouth."

Then the whole assembly of them arose and brought him before Pilate.
They brought charges against him, saying,
    "We found this man misleading our people;
    he opposes the payment of taxes to Caesar
    and maintains that he is the Christ, a king."
Pilate asked him, "Are you the king of the Jews?"
He said to him in reply, "You say so."
Pilate then addressed the chief priests and the crowds,
    "I find this man not guilty."
But they were adamant and said,
    "He is inciting the people with his teaching
        throughout all Judea,
    from Galilee where he began even to here."

On hearing this Pilate asked if the man was a Galilean;
    and upon learning that he was under Herod's jurisdiction,
    he sent him to Herod who was in Jerusalem at that time.
Herod was very glad to see Jesus;
    he had been wanting to see him for a long time,
    for he had heard about him
    and had been hoping to see him perform some sign.
He questioned him at length,
    but he gave him no answer.
The chief priests and scribes, meanwhile,

stood by accusing him harshly.
Herod and his soldiers treated him contemptuously and mocked him,
    and after clothing him in resplendent garb,
    he sent him back to Pilate.
Herod and Pilate became friends that very day,
    even though they had been enemies formerly.
Pilate then summoned the chief priests, the rulers, and the people
    and said to them, "You brought this man to me
    and accused him of inciting the people to revolt.
I have conducted my investigation in your presence
    and have not found this man guilty
    of the charges you have brought against him,
    nor did Herod, for he sent him back to us.
So no capital crime has been committed by him.
Therefore I shall have him flogged and then release him."

But all together they shouted out,
    "Away with this man!
    Release Barabbas to us."
—Now Barabbas had been imprisoned for a rebellion
    that had taken place in the city and for murder.—
Again Pilate addressed them, still wishing to release Jesus,
    but they continued their shouting,
    "Crucify him! Crucify him!"
Pilate addressed them a third time,
    "What evil has this man done?
    I found him guilty of no capital crime.
Therefore I shall have him flogged and then release him."
With loud shouts, however,
    they persisted in calling for his crucifixion,
    and their voices prevailed.
The verdict of Pilate was that their demand should be granted.
So he released the man who had been imprisoned
    for rebellion and murder, for whom they asked,
    and he handed Jesus over to them to deal with as they wished.

As they led him away
    they took hold of a certain Simon, a Cyrenian,
    who was coming in from the country;
    and after laying the cross on him,
    they made him carry it behind Jesus.
A large crowd of people followed Jesus,
    including many women who mourned and lamented him.
Jesus turned to them and said,
    "Daughters of Jerusalem, do not weep for me;
    weep instead for yourselves and for your children
    for indeed, the days are coming when people will say,
    'Blessed are the barren,
    the wombs that never bore
    and the breasts that never nursed.'
At that time people will say to the mountains,
    'Fall upon us!'
    and to the hills, 'Cover us!'
    for if these things are done when the wood is green
    what will happen when it is dry?"
Now two others, both criminals,
    were led away with him to be executed.

When they came to the place called the Skull,
    they crucified him and the criminals there,
    one on his right, the other on his left.
Then Jesus said,
    "Father, forgive them, they know not what they do."

They divided his garments by casting lots.
The people stood by and watched;
    the rulers, meanwhile, sneered at him and said,
    "He saved others, let him save himself
    if he is the chosen one, the Christ of God."
Even the soldiers jeered at him.
As they approached to offer him wine they called out,
    "If you are King of the Jews, save yourself."
Above him there was an inscription that read,
    "This is the King of the Jews."

Now one of the criminals hanging there reviled Jesus, saying,
    "Are you not the Christ?
    Save yourself and us."
The other, however, rebuking him, said in reply,
    "Have you no fear of God,
    for you are subject to the same condemnation?
And indeed, we have been condemned justly,
    for the sentence we received corresponds to our crimes,
    but this man has done nothing criminal."
Then he said,
    "Jesus, remember me when you come into your kingdom."
He replied to him,
    "Amen, I say to you,
    today you will be with me in Paradise."

It was now about noon and darkness came over the whole land
    until three in the afternoon
    because of an eclipse of the sun.
Then the veil of the temple was torn down the middle.
Jesus cried out in a loud voice,
    "Father, into your hands I commend my spirit";
    and when he had said this he breathed his last.

Here all kneel and pause for a short time.

The centurion who witnessed what had happened glorified God and said,
    "This man was innocent beyond doubt."
When all the people who had gathered for this spectacle
        saw what had happened,
    they returned home beating their breasts;
    but all his acquaintances stood at a distance,
    including the women who had followed him from Galilee
    and saw these events.

Now there was a virtuous and righteous man named Joseph who,
    though he was a member of the council,
    had not consented to their plan of action.
He came from the Jewish town of Arimathea
    and was awaiting the kingdom of God.
He went to Pilate and asked for the body of Jesus.
After he had taken the body down,
    he wrapped it in a linen cloth
    and laid him in a rock-hewn tomb
    in which no one had yet been buried.
It was the day of preparation,
    and the sabbath was about to begin.
The women who had come from Galilee with him followed behind,
    and when they had seen the tomb
    and the way in which his body was laid in it,
    they returned and prepared spices and perfumed oils.
Then they rested on the sabbath according to the commandment.

or Luke 23:1-49

The elders of the people, chief priests and scribes,
    arose and brought Jesus before Pilate.
They brought charges against him, saying,
    "We found this man misleading our people;
    he opposes the payment of taxes to Caesar
    and maintains that he is the Christ, a king."
Pilate asked him, "Are you the king of the Jews?"
He said to him in reply, "You say so."
Pilate then addressed the chief priests and the crowds,
    "I find this man not guilty."
But they were adamant and said,
    "He is inciting the people with his teaching
        throughout all Judea,
    from Galilee where he began even to here."

On hearing this Pilate asked if the man was a Galilean;
    and upon learning that he was under Herod's jurisdiction,
    he sent him to Herod who was in Jerusalem at that time.
Herod was very glad to see Jesus;
    he had been wanting to see him for a long time,
    for he had heard about him
    and had been hoping to see him perform some sign.
He questioned him at length,
    but he gave him no answer.
The chief priests and scribes, meanwhile,
    stood by accusing him harshly.
Herod and his soldiers treated him contemptuously and mocked him,
    and after clothing him in resplendent garb,
    he sent him back to Pilate.
Herod and Pilate became friends that very day,
    even though they had been enemies formerly.
Pilate then summoned the chief priests, the rulers, and the people
    and said to them, "You brought this man to me
    and accused him of inciting the people to revolt.
I have conducted my investigation in your presence
    and have not found this man guilty
    of the charges you have brought against him,
    nor did Herod, for he sent him back to us.
So no capital crime has been committed by him.
Therefore I shall have him flogged and then release him."

But all together they shouted out,
    "Away with this man!
    Release Barabbas to us."
—Now Barabbas had been imprisoned for a rebellion
    that had taken place in the city and for murder.—
Again Pilate addressed them, still wishing to release Jesus,
    but they continued their shouting,
    "Crucify him! Crucify him!"
Pilate addressed them a third time,
    "What evil has this man done?
    I found him guilty of no capital crime.
Therefore I shall have him flogged and then release him."
With loud shouts, however,
    they persisted in calling for his crucifixion,
    and their voices prevailed.
The verdict of Pilate was that their demand should be granted.
So he released the man who had been imprisoned
    for rebellion and murder, for whom they asked,
    and he handed Jesus over to them to deal with as they wished.

Gospel (cont.)

Luke 23:1-49

As they led him away
   they took hold of a certain Simon, a Cyrenian,
   who was coming in from the country;
   and after laying the cross on him,
   they made him carry it behind Jesus.
A large crowd of people followed Jesus,
   including many women who mourned and lamented him.
Jesus turned to them and said,
   "Daughters of Jerusalem, do not weep for me;
   weep instead for yourselves and for your children
   for indeed, the days are coming when people will say,
   'Blessed are the barren,
   the wombs that never bore
   and the breasts that never nursed.'
At that time people will say to the mountains,
   'Fall upon us!'
   and to the hills, 'Cover us!'
   for if these things are done when the wood is green
   what will happen when it is dry?"
Now two others, both criminals,
   were led away with him to be executed.

When they came to the place called the Skull,
   they crucified him and the criminals there,
   one on his right, the other on his left.
Then Jesus said,
   "Father, forgive them, they know not what they do."
They divided his garments by casting lots.
The people stood by and watched;
   the rulers, meanwhile, sneered at him and said,
   "He saved others, let him save himself
   if he is the chosen one, the Christ of God."
Even the soldiers jeered at him.

As they approached to offer him wine they called out,
   "If you are King of the Jews, save yourself."
Above him there was an inscription that read,
   "This is the King of the Jews."

Now one of the criminals hanging there reviled Jesus, saying,
   "Are you not the Christ?
   Save yourself and us."
The other, however, rebuking him, said in reply,
   "Have you no fear of God,
   for you are subject to the same condemnation?
And indeed, we have been condemned justly,
   for the sentence we received corresponds to our crimes,
   but this man has done nothing criminal."
Then he said,
   "Jesus, remember me when you come into your kingdom."
He replied to him,
   "Amen, I say to you,
   today you will be with me in Paradise."

It was now about noon and darkness came over the whole land
   until three in the afternoon
   because of an eclipse of the sun.
Then the veil of the temple was torn down the middle.
Jesus cried out in a loud voice,
   "Father, into your hands I commend my spirit";
   and when he had said this he breathed his last.

Here all kneel and pause for a short time.

The centurion who witnessed what had happened glorified God and said,
   "This man was innocent beyond doubt."
When all the people who had gathered for this spectacle
      saw what had happened,
   they returned home beating their breasts;
   but all his acquaintances stood at a distance,
   including the women who had followed him from Galilee
   and saw these events.

Gospel (cont.)

John 13:1-15; L39ABC

For he knew who would betray him;
    for this reason, he said, "Not all of you are clean."
So when he had washed their feet
    and put his garments back on and reclined at table again,
    he said to them, "Do you realize what I have done for you?
You call me 'teacher' and 'master,' and rightly so, for indeed I am.
If I, therefore, the master and teacher, have washed your feet,
    you ought to wash one another's feet.
I have given you a model to follow,
    so that as I have done for you, you should also do."

FIRST READING

Exod 12:1-8, 11-14

The LORD said to Moses and Aaron in the land
    of Egypt,
    "This month shall stand at the head of
        your calendar;
    you shall reckon it the first month of the
        year.
Tell the whole community of Israel:
    On the tenth of this month every one of
        your families
    must procure for itself a lamb, one apiece
        for each household.
If a family is too small for a whole lamb,
    it shall join the nearest household in
        procuring one
    and shall share in the lamb
    in proportion to the number of persons
        who partake of it.
The lamb must be a year-old male and
    without blemish.
You may take it from either the sheep or the
    goats.
You shall keep it until the fourteenth day of
    this month,
    and then, with the whole assembly of Israel
        present,
    it shall be slaughtered during the evening
        twilight.
They shall take some of its blood
    and apply it to the two doorposts and the
        lintel
    of every house in which they partake of
        the lamb.
That same night they shall eat its roasted
    flesh
    with unleavened bread and bitter herbs.

"This is how you are to eat it:
    with your loins girt, sandals on your feet
        and your staff in hand,
    you shall eat like those who are in flight.

It is the Passover of the LORD.
For on this same night I will go through
        Egypt,
    striking down every firstborn of the land,
        both man and beast,
    and executing judgment on all the gods of
        Egypt—I, the LORD!
But the blood will mark the houses where you
    are.
Seeing the blood, I will pass over you;
    thus, when I strike the land of Egypt,
    no destructive blow will come upon you.

"This day shall be a memorial feast for you,
    which all your generations shall celebrate
    with pilgrimage to the LORD, as a perpetual
        institution."

RESPONSORIAL PSALM

Ps 116:12-13, 15-16bc, 17-18

R⁄. (cf. 1 Cor 10:16) Our blessing-cup is a
        communion with the Blood of Christ.

How shall I make a return to the LORD
    for all the good he has done for me?
The cup of salvation I will take up,
    and I will call upon the name of the LORD.

R⁄. Our blessing-cup is a communion with the
        Blood of Christ.

Precious in the eyes of the LORD
    is the death of his faithful ones.
I am your servant, the son of your handmaid;
    you have loosed my bonds.

R⁄. Our blessing-cup is a communion with the
        Blood of Christ.

To you will I offer sacrifice of thanksgiving,
    and I will call upon the name of the LORD.
My vows to the LORD I will pay
    in the presence of all his people.

R⁄. Our blessing-cup is a communion with the
        Blood of Christ.

SECOND READING

1 Cor 11:23-26

Brothers and sisters:
I received from the Lord what I also handed
        on to you,
    that the Lord Jesus, on the night he was
        handed over,
    took bread, and, after he had given thanks,
    broke it and said, "This is my body that is
        for you.
Do this in remembrance of me."
In the same way also the cup, after supper,
    saying,
    "This cup is the new covenant in my blood.
Do this, as often as you drink it, in
        remembrance of me."
For as often as you eat this bread and drink
        the cup,
    you proclaim the death of the Lord until he
        comes.

Gospel (cont.)

John 18:1–19:42; L40ABC

So the band of soldiers, the tribune, and the Jewish guards seized Jesus,
   bound him, and brought him to Annas first.
He was the father-in-law of Caiaphas,
   who was high priest that year.
It was Caiaphas who had counseled the Jews
   that it was better that one man should die rather than the people.

Simon Peter and another disciple followed Jesus.
Now the other disciple was known to the high priest,
   and he entered the courtyard of the high priest with Jesus.
But Peter stood at the gate outside.
So the other disciple, the acquaintance of the high priest,
   went out and spoke to the gatekeeper and brought Peter in.
Then the maid who was the gatekeeper said to Peter,
   "You are not one of this man's disciples, are you?"
He said, "I am not."
Now the slaves and the guards were standing around a charcoal fire
   that they had made, because it was cold,
   and were warming themselves.
Peter was also standing there keeping warm.

The high priest questioned Jesus
   about his disciples and about his doctrine.
Jesus answered him,
   "I have spoken publicly to the world.
I have always taught in a synagogue
   or in the temple area where all the Jews gather,
   and in secret I have said nothing. Why ask me?
Ask those who heard me what I said to them.
They know what I said."
When he had said this,
   one of the temple guards standing there struck Jesus and said,
   "Is this the way you answer the high priest?"
Jesus answered him,
   "If I have spoken wrongly, testify to the wrong;
   but if I have spoken rightly, why do you strike me?"
Then Annas sent him bound to Caiaphas the high priest.

Now Simon Peter was standing there keeping warm.
And they said to him,
   "You are not one of his disciples, are you?"
He denied it and said,
   "I am not."
One of the slaves of the high priest,
   a relative of the one whose ear Peter had cut off, said,
   "Didn't I see you in the garden with him?"
Again Peter denied it.
And immediately the cock crowed.

Then they brought Jesus from Caiaphas to the praetorium.
It was morning.
And they themselves did not enter the praetorium,
   in order not to be defiled so that they could eat the Passover.
So Pilate came out to them and said,
   "What charge do you bring against this man?"
They answered and said to him,
   "If he were not a criminal,
   we would not have handed him over to you."
At this, Pilate said to them,
   "Take him yourselves, and judge him according to your law."

The Jews answered him,
   "We do not have the right to execute anyone,"
   in order that the word of Jesus might be fulfilled
   that he said indicating the kind of death he would die.
So Pilate went back into the praetorium
   and summoned Jesus and said to him,
   "Are you the King of the Jews?"
Jesus answered,
   "Do you say this on your own
   or have others told you about me?"
Pilate answered,
   "I am not a Jew, am I?
Your own nation and the chief priests handed you over to me.
What have you done?"
Jesus answered,
   "My kingdom does not belong to this world.
If my kingdom did belong to this world,
   my attendants would be fighting
   to keep me from being handed over to the Jews.
But as it is, my kingdom is not here."
So Pilate said to him,
   "Then you are a king?"
Jesus answered,
   "You say I am a king.
For this I was born and for this I came into the world,
   to testify to the truth.
Everyone who belongs to the truth listens to my voice."
Pilate said to him, "What is truth?"

When he had said this,
   he again went out to the Jews and said to them,
   "I find no guilt in him.
But you have a custom that I release one prisoner to you at Passover.
Do you want me to release to you the King of the Jews?"
They cried out again,
   "Not this one but Barabbas!"
Now Barabbas was a revolutionary.

Then Pilate took Jesus and had him scourged.
And the soldiers wove a crown out of thorns and placed it on his head,
   and clothed him in a purple cloak,
   and they came to him and said,
   "Hail, King of the Jews!"
And they struck him repeatedly.
Once more Pilate went out and said to them,
   "Look, I am bringing him out to you,
   so that you may know that I find no guilt in him."
So Jesus came out,
   wearing the crown of thorns and the purple cloak.
And he said to them, "Behold, the man!"
When the chief priests and the guards saw him they cried out,
   "Crucify him, crucify him!"
Pilate said to them,
   "Take him yourselves and crucify him.
I find no guilt in him."
The Jews answered,
   "We have a law, and according to that law he ought to die,
   because he made himself the Son of God."
Now when Pilate heard this statement,

he became even more afraid,
and went back into the praetorium and said to Jesus,
"Where are you from?"
Jesus did not answer him.
So Pilate said to him,
"Do you not speak to me?
Do you not know that I have power to release you
and I have power to crucify you?"
Jesus answered him,
"You would have no power over me
if it had not been given to you from above.
For this reason the one who handed me over to you
has the greater sin."
Consequently, Pilate tried to release him; but the Jews cried out,
"If you release him, you are not a Friend of Caesar.
Everyone who makes himself a king opposes Caesar."

When Pilate heard these words he brought Jesus out
and seated him on the judge's bench
in the place called Stone Pavement, in Hebrew, Gabbatha.
It was preparation day for Passover, and it was about noon.
And he said to the Jews,
"Behold, your king!"
They cried out,
"Take him away, take him away! Crucify him!"
Pilate said to them,
"Shall I crucify your king?"
The chief priests answered,
"We have no king but Caesar."
Then he handed him over to them to be crucified.

So they took Jesus, and, carrying the cross himself,
he went out to what is called the Place of the Skull,
in Hebrew, Golgotha.
There they crucified him, and with him two others,
one on either side, with Jesus in the middle.
Pilate also had an inscription written and put on the cross.
It read,
"Jesus the Nazorean, the King of the Jews."
Now many of the Jews read this inscription,
because the place where Jesus was crucified was near the city;
and it was written in Hebrew, Latin, and Greek.
So the chief priests of the Jews said to Pilate,
"Do not write 'The King of the Jews,'
but that he said, 'I am the King of the Jews.'"
Pilate answered,
"What I have written, I have written."

When the soldiers had crucified Jesus,
they took his clothes and divided them into four shares,
a share for each soldier.
They also took his tunic, but the tunic was seamless,
woven in one piece from the top down.
So they said to one another,
"Let's not tear it, but cast lots for it to see whose it will be,"
in order that the passage of Scripture might be fulfilled that says:
They divided my garments among them,
and for my vesture they cast lots.
This is what the soldiers did.

Standing by the cross of Jesus were his mother
and his mother's sister, Mary the wife of Clopas,
and Mary of Magdala.
When Jesus saw his mother and the disciple there whom he loved
he said to his mother, "Woman, behold, your son."
Then he said to the disciple,
"Behold, your mother."
And from that hour the disciple took her into his home.

After this, aware that everything was now finished,
in order that the Scripture might be fulfilled,
Jesus said, "I thirst."
There was a vessel filled with common wine.
So they put a sponge soaked in wine on a sprig of hyssop
and put it up to his mouth.
When Jesus had taken the wine, he said,
"It is finished."
And bowing his head, he handed over the spirit.

Here all kneel and pause for a short time.

Now since it was preparation day,
in order that the bodies might not remain
on the cross on the sabbath,
for the sabbath day of that week was a solemn one,
the Jews asked Pilate that their legs be broken
and that they be taken down.
So the soldiers came and broke the legs of the first
and then of the other one who was crucified with Jesus.
But when they came to Jesus and saw that he was already dead,
they did not break his legs,
but one soldier thrust his lance into his side,
and immediately blood and water flowed out.
An eyewitness has testified, and his testimony is true;
he knows that he is speaking the truth,
so that you also may come to believe.
For this happened so that the Scripture passage might be fulfilled:
Not a bone of it will be broken.
And again another passage says:
They will look upon him whom they have pierced.

After this, Joseph of Arimathea,
secretly a disciple of Jesus for fear of the Jews,
asked Pilate if he could remove the body of Jesus.
And Pilate permitted it.
So he came and took his body.
Nicodemus, the one who had first come to him at night,
also came bringing a mixture of myrrh and aloes
weighing about one hundred pounds.
They took the body of Jesus
and bound it with burial cloths along with the spices,
according to the Jewish burial custom.
Now in the place where he had been crucified there was a garden,
and in the garden a new tomb, in which no one had yet been buried.
So they laid Jesus there because of the Jewish preparation day;
for the tomb was close by.

FIRST READING

Isa 52:13–53:12

See, my servant shall prosper,
    he shall be raised high and greatly exalted.
Even as many were amazed at him—
    so marred was his look beyond human
        semblance
    and his appearance beyond that of the sons
        of man—
so shall he startle many nations,
    because of him kings shall stand
        speechless;
for those who have not been told shall see,
    those who have not heard shall ponder it.

Who would believe what we have heard?
    To whom has the arm of the LORD been
        revealed?
He grew up like a sapling before him,
    like a shoot from the parched earth;
there was in him no stately bearing to make
        us look at him,
    nor appearance that would attract us to him.
He was spurned and avoided by people,
    a man of suffering, accustomed to infirmity,
one of those from whom people hide their
        faces,
    spurned, and we held him in no esteem.

Yet it was our infirmities that he bore,
    our sufferings that he endured,
while we thought of him as stricken,
    as one smitten by God and afflicted.
But he was pierced for our offenses,
    crushed for our sins;
upon him was the chastisement that makes
        us whole,
    by his stripes we were healed.
We had all gone astray like sheep,
    each following his own way;
but the LORD laid upon him
    the guilt of us all.

Though he was harshly treated, he submitted
    and opened not his mouth;
like a lamb led to the slaughter
    or a sheep before the shearers,
    he was silent and opened not his mouth.
Oppressed and condemned, he was taken away,
    and who would have thought any more of
        his destiny?
When he was cut off from the land of the
        living,
    and smitten for the sin of his people,
a grave was assigned him among the wicked
    and a burial place with evildoers,
though he had done no wrong
    nor spoken any falsehood.
But the LORD was pleased
    to crush him in infirmity.

If he gives his life as an offering for sin,
    he shall see his descendants in a long life,
    and the will of the LORD shall be
        accomplished through him.

Because of his affliction
    he shall see the light
        in fullness of days;
through his suffering, my servant shall justify
        many,
    and their guilt he shall bear.
Therefore I will give him his portion among
        the great,
    and he shall divide the spoils with the
        mighty,
because he surrendered himself to death
    and was counted among the wicked;
and he shall take away the sins of many,
    and win pardon for their offenses.

RESPONSORIAL PSALM

Ps 31:2, 6, 12-13, 15-16, 17, 25

R̸. (Luke 23:46) Father, into your hands I
    commend my spirit.

In you, O LORD, I take refuge;
    let me never be put to shame.
In your justice rescue me.
Into your hands I commend my spirit;
    you will redeem me, O LORD, O faithful God.

R̸. Father, into your hands I commend my
    spirit.

For all my foes I am an object of reproach,
    a laughingstock to my neighbors, and a
        dread to my friends;
    they who see me abroad flee from me.
I am forgotten like the unremembered dead;
    I am like a dish that is broken.

R̸. Father, into your hands I commend my
    spirit.

But my trust is in you, O LORD;
    I say, "You are my God.
In your hands is my destiny; rescue me
    from the clutches of my enemies and my
        persecutors."

R̸. Father, into your hands I commend my
    spirit.

Let your face shine upon your servant;
    save me in your kindness.
Take courage and be stouthearted,
    all you who hope in the LORD.

R̸. Father, into your hands I commend my
    spirit.

SECOND READING

Heb 4:14-16; 5:7-9

Brothers and sisters:
Since we have a great high priest who has
        passed through the heavens,
    Jesus, the Son of God,
    let us hold fast to our confession.
For we do not have a high priest
    who is unable to sympathize with our
        weaknesses,
    but one who has similarly been tested in
        every way,
    yet without sin.
So let us confidently approach the throne of
        grace
    to receive mercy and to find grace for
        timely help.

In the days when Christ was in the flesh,
    he offered prayers and supplications with
        loud cries and tears
    to the one who was able to save him from
        death,
    and he was heard because of his reverence.
Son though he was, he learned obedience from
        what he suffered;
    and when he was made perfect,
    he became the source of eternal salvation
        for all who obey him.

FIRST READING
Gen 1:1–2:2

In the beginning, when God created the
    heavens and the earth,
    the earth was a formless wasteland, and
        darkness covered the abyss,
    while a mighty wind swept over the waters.

Then God said,
    "Let there be light," and there was light.
God saw how good the light was.
God then separated the light from the
    darkness.
God called the light "day," and the darkness
    he called "night."
Thus evening came, and morning followed—
    the first day.

Then God said,
    "Let there be a dome in the middle of the
        waters,
    to separate one body of water from the
        other."
And so it happened:
    God made the dome,
    and it separated the water above the dome
        from the water below it.
God called the dome "the sky."
Evening came, and morning followed—the
    second day.

Then God said,
    "Let the water under the sky be gathered
        into a single basin,
    so that the dry land may appear."
And so it happened:
    the water under the sky was gathered into
        its basin,
    and the dry land appeared.
God called the dry land "the earth,"
    and the basin of the water he called "the
        sea."
God saw how good it was.
Then God said,
    "Let the earth bring forth vegetation:
    every kind of plant that bears seed
    and every kind of fruit tree on earth
    that bears fruit with its seed in it."
And so it happened:
    the earth brought forth every kind of plant
        that bears seed
    and every kind of fruit tree on earth
    that bears fruit with its seed in it.
God saw how good it was.
Evening came, and morning followed—the
    third day.

Then God said:
    "Let there be lights in the dome of the sky,
    to separate day from night.
Let them mark the fixed times, the days and
    the years,

and serve as luminaries in the dome of the
    sky,
    to shed light upon the earth."
And so it happened:
    God made the two great lights,
    the greater one to govern the day,
    and the lesser one to govern the night;
    and he made the stars.
God set them in the dome of the sky,
    to shed light upon the earth,
    to govern the day and the night,
    and to separate the light from the darkness.
God saw how good it was.
Evening came, and morning followed—the
    fourth day.

Then God said,
    "Let the water teem with an abundance of
        living creatures,
    and on the earth let birds fly beneath the
        dome of the sky."
And so it happened:
    God created the great sea monsters
    and all kinds of swimming creatures with
        which the water teems,
    and all kinds of winged birds.
God saw how good it was, and God blessed
    them, saying,
    "Be fertile, multiply, and fill the water of
        the seas;
    and let the birds multiply on the earth."
Evening came, and morning followed—the
    fifth day.

Then God said,
    "Let the earth bring forth all kinds of living
        creatures:
    cattle, creeping things, and wild animals of
        all kinds."
And so it happened:
    God made all kinds of wild animals, all
        kinds of cattle,
    and all kinds of creeping things of the
        earth.
God saw how good it was.
Then God said:
    "Let us make man in our image, after our
        likeness.
Let them have dominion over the fish of the
    sea,
    the birds of the air, and the cattle,
    and over all the wild animals
    and all the creatures that crawl on the
        ground."
God created man in his image;
        in the image of God he created him;
        male and female he created them.
God blessed them, saying:
    "Be fertile and multiply;
    fill the earth and subdue it.
Have dominion over the fish of the sea, the
    birds of the air,

and all the living things that move on the
    earth."
God also said:
    "See, I give you every seed-bearing plant all
        over the earth
    and every tree that has seed-bearing fruit
        on it to be your food;
    and to all the animals of the land, all the
        birds of the air,
    and all the living creatures that crawl on
        the ground,
    I give all the green plants for food."
And so it happened.
God looked at everything he had made, and he
    found it very good.
Evening came, and morning followed—the
    sixth day.

Thus the heavens and the earth and all their
    array were completed.
Since on the seventh day God was finished
    with the work he had been doing,
    he rested on the seventh day from all the
        work he had undertaken.

or

Gen 1:1, 26-31a

In the beginning, when God created the
    heavens and the earth,
    God said: "Let us make man in our image,
        after our likeness.
Let them have dominion over the fish of the
    sea,
    the birds of the air, and the cattle,
    and over all the wild animals
    and all the creatures that crawl on the
        ground."
God created man in his image;
    in the image of God he created him;
    male and female he created them.
God blessed them, saying:
    "Be fertile and multiply;
    fill the earth and subdue it.
Have dominion over the fish of the sea, the
    birds of the air,
    and all the living things that move on the
        earth."
God also said:
    "See, I give you every seed-bearing plant all
        over the earth
    and every tree that has seed-bearing fruit
        on it to be your food;
    and to all the animals of the land, all the
        birds of the air,
    and all the living creatures that crawl on
        the ground,
    I give all the green plants for food."
And so it happened.
God looked at everything he had made, and
    found it very good.

RESPONSORIAL PSALM

Ps 104:1-2, 5-6, 10, 12, 13-14, 24, 35

R̸. (30) Lord, send out your Spirit, and renew
the face of the earth.

Bless the Lᴏʀᴅ, O my soul!
  O Lᴏʀᴅ, my God, you are great indeed!
You are clothed with majesty and glory,
  robed in light as with a cloak.

R̸. Lord, send out your Spirit, and renew the
face of the earth.

You fixed the earth upon its foundation,
  not to be moved forever;
with the ocean, as with a garment, you
  covered it;
  above the mountains the waters stood.

R̸. Lord, send out your Spirit, and renew the
face of the earth.

You send forth springs into the watercourses
  that wind among the mountains.
Beside them the birds of heaven dwell;
  from among the branches they send forth
  their song.

R̸. Lord, send out your Spirit, and renew the
face of the earth.

You water the mountains from your palace;
  the earth is replete with the fruit of your
  works.
You raise grass for the cattle,
  and vegetation for man's use,
producing bread from the earth.

R̸. Lord, send out your Spirit, and renew the
face of the earth.

How manifold are your works, O Lᴏʀᴅ!
  In wisdom you have wrought them all—
the earth is full of your creatures.
  Bless the Lᴏʀᴅ, O my soul!

R̸. Lord, send out your Spirit, and renew the
face of the earth.

or

Ps 33:4-5, 6-7, 12-13, 20 and 22

R̸. (5b) The earth is full of the goodness of
the Lord.

Upright is the word of the Lᴏʀᴅ,
  and all his works are trustworthy.
He loves justice and right;
  of the kindness of the Lᴏʀᴅ the earth is full.

R̸. The earth is full of the goodness of the Lord.

By the word of the Lᴏʀᴅ the heavens were
  made;
  by the breath of his mouth all their host.
He gathers the waters of the sea as in a flask;
  in cellars he confines the deep.

R̸. The earth is full of the goodness of the Lord.

Blessed the nation whose God is the Lᴏʀᴅ,
  the people he has chosen for his own
  inheritance.
From heaven the Lᴏʀᴅ looks down;
  he sees all mankind.

R̸. The earth is full of the goodness of the Lord.

Our soul waits for the Lᴏʀᴅ,
  who is our help and our shield.
May your kindness, O Lᴏʀᴅ, be upon us
  who have put our hope in you.

R̸. The earth is full of the goodness of the Lord.

SECOND READING

Gen 22:1-18

God put Abraham to the test.
He called to him, "Abraham!"
"Here I am," he replied.
Then God said:
  "Take your son Isaac, your only one, whom
  you love,
  and go to the land of Moriah.
There you shall offer him up as a holocaust
  on a height that I will point out to you."
Early the next morning Abraham saddled his
  donkey,
  took with him his son Isaac and two of his
  servants as well,
  and with the wood that he had cut for the
  holocaust,
  set out for the place of which God had told
  him.

On the third day Abraham got sight of the
  place from afar.
Then he said to his servants:
  "Both of you stay here with the donkey,
  while the boy and I go on over yonder.
We will worship and then come back to you."
Thereupon Abraham took the wood for the
  holocaust
  and laid it on his son Isaac's shoulders,
  while he himself carried the fire and the
  knife.
As the two walked on together, Isaac spoke to
  his father Abraham:
  "Father!" Isaac said.
"Yes, son," he replied.
Isaac continued, "Here are the fire and the
  wood,
  but where is the sheep for the holocaust?"
"Son," Abraham answered,
  "God himself will provide the sheep for the
  holocaust."
Then the two continued going forward.

When they came to the place of which God
  had told him,
  Abraham built an altar there and arranged
  the wood on it.

Next he tied up his son Isaac,
  and put him on top of the wood on the
  altar.
Then he reached out and took the knife to
  slaughter his son.
But the Lᴏʀᴅ's messenger called to him from
  heaven,
  "Abraham, Abraham!"
"Here I am," he answered.
"Do not lay your hand on the boy," said the
  messenger.
"Do not do the least thing to him.
I know now how devoted you are to God,
  since you did not withhold from me your
  own beloved son."
As Abraham looked about,
  he spied a ram caught by its horns in the
  thicket.
So he went and took the ram
  and offered it up as a holocaust in place of
  his son.
Abraham named the site Yahweh-yireh;
  hence people now say, "On the mountain
  the Lᴏʀᴅ will see."

Again the Lᴏʀᴅ's messenger called to
  Abraham from heaven and said:
  "I swear by myself, declares the Lᴏʀᴅ,
  that because you acted as you did
  in not withholding from me your beloved
  son,
  I will bless you abundantly
  and make your descendants as countless
  as the stars of the sky and the sands of the
  seashore;
  your descendants shall take possession
  of the gates of their enemies,
  and in your descendants all the nations of
  the earth
  shall find blessing—
  all this because you obeyed my command."

or

Gen 22:1-2, 9a, 10-13, 15-18

God put Abraham to the test.
He called to him, "Abraham!"
"Here I am," he replied.
Then God said:
  "Take your son Isaac, your only one, whom
  you love,
  and go to the land of Moriah.
There you shall offer him up as a holocaust
  on a height that I will point out to you."

When they came to the place of which God
  had told him,
  Abraham built an altar there and arranged
  the wood on it.
Then he reached out and took the knife to
  slaughter his son.

But the Lord's messenger called to him from
    heaven,
    "Abraham, Abraham!"
"Here I am," he answered.
"Do not lay your hand on the boy," said the
    messenger.
"Do not do the least thing to him.
I know now how devoted you are to God,
    since you did not withhold from me your
        own beloved son."
As Abraham looked about,
    he spied a ram caught by its horns in the
        thicket.
So he went and took the ram
    and offered it up as a holocaust in place of
        his son.

Again the Lord's messenger called to
    Abraham from heaven and said:
    "I swear by myself, declares the Lord,
    that because you acted as you did
    in not withholding from me your beloved
        son,
    I will bless you abundantly
    and make your descendants as countless
    as the stars of the sky and the sands of the
        seashore;
    your descendants shall take possession
    of the gates of their enemies,
    and in your descendants all the nations of
        the earth
        shall find blessing—
    all this because you obeyed my command."

RESPONSORIAL PSALM

Ps 16:5, 8, 9-10, 11

R℣. (1) You are my inheritance, O Lord.

O Lord, my allotted portion and my cup,
    you it is who hold fast my lot.
I set the Lord ever before me;
    with him at my right hand I shall not be
        disturbed.

R℣. You are my inheritance, O Lord.

Therefore my heart is glad and my soul
    rejoices,
    my body, too, abides in confidence;
because you will not abandon my soul to the
    netherworld,
    nor will you suffer your faithful one to
        undergo corruption.

R℣. You are my inheritance, O Lord.

You will show me the path to life,
    fullness of joys in your presence,
    the delights at your right hand forever.

R℣. You are my inheritance, O Lord.

THIRD READING

Exod 14:15–15:1

The Lord said to Moses, "Why are you crying
    out to me?
Tell the Israelites to go forward.
And you, lift up your staff and, with hand
    outstretched over the sea,
    split the sea in two,
    that the Israelites may pass through it on
        dry land.
But I will make the Egyptians so obstinate
    that they will go in after them.
Then I will receive glory through Pharaoh and
    all his army,
    his chariots and charioteers.
The Egyptians shall know that I am the Lord,
    when I receive glory through Pharaoh
    and his chariots and charioteers."

The angel of God, who had been leading
    Israel's camp,
    now moved and went around behind them.
The column of cloud also, leaving the front,
    took up its place behind them,
    so that it came between the camp of the
        Egyptians
    and that of Israel.
But the cloud now became dark, and thus the
    night passed
    without the rival camps coming any closer
        together all night long.
Then Moses stretched out his hand over the
    sea,
    and the Lord swept the sea
    with a strong east wind throughout the
        night
    and so turned it into dry land.
When the water was thus divided,
    the Israelites marched into the midst of the
        sea on dry land,
    with the water like a wall to their right and
        to their left.

The Egyptians followed in pursuit;
    all Pharaoh's horses and chariots and
        charioteers went after them
    right into the midst of the sea.
In the night watch just before dawn
    the Lord cast through the column of the
        fiery cloud
    upon the Egyptian force a glance that
        threw it into a panic;
    and he so clogged their chariot wheels
    that they could hardly drive.
With that the Egyptians sounded the retreat
    before Israel,
    because the Lord was fighting for them
        against the Egyptians.

Then the Lord told Moses, "Stretch out your
    hand over the sea,
    that the water may flow back upon the
        Egyptians,
    upon their chariots and their charioteers."
So Moses stretched out his hand over the sea,
    and at dawn the sea flowed back to its
        normal depth.
The Egyptians were fleeing head on toward
    the sea,
    when the Lord hurled them into its midst.
As the water flowed back,
    it covered the chariots and the charioteers
        of Pharaoh's whole army
    which had followed the Israelites into the sea.
Not a single one of them escaped.
But the Israelites had marched on dry land
    through the midst of the sea,
    with the water like a wall to their right and
        to their left.
Thus the Lord saved Israel on that day
    from the power of the Egyptians.
When Israel saw the Egyptians lying dead on
    the seashore
    and beheld the great power that the Lord
    had shown against the Egyptians,
    they feared the Lord and believed in him
        and in his servant Moses.

Then Moses and the Israelites sang this song
    to the Lord:
    I will sing to the Lord, for he is gloriously
        triumphant;
    horse and chariot he has cast into the sea.

RESPONSORIAL PSALM

Exod 15:1-2, 3-4, 5-6, 17-18

R℣. (1b) Let us sing to the Lord; he has covered
    himself in glory.

I will sing to the Lord, for he is gloriously
    triumphant;
    horse and chariot he has cast into the sea.
My strength and my courage is the Lord,
    and he has been my savior.
He is my God, I praise him;
    the God of my father, I extol him.

R℣. Let us sing to the Lord; he has covered
    himself in glory.

The Lord is a warrior,
    Lord is his name!
Pharaoh's chariots and army he hurled into
    the sea;
    the elite of his officers were submerged in
        the Red Sea.

R℣. Let us sing to the Lord; he has covered
    himself in glory.

The flood waters covered them,
they sank into the depths like a stone.
Your right hand, O Lord, magnificent in
power,
your right hand, O Lord, has shattered the
enemy.

R⁊. Let us sing to the Lord; he has covered
himself in glory.

You brought in the people you redeemed
and planted them on the mountain of your
inheritance—
the place where you made your seat, O Lord,
the sanctuary, Lord, which your hands
established.
The Lord shall reign forever and ever.

R⁊. Let us sing to the Lord; he has covered
himself in glory.

FOURTH READING
Isa 54:5-14

The One who has become your husband is
your Maker;
his name is the Lord of hosts;
your redeemer is the Holy One of Israel,
called God of all the earth.
The Lord calls you back,
like a wife forsaken and grieved in spirit,
a wife married in youth and then cast off,
says your God.
For a brief moment I abandoned you,
but with great tenderness I will take you
back.
In an outburst of wrath, for a moment
I hid my face from you;
but with enduring love I take pity on you,
says the Lord, your redeemer.
This is for me like the days of Noah,
when I swore that the waters of Noah
should never again deluge the earth;
so I have sworn not to be angry with you,
or to rebuke you.
Though the mountains leave their place
and the hills be shaken,
my love shall never leave you
nor my covenant of peace be shaken,
says the Lord, who has mercy on you.
O afflicted one, storm-battered and
unconsoled,
I lay your pavements in carnelians,
and your foundations in sapphires;
I will make your battlements of rubies,
your gates of carbuncles,
and all your walls of precious stones.
All your children shall be taught by the Lord,
and great shall be the peace of your children.

In justice shall you be established,
far from the fear of oppression,
where destruction cannot come near you.

RESPONSORIAL PSALM
Ps 30:2, 4, 5-6, 11-12, 13

R⁊. (2a) I will praise you, Lord, for you have
rescued me.

I will extol you, O Lord, for you drew me clear
and did not let my enemies rejoice over me.
O Lord, you brought me up from the
netherworld;
you preserved me from among those going
down into the pit.

R⁊. I will praise you, Lord, for you have
rescued me.

Sing praise to the Lord, you his faithful ones,
and give thanks to his holy name.
For his anger lasts but a moment;
a lifetime, his good will.
At nightfall, weeping enters in,
but with the dawn, rejoicing.

R⁊. I will praise you, Lord, for you have
rescued me.

Hear, O Lord, and have pity on me;
O Lord, be my helper.
You changed my mourning into dancing;
O Lord, my God, forever will I give you
thanks.

R⁊. I will praise you, Lord, for you have
rescued me.

FIFTH READING
Isa 55:1-11

Thus says the Lord:
All you who are thirsty,
come to the water!
You who have no money,
come, receive grain and eat;
come, without paying and without cost,
drink wine and milk!
Why spend your money for what is not bread,
your wages for what fails to satisfy?
Heed me, and you shall eat well,
you shall delight in rich fare.
Come to me heedfully,
listen, that you may have life.
I will renew with you the everlasting covenant,
the benefits assured to David.
As I made him a witness to the peoples,
a leader and commander of nations,
so shall you summon a nation you knew not,
and nations that knew you not shall run
to you,

because of the Lord, your God,
the Holy One of Israel, who has glorified
you.

Seek the Lord while he may be found,
call him while he is near.
Let the scoundrel forsake his way,
and the wicked man his thoughts;
let him turn to the Lord for mercy;
to our God, who is generous in forgiving.
For my thoughts are not your thoughts,
nor are your ways my ways, says the Lord.
As high as the heavens are above the earth,
so high are my ways above your ways
and my thoughts above your thoughts.

For just as from the heavens
the rain and snow come down
and do not return there
till they have watered the earth,
making it fertile and fruitful,
giving seed to the one who sows
and bread to the one who eats,
so shall my word be
that goes forth from my mouth;
my word shall not return to me void,
but shall do my will,
achieving the end for which I sent it.

RESPONSORIAL PSALM
Isa 12:2-3, 4, 5-6

R⁊. (3) You will draw water joyfully from the
springs of salvation.

God indeed is my savior;
I am confident and unafraid.
My strength and my courage is the Lord,
and he has been my savior.
With joy you will draw water
at the fountain of salvation.

R⁊. You will draw water joyfully from the
springs of salvation.

Give thanks to the Lord, acclaim his name;
among the nations make known his deeds,
proclaim how exalted is his name.

R⁊. You will draw water joyfully from the
springs of salvation.

Sing praise to the Lord for his glorious
achievement;
let this be known throughout all the earth.
Shout with exultation, O city of Zion,
for great in your midst
is the Holy One of Israel!

R⁊. You will draw water joyfully from the
springs of salvation.

SIXTH READING
Bar 3:9-15, 32–4:4

Hear, O Israel, the commandments of life:
   listen, and know prudence!
How is it, Israel,
   that you are in the land of your foes,
   grown old in a foreign land,
defiled with the dead,
   accounted with those destined for the
      netherworld?
You have forsaken the fountain of wisdom!
   Had you walked in the way of God,
   you would have dwelt in enduring peace.
Learn where prudence is,
   where strength, where understanding;
that you may know also
   where are length of days, and life,
   where light of the eyes, and peace.
Who has found the place of wisdom,
   who has entered into her treasuries?

The One who knows all things knows her;
   he has probed her by his knowledge—
the One who established the earth for all time,
   and filled it with four-footed beasts;
he who dismisses the light, and it departs,
   calls it, and it obeys him trembling;
before whom the stars at their posts
   shine and rejoice;
when he calls them, they answer, "Here we are!"
   shining with joy for their Maker.
Such is our God;
   no other is to be compared to him:
he has traced out the whole way of
      understanding,
   and has given her to Jacob, his servant,
   to Israel, his beloved son.

Since then she has appeared on earth,
   and moved among people.
She is the book of the precepts of God,
   the law that endures forever;
all who cling to her will live,
   but those will die who forsake her.
Turn, O Jacob, and receive her:
   walk by her light toward splendor.
Give not your glory to another,
   your privileges to an alien race.
Blessed are we, O Israel;
   for what pleases God is known to us!

RESPONSORIAL PSALM
Ps 19:8, 9, 10, 11

R̶/. (John 6:68c) Lord, you have the words of
   everlasting life.

The law of the LORD is perfect,
   refreshing the soul;
the decree of the LORD is trustworthy,
   giving wisdom to the simple.

R̶/. Lord, you have the words of everlasting life.

The precepts of the LORD are right,
   rejoicing the heart;
the command of the LORD is clear,
   enlightening the eye.

R̶/. Lord, you have the words of everlasting life.

The fear of the LORD is pure,
   enduring forever;
the ordinances of the LORD are true,
   all of them just.

R̶/. Lord, you have the words of everlasting life.

They are more precious than gold,
   than a heap of purest gold;
sweeter also than syrup
   or honey from the comb.

R̶/. Lord, you have the words of everlasting life.

SEVENTH READING
Ezek 36:16-17a, 18-28

The word of the LORD came to me, saying:
   Son of man, when the house of Israel lived
      in their land,
   they defiled it by their conduct and deeds.
Therefore I poured out my fury upon them
   because of the blood that they poured out
      on the ground,
   and because they defiled it with idols.
I scattered them among the nations,
   dispersing them over foreign lands;
   according to their conduct and deeds I
      judged them.
But when they came among the nations
      wherever they came,
   they served to profane my holy name,
   because it was said of them: "These are the
      people of the LORD,
   yet they had to leave their land."
So I have relented because of my holy name
   which the house of Israel profaned
   among the nations where they came.
Therefore say to the house of Israel: Thus
      says the Lord GOD:
   Not for your sakes do I act, house of Israel,
   but for the sake of my holy name,
   which you profaned among the nations to
      which you came.
I will prove the holiness of my great name,
   profaned among the nations,
   in whose midst you have profaned it.
Thus the nations shall know that I am the
      LORD, says the Lord GOD,
   when in their sight I prove my holiness
      through you.
For I will take you away from among the nations,
   gather you from all the foreign lands,
   and bring you back to your own land.
I will sprinkle clean water upon you
   to cleanse you from all your impurities,
   and from all your idols I will cleanse you.

I will give you a new heart and place a new
      spirit within you,
   taking from your bodies your stony hearts
   and giving you natural hearts.
I will put my spirit within you and make you
      live by my statutes,
   careful to observe my decrees.
You shall live in the land I gave your fathers;
   you shall be my people, and I will be your
      God.

RESPONSORIAL PSALM
Ps 42:3, 5; 43:3, 4

R̶/. (42:2) Like a deer that longs for running
   streams, my soul longs for you, my God.

Athirst is my soul for God, the living God.
   When shall I go and behold the face of God?

R̶/. Like a deer that longs for running streams,
   my soul longs for you, my God.

I went with the throng
   and led them in procession to the house of God,
amid loud cries of joy and thanksgiving,
   with the multitude keeping festival.

R̶/. Like a deer that longs for running streams,
   my soul longs for you, my God.

Send forth your light and your fidelity;
   they shall lead me on
and bring me to your holy mountain,
   to your dwelling-place.

R̶/. Like a deer that longs for running streams,
   my soul longs for you, my God.

Then will I go in to the altar of God,
   the God of my gladness and joy;
then will I give you thanks upon the harp,
   O God, my God!

R̶/. Like a deer that longs for running streams,
   my soul longs for you, my God.

or

Isa 12:2-3, 4bcd, 5-6

R̶/. (3) You will draw water joyfully from the
   springs of salvation.

God indeed is my savior;
   I am confident and unafraid.
My strength and my courage is the LORD,
   and he has been my savior.
With joy you will draw water
   at the fountain of salvation.

R̶/. You will draw water joyfully from the
   springs of salvation.

Give thanks to the LORD, acclaim his name;
   among the nations make known his deeds,
   proclaim how exalted is his name.

R̶/. You will draw water joyfully from the
   springs of salvation.

Sing praise to the Lord for his glorious
    achievement;
  let this be known throughout all the earth.
Shout with exultation, O city of Zion,
    for great in your midst
    is the Holy One of Israel!

R7. You will draw water joyfully from the
    springs of salvation.

or

Ps 51:12-13, 14-15, 18-19

R7. (12a) Create a clean heart in me, O God.

A clean heart create for me, O God,
    and a steadfast spirit renew within me.
Cast me not out from your presence,
    and your Holy Spirit take not from me.

R7. Create a clean heart in me, O God.

Give me back the joy of your salvation,
    and a willing spirit sustain in me.
I will teach transgressors your ways,
    and sinners shall return to you.

R7. Create a clean heart in me, O God.

For you are not pleased with sacrifices;
    should I offer a holocaust, you would not
        accept it.
My sacrifice, O God, is a contrite spirit;
    a heart contrite and humbled, O God, you
        will not spurn.

R7. Create a clean heart in me, O God.

EPISTLE
Rom 6:3-11

Brothers and sisters:
Are you unaware that we who were baptized
    into Christ Jesus
    were baptized into his death?
We were indeed buried with him through
    baptism into death,
    so that, just as Christ was raised from the
        dead
    by the glory of the Father,
    we too might live in newness of life.

For if we have grown into union with him
    through a death like his,
    we shall also be united with him in the
        resurrection.
We know that our old self was crucified with
    him,
    so that our sinful body might be done away
        with,
    that we might no longer be in slavery to sin.
For a dead person has been absolved from sin.
If, then, we have died with Christ,
    we believe that we shall also live with him.
We know that Christ, raised from the dead,
    dies no more;
    death no longer has power over him.
As to his death, he died to sin once and for all;
    as to his life, he lives for God.
Consequently, you too must think of
    yourselves as being dead to sin
    and living for God in Christ Jesus.

RESPONSORIAL PSALM
Ps 118:1-2, 16-17, 22-23

R7. Alleluia, alleluia, alleluia.

Give thanks to the Lord, for he is good,
    for his mercy endures forever.
Let the house of Israel say,
    "His mercy endures forever."

R7. Alleluia, alleluia, alleluia.

The right hand of the Lord has struck with
    power;
    the right hand of the Lord is exalted.
I shall not die, but live,
    and declare the works of the Lord.

R7. Alleluia, alleluia, alleluia.

The stone which the builders rejected
    has become the cornerstone.
By the Lord has this been done;
    it is wonderful in our eyes.

R7. Alleluia, alleluia, alleluia.

Gospel
Luke 24:1-12; L41C

At daybreak on the first day of the week
 the women who had come from Galilee with Jesus
 took the spices they had prepared
 and went to the tomb.
They found the stone rolled away from the tomb;
 but when they entered,
 they did not find the body of the Lord Jesus.
While they were puzzling over this, behold,
 two men in dazzling garments appeared to them.
They were terrified and bowed their faces to the ground.
They said to them,
 "Why do you seek the living one among the dead?
He is not here, but he has been raised.
Remember what he said to you while he was still in Galilee,
 that the Son of Man must be handed over to sinners
 and be crucified, and rise on the third day."
And they remembered his words.
Then they returned from the tomb
 and announced all these things to the eleven
 and to all the others.
The women were Mary Magdalene, Joanna, and Mary the mother of
 James;
 the others who accompanied them also told this to the apostles,
 but their story seemed like nonsense
 and they did not believe them.
But Peter got up and ran to the tomb,
 bent down, and saw the burial cloths alone;
 then he went home amazed at what had happened.

at an afternoon or evening Mass

Gospel
Luke 24:13-35; L46

That very day, the first day of the week,
 two of Jesus' disciples were going
 to a village seven miles from Jerusalem called Emmaus,
 and they were conversing about all the things that had occurred.
And it happened that while they were conversing and debating,
 Jesus himself drew near and walked with them,
 but their eyes were prevented from recognizing him.
He asked them,
 "What are you discussing as you walk along?"
They stopped, looking downcast.
One of them, named Cleopas, said to him in reply,
 "Are you the only visitor to Jerusalem
 who does not know of the things
 that have taken place there in these days?"
And he replied to them, "What sort of things?"
They said to him,
 "The things that happened to Jesus the Nazarene,
 who was a prophet mighty in deed and word
 before God and all the people,
 how our chief priests and rulers both handed him over
 to a sentence of death and crucified him.
But we were hoping that he would be the one to redeem Israel;
 and besides all this,
 it is now the third day since this took place.
Some women from our group, however, have astounded us:
 they were at the tomb early in the morning
 and did not find his body;
 they came back and reported
 that they had indeed seen a vision of angels
 who announced that he was alive.
Then some of those with us went to the tomb
 and found things just as the women had described,
 but him they did not see."
And he said to them, "Oh, how foolish you are!
How slow of heart to believe all that the prophets spoke!
Was it not necessary that the Christ should suffer these things
 and enter into his glory?"
Then beginning with Moses and all the prophets,
 he interpreted to them what referred to him
 in all the Scriptures.
As they approached the village to which they were going,
 he gave the impression that he was going on farther.
But they urged him, "Stay with us,
 for it is nearly evening and the day is almost over."
So he went in to stay with them.
And it happened that, while he was with them at table,
 he took bread, said the blessing,
 broke it, and gave it to them.
With that their eyes were opened and they recognized him,
 but he vanished from their sight.
Then they said to each other,
 "Were not our hearts burning within us
 while he spoke to us on the way and opened the Scriptures to us?"
So they set out at once and returned to Jerusalem
 where they found gathered together
 the eleven and those with them who were saying,
 "The Lord has truly been raised and has appeared to Simon!"
Then the two recounted
 what had taken place on the way
 and how he was made known to them in the breaking of the bread.

Easter Sunday, *April 21, 2019*

FIRST READING
Acts 10:34a, 37-43

Peter proceeded to speak and said:
"You know what has happened all over Judea,
beginning in Galilee after the baptism
that John preached,
how God anointed Jesus of Nazareth
with the Holy Spirit and power.
He went about doing good
and healing all those oppressed by the devil,
for God was with him.
We are witnesses of all that he did
both in the country of the Jews and in
Jerusalem.
They put him to death by hanging him on a tree.
This man God raised on the third day and
granted that he be visible,
not to all the people, but to us,
the witnesses chosen by God in advance,
who ate and drank with him after he rose
from the dead.
He commissioned us to preach to the people
and testify that he is the one appointed by God
as judge of the living and the dead.
To him all the prophets bear witness,
that everyone who believes in him
will receive forgiveness of sins through his
name."

RESPONSORIAL PSALM
Ps 118:1-2, 16-17, 22-23

R℣. (24) This is the day the Lord has made; let
us rejoice and be glad.
or:
R℣. Alleluia.

Give thanks to the LORD, for he is good,
for his mercy endures forever.
Let the house of Israel say,
"His mercy endures forever."

R℣. This is the day the Lord has made; let us
rejoice and be glad.
or:
R℣. Alleluia.

"The right hand of the LORD has struck with
power;
the right hand of the LORD is exalted.
I shall not die, but live,
and declare the works of the LORD."

R℣. This is the day the Lord has made; let us
rejoice and be glad.
or:
R℣. Alleluia.

The stone which the builders rejected
has become the cornerstone.
By the LORD has this been done;
it is wonderful in our eyes.

R℣. This is the day the Lord has made; let us
rejoice and be glad.
or:
R℣. Alleluia.

SECOND READING
Col 3:1-4

Brothers and sisters:
If then you were raised with Christ, seek what
is above,
where Christ is seated at the right hand of
God.
Think of what is above, not of what is on
earth.
For you have died, and your life is hidden with
Christ in God.
When Christ your life appears,
then you too will appear with him in glory.

or

1 Cor 5:6b-8

Brothers and sisters:
Do you not know that a little yeast leavens all
the dough?
Clear out the old yeast,
so that you may become a fresh batch of
dough,
inasmuch as you are unleavened.
For our paschal lamb, Christ, has been
sacrificed.
Therefore, let us celebrate the feast,
not with the old yeast, the yeast of malice
and wickedness,
but with the unleavened bread of sincerity
and truth.

SEQUENCE

Victimae paschali laudes
Christians, to the Paschal Victim
Offer your thankful praises!
A Lamb the sheep redeems;
Christ, who only is sinless,
Reconciles sinners to the Father.
Death and life have contended in that combat
stupendous:
The Prince of life, who died, reigns
immortal.
Speak, Mary, declaring
What you saw, wayfaring.
"The tomb of Christ, who is living,
The glory of Jesus' resurrection;
Bright angels attesting,
The shroud and napkin resting.
Yes, Christ my hope is arisen;
To Galilee he goes before you."
Christ indeed from death is risen, our new life
obtaining.
Have mercy, victor King, ever reigning!
Amen. Alleluia.

Second Sunday of Easter (or of Divine Mercy), *April 28, 2019*

Gospel (cont.)
John 20:19-31; L45C

Then he said to Thomas, "Put your finger here and see my hands,
and bring your hand and put it into my side,
and do not be unbelieving, but believe."
Thomas answered and said to him, "My Lord and my God!"
Jesus said to him, "Have you come to believe because you have seen me?
Blessed are those who have not seen and have believed."

Now Jesus did many other signs in the presence of his disciples
that are not written in this book.
But these are written that you may come to believe
that Jesus is the Christ, the Son of God,
and that through this belief you may have life in his name.

Gospel (cont.)
John 21:1-19; L48C

When they climbed out on shore,
  they saw a charcoal fire with fish on it and bread.
Jesus said to them, "Bring some of the fish you just caught."
So Simon Peter went over and dragged the net ashore
  full of one hundred fifty-three large fish.
Even though there were so many, the net was not torn.
Jesus said to them, "Come, have breakfast."
And none of the disciples dared to ask him, "Who are you?"
  because they realized it was the Lord.
Jesus came over and took the bread and gave it to them,
  and in like manner the fish.
This was now the third time Jesus was revealed to his disciples
  after being raised from the dead.

When they had finished breakfast, Jesus said to Simon Peter,
  "Simon, son of John, do you love me more than these?"
Simon Peter answered him, "Yes, Lord, you know that I love you."
Jesus said to him, "Feed my lambs."
He then said to Simon Peter a second time,
  "Simon, son of John, do you love me?"
Simon Peter answered him, "Yes, Lord, you know that I love you."
Jesus said to him, "Tend my sheep."
Jesus said to him the third time,
  "Simon, son of John, do you love me?"
Peter was distressed that Jesus had said to him a third time,
  "Do you love me?" and he said to him,
  "Lord, you know everything; you know that I love you."
Jesus said to him, "Feed my sheep.
Amen, amen, I say to you, when you were younger,
  you used to dress yourself and go where you wanted;
  but when you grow old, you will stretch out your hands,
  and someone else will dress you
  and lead you where you do not want to go."
He said this signifying by what kind of death he would glorify God.
And when he had said this, he said to him, "Follow me."

or John 21:1-14; L48C

At that time, Jesus revealed himself again to his disciples at the Sea of
    Tiberias.
He revealed himself in this way.
Together were Simon Peter, Thomas called Didymus,
  Nathanael from Cana in Galilee,
  Zebedee's sons, and two others of his disciples.
Simon Peter said to them, "I am going fishing."
They said to him, "We also will come with you."
So they went out and got into the boat,
  but that night they caught nothing.
When it was already dawn, Jesus was standing on the shore;
  but the disciples did not realize that it was Jesus.
Jesus said to them, "Children, have you caught anything to eat?"
They answered him, "No."
So he said to them, "Cast the net over the right side of the boat
  and you will find something."
So they cast it, and were not able to pull it in
  because of the number of fish.
So the disciple whom Jesus loved said to Peter, "It is the Lord."
When Simon Peter heard that it was the Lord,
  he tucked in his garment, for he was lightly clad,
  and jumped into the sea.
The other disciples came in the boat,
  for they were not far from shore, only about a hundred yards,
  dragging the net with the fish.
When they climbed out on shore,
  they saw a charcoal fire with fish on it and bread.
Jesus said to them, "Bring some of the fish you just caught."
So Simon Peter went over and dragged the net ashore
  full of one hundred fifty-three large fish.
Even though there were so many, the net was not torn.
Jesus said to them, "Come, have breakfast."
And none of the disciples dared to ask him, "Who are you?"
  because they realized it was the Lord.
Jesus came over and took the bread and gave it to them,
  and in like manner the fish.
This was now the third time Jesus was revealed to his disciples
  after being raised from the dead.

Fourth Sunday of Easter, May 12, 2019

SECOND READING
Rev 7:9, 14b-17

I, John, had a vision of a great multitude,
  which no one could count,
  from every nation, race, people, and tongue.
They stood before the throne and before the
    Lamb,
  wearing white robes and holding palm
    branches in their hands.

Then one of the elders said to me,
  "These are the ones who have survived the
    time of great distress;
they have washed their robes
and made them white in the blood of the
    Lamb.

  "For this reason they stand before God's
    throne
  and worship him day and night in his
    temple.
The one who sits on the throne will
    shelter them.
They will not hunger or thirst anymore,
  nor will the sun or any heat strike
    them.

For the Lamb who is in the center of the
    throne
  will shepherd them
  and lead them to springs of life-giving
    water,
  and God will wipe away every tear
    from their eyes."

Sixth Sunday of Easter, *May 26 2019*

SECOND READING
Rev 21:10-14, 22-23

The angel took me in spirit to a great, high
   mountain
   and showed me the holy city Jerusalem
   coming down out of heaven from God.
It gleamed with the splendor of God.
Its radiance was like that of a precious stone,
   like jasper, clear as crystal.
It had a massive, high wall,
   with twelve gates where twelve angels were
      stationed
   and on which names were inscribed,
   the names of the twelve tribes of the
      Israelites.

There were three gates facing east,
   three north, three south, and three west.
The wall of the city had twelve courses of
      stones as its foundation,
   on which were inscribed the twelve names
   of the twelve apostles of the Lamb.

I saw no temple in the city
   for its temple is the Lord God almighty and
      the Lamb.
The city had no need of sun or moon to shine
      on it,
   for the glory of God gave it light,
   and its lamp was the Lamb.

The Ascension of the Lord, *May 30 (Thursday) or June 2, 2019*

SECOND READING
Eph 1:17-23

Brothers and sisters:
May the God of our Lord Jesus Christ, the
      Father of glory,
   give you a Spirit of wisdom and revelation
   resulting in knowledge of him.
May the eyes of your hearts be enlightened,
   that you may know what is the hope that
         belongs to his call,
   what are the riches of glory
   in his inheritance among the holy ones,
   and what is the surpassing greatness of
         his power
   for us who believe,
   in accord with the exercise of his great
         might,
   which he worked in Christ,
   raising him from the dead
   and seating him at his right hand in the
         heavens,
   far above every principality, authority,
         power, and dominion,
   and every name that is named
   not only in this age but also in the one to
         come.

And he put all things beneath his feet
   and gave him as head over all things to the
      church,
   which is his body,
   the fullness of the one who fills all things
      in every way.

or

Heb 9:24-28; 10:19-23

Christ did not enter into a sanctuary made by
      hands,
   a copy of the true one, but heaven itself,
   that he might now appear before God on
      our behalf.
Not that he might offer himself repeatedly,
   as the high priest enters each year into the
      sanctuary
   with blood that is not his own;
   if that were so, he would have had to suffer
      repeatedly
   from the foundation of the world.
But now once for all he has appeared at the
      end of the ages
   to take away sin by his sacrifice.
Just as it is appointed that men and women
      die once,

and after this the judgment, so also Christ,
   offered once to take away the sins of many,
   will appear a second time, not to take away
      sin
   but to bring salvation to those who eagerly
      await him.

Therefore, brothers and sisters, since through
      the blood of Jesus
   we have confidence of entrance into the
      sanctuary
   by the new and living way he opened for us
      through the veil,
   that is, his flesh,
   and since we have "a great priest over the
      house of God,"
   let us approach with a sincere heart and in
      absolute trust,
   with our hearts sprinkled clean from an
      evil conscience
   and our bodies washed in pure water.
Let us hold unwaveringly to our confession
      that gives us hope,
   for he who made the promise is
      trustworthy.

301

SECOND READING
Rom 8:8-17

Brothers and sisters:
Those who are in the flesh cannot please
    God.
But you are not in the flesh;
    on the contrary, you are in the spirit,
    if only the Spirit of God dwells in you.
Whoever does not have the Spirit of Christ
    does not belong to him.
But if Christ is in you,
    although the body is dead because of sin,
    the spirit is alive because of righteousness.
If the Spirit of the one who raised Jesus from
    the dead dwells in you,
    the one who raised Christ from the dead
    will give life to your mortal bodies also,
    through his Spirit that dwells in you.
Consequently, brothers and sisters,
    we are not debtors to the flesh,
    to live according to the flesh.
For if you live according to the flesh, you
    will die,
    but if by the Spirit you put to death the
        deeds of the body,
    you will live.

For those who are led by the Spirit of God are
    sons of God.
For you did not receive a spirit of slavery to
    fall back into fear,
    but you received a Spirit of adoption,
    through whom we cry, "Abba, Father!"
The Spirit himself bears witness with our
    spirit
    that we are children of God,
    and if children, then heirs,
    heirs of God and joint heirs with Christ,
    if only we suffer with him
    so that we may also be glorified with him.

or

1 Cor 12:3b-7, 12-13

Brothers and sisters:
No one can say, "Jesus is Lord," except by the
    Holy Spirit.

There are different kinds of spiritual gifts but
    the same Spirit;
    there are different forms of service but the
        same Lord;
    there are different workings but the same God
    who produces all of them in everyone.
To each individual the manifestation of the
    Spirit
    is given for some benefit.

As a body is one though it has many parts,
    and all the parts of the body, though many,
        are one body,
    so also Christ.
For in one Spirit we were all baptized into one
    body,
    whether Jews or Greeks, slaves or free
        persons,
    and we were all given to drink of one Spirit.

SEQUENCE
Veni, Sancte Spiritus

Come, Holy Spirit, come!
And from your celestial home
    Shed a ray of light divine!
Come, Father of the poor!
Come, source of all our store!
    Come, within our bosoms shine.
You, of comforters the best;
You, the soul's most welcome guest;
    Sweet refreshment here below;
In our labor, rest most sweet;
Grateful coolness in the heat;
    Solace in the midst of woe.
O most blessed Light divine,
Shine within these hearts of yours,
    And our inmost being fill!
Where you are not, we have naught,
Nothing good in deed or thought,
    Nothing free from taint of ill.
Heal our wounds, our strength renew;
On our dryness pour your dew;
    Wash the stains of guilt away:
Bend the stubborn heart and will;
Melt the frozen, warm the chill;
    Guide the steps that go astray.
On the faithful, who adore
And confess you, evermore
    In your sevenfold gift descend;
Give them virtue's sure reward;
Give them your salvation, Lord;
    Give them joys that never end. Amen.
    Alleluia.

OPTIONAL SEQUENCE

Lauda Sion

Laud, O Zion, your salvation,
Laud with hymns of exultation,
　　Christ, your king and shepherd true:

Bring him all the praise you know,
He is more than you bestow.
　　Never can you reach his due.

Special theme for glad thanksgiving
Is the quick'ning and the living
　　Bread today before you set:

From his hands of old partaken,
As we know, by faith unshaken,
　　Where the Twelve at supper met.

Full and clear ring out your chanting,
Joy nor sweetest grace be wanting,
　　From your heart let praises burst:

For today the feast is holden,
When the institution olden
　　Of that supper was rehearsed.

Here the new law's new oblation,
By the new king's revelation,
　　Ends the form of ancient rite:

Now the new the old effaces,
Truth away the shadow chases,
　　Light dispels the gloom of night.

What he did at supper seated,
Christ ordained to be repeated,
　　His memorial ne'er to cease:

And his rule for guidance taking,
Bread and wine we hallow, making
　　Thus our sacrifice of peace.

This the truth each Christian learns,
Bread into his flesh he turns,
　　To his precious blood the wine:

Sight has fail'd, nor thought conceives,
But a dauntless faith believes,
　　Resting on a pow'r divine.

Here beneath these signs are hidden
Priceless things to sense forbidden;
　　Signs, not things are all we see:

Blood is poured and flesh is broken,
Yet in either wondrous token
　　Christ entire we know to be.

Whoso of this food partakes,
Does not rend the Lord nor breaks;
　　Christ is whole to all that taste:

Thousands are, as one, receivers,
One, as thousands of believers,
　　Eats of him who cannot waste.

Bad and good the feast are sharing,
Of what divers dooms preparing,
　　Endless death, or endless life.

Life to these, to those damnation,
See how like participation
　　Is with unlike issues rife.

When the sacrament is broken,
Doubt not, but believe 'tis spoken,

That each sever'd outward token
　　doth the very whole contain.

Nought the precious gift divides,
Breaking but the sign betides
　　Jesus still the same abides,
　　　still unbroken does remain.

The shorter form of the sequence begins here.

Lo! the angel's food is given
To the pilgrim who has striven;
　　See the children's bread from heaven,
　　which on dogs may not be spent.

Truth the ancient types fulfilling,
Isaac bound, a victim willing,
　　Paschal lamb, its lifeblood spilling,
　　manna to the fathers sent.

Very bread, good shepherd, tend us,
Jesu, of your love befriend us,
　　You refresh us, you defend us,
　　Your eternal goodness send us
In the land of life to see.

You who all things can and know,
Who on earth such food bestow,
　　Grant us with your saints, though lowest,
　　Where the heav'nly feast you show,
Fellow heirs and guests to be. Amen. Alleluia.

The Nativity of Saint John the Baptist, June 24, 2019

FIRST READING
Isa 49:1-6

Hear me, O coastlands,
    listen, O distant peoples.
The Lord called me from birth,
    from my mother's womb he gave me my
        name.
He made of me a sharp-edged sword
    and concealed me in the shadow of his arm.
He made me a polished arrow,
    in his quiver he hid me.
You are my servant, he said to me,
    Israel, through whom I show my glory.

Though I thought I had toiled in vain,
    and for nothing, uselessly, spent my
        strength,
yet my reward is with the Lord,
    my recompense is with my God.
For now the Lord has spoken
    who formed me as his servant from the
        womb,
that Jacob may be brought back to him
    and Israel gathered to him;
and I am made glorious in the sight of the
        Lord,
    and my God is now my strength!
It is too little, he says, for you to be my
        servant,
    to raise up the tribes of Jacob,
    and restore the survivors of Israel;
I will make you a light to the nations,
    that my salvation may reach to the ends of
        the earth.

RESPONSORIAL PSALM
Ps 139:1b-3, 13-14ab, 14c-15

R. (14a) I praise you, for I am wonderfully
    made.

O Lord, you have probed me, you know me;
    you know when I sit and when I stand;
    you understand my thoughts from afar.
My journeys and my rest you scrutinize,
    with all my ways you are familiar.

R. I praise you, for I am wonderfully made.

Truly you have formed my inmost being;
    you knit me in my mother's womb.
I give you thanks that I am fearfully,
    wonderfully made;
    wonderful are your works.

R. I praise you, for I am wonderfully made.

My soul also you knew full well;
    nor was my frame unknown to you
When I was made in secret,
    when I was fashioned in the depths of the
        earth.

R. I praise you, for I am wonderfully made.

SECOND READING
Acts 13:22-26

In those days, Paul said:
"God raised up David as their king;
    of him God testified,
    I have found David, son of Jesse, a man
        after my own heart;
    he will carry out my every wish.
From this man's descendants God, according
        to his promise,
    has brought to Israel a savior, Jesus.
John heralded his coming by proclaiming a
        baptism of repentance
    to all the people of Israel;
    and as John was completing his course, he
        would say,
'What do you suppose that I am? I am not
    he.
Behold, one is coming after me;
    I am not worthy to unfasten the sandals of
        his feet.'

"My brothers, sons of the family of Abraham,
    and those others among you who are God-
        fearing,
    to us this word of salvation has been sent."

FIRST READING
Ezek 34:11-16

Thus says the Lord GOD:
I myself will look after and tend my sheep.
As a shepherd tends his flock
    when he finds himself among his scattered
        sheep,
    so will I tend my sheep.
I will rescue them from every place where
        they were scattered
    when it was cloudy and dark.
I will lead them out from among the peoples
    and gather them from the foreign lands;
    I will bring them back to their own country
    and pasture them upon the mountains of
        Israel
    in the land's ravines and all its inhabited
        places.
In good pastures will I pasture them,
    and on the mountain heights of Israel
    shall be their grazing ground.
There they shall lie down on good grazing
        ground,
    and in rich pastures shall they be pastured
    on the mountains of Israel.
I myself will pasture my sheep;
    I myself will give them rest, says the Lord
        GOD.
The lost I will seek out,
    the strayed I will bring back,
    the injured I will bind up,
    the sick I will heal,
    but the sleek and the strong I will destroy,
    shepherding them rightly.

RESPONSORIAL PSALM
Ps 23:1-3a, 3b-4, 5, 6

R̸. (1) The Lord is my shepherd; there is noth-
    ing I shall want.

The LORD is my shepherd; I shall not want.
    In verdant pastures he gives me repose;
beside restful waters he leads me;
    he refreshes my soul.

R̸. The Lord is my shepherd; there is nothing
    I shall want.

He guides me in right paths
    for his name's sake.
Even though I walk in the dark valley
    I fear no evil; for you are at my side
with your rod and your staff
    that give me courage.

R̸. The Lord is my shepherd; there is nothing
    I shall want.

You spread the table before me
    in the sight of my foes;
you anoint my head with oil;
    my cup overflows.

R̸. The Lord is my shepherd; there is nothing
    I shall want.

Only goodness and kindness follow me
    all the days of my life;
and I shall dwell in the house of the LORD
    for years to come.

R̸. The Lord is my shepherd; there is nothing
    I shall want.

SECOND READING
Rom 5:5b-11

Brothers and sisters:
The love of God has been poured out into our
        hearts
    through the Holy Spirit that has been given
        to us.
For Christ, while we were still helpless,
    died at the appointed time for the ungodly.
Indeed, only with difficulty does one die for a
        just person,
    though perhaps for a good person
    one might even find courage to die.
But God proves his love for us
    in that while we were still sinners Christ
        died for us.
How much more then, since we are now
        justified by his blood,
    will we be saved through him from the
        wrath.
Indeed, if, while we were enemies,
    we were reconciled to God through the
        death of his Son,
    how much more, once reconciled,
    will we be saved by his life.
Not only that,
    but we also boast of God through our Lord
        Jesus Christ,
    through whom we have now received
        reconciliation.

FIRST READING
Acts 12:1-11

In those days, King Herod laid hands upon
     some members of the Church to harm
     them.
He had James, the brother of John, killed by
     the sword,
     and when he saw that this was pleasing to
        the Jews
     he proceeded to arrest Peter also.
—It was the feast of Unleavened Bread.—
He had him taken into custody and put in
     prison
     under the guard of four squads of four
        soldiers each.
He intended to bring him before the people
     after Passover.
Peter thus was being kept in prison,
     but prayer by the Church was fervently
        being made
     to God on his behalf.

On the very night before Herod was to bring
     him to trial,
     Peter, secured by double chains,
     was sleeping between two soldiers,
     while outside the door guards kept watch
        on the prison.
Suddenly the angel of the Lord stood by him,
     and a light shone in the cell.
He tapped Peter on the side and awakened
     him, saying,
     "Get up quickly."
The chains fell from his wrists.
The angel said to him, "Put on your belt and
     your sandals."
He did so.
Then he said to him, "Put on your cloak and
     follow me."
So he followed him out,
     not realizing that what was happening
        through the angel was real;
     he thought he was seeing a vision.
They passed the first guard, then the second,
     and came to the iron gate leading out to the
        city,
     which opened for them by itself.
They emerged and made their way down an
     alley,
     and suddenly the angel left him.
Then Peter recovered his senses and said,
     "Now I know for certain
     that the Lord sent his angel
     and rescued me from the hand of Herod
     and from all that the Jewish people had
        been expecting."

RESPONSORIAL PSALM
Ps 34:2-3, 4-5, 6-7, 8-9

R︎. (8) The angel of the Lord will rescue those
     who fear him.

I will bless the LORD at all times;
     his praise shall be ever in my mouth.
Let my soul glory in the LORD;
     the lowly will hear me and be glad.

R︎. The angel of the Lord will rescue those
     who fear him.

Glorify the LORD with me,
     let us together extol his name.
I sought the LORD, and he answered me
     and delivered me from all my fears.

R︎. The angel of the Lord will rescue those
     who fear him.

Look to him that you may be radiant with joy,
     and your faces may not blush with shame.
When the poor one called out, the LORD heard,
     and from all his distress he saved him.

R︎. The angel of the Lord will rescue those
     who fear him.

The angel of the LORD encamps
     around those who fear him, and delivers
        them.
Taste and see how good the LORD is;
     blessed the man who takes refuge in him.

R︎. The angel of the Lord will rescue those
     who fear him.

SECOND READING
2 Tim 4:6-8, 17-18

I, Paul, am already being poured out like a
     libation,
     and the time of my departure is at hand.
I have competed well; I have finished the race;
     I have kept the faith.
From now on the crown of righteousness
     awaits me,
     which the Lord, the just judge,
     will award to me on that day, and not only
        to me,
     but to all who have longed for his
        appearance.

The Lord stood by me and gave me strength,
     so that through me the proclamation might
        be completed
     and all the Gentiles might hear it.
And I was rescued from the lion's mouth.
The Lord will rescue me from every evil threat
     and will bring me safe to his heavenly
        Kingdom.
To him be glory forever and ever. Amen.

Gospel (cont.)
Luke 10:1-12, 17-20; L102C

Yet know this: the kingdom of God is at hand.
I tell you,
    it will be more tolerable for Sodom on that day than for that town."

The seventy-two returned rejoicing, and said,
    "Lord, even the demons are subject to us because of your name."
Jesus said, "I have observed Satan fall like lightning from the sky.
Behold, I have given you the power to 'tread upon serpents' and
       scorpions
   and upon the full force of the enemy and nothing will harm you.
Nevertheless, do not rejoice because the spirits are subject to you,
    but rejoice because your names are written in heaven."

or Luke 10:1-9; L102C

At that time the Lord appointed seventy-two others
    whom he sent ahead of him in pairs
    to every town and place he intended to visit.
He said to them,
    "The harvest is abundant but the laborers are few;
    so ask the master of the harvest
    to send out laborers for his harvest.
Go on your way;
    behold, I am sending you like lambs among wolves.
Carry no money bag, no sack, no sandals;
    and greet no one along the way.
Into whatever house you enter, first say,
    'Peace to this household.'
If a peaceful person lives there,
    your peace will rest on him;
    but if not, it will return to you.
Stay in the same house and eat and drink what is offered to you,
    for the laborer deserves his payment.
Do not move about from one house to another.
Whatever town you enter and they welcome you,
    eat what is set before you,
    cure the sick in it and say to them,
    'The kingdom of God is at hand for you.'"

Gospel (cont.)
Luke 10:25-37; L105C

But a Samaritan traveler who came upon him
    was moved with compassion at the sight.
He approached the victim,
    poured oil and wine over his wounds and bandaged them.
Then he lifted him up on his own animal,
    took him to an inn, and cared for him.
The next day he took out two silver coins
    and gave them to the innkeeper with the instruction,
    'Take care of him.
If you spend more than what I have given you,
    I shall repay you on my way back.'
Which of these three, in your opinion,
    was neighbor to the robbers' victim?"
He answered, "The one who treated him with mercy."
Jesus said to him, "Go and do likewise."

RESPONSORIAL PSALM
Ps 19:8, 9, 10, 11

℟. (9a) Your words, Lord, are Spirit and life.

The law of the LORD is perfect,
    refreshing the soul;
the decree of the LORD is trustworthy,
    giving wisdom to the simple.

℟. Your words, Lord, are Spirit and life.

The precepts of the LORD are right,
    rejoicing the heart;
the command of the LORD is clear,
    enlightening the eye.

℟. Your words, Lord, are Spirit and life.

The fear of the LORD is pure,
    enduring forever;
the ordinances of the LORD are true,
    all of them just.

℟. Your words, Lord, are Spirit and life.

They are more precious than gold,
    than a heap of purest gold;
sweeter also than syrup
    or honey from the comb.

℟. Your words, Lord, are Spirit and life.

Seventeenth Sunday in Ordinary Time, *July 28, 2019*

Gospel (cont.)
Luke 11:1-13; L111C

"And I tell you, ask and you will receive;
   seek and you will find;
   knock and the door will be opened to you.
For everyone who asks, receives;
   and the one who seeks, finds;
   and to the one who knocks, the door will be opened.
What father among you would hand his son a snake
   when he asks for a fish?
Or hand him a scorpion when he asks for an egg?
If you then, who are wicked,
   know how to give good gifts to your children,
   how much more will the Father in heaven
   give the Holy Spirit to those who ask him?"

SECOND READING
Col 2:12-14

Brothers and sisters:
You were buried with him in baptism,
   in which you were also raised with him
   through faith in the power of God,
   who raised him from the dead.
And even when you were dead
   in transgressions and the uncircumcision of your flesh,
   he brought you to life along with him,
   having forgiven us all our transgressions;
obliterating the bond against us, with its legal claims,
   which was opposed to us,
   he also removed it from our midst, nailing it to the cross.

Nineteenth Sunday in Ordinary Time, *August 11, 2019*

Gospel (cont.)
Luke 12:32-48; L117C

You also must be prepared, for at an hour you do not expect,
   the Son of Man will come."

Then Peter said,
   "Lord, is this parable meant for us or for everyone?"
And the Lord replied,
   "Who, then, is the faithful and prudent steward
   whom the master will put in charge of his servants
   to distribute the food allowance at the proper time?
Blessed is that servant whom his master on arrival finds doing so.
Truly, I say to you, the master will put the servant
   in charge of all his property.
But if that servant says to himself,
   'My master is delayed in coming,'
   and begins to beat the menservants and the maidservants,
   to eat and drink and get drunk,
   then that servant's master will come
   on an unexpected day and at an unknown hour
   and will punish the servant severely
   and assign him a place with the unfaithful.
That servant who knew his master's will
   but did not make preparations nor act in accord with his will
   shall be beaten severely;
   and the servant who was ignorant of his master's will
   but acted in a way deserving of a severe beating
   shall be beaten only lightly.
Much will be required of the person entrusted with much,
   and still more will be demanded of the person entrusted with more."

or Luke 12:35-40

Jesus said to his disciples:
"Gird your loins and light your lamps
and be like servants who await their master's return from a wedding,
ready to open immediately when he comes and knocks.
Blessed are those servants
   whom the master finds vigilant on his arrival.
Amen, I say to you, he will gird himself,
   have them recline at table, and proceed to wait on them.
And should he come in the second or third watch
   and find them prepared in this way,
   blessed are those servants.
Be sure of this:
   if the master of the house had known the hour
   when the thief was coming,
   he would not have let his house be broken into.
You also must be prepared, for at an hour you do not expect,
   the Son of Man will come."

SECOND READING
Heb 11:1-2, 8-19 *(cont.)*

So it was that there came forth from one man,
    himself as good as dead,
      descendants as numerous as the stars in
        the sky
      and as countless as the sands on the
        seashore.

All these died in faith.
They did not receive what had been promised
    but saw it and greeted it from afar
    and acknowledged themselves to be
        strangers and aliens on earth,
    for those who speak thus show that they
        are seeking a homeland.
If they had been thinking of the land from
      which they had come,
    they would have had opportunity to return.
But now they desire a better homeland, a
    heavenly one.
Therefore, God is not ashamed to be called
    their God,
    for he has prepared a city for them.

By faith Abraham, when put to the test,
    offered up Isaac,
    and he who had received the promises was
        ready to offer his only son,
    of whom it was said,
    "Through Isaac descendants shall bear
      your name."
He reasoned that God was able to raise even
    from the dead,
    and he received Isaac back as a symbol.

or Heb 11:1-2, 8-12

Brothers and sisters:
Faith is the realization of what is hoped for
    and evidence of things not seen.
Because of it the ancients were well attested.

By faith Abraham obeyed when he was called
      to go out to a place
    that he was to receive as an inheritance;
    he went out, not knowing where he was to
      go.
By faith he sojourned in the promised land as
      in a foreign country,
    dwelling in tents with Isaac and Jacob,
      heirs of the same promise;
    for he was looking forward to the city with
      foundations,
    whose architect and maker is God.
By faith he received power to generate,
    even though he was past the normal age
    —and Sarah herself was sterile—
    for he thought that the one who had made
      the promise was trustworthy.
So it was that there came forth from one man,
    himself as good as dead,
      descendants as numerous as the stars in
        the sky
      and as countless as the sands on the
        seashore.

Gospel (cont.)
Luke 1:39-56; L622

He has cast down the mighty from their
    thrones,
    and has lifted up the lowly.
He has filled the hungry with good things,
    and the rich he has sent away empty.
He has come to the help of his servant
    Israel
    for he has remembered his promise of
    mercy,
    the promise he made to our fathers,
    to Abraham and his children forever."

Mary remained with her about three months
    and then returned to her home.

FIRST READING
Rev 11:19a; 12:1-6a, 10ab

God's temple in heaven was opened,
    and the ark of his covenant could be seen
    in the temple.

A great sign appeared in the sky, a woman
    clothed with the sun,
    with the moon under her feet,
    and on her head a crown of twelve stars.
She was with child and wailed aloud in pain
    as she labored to give birth.
Then another sign appeared in the sky;
    it was a huge red dragon, with seven heads
    and ten horns,
    and on its heads were seven diadems.

Its tail swept away a third of the stars in the
    sky
    and hurled them down to the earth.
Then the dragon stood before the woman
    about to give birth,
    to devour her child when she gave birth.
She gave birth to a son, a male child,
    destined to rule all the nations with an iron
    rod.
Her child was caught up to God and his
    throne.
The woman herself fled into the desert
    where she had a place prepared by God.

Then I heard a loud voice in heaven say:
    "Now have salvation and power come,
    and the Kingdom of our God
    and the authority of his Anointed One."

RESPONSORIAL PSALM
Ps 45:10, 11, 12, 16

R⍫. (10bc) The queen stands at your right
    hand, arrayed in gold.

The queen takes her place at your right hand
    in gold of Ophir.

R⍫. The queen stands at your right hand,
    arrayed in gold.

Hear, O daughter, and see; turn your ear,
    forget your people and your father's house.

R⍫. The queen stands at your right hand,
    arrayed in gold.

So shall the king desire your beauty;
    for he is your lord.

R⍫. The queen stands at your right hand,
    arrayed in gold.

They are borne in with gladness and joy;
    they enter the palace of the king.

R⍫. The queen stands at your right hand,
    arrayed in gold.

SECOND READING
1 Cor 15:20-27

Brothers and sisters:
Christ has been raised from the dead,
    the firstfruits of those who have fallen asleep.
For since death came through man,
    the resurrection of the dead came also
    through man.
For just as in Adam all die,
    so too in Christ shall all be brought to life,
    but each one in proper order:
    Christ the firstfruits;
    then, at his coming, those who belong to
    Christ;
    then comes the end,
    when he hands over the Kingdom to his
    God and Father,
    when he has destroyed every sovereignty
    and every authority and power.
For he must reign until he has put all his
    enemies under his feet.
The last enemy to be destroyed is death,
    for "he subjected everything under his feet."

Twenty-Second Sunday in Ordinary Time, *September 1, 2019*

Gospel (cont.)
Luke 14:1, 7-14; L126C

Then he said to the host who invited him,
    "When you hold a lunch or a dinner,
    do not invite your friends or your brothers
    or your relatives or your wealthy neighbors,
    in case they may invite you back and you have repayment.
Rather, when you hold a banquet,
    invite the poor, the crippled, the lame, the blind;
    blessed indeed will you be because of their inability to repay you.
For you will be repaid at the resurrection of the righteous."

Gospel (cont.)

Luke 15:1-32; L132C

And when she does find it,
    she calls together her friends and neighbors
    and says to them,
    'Rejoice with me because I have found the coin that I lost.'
In just the same way, I tell you,
    there will be rejoicing among the angels of God
    over one sinner who repents."

Then he said,
    "A man had two sons, and the younger son said to his father,
    'Father give me the share of your estate that should come to me.'
So the father divided the property between them.
After a few days, the younger son collected all his belongings
    and set off to a distant country
    where he squandered his inheritance on a life of dissipation.
When he had freely spent everything,
    a severe famine struck that country,
    and he found himself in dire need.
So he hired himself out to one of the local citizens
    who sent him to his farm to tend the swine.
And he longed to eat his fill of the pods on which the swine fed,
    but nobody gave him any.
Coming to his senses he thought,
    'How many of my father's hired workers
    have more than enough food to eat,
    but here am I, dying from hunger.
I shall get up and go to my father and I shall say to him,
    "Father, I have sinned against heaven and against you.
I no longer deserve to be called your son;
    treat me as you would treat one of your hired workers."'
So he got up and went back to his father.
While he was still a long way off,
    his father caught sight of him,
    and was filled with compassion.
He ran to his son, embraced him and kissed him.
His son said to him,
    'Father, I have sinned against heaven and against you;
    I no longer deserve to be called your son.'
But his father ordered his servants,
    'Quickly bring the finest robe and put it on him;
    put a ring on his finger and sandals on his feet.
Take the fattened calf and slaughter it.
Then let us celebrate with a feast,
    because this son of mine was dead, and has come to life again;
    he was lost, and has been found.'
Then the celebration began.
Now the older son had been out in the field
    and, on his way back, as he neared the house,
    he heard the sound of music and dancing.
He called one of the servants and asked what this might mean.

The servant said to him,
    'Your brother has returned
    and your father has slaughtered the fattened calf
    because he has him back safe and sound.'
He became angry,
    and when he refused to enter the house,
    his father came out and pleaded with him.
He said to his father in reply,
    'Look, all these years I served you
    and not once did I disobey your orders;
    yet you never gave me even a young goat to feast on with my
        friends. But when your son returns,
    who swallowed up your property with prostitutes,
    for him you slaughter the fattened calf.'
He said to him,
    'My son, you are here with me always;
    everything I have is yours.
But now we must celebrate and rejoice,
    because your brother was dead and has come to life again;
    he was lost and has been found.'"

or Luke 15:1-10

Tax collectors and sinners were all drawing near to listen to Jesus,
    but the Pharisees and scribes began to complain, saying,
    "This man welcomes sinners and eats with them."
So to them he addressed this parable.
"What man among you having a hundred sheep and losing one of them
    would not leave the ninety-nine in the desert
    and go after the lost one until he finds it?
And when he does find it,
    he sets it on his shoulders with great joy
    and, upon his arrival home,
    he calls together his friends and neighbors and says to them,
    'Rejoice with me because I have found my lost sheep.'
I tell you, in just the same way
    there will be more joy in heaven over one sinner who repents
    than over ninety-nine righteous people
    who have no need of repentance.

"Or what woman having ten coins and losing one
    would not light a lamp and sweep the house,
    searching carefully until she finds it?
And when she does find it,
    she calls together her friends and neighbors
    and says to them,
    'Rejoice with me because I have found the coin that I lost.'
In just the same way, I tell you,
    there will be rejoicing among the angels of God
    over one sinner who repents."

Gospel (cont.)

Luke 16:1-13; L135C

The steward said to him, 'Here is your promissory note;
 write one for eighty.'
And the master commended that dishonest steward for acting
  prudently.

"For the children of this world
 are more prudent in dealing with their own generation
 than are the children of light.
I tell you, make friends for yourselves with dishonest wealth,
 so that when it fails, you will be welcomed into eternal dwellings.
The person who is trustworthy in very small matters
 is also trustworthy in great ones;
 and the person who is dishonest in very small matters
 is also dishonest in great ones.
If, therefore, you are not trustworthy with dishonest wealth,
 who will trust you with true wealth?
If you are not trustworthy with what belongs to another,
 who will give you what is yours?
No servant can serve two masters.
He will either hate one and love the other,
 or be devoted to one and despise the other.
You cannot serve both God and mammon."

or Luke 16:10-13

Jesus said to his disciples,
 "The person who is trustworthy in very small matters
 is also trustworthy in great ones;
 and the person who is dishonest in very small matters
 is also dishonest in great ones.
If, therefore, you are not trustworthy with dishonest wealth,
 who will trust you with true wealth?
If you are not trustworthy with what belongs to another,
 who will give you what is yours?
No servant can serve two masters.
He will either hate one and love the other,
 or be devoted to one and despise the other.
You cannot serve both God and mammon."

Gospel (cont.)

Luke 16:19-31; L138C

Moreover, between us and you a great chasm is established
 to prevent anyone from crossing who might wish to go
 from our side to yours or from your side to ours.'
He said, 'Then I beg you, father,
 send him to my father's house, for I have five brothers,
 so that he may warn them,
 lest they too come to this place of torment.'
But Abraham replied, 'They have Moses and the prophets.
Let them listen to them.'
He said, 'Oh no, father Abraham,
 but if someone from the dead goes to them, they will repent.'
Then Abraham said, 'If they will not listen to Moses and the prophets,
 neither will they be persuaded if someone should rise from the dead.'"

FIRST READING

Rev 7:2-4, 9-14

I, John, saw another angel come up from the
    East,
    holding the seal of the living God.
He cried out in a loud voice to the four angels
    who were given power to damage the land
        and the sea,
    "Do not damage the land or the sea or the
        trees
    until we put the seal on the foreheads of
        the servants of our God."
I heard the number of those who had been
        marked with the seal,
    one hundred and forty-four thousand
        marked
    from every tribe of the children of Israel.

After this I had a vision of a great multitude,
    which no one could count,
    from every nation, race, people, and tongue.
They stood before the throne and before the
        Lamb,
    wearing white robes and holding palm
        branches in their hands.
They cried out in a loud voice:

    "Salvation comes from our God,
        who is seated on the throne,
    and from the Lamb."

All the angels stood around the throne
    and around the elders and the four living
        creatures.
They prostrated themselves before the throne,
    worshiped God, and exclaimed:

    "Amen. Blessing and glory, wisdom and
        thanksgiving,
    honor, power, and might
    be to our God forever and ever. Amen."

Then one of the elders spoke up and said to
        me,
    "Who are these wearing white robes, and
        where did they come from?"
I said to him, "My lord, you are the one who
        knows."
He said to me,
    "These are the ones who have survived the
        time of great distress;
    they have washed their robes
    and made them white in the Blood of the
        Lamb."

RESPONSORIAL PSALM

Ps 24:1bc-2, 3-4ab, 5-6

R℟. (cf. 6) Lord, this is the people that longs to
    see your face.

The Lᴏʀᴅ's are the earth and its fullness;
    the world and those who dwell in it.
For he founded it upon the seas
    and established it upon the rivers.

R℟. Lord, this is the people that longs to see
    your face.

Who can ascend the mountain of the Lᴏʀᴅ?
    or who may stand in his holy place?
One whose hands are sinless, whose heart is
    clean,
    who desires not what is vain.

R℟. Lord, this is the people that longs to see
    your face.

He shall receive a blessing from the Lᴏʀᴅ,
    a reward from God his savior.
Such is the race that seeks him,
    that seeks the face of the God of Jacob.

R℟. Lord, this is the people that longs to see
    your face.

SECOND READING

1 John 3:1-3

Beloved:
See what love the Father has bestowed on us
    that we may be called the children of God.
Yet so we are.
The reason the world does not know us
    is that it did not know him.
Beloved, we are God's children now;
    what we shall be has not yet been revealed.
We do know that when it is revealed we shall
        be like him,
    for we shall see him as he is.
Everyone who has this hope based on him
        makes himself pure,
    as he is pure.

FIRST READING
Dan 12:1-3; L1011.7

In those days, I, Daniel, mourned
    and heard this word of the Lord:
At that time there shall arise
    Michael, the great prince,
    guardian of your people;
It shall be a time unsurpassed in distress
    since nations began until that time.
At that time your people shall escape,
    everyone who is found written in the book.

Many of those who sleep in the dust of the
      earth shall awake;
Some shall live forever,
    others shall be an everlasting horror and
      disgrace.
But the wise shall shine brightly
    like the splendor of the firmament,
And those who lead the many to justice
    shall be like the stars forever.

RESPONSORIAL PSALM
Ps 27:1, 4, 7, and 8b, and 9a, 13-14; L1013.3

℞. (1a) The Lord is my light and my
    salvation.
    or:
℞. (13) I believe that I shall see the good
    things of the Lord in the land of the
    living.

The LORD is my light and my salvation;
    whom should I fear?
The LORD is my life's refuge;
    of whom should I be afraid?

℞. The Lord is my light and my salvation.
    or:
℞. I believe that I shall see the good things of
    the Lord in the land of the living.

One thing I ask of the LORD;
    this I seek:
To dwell in the house of the LORD
    all the days of my life,
That I may gaze on the loveliness of the LORD
    and contemplate his temple.

℞. The Lord is my light and my salvation.
    or:
℞. I believe that I shall see the good things of
    the Lord in the land of the living.

Hear, O LORD, the sound of my call;
    have pity on me and answer me.
Your presence, O LORD, I seek.
    Hide not your face from me.

℞. The Lord is my light and my salvation.
    or:
℞. I believe that I shall see the good things of
    the Lord in the land of the living.

I believe that I shall see the bounty of the
    LORD
    in the land of the living.
Wait for the LORD with courage;
    be stouthearted, and wait for the LORD.

℞. The Lord is my light and my salvation.
    or:
℞. I believe that I shall see the good things of
    the Lord in the land of the living.

SECOND READING
Rom 6:3-9; L1014.3

Brothers and sisters:
Are you unaware that we who were baptized
      into Christ Jesus
    were baptized into his death?
We were indeed buried with him through
      baptism into death,
    so that, just as Christ was raised from the
      dead
    by the glory of the Father,
    we too might live in newness of life.

For if we have grown into union with him
      through a death like his,
    we shall also be united with him in the
      resurrection.
We know that our old self was crucified with
      him,
    so that our sinful body might be done away
      with,
    that we might no longer be in slavery to sin.
For a dead person has been absolved from sin.
If, then, we have died with Christ,
    we believe that we shall also live with him.
We know that Christ, raised from the dead,
      dies no more;
    death no longer has power over him.

Thirty-Second Sunday in Ordinary Time,
November 10, 2019

Gospel
Luke 20:27, 34-38; L156C

Some Sadducees, those who deny that there is a resurrection,
   came forward.

Jesus said to them,
   "The children of this age marry and remarry;
   but those who are deemed worthy to attain to the coming age
   and to the resurrection of the dead
   neither marry nor are given in marriage.
They can no longer die,
   for they are like angels;
   and they are the children of God
   because they are the ones who will rise.
That the dead will rise
   even Moses made known in the passage about the bush,
   when he called out 'Lord,'
   the God of Abraham, the God of Isaac, and the God of Jacob;
   and he is not God of the dead, but of the living,
   for to him all are alive."

Thirty-Third Sunday in Ordinary Time,
November 17, 2019

Gospel (cont.)
Luke 21:5-19; L159C

"Before all this happens, however,
   they will seize and persecute you,
   they will hand you over to the synagogues and to prisons,
   and they will have you led before kings and governors
   because of my name.
It will lead to your giving testimony.
Remember, you are not to prepare your defense beforehand,
   for I myself shall give you a wisdom in speaking
   that all your adversaries will be powerless to resist or refute.
You will even be handed over by parents, brothers, relatives, and
   friends,
   and they will put some of you to death.
You will be hated by all because of my name,
   but not a hair on your head will be destroyed.
By your perseverance you will secure your lives."

Thanksgiving Day, *November 28, 2019*
(Other options can be found in the Lectionary for Mass, L943–947.)

FIRST READING
Sir 50:22-24; L943.2

And now, bless the God of all,
   who has done wondrous things on earth;
Who fosters people's growth from their
     mother's womb,
   and fashions them according to his will!
May he grant you joy of heart
   and may peace abide among you;
May his goodness toward us endure in Israel
   to deliver us in our days.

RESPONSORIAL PSALM
Ps 138:1-2a, 2bc-3, 4-5; L945.3

℟. (2bc) Lord, I thank you for your
   faithfulness and love.

I will give thanks to you, O Lord, with all of
   my heart,
   for you have heard the words of my mouth;
   in the presence of the angels I will sing
     your praise;
I will worship at your holy temple.

℟. Lord, I thank you for your faithfulness and
   love.

I will give thanks to your name,
Because of your kindness and your truth.
When I called, you answered me;
   you built up strength within me.

℟. Lord, I thank you for your faithfulness and
   love.

All the kings of the earth shall give thanks to
    you, O Lord,
   when they hear the words of your mouth;
And they shall sing of the ways of the Lord:
   "Great is the glory of the Lord."

℟. Lord, I thank you for your faithfulness and
   love.

SECOND READING
1 Cor 1:3-9; L944.1

Brothers and sisters:
Grace to you and peace from God our Father
   and the Lord Jesus Christ.

I give thanks to my God always on your
     account
   for the grace of God bestowed on you in
     Christ Jesus,
   that in him you were enriched in every way,
   with all discourse and all knowledge,
   as the testimony to Christ was confirmed
     among you,
   so that you are not lacking in any spiritual
     gift
   as you wait for the revelation of our Lord
     Jesus Christ.
He will keep you firm to the end,
   irreproachable on the day of our Lord Jesus
     Christ.
God is faithful,
   and by him you were called to fellowship
     with his Son, Jesus Christ our Lord.

Lectionary Pronunciation Guide

Lectionary Word	Pronunciation
Aaron	EHR-uhn
Abana	AB-uh-nuh
Abednego	uh-BEHD-nee-go
Abel-Keramin	AY-b'l-KEHR-uh-mihn
Abel-meholah	AY-b'l-mee-HO-lah
Abiathar	uh-BAI-uh-ther
Abiel	AY-bee-ehl
Abiezrite	ay-bai-EHZ-rait
Abijah	uh-BAI-dzhuh
Abilene	ab-uh-LEE-neh
Abishai	uh-BIHSH-ay-ai
Abiud	uh-BAI-uhd
Abner	AHB-ner
Abraham	AY-bruh-ham
Abram	AY-br'm
Achaia	uh-KAY-yuh
Achim	AY-kihm
Aeneas	uh-NEE-uhs
Aenon	AY-nuhn
Agrippa	uh-GRIH-puh
Ahaz	AY-haz
Ahijah	uh-HAI-dzhuh
Ai	AY-ee
Alexandria	al-ehg-ZAN-dree-uh
Alexandrian	al-ehg-ZAN-dree-uhn
Alpha	AHL-fuh
Alphaeus	AL-fee-uhs
Amalek	AM-uh-lehk
Amaziah	am-uh-ZAI-uh
Amminadab	ah-MIHN-uh-dab
Ammonites	AM-uh-naitz
Amorites	AM-uh-raits
Amos	AY-muhs
Amoz	AY-muhz
Ampliatus	am-plee-AY-tuhs
Ananias	an-uh-NAI-uhs
Andronicus	an-draw-NAI-kuhs
Annas	AN-uhs
Antioch	AN-tih-ahk
Antiochus	an-TAI-uh-kuhs
Aphiah	uh-FAI-uh
Apollos	uh-PAH-luhs
Appius	AP-ee-uhs
Aquila	uh-KWIHL-uh
Arabah	EHR-uh-buh
Aram	AY-ram
Arameans	ehr-uh-MEE-uhnz
Areopagus	ehr-ee-AH-puh-guhs
Arimathea	ehr-uh-muh-THEE-uh
Aroer	uh-RO-er
Asaph	AY-saf
Asher	ASH-er
Ashpenaz	ASH-pee-naz
Assyria	a-SIHR-ee-uh
Astarte	as-TAHR-tee
Attalia	at-TAH-lee-uh
Augustus	uh-GUHS-tuhs
Azariah	az-uh-RAI-uh
Azor	AY-sawr
Azotus	uh-ZO-tus
Baal-shalishah	BAY-uhl-shuh-LAI-shuh
Baal-Zephon	BAY-uhl-ZEE-fuhn
Babel	BAY-bl
Babylon	BAB-ih-luhn
Babylonian	bab-ih-LO-nih-uhn
Balaam	BAY-lm
Barabbas	beh-REH-buhs
Barak	BEHR-ak
Barnabas	BAHR-nuh-buhs
Barsabbas	BAHR-suh-buhs
Bartholomew	bar-THAHL-uh-myoo
Bartimaeus	bar-tih-MEE-uhs
Baruch	BEHR-ook
Bashan	BAY-shan
Becorath	bee-KO-rath
Beelzebul	bee-EHL-zee-buhl
Beer-sheba	BEE-er-SHEE-buh
Belshazzar	behl-SHAZ-er
Benjamin	BEHN-dzhuh-mihn
Beor	BEE-awr
Bethany	BEHTH-uh-nee
Bethel	BETH-el
Bethesda	beh-THEHZ-duh
Bethlehem	BEHTH-leh-hehm
Bethphage	BEHTH-fuh-dzhee
Bethsaida	behth-SAY-ih-duh
Beth-zur	behth-ZER
Bildad	BIHL-dad
Bithynia	bih-THIHN-ih-uh
Boanerges	bo-uh-NER-dzheez
Boaz	BO-az
Caesar	SEE-zer
Caesarea	zeh-suh-REE-uh
Caiaphas	KAY-uh-fuhs
Cain	kayn
Cana	KAY-nuh
Canaan	KAY-nuhn
Canaanite	KAY-nuh-nait
Canaanites	KAY-nuh-naits
Candace	kan-DAY-see
Capernaum	kuh-PERR-nay-uhm
Cappadocia	kap-ih-DO-shee-u
Carmel	KAHR-muhl
carnelians	kahr-NEEL-yuhnz
Cenchreae	SEHN-kree-ay
Cephas	SEE-fuhs
Chaldeans	kal-DEE-uhnz
Chemosh	KEE-mahsh
Cherubim	TSHEHR-oo-bihm
Chislev	KIHS-lehv
Chloe	KLO-ee
Chorazin	kor-AY-sihn
Cilicia	sih-LIHSH-ee-uh
Cleopas	KLEE-o-pas
Clopas	KLO-pas
Corinth	KAWR-ihnth
Corinthians	kawr-IHN-thee-uhnz
Cornelius	kawr-NEE-lee-uhs
Crete	kreet
Crispus	KRIHS-puhs
Cushite	CUHSH-ait
Cypriot	SIH-pree-at
Cyrene	sai-REE-nee
Cyreneans	sai-REE-nih-uhnz
Cyrenian	sai-REE-nih-uhn
Cyrenians	sai-REE-nih-uhnz
Cyrus	SAI-ruhs
Damaris	DAM-uh-rihs
Damascus	duh-MAS-kuhs
Danites	DAN-aits
Decapolis	duh-KAP-o-lis
Derbe	DER-bee
Deuteronomy	dyoo-ter-AH-num-mee
Didymus	DID-I-mus
Dionysius	dai-o-NIHSH-ih-uhs
Dioscuri	dai-O-sky-ri
Dorcas	DAWR-kuhs
Dothan	DO-thuhn
dromedaries	DRAH-muh-dher-eez
Ebed-melech	EE-behd-MEE-lehk
Eden	EE-dn
Edom	EE-duhm
Elamites	EE-luh-maitz
Eldad	EHL-dad
Eleazar	ehl-ee-AY-zer
Eli	EE-lai
Eli Eli Lema Sabachthani	AY-lee AY-lee luh-MAH sah-BAHK-tah-nee

Lectionary Word	Pronunciation	Lectionary Word	Pronunciation	Lectionary Word	Pronunciation
Eliab	ee-LAI-ab	Gilead	GIHL-ee-uhd	Joppa	DZHAH-puh
Eliakim	ee-LAI-uh-kihm	Gilgal	GIHL-gal	Joram	DZHO-ram
Eliezer	ehl-ih-EE-zer	Golgotha	GAHL-guh-thuh	Jordan	DZHAWR-dn
Elihu	ee-LAI-hyoo	Gomorrah	guh-MAWR-uh	Joseph	DZHO-zf
Elijah	ee-LAI-dzhuh	Goshen	GO-shuhn	Joses	DZHO-seez
Elim	EE-lihm	Habakkuk	huh-BAK-uhk	Joshua	DZHAH-shou-ah
Elimelech	ee-LIHM-eh-lehk	Hadadrimmon	hay-dad-RIHM-uhn	Josiah	dzho-SAI-uh
Elisha	ee-LAI-shuh	Hades	HAY-deez	Jotham	DZHO-thuhm
Eliud	ee-LAI-uhd	Hagar	HAH-gar	Judah	DZHOU-duh
Elizabeth	ee-LIHZ-uh-bth	Hananiah	han-uh-NAI-uh	Judas	DZHOU-duhs
Elkanah	el-KAY-nuh	Hannah	HAN-uh	Judea	dzhou-DEE-uh
Eloi Eloi Lama	AY-lo-ee AY-lo-ee	Haran	HAY-ruhn	Judean	dzhou-DEE-uhn
Sabechthani	LAH-mah sah-	Hebron	HEE-bruhn	Junia	dzhou-nih-uh
	BAHK-tah-nee	Hermes	HER-meez	Justus	DZHUHS-tuhs
Elymais	ehl-ih-MAY-ihs	Herod	HEHR-uhd	Kephas	KEF-uhs
Emmanuel	eh-MAN-yoo-ehl	Herodians	hehr-O-dee-uhnz	Kidron	KIHD-ruhn
Emmaus	eh-MAY-uhs	Herodias	hehr-O-dee-uhs	Kiriatharba	kihr-ee-ath-AHR-buh
Epaenetus	ee-PEE-nee-tuhs	Hezekiah	heh-zeh-KAI-uh	Kish	kihsh
Epaphras	EH-puh-fras	Hezron	HEHZ-ruhn	Laodicea	lay-o-dih-SEE-uh
ephah	EE-fuh	Hilkiah	hihl-KAI-uh	Lateran	LAT-er-uhn
Ephah	EE-fuh	Hittite	HIH-tait	Lazarus	LAZ-er-uhs
Ephesians	eh-FEE-zhuhnz	Hivites	HAI-vaits	Leah	LEE-uh
Ephesus	EH-fuh-suhs	Hophni	HAHF-nai	Lebanon	LEH-buh-nuhn
Ephphatha	EHF-uh-thuh	Hor	HAWR	Levi	LEE-vai
Ephraim	EE-fray-ihm	Horeb	HAWR-ehb	Levite	LEE-vait
Ephrathah	EHF-ruh-thuh	Hosea	ho-ZEE-uh	Levites	LEE-vaits
Ephron	EE-frawn	Hur	her	Leviticus	leh-VIH-tih-kous
Epiphanes	eh-PIHF-uh-neez	hyssop	HIH-suhp	Lucius	LOO-shih-uhs
Erastus	ee-RAS-tuhs	Iconium	ai-KO-nih-uhm	Lud	luhd
Esau	EE-saw	Isaac	AI-zuhk	Luke	look
Esther	EHS-ter	Isaiah	ai-ZAY-uh	Luz	luhz
Ethanim	EHTH-uh-nihm	Iscariot	ihs-KEHR-ee-uht	Lycaonian	lihk-ay-O-nih-uhn
Ethiopian	ee-thee-O-pee-uhn	Ishmael	ISH-may-ehl	Lydda	LIH-duh
Euphrates	yoo-FRAY-teez	Ishmaelites	ISH-mayehl-aits	Lydia	LIH-dih-uh
Exodus	EHK-so-duhs	Israel	IHZ-ray-ehl	Lysanias	lai-SAY-nih-uhs
Ezekiel	eh-ZEE-kee-uhl	Ituraea	ih-TSHOOR-ree-uh	Lystra	LIHS-truh
Ezra	EHZ-ruh	Jaar	DZHAY-ahr	Maccabees	MAK-uh-beez
frankincense	FRANGK-ihn-sehns	Jabbok	DZHAB-uhk	Macedonia	mas-eh-DO-nih-uh
Gabbatha	GAB-uh-thuh	Jacob	DZHAY-kuhb	Macedonian	mas-eh-DO-nih-uhn
Gabriel	GAY-bree-ul	Jairus	DZH-hr-uhs	Machir	MAY-kihr
Gadarenes	GAD-uh-reenz	Javan	DZHAY-van	Machpelah	mak-PEE-luh
Galatian	guh-LAY-shih-uhn	Jebusites	DZHEHB-oo-zaits	Magdala	MAG-duh-luh
Galatians	guh-LAY-shih-uhnz	Jechoniah	dzhehk-o-NAI-uh	Magdalene	MAG-duh-lehn
Galilee	GAL-ih-lee	Jehoiakim	dzhee-HOI-uh-kihm	magi	MAY-dzhai
Gallio	GAL-ih-o	Jehoshaphat	dzhee-HAHSH-uh-fat	Malachi	MAL-uh-kai
Gamaliel	guh-MAY-lih-ehl	Jephthah	DZHEHF-thuh	Malchiah	mal-KAI-uh
Gaza	GAH-zuh	Jeremiah	dzhehr-eh-MAI-uh	Malchus	MAL-kuhz
Gehazi	gee-HAY-zai	Jericho	DZHEHR-ih-ko	Mamre	MAM-ree
Gehenna	geh-HEHN-uh	Jeroham	dzhehr-RO-ham	Manaen	MAN-uh-ehn
Genesis	DZHEHN-uh-sihs	Jerusalem	dzheh-ROU-suh-lehm	Manasseh	man-AS-eh
Gennesaret	gehn-NEHS-uh-reht	Jesse	DZHEH-see	Manoah	muh-NO-uh
Gentiles	DZHEHN-tailz	Jethro	DZHEHTH-ro	Mark	mahrk
Gerasenes	DZHEHR-uh-seenz	Joakim	DZHO-uh-kihm	Mary	MEHR-ee
Gethsemane	gehth-SEHM-uh-ne	Job	DZHOB	Massah	MAH-suh
Gideon	GIHD-ee-uhn	Jonah	DZHO-nuh	Mattathias	mat-uh-THAI-uhs

317

Lectionary Word	Pronunciation	Lectionary Word	Pronunciation	Lectionary Word	Pronunciation
Matthan	MAT-than	Parmenas	PAHR-mee-nas	Sabbath	SAB-uhth
Matthew	MATH-yoo	Parthians	PAHR-thee-uhnz	Sadducees	SAD-dzhoo-seez
Matthias	muh-THAI-uhs	Patmos	PAT-mos	Salem	SAY-lehm
Medad	MEE-dad	Peninnah	pee-NIHN-uh	Salim	SAY-lim
Mede	meed	Pentecost	PEHN-tee-kawst	Salmon	SAL-muhn
Medes	meedz	Penuel	pee-NYOO-ehl	Salome	suh-LO-mee
Megiddo	mee-GIH-do	Perez	PEE-rehz	Salu	SAYL-yoo
Melchizedek	mehl-KIHZ-eh-dehk	Perga	PER-guh	Samaria	suh-MEHR-ih-uh
Mene	MEE-nee	Perizzites	PEHR-ih-zaits	Samaritan	suh-MEHR-ih-tuhn
Meribah	MEHR-ih-bah	Persia	PER-zhuh	Samothrace	SAM-o-thrays
Meshach	MEE-shak	Peter	PEE-ter	Samson	SAM-s'n
Mespotamia	mehs-o-po-TAY-mih-uh	Phanuel	FAN-yoo-ehl	Samuel	SAM-yoo-uhl
		Pharaoh	FEHR-o	Sanhedrin	san-HEE-drihn
Micah	MAI-kuh	Pharisees	FEHR-ih-seez	Sarah	SEHR-uh
Midian	MIH-dih-uhn	Pharpar	FAHR-pahr	Sarai	SAY-rai
Milcom	MIHL-kahm	Philemon	fih-LEE-muhn	saraph	SAY-raf
Miletus	mai-LEE-tuhs	Philippi	fil-LIH-pai	Sardis	SAHR-dihs
Minnith	MIHN-ihth	Philippians	fih-LIHP-ih-uhnz	Saul	sawl
Mishael	MIHSH-ay-ehl	Philistines	fih-LIHS-tihnz	Scythian	SIH-thee-uihn
Mizpah	MIHZ-puh	Phinehas	FEHN-ee-uhs	Seba	SEE-buh
Moreh	MO-reh	Phoenicia	fee-NIHSH-ih-uh	Seth	sehth
Moriah	maw-RAI-uh	Phrygia	FRIH-dzhih-uh	Shaalim	SHAY-uh-lihm
Mosoch	MAH-sahk	Phrygian	FRIH-dzhih-uhn	Shadrach	SHAY-drak
myrrh	mer	phylacteries	fih-LAK-ter-eez	Shalishah	shuh-LEE-shuh
Mysia	MIH-shih-uh	Pi-Hahiroth	pai-huh-HAI-rahth	Shaphat	Shay-fat
Naaman	NAY-uh-muhn	Pilate	PAI-luht	Sharon	SHEHR-uhn
Nahshon	NAY-shuhn	Pisidia	pih-SIH-dih-uh	Shealtiel	shee-AL-tih-ehl
Naomi	NAY-o-mai	Pithom	PAI-thahm	Sheba	SHEE-buh
Naphtali	NAF-tuh-lai	Pontius	PAHN-shus	Shebna	SHEB-nuh
Nathan	NAY-thuhn	Pontus	PAHN-tus	Shechem	SHEE-kehm
Nathanael	nuh-THAN-ay-ehl	Praetorium	pray-TAWR-ih-uhm	shekel	SHEHK-uhl
Nazarene	NAZ-awr-een	Priscilla	PRIHS-kill-uh	Shiloh	SHAI-lo
Nazareth	NAZ-uh-rehth	Prochorus	PRAH-kaw-ruhs	Shinar	SHAI-nahr
nazirite	NAZ-uh-rait	Psalm	Sahm	Shittim	sheh-TEEM
Nazorean	naz-aw-REE-uhn	Put	puht	Shuhite	SHOO-ait
Neapolis	nee-AP-o-lihs	Puteoli	pyoo-TEE-o-lai	Shunammite	SHOO-nam-ait
Nebuchadnezzar	neh-byoo-kuhd-NEHZ-er	Qoheleth	ko-HEHL-ehth	Shunem	SHOO-nehm
		qorban	KAWR-bahn	Sidon	SAI-duhn
Negeb	NEH-gehb	Quartus	KWAR-tuhs	Silas	SAI-luhs
Nehemiah	nee-hee-MAI-uh	Quirinius	kwai-RIHN-ih-uhs	Siloam	sih-LO-uhm
Ner	ner	Raamses	ray-AM-seez	Silvanus	sihl-VAY-nuhs
Nicanor	nai-KAY-nawr	Rabbi	RAB-ai	Simeon	SIHM-ee-uhn
Nicodemus	nih-ko-DEE-muhs	Rabbouni	ra-BO-nai	Simon	SAI-muhn
Niger	NAI-dzher	Rahab	RAY-hab	Sin *(desert)*	sihn
Nineveh	NIHN-eh-veh	Ram	ram	Sinai	SAI-nai
Noah	NO-uh	Ramah	RAY-muh	Sirach	SAI-rak
Nun	nuhn	Ramathaim	ray-muh-THAY-ihm	Sodom	SAH-duhm
Obed	O-behd	Raqa	RA-kuh	Solomon	SAH-lo-muhn
Olivet	AH-lih-veht	Rebekah	ree-BEHK-uh	Sosthenes	SAHS-thee-neez
Omega	o-MEE-guh	Rehoboam	ree-ho-BO-am	Stachys	STAY-kihs
Onesimus	o-NEH-sih-muhs	Rephidim	REHF-ih-dihm	Succoth	SUHK-ahth
Ophir	O-fer	Reuben	ROO-b'n	Sychar	SI-kar
Orpah	AWR-puh	Revelation	reh-veh-LAY-shuhn	Syene	sai-EE-nee
Pamphylia	pam-FIHL-ih-uh	Rhegium	REE-dzhee-uhm	Symeon	SIHM-ee-uhn
Paphos	PAY-fuhs	Rufus	ROO-fuhs	synagogues	SIHN-uh-gahgz

Lectionary Word	Pronunciation	Lectionary Word	Pronunciation	Lectionary Word	Pronunciation
Syrophoenician	SIHR-o fee-NIHSH-ih-uhn	Timon	TAI-muhn	Zebedee	ZEH-beh-dee
		Titus	TAI-tuhs	Zebulun	ZEH-byoo-luhn
Tabitha	TAB-ih-thuh	Tohu	TO-hyoo	Zechariah	zeh-kuh-RAI-uh
Talitha koum	TAL-ih-thuh-KOOM	Trachonitis	trak-o-NAI-tis	Zedekiah	zeh-duh-KAI-uh
Tamar	TAY-mer	Troas	TRO-ahs	Zephaniah	zeh-fuh-NAI-uh
Tarshish	TAHR-shihsh	Tubal	TYOO-b'l	Zerah	ZEE-ruh
Tarsus	TAHR-suhs	Tyre	TAI-er	Zeror	ZEE-rawr
Tekel	TEH-keel	Ur	er	Zerubbabel	zeh-RUH-buh-behl
Terebinth	TEHR-ee-bihnth	Urbanus	er-BAY-nuhs	Zeus	zyoos
Thaddeus	THAD-dee-uhs	Uriah	you-RAI-uh	Zimri	ZIHM-rai
Theophilus	thee-AH-fih-luhs	Uzziah	yoo-ZAI-uh	Zion	ZAI-uhn
Thessalonians	theh-suh-LO-nih-uhnz	Wadi	WAH-dee	Ziph	zihf
Theudas	THU-duhs	Yahweh-yireh	YAH-weh-yer-AY	Zoar	ZO-er
Thyatira	thai-uh-TAI-ruh	Zacchaeus	zak-KEE-uhs	Zorah	ZAWR-uh
Tiberias	tai-BIHR-ih-uhs	Zadok	ZAY-dahk	Zuphite	ZUHF-ait
Timaeus	tai-MEE-uhs	Zarephath	ZEHR-ee-fath